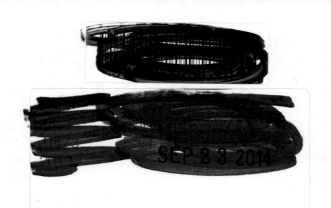

THE CONTEMPORARY
MIDDLE EAST

UNDERSTANDING

Introductions to the States and Regions of the Contemporary World

Donald L. Gordon, series editor

Understanding Contemporary Africa, 5th edition
edited by April A. Gordon and Donald L. Gordon

Understanding Contemporary Asia Pacific
edited by Katherine Palmer Kaup

Understanding the Contemporary Caribbean, 2nd edition
edited by Richard S. Hillman and Thomas J. D'Agostino

Understanding Contemporary China, 4th edition
edited by Robert E. Gamer

Understanding Contemporary India, 2nd edition
edited by Neil DeVotta

Understanding Contemporary Latin America, 4th edition
edited by Richard S. Hillman and Thomas J. D'Agostino

Understanding the Contemporary Middle East, 4th edition
edited by Jillian Schwedler

Understanding Contemporary Russia
edited by Michael L. Bressler

FOURTH EDITION

UNDERSTANDING

THE CONTEMPORARY

MIDDLE
EAST

EDITED BY
JILLIAN SCHWEDLER

LYNNE
RIENNER
PUBLISHERS

BOULDER
LONDON

Published in the United States of America in 2013 by
Lynne Rienner Publishers, Inc.
1800 30th Street, Boulder, Colorado 80301
www.rienner.com

and in the United Kingdom by
Lynne Rienner Publishers, Inc.
3 Henrietta Street, Covent Garden, London WC2E 8LU

Library of Congress Cataloging-in-Publication Data
Understanding the contemporary Middle East / edited by Jillian Schwedler. —
  Fourth edition.
      p. cm. — (Understanding: introductions to the states and regions of
the contemporary world)
   Includes bibliographical references and index.
   ISBN 978-1-58826-910-2 (alk. paper)
   1. Middle East. 2. Africa, North. I. Schwedler, Jillian.
   DS44.U473 2013
   956—dc23
                                                                   2013003036

British Cataloguing in Publication Data
A Cataloguing in Publication record for this book
is available from the British Library.

Printed and bound in the United States of America

      The paper used in this publication meets the requirements
  ∞   of the American National Standard for Permanence of
      Paper for Printed Library Materials Z39.48-1992.

   5   4   3   2   1

Contents

List of Illustrations   ix

Preface   xi

1 Introduction   *Jillian Schwedler*   1
What Is the Middle East?   *3*
The Arab Uprisings   *4*
Organization of the Book   *6*

2 The Middle East: A Geographic Preface   *Ian R. Manners,*
Barbara McKean Parmenter, and Ryan King   9
Boundaries   *13*
Aridity and Water   *19*
Cityscapes   *27*
Conclusion   *34*

3 The Historical Context   *Arthur Goldschmidt Jr.*   41
The Ancient Middle East   *41*
The Islamic Middle East as an Autonomous System   *45*
The Subordination of the Middle East to the West   *53*
The Middle East Since World War I   *62*
Popular Uprisings in Iran and the Arab Countries   *85*
Conclusion   *87*

4 Middle Eastern Politics   *Philip A. Schrodt and
   Deborah J. Gerner*   89
   The Colonial Legacy   *90*
   A Changing International Context   *92*
   Economic Development   *97*
   Informal Structures of Power   *99*
   The Myth of Political Instability   *100*
   The Arab Uprisings   *101*
   Prospects for Democratization   *104*
   The Role of the Military   *108*
   Government Legitimization and State Building   *110*
   Nationalist Revolutionary Republics   *112*
   Traditional and Parliamentary Monarchies   *117*
   Conditional Democracies   *125*
   Transitional Democracies   *132*
   Conclusion   *133*

5 International Relations   *Mary Ann Tétreault*   139
   Local Challenges to State Sovereignty: Boundary Disputes   *144*
   External Challenges: The Middle East and the Great Powers   *146*
   Middle East Regionalism   *150*
   The Middle East in the World   *153*
   The Gulf Wars   *159*
   Conclusion   *165*

6 The Israeli-Palestinian Conflict   *Simona Sharoni and
   Mohammed Abu-Nimer*   175
   The Parties: Two Peoples—Palestinians and Israeli Jews   *176*
   The History and Dynamics of the Conflict   *184*
   One Land, Two Peoples: Central Issues and Points of Contention   *202*
   The Rocky Road to Peace: Past and Present Attempts to
      Resolve the Conflict   *206*
   Conclusion   *213*

7 The Economies of the Middle East   *Agnieszka Paczynska*   223
   Middle East Economies Before World War II   *224*
   Economic Development Following World War II   *226*
   Labor Migration and Remittances   *230*
   Economic Crises and Structural Adjustment   *234*
   Trade   *239*
   The New Oil Boom   *244*
   The Global Financial Crisis and the Arab Uprisings   *245*
   Conflict and Regional Economies   *246*
   Conclusion   *255*

8 The Political Economy of Middle Eastern Oil
Mary Ann Tétreault 259
Industry Structure 260
The System Unravels 263
The Politics in Oil's Political Economy 266
The Oil Revolution 268
Oil Politics in the Middle East 269
Oil Politics and the Price Bust 271
The Iraq War: A New Oil Regime? 274
Oil, Climate Change, and World Order 277
Oil and Money in the Middle East 280
Conclusion 282

9 Population Growth, Urbanization, and the
Challenges of Unemployment *Valentine M. Moghadam* 287
Urbanization 288
Population Growth 291
Labor Force Growth and Employment Challenges 295
Rising Unemployment 298
Poverty and Inequality 302
Conclusion 309

10 Kinship, Class, and Ethnicity *Laurie King-Irani* 315
Key Concepts 318
The Historical Context of the Environment 320
Kinship 322
Ethnicity 329
The Historical Context of Identity Categories 333
Social Class 335
Kinship, Class, and Ethnicity in Context:
Strategies or Straitjackets? 338
Conclusion 340

11 The Role of Women *Lisa Pollard* 345
The Middle East and the Woman Question 347
Building the Nation Through Women 352
Middle Eastern Women Beyond the Woman Question 361
Conclusion 372

12 Religion and Politics in the Middle East
Jillian Schwedler 377
The Historical Role of Religion in the Middle East 378
The Experiences of Religious Minorities 383
Religion and States 386

Religious Activism   *391*
Islamist Groups Since the Arab Uprisings   *398*
Conclusion   *400*

13 Middle Eastern Literature   *miriam cooke*   403
European Colonialism and Its Discontents   *403*
Cultural Ferment at the Turn of the Twentieth Century   *406*
The Short Story as a Literary Pioneer   *409*
Francophone Novels in North Africa   *413*
The Arabic Novel   *414*
The Iranian Novel   *416*
The Turkish Novel   *417*
The Israeli Novel   *419*
Drama: Grafting the New onto the Old   *420*
Poetry and the Hold of the Desert   *423*
Independence and Postcolonial Struggles   *425*
Emigration and Exile   *431*
The Muslim State   *433*
Translation and Recognition   *436*

14 Trends and Prospects   *Jillian Schwedler*   439
The Arab Uprisings and Popular Mobilizations   *439*
New Media   *441*
Conclusion   *442*

List of Acronyms   445
Basic Political Data   449
The Contributors   463
Index   465
About the Book   487

Illustrations

Maps

2.1	Political Map of the Middle East	15
2.2	Extent of the Ottoman Empire	17
3.1	Extent of the Islamic Empire	49
6.1	Israel/Palestine, Showing the 1947 Partition Plan, 1948 Boundaries, and Borders After the 1967 War	187
6.2	The Oslo Accords: Areas A, B, and C Within the West Bank	200

Tables

4.1	Freedom House Classification of Countries Globally	102
7.1	Indicators of Development, 2011	224
7.2	Contributions of Agriculture and Industry to GDP	228
7.3	Estimated Migrants in Selected Host Countries, 2010	230
7.4	Official Remittances in Selected Countries During the First Oil Boom	231
7.5	Official Remittances, 2010	232
7.6	GDP Growth in the Middle East	237
7.7	Size of the Informal Economy as a Percentage of GDP	238
7.8	Middle East Exports by Destination	242
7.9	Middle East Imports by Origin	243
9.1	Population and Urbanization in the MENA Region	289
9.2	Cities in the MENA Region with Populations over 1 Million, 2010	290
9.3	Fertility Rates and Related Sociodemographic Features in the MENA Region	292
9.4	Unemployment Rates in the MENA Region	301
9.5	Poverty and Inequality in the MENA Region	305

Photographs

Palestinian checking Facebook	2
Revolutionary graffiti in le Kef, Tunisia	5
The pyramids of Giza	10
Cappadocia region in Turkey	12
Snowfall in Kandovan, Iran	20
Flag over Amman, Jordan	34
Petra monastery in Jordan	44
Milk Bar in Algiers	71
Palestinian woman talks to Israeli border guards	74
Revolution mural at the American University of Cairo	87
Revolution mural in Cairo	90
Workers at an oil production site	98
Women voters in Tunis	105
Riot police in Jordan	124
A Kurdish man relaxes in Iraq	159
Female soldiers in the Iran-Iraq War	162
Palestinian demonstrators	181
Palestinian man with key commemorating al-Nakbah	188
Israeli peace activist Uri Avnery	210
Israeli separation wall	214
Dress market in Cairo	240
Man harvesting olives in Palestine	252
Gasoline prices in New York City	260
Dhow and oil tanker in Bahrain	279
View of downtown Cairo and the Nile	291
Transporting bread by bicycle in Cairo	300
Teenagers in a gym in le Kef, Tunisia	307
Couple sharing laughs in Cairo	325
Women in Qom, Iran	358
Protesting violence against women	366
Palestinian women demonstrators	370
Women celebrating Tunisia's first free elections	373
Crusader castle in Syria	381
Mural of Jesus in Beirut	384
Young Orthodox Jew praying in Jerusalem	387
Mosque in Esphahan, Iran	390
Egyptian Nobel laureate Naguib Mahfouz	415
Syrian poet Nizar Kabbani and poem	423
Palestinian writer Ghassan Kanafani	432
Media at a protest in Amman	442

Preface

As this fourth edition of *Understanding the Contemporary Middle East* goes to press, the Middle East is once again front and center in the news. Since late 2010, millions of people in the region have taken to the streets in protest against corrupt and repressive regimes and to demand economic reforms that address the needs of the many rather than the few.

The "war on terrorism" continues largely through unarmed drone attacks, and US troops have finally withdrawn from Iraq. The administration of President Barack Obama has promised to help usher the Middle East into a new era, although many US policies seem unchanged from previous administrations. The Israeli-Palestinian conflict remains unresolved, with Israel expanding settlements into the last zones of the West Bank where it previously promised to never build. While scholars vie with pundits and politicians to explain what is happening in the Middle East, courses on all aspects of the region—including language classes—are filled to capacity.

Like earlier editions, this updated collection draws on the expertise of more than a dozen scholars from a variety of disciplines: history, economics, politics, international relations, demography, geography, anthropology, sociology, gender studies, conflict resolution, religion, and literature. The authors have taken time from their busy schedules to undertake extensive revisions because they believe in the value of making nuanced analyses accessible to a broader readership. Like most scholars of the Middle East, they have been pulled in many directions. Their families, like mine, have far too often been pushed to the back burner while they speak with yet another student group, community organization, or stranger about the Middle East. I am humbled and overwhelmed by their hard work in the face of such commitments and obstacles. Extraordinary photographs for this edition

xii   *Preface*

were generously donated by Kathleen Cavanaugh, Laryssa Chomiak, Geoff Hartmann, Thomas Hartwell, Anne Norton, Anne Paq, Robert P. Parks, Lynn Peterfreund, and Ella Wind. Tyler Schuenemann diligently updated the Basic Political Data, which required extensive revisions given the exciting developments that have resulted from the Arab uprisings. I am grateful to Ryan King for his invaluable research assistance at every stage, including during the hectic final days of pulling everything together. Finally, everyone at Lynne Rienner Publishers was wonderful, notably Lesli Brooks Athanasoulis, who oversaw production of the volume. Lynne's enthusiasm and insights are treasures, and her extraordinary friendship helped me finish this project under difficult personal circumstances.

The original authors of this volume were brought together under the inspiring leadership of Deborah J. (Misty) Gerner. The heart and soul of this edition, like the three before it, capture Misty's spirit and commitment to the peaceful resolution of conflicts globally and locally. I wish she could have seen the Arab uprisings, as she was unwavering in her belief that the peaceful mobilization of people could change the world. She was right.

—*Jillian Schwedler*

UNDERSTANDING

THE CONTEMPORARY

MIDDLE
EAST

1

Introduction

Jillian Schwedler

To many in the West, the Middle East has always been exotic: a land of endless deserts, warriors wielding sabers on camelback, and veiled women confined to harems. Touring exhibits of the treasures of King Tutankhamun attract long lines and command high ticket prices and, for many, a visit to the Great Pyramid of Giza and a boat ride down the Nile would be the trip of a lifetime. Many students are attracted to courses on the Middle East precisely because of these images, along with more immediate concerns about the global spread of terrorism and the looming energy crisis as oil and natural gas supplies are rapidly being depleted.

In this book we provide a broad but detailed overview of the geography, politics, history, cultures, economies, religions, and peoples of the Middle East. Written by area specialists from diverse disciplines, we addresse head-on the myths and realities of conventional wisdom about the region, aiming to unpack complex processes without romanticizing the region's cultures or downplaying the very real political violence with which many peoples of the Middle East must live and cope daily. Deserts, harems, tribes, camels, oil, and terrorist groups are all discussed, but so are gleaming skyscrapers, Nobel laureates, a feminist movement dating to the nineteenth century, and the rapid spread of new social media such as Twitter and Facebook. We also discuss in detail the Arab uprisings in which millions of citizens across the region demanded an end to decades of repression, corruption, and neglect by their regimes.

Observers might view the region as a land of inevitable conflict—where the traditional and premodern clash with the modern and global. Of course, tensions do emerge between old and new forms of political, economic, and social structures. But just as often, traditional elements such as

A young Palestinian checking his Facebook account.

tribes, patriarchy, and religious conservatism take on new forms and roles in their dynamic and changing environments. In many cases, the traditional and the modern turn out to not be the distinct categories we imagine. Traditional tribes have begun to hold internal primary elections prior to contesting national elections; conservative religious groups like the Muslim Brotherhood embrace social media; and virtually every political opposition group frames its grievances in terms of freedom, rights, and democracy—the dominant language of political legitimacy worldwide. The contributors to this volume unpack these various practices, taking a longer historical view but focusing on how the past has helped to shape the contemporary Middle East in an increasingly globalized world. In many ways, how we look at the Middle East has changed significantly since the publication of the previous edition of this book in 2008. We all watched the Arab uprisings in real time, viewing the same images as the protesters themselves and rooting alongside them for the fall of the dictators who had long held the region hostage.

The Middle East has never existed in a vacuum, with international trade routes, struggles from external powers to control the region and its resources, and cultural and scientific exchange dating back centuries. As the world becomes smaller through easy travel and new media, people everywhere are becoming increasingly aware of those connections. Popular Hollywood films such as *Syriana* and *Argo* address some of these complexities, emphasizing that many of the political problems of the region are the direct result of foreign meddling. At the same time, however, they reinforce notions of a region in turmoil with a future that likely will continue on a bloody and chaotic path. This book challenges that image by providing substantive explanations for the contemporary state of the region and by connecting the local to the regional and global.

What Is the Middle East?

The term *Middle East* refers to those countries that are members of the League of Arab States, plus Israel (with its Jewish and Arab populations), and the non-Arab countries of Turkey and Iran (both of which also have small Arab populations). These countries are clustered into three subregions. North Africa includes the countries of Algeria, Egypt, Libya, Morocco, and Tunisia as well as the sub-Saharan states of the Comoros Islands, Djibouti, Mauritania, Somalia, Sudan, and South Sudan. The area along the eastern Mediterranean is the Fertile Crescent (also called the Levant, its colonial name) and includes Syria, Lebanon, Jordan, Israel, and Palestine as well as non-Arab Turkey to the north. Finally, the oil-producing countries of the Gulf and Arabian Peninsula include Iraq, Saudi Arabia, Bahrain, Kuwait, Qatar, the United Arab Emirates, Oman, Yemen, and the non-Arab, Persian state of Iran.

Does it make sense to cluster countries as diverse historically and culturally as, for example, Iran, Turkey, Israel, Somalia, Yemen, and Morocco under the single category of Middle East? It might make more sense to cluster studies around the bodies of water that facilitated historical interactions such as the Mediterranean Sea (so that France, Italy, and Greece would be included in a category with Morocco, Algeria, Israel, Syria, and Lebanon, among others) or the Red Sea (Somalia, Sudan, South Sudan, Egypt, Israel, Jordan, Saudi Arabia, and Yemen). Similarly, non-Arab Iran is mostly connected to the Middle East as a result of its Islamic heritage and just as easily might be included with Central Asian states, or it might form the core of a cluster surrounding it (Turkey, Iraq, Afghanistan, Pakistan, and Turkmenistan). Yemen has strong historical ties not only to the Arabian Peninsula, but also to Malaysia as a result of centuries-old trade routes. Indeed, these connections remain salient today and are visible, for example, on the many commercial signs in the Malay language in Yemen's southern coastal cities.

Yet the category of Middle East does make considerable sense given the shared historical experiences of the spread of Islam, the reach of the Ottoman Empire, and the experiences of European colonialism. The Arab world shares linguistic as well as cultural similarities, although a Syrian, a Moroccan, and an Omani, for example, could easily find much that is different in terms of their actual life experiences. The Islamic world, similarly, has limitations as a category, even though Muslims globally identify themselves as part of a broader Muslim community, or *umma*. But Muslims—the followers of the Islamic faith—make up a fifth of the global population with some 1.65 billion. Of that number, only some 250 million—less than a sixth of the total—live in the Arab world. The point is not to settle on a better or more accurate category—favoring Middle East over Islamic world or Arab world—but to recognize the myriad ways in which the region coheres as a whole around some issues and less so around others.

As noted above, a common assumption is that Western nations had limited interest in the Middle East until the colonial period of the eighteenth and nineteenth centuries and the later discovery of oil. In this erroneous view, the Middle East was largely isolated from the outside world prior to the spread of European colonialism. However, the peoples of the Middle East in fact have been in contact with those in all geographic directions for centuries. Ancient trade patterns have persisted and changed with the advent of different forms of transportation, but pilgrims from all over the globe have trekked to visit the region's many holy sites.

Intellectually, the major works of Greek philosophy were lost to Europe for centuries, but survived in the Arab-Islamic world; they were reintroduced to the West by Arab scholars. During Europe's dark Middle Ages, Muslim as well as Jewish scholars in the Middle East were substantially more advanced in many fields, including science, medicine, mathematics, architecture, literature, the visual arts, and education. The decimal number system used widely today was developed by Arabs who later taught it to Europeans, introducing them to the concept of zero in the process. In terms of ordinary language, English words such as *alcohol* and *algebra* come from Arabic.

Middle Eastern cultural influences in the West extend well beyond science, religion, and mathematics. Since the early twentieth century, numerous Middle Eastern poets and philosophers have gained sizable followings. Edward FitzGerald's nineteenth-century English translation of *The Rubaiyat of Omar Khayyam* enthralled Western readers, just as the flower children and peace activists of the 1960s embraced the works of Lebanese poet Khalil Gibran. In the 1990s, the poetry of Jalal al-Din al-Rumi, the eleventh-century Persian mystic, found its way onto bestseller lists in the United States. The Egyptian novelist Naguib Mahfouz was awarded the Nobel Prize in 1988, an honor also bestowed on the Turkish novelist Orhan Pamuk in 2006. Yet the Middle East retains distinctive features, even as such global connections deepen. This book explains these connections.

The Arab Uprisings

The Middle East never seems to be out of the news, from the ongoing Israeli-Palestinian conflict to the spread of al-Qaeda during the past decade and its role in the attacks of September 11, 2001. Most recently, the Arab uprisings that spread across the region in 2011 have been among the most significant global happenings, with reverberations felt in many corners of the world. Like many major events in world politics—such as the outbreak of World War I or the fall of the Soviet Union—the Arab uprisings may have taken much of the world by surprise, but they did not come out of nowhere. In the way that the assassination of Austrian archduke Franz Ferdinand is said to have started World War I, the Arab uprisings are now commonly said to have begun with the self-immolation of Tunisian fruit cart vendor Mohamed Bouazizi on December 17, 2010. Protests spread throughout Tunisia within weeks, culminating in the resignation of President Zine Abidine Ben Ali on January 14, 2011. From there, the revolutionary spirit spread to Egypt, Libya, Yemen, Bahrain, and Syria, sparking serious challenges to repressive regimes that just months earlier appeared as stable as they had been for decades.

*This graffiti from Tunisia's January 14, 2011,
revolution in the town of le Kef portrays
the party and regime of Ben Ali as a rat.*

But the story is not so simple. In Tunisia, at least two other citizens had self-immolated in the months before Bouazizi, and yet those brutal deaths sparked nothing. In Egypt, protests and demonstrations had been escalating almost steadily since at least 2004, notably as more than a million organized laborers participated in strikes and marches that brought portions of the country to a standstill. While no one predicted the precise timing of the uprisings or that they would begin in Tunisia, many scholars of the region had been documenting what appeared to be growing expressions of dissent, particularly over the past decade. And despite common perceptions, virtually no regime escaped the Arab uprisings. Saudi Arabia, Jordan, Morocco, and Oman have all seen unprecedented challenges to their regimes, even though as of this writing they do not appear in imminent danger of falling. The chapters in this book unpack many of the dimensions that led to the uprisings—economic hardship, corrupt political elites, decades of severe repression and stifled political expression, and complex relations with external powers (including the United States) that supported those regimes.

Organization of the Book

In this book we explore the key themes and controversies of the Middle East in the fields of geography, history, politics, international relations, economics, sociology, demography, anthropology, gender studies, conflict resolution, religion, and literature. Each chapter can stand alone, but the authors also engage directly in the debates in other chapters, particularly when another chapter provides an expanded discussion of a given topic. In Chapter 2, Ian R. Manners, Barbara McKean Parmenter, and Ryan King ask a critical starting question, "What Is the Middle East?" Rather than considering the region as a single, geographical entity, the multiple and shifting boundaries of the region have been shaped (and continue to be shaped) by foreign interventions, cultural change, language, urbanization, the flow of migrant workers and refugees, and the rapid decline in water resources. In Chapter 3, Arthur Goldschmidt Jr. examines the history of the region (and its shifting geographies), from the ancient empires of Egypt and Sumer more than 5,000 years ago to the Middle East we know today. He elaborates on a central theme of the book; namely, that the Middle East has never been a closed or isolated unit.

In Chapter 4, Philip A. Schrodt and Deborah J. Gerner focus on the domestic politics of Middle Eastern countries, emphasizing the ongoing effects of the colonial legacy as well as contemporary forms of political organization and the various ideologies that offer competing visions of political reform. In Chapter 5, Mary Ann Tétreault explores international intervention, regional alliances, and various regional subsystems. From the colonial period to the Cold War to the Iraq War, the politics of the Middle

East has been intimately connected—in mostly negative ways—with the political agendas and ambitions of the great powers. Chapter 6, by Simona Sharoni and Mohammed Abu-Nimer, is unique to this volume in providing a detailed analysis of a single conflict; it is also unusual in being coauthored by an Israeli Jew and a Palestinian citizen of Israel. Their nuanced discussion of the Israeli-Palestinian conflict examines the history of the conflict through the lens of conflict resolution, a forward-looking perspective that rejects the idea that the conflict is intractable and cannot be solved.

In Chapter 7, Agnieszka Paczynska discusses the economies of the Middle East, with particular attention to contemporary challenges. She examines structural adjustment, trade patterns, and economic trends in light of regional politics and the long history of foreign involvement in the region. In Chapter 8, Mary Ann Tétreault explores the profound ways in which the discovery of oil in the early twentieth century ensured the continued and deep involvement of foreign governments after the end of the colonial period. The first multinational corporations were oil companies, and their heavy-handed efforts to ensure their interests shaped domestic politics in the region.

In Chapter 9, Valentine M. Moghadam looks at the ways in which these economic processes have affected the region's populations. She emphasizes the connections between population growth, urbanization, labor and immigration, (un)employment, poverty, and income inequality, with particular attention to the striking differences that emerge between countries of the region as well as between men and women. In Chapter 10, Laurie King-Irani explores the ways in which kinship networks, class, and ethnicity affect the daily social realities of the peoples of the region. She provides insights into the gender and family relationships that are often a source of confusion to outsiders. Chapter 11 further develops questions of gender, as Lisa Pollard presents a history of complex gender relations and the struggles of women (and men) in the region to reshape gender hierarchies. She emphasizes the diversity of experiences among women in the region, from harem life to participation in high political offices.

In Chapter 12, I examine the historical role of Judaism, Christianity, and Islam in the Middle East, and the ways in which religion and politics have been interconnected historically. I then discuss the role of religion in the contemporary politics of the region, from the emergence of religious extremism to the many and varied ways in which moderate religious activists have engaged peacefully in the pluralist political processes before and after the Arab uprisings. In Chapter 13, miriam cooke describes beautifully the historical and cultural underpinnings of Middle Eastern literature: poetry, short stories, novels, and plays. She shows that literature reflects, as well as influences, its environment—the cultural ferment, the impact of colonization and struggles for independence, and the experience of exile and emigration.

As the richness of Middle Eastern literature remains unknown to most Westerners, this chapter also provides an introduction to the large and growing body of material available in English translations. Finally, in Chapter 14, I outline the challenges facing the region in the twenty-first century, particularly since the outbreak of the Arab uprisings.

The authors seek to challenge some of your existing perceptions about the Middle East while confirming and fleshing out others. Like any region of the world, "reality" is a complicated notation that cannot be fully understood outside of local perspectives. The politics of the region dominate most of the West's common knowledge, and these chapters aim to make accessible a rich understanding of these complexities. At the same time, a primary goal of this book is to bring to life the lived experiences of Middle Eastern peoples—and many of these will feel surprisingly familiar to you. We hope that you enjoy your exploration of the contemporary Middle East.

2

The Middle East:
A Geographic Preface

Ian R. Manners, Barbara McKean Parmenter, and Ryan King

A camel caravan crossing desert dunes, oil derricks pumping
thick black crude, rows of men kneeling in prayer, bearded protesters shouting slogans—more than likely these are some of the images conjured up
when the outside world thinks of the Middle East. This was how we began
our chapter for the first edition of *Understanding the Contemporary Middle
East* appearing in 2000. Over a decade later, these images of the region,
though retaining considerable power in shaping a geographical view of the
Middle East, have been overlain by more recent and more visceral images
brought to us through cable television and the Internet. Many of these
newer images are the result of direct US military engagement in the region
as experienced through war in Iraq and Afghanistan. Explosions illuminating the night skies during the initial US-led aerial assault on Baghdad, the
carnage of roadside bombs in the course of a growing insurgency in Iraq,
and the natural caves and deep gorges of Tora Bora on the Afghanistan-
Pakistan border are now part of a more complicated regional landscape. As
we revised this chapter, Arab uprisings epitomized in dramatic aerial views
of massive crowds in Cairo's Tahrir Square reminded us of the ways in
which the large public squares of cities, originally designed and built as expressions of modernity and Westernization, quickly became spaces of
protest as women, students, tradespeople, and street vendors expressed political and economic grievances and challenged some of the region's most
authoritarian regimes. In the Gulf, the past decade has seen the emergence
of global cities, symbolized by Dubai's Burj Khalifa skyscraper, where oil
and natural gas no longer drive the economy or shape the cityscape but
rather technological connectivity to a wider world, the provision of financial services, and the promotion of real estate development and cosmopolitan

tourism. Thus, our geographical imagery today draws from and is shaped by a much more diverse set of experiences and images while social media and news sources such as Al Jazeera allow many more Middle East voices to be heard around the world.

We start with these images because each of us carries our own geography of the world and its places in our minds, our own way of visualizing and interpreting the earth on which we live. Professional geographers attempt to correct preconceived notions and present a broader perspective. Typically, a geographical description of the Middle East, like that of any other region, begins with an overview of the physical environment—geology, geomorphology, climate, flora, and fauna—as a backdrop for a discussion of human activities in the region, land use, resource development, population distribution, urbanization, and political organization. Yet even the best of these descriptions often fail to convey what the Middle East is "really" like.

The Middle East cannot be easily compartmentalized into book chapters or neatly divided by border lines on a map. Sharp boundaries are blurred, discontinuities appear unexpectedly, the familiarity of everyday life surprises us in our anticipation of the exotic and dangerous. Timothy Mitchell (1988) describes how European travelers to Egypt in the nineteenth century were frequently confused by what they saw when they reached Egypt. They had seen the ancient Egyptian artifacts that had been

Jillian Schwedler

Images like this one of the pyramids of Giza and the lush palms of an oasis dominate many perceptions of the geography of the Middle East.

collected and displayed in Europe's capitals, some had even visited the Egyptian Hall at the Exposition Universelle held in Paris, and others had read the *Description de l'Egypte,* the twenty-two-volume work prepared by the French artists and scholars who had accompanied Napoleon to Egypt— but nothing they saw or experienced quite matched up to what they had been expecting to see. There was often a palpable sense of disappointment. Where was the "real Egypt"? In a similar way, contemporary visitors to the Middle East are likely to find that their geographical knowledge has to be reformulated as they encounter a world that challenges many of their expectations.

The difficult path to understanding the Middle East in all of its complexity is not traveled only by outsiders. In the Iranian film *Bashu,* director Bahram Bayza'i tells the story of a boy from the deserts of Khuzistan in southwestern Iran whose village is caught in a bombardment. Bashu understands little of the reasons for the conflict between his government and its neighbor, Iraq; he knows only that he is now both homeless and orphaned. Seeking refuge in the back of a truck, he falls asleep. When he awakes, he is bewildered to find himself in a quiet world of cool, deep green forests, a paradise he never dreamed existed. The truck has brought him to Gilan province in northwestern Iran, where he is taken in by a peasant woman despite the disapproval of her neighbors. Bashu is of Arab descent and speaks a mixture of Arabic and Persian common to the borderlands of Khuzistan; the woman speaks Gilaki, a dialect of Persian. Unable to communicate with either his caregiver or her neighbors, Bashu struggles against their prejudices. But he is not alone in being different. The woman who has taken him in is struggling to manage the farm on her own while her husband is away fighting in the war. When her husband returns and demands that the boy be sent away, she refuses to comply. In a very real sense, the film is a small reflection of much larger issues in Middle Eastern society, exploring the ways in which people deal with differences and face changes related to environment, culture, government, religion, and gender.

Thus, although the term *Middle East* may appear to suggest a degree of homogeneity, the region is extraordinarily diverse in its physical, cultural, and social landscapes. For many, the desert seems the central physical metaphor for the Middle East, an image frequently repeated in films and novels. The sand seas of the Rub'al-Khali (the Empty Quarter) in Arabia perhaps best fit this image. Yet the landscapes of the Middle East also encompass the coral reefs that draw scuba divers to the Red Sea, permanent snowfields and cirque glaciers on the slopes of the great volcanic peaks of Mount Ararat (5,165 meters) in eastern Anatolia and Mount Damavand (more than 5,600 meters) in the Elburz Mountains of Iran, the salt-crusted flats and evaporation pans of the Dasht-e Kavir in central Iran, and the coastal marshes and wetlands of the Nile Delta. Most emphatically, and

Geoff Hartmann

The Cappadocia region, in central modern-day Turkey, is characterized by dramatic rock spires that protrude from the bottom of the drainage basin.

despite the vast expanses of desert and steppe, the Middle East is also very much an urban society, with more than half the population living in cities that face much the same environmental, infrastructural, and social problems of cities around the world.

The Middle East is likewise culturally diverse. Much of the area came under Arab Muslim influence during and after the seventh century. At various times, Persian and Central Asian peoples and influences flowed westward into the lands around the eastern Mediterranean. Most people in the region are Muslims, but Christians and Jews constitute significant communities. The three major languages are Arabic, Turkish, and Persian, all of which are quite distinct linguistically (Arabic is a Semitic language, Persian is Indo-European, and Turkish is Ural-Altaic). Nonetheless, they have been heavily influenced by each other. Persian is written in Arabic script, as was Ottoman Turkish; only since 1928 has Turkish used a modified Latin alphabet. All three languages contain numerous words from the others, and each has a subset of distinct dialects. In addition, other peoples with their own languages are found throughout the region. There are, for example, Berber speakers in Morocco and Algeria and Baluchi speakers in southeastern Iran. Kurdish-speaking people probably constitute the fourth-largest linguistic group in the region, and the revived Hebrew language has been a central integrating force among Jews in Israel.

Increasingly over the past twenty years, the Middle East, like most regions of the world, has been transformed by globalizing markets, the rising power of the financial sector, and the widespread diffusion of information technology. Many governments embarked on schemes to privatize sectors of the economy, but in ways that kept these under control of government-supported elites. The surplus capital created by this transformation, along with capital flows from newly emerging global economic powers like China, fueled a wave of new urbanization. This more recent urbanization took the form of massive real estate developments in satellite cities outside of the region's historical urban centers and in the breathtakingly rapid development of cities in the Arab Gulf as these positioned themselves as global financial centers in the postoil economy. A region already marked by inequality saw inequality increase. With a burgeoning youth population, the Iraq War and the regional tensions created by the US policy, and the concomitant rise of twenty-four-hour cable news and digital social media that enabled communication outside of government-controlled means, the stage was set for conflict. Perhaps the only surprise is how completely astonished the world was by the wave of urban uprisings that occurred across the Middle East starting in 2010. The failure to foresee what now seems so obvious argues for new ways of understanding the geography of the region, its borders, resources, and changing cityscapes in a globalized world.

How, then, can the geography of the Middle East be described? In this chapter we present multiple geographies of the Middle East that suggest different ways of seeing and depicting the region. In this way, we hope to provide a richer description of the area than would normally be possible in a few pages, although one that is far from comprehensive.

Boundaries

A geography of the Middle East must first come to grips with how to define the *Middle East*. Compared to the area portrayed in any Western atlas published in the late nineteenth century, the political landscape of the region we know today as the Middle East is virtually unrecognizable. The *Times* (London) published *The Times Atlas* in 1895, for example, that provides a series of maps entitled "The Balkan Peninsula," "The Caucasus," "Asia Minor and Persia," "Egypt," and "Palestine" (69–76, 103). Neither would these places, as depicted in the atlas, have been any more familiar to those living in the region, who would have recognized no unified geographical entity but rather a mosaic of regions. Al-Iraq referred to the area around the Shatt al-Arab waterway, and al-Jazira was the lands between the Tigris and Euphrates rivers, including Baghdad. Sham indicated the area immediately around Damascus, and Bilad al-Sham (or country of Sham) the larger region now comprising Syria, Lebanon, Jordan, and Palestine. Egyptians still call their country Misr, but originally the term referred only to the Nile Delta and its narrow valley, not to the vast territory contained within its present-day boundaries. Today's map reveals a very different geography. As discussed in Chapters 3, 4, and 5, the present sovereign states are almost without exception creations of the twentieth century, in large measure the products of European intervention and the dismemberment of the Ottoman Empire.

The term *Middle East* is itself an unabashedly Eurocentric term. It seems to have been used first in 1902 in reference to British naval strategy in the Gulf at a time of increased Russian influence around the Caspian Sea and German plans for a Berlin-to-Baghdad railway. Largely through the columns of the *Times* (London) the term achieved wider circulation and came to denote an area of strategic concern to Britain lying between the Near East (another Eurocentric designation, essentially synonymous with the area remaining under the control of the Ottoman Empire), the expanding Russian Empire in Central Asia, and the Indian Raj (Chirol, 1903). During World War I, the British expeditionary force to Mesopotamia was generally referred to as "Middle East Forces," as distinct from Britain's "Near East Forces," which operated from bases in Egypt. After the war, these two military commands were integrated as an economy measure, but the "Middle East" designation was retained.

With the passage of time, the name became both familiar and institutionalized, first in the military commands of World War II and later in the specialist agencies of the United Nations (Smith, 1968). Yet there remain ambiguities and uncertainties in terms of its more precise delimitation. Does the Middle East include Afghanistan to the east? With the demise of the Soviet Union, should the region be reconstituted to include the new sovereign states of Armenia and Azerbaijan? Frequently, the Maghreb states of Morocco, Tunisia, and Algeria are included in discussions of the Middle East based on the fact that they share so much of its culture and history. In this book, we opted for a broad interpretation by including in its discussion Turkey, Iran, and Israel, together with all the states that belong to the Arab League.

What is surprising is that the term *Middle East* is also used by people within the region. The literal Arabic translation, *al-sharq al-awsat,* and the Turkish, *orta dogu,* can be found in books, journals, and newspapers. Interestingly, the term is most widely used in discussions of geopolitical strategies in the region. Arab commentators, for example, might discuss "US policy in the Middle East" or "Israel's relationship to the Middle East." Thus, the term is perhaps more a reference to how others, either outside the region or outside the predominant culture, view the region and is less a self-description.

The "map view" of a region is the most skeletal of possible geographies, but it is both formative and informative. Looking at a contemporary political map of the Middle East, the predominance of long, straight boundary lines stretching across hundreds of miles of desert is striking (see Map 2.1). Another revealing feature of the twentieth-century map, as Bernard Lewis points out, is that the names of countries are, for the most part, restorations or reconstructions of ancient names (1989:21–22). *Syria,* for instance, is a term that first appears in Greek histories and geographies and was subsequently adopted by the Romans as the name for an administrative

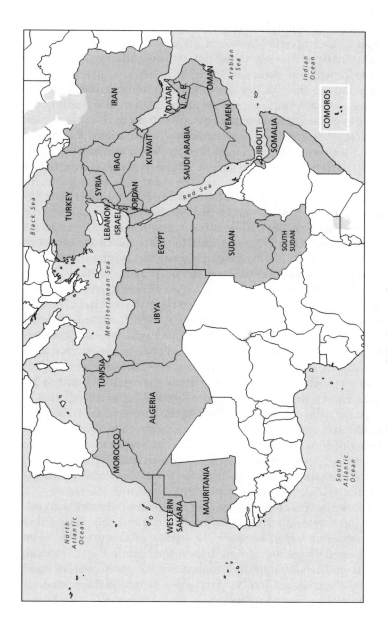

Map 2.1 Political Map of the Middle East

province. But from the time of the Arab-Islamic conquest of the seventh century, the name virtually disappeared from local use. Its reappearance dates from the nineteenth century, largely through the writing and influence of Western scholars. Similarly, although Europeans have been referring to the lands of Anatolia and Asia Minor as Turkey since the time of the Crusades, the inhabitants of this region did not use this name until the establishment of the Republic of Turkey in 1923.

To understand the changes that have occurred in the political map of the Middle East, it is helpful to recall that at the end of the sixteenth century the authority of the Ottoman Empire extended from the borders of Morocco in the west to the borders of Iran in the east, and from the Red Sea in the south to the northern and eastern shores of the Black Sea (see Map 2.2). In Europe, the Ottomans twice laid siege to Vienna. But the eighteenth and nineteenth centuries saw a gradual retreat from these high-water marks. In the Tartar and Turkish principalities from the Crimea to the Caucasus, Ottoman sovereignty was replaced by Russian domination; in the Balkans, the Ottomans confronted growing nationalist aspirations and a concerted assault by Austria and its allies; in North Africa, the Ottomans had to deal with the expansion and imposition of colonial authority involving the French in Algeria (1830) and Tunisia (1881) and the Italians in Libya (1911).

In other areas, Ottoman power was greatly weakened by the emergence of strong local rulers. In the aftermath of Napoleon's unsuccessful invasion of Egypt, for example, an Ottoman military officer named Mehmet (Muhammad) Ali established a dynasty that made Egypt virtually independent of Ottoman rule. The bankruptcy of the Egyptian administration after efforts to modernize the country's economy and infrastructure in turn opened the way to more direct European intervention in the country's affairs through a French-British Debt Commission and British occupation in 1882, although the country remained nominally under Ottoman sovereignty. In Lebanon, following a massacre of Maronite Christians by Druze in 1860 and the landing of French troops in Beirut, Britain and France forced the Ottoman sultan to establish the semiautonomous province of Mount Lebanon with a Christian governor to be appointed in consultation with European powers (Drysdale and Blake, 1985:196).

Thus, even where European powers did not control territory outright, by the end of the nineteenth century they had become deeply involved in the region's commerce and governance. The defeat of Ottoman Turkey in World War I helped create the current map of the Middle East (Fromkin, 1991). In the final dissolution of the Ottoman Empire, the remaining Arab provinces were reconstituted into the territories of Iraq, Syria, Lebanon, Transjordan, and Palestine and subjected for a brief period to direct British and French administration, albeit under the guise of a League of Nations mandate.

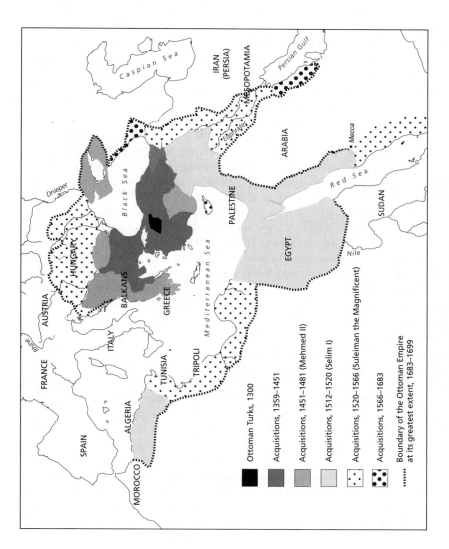

Map 2.2 Extent of the Ottoman Empire

■ Ottoman Turks, 1300

■ Acquisitions, 1359–1451

■ Acquisitions, 1451–1481 (Mehmed II)

□ Acquisitions, 1512–1520 (Selim I)

⬚ Acquisitions, 1520–1566 (Suleiman the Magnificent)

⬚ Acquisitions, 1566–1683

⋯⋯ Boundary of the Ottoman Empire at its greatest extent, 1683–1699

The map of the Middle East, then, is both very recent and frequently a cause of conflict. From a resource perspective, the lack of correspondence between political and hydrological boundaries has complicated the development of scarce water resources. New conflicts have arisen particularly over claims to offshore resources such as oil and natural gas. In the shallow, hydrocarbon-rich waters of the Gulf, where numerous small islands, sandbanks, and reefs with contested histories of settlement and occupation provide a basis for rival claims to sovereignty, the extension of land boundaries offshore has proven to be complicated and contentious. Such a dispute between Bahrain and Qatar, regarding sovereignty over the Huwar Islands and other coastal territories, became the subject of the longest arbitration case in international legal history, being finally resolved by the International Court of Justice in The Hague in March 2001 after nine years of litigation. In its adjudication of claims that drew from long-standing family and tribal disagreements over fishing and pearling rights dating back to the nineteenth century, the court essentially upheld a 1939 determination of boundaries by Britain, then the protectorate power in the region.

From a cultural perspective, boundaries are also problematic. The Kurds, for example, a non-Arab, predominantly Muslim people numbering several million, are spread across Turkey, Syria, Iraq, and Iran. Their quest for autonomy has at one time or another involved the Kurds in clashes with all four of these states. The distribution of Sunni and Shi'i Muslims, the two major subgroups of Islam, likewise does not adhere to national boundaries. The fault lines of this division cross the oil fields of southern Iraq and northern Arabia. The US incursion into Iraq starting in 2003 inflamed divisions between Sunni and Shi'i Muslims there, and these divisions have fueled both regional tensions (e.g., over Iran's influence in Iraq, Syria, Lebanon, and the Gulf) and internal conflict (e.g., in Bahrain and Lebanon).

From a political perspective, the appearance, disappearance, and tentative reappearance of Palestine demonstrate that borders are still in flux. Assigned the mandate for Palestine in 1921, Britain sought to fulfill its 1917 promise to facilitate the establishment of a national home for the Jewish people while simultaneously ensuring that, as stated in the Balfour Declaration, the civil and religious rights of non-Jewish communities in Palestine were safeguarded. The establishment of Israel in 1948 realized the Zionist vision of an independent homeland in which the Jewish people could live free of persecution, a return to the land from which they had been physically separated during nearly 2,000 years of exile. A consequence of these events has been the departure, through emigration to Israel, of large numbers of Jews whose families had lived for centuries in cities and towns throughout the Middle East and the displacement of another people, the Palestinian Arabs, who fled or were forced from their homes and lands during the fighting and sought refuge in Egypt, Jordan, Syria, Lebanon, and elsewhere in the region.

In such ways have the cartographies of the region been reimagined and refashioned in the course of the twentieth century. As the century progressed, a complex body of interests grew up around the new states of the Middle East. Up into the 1990s, Western scholars like Bernard Lewis continued to see a hardening of the boundaries created by colonial administrators and the emergence of new identities based on a sense of loyalty and attachment to country (1989:38). Yet the revived vitality of Islam, expressed differently throughout the region, is an eloquent reminder that the issue of identity is still being worked out. Likewise the rise of satellite cable news networks in the 1990s challenged the "borders" of communication controlled by the nation-state. Cable News Network (CNN) gained its worldwide following with coverage of the Gulf War and Arab networks like Al Jazeera followed a few years later. In the 2000s, the widespread adoption of Internet-based social networks, combined with media coverage by networks like Al Jazeera, made possible the wildfire-like spread of protest movements.

Likewise, the movement of people across borders should remind us that these states are not disconnected spaces. Labor migration, for instance, has played and continues to play a major role in shaping social and economic structures throughout the area, through the remittance of foreign earnings and through the direct experience of living and working overseas. Both inter- and intraregional migrations occur: there are Turkish *gastarbeiter* (guest workers) in Germany and laborers from the Maghreb in France. Prior to the 1990–1991 Gulf War, Egyptians, Yemenis, and Jordanians made up the majority of the labor force in Saudi Arabia and the Gulf states. More recently, migrants from Asia have come to make up large portions of the labor force in these countries, joined by Westerners in the professional classes. Across the region, workers from the former Soviet Union can be found in various occupations. Finally, the Iraq War and civil wars in Libya and Syria have created large numbers of refugees and exiles. It is often those who are forced to leave that write most eloquently about the attachments that exist between people and places (Parmenter, 1994). In such ways, migration, whether forced or voluntary, touches on the experience of many of us and raises questions that are central to much writing in contemporary cultural geography about the nature of place and identity in the midst of globalization (Massey and Jess, 1995).

Aridity and Water

Imagine now that we move from our map view of the region to a closer scale. Other geographical phenomena come into focus, perhaps none so important as the presence or absence of water. Aridity is a pervasive element in land and livelihood throughout the Middle East. This is perhaps most evident during the long, hot summer drought when only the lush greenery of irrigated fields interrupts the hazy brown landscape of bare hillsides and steppes, roads, and dusty towns. Palestinian writer Laila Abou-Saif describes Cairo as "sand-colored, and the people's faces are of the same color, as if they had been sculpted and layered out of the surrounding intertwining desert. . . . Even the trees are dusty and layered with the golden sand. Cairo is always beige" (1990:6).

Yet the degree of aridity varies enormously within the region. The winter months bring rainfall to many areas, particularly the higher elevations of Asia Minor, the Zagros and Elburz mountains of Iran, and the hills of Lebanon, Israel, and the West Bank. Heavy snowfalls occur as far south as Amman and Jerusalem, and the melting of winter snows has historically contributed to heavy spring flooding in the Tigris and Euphrates river basins. In these areas, the rainfall associated with midlatitude depressions moving through the Mediterranean basin during the winter months is prolonged, abundant, and reliable. It is sufficient for successful long-term cereal cultivation relying exclusively on dryland farming, or rain-fed methods.

Kandovan, a mountain village in northwestern Iran, is among the many parts of the Middle East that regularly see heavy snowfall.

In the more mountainous areas, poorer soils and steeper slopes may restrict the opportunities for farming, but elsewhere villages are clustered closely together, and the onset of the winter rains marks the beginning of the agricultural cycle of plowing, sowing, and harvesting.

As one moves southward across the region, however, the winter storms occur less frequently. Alexandria receives an average of less than 200 millimeters of rainfall a year, only a fifth of that recorded at Antalya, 200 miles to the north on the Turkish coastline. Rain-fed agriculture becomes an increasingly precarious and risky proposition. In southern Jordan and in the northern desert of Saudi Arabia, rainfall is likely to be in the form of intense and highly localized storms when it does occur. Here, the steppe merges imperceptibly into desert, traditionally the domain of nomadic pastoralists. In this zone, any form of agricultural activity other than herding is possible only where major rivers transport water from better-watered regions, as in the Nile and the Tigris and Euphrates basins, or where springs and groundwater provide a supplementary water supply for irrigation.

In an immediate sense, water has been and remains the critical "life-sustaining resource." The Quran states that every living thing is made from water, and everyone from the nomadic pastoralist to the sophisticated city dweller shares an interest in its availability and distribution. Over the centuries, Middle Eastern societies developed a range of techniques for dealing with water scarcity, many of which revealed a close adjustment to the conditions of supply (Manners, 1990). Along the Nile, for instance, traditional basin irrigation permitted effective use of the river's floodwaters for millennia. Each year farmers constructed mud embankments in the river's floodplain, dividing the land into a series of basins. Drawings and paintings from Pharaonic Egypt suggest that similar methods of water management were in use as early as the fourth millennium BCE.[1] As the Nile rose in summer, the silt-laden floodwaters were diverted into the basins and retained there for several weeks. Once the level of the Nile dropped, surplus water could be drained back into the river and a winter crop—wheat, barley, lentils, beans, berseem (Egyptian clover)—cultivated in the saturated alluvial soils. Harvesting took place in March or April, after which the land lay fallow until the next flood season. By ensuring a reliable and controlled flow of water and by contributing to the maintenance of soil fertility, basin irrigation allowed for the development of a highly productive agricultural system. Equally critical from the point of view of long-term stability, the flushing action of the annual flood prevented the buildup of salts harmful to crop growth. Basin irrigation remained the dominant method of irrigation in the Nile valley until the end of the nineteenth century, by which time the modern phase of water development had begun to take shape through the construction of barrages, annual storage reservoirs, and summer canals intended to allow for year-round irrigation and multiple cropping.

Like the basin irrigation system developed in the Nile valley, other traditional water management devices such as the *qanats* of Iran, the *shadufs* of Egypt, and the *norias* of the Orontes River in Syria had a common purpose: to make effective use of a critical resource and thereby enable societies to survive and flourish under conditions of scarcity and uncertainty. The *qanat,* a sophisticated technique for developing, collecting, and distributing groundwater through a network of underground tunnels, may well have been in use in Iran as early as the first millennium BCE: that it represented an extremely successful adaptation to a variety of local conditions is evident in the diffusion of this technique to other parts of the Middle East and North Africa, particularly during the early Arab caliphates, and from North Africa to Spain and later the New World.

As the demand for water has grown, however, newer technologies of water development intended to make more productive use of both surface water and groundwater have frequently disrupted and displaced traditional systems. Several newly independent states in the mid–twentieth century embarked on dam projects. The construction of the Aswan High Dam in the 1960s, for example, enabled all of Egypt to be irrigated on a perennial basis; made possible two, and in some cases even three, crops per year; and generated power for countrywide electrification projects. These benefits came with environmental side effects, however, including serious problems of soil salinization (White, 1988).

Herein lies one of the major challenges facing the region today. The burgeoning demand for water to meet agricultural, industrial, transportation, and urban needs would be difficult enough to satisfy even if water supplies were more abundant. In the Middle East, the problem is greatly complicated by the uneven distribution of water resources and by the lack of correspondence between political and hydrological boundaries. As a result, those countries where irrigated agriculture is of paramount importance (Egypt, Iraq, and, to a lesser extent, Israel, Jordan, and Syria) are unable to control the sources of water on which their populations and their economies depend. Roughly two-thirds of the water supply available to Arab countries has its source in non-Arab countries (Gleick, 1994). In Israel, by some estimates, between one-half and two-thirds of the water currently used for irrigation and domestic and industrial purposes actually originates outside the country's pre-1967 boundaries. In particular, the major aquifers that supply groundwater to municipalities and farms in Israel's coastal plains are actually recharged through rainfall occurring over the West Bank.

In such circumstances, it is hardly surprising that water rights and allocations became a key issue in the post-Oslo negotiations between the Israelis and the Palestinians over the future status of the West Bank. Certainly it would be quite wrong to see the conflict between Israelis and Palestinians and between Israel and neighboring Arab states as primarily a struggle over water (Libiszewski, 1995; Wolf, 2000). Nevertheless, in conjunction with other imperatives, particularly national security considerations, access to water resources is certainly a factor in strategic thinking. In 1964, for example, the Arab states made plans to divert the flow of the Hasbani and Banias headwaters of the Jordan River away from Israel. (The Hasbani, which originates in Lebanon, was to be diverted into the Litani River and from there to the Mediterranean Sea, and the Banias, originating in Syria, to a storage reservoir in Jordan on the Yarmuk River via a canal along the western edge of the Golan Heights.) These plans were brought to a halt by an Israeli attack on the construction works (Manners, 1974). And while water was not an overriding issue in the subsequent Six Day War of June 1967, the occupation by Israel of Syrian territory on the Golan Heights, a strategic plateau in southern Syria that included the Banias Springs during that war, effectively extended Israel's hydrostrategic control over this part of the Jordan drainage basin and cut Syria off from a major aquifer.

More recently, in October 2002, Lebanon's completion of a pumping project involving the Wazzani Springs, an important contributor to the flow of the Hasbani particularly during the dry summer months, provoked threats of retaliatory action from Israel and resurrected old arguments and animosities over rights to use the Jordan waters. That a relatively minor development project intended to provide a water supply to local villages should have necessitated the dispatch of UN and US mediators is perhaps an indication of the severity of the water crisis that confronts all states in the Jordan basin. More discouraging in the long term is the extent to which efforts, begun in the aftermath of the Oslo Accords, to build trust and to create joint management institutions for equitable, sustainable use of the Jordan River waters (Wolf, 1995) have been undermined by the breakdown in the peace process since 2000.

The extent to which control over water resources empowers some countries at the expense of others is well illustrated in the case of the Euphrates River. The Euphrates rises in eastern Turkey, punches its way through the edge of the Anatolian Plateau in a series of dramatic gorges, then flows across the increasingly arid steppes of Syria and Iraq to a confluence with the Tigris River (which also originates in Turkey) just above Basra, Iraq. From there, the two rivers flow together as the Shatt al-Arab to the Gulf. Although most of the huge drainage basin of the Euphrates is actually in Iraq, nearly 90 percent of the annual flow of the river is generated within Turkey. This means that the downstream users, Syria and Iraq, are vulnerable to Turkey's future development plans for the Euphrates.

Iraq has long-established claims to the Euphrates; indeed, Mesopotamian power and culture was linked to effective control over the waters of these rivers (Jacobsen and Adams, 1958). The later Sassanian and Abbasid periods (fourth to twelfth centuries) were marked by a considerable expansion of the irrigation system. In the twentieth century, first during the British Mandate and later after independence, the irrigation systems were rehabilitated and new control structures erected. In the 1970s, Iraq began planning a major storage reservoir that, like the Aswan High Dam, was intended to provide long-term storage. Despite setbacks caused by war, Iraq's long-term plans envision greater use of Euphrates water. Syria, like Iraq, is steadily making greater use of Euphrates water for irrigation development and power generation and in 1973 completed the huge al-Thawra Dam.

But it is Turkey that holds the real key to what happens in the future, and Turkey is currently in the process of implementing a truly massive water development project in southeastern Anatolia, the Güneydoğu Anadolu Projesi (GAP), that involves both the Tigris and the Euphrates rivers. If fully implemented, the GAP would involve as many as fourteen dams and storage reservoirs on the Euphrates and eight on the Tigris, plus additional power-generating facilities. This immense undertaking is intended to pump new life into Turkey's hardscrabble, semiarid southeast provinces where living standards are far below the national average, but it is clearly more than just another water development project. These provinces are home to the majority of Turkey's Kurdish population. By providing people with a more secure and comfortable livelihood, the government hopes to undercut support for the Kurdish separatist movement and bring an end to a costly and bloody conflict.

In 1990 Turkey began filling the reservoir behind the Atatürk Dam, triggering protests from both Syria and Iraq. By some estimates, the Atatürk Dam and other proposed storage and diversion projects on the Euphrates could reduce downstream flows to Syria by 40 percent and to Iraq by as much as 80 percent, especially during the dry years. Clearly, if all the proposed water projects are carried out, the total water demand will be well in excess of the normal flow of the river. Moreover, water quality is likely to be an issue for downstream users since an increasing proportion of the available flow will consist of return irrigation flows containing high concentrations of agricultural chemicals and salts.

Some see the potential for future conflict in this situation of growing competition for limited water supplies. Unfortunately, in none of the major river basins do there exist formal agreements among all riparian states (those bordering on rivers) over water rights; there is no such agreement for the Jordan River or for the Tigris and Euphrates rivers, and legal agreements for the Nile River involve only Egypt and Sudan. Since its independence, South Sudan has taken the position that it is not bound by the terms of the 1959 Nile Waters Treaty that in essence allocated the entire annual flow of the Nile between Egypt and Sudan. Instead South Sudan has indicated that it will join other upstream riparian states in the Cooperative Framework Agreement (already signed by Ethiopia, Kenya, Uganda, Rwanda, Tanzania, and Burundi), which is intended to promote their own water development needs and secure what they believe would be a more equitable distribution of the basin's water resources (Agreement on the Nile River Basin Cooperative Agreement, 2010). Boutros Boutros-Ghali's comment when he was Egypt's foreign minister to the effect that "the next war in our region will be over the waters of the Nile, not politics," has been widely repeated (for example, see Klare 2001). An alternative, more hopeful view, is that water could be a vehicle for regional cooperation. Sharing of knowledge and experience with regard to using water less wastefully—for instance through drip and subsurface irrigation systems and the recycling and reuse of wastewater, or the transfer of water from water surplus to water deficit states, as in the case of the proposed peace pipeline from Turkey through Syria to Jordan, the West Bank, Israel, and Gaza—are the kind of cooperation that could transform regional geographies.

As Will D. Swearingen describes in *Moroccan Mirages,* for many hydraulic engineers and government administrators, the ideal vision of water development has been "not a drop of water to the sea" (1987:39). Likewise, the region's marshes and wetlands have often been targets for major hydraulic engineering projects because they are perceived as empty spaces that waste potentially valuable land and water resources. But water is more than just a commodity with economic value to society, a resource to be developed, and its flow regulated on a liter-by-liter basis: water has other values and meanings to those living in the region.

People are increasingly recognizing that water sustains a range of ecological processes, which in turn support communities of fishers, hunters, reed gatherers, salt producers, and the like. The coastal lagoons of the Nile Delta, the marshes of the Shatt al-Arab, Lake Hula in Israel, Jordan's Azraq oasis, Lake Ishkeul in Tunisia, and other wetlands scattered throughout the region were once highly productive ecosystems that provided habitat and sustenance for diverse communities of plants and animals. Those living around wetlands traditionally exploited these resources, maintaining a diverse and relatively sustainable livelihood. Other nonconventional values of wetlands include absorbing and treating human sewage and other organic wastes, recharging groundwater aquifers, and acting as vital resting and feeding sites for waterfowl and shorebirds migrating between breeding grounds in northern Eurasia and wintering grounds in Africa. In many cases, these wetlands have been drained, severely polluted, or dried out as a result of groundwater withdrawals, with devastating impacts on local communities. Fishing villages around Lake Maryut near Alexandria, Egypt, have seen livelihoods destroyed due to dumping of industrial wastes. The marshes of the Azraq oasis in Jordan have been largely drained to supplement the municipal water supply of Amman. In Iraq, the government of Saddam Hussein drained portions of the Shatt al-Arab marshes at least in part for political reasons: to exercise greater control over the Marsh Arabs, a largely Shi'i people opposed to Hussein's rule. After the US invasion in 2003 and the toppling of Hussein's regime, Iraqi conservationists worked to restore the marshes, with limited success (Nature Iraq, 2011). Israelis drained the Hula marshes in the 1950s for agriculture, but later discovered that the high amount of fertilizer required to farm the drained and eroding peat was polluting the nearby Sea of Galilee. In the 1990s, the Jewish National Fund undertook a project to restore a portion of the marshes. Since the restoration was completed in 1998, the area has seen an increase in migratory waterfowl, including cranes and pelicans (Shapiro, 2002).

The Convention on Wetlands of International Importance (commonly known as the Ramsar Convention), signed in 1971, signaled a turn toward environmental conservation. To date, nineteen of the countries covered in this book are contracting parties to the convention, protecting 180 wetland areas totaling over 15 million hectares (60,000 square miles), and are committed to following the convention's guidelines of wise use in the management of these sites (Ramsar Convention Bureau, 2012). These guidelines include setting up the legal framework for protection and participatory processes to involve local communities (Parmenter, 1996). The existence of these initiatives testifies to an awareness of the complexity of water issues.

The case of Egypt offers a glimpse of the ways in which applied market forces are shaping the issues of aridity and water. Egypt, with a population over 80 million, ranks below the UN water poverty indicator of 1,000 cubic meters of water per person a year. In recent years, the state water utility has raised rates for residents in downtown Cairo. In 2004, the Egyptian government privatized its water utility under direction from the World Bank on the grounds that privatization increases "efficiency" and as a condition for loans. To be a profit-generating entity, the utility ensures that water flows uninterrupted to paying customers largely in wealthy neighborhoods, but provides less reliable service to other neighborhoods (Piper, 2012).

There are connections here between water and life that are crucial to any understanding of environment, culture, markets, and politics in the Middle East. The Quran holds out to all believers the promise of a paradise that is filled with fountains and cool, shaded watercourses, "gardens beneath which rivers flow" (Schimmel, 1985:6). Images of gardens and water, inspired by descriptions of paradise in the Quran, have had a profound influence on Islamic art and poetry (MacDougall and Ettinghausen, 1976). This promise was not limited to literary and artistic representations; it also found expression in a love of gardens that were imagined and conceived as a reflection of the beauty and serenity of paradise on earth.

This linking of the sacred and the secular, of water and life, is eloquently conveyed in a story Annemarie Schimmel relates about the puzzling question she was first asked in Anatolia by an old woman, *"Ankara'da rahmet var mı?"* [Is there mercy in Ankara?] I wondered what the question might mean in a casual conversation with some unknown person. But it meant "Is there rain in Ankara?" In Turkish, *rahmet* means both God's mercy and the blessing of rain, for it is through the blessing of rain that everything that is seemingly dead is made alive again. (1985:6)

Cityscapes

Closing in on our scale further, we move from regional phenomena like water to local environments and to the most important node of Middle East geography historically and today, its cities. In the film *Raiders of the Lost Ark,* Indiana Jones stands on a rooftop overlooking an assemblage of small white-domed houses. His Egyptian host gestures toward the scene. "Cairo," he says. "City of the living. A paradise on earth." The scene that they are looking at is more likely a small village in Tunisia. Cairo, even in the 1930s when the story takes place, was a large sprawling metropolis filled with apartment buildings, factories, government offices, theaters, museums, and all the other accoutrements of modern urban life. The film confirmed Western imaginative expectations and our own assumed position vis-à-vis this Arab city in the later twentieth century. It is exotic, alluring, and inscrutable—we gaze comfortably at this fantasy place from a high vantage point and leave it to the intrepid Indy to plunge into the labyrinthine alleyways and bazaars of Cairo itself. At the turn of the twenty-first century, with the rapid urban development of Arab Gulf cities, the US invasion of Iraq and the urban warfare that ensued, and the coverage of Arab uprisings in Tunisia, Egypt, Libya, and Syria, Westerners encountered new images of Arab cities and their citizens, images that both reinforced and challenged what outsiders thought they knew about life in the Arab world.

The Cairo of the 1930s that *Raiders of the Lost Ark* did not show might have seemed rather mundane: a vibrant, bustling city, home at that time to just over 1 million people carrying on their daily lives in ways that were far from mysterious. But vision and imagination are powerful weapons, and Middle Eastern cities have been the object of intense imagining over the course of their history. Nowhere in the Middle East is this more evident than in Jerusalem, a city sacred to three religions. Jews, Christians, and Muslims have struggled for centuries to make Jerusalem "their" city. "The chronicles of Jerusalem," Meron Benvenisti writes, "are a gigantic quarry from which each side has mined stones for the construction of myths—and for throwing at each other" (1996:4).

Cities have always been important in the history of the region, frequently developing as nodes connecting the well-traveled routes of armies and traders. To rulers, cities were constituted as centers of power and authority. In the eyes of travelers and traders, cities were almost literally oases of security, walled and protected, centers of commerce, learning, and entertainment. Al-Hariri, in a famous twelfth-century adventure story, *al-Maqamat (The Assemblies)*, wrote admiringly of Basra in present-day Iraq: "Thy heart's desire of holy things and worldly thou findest there" (1898: 164). Today the old walled cities of the region are, in most cases, small fractions of the larger urban fabric that changes with each passing day. As Janet Abu-Lughod observes, "A city at any one point in time is a still photograph of a complex system of building and destroying, of organizing and reorganizing" (1987:162). This system includes both the formal visions imposed by governors, conquerors, and administrators and the vernacular forces of ordinary citizens working to establish their own territories and routines.

Istanbul is a prime example of this dialectic between formal and vernacular. In the fourth century, the emperor Constantine moved the seat of the Roman Empire from Rome to the site of a former Greek settlement, Byzantium, located on a promontory bordered on one side by the Golden Horn and on the other by the Sea of Marmara. Although the city's official name was always Konstantinoupolis Nea Rome, "the city of Constantine that is the new Rome," it quickly became known as Constantinople, a name that retained currency even among Turks, whose documents and coins frequently referred to the city as Konstaniniye until the end of the Ottoman Empire (Çelik, 1986:12). Christianity enjoyed a special status in this new Rome, which was seen as a sacred city, its churches and monasteries housing a unique collection of holy relics and shrines that symbolized God's special favor. Justinian's great church of Haghia Sophia, its domed basilica rising above the city, epitomized the close relationship between the Byzantine state and the Christian church. But other buildings and monuments—palaces, walls, columns, churches, and aqueducts—remain embedded within today's urban fabric to recall more than 1,000 years of Roman-Byzantine rule.

When the Ottomans finally captured the city in 1453 after an eight-week siege, Sultan Mehmet II inherited a prized imperial city but one in a sad state of dilapidation. The sultan initiated a massive program of repopulation and reconstruction intended to restore the city to its past grandeur and prosperity. Thousands of people were relocated to the city, since 1930 known popularly as Istanbul, from all quarters of the empire. These included skilled artisans and craftspeople to assist in the immense task of reconstruction. Transforming the city were new palaces; great mosques with their schools, libraries, and charitable institutions; extensive bazaars and markets; and improved systems of water supply. These were the symbols of power and prosperity befitting the capital of a great empire.

In the twentieth century, with the final collapse of the Ottoman Empire, Turkish nationalists desiring to establish a secular republic along European lines made their own statement through urban planning and design. Turning their backs on Istanbul, they decided to construct a new capital in central Anatolia, hundreds of miles to the east of Istanbul, adjacent to the small town of Ankara. The design of the new Ankara was carefully planned to create an entirely different way of public life, one divorced from the Ottoman and Islamic past (Keleş and Payne, 1984). A German urban planner and architect, Hermann Jansen, was engaged to lay out a master plan for the city along the lines of a garden city, a scheme popular in Europe at the time and considered to embody the "rational" approach to urban planning. The plan specified separate zones for residences, businesses, and industry, separated by wide boulevards and interspersed with parks and public squares. The government encouraged new styles of architecture that were intended to give public expression to the nation's modern image (Bozdocan, 1994). These styles applied even to the design of ordinary residences, symbolizing the desire to shape not only the structure of the city but also the fundamentals of private life.

Istanbul and Ankara are only two examples of how visions backed up by political power organize and reorganize urban landscapes. Cairo was originally laid out by the Fatimid ruler Mu'izz al-Din in the tenth century to serve as a formal, ordered imperial capital next to the bustling commercial town of Fustat. Fustat itself had grown from the encampment of the Arab army that laid siege to the fortified Byzantine settlement of Babylon during the Arab conquest of Egypt in 640 CE.[2] In her study of Cairo, Janet Abu-Lughod relates that by one account the conquering Fatimid general "carried with him precise plans for the construction of a new princely city which Mu'izz envisaged as the seat of a Mediterranean Empire" (1971:18). The new city was named al-Qahira, the victorious city, and its monumental architecture was to become a favorite subject of European artists.

As in other cities in the Middle East, the nineteenth and twentieth centuries saw many attempts to "modernize" and "improve" Cairo. In 1867, the ruler of Egypt, Isma'il Pasha, who already had a keen interest in urban development, attended the Exposition Universelle in Paris. There he reportedly met with Baron Georges-Eugène Haussman, the urban planner who had remade Paris into the city of broad boulevards and gardens we know today. Eager to create a modern capital before the deluge of foreign visitors who would arrive following the completion of the Suez Canal, Isma'il quickly translated Haussman's principles into a new plan for Cairo. With no time to waste, Isma'il chose to leave the medieval city essentially as it was, without gas, water, sanitation, or paved streets. Instead, he concentrated on building a new European-style city to the west, complete with Haussman-style boulevards, parks, squares, villas, theaters, and an opera house (Ghannam, 1997:27). This was the city foreigners would see, and their only forays into the old Cairo would be as tourists viewing the scattered monuments of a distant past (Abu-Lughod, 1971:98–111).

On the other side of this dialectic between formal and vernacular is the sheer persistence and energy of ordinary citizens. Life grows up and around, through and between, formal plans like vines on a trellis. No urban paradigm shift is ever total. Instead, multiple layers of community and urban fabric coexist and intertwine.

Abu-Lughod (1987:163) notes how residential neighborhoods formed a crucial building block of cities in the Islamic world during medieval and even later times. These neighborhoods, which often housed people related to each other or with common ethnic or religious backgrounds, enjoyed a large measure of autonomy. The state was concerned primarily with regulating the commerce and ensuring the defense of the city. Thus, meeting the needs and protecting the interests of the neighborhood was primarily a local community responsibility. This involved such things as cleaning and maintaining the streets, providing lighting, and supervising and sanctioning behavior. A wealthier neighborhood might have its own charitable institutions, organize its own water supply with public fountains, or appoint night watchmen for internal security, often paid for through endowments to religious foundations.

When Europeans tried to penetrate these neighborhoods, they were confused and threatened by what they saw as a chaotic warren of streets that frequently ended in culs-de-sac. Yet the intent in the layout and structure of neighborhoods and even individual buildings was to minimize physical contact and protect visual separation. Thus, Islamic building laws regulated the placement of windows, the heights of adjacent buildings, and the mutual responsibilities of neighbors toward one another so as to guard and protect privacy (Abu-Lughod, 1987:167). Of course, the majority of the urban population lived in modest circumstances that bore little resemblance to the luxurious lifestyles of the rich and powerful, and this reality was reflected in the shabby construction and cramped quarters of many neighborhoods.

Neither was urban life free of hazards. The common use of wood construction in Istanbul, for example, made the city particularly vulnerable to fires. Between 1633 and 1839 the city suffered as many as 109 major conflagrations, many of which wiped out entire neighborhoods; between 1853 and 1906, this number reached 229 as fires increasingly came to play a major role in reshaping and redesigning urban architecture (Çelik, 1986: 52–53). Diseases were another harsh aspect of city life, particularly bubonic plague, which until the nineteenth century periodically reappeared to carry off large numbers of the city's population.

As in many other parts of the world, the experience in Middle Eastern cities in recent years has been one of rapid urbanization, largely as a result of the influx of rural migrants in search of employment and better living conditions. These demographic shifts have dramatically transformed not only the physical appearance of cities, but also the daily lives and routines of millions of people. In 1900, perhaps 10 percent of the region's population lived in urban settlements; by 2000, an estimated 59 percent resided in urban communities (Population Reference Bureau, 2001:4). The dominant impression of urban life in the region today is one of incessant construction and a struggle to deal with the consequences of unrestrained growth. Everywhere one looks, there are sprawling housing projects and lines of apartment blocks alongside new highways. In older neighborhoods, residents add more floors to buildings, squeezing space out of places where there seems to be none available.

The most explosive phase of urban growth has occurred within the past forty years, but many cities in the region began to experience an increase in growth in the late nineteenth century as improvements in sanitation and hygiene were reflected in declining mortality rates. By the beginning of the twentieth century, for instance, Istanbul had already begun to spread beyond the land walls that delimited the Byzantine-Ottoman city at the head of the Golden Horn. Today, the city's boundaries extend for miles along the Bosporus and along the European and Asian shores of the Sea of Marmara. Villages that in the 1950s retained a distinctive identity now remain only as names on a map, submerged beneath a tidal wave of immigrants. The construction during the 1970s and 1980s of two bridges across the Bosporus, linking Europe and Asia, symbolized the emergence of this new greater metropolitan Istanbul. In 2012, plans for a new bridge sparked a backlash from environmentalists, who worried about traffic and the further loss of green space (Letsch, 2012).

Cairo, which at the beginning of the nineteenth century had a population of around 250,000, had grown to a city of 1 million people by the mid-1930s. By 1960 Greater Cairo's population had reached 3.6 million, and by 1970 more than 7 million. In the 2006 census, the population of the metropolis (made up by the governorates of Cairo, Giza, and Qalubiya) is estimated to be near 20 million people. Put slightly differently, in the past forty years, Cairo has added to its population three cities comparable to the one that existed in 1960.

Clearly, the pace of urbanization has overwhelmed planners. Traffic congestion, lack of services, loss of amenities and open space, air pollution, inadequate water supply, and overloaded sewage treatment systems have become an all-too-familiar experience in many cities. Housing construction in many cities failed to keep pace with urban growth. Many newcomers to the cities live in "temporary" housing, often referred to as squatter settlements. By one estimate the *ashwa'iyyat* (spontaneous communities) areas of Cairo house more than 11 million people in Greater Cairo (Sims, 2010; Bayat and el-Gawhary, 1997:5–6). In Turkey, such spontaneous settlements are called *gecekondus*—literally, "placed there at night"—reflecting the speed with which houses are illegally erected on vacant land. For those of us who see such settlements only from the outside, Latife Tekin's compelling novel *Berji Kristin: Tales from the Garbage Hills* (1996) conveys some sense of what life must be like in a squatter settlement on the edge of Istanbul, the experiences, the fears, the rumors, the wind, and the dust.

Although governments on occasion have attempted to demolish illegal settlements, they also periodically have offered construction pardons and provided title to land. Over time, therefore, many of these squatter settlements have acquired legal status and become functionally and administratively integrated into the urban fabric. Makeshift houses have been replaced by more permanent residences and modest apartment blocks. Thus, temporary housing has been transformed into a more permanent feature of most large Middle Eastern cities, with numerous local variations such as Cairo's City of the Dead, where families have taken over the aboveground tombs for housing. In these new neighborhoods, where public services remain inadequate, residents often organize themselves or seek assistance from nongovernmental or religious organizations to pave streets, install water lines, organize garbage collection, establish a health clinic, or start a bus service. Neighborhood self-help and improvement associations play an important, albeit often unacknowledged, role in transforming neighborhoods and nurturing a sense of community and identity among recent migrants to the city. Thus, for many urban residents, the neighborhood has continued to constitute the most important element, both spatially and socially, in their conception of the city and has played a crucial community role in the struggles of the Arab uprisings.

The past twenty years have seen a parallel dramatic transformation of urban spaces in the development of wealthy enclaves and, in the case of the Arab Gulf states, of entire cities devoted to the support of and consumption by wealthy elites, both local and global. This shift reflects reconfigurations of power relations in the region. Neoliberal economic policies, encouraged by world financial institutions, and which in theory liberate entrepreneurial practices based on free trade, free markets, and private property rights, have been partially adopted by many authoritarian regimes in the Middle East in a way that has cemented the power of these regimes and rewarded supportive behavior by institutions, companies, and individuals who had sufficient wealth to participate in the new economy and reinforce the system.

Within Cairo, for example, government-owned land has been opened for real estate development in the form of upscale residential subdivisions, shopping malls, and office space. Planners have elected to build elevated highways through neighborhoods, facilitating movement between the new high-end residential suburbs on the city's periphery and the banks, offices, and ministries in the center (Sims, 2010; Denis, 1997:9). Older neighborhoods near the center have been cleared away to make room for modern luxury apartments, conference centers, and five-star hotels, and the former residents relocated in public housing projects.

Despite the dislocation and disruption that this entails in daily living and working arrangements, the government's efforts to transform and "improve" the appearance of the city are matched by the practices and resolve of those who have been relocated, as they reconstruct the housing the state has built for them by illegally erecting partitions, adding balconies, and creating new public and private spaces to suit their needs (Ghannam, 1997:17–20). David Sims, an urban planner at the American University in Cairo, celebrates the resiliency of Cairo's residents for their ability to create and manage the "informal" city despite government policy indifferent to their needs. He notes that after thirty years of development, the carefully planned satellite cities developed around Cairo house only 800,000 people while 11 million Egyptians live in the informal *ashwa'iyyat* (spontaneous communities) (Sims, 2010). Even in Dubai, the epicenter of global financial-based real estate development and "starchitecture" (development through the creation of eye-popping buildings designed by star architects), Yasser Elsheshtawy (2008) documents how Asian migrant laborers who make up the vast majority of Dubai's population have created an informal city of their own that rivals central planning.

Under these new conditions, the cityscapes of the Middle East are competing on a global field. For example, the city of Amman "is being remade and presented to investors as a new city that conforms to [the] globalized benchmarks" of speed (C. Parker, 2009:110). Networks of highways, tunnels, and bridges are serving to restructure cites in a way that advances global connections. Privileging cars and customers, new patterns of urban circulation are emerging. Sims (2010) points out that only 14 percent of Cairo's population owns cars, yet transportation investments by the government have been almost wholly in new roads and highways. Infrastructure that privileges automobiles generates an urban landscape that is hostile to pedestrians. Yet as with housing, urban residents without cars have started to appropriate these spaces. David Kendall (2012) observes how migrant construction workers in Dubai use the marginal spaces created by road infrastructure for walking, informal gatherings, and unofficial soccer and cricket games. Economic reform applied spatially creates new sites of engagement as well as exclusion between citizens. New appendages to cities in the Middle East often carry an entrance fee, whether it is actual money or a proper dress code or a car; inequality is inscribed into the infrastructure itself and development is uneven. Thus, restructuring can be said to create enclaves that bypass the city itself and hide the poor, the dispossessed, and the migrant from the eye of the motorist (Schwedler, 2012).

In order to understand the unrest brought on by the Arab uprisings, it is crucial to consider not only the production of space dedicated to consumption and economic activity, but also the impact of colonial rule on urban form. Traditionally, public space in Middle Eastern cities was found in and

Amman, set amid seven steep hills, has been expanding rapidly in recent decades.

around mosques and markets. Urban redevelopment that copied the Western styles of straight, wide streets also brought additional public spaces to the city. The Arab uprisings symbolize a moment of reclaiming these spaces and utilizing them as an active political space. There is a multitude of causes for the uprisings, but through them we see a connecting link between borders, economics, land, water, and the changing cityscapes of the Middle East.

Conclusion

In his essay "Geography Is Everywhere," Denis Cosgrove writes about "the real magic of geography—the sense of wonderment at the human world, the joy of seeing and reflecting upon the richly variegated mosaic of human life and of understanding the elegance of its expression in the human landscape" (1985:120). We hope this chapter reflects that rich mosaic and conveys a sense of interconnectedness: the ways in which water links politics, economy, and religion; the ways in which cities are shaped by global trading connections, colonial experiences, labor migration, and flows of capital as well as local practices and imaginings; and the ways in which species, water, people, goods, capital, and ideas move across political boundaries. We would also like to emphasize the connections that places have with their pasts (Massey, 1995). By this, we mean not simply the ways in which the past is present materially in the present-day landscape of the Middle East, but the ways in which the past may be present in the memories of people and in the conscious and unconscious constructions of the histories of places (Massey, 1995:187).

All of this suggests that we need to think about a borderless world as much as we do about borders in terms of understanding people's knowledge and experience of place. Clearly, the events of the early twenty-first century in the Middle East—US military interventions, transformative urban development, popular democratic uprisings—all speak to global linkages and flows. But the region has a long history of these global linkages and, through a historical understanding of these, we might come to a clearer understanding of the region. Connections between past and present and the absence of boundaries are brilliantly evoked in Amitav Ghosh's *In an Antique Land: History in the Guise of a Traveler's Tale* (1994), in which the writer, a Hindu researcher from India, reconstructs the journey and experience of a former Indian slave who, early in the twelfth century, had traveled to Cairo on behalf of Abraham Ben Yiju, a Jewish trader from Tunisia living in Mangalore. At one level, the writer parallels the slave's journey, traveling to Tunisia and Egypt, living with a Muslim family in a small village outside Cairo, and learning a form of spoken Arabic that later proved helpful in reading medieval documents. At another level, the research, based on the Genizah Documents (letters and other items found in the genizah, or storeroom, of a Cairo synagogue), "bears witness to a pattern of movement so fluent and far-reaching that they make the journeys of later medieval travelers, such as Marco Polo and Ibn Battuta seem unremarkable in comparison" (Ghosh, 1994:157).

As the letters between Ben Yiju and other merchants indicate, travel between Morocco, Egypt, Syria, Yemen, and India, although not free of risk (one letter describes how a merchant had been captured by pirates off the coast of Gujarat), was frequent and regular. Here is a very different construction of the geography of the region. Looking at today's political map and the divided world of the Middle East, it is difficult for us to step back and imagine the possibility of a world in which frontiers were not clearly or precisely defined, a place where Muslims and Jews and Christians traveled freely and crossed paths frequently in the course of everyday life and commerce. S. D. Goitein describes this period, roughly from the tenth through the thirteenth centuries, as the High Middle Ages when the Mediterranean area "resembled a free-trade community [in which] the treatment of foreigners, as a rule, was remarkably liberal" (1967:66). Goitein notes that, with few exceptions, the hundreds of documents and letters in the genizah archive describing travels to or in foreign countries "have nothing to say about obstacles put in the way of the traveler for political reasons" (1967:59).

Not only merchants and traders, but also artisans, scholars, and craftspeople were involved in this "continuous coming and going." Added to this were the many Muslims who made the hajj (pilgrimage to Mecca). Until the advent of the steamship in the nineteenth century, most hajjis traveled to Mecca with one of the great overland caravans that set out each year from Cairo, Damascus, and Baghdad. But even in the fifteenth and sixteenth centuries, caravans could consist of several thousand camels, hundreds of horses, and 30,000 to 40,000 people (Peters, 1994), giving some sense of the large numbers of people involved. In earlier centuries, the round-trip journey could take several years for people from North and West Africa, China, and Southeast Asia. From India, the seventeenth-century pilgrim Safi ibn Wali Qazvini spent a year getting to and from Mecca (Pearson, 1994:45–46). Like other literate pilgrims, Qazvini wrote an account of his travels that was intended at least in part as a guide for others, providing a wealth of details about the pilgrimage route and practical information about rest stations, watering points, and the costs of purchasing supplies.

The hajj is still an extraordinary undertaking for many Muslims in terms of both logistics and financing. But for the 2 million who now make the hajj each year, the same sort of information contained in Qazvini's narrative, together with visa application forms, is to be found on the Internet. And once again, through such experiences as the hajj, local places and communities are linked to and become part of the world beyond. Tourists traveling along the Nile may be surprised to see paintings of jumbo jets adorning the mud brick walls of humble houses. Here is a poignant and elegant reminder of the significance of the hajj in the lives of these villagers, conveyed in a tradition that has evolved over the past century whereby the experience of a lifetime—circling the Ka'ba, praying at Ararat, and making a joyful homecoming—is graphically captured and portrayed in folk art and architecture (A. Parker and Neal, 1995).

In contemporary atlases, the Middle East is usually divided into a familiar mosaic of nation-states, each nation with its distinctive color like detachable pieces of a jigsaw puzzle as if each were a discrete object. Benedict Anderson sees nations as "imagined political communities" in the sense that members of the nation do not know most of their fellow members, yet imagine themselves part of a broader community sharing a deep sense of fraternity and comradeship (1991:6–7). For Anderson, the "map-as-logo" contributes to this imaginative process, not least because as "this 'jig-saw' effect became normal, each 'piece' could be wholly detached from its geographic context" (1991:175). Today that jigsaw is becoming less clear-cut, and the people of the region continue to remake their communities in ways that harken back to the past and reflect contemporary global connections. Our desire is that this chapter will encourage people to explore what lies beneath the surface of the map, to reconnect the map with its geographic context, to ask critical questions about how maps and knowledge of the region have been constituted, and to imagine alternative geographies.

Notes

This chapter was written by Ian R. Manners and Barbara McKean Parmenter and updated for this edition with assistance from Ryan King. We would like to express particular thanks to Kay Ebel and Zjaleh Hajibashi for helpful comments on an early version of this chapter.

1. BCE (before the common era) is viewed by non-Christians as a more neutral term for marking history than BC (before Christ).

2. CE (of the common era) is a neutral term for AD (*anno Domini* or in the year of the Lord).

Bibliography

Abou-Saif, Laila. 1990. *Middle East Journal: A Woman's Journey into the Heart of the Arab World*. New York: Charles Scribner's Sons.

Abu-Lughod, Janet. 1971. *Cairo: 1001 Years of the City Victorious*. Princeton: Princeton University Press.

———. 1987. "The Islamic City—Historic Myth, Islamic Essence, and Contemporary Relevance." *International Journal of Middle Eastern Studies* 19, no. 2: 155–176.

Agreement on the Nile River Basin Cooperative Agreement. 2010. International Water Law Project. http://www.internationalwaterlaw.org/documents/regional-docs/Nile_River_Basin_Cooperative_Framework_2010.pdf.

Anderson, Benedict. 1991. *Imagined Communities*. London: Verso.

Bayat, Asef, and Karim el-Gawhary (eds.). 1997. "Cairo: Power, Poverty and Urban Sprawl." *Middle East Report,* no. 202:2–30.

Benvenisti, Meron. 1996. *City of Stone: The Hidden History of Jerusalem*. Trans. Maxine Kauffman Nunn. Berkeley: University of California Press.

Blake, Gerald, John Dewdney, and Jonathan Mitchell. 1987. *The Cambridge Atlas of the Middle East and North Africa*. Cambridge: Cambridge University Press.

Bozdocan, Sibel. 1994. "Architecture, Modernism and Nation-Building in Kemalist Turkey." *New Perspectives on Turkey* 10:37–55.

Çelik, Zeynep. 1986. *The Remaking of Istanbul*. Seattle: University of Washington Press.

Chirol, V. 1903. *The Middle East Question, or Some Political Problems of Indian Defence*. London: John Murray.

Cosgrove, Denis. 1985. "Geography Is Everywhere: Culture and Symbolism in Human Landscapes." Pp. 118–135 in Derek R. Gregory and Rex Walford (eds.), *Horizons in Human Geography*. London: Macmillan.

Denis, Eric. 1997. "Urban Planning and Growth in Cairo." *Middle East Report,* no. 202:8–12.

Drysdale, Alasdair, and Gerald Blake. 1985. *The Middle East and North Africa: A Political Geography*. New York: Oxford University Press.

Elsheshtawy, Yasser. 2008. "Transitory Sites: Mapping Dubai's 'Forgotten' Urban Spaces." *International Journal of Urban and Regional Research* 32, no. 4: 968–988.

Fromkin, David. 1991. May. "How the Modern Middle East Map Came to Be Drawn." *Smithsonian,* pp. 132–146.

Ghannam, Fara. 1997. "Relocation and the Use of Urban Space in Cairo." *Middle East Report,* no. 202:17–20.

Ghosh, Amitav. 1994. *In an Antique Land: History in the Guise of a Traveler's Tale*. New York: Vintage Books.

Gleick, Peter H. 1994. "Water, War and Peace in the Middle East." *Environment* 36, no. 3:6–15, 35–42.

Goitein, S. D. 1967. *A Mediterranean Society: Economic Foundations.* Berkeley: University of California Press.

al-Hariri. 1898. *The Assemblies of al Hariri: Translated from the Arabic, with an Introduction and Notes Historical and Grammatical,* edited by Thomas Chenery. London: Williams & Norgate.

Jacobsen, Thorkild, and Robert M. Adams. 1958. November. "Salt and Silt in Ancient Mesopotamian Agriculture." *Science,* pp. 1251–1258.

Keleş, Ruşen, and Geoffrey Payne. 1984. "Turkey." Pp. 165–197 in Martin Wynn (ed.), *Planning and Urban Growth in Southern Europe.* London: Mansell.

Kendall, D. 2012. "Always Let the Road Decide." *South Asian Diaspora* 4, no. 1:45–54.

Klare, M. T. 2001. "The New Geography of Conflict." *Foreign Affairs* 80, no. 3: 49–61.

Letsch, Constanze. 2012. June 8. "Plan for New Bosphorus Bridge Sparks Row over Future of Istanbul." *The Guardian.*

Lewis, Bernard. 1989. "The Map of the Middle East: A Guide for the Perplexed." *American Scholar* (Winter), pp. 19–38.

Libiszewski, Stephan. 1995. *Water Disputes in the Jordan Basin Region and Their Role in the Resolution of the Arab-Israeli Conflict.* Zurich: Center for Security Studies and Conflict Research.

MacDougall, Elisabeth B., and Richard Ettinghausen (eds.). 1976. *The Islamic Garden.* Washington, DC: Dumbarton Oaks Trustees for Harvard University.

Manners, Ian R. 1974. "Problems of Water Resource Management in a Semi-Arid Environment: The Case of Irrigation Agriculture in the Central Jordan Valley." Pp. 95–114 in B. S. Hoyle (ed.), *Spatial Aspects of Development.* London: Wiley.

———. 1990. "The Middle East." Pp. 39–66 in Gary A. Klee (ed.), *World Systems of Traditional Resource Management.* New York: Halstead Press.

Massey, Doreen. 1995. "Places and Their Pasts." *History Workshop Journal* 39: 182–192.

Massey, Doreen, and Pat Jess (eds.). 1995. *A Place in the World? Places, Cultures, and Globalization.* Oxford: Oxford University Press for the Open University.

Mitchell, Timothy. 1988. *Colonising Egypt.* Cambridge: Cambridge University Press.

Nature Iraq. 2011. August. *Nature Iraq Progress Report: Mesopotamian Marshlands National Park and Other Marshland Issues.* www.natureiraq.org.

Parker, Ann, and Avon Neal. 1995. *Hajj Paintings: Folk Art of the Great Pilgrimage.* Washington, DC: Smithsonian Institution Press.

Parker, Christopher. 2009. "Tunnel-Bypasses and Minarets of Capitalism: Amman as Neoliberal Assemblage." *Political Geography* 28, no. 2:110–120.

Parmenter, Barbara. 1994. *Giving Voice to Stones: Place and Identity in Palestinian Literature.* Austin: University of Texas Press.

———. 1996. "Endangered Wetlands and Environmental Management in North Africa." Pp. 155–174 in Will D. Swearingen and Abdellatif Bencherifa (eds.), *The North African Environment at Risk.* Boulder: Westview Press.

Pearson, M. N. 1994. *Pious Passengers: The Hajj in Earlier Times.* London: C. Hurst.

Peters, F. E. 1994. *The Hajj: The Muslim Pilgrimage to Mecca and the Holy Places.* Princeton: Princeton University Press.

Piper, Karen. 2012. July 12. "Revolution of the Thirsty." *Places.* http://places.design observer.com.

Population Reference Bureau. 2001. *Populations Trends and Challenges in the Middle East and North Africa.* www.prb.org/pdf.

Ramsar Convention Bureau. 2012. *Contracting Parties to Ramsar Convention on Wetlands.* www.ramsar.org.

Schimmel, Annemarie. 1985. "The Water of Life." *Environmental Design* 2:6–9.

Schwedler, Jillian. 2012. "Amman Cosmopolitan: Spaces and Practices of Aspiration and Consumption," *Comparative Studies of South Asia, Africa and the Middle East* 30, no. 3:947–962.

Shapiro, Haim. 2002. November 1. "For the Birds." *Jerusalem Post,* p. 20.

Sims, David. 2010. *Understanding Cairo: The Logic of a City Out of Control.* Cairo: American University in Cairo Press.

Smith, Gordon C. 1968. "The Emergence of the Middle East." *Journal of Contemporary History* 3, no. 3:3–17.

Swearingen, Will D. 1987. *Moroccan Mirages: Agrarian Dreams and Deceptions, 1912–1986.* Princeton: Princeton University Press.

Tekin, Latife. 1996. *Berji Kristin: Tales from the Garbage Hills.* Trans. Ruth Christie and Saliha Parker. London: Marion Boyars.

Times (London). 1895. *The Times Atlas.* London: Printing House Square.

White, Gilbert. 1988. "The Environmental Effects of the High Dam at Aswan." *Environment* 30, no. 7:4–11, 34–40.

Wolf, Aaron T. 1995. "International Water Dispute Resolutions: The Middle East Multilateral Working Group on Water Resources." *Water International* 20, no. 3:141–150.

———. 2000. "Hydrostrategic Territory in the Jordan Basin." Pp. 63–120 in Hussain A. Amery and Aaron T. Wolf (eds.), *Water in the Middle East: A Geography of Peace.* Austin: University of Texas Press.

3

The Historical Context

Arthur Goldschmidt Jr.

History is the study of humanity's recorded past; that of the Middle East is the world's longest. In this area many staple crops were first cultivated, most farm animals were first domesticated, and the earliest agricultural villages were founded. Here, too, were the world's oldest cities, the first governments and law codes, and the earliest ethical monotheistic systems. A crossroads for people and ideas, the Middle East has sometimes contained only one state or a single culture, but usually it has split into competing fragments. During eras of internal cohesion and power, Middle Easterners controlled remote parts of Europe, Asia, and Africa. At times of dissension and weakness, however, they were invaded and ruled by outsiders. When they could not drive out the interlopers, they adjusted to them and subtly made their rulers adapt to their own ways. The interplay between invasion and accommodation is characteristic of the region. In this chapter, I will summarize Middle East history: the ancient empires, the rise of Islam and its civilization, the area's subordination to European control, and its struggle for political independence.

The Ancient Middle East
Environment has shaped much of the region's history. As polar ice caps receded and rainfall diminished, hunters and food gatherers had to find ways to control their sources of sustenance. Hunting and gathering as a way of life died out in the Middle East some 5,000 years ago, giving way to pastoral nomadism and settled agriculture. Archaeologists have found the world's oldest farming villages in northeastern Africa and in the highlands of Asia Minor. Many people migrated to the Nile, Euphrates, and Tigris

river valleys where they learned how to tame the annual floods to water their fields.

As grain cultivation spread, farmers improved their implements and pottery. They needed governments to organize the building of dams, dikes, and canals for large-scale irrigation, to regulate water distribution, and often to protect farmers from invading herders. Although the nomads at times served the settled people as merchants and soldiers, they also pillaged their cities and farms. Even though sedentary farmers and nomadic herders often fought against each other, they and the city dwellers built the civilizations of the Middle East.

The first states based on agriculture were the kingdoms of the Upper and Lower Nile, conjoined around 3000 BCE to form Egypt; and the Kingdom of Sumer, which had arisen a bit earlier in Mesopotamia, the land between the Euphrates and Tigris rivers. Both developed strong monarchies supported by elaborate bureaucracies, codes of conduct, and religious doctrines that integrated the government system into a cosmological order. Their rulers marshaled large workforces to protect the lands from floods and invaders. A complex division of labor facilitated the development of writing, calculation, architecture, metallurgy, and hydraulic engineering.

Semitic and Indo-Iranian Invasions

The river states were disrupted and partially transformed by outside infiltrators and invaders. Sumer was conquered by peoples who spoke Semitic languages, producing Babylonia, which reached its height during the reign of the lawgiver Hammurabi (r. 1792–1750 BCE). Meanwhile, Indo-European invaders from the north mixed with local peoples in Anatolia and Persia and introduced the horse into the region. The horse-drawn chariot enabled the Hyksos, another Semitic people, to occupy the Nile Delta from 1720 BCE to 1570 BCE. The Babylonians absorbed their invaders, but the Egyptians expelled theirs and extended their empire into Syria.

Internal dissension and external pressures finally weakened Egypt and Babylonia, leading to a bewildering series of invasions and emerging states around 1000 BCE. As the Middle East's climate grew drier, Semitic peoples, including the Phoenicians and the Hebrews, migrated from the Arabian Desert into the better-watered lands of Syria and Mesopotamia. The Phoenicians of Syria's coast became the ancient world's main mariners, traders, and colonizers. They also invented the phonetic alphabet. Under King David, who ruled in the early tenth century BCE, the Hebrews set up a kingdom in Palestine, with its capital at Jerusalem; later this state split and fell to mighty conquerors. The Hebrews developed a faith in one God, who according to the Bible appeared to Moses on Mount Sinai and later to the prophets. Elements of this ethical monotheism had existed in earlier Middle

Eastern religions, but the Hebrews' ideas, crystallized in Judaism, profoundly shaped the intellectual history of both the Middle East and the West.

As people learned how to forge iron tools and weapons, they could form larger and longer-lasting empires. About 1350 BCE, Babylonia gave way to Assyria, centered in northern Mesopotamia. At its height (around 700 BCE), Assyria ruled Syria and even Egypt. Its Semitic successor, Chaldea, upheld Babylon's glory for another century. Then Mesopotamia—indeed the whole Middle East, came under the rule of Persia's king Cyrus (r. 560–530 BCE).

From Cyrus's reign to modern times, the political history of the Middle East has centered on the rise and fall of successive multinational empires: Persia, Greece, Rome, the Arabs, the Seljuk Turks, the Mongols, and the Ottomans. Like Babylon, most of these empires were formed by outside invasions. External rule stirred up local resistance forces that eventually sapped the rulers' strength, causing the states to break up and fall prey to new invaders. Often the conquerors adopted the institutions and beliefs of their Middle Eastern subjects; rarely could they impose their own uniformly.

The Persian empire of Cyrus and his heirs, the Achaemenids, was the prototype of this multicultural system. Sprawling from the Indus valley to the Nile, the empire could not make its subjects think and act alike. Instead, it accepted their beliefs and practices so long as they obeyed its laws, paid their taxes, and sent men to the Persian army. The satraps (provincial governors) were given broad civil, judicial, and fiscal powers by the Persian emperor. A feudal landownership system kept the local aristocrats loyal, and a postal system and road network—along with a uniform coinage, calendar, and administrative language—also helped to unite the empire. Achaemenid Persia survived two centuries before it fell to Alexander the Great.

Greek and Roman Rule

Alexander's whirlwind conquest of the Middle East between 332 BCE and 323 BCE marks a critical juncture in the area's history. For the next millennium, it belonged to the Hellenistic world. Alexander wanted to fuse Greek culture with that of the Middle East, taking ideas, institutions, and administrators from the Egyptians, Mesopotamians, and Persians. This fusion did not occur in his lifetime, nor was it ever complete, but from Alexander to Muhammad the Mediterranean world and the Middle East shared a common civilization. The centers of its cultural blending were the coastal cities, of which the greatest was Alexandria. Alexander's descendants in Egypt, the Ptolemies, ruled the country for three centuries. They erected monumental buildings, such as the Alexandria Lighthouse, one of the seven wonders of the ancient world, and the Museum (academy of scholars), which housed the largest library in antiquity.

Southern Anatolia, Syria, and Mesopotamia were ruled for two centuries by the Seleucids, who were the descendants of one of Alexander's generals. In the third century BCE, the Seleucids lost control of their eastern lands to another dynasty descended from some of Alexander's soldiers, and Persia regained its independence as Parthia.

Meanwhile, a new state was rising farther west: Rome. Having taken Carthage, Macedonia, and Greece by 100 BCE, the Roman legions marched eastward, conquering Asia Minor, Syria, and Egypt. Once again most of the Middle East was united under an ecumenical empire; only Persia and part of Mesopotamia were ruled by Parthia. Like earlier states, Rome absorbed much from its Middle Eastern subjects, including several religions, two of which, Mithraism and Christianity, vied for popular favor throughout the Roman Empire. Christianity finally won. After his conversion, the emperor Constantine (r. 306–337 CE) moved the capital—and Rome's economic and cultural center—to Byzantium, renamed Constantinople. But the city gave its old name to Rome's successor state, the Byzantine Empire.

Under Roman rule, commercial cities flourished. Syrian and Egyptian merchants grew rich from the trade between Europe, Asia, and eastern Africa. Arab camel nomads (bedouin) prospered as carriers of cloth and spices. Other Middle Easterners navigated the Red Sea, the Gulf, and the Indian Ocean. But Roman rule was enforced by a large occupying army, and grain-producing Syria and Egypt were taxed heavily. Rome's leaders did not always tolerate their subjects' beliefs. Roman soldiers destroyed the Jewish temple in Jerusalem, and many of Jesus' early followers were martyred. Christian Rome proved even less tolerant. Many Christians in North

A people known as the Nabataeans carved this monastery into solid rock in Petra, Jordan, an ancient city that was annexed by the Roman Empire in the first century BCE.

Africa and Egypt espoused heterodox beliefs that the emperors viewed as treasonous. Their efforts to suppress heresy alienated many of their Middle Eastern subjects in the fifth and sixth centuries CE.

Rome (and later Byzantium) had one major rival: Persia. There the Parthians gave way in the third century CE to the Sassanid dynasty. Bolstered by a powerful military aristocracy and the resources of many Hellenized religious refugees from Byzantium, Sassanid Persia threatened Byzantine rule in the Middle East. Early in the seventh century, the Sassanids briefly overran Syria, Palestine, and Egypt. The Hellenistic era of Middle Eastern history was coming to an end.

The Islamic Middle East as an Autonomous System

The revelation of Islam to an unlettered Meccan merchant in the early seventh century, the unification of hitherto feuding Arab tribes under this new religion, the rapid conquest of the Middle East and North Africa, the conversion of millions of Asians and Africans to Islam, and the development of Islamic civilization under a succession of empires marked a new epoch. Egyptians, Syrians, and Persians influenced the beliefs of their Arab conquerors just as they had transformed and absorbed earlier invaders. Yet the rise of Islam led to new ideas and institutions, monuments, and memories, which continue to affect Middle Eastern peoples profoundly.

The Arabs Before Islam

Once the camel had been domesticated around 3000 BCE, bands of people began roaming the Arabian Peninsula in search of water and forage for their flocks. These early Arabs composed poems that embodied their code of values: bravery in battle, patience in misfortune, persistence in revenge, protection of the weak, defiance of the strong, loyalty to the tribe, hospitality to the guest, generosity to the needy, and fidelity in carrying out promises. These were the virtues that people needed to survive in the desert. Their poems, recited from memory, expressed the joys and sorrows of nomadic life, hailed the bravery of their heroes, lauded their own tribes, and lampooned their rivals. Even now Arabs recite these poems and often repeat their precepts.

In Roman times, the southern Arabs played a larger role in the world; they developed Yemen, colonized Ethiopia, and crossed the Indian Ocean. The northern Arabs were relatively isolated. Some adopted Judaism or Christianity, but most practiced animism (the belief that every object, whether animate or inanimate, has a spirit). One of their tribes, the Quraysh, built a shrine, the Ka'ba, at a small desert city called Mecca on the main trade route between Syria and Yemen. Once a year, the pagan tribes of northwestern Arabia suspended their quarrels to make pilgrimages to the Ka'ba, which housed idols representing tribal deities.

Muhammad

In Mecca, around 570 CE, one of the world's greatest religious leaders, Muhammad, was born to a minor branch of the Quraysh. Orphaned as a child, Muhammad was reared by an uncle as a caravan trader. Upon reaching manhood, he became the agent for a rich merchant widow, Khadija, whom he married. Until he was forty years old, Muhammad was simply a Meccan trader. But he was troubled by the widening gulf between the accepted Arab virtues of bravery and generosity and the blatantly acquisitive practices of Mecca's business leaders. Often he went to a hill near Mecca to meditate.

One day in the Arab month of Ramadan, Muhammad heard a voice exhorting him to recite. Despite his protest that he could not read, the voice (later identified as the angel Gabriel) ordered him to testify to the existence of a creator god, called Allah, to proclaim God's existence to the Arabs, and to warn them of an imminent judgment day when all people would be called to account for what they had done. As he received new revelations, he began to share them in the community. Those who accepted Muhammad's message called themselves Muslims and their religion Islam, or submission to the will of God, the creator and sustainer.

Muhammad's public recitation of his revelations disturbed the Meccan leaders. If the Arabs accepted Islam, would they stop their annual pilgrimages to the Ka'ba, so lucrative to local merchants? Why did God reveal his message to Muhammad, rather than to one of the rich and powerful Quraysh leaders? The pagan Meccans persecuted the Muslims. After Muhammad's uncle and protector died, they could no longer live in Mecca. Finally the Arabs of Medina, a city north of Mecca, asked Muhammad to arbitrate their tribal disputes and accepted Islam as the condition for his coming there.

The hijra (emigration) of Muhammad and his followers from Mecca is, for Muslims, the crucial event in history. The Muslim calendar begins in the year in which it occurred, 622 CE, for it was in Medina that Muhammad formed the Islamic *umma* (a community ruled by a divine plan). Politics and religion are united in Islam; God, speaking to humanity through Muhammad, is the supreme lawgiver. Thus the Prophet became a political leader and, when the Meccans tried to destroy the *umma,* a military commander as well. Buttressed by their faith, the Muslims of Medina defeated Meccan armies larger and stronger than their own, converted most of the pagan Arab tribes, and finally won Mecca over to Islam. In 630 CE, Muhammad made a triumphal pilgrimage to the Ka'ba, smashed its pagan idols, and declared it a Muslim shrine. Two years later, having united much of Arabia under Islam, he died.

Islamic Beliefs and Institutions

Muslims believe in one God, all powerful and all knowing, who has no partner and no offspring. God has spoken to a succession of human messengers, of whom the last was Muhammad. To the Jewish prophets God imparted the Torah, and to Jesus and his disciples the Gospels. Muslims believe that Jews and Christians corrupted their scriptures so God sent a perfected revelation, the Quran, to Muhammad. Although Muslims regard the Quran as truer than the Bible in its present form, they do not deny any of God's prophets, honoring Abraham, Moses, and Jesus. Muslims also believe in a judgment day when God will assess all people and consign them to heaven or hell.

Muslim duties are summed up as the "five pillars of Islam": statement of belief in God and in Muhammad as his Prophet; ritual prayer five times daily; fasting in the daylight hours of the month of Ramadan; payment of part of one's property or income to provide for the needy; and the pilgrimage to Mecca. Muslims also abstain from drinking alcoholic beverages, eating pork, gambling, and all licentious and dishonest acts. Standards of sexual morality are strict, limiting relations between men and women outside marriage. Muslims ascribe human misdeeds to ignorance or forgetfulness; God forgives those who repent.

Islam is a way of life. It prescribes how people relate to one another as well as their duties to God. Muhammad's *umma* aspired to serve as the ideal earthly setting in which believers could prepare for the judgment day. In the centuries after Muhammad's death, ulama (scholars of Islam) developed an elaborate legal code, sharia, to regulate all aspects of human behavior. Sharia was derived from the Quran, the words and deeds of the Prophet (or those actions by his followers that he sanctioned), the consensus of the *umma,* analogical reasoning, and judicial opinion. Dynastic and doctrinal schisms soon divided the *umma;* however, sharia, upheld by the ulama, united Muslims of diverse races, cultures, regions, and political allegiances.

The Right-Guided Caliphs and the Early Arab Conquests

When Muhammad died, his followers needed a new leader for the *umma,* although no one could succeed Muhammad as the Prophet. Abu Bakr was chosen as the first caliph (successor). During his caliphate, the Muslims won back the rebellious tribal Arabs and deflected their energies outward against Byzantium and Persia. Under Umar ibn al-Khattab, the second caliph, the Arabs routed armies mightier than their own, wresting Syria and

Egypt from Byzantine control and absorbing Sassanid Persia. The Arabs conquered most of the Middle East in a generation and much of the Old World in a century. Many Syrians, Egyptians, and Persians welcomed Arab rule as a respite from Byzantine intolerance and Sassanid exploitation. These subjects were forced neither to speak Arabic nor to become Muslims, although gradually some chose to do one or both. The new rulers, often called the right-guided caliphs, retained local administrative customs and languages and even the bureaucrats themselves; the Arabs lacked the numbers and the experience to govern their new empire unaided. Men who did not convert were required to pay a head tax in return for exemption from military service. Jerusalem under Arab rule remained a religious center and pilgrimage site for Jews and Christians as well as for Muslims.

Although Arab toleration of local customs promoted stability, the conquests strained the *umma* itself. The caliphs set aside some of the captured booty for charitable or communal use and put the troops on a payroll, but the sudden influx of wealth led to unrest. In 656 CE the third caliph, Uthman, was murdered. His friends suspected his successor, Ali (Muhammad's son-in-law), of aiding his assassination. Seeking revenge, Uthman's supporters fought Ali's backers in a battle that ended in a mediation that favored Uthman's cousin, Mu'awiya, the governor of Syria. He proceeded to name himself caliph, moved the capital to Damascus, pacified dissident Muslims, and made the caliphate hereditary in his own family, the Umayyad branch of the Quraysh tribe.

The Umayyad caliphs, who ruled in Damascus from 661 to 750, were more political than pious. They crushed their opponents and spread Arab rule to northern Africa and Spain, Central Asia, and what is now Pakistan (see Map 3.1). Many Muslims resented the Umayyads. One of these dissidents was the Prophet Muhammad's grandson and Ali's son, Husayn, who died during a revolt at Karbala (Iraq) in 680 CE. Husayn's martyrdom led to a political and religious opposition movement known as Shiism. Even now Islam remains split between the Shi'a, who accept only Ali and his descendants as rightful leaders of the *umma,* and the Sunnis, who accept as legitimate the caliphs who actually ruled. Sunnis now outnumber Shi'a in most of the Muslim world, but Shi'ism dominates in Iran and plays a growing role in the politics of nearby Arab countries.

The First Islamic Empire

The Umayyads' power depended on their main fighting force, the Arab tribes, which the caliphs favored even after many non-Arabs converted to Islam. Some non-Arab Muslims joined revolutionary movements, often pro-Shi'a, against Umayyad rule. One such rebellion was led by the Abbasid family, who ousted the Umayyads in 750 and set up its own caliphate

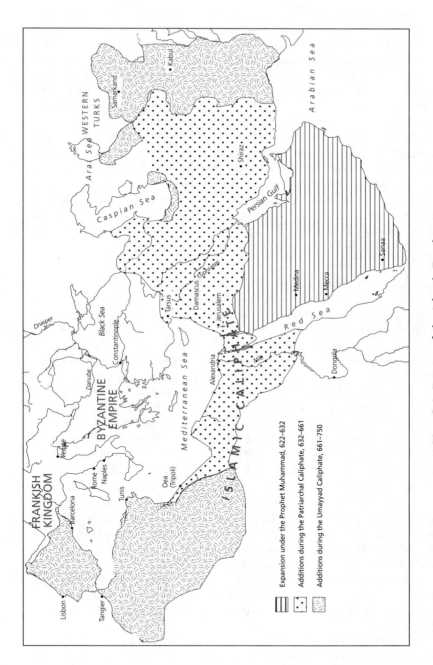

Map 3.1 Extent of the Islamic Empire

Expansion under the Prophet Muhammad, 622–632

Additions during the Patriarchal Caliphate, 632–661

Additions during the Umayyad Caliphate, 661–750

in Baghdad. At this point, the *umma* ceased to be united, for the Umayyads kept control over Spain. The North African Berbers, tribal peoples who converted from Christianity and Judaism to Islam but did not accept Arab political dominance, soon cast off Abbasid rule. A Shi'i movement, the Fatimids, took power in Tunisia and later in Egypt. Elsewhere, ambitious governors, warlords, and religious leaders carved out their own states. Most Arabs reverted to nomadism or intermarried with their conquered peoples, many of whom adopted the Arabic language and culture.

Despite its turbulent politics, the Abbasid era (which lasted at least nominally until 1258) was one of agricultural and commercial prosperity. As industry and trade flourished, so did science and letters. Rulers competed with one another to pay for the translation of scientific and philosophical works from Greek into Arabic, support court poets and historians, build mosques and palaces, and sponsor astronomical and medical research. Thus, Muslims preserved and improved their classical patrimony, which they passed on to Europe, helping to spark the Renaissance.

Invasions from the East and the West

The large-scale influx of Turks from Central Asia began in the tenth century. Some had already been imported as slave soldiers and bureaucrats for the Abbasid caliphs; others served the Abbasids or local Muslim rulers as frontier guards against non-Muslims farther east. Schooled in the arts of government and war, the Turkish *ghazis* (border raiders) proved more reliable than the caliphs' other subjects and rose to positions of power.

One Turkish family serving a Persian dynasty earned an *iqta'* (land granted for military or administrative service to the state) in Ghazna, in what is now Afghanistan, around 960. This family, the Ghaznavids, built up an empire spanning eastern Persia, Central Asia, and northern India. The Ghaznavids in turn gave *iqta's* to Turkish clans from Central Asia. One of these, the Seljuks, proceeded to conquer lands westward across Persia and Mesopotamia and into Anatolia, where they defeated the Byzantines in 1071. The military gains of these families attracted other Turks to serve as *ghazis,* opening the way for large-scale immigration of Turkish tribes with their horses, two-humped camels, sheep, and goats. Azerbaijan (northwestern Persia), northern Iraq, and much of Anatolia, highland areas that the Arabs had never taken, soon became mainly Turkish.

The Turks were devout Sunni Muslims who built new cities and refurbished old ones. They rescued the Abbasid caliph, who had been taken hostage by Shi'i bureaucrats, and restored his authority, although not his power. For several generations, the caliph ruled in Baghdad beside a Seljuk sultan (holder of power). The Turks strengthened Sunni schools, promoted Sufism (organized Islamic mysticism), and limited reinterpretation of sharia.

Sufism involved Muslims more deeply in their faith, but caused some to withdraw from worldly pursuits. Once Sunni Muslims could not revise sharia, changing social needs led rulers and subjects to bypass it, and practices diverged ever further from Islamic precepts.

As Turkish nomads poured in from the East, a different group of invaders came from the West. In 1096, the pope proclaimed a Crusade to regain the Holy Land for Christianity. Muslims had ruled Jerusalem for more than four centuries without harming Christian interests, but the Seljuk invasion of Anatolia had weakened the Byzantine Empire and threatened the Christian pilgrimage routes to the Holy City. The Seljuks had started to disintegrate in 1092, and seven years later the Crusaders took coastal Syria and Palestine from divided and weak Muslim rulers. For almost a century, Jerusalem, purged of its Muslim and Jewish inhabitants, was the capital of a European Christian kingdom.

Outside Jerusalem, however, the Crusaders rarely uprooted the local population, and they never took the Muslim power centers: Cairo, Damascus, Aleppo, and Mosul. Once Egypt and Syria were united under a strong Sunni Muslim ruler, Saladin, the Muslims retook Jerusalem in 1187. The Crusaders held part of coastal Syria for another century and twice invaded the Nile Delta, but Saladin's descendants, the Ayyubids, kept them in check.

Far more harmful to the Middle East were the thirteenth-century invasions by the Mongols, who came from the lands north of China. Mongol armies led by Genghis Khan (r. 1206–1227) defeated weak Muslim rulers and conquered Central Asia and eastern Persia. His grandson, Hülegü, pressed farther into Persia and Mesopotamia and in 1258 took Baghdad and wiped out the Abbasid caliphate. The Mongols were not Muslims. Horse nomads accustomed to grassy steppes, they saw no need for cities or the farmers who supported them. They destroyed irrigation works in Persia, Mesopotamia, and Syria, impoverishing the land and its people. Many Muslim rulers, even Anatolia's surviving Seljuks, became Mongol vassals. But in 1260 the Mongols failed to take Palestine and Egypt, where the Ayyubids had recently been overthrown by their Turkish slave soldiers, the Mamluks. The Mamluk rulers went on to build a prosperous empire in Egypt and Syria, the bulwark of Muslim power until their conquest by the Ottoman Turks in 1516–1517. Meanwhile, Persia's Mongol rulers soon adopted Islam, accepted Persian culture, and rebuilt much of what they had earlier destroyed.

The harnessing of gunpowder by Europe in the fourteenth century altered the West's relationship with the rest of the world. Firearms and long-distance sailing ships soon enabled Europeans to explore and conquer distant lands and, finally, to encircle the Muslim world. States using gunpowder as their main weapon require disciplined infantries rather than the feudal cavalries of the Middle Ages. The West's adoption of firearms engendered strong monarchies, a mercantile class, and eventually the Industrial Revolution. In the Middle East, some Muslim states learned how to use firearms, but others never did. The gunpowder revolution weakened the feudal landowners there, too, but failed to stimulate European-style modernization.

The Ottoman Empire

The Ottoman Empire was the archetypal Muslim state built on the use of firearms. From their humble origins in the thirteenth century as Turkish *ghazis* for the Seljuks, the Ottomans expanded their landholdings into an empire that stretched—at its height in the seventeenth century—from Central Europe to the Gulf and from Algeria to Azerbaijan. Like most *ghazis,* the early Ottomans raided peasant lands on horseback. During the fourteenth and fifteen centuries, however, they developed a disciplined corps of professional foot soldiers, the famous janissaries, who used siege cannon and lighter firearms against the Europeans or their Muslim neighbors. The Ottoman state took boys as tribute from their Christian subjects. Converted to Islam, the boys were taught Turkish and Arabic and trained as soldiers or, less often, as administrators. As the Ottoman sultan's slaves, the janissaries were forbidden to marry or to own land. They lived in barracks in order to be ready to fight whenever they were needed. This system of recruitment and training was called *devshirme,* as were, collectively, the Ottoman soldiers and bureaucrats that it produced.

Backed by well-equipped armies and competent administrators, the Ottoman sultans, the first ten of whom were energetic and competent, conquered the Christian peoples of the Balkans and surrounded Constantinople. In 1453, they took the city and ended the 1,000-year Byzantine Empire. Once the world's greatest Christian city, Constantinople (now Istanbul) became a Muslim center. During the following century, the Ottomans subdued most of their Muslim neighbors, including the Mamluks of Egypt and Syria. Only the Persians, ruled after 1501 by the Safavids, remained independent, for they, too, learned to use firearms.

The first ten Ottoman sultans competed for the succession, supervised the bureaucracy, and led their troops into battle. Their rule, however, rested on two principles: (1) the ruling class's power was balanced between the landowning aristocrats and the *devshirme* soldiers and administrators; and (2) the subject peoples were organized into religious communities, called *millets,* that had autonomous control over their laws, schools, and welfare. These divisions strengthened the sultan. So long as the sultan could play off the aristocracy against the *devshirme* class, both ruling groups performed their tasks as defenders and managers of the Ottoman Empire. The *millets* were self-sufficient, but geographically scattered, unable to combine against their Ottoman overlords. These subjects looked to their communal leaders (rabbis, priests, and ulama), whose top members were named by and responsible to the sultan, to mediate between them and the government. For centuries, this political and social organization endured; even now, some Middle Easterners identify with their religion more than their nationality.

Of all the factors that weakened the Ottoman Empire, the most significant was the triumph of the *devshirme* bureaucrats and janissaries over the aristocracy. This happened under the greatest Ottoman sultan, Suleyman the Magnificent (r. 1520–1566), when he appointed a series of chief ministers who had risen from *devshirme* origins. Not checked by either the weaker succeeding sultans or the declining aristocracy, these former slaves used the Ottoman government to serve their own interests. Janissaries won the sultan's permission to leave the barracks, marry, buy property, and enroll their sons in the corps, which stopped training and degenerated into a hereditary, privileged caste. Military failure and corrupt government ensued. Taxes rose, especially for those unable to avoid paying them. Agrarian and commercial prosperity declined, partly because the trade routes between Asia and Europe shifted away from the Middle East. Once loyal subjects rebelled against Ottoman misrule. By the late seventeenth century, the Ottoman Empire was no longer the scourge of Europe.

The Subordination of the Middle East to the West

During the eighteenth and nineteenth centuries, the West gained military, political, and economic superiority over the Middle East. Whereas Arabs and Turks had once mastered the routes between Europe and Asia, by 1800 Europe sold its manufactured goods to the Middle East in exchange for raw materials and agricultural products. Europeans in Muslim lands were exempted from local taxes and legal jurisdiction; this exemption was guaranteed by treaties called the capitulations. Whereas once the Mediterranean Sea and the Indian Ocean were controlled by Muslim navies, now European sailing ships dominated the high seas. Whereas once the Ottoman sultan could choose the time and place for an attack on Europe and then dictate the peace terms, now the sultan's armies feared the mighty forces of Habsburg Austria and czarist Russia. The greatest shock came when Napoleon occupied Egypt in 1798, for France had long been an Ottoman ally.

Westernizing Reforms

As early as the seventeenth century, some Ottoman sultans and their ministers saw the need for internal change. At first, they regarded reform as the restoration of the institutions and practices that had made their empire strong in the past. But defeat by Western armies showed that conditions had altered, necessitating more drastic modifications. Reforms began in the military. Sultan Selim III (r. 1789–1807) tried to set up a new army corps trained and equipped in the European fashion. Afraid that these interlopers would take away their power, the janissaries rebelled, destroyed the new corps, and deposed Selim. The conservative ulama and trade guilds blocked economic reforms. Even the introduction of printing was long opposed by the ulama and scribes, the former condemning innovation and the latter fearing the loss of their jobs.

The failure of early reform efforts taught Muslim rulers that change could not be confined to the military. Only by centering power in the state could they resist European expansion. Reform meant autocracy, not democracy. Three Middle Eastern reformers serve as examples: Muhammad Ali (r. 1805–1849) of Egypt, Sultan Mahmud II (r. 1808–1839) of the Ottoman Empire, and Nasir al-Din Shah (r. 1848–1896) of Persia. Each tried to concentrate power in his own hands; each became hamstrung by European actions serving imperialist interests.

The ablest was Muhammad Ali, an Ottoman officer commanding an Albanian regiment sent to Egypt. He took control of that Ottoman province after Napoleon's forces withdrew in 1801 and proceeded to eliminate every rival for power. He massacred the Mamluks and curbed the ulama, who had enjoyed special power and prestige in Egypt, by exploiting their rivalries and seizing the endowments that supported them. Advised and equipped by France, he built the region's strongest army and navy. He subordinated the rural aristocracy to the state by taking control of all farmland.

Under Muhammad Ali's rule, Egypt became the first Middle Eastern country to complete the change from subsistence to market agriculture. Tobacco, sugar, indigo, and cotton became Egypt's cash crops, earning revenues to fund his ambitious projects for industrial development and military expansion. The first non-Western ruler to recognize the Industrial Revolution, he set up textile mills and weapons factories, sent hundreds of his subjects to Europe for technical or military training, and imported European instructors to staff schools and military academies in Egypt. He even conscripted Egyptian farmers as soldiers. Officered by Turks, they became such a potent force that Muhammad Ali's son, Ibrahim, conquered Syria in 1832 and would have taken over the whole Ottoman Empire in 1839 if Britain had not intervened. Although the Ottoman Empire recognized Egypt's autonomy in 1841, Muhammad Ali felt that his ambitions had been thwarted and let his reforms lapse. However, his heirs ruled Egypt, with only nominal Ottoman control, up to the British occupation in 1882, and Egypt remained a monarchy until Farouk abdicated in 1952.

Muhammad Ali's Ottoman contemporary, Sultan Mahmud II, tried to reform his state but first had to destroy the janissary corps, the main obstacle to change. His efforts were hampered by the diversity and extent of his domains, local revolts, the lack of a loyal and trained bureaucracy, the Greek independence war (backed by Britain, France, and Russia), and the growing need of industrialized states to buy Ottoman raw materials and sell their own manufactures. Mahmud laid the groundwork for the great decree issued by his son and successor that began the Tanzimat (reorganization) era, one of intense centralization and Westernization. The Tanzimat alone could not block Russian expansion in the Balkans, so Britain and France helped the Ottomans defeat Russia in the Crimean War (1853–1856). The Europeans then made the Ottomans issue another decree that gave Christians and Jews legal equality with Muslims.

Persia was the only core Middle Eastern state never to fall under Ottoman rule. Its rulers' adherence to ancient Persian customs preserved a national identity. This was reinforced by their adherence to Shi'ism whereas the Ottomans were Sunni Muslims. In the sixteenth and seventeenth centuries, Persia flourished under the Safavid shahs, who adorned their capital at Isfahan and formed commercial and diplomatic ties with the European countries needing allies against the Ottoman Empire.

Persia, too, declined. The Qajar dynasty (1794–1925) resisted dissolution from within and Russian and British encroachments from without. During the first three years of Nasir al-Din Shah's reign, his energetic chief minister began a series of military, financial, and educational reforms. But in 1851 the shah executed his minister, followed by new tribal and religious uprisings. Later on, Nasir al-Din began selling concessions to British investors and hiring Russian officers to train his army. Instead of reforming his government to protect Persia from foreigners, the shah let them take over. His subjects rejected his policies; a nationwide tobacco boycott made him cancel his most lucrative concession, and he was finally assassinated. Later Qajar shahs submitted to even more foreign interference.

European Imperialism in the Nineteenth Century

If Western power inspired Middle Eastern reform, European policies and actions kept it from succeeding. From 1815 to 1914, European governments preserved peace among themselves by keeping a balance of power. For the Middle East, this meant that neither Britain nor Russia could let the other become supreme. Fearing that breaking up the Ottoman Empire would give Russia control of the Balkans and of the straits linking the Black Sea to the Aegean, Britain usually tried to uphold the empire's territorial integrity. Thus, the British led European opposition to Muhammad Ali's takeover of Ottoman Syria in 1839, Russia's occupation of the Romanian principalities in 1853 (which led to the Crimean War), and Russia's frequent efforts to exploit nationalism in the Balkans. Britain also backed reforms that enabled the Ottoman Empire to resist Russia, especially those during the Tanzimat era that promised equality to non-Muslims. By contrast, Russia's expansionist aims, its claim to protect the sultan's Orthodox Christian subjects, and its promotion of Balkan nationalist movements served to thwart Ottoman reform efforts.

While guarding its routes to India, Britain also vied with France for power in the eastern Mediterranean; it fought to expel Napoleon from Egypt and later to remove Muhammad Ali from Syria. Britain signed treaties with tribal leaders in the Gulf and occupied Aden in order to outflank Muhammad Ali and his French allies and to guard its sea route to India. A British company started steamship navigation on the Euphrates River in the 1830s; another built the first railroad from Alexandria to Cairo in 1851. But it was a French diplomat, Ferdinand de Lesseps, who won a concession from Egypt's viceroy to cut a canal across the Isthmus of Suez, joining the Red Sea to the Mediterranean and slashing travel time between Europe and southern Asia. Britain tried at first to block this mainly French project, but it became the Suez Canal's main user after it was opened in 1869. France expanded across North Africa, taking Algeria in a protracted war (1830–1847) and establishing protectorates over Tunisia in 1881 and Morocco in 1912. A mainly Christian part of Syria became an international protectorate as the autonomous governorate of Mount Lebanon from 1864 to 1914.

The Middle Eastern Reaction to the West

Some Middle Easterners thought, then as now, that Westernization had gone too far. In the Ottoman Empire, a few Muslims adopted pan-Islam, the idea that all Muslims should unite behind the sultan to counter outside threats and the divisive nationalist movements of non-Muslim Balkan subjects. Pan-Islam reaffirmed the tradition of Muslims uniting to defend the *umma,* but this doctrine took on a new meaning: the Ottoman sultan claimed for himself the caliphate, hence the allegiance of all Muslims, regardless of who actually ruled them. Because Britain, France, and Russia all had Muslim subjects within their empires, Europeans soon saw the fearsome potential of pan-Islam.

Westernizing reforms, especially in education and military training, led to the growth of liberal and nationalist movements among young Egyptians, Ottomans, Arabs, Persians, and Tunisians. These new groups challenged their rulers' monopoly on power and called for constitutional government. None wholly succeeded.

The Beginnings of Egyptian Nationalism

Muhammad Ali's grandson, Isma'il (r. 1863–1879), adopted new Westernizing reforms and secured Egypt's autonomy from the Ottoman Empire. He sent explorers to find the sources of the Nile River and army expeditions to conquer the Red Sea coast and southern Sudan. Sections of Cairo and

Alexandria were transformed by broad boulevards, parks, gardens, and mansions. Factories and public works built up the economy as a cotton boom caused by a drop in US exports during the American Civil War, the growing availability of European capital, and the construction of the Suez Canal made Egypt an attractive field for investment.

Egypt's economy boomed, but so did Isma'il's problems. In 1866, he convened a representative assembly to advise his regime and impose new taxes. Timid at first but later incited by a burgeoning press, this new body began calling for constitutional government. Isma'il borrowed vast sums from foreign banks to cover his expenditures. Unable to repay his debts, he sold his government's Suez Canal shares to Britain, accepted British and French control over Egypt's finances, and finally admitted representatives of these two creditor states into his cabinet. Egyptians resented these changes. The assembly demanded a council of ministers responsible to itself and purged of Europeans, control of the government's budget, and an end to the economies that harmed many Egyptians. In 1879, Isma'il dismissed his "European cabinet" and named one that heeded the assembly's call for constitutional government. The European powers ordered the Ottoman sultan to replace Isma'il with his son, Tawfiq.

Tawfiq obediently purged his regime of dissidents and tried to pay back some of his father's debts. But many Egyptians, harmed by European meddling, demanded independence. Their main backers were Egyptian army officers led by Colonel Ahmad Urabi, who founded Egypt's first nationalist movement. In 1881, Urabi's troops surrounded the palace and called for a new cabinet responsible to an elected parliament. Tawfiq gave in, and soon Egypt had a constitution. Nationalism's triumph was brief; its leaders were split, the Europeans threatened to intervene, and Tawfiq turned against the nationalists. Landing in Alexandria, British troops invaded the Suez Canal, defeated Urabi, and occupied Cairo.

When Britain occupied Egypt in 1882, it promised to pull its troops out as soon as order was restored to the country. It was easy to defeat the nationalists and prop Tawfiq back on his throne. It was harder to remedy the causes of Egypt's disorder: huge debts, a peasantry burdened by high taxes, and a revolt in Sudan. The longer Britain stayed on to tackle Egypt's problems, the harder it was to leave. A skilled administrator, Sir Evelyn Baring, commonly known as Lord Cromer, became Britain's diplomatic representative in Cairo. Backed by British troops, he reformed Egypt's finances and administration and gradually became its ruler in all but name.

Although the country prospered, British advisers sapped the authority of the Egyptian ministers. The British claimed to be preparing the Egyptians for self-rule, but in fact Egypt became a training ground for British colonial administrators. The extension of irrigation under British rule was not paralleled by expanded education or industrial development. After Tawfiq was succeeded by his son Abbas in 1892, a cabal of young Egyptians helped Abbas thwart Cromer's power. Their spokesman, a young lawyer named Mustafa Kamil, founded the National Party. Its members urged Britain to withdraw its forces from Egypt and later demanded a new constitution. Cromer ignored them, but his successor promised to hasten Egypt's progress toward self-rule. Mustafa Kamil died prematurely in 1908, and his followers split between the moderate reformers and the radical pan-Islamists. A more repressive British policy forced the leaders into exile. After World War I began, Britain deposed Abbas, declared a protectorate, and severed Egypt's ties with the Ottoman Empire.

Liberalism and Nationalism Within the Ottoman Empire

As the Tanzimat era wound down, a group of Westernized Turkish intellectuals and army officers known as the New Ottomans called for a constitution that would limit the sultan's autocracy. In 1876, amid Balkan revolts, growing state indebtedness to Europe, and threats of a Russian invasion, an officers' coup placed a liberal sultan on the throne. He was soon replaced by Abdülhamid II, who proclaimed a constitution in December of that year to forestall a Russian attempt to break up his empire. For about a year, the Ottoman Empire had a popularly elected parliament. But when Russia invaded the Balkans and threatened to take Istanbul, Abdülhamid closed parliament and suspended the constitution. For thirty years, the sultan further centralized state control and stifled Ottoman liberal and nationalist movements. A group of Westernized students and army officers, convinced that the empire could survive only as a constitutional monarchy, formed the Committee of Union and Progress (the Young Turks). In 1908, it forced the sultan to restore the 1876 Constitution and hold elections; in 1909, after an abortive countercoup, it deposed him. But the Young Turk regime soon became a military junta. As Balkan revolts and Western imperialism took one Ottoman province after another, the leaders espoused Turkish nationalism, which alienated subjects who did not regard themselves as Turkish such as the Kurds and the Armenians.

Among the Ottoman subjects who resisted Turkish nationalism were those who spoke Arabic. Long divided by local, sectarian, or family rivalries, the people of Syria, Mesopotamia, and Arabia began to view themselves as one Arab nation. Arabic-speaking lawyers, teachers, students, and army officers formed nationalist societies in the main Ottoman cities. Some wanted internal autonomy and equal status with the Turks as Ottoman subjects; others demanded Arab independence from Turkish rule. A few hoped to restore the caliphate to an Arab ruler. Although Arab nationalism had only a few adherents at first, its ideas helped spark the Arab Revolt during World War I.

Persian Constitutionalism

Persia's Qajar shahs were autocratic and weak. They could not protect the farmers and city dwellers from nomadic tribes, nor could they stop Russian military incursions or the commercial ascendancy of the British and other Europeans. In reaction, the idea of constitutional government arose within three groups: merchants, Shi'i ulama, and Westernized intellectuals. The merchants resented the shahs' concessions to foreign companies, which threatened their livelihood; the ulama feared that Westernization would undermine Islam generally and their own influence in particular; and the intellectuals, influenced by Western liberalism and nationalism, viewed the shah, backed by foreign advisers and funds, as an obstacle to reform.

These groups wanted different things. United by nationalism, however, they engineered the 1892 tobacco boycott and a national revolution in 1906. In response to the latter event, the shah granted a constitution that provided for a popularly elected majles (parliament). But in 1907, his successor called in Russian troops to suppress the majles and its revolutionary backers. However, outside the capital the Constitutionalists continued their struggle. A prominent tribal leader helped them retake Tehran, and they replaced the shah with a more docile relative.

Once in power, though, the Constitutionalists failed to implement their reform program. Their political revolution did not change social and economic conditions, they were split into factions, and outsiders exacerbated their problems. Britain cared about protecting commerce and defending India. Russia, having earlier taken Central Asia, hoped to expand into Persia. Meanwhile, a British firm won a concession to explore southern Persia for oil. The first major discovery came in 1908, and the Anglo-Persian Oil Company was formed the next year. Soon, it built a refinery at Abadan. When Britain's fleet switched from coal to oil in 1912, Persia's new role as an oil producer made it central to British imperial strategy.

Britain and Russia had agreed in 1907 to define spheres of influence within Persia. Russia's sphere covered the country's northern third, including Tehran. Britain, whose area bordered on northwestern India, allowed the Russians to tighten their grip on Persia's government before and during World War I. The 1917 Bolshevik Revolution would cause the withdrawal of Russian troops, but Britain still hoped to control Persia.

World War I, the Ottoman Jihad, and the Arab Revolt

World War I completed the ongoing subordination of Middle Eastern peoples to Western domination. Since the eighteenth century, Russia had won control over the lands north of the Black Sea, the Caucasus Mountains, most of the Caspian Sea coast, and vast stretches of Muslim Central Asia. Persia was virtually a Russian protectorate. The czarist regime hoped to gain Istanbul and the Bosporus and Dardanelles straits in the war. France ruled North Africa. Britain held Egypt, Cyprus, and Aden; it also had treaties empowering it to protect most of the Gulf rulers. British and French capitalists had huge investments in Middle Eastern land, buildings, factories, railroads, and utilities. In 1914, Germany had become the protector of what remained of the Ottoman Empire; a German military mission reorganized its army, and German capital financed construction of a rail line from Istanbul to Baghdad, raising its influence in the Ottoman interior.

Istanbul's decision to enter World War I as Germany's ally sealed the fate of the Ottoman Empire. Russian expansionism threatened its eastern provinces, and the Young Turk leaders came to fear their Armenian subjects as a fifth column, though most had remained loyal to the Ottoman Empire. The government deported most of the Armenians from their homes, causing an estimated 1.5 million deaths and much economic dislocation.

The Ottoman proclamation of jihad (struggle for Islam) failed to rally the Muslims under Allied rule to rebel. As Britain repulsed Turkish attacks against the Suez Canal and sent forces to invade Mesopotamia and Palestine, the Arabs' loyalty to the Ottoman sultan waned. Husayn ibn Ali, the emir (prince) of Mecca and sharif (leading descendant of Muhammad) of the prestigious Hashemite family, negotiated secretly with Sir Henry McMahon, Britain's high commissioner in Egypt. McMahon's letters seemed to offer British support for an independent Arab kingdom under the Hashemites if Husayn rebelled against the Turks. He reserved Baghdad and Basra for separate administration, however, and excluded Mersin, Alexandretta, and "portions of Syria lying to the west of the districts of Damascus, Homs, Hama, and Aleppo" from the areas to be ruled by Husayn. These terms fell short of the nationalists' dream of independence for all the Arabic-speaking Ottoman lands. Although Husayn was disappointed, the Ottoman government's repression of the Arabs in Syria goaded him to proclaim the Arab Revolt in 1916. Together, the Arabs and the British drove the Turks from Palestine and Syria while Anglo-Indian troops took Mesopotamia (Iraq). The Ottoman Empire surrendered in October 1918.

Because the Arabs predominated in Palestine, Syria, and Iraq, they expected to win independence in return for their support during the Arab Revolt. US president Woodrow Wilson proposed autonomy for these former Ottoman lands in the twelfth of his Fourteen Points, which Britain and France accepted as the basis for making peace. The British and French gave new assurances to the Arabs in 1918 that the Fertile Crescent and the Hejaz would be ruled by the Hashemites after the war.

But this was not to be. During the war, Britain had made conflicting promises to other interested parties. In a series of secret pacts, the Allies had agreed that the Bosporus and Dardanelles straits, Istanbul, and eastern Anatolia were to go to czarist Russia, portions of western Anatolia to the Greeks and the Italians, and most of the Arab lands to Britain and France.

The 1916 Sykes-Picot Agreement designated part of the Syrian coast for direct French control and a larger zone of French influence in the Syrian hinterland as far east as Mosul. Britain was to rule lower Iraq and to have a sphere of influence over the rest of Iraq and Palestine, except that the Christian holy places would be under an international administration. Only in the desert were the Arabs to be free from Western rule.

Meanwhile, there was another group, the Jewish nationalists (Zionists), that was pressing the Western powers to recognize its claim to Palestine (Eretz Yisrael). Beginning in the 1880s partly due to anti-Jewish pogroms in Russia, some European Jews settled in Palestine, which was then under Ottoman rule and inhabited mainly by Arabs. During World War I, Chaim Weizmann, an eminent chemist and Zionist leader living in England, convinced members of the British cabinet, which authorized Foreign Secretary Sir Arthur Balfour to declare his government's support for the establishment in Palestine of a national home for the Jewish people. He cautioned that this should not prejudice the civil and religious (but not political) rights of Palestine's "existing non-Jewish inhabitants," who comprised over nine-tenths of its population. The 1917 Balfour Declaration was a major victory for the nascent Zionist movement.

The Post–World War I Peace Settlement

All of these contradictory commitments were aired at the 1919 Paris Peace Conference. Husayn's son, Faisal, spoke for the Arab provisional government that the Hashemites had set up in Damascus. Seeking to learn what Arabs in Syria and Palestine wanted, Wilson sent out the King-Crane Commission, which found that the Arabs opposed French rule and Zionist colonization and craved independence. Its report was ignored. The British let the French troops occupy Beirut and later acceded to French control over Syria, including Mount Lebanon but not Palestine. Arab nationalists in Damascus declared Syria independent in March 1920 and vowed to resist, but the French defeated them in July and toppled the Arab provisional government.

By then, the Allies had agreed on how to rule the conquered Ottoman provinces. Owing to Wilson's self-determination policy, Britain and France did not annex these lands. Rather, under the League of Nations Covenant, Ottoman territories captured during the war were divided into small states that had developed enough to be recognized as nearly ready for independence, subject to a brief period of foreign tutelage under the League's supervision. Accordingly, France became the mandatory power in Syria and Britain in Iraq and Palestine. In principle, the powers were to govern these mandates to benefit the inhabitants and to prepare them for self-rule. In practice, the mandates benefited Britain and France, not their new and resentful subjects.

France split Syria into smaller administrative units to ensure its control, further embittering the nationalists. One result was the enlargement of prewar Mount Lebanon to include most of the Syrian coast, forming the Republic of Lebanon, which in 1920 had a slight Christian majority. Syria has never recognized this separation, and Lebanon's people are now predominantly Muslim.

Faisal, ousted from Damascus, was crowned in Baghdad in 1921 as the British sought to suppress a general revolt in the new Kingdom of Iraq, an awkward combination of the Ottoman provinces of Mosul, Baghdad, and Basra, minus the emirate (principality) of Kuwait. For Faisal's brother Abdullah, who had been promised the Iraqi throne, the British carved from Palestine the emirate of Transjordan, a desert land inhabited by bedouin tribes. Britain helped Abdullah weld his new state into a cohesive unit by forming the Arab Legion, a camel corps made up of men from most of the tribes and led by British officers. The Zionists in Palestine protested that Abdullah's kingdom was not open to Jewish colonization while Arab nationalists objected to the fragmentation of what they felt should have been a unified Syria. Abdullah himself hoped that, once the French left Syria, he could move from dusty Amman to historic Damascus.

The Middle East Since World War I

When Europe's armies laid down their weapons at the war's end, Britain seemed to dominate the Middle East. Its troops patrolled western Arabia, Palestine, Syria, Iraq, some of Persia, parts of the Caucasus long under czarist rule, and the Turkish straits. But the rise of nationalism checked Britain's control of the area. Egypt and Iraq were soon convulsed by nationwide rebellions against the British occupying forces. The Arabs rioted in Palestine against the Jewish immigrants and in Syria against the French colonists, for they viewed both groups as serving British imperial interests.

Deserted by its Young Turk leaders, the defeated Ottoman government let the British and French occupy the straits, but Ottoman attempts to demobilize the Turkish army as Greek forces invaded western Anatolia set off a mutiny led by its ablest general, Mustafa Kemal, later named Atatürk (Father of the Turks). Soon Kemal's followers set up in Ankara a nationalist government that replaced the Ottoman sultanate. The new Republic of Turkey rejected the 1920 Treaty of Sèvres, imposed on the Ottomans by the Allies, and drove out the Greeks.

In Persia, Britain drafted a treaty with the Qajar rulers that would have turned their country into a British protectorate, but the majles rejected the pact and revolts broke out in various parts of Persia. In 1921 an officer in the shah's guard, Reza Khan, took control and set up a military dictatorship, reducing Britain's role to protecting its oil fields in southwest Persia.

Western Imperialism in the Arab Lands

Despite this resistance, the British did manage to protect their communication links across the region to India. Egypt's revolutionaries did not win the independence they had sought in 1919, but the British did agree in 1922 to end the protectorate and let the Egyptians draw up a formal constitution, creating a parliament that would vie with the king for power. British troops remained to guard Cairo, Alexandria, the Suez Canal, and such vital infrastructure as airports and radio transmitters. Sudan remained under a formal Anglo-Egyptian condominium, but the British held almost all the power. London also reserved the right to defend Egypt against outside aggression and to protect foreign residents and minorities from nationalists or Muslim extremists. Under the new constitution, the Egyptians held parliamentary elections in 1923. Egypt's purported delegation (wafd) to the Paris Peace Conference turned into the Wafd Party, which could win any election not rigged by the king.

Palestine came under the direct control of Britain's Colonial Office, with a high commissioner governing in Jerusalem. The Jewish community had a Jewish Agency and an elected assembly to manage its internal affairs. The Muslim and Christian Arabs had no such organizations, and their leaders rejected a proposed legislature. Jews and Arabs spoke different languages, lived in distinct villages or separate neighborhoods, and related as little as possible to each other as communities, although some individuals or families got along well with their rivals. Jewish immigrants from war-torn revolutionary Russia or Central Europe viewed local Arabs as threatening brigands, greedy landlords, or backward peasants. The Palestinian Arabs feared that the Zionist movement would take away their lands and their homes. Jews and Arabs, both having long memories of powerlessness, showed scant sympathy for each other as they began competing for Palestine.

The French accepted control over Syria, but resented having to forgo Palestine and oil-rich western Iraq. France was determined to turn its League of Nations mandate over Syria into a colony. Soon after French troops had driven out the Arab nationalists, France divided the country into districts: Damascus, Aleppo, the north Mediterranean coast for the Alawites (a breakaway Shi'i sect), the highlands south of Damascus for the Druze (also a past offshoot of Shi'ism), and the special Republic of Lebanon already mentioned. French rule in Syria benefited farmers and merchants, as the mandatory regime invested in roads and other public works, but did not allay the chagrin of the nationalists who had craved Arab independence.

In North Africa, the French treated Algeria as an integral part of France. European settlers held most of the cultivable land, dominated political life, and controlled Algiers and the other major cities. The Algerian Muslims, mainly Berber but including many Arabs, had no political rights and only belatedly formed a secular nationalist party. A Muslim bey (governor) ruled in

Tunisia and had Muslim ministers, but real power was held by the French governor-general and his advisers. European settlers were less numerous than in Algeria, though. An emerging professional class formed the Destour (Constitution) Party to seek Tunisia's independence.

Morocco, which unlike the rest of North Africa had never been under Ottoman rule, was now divided between a Spanish enclave in the north, the international city of Tangier, and a French protectorate over most of the country. A French governor-general advised the sultan and his ministers, who normally obeyed. A large-scale rural rebellion was suppressed in 1925 after a fierce struggle. Although Morocco's urban nationalists formed the Istiqlal (Independence) Party, the French invested heavily in agriculture and mining, expecting to remain. Italy, which had seized Tripolitania from the Ottoman Empire in 1911, slowly took Cyrenaica and the Fezzan, creating what is now Libya. Its administration was especially brutal. Efforts to colonize Libya with Italians displaced many Arabs, but attracted few settlers.

Independence in Turkey, Iran, and the Arabian Peninsula

It is one of the great ironies of Middle Eastern history that most of the Arabs, who had thrown in their lot with the Allies during World War I, did not achieve their political goals after 1918 whereas the Turks, who had joined the Central Powers and shared in their defeat, managed to retain their independence once the war was over. The Turkish-speaking lands of Anatolia and Thrace could have been divided among Britain, France, Italy, Greece, and possibly even the United States. The Sèvres Treaty might have given lands to Armenians and Kurds. Instead, Kemal led a nationwide revolt that gradually won the support of the Union of Soviet Socialist Republics (USSR), France, and Italy, expelled the Greek invaders who had occupied much of western Anatolia, and persuaded the British to withdraw their troops from the straits. A new treaty signed at Lausanne in 1923 freed Thrace and Anatolia (with no enclaves for the Armenians or the Kurds) from foreign rule and accepted Turkey's abolition of the capitulations that had exempted Europeans from Ottoman control.

Kemal also abolished the sultanate and the other political institutions of the moribund Ottoman Empire in 1923. Ankara was the new capital of Turkey, the first republic in the modern Middle East. More drastic reforms followed, as Kemal ended the Islamic caliphate and dismantled Turkey's Muslim institutions, including its sharia courts and schools, its dervish and Sufi orders, and even its holidays. The Arabic alphabet, in which Turkish had been written for a thousand years, was replaced by a Roman one. The Gregorian calendar and Western clocks became standard, as did the metric system of weights and measures. Kemal discouraged women from veiling their faces and ordered men to wear hats with brims in place of the fezzes that had become the customary head covering for Muslim officers and officials. The ulama lost most of their power as judges and educators. Kemal wanted to wrest Turkey out of the Middle East and make it a part of Europe. Because he had saved his country from a hated Allied occupation, most Turks obeyed him.

Kemal had an imitator in Persia, where Reza Khan had seized control in 1921. When civilian politicians quarreled and the Qajar shah dithered, Reza crowned himself as the new shah in 1925. He founded the Pahlavi dynasty and decreed that Persia should be called Iran (land of the Aryans). Like Kemal, Reza Shah weakened the ulama and secularized their courts, schools, and welfare institutions. He outlawed the veiling of women and required both sexes to dress like Europeans. The new shah also curbed the nomadic tribes that had dominated rural Persia by forcing them to settle down as farmers. Trying to strengthen state control over the countryside, he extended the telegraph and road networks and decreed the construction of the Trans-Iranian Railway. The presence of the Anglo-Iranian (formerly Anglo-Persian) Oil Company, owned and managed by the British, limited Iran's economic sovereignty, but Reza Shah did manage to renegotiate its concession to the host country's benefit. As oil output expanded, more and more Iranians went to work for the company. As nationalist feelings spread, Iranians began to ask why such a vital resource should be controlled by foreigners.

Petroleum exploration began in other Middle Eastern countries as well. British companies found deposits in Iraq and Kuwait, as did US companies operating in Bahrain. A coalition of US firms that became the Arabian American Oil Company (ARAMCO) prospected for oil in the deserts of Arabia. This peninsula had long been dominated by feuding Arab tribes, but in the early twentieth century a remarkable military leader named Abdul Aziz ibn Saud took much of Arabia. Having subdued most of the tribes in central and eastern Arabia, Ibn Saud managed to take Mecca and Medina from the Hashemites in 1925. After conquering Asir, Ibn Saud proclaimed the Kingdom of Saudi Arabia in 1932. His country remained poor until ARAMCO struck oil; it was only much later that Saudi Arabia evolved into an economic giant.

Yemen remained a separate state under a dynasty of Zaydi Shiʻi imams (religious leaders), mountainous and colorful but lacking education, health care, industry, and oil. To the south of Yemen, where the Red and Arabian seas meet, lay the British colony of Aden. The tribal shaikhs near the coasts of the Arabian Sea and the Gulf had made treaties that placed them under British protection. Oman, which in previous centuries had been an autonomous actor in regional affairs, had also become a British protectorate.

Oil was also found in some of these areas, but little was extracted or sold until the 1960s.

The Retreat of Western Imperialism

With the spread of education and communications, nationalism grew among the Arabic-speaking peoples under British and French control. This feeling was expressed either as Arab nationalism, the idea that all people who speak Arabic should be united in one nation-state, or as a more localized patriotism. As more Arabs attended schools and colleges and as a burgeoning press fueled their desire for independence and unity, they openly attacked the British and French mandates in the Fertile Crescent and the prolonged British domination over Egypt and Sudan. Indeed, the British meant to prepare Iraqis, Transjordanians and Palestinians, and Egyptians and Sudanese for self-rule and eventual independence, but as separate countries, not as a single united state (as Arab nationalists wanted).

Leading the Arabs' march to independence was the Kingdom of Iraq. Although its subjects were less advanced than the Syrians or Egyptians, the British certified that Iraq was ready for sovereign statehood. In 1932, Iraq achieved formal independence and was admitted to the League of Nations. The next year, King Faisal I died suddenly and was succeeded by his minor son. A rebellion by the Assyrian Christians was suppressed by Iraqi troops who massacred many villagers. Other ethnic minorities (mainly non-Arab Kurds and Turcomans living in the north who made up one-fifth of Iraq's population, but also Jews in Baghdad) were barred from power. Most of Iraq's Arab Muslims were Shi'a who also suffered from discrimination.

Iraq's parliament was dominated by landowning tribal leaders, and a few aristocratic families monopolized cabinet posts. Then, several military coups brought a succession of army officers to power. This succession culminated in an Arab nationalist government that was toppled by Britain's military intervention in 1941, leaving a legacy of anti-Western hostility that would resurface under Abd al-Karim Qasim (r. 1958–1963) and Saddam Hussein (r. 1979–2003).

The brother of Iraq's King Faisal I, Abdullah, managed to unite Transjordan, which gained its independence in 1946. Its most viable institution, the Arab Legion, had helped the British suppress riots in Palestine west of the Jordan, the area subject to the Jewish-Arab contest for the "twice-promised land."

As detailed in Chapter 6, the Zionist movement aimed to persuade enough Jews to migrate to Palestine to form a Jewish state. Few came during the 1920s, lulling the Arab majority. But in 1929, a quarrel at Jerusalem's Western Wall sparked large-scale rioting in which many Arabs and Jews were killed or injured. A British investigating commission reported that sales of Arab-owned lands to Jewish settlers were taking many Palestinian Arab farmers' tenancy rights and, hence, their livelihoods. The Jewish settlers blamed Arab agitation for the riots and claimed they had brought prosperity to Palestine.

The Nazi takeover in Germany speeded up Jewish immigration in the 1930s, fueling Arab fears that they would soon become a minority. In 1936 their political parties, hitherto divided on family and religious lines, united as the Arab Higher Committee, which organized a general strike against the mandate. A three-year civil war ensued. A British commission of inquiry visited Palestine in 1937 and recommended forming separate enclaves in Palestine for Jewish immigration and settlement. Neither the Palestinians (backed by newly independent Iraq and Egypt) nor the Zionists favored this partition. The British revised their proposal and then, anxious about their strategic bases in Egypt and Iraq in case war with Germany broke out, issued the May 1939 White Paper, which limited Jewish immigration and land purchases in Palestine. The Zionists felt betrayed, for Europe's Jews were in mortal peril and no other country would admit them. The Arabs doubted British promises of independence, even though they were the majority in Palestine, and argued that Zionism was another manifestation of Western imperialism.

If the British were distrusted in Palestine, the Arabs hated France's mandates in Syria and Lebanon. Only Lebanon's Maronites wanted the French presence; most other Christians and virtually all Muslims in Syria wanted Arab unity and independence. During an interval when a leftist government held power in Paris, the French offered independence, only to retract it when a more conservative cabinet took over. France's sudden defeat by Nazi Germany in 1940 enabled Britain and the United States to pressure the anti-Nazi Free French to recognize the independence of Syria and Lebanon in 1943, but it was another three years before the last French troops left.

In the 1920s and 1930s, Egypt was the most populous Arab state. It had the most newspapers and magazines, the leading universities, the largest cinema and record companies, and the most influential writers. Yet it lagged behind the other Arab countries in gaining independence because of competition between King Fuad and the Wafd Party and due also to Britain's continued occupation of the Nile valley. Finally Britain and Egypt signed a treaty in 1936 because both feared Italy's expansion in Libya and Ethiopia, countries that bordered on Egypt and Sudan. Britain agreed to limit its forces to the Suez Canal Zone, Cairo, and Alexandria, reducing them to 10,000 men in peacetime. Sudan remained under an Anglo-Egyptian condominium.

Egypt's King Fuad died in 1936 and was succeeded by his young and initially popular son, Farouk. But he lost his popularity in 1942 when the British made him appoint a cabinet that would back their wartime presence in Egypt. Egypt was occupied by even more British imperial troops during World War II than in World War I, as Fascist Italy and Nazi Germany invaded from Libya, and the Suez Canal had to be defended at all costs. Antidemocratic groups such as pro-fascist Young Egypt, communists, and the Muslim Brotherhood vied for Egyptian support while parliamentary parties seemed outdated. Once the war ended, Egyptians demanded that British troops leave their country, including Suez and Sudan.

The Struggle Between Arab Nationalism and Zionism

The idea of Arab unification gained support in the Fertile Crescent, Egypt, and the Arabian Peninsula during World War II. Nuri al-Said, Iraq's prime minister, proposed a union of Syria, Lebanon, Transjordan, and Palestine with his own country. But King Farouk of Egypt and King Ibn Saud of Saudi Arabia also wanted to lead the Arabs. Egypt therefore proposed a looser organization for all sovereign Arab states. The Arabs accepted the latter alternative, and the Arab League came into being in 1945, with its headquarters in Cairo and an Egyptian as its secretary-general. The Arab countries also joined the United Nations (UN) that same year. Although Arab peoples still craved unity, their governments went their separate ways.

The issue that seemed to unite all Arabs was Palestine. Europe's Jews, decimated by the Nazi Shoah (Holocaust), sought a safe haven. Palestine's Arab majority feared a flood of refugees who would demand statehood at their expense. As Britain enforced its White Paper immigration restrictions even after World War II, some Jews resorted to terrorism. The British government became ever more hostile to Zionism and to Jewish settlement, and fighting intensified among Jews, Arabs, and British troops.

In 1947, Britain announced that it could no longer govern its mandate and submitted the Palestine issue to the United Nations. The UN General Assembly set up a special committee, which went to Palestine to look into the problem and recommended that its lands be divided into seven parts, three for the Jews and three for the Arabs, leaving Jerusalem and Bethlehem as a separate area under UN control. The Arab states opposed this plan, which would award more than half the territory (including the fertile coastal area) to the Jews, who made up only a third of the population and owned about 7 percent of the land. Pressured by the United States, more than two-thirds of the General Assembly members voted for the partition proposal.

Despite military threats by the Arab states to block partition, British troops prepared to pull out of Palestine, and the UN debated how to restore order. On May 14, 1948, the day before Britain's mandate was to end, the Jewish Agency met in Tel Aviv to declare the independent State of Israel in the lands that they controlled. The United States and the USSR recognized the Jewish state, even as the Arab states sent their armies to destroy it.

Israel's creation was a revolutionary event for both Jews and Arabs. There had been no Jewish state for millennia; now one existed as an enclave in a predominantly Arab region. As the armies of Egypt, Iraq, Syria, Lebanon, and Transjordan failed to take Palestine, most Palestinian Arabs fled from their homes, driven by the realistic fear that the Israelis would drive them out and consoled by the fatuous hope that the Arab armies would bring them back. More than 750,000 Arabs became refugees. They were placed in camps in those areas of Palestine—the West Bank and the Gaza Strip—not captured by the Israelis or in the neighboring countries, mainly Syria, Lebanon, and Jordan. These Palestinian refugees refused assimilation into the Arab states and demanded the right under international law to return to their homes. Israel offered to readmit a few refugees, but only as part of a general peace settlement. The Arab states signed separate armistice agreements with Israel in 1949, but did not recognize the new state. Israel declared that all Jews had the right to become citizens, took in survivors of the Shoah, and gave refuge to Jews from Arab lands.

Political Changes in the Arab Countries

The defeat of the Arab armies in the 1948 Palestine war was one of the causes of the army coups that afflicted many Arab states, starting in 1949 with three successive revolts in Syria. Arab monarchies were toppled in Egypt in 1952, Iraq in 1958, Yemen in 1962, and Libya in 1969. The major causes of these revolutions were the demands for greater popular participation and for a fairer distribution of each country's resources. The trend was toward government by an officer corps coming from middle-class (as opposed to landowning) backgrounds and committed to reform. The presence of Palestinian refugees also reminded Arabs in many countries of their old regimes' failure to defend them against Zionism and imperialism. The Palestinians themselves, ever more educated and politicized, often pressed the Arab governments to restore their rights by continuing the fight against Israel.

As discussed in Chapter 4, revolutionary Arab regimes espoused socialism, a policy viewed as halfway between the communism of the USSR and the capitalism of the West, and Arab unification. The leading spokesman for these policies was Egyptian president Gamal Abdul Nasser. Nasser had led the officers' conspiracy that overthrew Farouk in 1952, negotiated a new pact with Britain in 1954 securing the latter's evacuation of the Suez Canal Zone, and renounced Egypt's claims to rule Sudan, which became independent in 1956.

As the United States tried to fill the power vacuum caused by the British retreat from the Middle East, Nasser resisted efforts to draw him into an anticommunist alliance that was being formed by Iraq, Britain, Turkey, Iran, and Pakistan in 1955. He chose instead to buy $200 million worth of arms from the Soviet bloc, a move that aroused Western fears of communist gains in the Arab world. The US government, working with Britain and the World Bank, offered to lend Egypt the money to build a new dam near Aswan that would control the Nile floodwaters and increase the country's farmland and hydroelectric generating capacity, but it later withdrew its offer due to Nasser's perceived procommunist policies. Nasser responded in July 1956 by nationalizing the Suez Canal Company. The British and French governments denounced the seizure and conspired with Israel to attack Egypt. Although the attackers retook the canal, they were opposed by nearly every UN member, including the United States. Ultimately, they had to withdraw, and Nasser emerged as an Arab hero for standing up to the West.

Early in 1958, Egypt acceded to Syria's request to form an organic union of the two countries, which they called the United Arab Republic (UAR). Many Arab nationalists hoped that other governments would join the new political entity. Instead, Jordan and Iraq formed their own federation, which soon foundered when a coup overthrew the Iraqi monarchy. A civil war broke out in Lebanon between Arab nationalists (mainly Muslim) who sought closer ties with the UAR and Lebanese particularists (mainly Christian) who wanted independence from the Arabs. US troops occupied Lebanon in July 1958 and helped restore order.

The general trend seemed to be toward pan-Arabism, as north Yemen federated with the UAR, the army seized power in Sudan, and even Saudi Arabia replaced a weak king with a brother who was thought to favor Nasser. Not only was Arab unity strong in the late 1950s, but many governments followed Nasser's lead in redistributing large estates to hitherto landless farmers, nationalizing companies owned by foreign or local capitalists, and expanding public education and welfare institutions. The watchwords of the day were "neutralism" and "Arab socialism."

Like the eastern Arab world, North Africa was also emerging from colonialism. Libya, ruled by Italy up to World War II and by Britain under a temporary trusteeship after the war, was the first to gain independence, in 1951. France gave up its protectorates over both Tunisia and Morocco in 1956, but resisted in Algeria. More than a million European settlers wanted to keep Algeria a part of France while Algerian Muslims chafed under oppressive colonial rule. A few formed the National Liberation Front (FLN) to gain greater autonomy.

A small FLN uprising, begun in 1954, escalated into a major insurgency, which became an eight-year civil war marred by terrorism and torture by both colonists and nationalists. The French government and army grew tired of fighting rearguard colonial wars, and in 1962 President Charles de Gaulle granted independence to Algeria. The Algerian revolution, the sole instance where an Arab people successfully overthrew a colonial rule, became an inspiration to third world liberation movements, but at a cost of 18,000 French and 1 million Algerian lives. More than 2 million Algerians were displaced during the fighting, and after Algeria became independent more than a million Europeans, Jews, and Muslim supporters of French rule fled. The new leaders soon declared their support of Nasser and Arab socialism but later, as Algeria grew rich from its oil, the FLN turned into an authoritarian, secular, ruling party. When the FLN voided an election in 1992 that would have brought a Muslim party to power, another civil war erupted that lasted for a decade and cost 150,000 Algerian lives.

The Northern Tier
As stated in the introduction to this book, not all Middle Eastern states are Arab. Turkey and Iran, although predominantly Muslim, are proud of their

The Milk Bar in Algiers, where twenty-two-year-old Zohra Drif (now Senator Drif) planted a bomb on September 30, 1956, during the Battle of Algiers. She was tortured and sentenced to twenty years hard labor.

distinctive cultures and heritages. Both stood up to the British and kept their independence after World War I. Both bordered the USSR and had to come to terms with it. Ismet Inönü, who had succeeded Atatürk as president, kept Turkey out of World War II and prevented the Allies from using the Bosporus and Dardanelles straits to supply the USSR. Stalin's postwar demand to station Soviet troops on the straits led the United States to back Turkey in the 1947 Truman Doctrine, the first step toward a US policy of defending the Middle East. In 1952 Turkey joined the North Atlantic Treaty Organization (NATO), having sent troops to Korea to fight the communists.

Turkey took the lead in moving toward democratic government. Inönü's government consented to the formation of a rival party that ousted the Kemalists from power in 1950. Gradually, other parties with strong socialist and Islamist agendas have entered the political arena, but the Turkish army remains strong. Turkey has continued to industrialize its economy and modernize its society, but its recent history has been punctuated by military coups and by challenges from militant Marxists, Muslims, and Kurdish separatists. Turkey remains a bridge between the West and the Middle East and has become a link to the former Soviet republic of Azerbaijan and to Central Asia. It has for years sought to join the European Union, so far unsuccessfully.

Iran also had to protect its independence from the Soviet Union. Even though the two countries had signed a pact that authorized the Soviets to enter Iran whenever it was occupied by troops hostile to the Soviets, Moscow had little influence as long as Reza Shah reigned. In the 1930s, his regime drew close to Nazi Germany, whose doctrines of Aryan supremacy appealed to local pride and offered a means to fight Anglo-Russian control. When the Nazis invaded the USSR in 1941, the Soviet and British governments demanded the expulsion of German advisers from Iran and seized control of the Trans-Iranian Railway to ship Western munitions to the beleaguered Soviets. They also forced Reza Shah to abdicate in favor of his son Mohammad. At the war's end, British troops left Iran, but the Soviets tried to set up puppet regimes in Kurdistan and Azerbaijan. It took a general UN condemnation, US threats, and clever Iranian diplomacy to oust the Soviet army.

But Britain still controlled Iran's oil, and in 1951 a cabinet headed by Mohammad Mosaddeq nationalized the Anglo-Iranian Oil Company. Iran's nationalists were elated, but Western countries supported Britain by refusing to buy any oil from Iran. In 1953 an army coup, engineered in part by British and US intelligence agencies, overthrew Mosaddeq's government. The shah, who had fled from Iran during the turmoil, regained his throne. He began a policy of concentrating control in his own hands at the expense of Iran's landowners, merchants, and ulama. He also joined the anticommunist alliance with Turkey, Pakistan, Britain, and Iraq. Britain and the United States viewed Iran, Turkey, and Pakistan as a bulwark against a possible

Soviet drive toward the oil-rich Gulf. The West sold vast quantities of arms to these countries, but skeptics said that these weapons would be used just to keep their regimes in power.

The Intensification of the Arab-Israeli Conflict

In the late 1950s and early 1960s, Israel's conflict with its Arab neighbors seemed to die down as Arab states tried to unite and leaders struggled for power. The UAR lapsed when Syria broke away in 1961. A popular nationalist movement, the Baath Party, committed to Arab unification and socialism, seized power in Iraq and then Syria early in 1963. The Baath tried to form a new Arab union with Egypt, but the talks broke down. An army coup had ousted the Yemeni monarchy in 1962, but the new republican regime needed Egyptian military aid and troops to stay in power while Saudi Arabia began backing tribes loyal to the overthrown imam. A draining civil war ensued in Yemen.

What brought the Arabs back together was Israel's completion of a development scheme that drew water from the Jordan River to irrigate new agricultural lands within the Jewish state. Early in 1964, Nasser invited the other Arab heads of state to Cairo to discuss ways of countering the Israeli scheme, which would deprive Jordan and other Arab states of freshwater needed for their irrigation projects. The Arabs agreed to prepare for future action against Israel and formed the Palestine Liberation Organization (PLO) to unite the Palestinian Arabs politically. Meanwhile, Fatah, led by Yasser Arafat, launched commando raids inside Israel. Although abetted by Syria, these attacks tended to come from the West Bank, which was controlled by Jordan. To deter future raids, Israel's army attacked West Bank villages late in 1966, though some Israelis blamed Syria.

An aerial dogfight broke out between Israel and Syria in April 1967. The USSR told Egypt that Israeli troops were massing to attack Syria. Nasser, anxious to remain the champion of Arab nationalism, ordered the UN to withdraw its peacekeeping forces, which had patrolled the Sinai Peninsula (the Sinai) and the Gaza Strip since the 1956 war. As Israel mobilized its reserves, Egypt declared a blockade in the Gulf of Aqaba against Israeli shipping. Arab governments, their press and radio stations, and their people all called for defeating Israel and restoring the Palestinians to their homes.

Although many Americans and Western Europeans favored Israel, their governments hoped to avoid war by taking the issue to the UN. Israel, fearing an Arab offensive, launched a preemptive strike. On June 5, 1967, Israeli fighter planes bombed Egypt's military airfields and wiped out most of the Egyptian air force. Before the Arabs could hit back, the Israelis annihilated the other Arab air forces. They invaded the Sinai, Gaza, the Jordanian-ruled sector of Jerusalem and the West Bank, and finally Syria's Golan

A Palestinian woman talking to Israeli border guards.

Heights. In six days, Israel used its superior technology, organization, and airpower to defeat Egypt, Syria, and Jordan, tripling the area under its control.

The Arab states accepted UN-mediated cease-fires, but they refused to make peace. At a summit held in Khartoum, Sudan, the Arab leaders agreed not to negotiate with Israel, but to rearm and regain their lost lands by force. The PLO tried but failed to mobilize the Palestinians of the Gaza Strip and the West Bank, numbering more than 1 million people, to resist Israeli military rule. After a lengthy debate, the UN Security Council unanimously passed Resolution 242, calling on Israel to withdraw from lands occupied in the recent war, but ordering all countries to recognize the right of "every state in the area" to exist "within secure and recognized boundaries." Israel, Egypt, Jordan, and Syria, as UN members, were all bound under its Charter to accept Security Council resolutions, but each made its own interpretation of this one, to which all member states have paid lip service since 1967. Resolution 242 did not mention the Palestinians, who felt that neither the superpowers nor the Arab governments protected their interests.

In 1969, Arafat was elected chairman of the PLO, the umbrella group for most Palestinians. Some became guerrillas and resorted to attacking not only Israel but also pro-Western Arab states, notably Jordan and Lebanon. Palestinian guerrilla groups seemed to resist Israel more effectively than had the armies of Egypt, Syria, and Jordan in 1967. While Israeli propaganda assailed "Arab terrorism," most Arabs flocked to support the PLO.

Nasser launched his War of Attrition against Israel's troops in the Sinai in 1969 partly to counter PLO claims to lead the struggle. Israel's counterattacks obliged Egypt to seek more military aid from the USSR, leading to aerial dogfights over the Suez Canal. US secretary of state William Rogers proposed a peace plan that would halt the War of Attrition and set up indirect talks to bring Egypt and Israel to a peace settlement based on Security Council Resolution 242. Nasser accepted the Rogers Peace Plan, but indirectly undercut it by positioning Soviet missiles near the Suez Canal. Meanwhile, Palestinian guerrillas threatened to take over Jordan, but the Jordanian army, loyal to King Hussein, crushed them. Nasser's efforts to restore peace among the Arabs led to his fatal heart attack on September 28, 1970. His funeral in Cairo inspired demonstrations of grief throughout the Arab world because of his heroic stand against Western imperialism. Nasser's successor, Anwar Sadat, vowed to continue the fallen leader's policies of Arab nationalism, opposition to Israel, neutralism, purchases of communist arms, and socialism. Soon, however, Sadat set his own course, liberalizing Egypt's economy and society, and expelling most Soviet advisers in 1972.

The Rogers Peace Plan had collapsed in 1971 because neither Israel nor the Arabs would make the concessions needed. Sadat threatened to renew war against Israel if it did not withdraw from the Sinai and recognize Palestinian political rights. He also tried to cement a union with Syria, Libya, and Sudan. Neither his threats nor his union scheme worked. Palestinian commando groups committed terrorist actions against civilian Israelis and foreigners, hoping to convince Israel and its backers that the Arab lands captured in 1967 were not worth keeping. But Israel argued that it had to retain the territories until the Arabs agreed to negotiate for peace. Since the Arabs quarreled among themselves and Egypt distanced itself from its erstwhile Soviet backers, Israel and its supporters became overconfident.

Israel's complacency was shaken on October 6, 1973, when Egypt and Syria attacked Israeli positions in the Sinai and the Golan Heights. Taken by surprise, the Israelis called up their reserve soldiers and brought them to both fronts. By the second week, Israel was driving back the Syrians and Egyptians. The Soviets and the United States rushed to rearm their Middle Eastern clients on a massive scale. Then, the Arabs decided to unsheathe an economic weapon. In 1960, the leading nonindustrialized oil producers had formed the Organization of Petroleum Exporting Countries (OPEC), which tried to limit oil output and set common prices. OPEC had begun to affect the world oil market in 1971, and the October 1973 war gave it a pretext to raise prices 400 percent. The Arab members of OPEC announced that they would sell no oil to the United States and the Netherlands and would reduce supplies to other oil importers (Spain, France, and Muslim countries were exempted) until Israel pulled out of all occupied lands and recognized the Palestinians' political rights. So vital had Arab oil become to Europe and

Japan that many countries made political promises to ensure winter supplies. The UN Security Council adopted Resolutions 338 and 340, calling for a cease-fire and for immediate negotiations between Israel and the Arabs.

The Israelis had won the war, but as other governments turned against them, they felt that they had lost politically. US secretary of state Henry Kissinger worked to disentangle the Egyptian and Israeli armies and to organize a general peace conference that met briefly in Geneva in December 1973. Then Kissinger began flying between Jerusalem and Cairo, dealing with Egypt's and Israel's leaders separately. Finally, they agreed to separate the two armies by creating demilitarized zones between them. After that, tensions lessened and the oil embargo ended. Kissinger engineered a similar agreement between Israel and Syria. Both agreements enabled the Arab states to regain some of the lands that Israel had taken in 1967 and 1973. Both sides took steps that, it was hoped, would lead toward future peace talks.

A second agreement between Egypt and Israel in 1975, again brokered by Kissinger, led to a further Israeli pullback and to an Egyptian renunciation of force to settle the Arab-Israeli conflict. Both sides feared political deals: Israel feared it might jeopardize its security by conceding too much to the Arabs; Egypt and Syria feared making concessions that might anger other Arabs, especially the Palestinians. In 1974, the Arabs agreed that only the PLO could speak for the Palestinians, but Israel refused to talk to what it viewed as a terrorist group. When a nationalist coalition, headed by Menachem Begin (who had led the underground paramilitary group Irgun Zvai Leumi up to 1948), won Israel's 1977 elections, the country seemed to be on a collision course with the Arabs. US president Jimmy Carter wanted to reconvene the Geneva Conference (with the Soviet Union) and include Palestinians in the new talks, to Israel's dismay.

Egyptian president Anwar Sadat surprised everyone by announcing that he would go to Jerusalem to parley with Israel's government. Although startled, Begin agreed to receive him and a new peace process began, leading to US mediation and finally to an extraordinary summit held at Camp David, with Carter as host and Sadat and Begin as chief negotiators. A tentative agreement was reached for peace between Egypt and Israel, and the three leaders signed the pact in September 1978. Diplomats ironed out the details, and the final Egyptian-Israeli peace treaty was signed in March 1979. The treaty provided for Israel's phased withdrawal from the Sinai, full diplomatic relations between Jerusalem and Cairo, and ongoing negotiations on the status of Palestinians under Israeli occupation. The other Arab states and the PLO denounced Sadat's policy, broke diplomatic ties with Egypt, and vowed to continue their opposition to Israel.

The Islamic Revolution in Iran

While the West watched the Egyptian-Israeli peace talks, a revolution was brewing against the government of Mohammad Reza Shah, who had ruled Iran for almost thirty-seven years. The US and most European governments had long backed the shah as a bulwark against Soviet expansionism and pan-Arabism, selling Iran billions of dollars worth of Western arms. Iran's surging income caused by the oil price hikes in 1973 drew US and European investors to Tehran where the shah proclaimed grandiose development schemes. These plans, run from the top down, gave little attention to what the Iranian people needed. They stressed showcase projects instead of making basic changes in the villages where most Iranians lived or in the factories or on the farms where most Iranians worked. The shah tolerated no opposition to his policies; a large intelligence bureau, Sazman-e Ettelaat va Amniyat-e Keshvar (SAVAK), spied on dissidents and jailed or tortured his critics.

Opposition to the shah came from nationalists who had backed Mosaddeq in 1951–1953, Marxists, labor leaders, intellectuals, and students. None of these groups could withstand threats of imprisonment, torture, or even death at the hands of SAVAK agents. The best-organized and most popular opposition came from Muslim leaders, for Iran is a Shi'i country and Shi'ism empowers its ulama to reinterpret Islamic law. One such leader was the Ayatollah Ruhollah Khomeini, who in his sermons and writings attacked the shah's tyranny and US interference in Iranian affairs. Exiled from Iran in 1964, Khomeini continued to stir up opposition from Iraq and later from Paris. His sermons were smuggled into Iran and passed from hand to hand; some were even read aloud in the mosques.

An attack on Khomeini in the Iranian press sparked popular demonstrations early in 1978, and government efforts to suppress them led instead to larger protests. Growing numbers of Iranians turned against the shah's government, demanding the liberties and human rights advocated by President Carter. Many Americans, fearing the shah's regime would fall, called for a nationalist government that would unite all Iranians. The shah, stricken with cancer and cut off from the people, appointed a nationalist premier and left Iran in January 1979, expecting the United States to restore his regime as it had done in 1953. This did not occur.

The Iranian people, elated at the shah's departure, staged demonstrations to bring back the ayatollah. In February Khomeini returned, the shah's army defected to the ayatollah's side, and the government turned over its power to the revolutionaries. A cabinet whose members held opinions ranging from nationalist to Marxist to ultra-Islamic temporarily took charge of Iran, and revolutionary *komiteh*s (committees) rounded up SAVAK agents and the shah's supporters, trying many and executing some of them. A popular plebiscite backed Khomeini's demand that Iran become an Islamic republic.

The Iranian Revolution was a turning point in modern Middle Eastern history. A government committed to rapid Westernization was toppled by a populist regime dedicated to making Islam the basis of its policies and the guide for its economy, society, and culture. The new leaders vowed to export the revolution throughout the Muslim world. The emirates and shaikhdoms of the Gulf, with their vast oil revenues and wide disparities between rich and poor, were vulnerable. Some had Shi'a likely to be influenced by Iran. Iran's seizure of the US embassy and the taking of fifty-two hostages outraged Westerners, but it also encouraged Muslims to criticize the United States and other Western governments viewed as hostile to Islam.

US diplomatic and military efforts to secure the release of the hostages failed. Soviet troops, observing US weakness after the Iranian Revolution, occupied Afghanistan in December 1979. Military aggression seemed to be in fashion, as Iraqi president Saddam Hussein renounced a treaty he had signed with the shah's government in 1975 letting Iran share control with Iraq over the confluence of the Euphrates and Tigris rivers, the Shatt al-Arab waterway, and proceeded to invade southwestern Iran in 1980. This dispute was a pretext for deeper antagonisms between the two countries: Iraq wanted to replace Egypt as the Arabs' leader; Iran urged all Muslims, especially Shi'a, to replace their secularized regimes with Islamic republics.

Iraq made huge inroads into Iran at first, but the Iranians fought back and eventually regained the captured lands and even seized strategic points near Iraq's second-largest city, Basra. Neither the Shi'i majority in Iraq nor the Arab minority in Iran rebelled against its government, but each state spent billions on weapons and suffered heavy losses of personnel and equipment as well as destruction of oil refineries, homes, shops, and factories. Both sides drafted what males they could find, even foreign workers and young boys, into their armies to replenish their fallen soldiers. Both, especially Iraq, fired missiles at the enemy's cities and used poison gas in combat.

Iran soon realized that it would have to release the US hostages to gain international support for its war effort. Algerian diplomats mediated the dispute and secured the release of all fifty-two hostages after 444 days in captivity. Although President Ronald Reagan's administration may have encouraged Iraq to attack, offered its regime credits to buy US grain, and provided military intelligence, it sold US missiles and spare parts to Iran for secret funds that could later be used to finance anticommunist rebels in Nicaragua. When Iran and Iraq attacked each other's oil tankers in the Gulf and then started firing on the ships of other countries, the US government took to reflagging Kuwaiti tankers and using its warships to escort them. In

1988, the United States and Iran almost went to war with each other when a US naval officer accidentally shot down an Iranian passenger plane over the Gulf, but Tehran found that almost no country would back it. The UN Security Council had passed a resolution calling for a cease-fire between the warring states. Iraq had already accepted the resolution and, in July 1988, Iran reluctantly followed suit.

The Iranian Revolution had many repercussions beyond the war with Iraq. Between 1979 and 1987, Tehran tried to foment revolts throughout the Muslim world, using its Islamic Republican Party to export its ideology. Iranian guerrillas set up training camps for revolutionaries as remote as the Moros in the Philippines and the Polisario rebels opposing Moroccan control of the Western Sahara. Especially important, however, was Iran's aid to Lebanon's Shi'a, once poor and unheeded but emerging in the 1980s as major players in that country's civil war.

Lebanon: A Cockpit of Middle Eastern Rivalry

Ever since independence, Lebanon had presented one face to the West: that of a democratic, urbane society, the "Switzerland of the Middle East." To many of its own inhabitants, and certainly to other Arabs, however, it showed another face: one of unfair privileges enjoyed by its Christians at the expense of Lebanon's Muslims (both Sunni and Shi'i) and Druze. As more Lebanese moved to the cities, where disparities of wealth and power were visible, and as the Muslim percentage of Lebanon's population rose relative to that of the Christians, discontent mounted. Economic and social conditions improved after the 1958 civil war, but Lebanese Muslims and Palestinian refugees still resented their inferior status. Skirmishes sometimes broke out between Muslims and Christians or between Palestinians and Lebanese. Usually they were settled quietly, but in 1975 Sunni Muslim and Maronite Christian militias started fighting in earnest, the PLO soon joined in, and a major civil war began. In 1976, the Lebanese government invited Syria into the country to help suppress Muslim and Palestinian militias. Syrian troops did indeed buttress the Maronite-dominated government in 1976, but they stayed in Lebanon and soon shifted to the Muslim side. Early in 1978, Israel invaded southern Lebanon, partly to keep the Syrian army away from their northern border, but withdrew after the UN stationed a buffer force in the parts of Lebanon bordering Israel.

But low-intensity conflict dragged on. Ignoring the UN buffer, Palestinian commandos sometimes raided northern Israel; Israeli troops bombed suspected PLO bases in Lebanese villages and even Beirut neighborhoods. In 1982 Israel invaded southern Lebanon, repulsed the Syrian army and PLO militias, bypassed the UN force, and besieged Beirut. Lebanon's parliament elected a Maronite president aligned with Israel against the Palestinians and their Arab backers. When he was killed in an explosion, Israel's troops invaded Beirut. While they were there, Maronite militias invaded the mainly Palestinian neighborhoods of Sabra and Shatilla where they killed hundreds of old men, women, and children. Appalled by the massacre, which Israel's army abetted, the Western powers sent a multinational force into Lebanon.

The United States hoped to persuade Syria and Israel to leave Lebanon and the various militias to hand over their arms and their powers to a reconstituted Lebanese government. Instead, the Israelis and the multinational force angered not just the Sunni Muslims and Palestinians, but also Lebanon's hitherto quiet Shi'i citizens. Some young Shi'a, trained by the Iranians, drove trucks loaded with explosives into Western embassies, the barracks of the foreign armies, and Maronite strongholds, killing and injuring hundreds. These suicide squads wrought such havoc among the European, US, and Israeli forces that they withdrew, although Israel continued to occupy southern Lebanon for fifteen more years. These militant Muslims gained prestige from ousting Western foreign troops from Lebanon.

Meanwhile, Palestinians under Israeli occupation launched a general uprising, or intifada, that lasted from 1987 until 1993 and caused 160 Israeli and 1,162 Palestinian deaths. The intifada did not shrink or enlarge the lands controlled by Israel, but it raised the prestige of the Palestinians living in Gaza (where the uprising began) and the West Bank in the eyes of other Arabs. The PLO formally declared the "independence" of the State of Palestine, Chairman Arafat denounced terrorism, and US-Palestinian talks occurred briefly in 1989, but US attention was soon drawn away to a crisis in the Gulf.

The Iraq-Kuwait Crisis and Israeli-Arab Negotiations

Iraq long felt overshadowed by Egypt as the Arabs' cultural center and second to Saudi Arabia as the area's largest oil producer. The Iran-Iraq War in the 1980s left it heavily indebted to the Gulf states. Iraqis also viewed Kuwait as a dynastic enclave beneficial to Western oil importers. At times Iraq even tried to annex Kuwait, hoping to enlarge its coastline and become the leading power on the Gulf. In July 1990, Iraq accused Kuwait of slant drilling for oil under Iraqi territory and of demanding that loans it had made to Iraq during the war against Iran be repaid. Other Arab governments tried to mediate the dispute, but Hussein ordered Iraqi troops to occupy Kuwait on August 2, 1990.

Hussein did not expect serious opposition to Iraq's annexation of Kuwait. When the Arab leaders failed to make the Iraqis withdraw, President George H. W. Bush's administration launched an intense campaign to liberate Kuwait, initially by diplomacy and later by sending troops and matériel to Saudi Arabia in what became known as Operation Desert Shield.

Economic sanctions, backed by increasingly strident UN Security Council resolutions, warned Iraq to remove its troops from Kuwait. Kuwaitis who escaped to other Arab lands called for military measures. Saudi Arabia, hitherto opposed to having any foreign troops in its territory, which includes Mecca and Medina, became a base for a US-led coalition of Arab and foreign forces prepared to attack Iraq's forces in Kuwait.

Undaunted, Hussein warned that such invasion would lead to the torching of Kuwait's oil fields. Nevertheless, the coalition attacked Iraq on January 16, 1991, launching Operation Desert Storm. When six weeks of intense aerial bombing did not dislodge Iraq from Kuwait, the coalition forces began a ground war that soon expelled the Iraqis. George H. W. Bush stopped the hostilities, even as the allied coalition was entering southern Iraq, for the UN resolutions called for only the liberation of Kuwait.

Shi'a in the south and Kurds in the north revolted against Iraq's central government, but never got the help they needed from the United States and its allies. Both uprisings were crushed. Any dissident officers in the Iraqi army hoping to oust their leader were killed, jailed, or expelled. UN sanctions remained in effect, keeping Iraq from importing consumer goods. Hussein stymied the UN inspectors who might have proved that his weapons of mass destruction were destroyed. The allied coalition had won a hollow victory.

Fulfilling a promise made to the Arab states to gain their support for the war against Iraq, the George H. W. Bush administration convened a conference, initially in Madrid, later in Washington, and then Moscow, at which Israeli and Arab delegations met to negotiate peace. Although Israel would not talk with the PLO, representatives from the Occupied Territories were admitted into a joint Jordanian-Palestinian delegation. While public talks dragged on, Israeli and PLO representatives met secretly in Oslo, forging an agreement that surprised everyone when it was announced in 1993. The public signing of a Declaration of Principles by Israel and the PLO in the presence of President Bill Clinton ended the intifada, leading to intense negotiations, focused initially on how to withdraw Israeli troops from Gaza and Jericho.

After many delays, Israel reached an agreement in May 1994 with Palestine's "self-governing authority," allowing Arafat to return to Gaza. Israel could still control the purportedly autonomous Palestinians by retaining troops in Gaza and the West Bank and by barring Palestinian workers from entering Israel during times of crisis. Few jobs were available to them in the autonomous areas. Some frustrated Palestinians forsook the PLO for a radical Muslim movement called Hamas. Jordan and Israel signed a peace treaty in October 1994, and several North African and Gulf states entered into diplomatic or commercial relations with the Jewish state. Israel reached a second agreement with the PLO in September 1995, providing for troop withdrawals from major West Bank population centers. Jerusalem's status was left for later negotiations, however, and most Palestinian lands remained under Israel's control. Prime Minister Yitzhak Rabin was murdered by an Israeli who believed that his government had already conceded too much. A new government, headed by Benjamin Netanyahu, was elected in 1996. It stepped up Jewish settlements in the West Bank and repressive policies against the Palestinians. Only intense US pressure made Netanyahu give up part of Hebron in 1997 and a few other occupied lands in 1998. When his fragile coalition collapsed, he called for early elections.

In 1999, the Labor Party leader, Ehud Barak, won by a narrow margin. He offered to cede most of the West Bank and Gaza to Arafat during negotiations at Camp David and Sharm al-Shaikh in 2000, but the Palestinians rejected an offer that would have left Israel in control of key points of the West Bank and obliged them to give up their right of return to other lands now part of Israel. Palestinians and Israelis stepped up attacks on each other, and a new intifada broke out in September 2000. The hawkish general, Ariel Sharon, accused of inspiring the 1982 Palestinian massacre at Sabra and Shatilla, defeated Barak in a special election in 2001 and reoccupied most of the West Bank and Gaza.

In 2002, the European Union, the United Nations, and the Russian and US governments proposed a Road Map to peace. In mid-2003, however, the plan foundered on the intransigence of the Jewish settlers in the Occupied Territories; Israel's construction of a "security fence" on the West Bank, its "targeted killings" of Palestinians, and its armed incursions into Palestinian-controlled areas; and the failure of the Palestinian Authority to stop attacks on Israeli civilians by Palestinian suicide bombers.

Terrorism and Democracy in the Middle East

Terrorism became the last resort of ever more desperate Arabs who sent suicide bombers into Israel to kill civilians, blew up US embassies in Kenya and Tanzania, damaged a US Navy warship in Yemen, and on September 11, 2001, hijacked four US civil airliners to attack New York's World Trade Center and the Pentagon in Washington, DC. The group behind these attacks was al-Qaeda (the Base). Although its headquarters was in Afghanistan, from which it had driven the Soviet forces in the late 1980s, most of its members were Arab. Its leader, Osama bin Laden, was a Saudi national. Indeed, the nineteen hijackers involved in the September 11 attacks were all Arabs, citizens of Egypt and Saudi Arabia. They protested US favoritism toward Israel, the US preference for dictatorial regimes over Islamist ones (notably in Algeria), and the domination of US culture in much of the Muslim world. US president George W. Bush declared a "war on terror" and directed US forces to bombard and occupy Afghanistan to capture bin Laden and destroy al-Qaeda.

His administration identified Iraq as a major supporter of terrorism and demanded that it fulfill the UN Security Council's Gulf War resolutions to destroy its nuclear, chemical, and biological weapons. If Iraq's government failed to prove it had done so, and the UN inspectors could not verify their absence, the US armed forces, aided if possible by its allies, would invade Iraq and oust Hussein's regime. On March 20, 2003, the "coalition of the willing"—forty nations led by the United States and Britain—attacked Iraq, occupied the country, and drove Hussein's regime from power on April 9.

Yet in the ensuing months, coalition forces failed to protect government buildings, museums, and libraries from looters. They could not ensure supplies of electricity, gasoline, food, and medicine to most Iraqis, or create a stable political system. The George W. Bush administration dissolved the Iraqi armed forces and the Baath Party, which had been the mainstay of the old political system. Creating a new government to represent Iraq's diverse mix of Sunni and Shi'i Muslim Arabs, Kurds, Turcomans, and Christians took longer than expected; meanwhile, dissidents attacked coalition forces, exploded bombs aimed at local and foreign targets, and sabotaged oil installations. The US-led coalition became frayed as Iraqi insurgents took soldiers from some of the smaller armies as hostages, and as al-Qaeda in Europe attacked public transportation in Madrid and London. Coalition forces in Iraq imprisoned thousands of civilians suspected of terrorism. Some were tortured by US soldiers in Abu Ghraib prison near Baghdad. The dissemination of digital photos taken by the tormentors infuriated the whole Muslim world and discredited the Iraq War among many in the United States.

In 2005 the United States arranged three Iraqi elections: one in January for a transitional assembly to write a constitution, one in October to ratify the document thus drafted, and one in December to elect representatives to parliament under its terms. Although most Iraqis welcomed the chance to vote, many Sunnis boycotted the first two elections, causing the new constitution to favor Shi'a and Kurds. The new parliament, whose elected members knew little about democratic procedures, took months to choose a cabinet and could not pass a law to share oil revenues fairly throughout Iraq.

During this time, the United States along with other coalition troops had to battle insurgents in Iraq's cities, causing heavy loss of civilian life and uprooting many, both internally displaced persons fleeing from one part of Iraq to another, and Iraqi refugees who fled, mainly to Syria and Jordan. For those Iraqis who were fighting a foreign occupation, there were no clear battle lines and no united resistance force. The Kurdish region of northern Iraq functioned independently of Baghdad, even though Iraq's president is a Kurd and Kurds also serve in the cabinet and parliament. Sunni and Shi'i militias opposed the Iraqi government, which most foreign countries recognized as legitimate and constitutional, but which many

Iraqis claimed was imposed on them by the occupying armies. Some local and foreign observers asked whether Iraq was even a nation and proposed dividing the country into Kurdish, Sunni, and Shi'i autonomous regions.

Neighboring Iran did benefit from the Iraq War, which empowered Iraqi Shi'a over the once dominant Sunnis, but the presence of large numbers of US troops in both Iraq and Afghanistan made Iranians fear for their own security. Both Israel and the United States have expressed concern about Iran's efforts to develop nuclear energy and to enrich uranium, which could lead to an Iranian nuclear bomb. The Iranians elected a conservative Islamist majority in the majles in 2004 and chose Tehran mayor Mahmood Ahmadinejad as their president in 2005. His public statements advocating Israel's destruction and questioning the Shoah (Holocaust) added to Israeli fears and to the urgent desire of its supporters and some US politicians to launch a preventative attack against Iran's nuclear facilities before its regime has nuclear weapons. Such an attack would lead to Iranian counterattacks against nearby US forces (they withdrew from Iraq in 2011) and possibly the oil installations of pro-Western countries. It would certainly stir up in such Muslim countries as Pakistan and Egypt.

Iran and its supporters have played a growing role in both Lebanon and Palestine. Lebanon did recover from its civil war of 1975–1991, but power within the country remained unevenly distributed among the various sects. Israel withdrew its remaining troops from southern Lebanon in 2000, but 25,000 Syrian troops still occupied the country and tended to favor Shi'i Muslim interests while Israel and the West still supported the Maronites and other Christians. Lebanon's most prominent leader was its Sunni Muslim prime minister, Rafiq Hariri, who had spearheaded the country's economic revival. He was killed in February 2005, an act widely ascribed to Syrian intelligence. Popular revulsion to his assassination led to a coalition of Christian and Sunni Muslim parties that made Syria withdraw its troops from Lebanon. Lebanon's unrest did not abate, however. Its Shi'a, who constituted a plurality of the population, threw their support to Hizbullah, a militant Islamist movement that accumulated Syrian and Iranian weapons and increasingly used them against Israel, whose troops retaliated in kind. When Hizbullah captured two Israeli soldiers in July 2006, Israel attacked its Lebanese bases by air, land, and sea, which killed, maimed, and displaced thousands of civilians as well as Hizbullah fighters. Hizbullah rockets struck northern Israel and caused damage to Haifa and some Jewish and Arab villages in Galilee. The fighting ended after thirty-four days under UN Security Council Resolution 1701, which dispatched a new peacekeeping force to southern Lebanon. Neither side really won, and tension persists on the Israeli-Lebanese border.

The Arab-Israeli conflict has gradually turned in the past quartercentury into a struggle between Israel and the Palestinians (or, more accurately, descendants of the Arabic-speaking refugees of the 1948 Arab-Israeli war). Israel and its backers had gradually come to accept the need for a Palestinian state, and the Arab governments offered to recognize Israel in return for its withdrawal from the Golan Heights, the West Bank, and the Gaza Strip, lands Israel had taken in the 1967 war. But the Palestinians and Israel still fought against each other. The second intifada, or Al-Aqsa Intifada, which followed the failure of the 2000 Camp David talks, dragged on, as the Palestinians resorted to suicide bombings against civilians in Israel and the Israeli army raided and occupied large swaths of the West Bank and Gaza, destroying houses and killing or maiming Palestinians. The number of Jewish settlers in the West Bank and Gaza doubled between 1993 and 2004, further dimming hopes for peace. The Road Map, an Israeli-Palestinian peace plan put forth in July 2002 by the United States, the European Union, Russia, and the United Nations, led to brief peace talks, which were soon suspended. The plan had proposed creating a Palestinian state to exist side-by-side with the Israeli state.

Realizing that the Jewish state faced a demographic challenge if it occupied Palestinian lands indefinitely, Israel decided to pull back from areas in which it had no long-term interest, starting with the Gaza Strip in 2005. Israel withdrew its settlers and soldiers, hoping for peace with the Palestinians—but, in part because it continued to control land, water, and air access to Gaza, dissatisfied Palestinians attacked southern Israel with rockets and Israel retaliated with targeted killings and military invasions. The 2006 war in Lebanon overshadowed a concurrent deadly conflict in Gaza. Another war, deadlier still, would break out in January 2009. As for the West Bank, Israel had begun building a "security fence" in 2002. Intended to keep raiders and suicide bombers out of Israel, it impeded Palestinian movement within the West Bank and cut off some of the captured lands, especially those occupied by Jewish settlers, from Palestinian areas. Not surprisingly, when Palestinians could elect representatives to their parliament in January 2006, most chose Islamist deputies loyal, not to Fatah, but rather to Hamas, which formed a new cabinet that openly opposed the Oslo Accords and recognition of Israel. As Israel blockaded Gaza, Hamas militias began fighting forces loyal to Fatah. In June 2007 the PLO president, Mahmoud Abbas, dismissed the Hamas government. Hamas took over in Gaza while Fatah retained control of the West Bank. Neither the George W. Bush administration nor Egypt's Hosni Mubarak could bring Hamas and Fatah back together.

Popular Uprisings in Iran and the Arab Countries

As other chapters in this book show, few Middle Eastern governments have much legitimacy in the early twenty-first century. In Iran, which has a functioning constitution and regular elections for both the majles and the presidency, real political power lies in the hands of the Council of Guardians and the supreme leader, who holds that position for life. Even so, the office of president is hotly contested every four years. When President Ahmadinejad ran for reelection in 2009, three candidates opposed him. Despite widespread reports of fraud, Ahmadinejad claimed victory, leading thousands of Iranians to demonstrate in a protest commonly called the Green Revolution. State security forces killed and injured thousands while other opponents were imprisoned. The Islamic Republic seemed as authoritarian as the shah's government had been, but the very fact that Iranians rebelled against it set an example for the Arab world.

The Arab uprisings that spread throughout the region in 2011 were inspired in part by Iran's Green Revolution and by hundreds of small uprisings in Algeria, whose people have never accepted the military dictatorship that suppressed the Islamists who won an election in 1991. Rising prices for food and fuel, coupled with widespread unemployment of young people, notably university graduates, also fed discontent in the Arab countries. When Mohamed Bouazizi, a Tunisian street vendor who was fined and humiliated by a policewoman, set himself on fire in December 2010, he is said to have lit the flame of revolution in his country, leading within a month to the fall of its dictatorial government on January 14, 2011. As Chapters 4 and 7 illustrate, however, protests throughout the region had been escalating in recent years, particularly around economic grievances. In Egypt, for example, laborers had been protesting in increasing numbers since 2004, so that by 2009 nearly 2 million of them had participated in marches and demonstrations. In almost every Arab state, citizens had long experienced similar abuse from police, bureaucrats, or others who wielded unchecked power over them. In Egypt, where Mubarak had ruled for almost thirty years, demonstrators gathered in various towns and urban neighborhoods beginning January 25, 2011. They converged in Tahrir Square in ever growing numbers, until Mubarak resigned on February 11, 2011. Soon large-scale rebellions broke out in Libya, Bahrain, Syria, and Yemen; lesser ones in Jordan, Oman, Morocco, Lebanon, Saudi Arabia, and Kuwait. The diverse protesters expressed a range of demands, primarily for economic reforms and pay increases, but also for dignity, democratic reforms, and freedom from the harsh repression of the state. The protests grew in numbers and zeal, with the chant "The people demand the downfall of the regime" adopted in various forms in many countries. The UN Security Council passed a landmark resolution on Libya that for the first time articulated a justification for violating a nation's sovereignty for the purpose of protecting citizens; promptly, the European countries, with US backing, sent arms and troops to help the rebels oust the regime of Muammar Qaddafi. In Yemen, a combination of massive nationwide protests and a coalition of opposition parties and military leaders led to the resignation of its long-ruling president, Ali Abdallah Salih, who nevertheless remains a powerful figure in the country. Other regimes, especially those of Syria and

Large murals on the new campus of the American University of Cairo commemorate the January 25, 2011, revolution.

Bahrain, resorted to draconian methods to intimidate and repress their opponents, and Syria ended up embroiled in a protracted and bloody civil war.

As of this writing, no one can say that the new regimes will solve their countries' economic and social problems. Tunisia and Egypt now have governments dominated by moderate Islamist groups, although in Tunisia the Islamists are working closely with secular and leftist parties while in Egypt they are not. The Libyans elected a secularist liberal government, but power remains dispersed among various tribes. Yemen's new regime resembles the old one, with former president Salih continuing to lead the ruling party. That regime continues to face challenges from rebels tied to al-Qaeda. Syria's civil war has begun to threaten the stability of Lebanon, and hundreds of thousands of Syrian refugees are flooding into neighboring Turkey and Jordan.

Conclusion

The peoples and the countries of the Middle East are not at peace, either with one another or, indeed, with themselves. Secular nationalism competes with Islam as the leading ideology for many Middle Eastern Arabs, Iranians, and Turks. The breakup of the Soviet Union has drawn some Middle Eastern countries into competition over the new republics of the Caucasus and Central Asia. The Cold War may have ended, but the United States articulates its Middle East policy goals not by diplomacy, but by force. Borders between countries, drawn mostly by Western imperialists for their own interests, rarely reflect natural frontiers and are often violated by the armies of strong states preying on weaker ones. Many Middle Easterners have moved to burgeoning cities, acquired years of schooling, and been exposed to radio and television propaganda, swelling their ambitions beyond what their societies actually have to offer. Young adults feel especially frustrated, a feeling often enhanced by their migration from countries of high population and little oil (such as Egypt) to others that are poor in labor but rich in oil (such as Saudi Arabia), separating them from their parents, spouses, children, and friends. Other chapters will show that no other area now poses so great a danger to world peace as the volatile Middle East.

Bibliography

Cleveland, William L., and Martin Bunton. 2013. *A History of the Modern Middle East.* 5th ed. Boulder: Westview Press.

Daniel, Elton. 2012. *The History of Iran.* 2nd ed. Westport, CT: Greenwood Press.

Findley, Carter V. 2005. *The Turks in World History.* Oxford: Oxford University Press.

Gelvin, James L. 2011. *The Modern Middle East: A History.* 3rd ed. Oxford: Oxford University Press.

———. 2012. *The Arab Uprisings: What Everyone Needs to Know.* Oxford: Oxford University Press.

Goldschmidt, Arthur, Jr., and Lawrence Davidson. 2013. *A Concise History of the Middle East.* 10th ed. Boulder: Westview Press.

Kamrava, Mehran. 2011. *The Modern Middle East: A Political History Since the First World War.* 2nd ed. Berkeley: University of California Press.

Lapidus, Ira M. 2002. *A History of Islamic Societies.* 2nd ed. New York: Cambridge University Press.

Reich, Bernard. 2012. *A Brief History of Israel.* 2nd ed. New York: Checkmark Books.

Roberson, Barnaby. 2012. *North Africa: A History from the Mediterranean Shore to the Sahara.* London: Duckworth.

Rogan, Eugene. 2009. *The Arabs: A History.* New York: Basic Books.

4

Middle Eastern Politics

Philip A. Schrodt and Deborah J. Gerner

Morocco reinforces security in Marrakech after protests . . . Saudi Royal
Court announces death of 84-year-old princess . . . Turkish aid organization sends flour to Syria . . . UAE paper urges Syrian warring parties to
stop fighting . . . Palestinian paper interviews Hamas official on agreement with Israel . . . Rebels reportedly take over "one of Syria's largest"
oil wells . . . Iraq marks withdrawal of foreign forces . . . Saudi cleric criticizes Egyptian president, Muslim Brotherhood . . . Tunisian Ennahdha
party head interviewed on Arab Spring developments . . . Two killed, four
injured in clashes southwest of Sabha in southern Libya.
—*BBC Middle East Monitor,* December 30–31, 2012

Viewed from the perspective of daily headlines, politics in the Middle East
appear confused, chaotic, and often violent. When asked why they are interested in taking a course in Middle Eastern politics, students often say they
want to be able to understand the news stories but do not know where to
begin. In this chapter we focus on the current political situation of the Arab
world, Iran, Israel, and Turkey. First we describe several general factors
that influence the contemporary Middle East such as its colonial legacy, the
evolving international context, its level of economic development, and the
recent series of political changes of the Arab uprisings. We then review a
variety of political institutions and ideologies that function in the region.
Particular attention is given to distinguishing those characteristics of Middle Eastern domestic politics that are relatively unusual, for example, the
prevalence of ruling monarchies, from those attributes that are more common such as close relations between the state and the military establishment. The critically important issue of gender, which is only touched on
here, is treated more comprehensively in Chapters 9, 10, and 11.

No discussion of Middle East politics can ignore the Arab uprisings, which have been commemorated in murals like this one in Cairo.

The Colonial Legacy

Domestic politics in the Middle East are influenced by a paradox: this ancient region, with a history that dates back to the earliest years of human settlements, has only recently been organized politically into modern states, that is, centralized political units with sovereignty over a fixed territory and population. Arthur Goldschmidt describes in Chapter 3 the paths these countries took to reach the beginning of the twenty-first century. In this section we briefly summarize one of the most significant aspects of that history for understanding contemporary politics: the impact of European imperialism in the region.

The term *imperialism* refers to the establishment of political and economic control by one state or empire over a foreign territory. In the context of the Middle East, the involvement of European powers, particularly Britain and France, was highly interventionist and, from the perspective of regional history, often arbitrary. At the same time, the extent and nature of European control varied considerably, both between subregions (e.g., North Africa vs. the Arabian Peninsula) and between adjacent areas within a single region (e.g., Syria vs. Jordan). Decisions made during the colonial era brought about effects that persist today and continue to influence the Middle East's political development.

In contrast to the Americas, sub-Saharan Africa, and Asia, which were subjected to colonial exploitation after being "discovered" by Europeans, the geographical extent and the resources of the Middle East were known to the political powers of Europe since antiquity. Prior to the middle of the nineteenth century, however, widespread colonial activity by Europe was blocked by the military power of the Ottoman Empire. When Ottoman control weakened and Europeans opportunistically began to assert authority, that expansion occurred in the context of competing European imperial systems. The pattern of a single colonizer exercising control over a large contiguous territory—as with the British in North America and southern Asia or the Spanish in Latin America—did not occur, and so the colonial experience of states in the Middle East varied substantially across time and place.

Egypt provides an illustration of the political complexities of colonialism. As detailed in Chapter 3, Egypt was occupied by Napoleonic France at the beginning of the nineteenth century. French forces were defeated by the British who restored Ottoman control to Egypt. However, Ottoman rule was soon challenged by Muhammad Ali—a soldier originally appointed by the Ottomans to administer Egypt—who began to develop Egypt as a powerful and autonomous state. His successors were unable to continue this independence and, in conjunction with construction of the Suez Canal, the country fell into deep debt to European financiers. These financial problems provided the pretext for a British invasion in 1882 and the consolidation of forty years of direct British control. In 1923, Britain granted nominal independence to Egypt, but maintained the pro-British monarchy and reserved the right to station troops in the country, which it did during World War II to counter Nazi Germany's attempts to gain control of the Suez Canal. Even after the British-imposed monarchy was overthrown in 1952, Britain and France briefly invaded Egypt in 1956 in a final attempt to reassert European authority over the canal.

Although the details vary, a similar intensity and intricacy of colonial involvement can be found in most of the major countries of the region. Most significantly, British and French colonial interests competed throughout the region. On occasion this caused conflict between the European states, as with the Fashoda dispute in Sudan in 1898 and the Agadir Crisis in Morocco in 1911; at other times Britain and France agreed to sweeping divisions of authority, as with the Sykes-Picot Agreement in 1916, which divided up former Ottoman districts into modern-day Syria, Lebanon, Iraq, Jordan, Israel, and the Palestinian Territories. Algeria was actually made an administrative part of France and won independence only through a long and brutal war. Europe and the United States considered the Gulf region peripheral—allowing Abdul Aziz ibn Saud to assemble an independent state on the Arabian Peninsula without external interference—until the 1930s with the discovery of oil. Although Britain and France were responsible for most of the colonial activity in the region, other European states—notably, Italy in Libya and Russia in Iran and Turkey—also exercised substantial influence.

These diverse colonial interactions left a patchwork of widely differing political circumstances, as illustrated by comparing the experiences of Israel, Jordan, and Lebanon. The heavily populated parts of these countries occupy a small geographical area that, in the absence of borders, could be easily driven around by car in a day. But in the second half of the twentieth century, the experiences of the three countries could not be more different. Lebanon—in the French sphere of influence under the Sykes-Picot division—developed as a confessional parliamentary democracy that attempted to balance Muslim and Christian interests while maintaining the dominant position of the latter. Modern Israel developed out of a League of Nations mandate for Palestine—itself a relic of the Ottoman Empire—that under British control was promised as a "homeland" to the Zionist movement in the 1917 Balfour Declaration. Jordan was forged from another area under British control and politically constituted as an Arab monarchy ruled by the Hashemite family from the Arabian Peninsula to whom Britain owed a favor. At the beginning of the twenty-first century, still another political entity—some form of Palestinian state situated between Israel and Jordan and between Egypt and Israel—struggled to emerge. Consequently, three (and potentially four) very different states have been established in an area that for most of its history was intertwined economically and culturally.

As this example shows, the colonial experience has been critically important in determining the contemporary political environment. Differences between the North African states of Morocco, Algeria, Libya, and Egypt reflect in part the fact that they were, respectively, under Arab, French, Italian, and British authority during the early twentieth century. When British prestige in the Gulf waned, it was smoothly replaced with US influence whereas the Algerian political system was strongly influenced by its bloody war for independence from France. A few countries—Morocco, Turkey, Saudi Arabia, and Oman—escaped direct European domination almost entirely (although they were profoundly affected by the threat of this control) whereas others—Djibouti, for instance, or the Western Sahara, whose referendum on independence has been delayed repeatedly—are among the last areas in the world to achieve political sovereignty. As was true in Africa, the boundaries imposed by European powers often had little correspondence to the distribution of ethnic groups on the ground—most notably in the division of the Kurdish region between Turkey, Iraq, and Iran—or created states whose legitimacy could be called into question, as with Iraq's claims on Kuwait and Syria's claims on Lebanon. The colonial empires are gone, yet their effects not only linger but continue to have substantial influence.

A Changing International Context

Following European decolonization during the 1940s, 1950s, and 1960s, the foreign affairs of the Middle East have been dominated by four major conflicts: the Cold War prior to the 1990s, the Arab-Israeli dispute, a series of wars involving Iraq, and, after 1990, the religiously oriented conflicts involving both the Sunni/Shi'i split within Islam and the conservative Sunni militant movement al-Qaeda.

The end of the Cold War and the dissolution of the Soviet Union in 1991 had profound effects on Soviet allies such as Syria, Iraq, Libya, and particularly the former People's Democratic Republic of Yemen (PDR Yemen). Those countries could no longer count on the former superpower for military or economic assistance (although Russia will still gladly sell arms for hard cash), nor is Russia interested in providing the preferential trade arrangements that were often used by the Soviet Union to secure alliances. Allies of the United States faced an equally difficult situation. In the absence of the communist threat and in an environment of growing public disdain for US policies with respect to Israel, the eight-year US occupation of Iraq, and the escalating use of drone attacks in the territories of Muslim states in the Middle East and elsewhere, governments that are seen as too dependent on US support find that this policy generates significant domestic opposition.

During the first decade of the twenty-first century, foreign relations in the eastern half of the Middle East were dominated by the US occupation of Iraq that had been initiated by the administration of President George W. Bush. Following a year of increasing hostilities, this culminated in a relatively quick invasion of Iraq by the United States, Great Britain, and some additional allies in March and April of 2003. While a clear military victory was achieved over the regular Iraqi forces, the Bush administration went against the advice of its senior military officers and sent inadequate forces to ensure stability of the country following the dissolution of the regime of Saddam Hussein (Woodward, 2004; Chandrasekaran, 2006; Ricks, 2006). Postinvasion Iraq was plunged into a state of widespread internal conflict involving both Iraqi attacks on the forces of the United States and its allies; extensive ethnic conflict between Sunni, Shi'i, and Kurdish groups within Iraq itself; and attacks on both military and civilian targets by Islamic groups loosely affiliated with al-Qaeda (Galbraith, 2006; Woodward, 2006).

In early 2007, a new US commander, General David Petraeus, implemented a counterinsurgency strategy developed in response to these earlier failures (Petraeus, 2006), combined with a temporary increase in the number of US troops. With the financial support of the United States, Sunni tribes in western Iraq mobilized as the National Council for the Awakening of Iraq to defeat various al-Qaeda groups that had been responsible for widespread violence. Ethnic violence in urban areas was gradually reduced through a policy of increased military presence and physical separation, at the cost of imposing a high level of ethnic segregation in most areas. President Barack Obama was elected in 2008 in part on a promise to remove US troops from Iraq; after a period of gradual withdrawal to isolated bases, the final US troops left the country in December 2011.

Although the Iraqi government achieved a few early benchmarks toward democratic government, notably national legislative elections in 2005 and 2010, the parliamentary system quickly became stalemated as it divided along ethnic lines. Transparency International's Corruption Perceptions Index has consistently ranked Iraq as the most corrupt government in the Middle East, and postwar reconstruction has proceeded only gradually (Transparency International, 2012).

The US invasion of Iraq continues to leave numerous long-term consequences for the region. The war and subsequent ethnic violence generated an estimated 2 million international refugees, and more than 1 million internally displaced persons (Peteet, 2007). While these numbers have declined as postoccupation Iraq stabilizes, internal population changes may be moving Iraq toward a situation where an ethnically mixed central state is no longer possible, leading instead to either a confederation with a weak central state or even outright division of the country. The northern Kurdish area—which has generally avoided the violence plaguing Sunni and Shi'i Iraq—is already essentially an autonomous state; this, in turn, however, is causing considerable tensions with Turkey, which also has a large Kurdish minority.

As Iraq's Shi'i population asserts political control proportional to its numbers, relations between Iraq and predominantly Shi'i Iran may improve. A reversal of the antagonism between these states during the Sunni-dominated regime of Hussein, in turn, may affect Iraq's relations with Saudi Arabia and possibly the United States. Finally, the United States has now established an extensive long-term military presence in the region, with bases in most of the Gulf states (Global Security, 2013) and a large ongoing naval presence. While this has been justified primarily as a counter to Iran, these forces potentially could intervene quickly if some of these countries, particularly Saudi Arabia, were to experience domestic instability.

As discussed in Chapters 5 and 6, the Arab-Israeli conflict also continues, primarily between Palestinians and Israel. Egypt and Jordan have officially normalized relations with Israel, and visitors can now pass freely, if not easily, among these three countries. Egyptian-Israeli relations will almost certainly be altered with the replacement of Israel's strong ally Hosni Mubarak with a parliamentary government led by the Muslim Brotherhood, but as of this writing neither country has made dramatic changes to the Mubarak-era arrangements. To the northeast Syria, crippled by a devastating civil war, is irrelevant until that is resolved. Southern Lebanon, meanwhile, remains a source of tension. Israel withdrew from Lebanon in 2000 after nearly two decades of occupation, but the Israeli-Lebanese border remains a major flash point in the conflict between the Shi'i Hizbullah movement and Israel. A war ensued in the summer of 2006, with Hizbullah firing missiles that reached the Israeli northern city of Haifa and Israel bombing Lebanese territories as far north as Beirut.

With the Oslo Accords of 1993 and establishment of the internationally recognized Palestinian Authority with an elected president and assembly, rapprochement between Palestinians and Israelis briefly appeared likely. The disastrous Camp David talks in 2000 and the subsequent outbreak of the second intifada (sparked by Ariel Sharon's provocative visit to the Haram al-Sharif/Temple Mount in September 2000) ended these hopes.

As of June 2013, the peace process of the 1990s is in complete disarray. Israel has reoccupied much of the land it ceded to the Palestinians as part of the Oslo peace process and has constructed a separation wall—a structure that is merely a well-patrolled fence in rural areas and a massive ten-meter-high concrete wall with guard towers and fortified gateways in major urban areas—to separate West Bank Palestinians from Israel and, in many instances, from their ancestral farmland and water resources. Israel withdrew its military forces and settlements from the Gaza Strip in the summer of 2005, but the combination of rocket attacks launched from Gaza into Israel and retaliatory Israeli air strikes and economic blockades have meant that Gaza has seen nearly continuous military activity, including intense attacks from Israel in January 2009 and November 2012 that caused hundreds of casualties in Gaza.

The prospects for a resolution of the Israeli-Palestinian situation are further hampered by major political changes in nearly all of the major actors involved. Palestinian president Yasser Arafat died in November 2004, after having been weakened by illness for some years prior. Mahmoud Abbas is his nominal successor, but Abbas has not had the skill in balancing the competing constituencies in the West Bank, Gaza, and the Palestinian diaspora. In June 2007 a brief civil war in Gaza resulted in a takeover by Hamas and, since that time, Hamas and the Palestinian Authority have essentially been operating parallel Palestinian governments in Gaza and the West Bank.

While the security and economic situation is better on the Israeli side, the political situation has not been conducive to diplomacy. The Labor Party, which historically was more sympathetic to a peace agreement with the Palestinians, has declined in power—in the 2009 election it won only 8 seats in the 120-member Knesset (Israel's parliament)—and recent governments have involved coalitions of conservative and nationalist parties with little interest in negotiations. The United States, which historically played a major role in facilitating agreements, was focused on the wars in Iraq and Afghanistan during most of the George W. Bush administration, and the Obama administration has shown little interest in becoming involved in new negotiations. This might open up the possibility of peace negotiations facilitated by the European Union (EU), but whether the EU is willing to increase its involvement and how effective it can be remain to be seen.

The final major factor that has arisen in the past decade is the emergence of two significant transnational military movements that challenge the established governments in the region. The Shiʻa of Iran, Iraq, and Lebanon, who for most of the modern period had occupied positions of limited political power, have emerged as a significant military force in the region (Nasr, 2006; *Middle East Report*, 2007). This has resulted from the confluence of a number of events, including Hizbullah's unexpectedly effective attacks against Israel during the later phases of Israel's occupation of Lebanon and in the summer of 2006, as well as the establishment of a state-within-a-state in southern Lebanon under Hizbullah's control. The period of ethnic conflict in Iraq saw the creation of large Shiʻi militias, most notably the Mahdi Army of Muqtada al-Sadr, and subsequent elections gave Shiʻi parties considerable parliamentary power, including the prime ministership. The Iranian government of Mahmood Ahmadinejad has developed advanced capabilities in long-range ballistic missiles and has embarked on a program to develop nuclear weapons as well as providing weapons to groups such as Hamas and Hizbullah.

The implications of these developments are unclear. Sunni-Shiʻi divisions are not a new phenomenon in the Middle East, though for most of recent history these were always resolved in favor of Sunni-dominated political institutions except in Iran, which was culturally as well as religiously distinct from the Arab world. As the Shiʻi majority gains political power in Iraq, a semiautonomous Shiʻi area is established in southern Lebanon, and the large Shiʻi populations in states such as Saudi Arabia and Bahrain assert claims for greater political participation, the issue moves into key areas of the Arab world itself. This is further complicated, as discussed in Chapter 12, by the fact that conservative Sunni movements such as al-Qaeda regard Shiism as heretical, a distinction frequently lost on Western commentators who lump together al-Qaeda, Saudi Wahhabism, and the Shiʻi Islamic Republic of Iran as "Islamic fundamentalists."

The second major factor in the past decade has been the extension of the loosely organized militant movement al-Qaeda into a variety of internal conflicts in the region. Al-Qaeda initially was associated with veterans of the successful campaign against the Soviet occupation of Afghanistan in 1979–1989, and then a series of terrorist attacks against the United States and other Western targets, most notoriously the attacks of September 11, 2001. Now a variety of armed groups ideologically and religiously aligned with al-Qaeda's program that emphasizes the rigorous imposition of extreme versions of religious law and a desire to see Muslim countries completely free of Western influence have had significant influence in conflicts within the Middle East, most conspicuously in Iraq, Yemen, Libya, and

Syria. As with earlier Islamic extremist movements, in these countries their targets primarily have been other Muslims such as Shi'a, secular modernists, and Western-aligned governments as well as people who were simply in the wrong place when a bomb was detonated.

Al-Qaeda has been declining in power—and may have essentially ended as a distinct organization when the United States killed its founder, Osama bin Laden, in May 2011—and its associated groups have attracted little popular support. Nonetheless, these groups can be a significant factor in areas experiencing civil war due to their military experience, access to weapons, and tendency to spill over to adjacent areas after suffering defeats. For example, the end of the Libyan civil war in 2011 led to an upsurge in extremist violence in neighboring Mali in 2012, and Somalia has attracted Islamic extremists from Yemen and Sudan. In addition, the US opposition to al-Qaeda as part of its global war on terror has led to substantial US military involvement through the use of robotic drone aircraft to kill individuals, particularly in Yemen. The long-term implications of these activities for continued US involvement in the region are unclear.

Economic Development

Like all decolonized areas, the states of the Middle East are confronting the problem of economic development. This issue will be covered in detail in Chapters 7, 8, and 9; here, we point out several aspects that are most salient to domestic politics. (See Richards and Waterbury, 2007, and Rivlin, 2009, for an extensive treatment of the Middle East's political economy.)

Any discussion of economics must deal separately with states that have significant oil revenues and those that do not. As discussed in Chapter 8, the oil wealth of the boom era of the Organization of Petroleum Exporting Countries (OPEC) made possible policies of almost unimaginable extravagance such as growing wheat in the desert using desalinated water. The subsequent instability of oil prices, however, has left a series of new problems for the petroleum-based economies. In contrast, states that have little or no oil face a fairly conventional set of development issues similar to those of any newly industrializing country.

Under the control of the OPEC cartel, the price of oil increased dramatically during the 1970s. But in the 1980s and 1990s, it slowly declined as sources developed in areas outside of OPEC's control such as the North Sea and Mexico and briefly fell below its pre-1973 levels when measured in inflation-adjusted dollars. The drop in oil revenues, in turn, created several sources of domestic instability as governments had fewer funds available to deal with potential opponents of the regime, either by co-opting them or paying for the coercive power required to suppress them. In a number of countries, economic restructuring programs mandated by the International

Monetary Fund (IMF) in the 1980s and 1990s led to civil unrest as governments began eliminating social services and subsidy programs on which poorer citizens relied.

The oil price decline reversed around 2000, and prices have steadily increased to the point where, by 2012, they were at an all-time high. This increase was initially caused by supply disruptions and instability in Iraq, but persisted due to the demand for oil by the rapidly growing economies of Asia, notably China and India. Despite the development of renewable energy resources and alternative sources such as the use of hydraulic fracking to extract natural gas and shale oil, it appears that Middle Eastern petroleum will remain a significant part of the global energy budget for several decades.

The response of oil-rich Middle Eastern states to this most recent upward trend in oil prices is likely to be different from what it was in the 1970s. The oil price decline of 1980–2000 led to a realization that oil-derived wealth was not permanent and a sense that, once oil revenues again became abundant, they needed to be used more prudently to develop a diversified, sustainable economy, based on professional services such as trade, banking, engineering, information technology, and education. This requires a well-educated indigenous middle class, which, if the Middle East follows the pattern of numerous other countries, will result in pressures for greater democratic openness. Alternatively, these states may be able to use these renewed revenues to follow the "Confucian capitalism" model of China and Singapore where a world-class technological elite accommodates a nondemocratic central authority that maintains its legitimacy through the provision of political stability and economic growth, but not liberal democracy. This possibility is discussed in greater detail later in this chapter.

Courtesy of World Oil

Local workers at an oil production site take a break to brew tea.

Outside the oil-rich states, the political problems of development differ little from those found elsewhere in the world. On average, the Middle East is neither unusually wealthy nor unusually poor, although there are extremes on either end. Turkey and Israel have achieved economic growth comparable to that of the most successful Asian industrializing countries whereas resource-poor Djibouti, Mauritania, Sudan, and Somalia have limited prospects for development. International war and international sanctions due to its nuclear program have disrupted economic expansion in Iran; civil war has had the same effect in Algeria, Syria, and Yemen; and Lebanon and Iraq have faced the dislocations of both civil and international wars.

Informal Structures of Power

To fully understand the processes of Middle Eastern politics, one must look beyond the formal structures of governance—kings, emirs, parliaments, presidents, and prime ministers—which are discussed below. Of particular importance are the informal structures of family and social networks: the average citizen in the Middle East, whether Arab, Israeli, Turkish, or Persian, finds these far more important in influencing political loyalties than typically is the case for a citizen of North America or Western Europe.

The word that many Western analysts have attached to these networks is *tribes,* but this term is not particularly accurate since Middle Eastern political networks frequently do not differ in language, religion, or cultural traditions, attributes that are distinguishing characteristics of a tribe as the word is commonly used. (When such distinctions do exist—for instance, with the complex religious differences within Lebanon or the linguistically distinct Kurds—they usually translate into politically salient alignments.) Instead, as discussed in Chapter 10, the networks are usually based on extended families and geographical connections to a region or village.

Within these networks, linkages are first and foremost social or economic and only then political. However, as politics become more local, the strength of the existing social networks increases. As a consequence, political control can change at the top of the system with relatively little change at the bottom. Egypt was under foreign political control for 2,284 years— from the defeat of the last Pharaonic dynasty by Alexander the Great in 332 BCE to the overthrow of British-supported King Farouk in 1952 CE—yet in the villages of the Nile Delta or the neighborhoods of Cairo, local politics persisted. The Ottoman Empire recognized this aspect of Middle Eastern life and guaranteed local control of local issues through its *millet* system (which placed each religious community under the jurisdiction of its own religious authorities for most legal, social, and cultural affairs). In contrast, the efforts by European colonial powers to develop centralized and uniform governance frequently caused chaos and inefficiency since Western bureaucratic institutions created extensive—and usually corrupt—systems of patronage and nepotism, much as they had done in most of Europe until the past century or so.

At the same time, the old systems of social networks are less pronounced today than a century ago. Within the Middle East, rapid urbanization has disrupted and weakened centuries-old alliances based in isolated villages. Although immigrants to major cities such as Beirut, Cairo, Istanbul, and Tehran are still influenced by family and village, new loyalties and affiliations challenge the older bonds. These traditional loyalties are further eroded by the migration of many expatriate workers—often the best and brightest young people of a generation—to jobs in the Gulf, Europe, or North America where the old ties are difficult to maintain, particularly for an immigrant's daughters and sons born in a distant land.

Consequently, the contemporary Middle East sees a mix of old and new political structures. The royal family of Saudi Arabia and King Abdullah of Jordan, for instance, continue to base much of their power—particularly in the military and security services—on systems of loyalty based on family and village. Desert bedouin, not the Palestinians who form the majority of the population, dominate the Jordanian monarchy's security services while tribal groupings put forth political candidates to represent their distinct interests. Most of former Iraqi leader Hussein's inner circle of advisers and administrators came from his home village of Tikrit. In contrast, the urban economic elites of Beirut and Istanbul are more likely to follow a European model of social relationships and some may, in fact, feel more comfortable in European circles than in Arab or Turkish social groups.

However, the systems can coexist. Within Israel, the Labor Party, which historically attracted individuals whose parents or grandparents immigrated to Israel from Europe, has a European-style system of flexible loyalties based on ideology, albeit one that has declined in importance as that founding generation has aged. In contrast, the Shas Party, which emerged in the 1990s as a major player in Israeli politics, attracts voters from the ethnically Arab Jewish communities who immigrated from Morocco, Yemen, and Iraq, and places far greater importance on traditional relationships and political guidance from conservative rabbinical leaders. The more secular, but politically conservative Yisrael Beiteinu has a basis in Israel's large community of Russian immigrants. This tension between various styles of political organization is likely to be a pervasive factor in Middle Eastern politics for the foreseeable future.

The Myth of Political Instability

Any discussion of the domestic politics of the Middle East that is directed to a Western audience must confront one of the most pervasive—but, at the same time, most conspicuously untrue—myths about the region: that governments in the Middle East are precarious and extremely changeable. Nothing could be further from the truth. In the past several decades, prior to the Arab uprising, many have been extraordinarily stable. Until his death from cancer in 1999, King Hussein of Jordan was the longest-ruling leader in the region, having served as king for nearly five decades. King Hassan II, who also died in 1999, had governed Morocco since 1961. Despite predictions of a chaotic transition, power passed smoothly to their sons. Djibouti has had only two leaders since gaining independence in 1977. Egypt's Mubarak had been in power for almost thirty years before his overthrow in 2011.

Egypt, Saudi Arabia, and Israel have handled transfers of power smoothly under the difficult conditions of assassination. Oman and Tunisia have replaced, more or less gracefully, leaders whose mental or physical condition had deteriorated. Jordan, Morocco, Syria, and Bahrain each dealt with the death of a longtime leader and the transition to a new generation with apparent ease, even though both Syria and Bahrain subsequently experienced instability in the Arab uprisings. The political system established in Turkey in the 1920s has survived to the present day and has been far more stable than the governments of such European Mediterranean states as Spain, Italy, Yugoslavia, and Greece during the same ninety-year period, notwithstanding three coups by the Turkish military. Significant revolutionary transformations have occurred—conspicuously, in Iraq (1958), Libya (1969), and Iran (1979) with the overthrow of Western-imposed monarchies—but even these changes were arguably no more dramatic than those that occurred in Eastern Europe and the Soviet Union in the late 1980s and early 1990s. The Middle East probably did experience an unusual number of political upheavals in the years immediately following decolonization (as did almost every other newly independent region) and in the period since 2011, but continuity has been the norm during most of the period of independence.

The Arab Uprisings

On December 17, 2010, Mohamed Bouazizi, a fruit vendor in the obscure Tunisian town of Sidi Bouzid, set fire to himself following humiliating treatment from the police and local authorities. By the time of his death eighteen days later, Tunisia had erupted in protests against Tunisian president Zine Abidine Ben Ali, who fled the country on January 14, 2011, ending a twenty-three-year period of rule.

From these decidedly unexpected origins, the Arab uprisings spread throughout the region in one of the most systematic sequences of rapid political change that the world had seen since the disintegration of Soviet control in Eastern Europe in 1989–1991. By the time of this writing—June

2013—Tunisia and Egypt had experienced largely peaceful transitions; Libya, Yemen, and Syria had undergone large-scale civil wars (ending in a thus far democratic transition in Libya and a quasi-transition in Yemen); the Moroccan monarchy had undertaken significant liberal reforms; and Bahrain was experiencing ongoing protests despite substantial government repression.

It is clearly too early to provide a definitive analysis of the Arab uprisings, but several factors are worth considering. The first factor is the global trend toward democratization. As shown in Table 4.1, the human rights monitoring group Freedom House rated sixty countries as "Free" (democratic) and sixty as "Not Free" (authoritarian) in 1990; by 2010, eighty-nine countries were "Free" and only forty-seven "Not Free."

These democratic transitions tend to occur with rising income levels and the emergence of a middle class that has substantial communication and organizational skills, as has been occurring in the Middle East in recent decades, particularly in urban areas such as Cairo. The success of popular uprisings against authoritarian regimes in the color revolutions in the Philippines, Serbia, Georgia, and Ukraine, and tactical innovations building on the work of the theorist of nonviolence, Gene Sharp (2010), were particularly important in Egypt and are probably also a factor in the still unsuccessful protest movements in Bahrain and Jordan.

The Arab uprisings were further encouraged by the presence of several aging leaders who were supported by egregiously corrupt bureaucracies and a small circle of cronies who were becoming fabulously wealthy while most of the population saw their economic circumstances steadily worsening. In previous editions, this chapter included a section on long-standing single-party and personalist rulers: Hussein of Iraq, Ben Ali of Tunisia, Mubarak of Egypt, Muammar Qaddafi of Libya, Ali Abdallah Salih of Yemen, and the Assad family of Syria. Of that list, only Bashar al-Assad remains in power, but could well be gone by the time this book appears in print.

In contrast to the 1979 revolution in Iran or the Taliban takeover of Afghanistan in 1996, the influence of Islam in the Arab uprisings has been

Table 4.1 Freedom House Classifications of Countries Globally

Year	Free	Partly Free	Not Free
1990	60	50	60
2000	86	58	48
2010	89	58	47

Source: Freedom House, *Freedom in the World, Country Ratings 1973–2012* (Washington, DC: Freedom House, 2012), www.freedomhouse.org.

relatively muted. Islamic groups have played an important role in providing preexisting social and political structures around which opposition can organize—a major advantage in the Egyptian elections in 2012 for the Muslim Brotherhood, the long-established opposition group—as well as emphasizing Islamic norms, particularly against corruption, but there appears to be little popular interest in a radical transition. Similarly, while various Islamic jihadi military groups have played a role in the civil wars in Libya, Yemen, and Syria, those wars generally have been characterized by loosely organized militias motivated variously by regional, ethnic, and tribal identity rather than by a dominant Islamic focus.

The new electronic media, in particular the wide availability of cell phones, satellite television networks such as Al Jazeera and al-Arabiya in Arabic, and global media such as the British Broadcasting Corporation (BBC) and Cable News Network (CNN) in English, may also have had a significant impact by opening lines of communication that could not be controlled by the centralized regimes. In the protests in Cairo (and earlier in the 2009 election protests in Iran), new social media such as YouTube, Twitter, and Facebook may also have played some role, though the open nature of these meant that they could be easily monitored and manipulated once authorities became aware of their importance.

In contrast to the collapse of communism in Eastern Europe in 1989–1991, particularly the rapid collapse of Soviet-allied governments in the five months of August to December 1989, the spread of the Arab uprisings has been relatively slow, though it seems unlikely that it has completely finished. The long-established regimes in Tunisia and Egypt collapsed rapidly following generally nonviolent street demonstrations, but subsequent developments have taken different forms. Government suppression of nonviolent protests in Libya, Yemen, and Syria spawned decentralized military movements that gradually weakened the control of the central government and in Libya and Yemen, the eventual deposing of the old regime, an outcome that also seems likely in Syria. Bahrain also saw major protests—largely along ethnic lines by the majority Shi'i population against the Saudi-supported Sunni ruling family—but to date these have not resulted in regime-level political change. Morocco experienced major urban protests and undertook substantial political reforms, including a new constitution approved by popular referendum in July 2011 and elections in November 2011 that resulted in a moderate Islamist party gaining the largest number of seats in parliament. While the Moroccan system continues to allocate significant power to the king, these reforms move it closer to a constitutional monarchy with meaningful democratic institutions.

These have been the major changes to date, though others seem possible. Jordan has not followed the Moroccan example of using constitutional reform to deflate protest momentum, though it would seem a likely candidate in the future. In October 2012 King Abdullah dissolved parliament with the expectation of new elections in 2013, but large-scale protests in favor of reform broke out in every governorate just weeks later. Kuwait is a similar candidate for reform, with long-standing popular grievances against the al-Sabah ruling family and an increasingly sophisticated popular opposition (Tétreault, 2012). With the exception of Bahrain, the Gulf states seem to have been insulated by their relatively small populations and, along with Saudi Arabia, the buffer of high oil revenues. Qatar, however, openly supported the Libyan rebels, sending aircraft to assist in the enforcement of the no-fly zone led by the North Atlantic Treaty Organization (NATO), and both Qatar and Saudi Arabia are reported to be providing arms to Syrian rebels (Vela, 2012). Finally, states with recent civil wars—Algeria, Lebanon, Palestine, and Iraq—seem to have little appetite for further conflict, particularly in view of the experiences of Libya and Syria.

Prospects for Democratization

With the virtual demise of Marxist-Leninist governments around the world, liberal democracy, characterized by the regular, open, honest electoral competition of political parties and protection of rights to organize politically, has become the dominant ideological basis for legitimizing political power globally. In contrast to many areas of the world that have successfully adapted Western liberal democratic structures and norms to local conditions (e.g., Japan, India, and Latin America), democratization has posed several problems in the Middle East.

Perhaps the most fundamental challenge lies in the preexistence of many democratic—but not liberal democratic—institutions in the region. The successful monarchies have maintained and expanded extensive consultative structures and in Bahrain, Jordan, Kuwait, and Morocco have even established liberal democratic institutions, albeit with highly constrained powers. Most countries in the region also have a constitution and hold regular elections for a nationally elected assembly. The importance of these representative institutions for governance varies considerably from state to state, but in countries as diverse as Morocco, Lebanon, Palestine, Turkey, Bahrain, Iran, and Yemen, citizens remain willing to stand in long lines to cast their ballots on election day.

Consequently, much of the Middle East is far from devoid of structures for political participation (in contrast, for instance, to the military regimes of Latin America in the 1970s). The claim of a regionally constructed "Arab democracy" has some credibility, and will become more so as the transitional democracies established by the Arab uprisings mature. Nevertheless, the current Middle Eastern models for liberal democracy have significant flaws. The extreme secularism of Mustafa Kemal Atatürk's constitution for

Turkey is not acceptable in the current environment of Islamic revivalism and was eventually successfully challenged even in Turkey itself with the emergence of the Justice and Development Party (AKP)—a loosely Islamic center right coalition—as the majority ruling party in the 2000s. Lebanon's initial attempts at confessional democracy—a system that assumes religious affiliation is the primary factor in how society is organized politically and constitutionally, which ensures the power of various groups—led to a devastating civil war in the 1970s and strongly contributed to the current governmental weakness. Surprisingly, public opinion polls have repeatedly shown that Israel's model of government is widely admired by Arabs in countries as diverse as Jordan, Kuwait, and Egypt, despite popular opposition to Israel itself, though in recent years Israel has been moving toward restricting the rights of the 20 percent Arab population within Israel as well as leaving unresolved the issue of Palestinian rights in the areas it controls militarily.

Women voters in Tunis, Tunisia.

Moreover, the major liberal democratic powers have done little to encourage democracy in the region. In the mid–twentieth century, Britain left absolute monarchies in place as it retreated. The United States has consistently tolerated undemocratic policies in its allies—including the monarchies of Saudi Arabia, Bahrain, and Oman; the police state of Iran's Mohammad Reza Shah; and single-party rule in Egypt—despite its eight-year occupation of Iraq that left the country with only a fragile and ethnically divided regime. Hamas's parliamentary victory in a well-supervised election in January 2006 led to retaliation, rather than acceptance, by the democratic states of North America and Western Europe; those democracies also did little to discourage the violent suppression by the Algerian military of the Islamic Salvation Front (ISF) after its electoral victory in 1991.

However, at least three factors suggest that democratization will continue to develop in the Middle East, and the democratic openings of the Arab uprisings are probably more than temporary. First, the creation of a literate, urbanized middle class has consistently, in a variety of cultures, led to prodemocratic political movements, even in the most repressive states. Second, the most dynamic economies of the region (Turkey, Israel, and pre–civil war Lebanon) have thrived under democratic regimes. Third, the conditions that legitimized nondemocratic regimes—notably, postcolonial politics and the Cold War competition—are declining in importance.

Most contemporary democratic theory emphasizes the importance of the institutions of civil society in buttressing liberal democracy. As Egyptian sociologist Saad Eddin Ibrahim explained sixteen years before the successful popular overthrow of the Mubarak regime in Egypt:

> While there are a variety of ways of defining [the concept of civil society], they all revolve around *maximizing volitional, organized, collective participation in the public space between individuals and the state.* In its institutional form, "civil society" is composed of non-state actors or non-governmental organizations (NGOs), including political parties, trade unions, professional associations, community development associations, and other interest groups. Normatively, "civil society" implies values and behavioral codes of tolerating—if not accepting—others and a tacit or explicit commitment to the peaceful management of differences among individuals and collectivities sharing the same "public space"—that is, the polity. (1995:29; emphasis in original)

As discussed in Chapter 10, traditional Middle Eastern society has a rich set of institutions and nonstate actors, including labor unions and political parties that mediate between public and private space. These often exist in the nondemocratic context of the mosque, family, or clan but are not less valid (nor less valuable) for that reason. Informal arrangements also serve many of the same functions as formal civic institutions. A farmer does not need to form a cooperative when his village has been sharing in the task of the olive harvest for generations and a mother has less interest in forming a parent-teacher association when her child's instructor is a cousin she has known since birth. In many instances, transplanting Western institutions of civil society into the Middle East—an objective of many North American and European development projects—is like trying to pour coffee into a cup that is already full: little new coffee will remain in the cup and, in the meantime, one has created a mess.

This suggests the possibility that a distinctly Middle Eastern model of democratic accommodation could develop, much as Confucian capitalism has developed in lieu of Western liberal democracy in China and parts of Southeast Asia (Yao, 2002). While the Confucian cultural element is obviously irrelevant to the Middle East, the model is applicable in the sense of a strong, oftentimes paternalistic leadership providing a path that satisfies a growing professional class through modification of existing norms and political structures rather than through the importing of Western institutions such as competitive political parties.

This experiment is most evident in the small Gulf states such as Qatar and the United Arab Emirates (UAE), which have embarked on policies seeking a high level of economic liberalization and integration into the global capitalist economy without political liberalization. It is less clear whether this approach can be sustained over the long haul or whether, as occurred in the culturally Confucian states of South Korea and the Republic of China (Taiwan), the middle class will eventually force democratic reforms. It is also unclear whether a model that works in oil-rich city-states will generalize to larger or less wealthy states such as Egypt, Tunisia, Syria, and Morocco. Somewhat improbably, however, the Confucian capitalism model has thus far been successfully transplanted from the city-state of Singapore to the vastly larger People's Republic of China, albeit with a strong central leadership that may not be present in countries such as Saudi Arabia and Iraq.

However, the Western political models also face significant challenges. Clearly, any liberal democratic movement will need to accommodate Islam explicitly in some form. According to Arab democratic theorists, this presents few problems: many interpretations of Islamic theology are at least as sympathetic to democratic ideals as is Christianity (and are more so than the Hinduism of India, where nonetheless a thriving liberal democracy has been established). However, many of the most politically powerful trends in contemporary Islam are highly conservative (e.g., regarding the role of women).

Furthermore, any democratic movement must deal with the unresolved issues of ethnonational and religious minorities in Turkey, Iran, Iraq, Lebanon, Israel, Syria, and elsewhere. In addition to indigenous groups such as the Egyptian Coptic Christians and the Kurds, many of the smaller states have large populations of "foreign" workers, some of whom have been residents for generations. Refugee flows also create complex problems concerning political rights, as illustrated by the ongoing problems of Palestinian refugees in Jordan, Lebanon, and Syria (and elsewhere), and the refugees from the conflicts in both Syria and Iraq who have made their way to Jordan and Turkey. Establishing the rights and roles of such groups is a problem even for established democracies, as the experiences of the United States, France, and Germany illustrate; it is even more difficult in states for which political independence is relatively new and liberal democracy is an experiment some already regard with skepticism.

The Role of the Military

The Middle East is the most highly militarized region in the world. Even after the Arab uprisings, the military continues to play a critical role in both the construction and the implementation of domestic policy. Several factors, some specific to the area, others more generally applicable to newly independent states, explain this continuing trend.

First, neither the period of European colonization and occupation nor the political situation immediately after independence was conducive to the establishment of formal civic groups. Colonial powers, intent solely on exploiting the resources of the region, discouraged or suppressed indigenous institutions for fear that these would be used as centers of opposition to colonial rule. Many of these policies continued after independence, particularly when rulers had been installed by the departing European power or were supported through the anticommunist agenda of the United States. When states were allied with the Soviet Union, the opposite problem occurred: most grassroots civic activity was channeled into officially recognized, state-controlled institutions, leaving little room for independent action.

Thus, the focus of social organization was on rapid modernization and the creation of a military capable of addressing internal and external threats to the fragile regimes. In both Turkey under Atatürk and Iran under the Pahlavi dynasty, the government claimed its authoritarian rule was necessary for the country's economic development. Elsewhere, civil and international conflicts—the Iran-Iraq War, invasion of Kuwait, long-standing Arab-Israeli tensions, civil war in Sudan, Kurdish autonomy movements, and so on—provided a justification (some would argue an excuse) for a massive buildup of military forces throughout the region.

In 1999, the Middle East (including North Africa), with just over 5 percent of the world's population, accounted for more than 13 percent of the world's armed forces with 2.8 million soldiers (US Department of State, 2003:5). Through the 1980s and 1990s, the region accounted for an astonishing 40 percent of global arms imports, although most of these purchases were concentrated in a small number of countries: Saudi Arabia, Egypt, Israel, Kuwait, Iran, and the UAE. Saudi Arabia was by far the largest arms importer during this period, followed by Israel (which also has an indigenous arms industry). By the end of the 1990s, Middle East arms imports had declined somewhat, but still accounted for over 26 percent of total world imports in 1999 (US Department of State, 2003:9).

Second, military power frequently played a key role in the origins of the ruling regimes, resulting in a significant intertwining of the political and military elites. For instance, the unification of the central Arabian territory into the Kingdom of Saudi Arabia during the first three decades of the twentieth century can be attributed almost entirely to the military prowess of Ibn Saud (although Ibn Saud also deserves credit for the political consolidation of the areas he conquered). In Algeria, the eight-year war of independence left the country virtually demolished, with the National Liberation Front (FLN) the one political-military institution that was intact and able to rule. Qaddafi came to power in Libya in 1969 through a military coup, and the military remained a key source of his power until his overthrow in the civil war of 2011.

Over the past two decades, Middle Eastern militaries have at times fueled tremendously destructive civil wars, notably in Algeria in 1992–1998 and Syria 2011 to the present, each resulting in more than 100,000 deaths, mostly civilian. In other countries such as Libya, Yemen, Iraq following the defeat of Hussein in 2003, and Lebanon 1975–1990, military control has been so weak that the national arsenals were simply looted to supply local militias in the wake of the collapse of central authority. This mixed record on the efficacy of military power may lead to more caution in the future as many of these countries democratize, much as the countries of Latin America reduced the power of their militaries following reassertion of democratic control in the 1980s.

During Israel's early years, the military was clearly associated with the Mapai (which later evolved into the Labor Party); thus, the political and the military were inextricably associated. In recent years, the military has become more autonomous (especially with Labor's political decline), but remains quite powerful. The common military experience of the majority of Jewish Israeli citizens has left an indelible mark on that country's politics: high rank, preferably in a selective army unit, and combat experience in one or more of Israel's many wars are attributes for success in the political arena; and, until recently, most prime ministers had impressive military credentials.

Finally, in a number of countries, elite military units, combined with effective secret intelligence forces (*mukhabarat*), are essential in securing the regime against political opposition. For example, in Iraq under Hussein some sixteen divisions of military intelligence, with varying degrees of power, were each responsible for a specific type of crime (Makiya, 1993:

339). Admittance into the military academies required membership in the Iraqi Baath Party; once accepted, military personnel were expected to show an absolute commitment to Iraq and to the dictates of the president.

Often, a leader assigns relatives or long-term allies to handle critical security functions. Within the Saudi military establishment, close family members hold all the significant positions and King Abdullah has retained command of the National Guard, which he has been head of since 1962. Similarly, in Jordan an overwhelming majority of the military officers are from East Bank families with links to the royal family that can be traced back to the earliest days of the state.

The implications of extensive military involvement in the governance of Middle Eastern countries can be profound. When a regime must rely on the military to protect it from opposition movements, terrorism, or civil unrest, that regime becomes vulnerable to *praetorianism*, a situation in which "the civil authorities face constant threats from powerful military forces who try to shape all kinds of political decisions while remaining formally out of government" (Wilson, 1996:135). The repeated ultimatums given by the Turkish military in 1997 to force the resignation of Prime Minister Necmettin Erbakan, head of the Islamic Refah Party, illustrate how these pressures operate. Furthermore, "once they begin to perform the functions typically associated with parties, legislatures, and interest groups, . . . militaries render those political institutions irrelevant" (Bill and Springborg, 1994:235), which makes political liberalization all the more difficult. In the Arab uprisings, the decision of the Egyptian military to not support the regime of Mubarak led to a rapid and largely peaceful end to that regime whereas the loyalty of the military in Libya and Syria resulted in protracted civil wars with tens of thousands of casualties.

Government Legitimization and State Building

As is true for most newly independent countries, the basic political challenge for the Middle East in the post–World War II era has been the task of *state building*: the creation of governments that are legitimate, stable, and capable of acting autonomously both regionally and globally (Hudson, 1977; Luciani, 1990). For a variety of reasons, this has not been easy. First, the political structures of many Middle Eastern countries were imposed by outside powers, rather than resulting from a gradual, internally driven process. Thus, the governments of these newly independent countries often lacked the political, economic, and social institutions and the widespread legitimacy that would have existed had the state-building activity begun at the grassroots level. In many countries, the presence of powerful multinational corporations (notably, international petroleum companies) meant that the new states were immediately drawn into the global political economy without having the opportunity to determine the type of relationship that would be of greatest benefit to their own development (Henry and Springborg, 2010). This, too, has made the tasks of governance more difficult.

A further complication has been "the blurred boundaries between [the] state and [the] collective, supra-state identity inspired by common Arab-Islamic culture, history, and vision" (Sela, 1998:4). As a result, the utopian dream of a united pan-Arab nation with a shared history, culture, and sense of common identity stretching from the Strait of Hormuz to the Atlantic is in tension with the practical dictates of more than twenty politically sovereign Arab states. In a different world, a single Arab nation-state might have emerged. The region is at least as ethnically cohesive as India, Russia, or Indonesia and is comparable in size. However, European colonial involvement and the competing interests of both indigenous and international elites prevented this outcome. Nonetheless, some Arabs view the existing political divisions as illegitimate and reject, for instance, the separation of Lebanon from Syria, or at an even more extreme level, embrace al-Qaeda's dream of an Islamic caliphate spanning the entire region. In this context, they believe it is perfectly appropriate for one state to intervene in the internal affairs of another since all are part of the greater Arab (or even more expansively, Muslim) nation.

Throughout the 1950s and 1960s, Arab leaders attempted to gain legitimacy in a variety of ways and with considerable ideological innovation (e.g., Baathism, discussed below), balancing state-based claims with the aspirations of the Arab nation as a whole. By the early 1970s, two forms of governance—conservative monarchies and military or single-party revolutionary republics—dominated the political landscape. The monarchies, such as those of the Arabian Peninsula, were strongly patriarchal with the king or emir taking on the role of a domineering yet benevolent father doing what he believes is best for his family. Constitutional monarchies like those of Jordan, Morocco, and Iran under the shah maintained the monarch as the ultimate political authority, but also established elected legislatures with modest amounts of authority and developed significant governmental bureaucracies.

In contrast, some of the revolutionary states functioned under authoritarian personalistic leadership (most notably, Libya, Syria, and Iraq) whereas others (e.g., Algeria, Egypt, Mauritania, Tunisia, and PDR Yemen) relied on the strength of a dominant political ideology, as expressed through a single political party, to provide support and legitimacy for the state leadership. These models, however, overlap in a variety of ways (see Anderson, 1991). Lebanon stands out as the one Arab country that had neither a king nor revolutionary leadership in the twentieth century. Its creation as an explicitly Christian-dominated Arab state, codified in the 1943 National Pact, made it unique.

Turkey and Israel also do not fit neatly into either a monarchical or a revolutionary model. Yet they reflect the same pressures of political development that have influenced the entire region. The governments of both Turkey and Israel are products of late-nineteenth-century and early-twentieth-century liberal European ideologies such as nationalism. In the creation of their political structures, both countries were inspired by Western-style political modernization approaches (in the case of Turkey, due to its proximity to Europe; in Israel, as a consequence of its initial origins as a diaspora nationalist movement originating in Europe) rather than by the family-oriented, personalistic style of rule present in much of the region. Consequently, the Israeli and Turkish regimes are based on secular and formally democratic norms—although without complete political integration of ethnic or religious minorities—and accept the principle of public accountability for the political leadership. In the 2000s, however, both countries were dealing with substantial challenges from groups seeking to redefine the role of religion within these states as well as to challenge their liberal democratic nature and treatment of minorities.

Nationalist Revolutionary Republics

For much of the twentieth century, the nationalist revolutionary state was one of the most important political models for the Middle East. Although the region suffered from its proximity to Europe by experiencing two centuries of colonial intervention and interference in the development of regional politics, this proximity provided at least one possible compensating advantage: intense exposure to the intellectual currents that accompanied the consolidation of the modern industrialized state in Europe, notably nationalism, political liberalism, and socialism.

As outlined in Chapter 3, the "Arab awakening" (Antonius, 1946) began in the early to middle 1800s and culminated in a series of independence and self-determination movements in the twentieth century. Due to the constraints of colonialism, few of these ideas could be implemented prior to the 1950s, but the intellectual groundwork existed, at least some of the relevant political writings were in Arabic, and the literature spoke to the region's history (Khalidi, 1991; Tibi, 1997). In this respect, the Middle East was in a quite different situation than Asia or sub-Saharan Africa, which were relatively isolated from European political developments by the constraints of physical distance in the days before telecommunications.

The first successful twentieth-century nationalist movement in the Middle East, that of Atatürk following the end of World War I, shows the effects of these influences. Atatürk's single most dramatic innovation—the secularization of Turkey—was completely consistent with liberal revolutionary movements from the American and French revolutions forward.

Although he was reluctant to share power, he did support the adoption of European political forms such as a parliamentary system with a prime minister and cabinet chosen from the unicameral Grand National Assembly. This meant that the necessary structures for participatory government were in place after Atatürk's death.

In contrast, early efforts by the intelligentsia and the middle classes in Iran failed to limit the power of the Qajar monarchy and give control to an elected assembly. By the mid-1920s, Reza Khan, who founded the Pahlavi dynasty, had replaced the Qajar ruler and taken the name Reza Shah. Reza Shah and his son Mohammad Reza Shah combined social, economic, and military modernization with repression and authoritarian rule. Little was done to nurture the nascent parliament or develop other democratic institutions (Halliday, 1979).

Another three decades passed before the process of state building commenced in the Arab Middle East, but when decolonization began in earnest in the 1950s, significant ideological movements were ready and waiting to challenge the immediate postcolonial political structures imposed by Britain, France, and the United States. Thus, the 1950s and 1960s saw a proliferation of alternative political approaches, often incorporating Islamic political values and histories into a formally secular framework. Much to the distress of the former colonizers, most of these new ideologies drew as much from the theories of Karl Marx and Vladimir Lenin as from those of Thomas Jefferson and John Locke. As a consequence, they emphasized a strong, centralized, and bureaucratized state, a characteristic that persists to this day even in countries that have in other ways moved away from this approach.

When viewed in the context of the 1950s and 1960s, there are several reasons for the appeal of centralized approaches to politics, none of which have anything to do with "Arab exceptionalism" or a distinctly Middle Eastern respect for strong leadership. First, the consolidation of state power was consistent with the prevailing Western political trends in government. During the previous two decades, the liberal democracies of Western Europe and North America had increasingly centralized authority, initially to counter the effects of the Great Depression and then to mobilize their economies for World War II. Both Marxists and progressive political theorists argued that such an expansion in central governmental authority was necessary to counter the economic power of industrialized capitalism.

Second, elements of the Soviet Union's communist model were initially quite attractive. In a mere twenty-five years, the Soviet Union had gone from a quasi-feudal society to an industrialized power capable of withstanding the military assault of Nazi Germany, one of the most advanced European economies, during World War II. It had survived the Great Depression, which had devastated most of the capitalist world and, in the 1950s, the toll that Stalin's brutal policies had extracted from the Soviet people was not widely known or understood. Thus, varieties of socialism were appealing not just in the Arab world, but also in every area undergoing decolonization (e.g., China, Vietnam, Cuba, and parts of Africa). Indeed, socialism might have been widely implemented had it not been for the efforts of the US Central Intelligence Agency (CIA) and other Cold War agents of containment.

Finally, the political left rather than the right had consistently opposed colonialism. As discussed below, the monarchies, without exception, allied themselves with the colonial powers or their successor, the United States. Even in the era of colonialism, progressive and socialist groups had provided greater assistance in the anticolonial cause than had the liberal democracies. Indeed, two of the most conspicuous of the European liberal democracies—Britain and France—had been the two most conspicuous meddlers in Arab affairs. Although the United States might have been able to exploit its anticolonial policies to promote a liberal democratic agenda (as it did briefly during the 1956 Suez crisis), it generally subordinated this goal to the pursuit of a simple anticommunist agenda. The CIA overthrow of Iran's Mohammad Mossadeq in 1953, anti-Nasserist policies following the Suez crisis, the 1958 military intervention in Lebanon, and the deepening US military activity in Indochina by the mid-1960s ended any anticolonial credibility the United States might once have had.

A full discussion of the diverse intellectual currents in Arab political thought during this period would fill several dozen books (and has). Here, we summarize the tenets of two ideological approaches that had a significant impact in the Middle Eastern political arena, Baathism in the postcolonial period and the recent impact of political Islam.

Baathism

The Baath Party is one of the only political movements truly indigenous to the Arab world. In the 1940s, the Arab Baath Party was founded by two Syrians, Greek Orthodox Michel Aflaq (the group's intellectual leader) and Sunni Muslim Salah al-Din al-Bitar (its political strategist). This group merged in 1953 with a second organization, the Arab Socialist Party, to create the Arab Socialist Resurrection Party, also known as the Baath Socialist Party. The first members of the Baath Party came primarily from the intellectual elite, but the Baath quickly gained support among disadvantaged groups and established itself as a mass movement.

The basic Baathist ideology embraced a set of principles that drew on multiple sources of legitimacy in the Arab world: history, religion, nationalism, development, freedom, and socialism. Most importantly, Baathism called for social reform and economic justice, to be achieved through Arab socialism. In his writings, Aflaq resisted the temptation to rely exclusively on European socialist thinkers with their emphasis on class struggle. Instead, he emphasized that the Baathist economic model was neither capitalist nor communist: it was a middle way that was the product of the Arab world's unique history. A second key element of Baathism was its emphasis on pan-Arab unity, which was understood to involve the unification of existing Arab states into a single political entity as a replacement for patriotism centered on a specific state. Third, Baathism was anti-imperialist and anti-Zionist; it stressed the achievement of true Arab independence from all forms of colonialism.

Finally, Baathism called for a toleration of religious minorities within an overall Arab-Islamic political framework that included representative government and civil rights. As a result, Baathism could appeal both to the majority Muslim population and to Christians who would be left out of a more explicitly Islamic formulation of nationalism. The Baath Party became the dominant political actor in Syria, albeit eventually secondary to a cult of personality around the Assad family; remains important in post-Hussein Iraq; and plays a more minor role in Jordan, Lebanon, and elsewhere. Even with the decline of institutional Baath parties, many of the concepts developed by Aflaq continue to influence the search for a modern secular Arab ideology.

Political Islam

Many of the political patterns established in the initial years of independence continue to exist today, although with some modifications in response to pressures for increased political liberalization (Norton, 1995; Ayoob, 2007). As discussed in Chapter 12, in recent decades a new model—the Islamic republic—has mounted an increasingly significant challenge to the secular, nationalist ideologies used to legitimize both existing regimes and opposition movements in the revolutionary states. This mirrors two global patterns.

First, people who see their world changing and feel that the values they hold dear are threatened, but believe that the government is not responding to their concerns, often turn to religion as a source of tradition and stability. For instance, the twentieth-century founder of the Muslim Brotherhood, Hassan al-Banna (1906–1948), argued that the colonial domination of the region in the nineteenth and twentieth centuries was a direct result of the declining importance of Islam in the lives of ordinary people; a return to Islam would allow for an improved political situation. Second, individuals often focus on the political dimensions of religion when they perceive themselves as oppressed by the existing secular government, and religious expression thus becomes a way to articulate frustration with the existing political structures.

Both elements were present in Iran under the rule of Mohammad Reza Shah. The shah combined extreme repression of opponents and claims of a historical right to rule with strongly Western-oriented modernization policies such as the land reforms of the White Revolution. Yet a few years before the Iranian Revolution, the shah held an incredibly expensive celebration linking his rule to that of the ancient Persian Empire. The Iranian population viewed this spectacle with skepticism and, in retrospect, the celebration illustrated the fragility of his position.

Although the most successful contemporary implementation of political Islam occurred at the edge of the Arab world, in Iran, and later temporarily in Sudan and Mauritania, the role of Islam in contemporary systems has influenced political dynamics across the entire region, including in Iraq, among Palestinians, in Egypt, and in previously Christian-dominated Lebanon. Islam's grounding in the impressive history of the region; its emphasis on the socioeconomic equity and justice promised, but not achieved, by the nationalist revolutionary ideologies; its comprehensive belief system, which gives guidance on virtually all aspects of life; and its extensive critique of Western goals and values are all crucial to understanding the success of groups using Islam as an instrument of political action.

While the phrase *political Islam* typically invokes the image of the complex intermixing of religious and political institutions of the Islamic Republic of Iran, or even the utopian caliphate espoused by al-Qaeda, the twenty-first-century reality is probably much more in line with the reconciliation of religion and liberal democracy that developed in Europe during the nineteenth century. The separation of religion and the state found in the US Constitution was the exception in early democratic developments and, even after two centuries, social conservatives refer to the United States as a "Christian nation." In Europe, the role of religion in the modern state was determined through a long set of experiments with various models, ranging from the extreme anticlericalism of the French and Russian revolutions to the church as effectively a parallel governing structure in Ireland and Spain. Even today in largely secular Great Britain, where only about 3 percent of the population attends the state-supported Anglican Church even once a month, Anglican bishops are granted 26 seats in the 775-member House of Lords. Many of the European democracies still retain taxpayer-funded churches and Christian democratic political parties.

A similar process of experimentation is likely to occur throughout the Middle East, particularly in the emerging democracies. The secularism of Atatürk and Nasser has not proven robust—much as the Russian Orthodox Church quickly reemerged after seven decades of communist atheism—and, by virtue of their independent base of operations in mosques and a generally well-deserved reputation for standing against corruption and the excesses of the elite, Islamic parties usually emerge as the earliest alternatives to established regimes as we are currently seeing in Egypt, Jordan, and Morocco. The issue over the next several decades, as it was in Europe, will be adapting these early positions to the requirements of a modern liberal state, and the answers to this issue are likely to vary across countries.

Traditional and Parliamentary Monarchies

The Middle East is the only area of the world where traditional monarchies (as distinct from constitutional monarchies, which exist in parts of Europe) have persisted in a number of states. At times, this fact has been used to label the domestic politics of the region "medieval" or even "primitive." A closer look suggests that the monarchical regimes might better be characterized as an adaptation of established forms of patrimonial leadership to the contemporary nation-state system. Drawing on a variety of traditional sources of legitimacy such as custom, a history of family governance, ancestral ties to the Prophet Muhammad, a leader's personal attributes, and the royal family's role as a symbol of nationalism, the current Arab monarchies have proved remarkably resilient.

This persistence is particularly striking in light of the fact that, in the 1950s and 1960s, six monarchies were unable to survive the critical postcolonial period and were removed from power: Egypt (1952); Tunisia (1956); Iraq (1958); Yemen (1962); South Arabia, which became PDR Yemen (1967); and Libya (1969). Yet since 1969, only a single additional monarchy—the Pahlavis of Iran—has been overthrown, even during the Arab uprisings, suggesting that the remaining royal rulers have found ways to repress democratic sentiment, co-opt opposition movements, or otherwise adapt their rule to address popular pressures for political reform.

Thus, the challenge for the Arab monarchies today is less one of validating their political control through tradition and more one of "establishing a linkage with modernity," as Michael C. Hudson argued over thirty years ago (1977:230). Sociopolitical structures such as the *diwan* (informal gatherings in the homes of elites at which there is wide-ranging discussion regarding contemporary issues), along with the Islamic concept of shura (consultation), have allowed for a fair amount of grassroots input without moving to a liberal democratic model. Furthermore, significant economic resources have made it possible in some instances to buy off the opposition (Gause, 2000). In addition, all of these states have chosen to align themselves politically with the West. In the name of anticommunism (originally) or anti-Islamic revivalism (currently), the United States in particular has been willing to supply the Arab ruling elites with whatever weapons and expertise they require to maintain internal security.

In four countries—Bahrain, Kuwait, Morocco, and Oman—the same extended family has held political power for more than 200 years, albeit over territories much different (and smaller) than those they control today. The current ruling family in Oman has governed the coast of the country (although not the interior) since 1749; Sultan Qaboos ibn Said al-Said became the leader in 1970 when he overthrew his father in a bloodless coup that was supported by the British. The al-Sabah family of Kuwait traces its rule to the early 1700s, when a group of formerly nomadic clans settled along the northeastern Arabian coast; the related al-Khalifah family established its authority in Bahrain in 1782 after defeating the Iranians who had previously controlled the islands.

The most enduring Arab regime is found in Morocco. Monarchical government in that country dates back twelve centuries. The Alawi family, which traces its roots to the Prophet Muhammad, came to power in the 1660s and consolidated its control over virtually all of modern-day Morocco in the early 1700s. Unlike most of the Arab world, Morocco largely escaped both European and Ottoman colonialism. After a brief period of Spanish and French control in the early twentieth century, Morocco regained its independence in 1956 and is now governed by King Mohammed VI, who succeeded his father, King Hassan II, in July 1999. The Moroccan regime consequently fits into a small set of states in which a long-standing monarchy has been able to resist the inroads of colonialism and emerge intact in the postcolonial period. (Ethiopia prior to the overthrow of Haile Selassie, Siam/Thailand, and Japan are three other examples of this unusual pattern.)

The other Arab monarchies are either the result of twentieth-century consolidations of power, as in the case of Saudi Arabia, or are relatively recent "dynasties" that gained their political position either in part (Qatar, the UAE) or entirely (Jordan) from the assistance of the retreating colonial powers. In the 1800s, the British signed treaties with a variety of local leaders in the Gulf, adopting a policy of indirect rule and support for the specific families with whom they negotiated agreements. This reinforced the position of the Gulf's ruling families and converted them into "royalty" who took full control of the newly independent countries when the British withdrew from the Gulf.

Some of these new dynasties failed due to incompetence, as in Iraq, where neither of the two successors to King Faisal I were able to hold the country's diverse population together. Others, such as the Idris regime in Libya, were never accepted by the population on whom they were imposed and could not survive in power once European support was withdrawn. In non-Arab Iran, the Pahlavi dynasty, which replaced the Qajar dynasty in a bloodless coup in the 1920s, maintained control only with the support of the CIA and was eventually overthrown.

Aspects of Arab Kingship

The Arab concept of kingship differs significantly from the European model in two significant ways. First, the conflict between the monarchy and the political power of the church that characterized so much of European history between the end of the Roman Empire and the Protestant Reformation has no counterpart in the Arab world. The authority of an Arab monarch nevertheless can be challenged on religious grounds, as occurred with the revolt in Arabia of the religiously fundamentalist Ikhwan (Muslim Brethren; not to be confused with the Muslim Brotherhood founded in Egypt in 1928) against Ibn Saud in the late 1920s.

Second, the absence of a widely recognized succession procedure limits the development of the extended family dynasties such as the Hapsburgs in Austria (r. 1282–1918) and the German-British House of Hanover. The status of sharif—a descendant of the Prophet Muhammad—enhances the legitimacy of a ruler, but tens of thousands of individuals carry this designation. Consequently, being a sharif does not carry the same power as would being the eldest son of a king in Europe, and marriage into such a family does not by itself guarantee that someone can claim political control.

As a result, Arab monarchies do not generally show the pattern—once common in Europe—of a weak or decadent leader being kept in power in order to preserve the traditions that also legitimize the power of organized religion and the lower nobility. An ineffective or otherwise problematic ruler can be replaced by a family member—as happened in modern times in Oman and Qatar—without threatening the legitimacy of the entire regime.

Furthermore, because rulers must demonstrate leadership and piety, they must be accessible to the population through a wide range of traditional institutions. For instance, shortly after he became king in 1999, Abdullah II of Jordan is said to have disguised himself as a taxi driver, left behind his bodyguards, and driven around Amman listening to ordinary citizens complain about the government. This unusual action, reminiscent of Abdullah's father, King Hussein, in the early years of his reign, was widely acclaimed and echoed the legends of great Arab monarchs in classical times who would leave their palaces disguised as beggars and roam the streets and marketplaces to assess public opinion. In contrast to Orientalist images that ascribe to the unfettered power of Arab monarchs, the absolutism of the Bourbons of France or the Romanovs of Russia (who ruled in nearly complete isolation from the populations of their territories) has no counterpart in Arab tradition.

One disadvantage of this system is that Arab monarchies are potentially more vulnerable than European monarchies to leadership crises upon the death of a ruler because the line of succession may be less well established. Furthermore, because the system is entirely patrilineal, half the population is excluded from direct power. Although the Arab system has avoided weak kings such as George III of England and Nicholas II of Russia, it has also never produced strong queens such as Elizabeth I and Victoria of England or Catherine the Great of Russia.

Saudi Arabia

Among the Gulf states, Saudi Arabia is clearly the most powerful; it is also the most inscrutable due to its tight control of access by non-Saudis and non-Muslims, rendering scholarly research highly difficult. Widespread restrictions on civil rights and political freedoms further limit knowledge about the kingdom. King Abdullah, a son of the country's founder Ibn Saud, serves as monarch and rules Saudi Arabia; he succeeded his half-brother Fahd upon the latter's death in August 2005, and as crown prince he held substantial power in the decade after Fahd suffered a stroke in 1995.

Drawing on its considerable political and economic resources, the Saudi leadership has consistently argued that it has pursued domestic policies in support of modernization with an emphasis on cooperation, negotiation, and compromise that is consistent with the Quran. Nonetheless, the royal family has not been immune to criticism and threats to its political legitimacy. Opponents of the regime—whether secular or religious—maintain that the oil wealth has been used to enrich the Saudi royal family more than the country as a whole, that the government is corrupt, and that the refusal of the House of Saud to share power is non-Islamic. There is also dissatisfaction among many with the close ties between Saudi Arabia and the United States: Osama bin Laden, the founder of al-Qaeda, was an intense opponent of the Saudi regime despite—or perhaps because of—coming from an elite family with close connections to that regime. Shortly after the 1991 Gulf War, a group of Western-educated intellectuals tried to persuade King Fahd to introduce democratic reforms in Saudi Arabia: the creation of a constitutional monarchy, greater respect for human rights, and the opportunity for political parties and universal suffrage. In response, a number of religious leaders urged Fahd instead to transform Saudi Arabia into a fully Islamic state along the lines of Iran. In an attempt to quell this nascent dissent, in February 1992 King Fahd announced the establishment of a sixty-man majlis al-shura (consultative council) whose appointed members were drawn from the professional, academic, religious, business, and retired military elites of the country. The majlis has subsequently expanded its membership from 60 to 150 persons representing a variety of sectors of Saudi society including academics (from both religious and secular institutions), bureaucrats and professionals, businesspeople, police, diplomats, and military personnel. The council can propose legislation but its actions have no binding force.

The question of Saudi succession following the end of line of sons of Ibn Saud—who are reaching the absolute limits of human longevity—is arguably one of the single greatest uncertainties in the Middle East. The list of potential successors among the grandsons is large, and the contenders for power will vie for support between the religious traditionalists and the modernizers, as well as within the extended royal family itself, and quite possibly will deal with domestic instability from the large Shi'i minority in the northeast and the large expatriate population. Instability in Saudi Arabia would almost certainly have a serious impact on global oil prices, and could potentially lead to a US-led intervention, though in the wake of the occupation of Iraq, and projections of US energy independence for a period in the 2020s (Daily Finance, 2013), there might be little domestic support for such an endeavor.

States of the Arabian Peninsula

The remaining monarchies of the Arabian Peninsula have several attributes in common. They are all relatively small in terms of both land and population, with little arable land; each has a significant expatriate population that is responsible for much of the economic activity; and all rely on petroleum and natural gas for a significant portion of their export revenue. The rulers of each country face internal pressures for political liberalization; most have chosen to respond cautiously by lifting some restrictions on speech and the media, decentralizing the government and giving greater power to individual ministries, establishing elected or appointed consultative councils, and introducing constitutions.

Qatar, Oman, and the UAE. Similar to Saudi Arabia in some ways, Qatar is a religiously conservative, traditional emirate, ruled by Hamad ibn Khalifah ibn Hamad al-Thani, who ousted his father, Khalifah, in a nonviolent coup on June 27, 1995. In this wealthy emirate, the decisions of the monarch are binding, and members of the al-Thani family hold many of the significant political positions. Hamad, who is significantly younger than the other Gulf leaders (except for Bahrain's Hamad ibn Isa al-Khalifah), sees himself as a modernizing ruler. He has allowed for increased political debate in the public arena and has begun to enfranchise the population: on March 8, 1999, some 23,000 Qatari women and men voted in the first-ever elections for a twenty-nine-member advisory Municipal Council. (The number of voters was small because individuals who were in the military or police and those who had been Qatari citizens for less than fifteen years were ineligible to participate, as was the more than 75 percent of the population that was expatriate.) Six women were among the more than 200 candidates, although none were elected.

Oman, too, has begun to move slowly toward constitutional rule and limited popular political participation. In September 2000, Oman held elections for an eighty-two-person Consultative Assembly. Both men and women were granted suffrage rights, and close to two dozen women were among the more than 550 individuals who stood for office (2 women were elected). Previously, membership in the council was determined by Sultan Qaboos, and he still exercises some control over who is permitted to run. The assembly advises the government, reviews legislation, and provides a formal means for community leaders to provide input to the government.

The third of the small, traditional Gulf states is the UAE, a union of seven shaikhdoms formed when Britain withdrew from the Gulf in the early 1970s. Independence was to be followed by the creation of a permanent constitution and elections, but even limited elections—for half of the council through a 6,689-member electoral college—did not occur until December 2006. Thus, although the UAE is technically a republic, in reality it is a federation of emirates with no suffrage and no political parties. Governance of the 4.4 million residents (only about 20 percent of whom are indigenous to the area) is by the Supreme Council, composed of the leader of each emirate and headed by Shaikh Khalifa ibn Zayid al-Nuhayyan of Abu Dhabi. There is also a forty-person Federal National Assembly, whose membership reflects the power distribution of the UAE: Abu Dhabi and Dubai have eight representatives each; Sharjah and Ras al-Khaimah have six each; and Umm al-Quaiwan, Fujairah, and Ajman have only four each. Periodically, tensions erupt among the emirates over the dominance of Abu Dhabi and Dubai; however, because these are the largest and wealthiest regions, the federation could not easily exist without their involvement and criticism is constrained.

Bahrain and Kuwait. The constitutions of both Bahrain and Kuwait call for a legislative body; however, until recently in the multi-island country of Bahrain, parliamentary rule was a legal fiction. The thirty-person National Assembly, partially elected by a small number of male Bahraini citizens in 1973, was suspended in 1975 after it "balked at endorsing a broadly written decree that would enable the government to detain critics and opponents at will for 'statements' or 'activities' deemed to threaten the country's 'internal or external security'" (Stork, 1997:34). Emir Isa ibn Salmon al-Khalifah, who ruled Bahrain from independence until his death on March 6, 1999, then suspended the constitution and dismissed the parliament.

More than two-thirds of the Bahraini population is Shi'i and, over the years, there have been allegations of Iranian-supported plots to overthrow the Sunni-controlled government. Demands of the opposition members include political rights for women, the restoration of the constitution and parliament, and more economic opportunities. The response of Isa's government was to increase political repression: detaining dissidents without charge, using torture, and increasing restrictions on freedom of expression (Human Rights Watch, 1997).

Government policy changed significantly with the accession of Hamad ibn Isa al-Khalifah in 1999. The new emir called for a national plebiscite and, in February 2002, Bahrain became a constitutional monarchy. The first elections for the parliament were held on October 24, 2002. In parliamentary elections in 2006, Al Wifaq, the largest Shi'i "political society," won the greatest number of seats. Bahrain appointed a female cabinet minister in 2004 and, when Bahrain was elected to head the UN General Assembly in 2006, it appointed a woman as president of that body, only the third woman in history to hold the position.

Since the beginning of the Arab uprisings, Bahrain has faced large-scale protests, which have been harshly repressed with the assistance of Saudi Arabia—which fears a spillover to its own Shi'i minority that is concentrated near Bahrain—and other Gulf states. Since Bahrain has shown little signs of undertaking serious political reform, the long-term effect of these protests is unclear, but they constitute a serious source of uncertainty in the region.

In contrast, of all the Gulf states, Kuwait has arguably been the most successful in preempting revolutionary pressures. This is due in large part to

> the massive and successful program of the al-Sabah dynasty . . . to preserve its power by building the region's first modern welfare state. . . . For decades, the Kuwaiti government has lavishly subsidized everything from electricity to housing, has underwritten travel abroad for those seeking education or medical treatment, and has created comfortable, well-paying, white collar jobs for 96 percent of its working citizens. (Sadowski, 1997:7)

Kuwait liberalized its laws on female suffrage in May 2005. In the parliamentary elections that followed in June 2006, none of the women candidates were successful. But in the election of May 2009, four women were elected. Until 1996, suffrage was granted only to adult males who were residents of Kuwait prior to 1920 and their male descendants. The vote has since been extended to the (few) naturalized citizens who have been citizens for at least twenty years, but the electorate remains tiny compared with the total population. The fifty-person National Assembly has a checkered history: the emir suspended the assembly and ruled by decree during 1975–1981 and 1986–1992, arguing that Kuwait could not afford the divisiveness facilitated by democracy, and he dissolved it and called for new elections in two other instances, in 1999 and in 2006. But subsequently elections have been held on a fairly regular basis, in 2008, 2009, and 2012.

Jordan and Morocco

The role of parliament in Jordan and Morocco is more substantial than in the other Middle Eastern monarchies: they are popularly elected and political parties are legal. Jordan, the only royal kingdom remaining in the Levant, has been a constitutional monarchy since the 1928 Constitution established an elected legislative council (although ultimate responsibility still rested with the Hashemites). A new constitution promulgated in February 1947 called for a bicameral National Assembly, with an 80-person lower house elected by popular vote that has been expanded over the years to 120 seats, including 12 seats guaranteed to women; a smaller upper house appointed by the king currently has 60 seats. However, internal instability and dislocations surrounding Jordan's loss of the West Bank in its 1967 war with Israel led to parliamentary institutions being suspended from 1967 to 1984. In the wake of riots through the country in April 1989, King Hussein decided to reliberalize the political system, adopting a new parliamentary system for the elections held in November 1989.

In reopening the political process, King Hussein was attempting to deflate dissent around poor economic conditions. Faced with a strong Islamic movement, he chose to integrate Islamists into the government rather than banning them, as occurred in Algeria, Egypt, and Tunisia. In fact, Jordan's Islamists had long been allies of the monarchy in the conflict with leftists in the 1950s and 1960s, and the Palestine Liberation Organization in 1970. When Islamists held five cabinet positions in the early 1990s, those ministers sought (mostly unsuccessfully) to introduce laws restricting activities such as the consumption of alcohol or requiring gender separation in public

Political protests in Jordan are legal, but carefully monitored. These riot police are lined up to prevent an anti-Israel protest from marching any closer to the Israeli embassy.

swimming pools and sports facilities. At the same time, participation in the government required the Islamists to compromise and forge alliances with other political entities (Schwedler, 2006).

Subsequent multiparty elections were held in 1993, 1997, 2003, 2007, and 2010. In 1993, some two dozen parties reflecting a diversity of views contended for representation. By the November 1997 elections, however, Human Rights Watch reported with dismay that there was "a clear intent to discourage Jordanians from organizing and participating in public discussion of political issues that segments of the civil society deem to be of national importance" and questioned whether, under these circumstances, any elections could be considered free and fair (cited in Andoni, 1997:19). Changes in the election law clearly strengthened the position of traditional regime loyalists at the expense of opposition groups, which led nine opposition parties, including the large Islamic Action Front, to boycott the election. Elections in 2003 (held more than eighteen months late), 2007, and 2010 also returned strong progovernment assemblies, even with the participation of opposition parties. Elections in 2003 (held more than eighteen months late), 2007, 2010, and 2013 also returned strong progovernment assemblies, even with the participation of opposition parties. By the 2013 election, the Islamic Action Front had resumed its boycott, again on the grounds of unfair election laws.

As noted earlier, the Kingdom of Morocco has made more substantial reforms in response to the Arab uprisings, which have periodically produced large demonstrations in Casablanca, Marrakesh, and Rabat focusing on corruption and economic issues as well as general demands for political reform. Recent changes in Morocco have included the accommodation of the previously banned Islamist Justice and Development Party, which is now the ruling party in parliament, and constitutional reform that shifts the power to dissolve parliament from the king to the prime minister. At present, Morocco has a two-tiered legislative body: a 395-member Chamber of Representatives, which is directly elected for a five-year term, and a Chamber of Councilors, which is indirectly elected by local councils, professional organizations, and labor groups for staggered nine-year terms. Both women and men have suffrage; women are guaranteed 30 seats in the Chamber of Representatives.

Conditional Democracies

Not considering the democratic transitions that resulted from the Arab uprisings, four states in the Middle East—Israel, Lebanon, Turkey, and Iran—can be considered at least nominally democratic as a function of their formal political institutions. Yet due to the emphasis on religion and ethnicity that is inherent in their political structures, all four are better labeled "conditional" democracies. Arguably, the first three countries used variations on the liberal democratic model—adopting European norms and appealing for European assistance—to make the best of a bad situation: Turkey because it needed to recover what it could from the remains of the Ottoman Empire, Lebanon because it was small and divided, and Israel because it was considered illegitimate by its Arab neighbors. Iran, in contrast, invented an entirely new system, but one with substantial democratic elements.

A comparison between Turkey and Iran is particularly interesting. Neither is a fully consolidated democracy. In both cases, sovereignty is divided, with an elected president and legislature constrained by either the military (in the case of Turkey) or religious authorities (in Iran). This requires an incredibly detailed constitution, which both countries have, and an active judiciary to interpret the laws while following a clear ideological position. As illustrated below, the challenges facing Israel and Lebanon have less to do with divided sovereignty and more with attempting to maintain certain positions of privilege for a portion of the population based on religion.

Turkey

In Turkey's parliamentary system, formal power rests with the 550 members of the Grand National Assembly, elected to four-year terms. The largely ceremonial president traditionally was elected by the assembly, but a recent constitutional amendment requires that the position be filled via popular elections every five years. Political parties are permitted; however, the government consistently denies the right of Kurds to organize an ethnically based political party and attempts to limit their power as a distinct ethnic group through an unusually high electoral quota (10 percent) that makes it difficult for a Kurdish-oriented party to join the assembly. The government's position is that Kurds may have full civil rights as Turks, but cannot express these in the context of Kurdish self-determination. Historically, Turkey has moved to restrict political expression by Islamic movements and the repeated, although short-lived, interventions by the military to preserve the Atatürk model, as well as long-term suppression of the civil liberties of the Kurds and of religious liberties in the name of secularism, weaken Turkey's democratic credentials.

A major transformation in Turkish politics started to take place with the overwhelming victory of the Justice and Development Party (AKP), headed by Recep Tayyip Erdoğan, in the November 2002 elections. For the first time in decades, a single political party—one that was a successor to a long line of banned Islamic parties—gained a majority of seats in the parliament and was able to form a stable and functioning administration; its success was replicated in subsequent elections in July 2007 and June 2011. Given AKP's moderate agenda—it made no attempts to implement sharia and retained Turkey's pro-Western foreign policies—and the strong public support it maintained, the military could no longer challenge the party and its administration without risking its own legitimacy. The AKP government was reaffirmed in 2007 and 2011 and has continued to pursue Turkey's gaining membership to the EU, although the exceedingly slow progress of these negotiations, as well as financial instability within the EU itself, has made this less of a priority than in the past.

Israel

For its Jewish citizens, Israel is the most open political system in the Middle East. However, its founding principle of maintaining the Jewish character of the state and its failures in dealing with the political rights of the Palestinians, both within Israel, where there is systematic legal and budgetary discrimination (Ghanem, 2001), and particularly in the Occupied Territories, limit the extent to which it can be called fully liberal. Furthermore, by the 1990s a substantial challenge to democratic norms by "Jewish revivalism"—efforts, particularly by Israeli Orthodox Jews, to increase the importance of Jewish religious observances in Israel—had emerged.

Israel's political system is based directly on democratic norms. Most of the Zionist leaders who helped found Israel were advocates of democratic socialism, and Israel has had liberal democratic institutions from the very beginning. Although military service is critical to advancing a political career, the Israeli military has never intervened to overthrow a government, and non-Jewish citizens—notably the sizable Palestinian minority within Israel—are permitted to vote and stand for election, although non-Jewish members of the Knesset were not included in governing coalitions until quite recently.

The structure of power in Israeli politics has gone through three distinct phases. In the early years of the state, politics were dominated by a single party, Labor, whose leadership consisted almost entirely of individuals of European descent. The Labor Party exercised control not only through the legislative mechanisms of the Knesset, but also through interlocking control of the labor unions and state enterprises, which provided ample opportunities for patronage.

In 1977, the Labor Party's dominance was challenged by a group of conservative parties that coalesced under the name Likud. In addition to providing alternatives to Labor policies—for example, Likud was interested in restraining the Labor-dominated state enterprises—Likud appealed to a number of Jewish voters who had emigrated from Arab countries such as Morocco, Yemen, and Iraq. Likud broke the Labor monopoly on political control of Israel and held power for a number of years, either alone or in "national unity" coalitions with Labor.

The third phase began with a change in electoral laws—effective in 1996—that provided for the direct election of a prime minister. Although intended to make the prime minister less dependent on the unstable parliamentary coalitions within the Knesset, direct election had the unexpected effect of encouraging the growth of a number of small, single-interest parties in the elections of 1996 and 1999. Both Labor and Likud lost substantial numbers of seats to new, ethnically oriented parties, notably Yisrael Beiteinu and Shas. Labor and Likud both supported a repeal of the Direct Election Law in February 2001 and the country returned to a more traditional parliamentary system in which the prime minister is the head of the party that is able to form a government after single-ballot general elections. Nonetheless, the ethnically-oriented parties continued to be successful at the parliamentary level: in the 2009 election, Yisrael Beiteinu and Shas had the third- and fifth-largest numbers of seats in the Knesset.

In November 2005, the right wing split over the issue of partial disengagement from the Occupied Territories, with Sharon forming the prodisengagement Kadima Party, while the remainder of Likud remained under the leadership of former prime minister Benjamin Netanyahu. Likud suffered a major electoral defeat in March 2006, receiving only twelve seats whereas Kadima achieved a plurality with twenty-nine seats and formed a coalition government with Labor and Shas. Sharon's subsequent incapacitation by a stroke in January 2006, however, left Kadima without clear leadership. In the 2009 elections, Likud regained the top position with twenty-seven seats to Kadima's twenty-one, and again formed a government under Netanyahu.

In addition to the potential parliamentary instability caused by the proliferation of small parties, the liberal character of Israeli democracy is also openly questioned by some of the religious parties that wish to see much more power granted to religious authorities. For example, the relative domains of secular and religious courts are being sharply contested, despite the fact that religious councils already have considerably greater power in Israel than they have in most other liberal democracies. Consequently, Israel is confronting many of the same issues of balancing secular and religious power that Muslim states in the region are facing.

Lebanon

Constitutionally, Lebanon is a parliamentary republic with an elected 128-member Chamber of Deputies reflecting confessional divisions of at least eighteen separate entities designed to create a form of sectarian proportional representation. By law and tradition, the president is a Maronite Christian while the prime minister is a Sunni Muslim and the speaker of the parliament is a Shi'i Muslim. The assembly provides for equal representation of Christians and Muslims based on the 1989 Taif Accords, which were negotiated to end the civil war that began in 1975.

The return to democracy after fifteen years of civil and international conflict has not been easy. Relationships with Syria, questions surrounding the legitimacy and the efficiency of the Taif system—due to changing demographics, Muslims now almost certainly have a substantially larger population than Christians and consequently are underrepresented—and Hizbullah activities in southern Lebanon continue to pose serious challenges to the country's stability. This became apparent in September 2004, when an effort to change the constitution to extend the term of pro-Syrian president Emile Lahoud led to a parliamentary deadlock. In February 2005, former prime minister Rafiq al-Hariri, a leader of the anti-Syrian faction, was assassinated by a car bomb. Although the perpetrators have not been identified, Syria was widely suspected of involvement, forcing it to withdraw from Lebanon in April 2005 following massive demonstrations.

Since the Syrian withdrawal, Lebanon has had a series of relatively weak coalition governments, typically established only after months of negotiations. With Syria now engaged in a protracted civil war, its direct political influence in Lebanon has declined, but the country has considerable concern about possible spillover effects, including large-scale refugee movements and militia groups establishing enclaves along its border. Hizbullah's dominance in southern Lebanon poses multiple issues, including the ability of the Beirut government to exercise full territorial control, the possibility of renewed military hostilities with Israel, and Hizbullah's promotion of Shi'i political power proportional to their true percentage of the population, which would upset the earlier confessional arrangements. While the Lebanese democratic system has avoided collapse, it continues to face serious challenges.

Iran

In February 1979, following months of increasingly widespread civil unrest, the staunchly pro-Western, authoritarian Pahlavi monarchy in Iran was overthrown. Much to the surprise of Western observers—although not to many in the region—the government that eventually gained control came not from Iranian elites, nor from leftist movements that the shah had brutally suppressed, but from a conservative Islamic movement led by Ayatollah Ruhollah Khomeini, a prominent Shi'i cleric who returned from exile in Paris.

Khomeini's "Islamic Republic" was a radical departure from earlier revolutionary movements in the Middle East. In contrast to Baathism, which combined a variety of anticolonial, Western, and Arab ideas, Khomeini and his followers implemented a conservative political agenda derived almost entirely from traditional Islamic thought and practice. Although the details of the nature of Islamic governance are complex and hotly debated (including—in fact, particularly—within the Islamic Republic itself), three characteristics distinguish it.

The first is the use of Islamic law—sharia—in place of various systems of civil law. This went directly against the twentieth-century tendency in the Middle East and other postcolonial regions to replace, at least in part, traditional legal systems based on religion and custom with uniform secular legal codes, often derived from the legal systems of former colonial powers. In practice, the implementation of sharia also involves the imposition of additional conservative social norms that are not actually addressed in the Quran, most conspicuously regarding restrictions on the behavior of women.

Second, the Islamic Republic of Iran placed the supreme authority of the state in the hands of religious councils. These councils also chose a supreme religious leader, a post held by Khomeini until his death in 1989. However, the remaining familiar structures of a modern state—a president, popularly elected parliament, court system, and so forth—remained intact and play an important role in ruling the state. The religious authorities can overturn the decisions of these secular structures, but such decisions must be made on the basis of Islamic law and tradition rather than personal whim. Candidates for election to the secular government require approval from the religious authorities and, during his lifetime, Khomeini retained absolute authority on issues regarding war and other foreign policy matters, although he often chose not to exercise his power.

Finally, Khomeini followed an approach to Islam that placed a high priority on missionary efforts. Consequently, the Islamic Republic saw itself in the vanguard of an international revolution and immediately sought to export its model of conservative political Islam to other states. (In this regard, the agenda of Iranian fundamentalism appeared to the West to be similar to that of international communism, and was treated similarly.) Iran has had only limited success in its effort to promote this specific version of political Islam, but the general concept of a conservative Islamic state following sharia has had tremendous influence throughout the Middle East, in particular among militant groups affiliated with al-Qaeda, even as these conservative Sunni groups fiercely oppose Shi'i theology and institutions.

Almost thirty-five years after Khomeini's triumphant return to Iran, the experiment of the Islamic Republic can be regarded as a mixed success. Contrary to the predictions of many skeptics who expected an early end to a "medieval" governing structure imposed on an industrializing, urbanizing state, the Islamic Republic has survived, has been generally stable, and has thus far successfully coped with several major difficulties, including a devastating war with Iraq, the collapse of the price of oil in the 1990s, and substantial refugee inflows from Iraq and Afghanistan.

In contrast to many depictions in the West, the Iranian model is not one of a totalitarian religious state. A functioning secular government remains in place, both for theological reasons (Islam emphasizes the importance of the *umma,* the Muslim community as a whole, and not merely the ulama, the religious elites) and presumably because the Shi'i clerics have little interest in taking on the responsibility for filling potholes and collecting garbage. These secular political institutions provide a natural source of opposition to the power of the religious authorities, particularly in urban areas. Furthermore, the religious authorities derive their power from the approval and respect of their followers, not from any intrinsic divine right. No leader with Khomeini's broad support has emerged since his death, and competition for leadership within the religious councils has somewhat weakened their control.

For a period of time, in fact, it appeared that the hold of the religious authorities in Iran was weakening substantially. The February 2000 parliamentary elections were extremely competitive, with 6,000 candidates vying for the 270 seats, and ended with a major victory for the leftist, reform-oriented Islamic Participation Front.

However, this sixth parliament was still constrained by the Council of Guardians, which limited its ability to implement the types of changes that its supporters had hoped to see (Rezaei, 2003; Ehteshami and Zweiri, 2007). In February 2004, conservatives reasserted control of parliament in elections after thousands of reformist candidates were disqualified by the Council of Guardians prior to the vote. This control was solidified in June 2005 when Mahmood Ahmadinejad, Tehran's ultraconservative mayor, won a run-off vote in presidential elections, defeating the more moderate cleric and former president Hojatolislam Ali Akbar Hashemi Rafsanjani.

Islamic control was again contested in 2009 in massive protests following the disputed reelection of Ahmadinejad. These protests in many ways presaged the later protests of the Arab uprisings: one of the most dramatic incidents was a video of the shooting death of a young woman demonstrator that was uploaded to YouTube and viewed millions of times. By early 2010, however, the movement had been successfully suppressed by police and proregime paramilitary groups. Despite this setback, Iran has a young, educated population that appears ready to reduce the control of religious authorities on Iran's political institutions (*Middle East Report,* 2006).

At the time of this writing, the most important international issue involving Iran concerns its nuclear weapons program. This program, one of the hallmarks of the Ahmadinejad regime, has been widely condemned internationally—to date, it has been the subject of seven UN Security Council resolutions, beginning in July 2006 to the most recent in June 2012—and has involved economic sanctions of increasing severity. While these initially involved only embargos on materials related to weapons production, they have expanded considerably: the EU's restrictions on Iranian financial institutions and energy exports, imposed in the summer of 2012, appear to be particularly damaging to the Iranian economy. More active measures have included the assassination of Iranian nuclear scientists, and the use of a highly sophisticated computer virus named Stuxnet—generally assumed to be a project of the United States and Israel—to disable some of the equipment used in the nuclear program.

By the autumn of 2012, there were increasing concerns that Israel would preemptively attack Iran's nuclear facilities, following the model of Israel's attacks on Iraq's Osirak reactor in 1981 and Syria's al Kibar facility in 2007. Despite considerable rhetoric by Israel's civilian leadership, the prospects of a successful attack are viewed with great skepticism by the Israel military and intelligence services, and would almost certainly require the assistance of the United States, which under President Obama's second term appears to show little enthusiasm for this project. At present, it appears more likely that the rising economic costs of the sanctions will force the Ahmadinejad regime to either stop or severely curtail the nuclear program much as sanctions ended the Iraqi nuclear program in the 1990s.

Transitional Democracies

The final category are the transitional democracies emerging out of earlier authoritarian states due to the Arab uprisings—Tunisia, Egypt, Libya, and probably Syria in the near future—as well as the Palestinian Authority, Iraq following the US occupation, and Algeria following the civil war of 1992–1998. While most of these states are in the very early stages of this process, based on the experience of other countries that have gone through the process (as Table 4.1 shows, transitions from authoritarian to democratic rule have been quite common in the past two decades) it should be possible to make some generalizations about their future.

The transitional democracies all face a common set of problems in developing institutions that can provide wide and fairly distributed political and economic opportunity despite building on a history where political and economic power was highly concentrated and structures such as legal opposition parties were generally absent. Several of these countries are also dealing with unresolved ethnic divisions and a recent history of high levels of violent conflict; all of them are dealing with the issue of reconciling the competing models of political Islam and secular liberalism. Corruption, one of the key issues in the Arab uprisings, has proven difficult to uproot even in countries such as Mexico, Russia, and India with strong central governments, as is changing the concentration of wealth in a small number of elite families who benefited from the authoritarian regime.

In all likelihood, this will be a slow, uneven, but ultimately successful process. The US advisers of the Coalition Provisional Authority arrived in Iraq in 2003 thinking that they would easily replicate the rapid reestablishment of democracy in Germany, Italy, and Japan following the defeat of those countries in World War II (Ricks, 2006), ignoring the fact that Germany, Italy, and Japan had already been democratic prior to their prewar takeover by military regimes. Iraq—and the other Arab transitional democracies—had no such history.

A more accurate model for Arab democratization might well be the United States itself, which went through a variety of experiments, including the flawed Articles of Confederation that were discarded entirely, before settling on a set of workable institutions, and even then experienced a devastating civil war and a lag of nearly two centuries before fully empowering its ethnic minorities. Arab democracies are unlikely to require that much time to develop. A mature set of international democratic norms has emerged and been applied successfully in transitions from authoritarian to democratic regimes, including in cases such as predominantly Muslim and highly multiethnic Indonesia, whereas the United States was often inventing institutions in isolation. Nonetheless, these processes are likely to see successes and failures.

There are no simple answers to such issues, and they will likely take years to resolve. The variety of experiences in post-Soviet Eastern Europe may also be instructive: while some states, particularly those in geographical proximity to Western Europe, quickly adopted robust democratic systems, others reverted to single-party rule with only weak democratic institutions—arguably the current situation in Algeria—or simply replaced Soviet authoritarianism with a more local variety. To date, the transitional democracies have avoided the last outcome, but it is unrealistic to assume the path to full democracy will be straightforward and problem free.

Conclusion

At the beginning of a new millennium in the Christian calendar, the states of the Middle East are confronting several major political challenges. First, the region is undergoing a generational change in both its leaders and its political issues: the faces and agendas that dominated the last three decades of the twentieth century are unlikely to be as critical in the early decades of the twenty-first century. Until recently, most governments in the Middle East were remarkably stable, with individual leaders in power for decades. However, many pivotal figures in the region have recently died or are likely to do so in the near future, and the Arab uprisings have triggered a series of political changes that are likely to continue for some time.

As the leaders of the older generation are fading, so are many of the older issues. The Cold War, during which the superpowers both used and were used by many states in the region, ended at the beginning of the 1990s. The revolutionary secular ideologies of the postcolonial period have faded and no longer inspire serious intellectual debate. In place of these concerns, a new domestic issue clearly dominates: the often competing pressures for either democratic or religious governance that would provide increased popular involvement in government. This has affected the full range of states, including countries with strong parliamentary traditions such as Turkey and Israel, and the Arab Gulf states, several of which have recently established consultative councils and held elections, as well as the transitional democracies emerging from the Arab uprisings. Such moves toward greater democratization are consistent with trends in most of the world.

A major open issue is whether the strong centralized states established in the postcolonial period will remain territorially intact in the twenty-first century. This again reflects global trends: the period of state consolidation that occurred in the nineteenth and twentieth centuries seems to have reversed since the early 1990s with dramatic breakups such as the Soviet Union and Yugoslavia, as well as smaller ones such as the former Czechoslovakia, Eritrea, South Sudan, and Timor-Leste. The Kurdish area of Iraq has now been effectively independent for a decade; political control in Palestine is split across the West Bank and Gaza; central government control in Yemen is tenuous in much of the territory; and one possible outcome of the Syrian civil war would be the division of the state along ethnic lines. Loosely federated states are not necessarily a bad thing—ethnically divided Switzerland has been stable for centuries and highly prosperous in recent decades—but this would present a very different Middle East than was seen in the twentieth century.

Tensions involving Israel and its neighbors also remain a critical concern. While aspects of the Arab-Israeli conflict have been addressed successfully (most notably, the Egyptian-Israeli and Jordanian-Israeli peace treaties), relations between Israelis and Palestinians remain unresolved, and the brief war with Hizbullah in June 2006 showed that Lebanon remains a flash point despite Israel's 2000 withdrawal from Lebanese territory. The Palestinian National Authority is now both geographically and politically split and faces the long-term ghettoization of Palestinian cities and villages due to Israeli military closures, roadblocks, the separation wall, and Jewish-only housing settlements. These and other factors have left the economy in tatters and much of it dependent on international aid.

With such a tense and violent situation, where mutual trust is all but nonexistent, one might be tempted to conclude that this conflict will never be resolved. However, people feared the same dire future for South Africa, which has became a vibrant pluralist society despite the horrific legacy of apartheid. The conflict between Israeli Jews and Palestinians is extremely difficult, to be sure, but there is no inevitability to its continuance.

Finally, governments throughout the region are under increasing pressure to implement policies that will improve economic performance and respond to a global economy that, due to concerns about the effects of fossil fuels on climate change and the rising price of oil, will be increasingly looking for alternative energy sources. While the short term has seen an increase in oil revenues, in the long term there will be greater pressure on Middle Eastern regimes to industrialize and diversify their economies. The professional class of accountants, engineers, and doctors who once lived as politically powerless expatriates is likely to demand a greater share of political power. The Middle East will also need to reassess its role in the global economy to decide, for instance, whether or not to pursue regional economic integration, link with the more developed economies of Europe, or join with the less developed economies of Africa and southern and Central Asia. These will be difficult questions for the new generation of Arabs, Iranians, Israelis, and Turks as the twenty-first century progresses.

Note

We owe so much to the late Deborah J. Gerner for her authorship of the original chapter. An earlier version of this chapter benefited enormously from the comments of Donald L. Gordon, Gwenn Okrulick, and Ömür Yilmaz. Jillian Schwedler and several outside reviewers made excellent suggestions for this and earlier revisions. None of them should be held responsible for whatever errors of fact or interpretation remain despite their wise counsel.

Bibliography

Anderson, Lisa. 1991. "Absolutism and the Resilience of the Monarchy." *Political Science Quarterly* 106, no. 1:1–15.

Andoni, Lamis. 1997. December 5. "Jordanian Elections: Setback for Democratisation." *Middle East International,* p. 19.

Antonius, George. 1946. *The Arab Awakening: The Story of the Arab National Movement.* New York: G. P. Putnam's Sons.

Ayoob, Mohammed. 2007. *The Many Faces of Political Islam: Religion and Politics in the Muslim World.* Ann Arbor: University of Michigan Press.

Bill, James A., and Robert Springborg. 1994. *Politics in the Middle East.* 4th ed. New York: HarperCollins.

Chandrasekaran, Rajiv. 2006. *Imperial Life in the Emerald City: Inside Iraq's Green Zone.* New York: Alfred A. Knopf.

Daily Finance. 2013. "Daily Finance." www.dailyfinance.com.

Ehsani, Kaveh. 2006. "Iran: The Populist Threat to Democracy." *Middle East Report,* no. 241:4–9.

Ehteshami, Anoushiravan, and Mahjoob Zweiri. 2007. *Iran and the Rise of Its Neoconservatives: The Politics of Tehran's Silent Revolution.* London: I. B. Tauris.

Freedom House. 2012. *Freedom in the World: Country Ratings 1973–2012.* Washington, DC: Freedom House. www.freedomhouse.org.

Galbraith, Peter W. 2006. *The End of Iraq: How American Incompetence Created a War Without End.* New York: Simon & Schuster.

Gause, F. Gregory, III. 2000. "The Persistence of Monarchy in the Arabian Peninsula: A Comparative Analysis." Pp. 167–186 in Joseph Kostiner (ed.), *Middle East Monarchies: The Challenge of Modernity.* Boulder: Lynne Rienner.

Ghanem, As'ad. 2001. *The Palestinian-Arab Minority in Israel, 1948–2000.* Albany: SUNY Press.

Global Security. 2013. "Global Security." www.globalsecurity.org.

Halliday, Fred. 1979. *Iran: Dictatorship and Development.* 2nd ed. New York: Penguin Books.

Henry, Clement Moore, and Robert Springborg. 2010. *Globalization and the Politics of Development in the Middle East.* 2nd ed. New York: Cambridge University Press.

Hudson, Michael C. 1977. *Arab Politics: The Search for Legitimacy.* New Haven: Yale University Press.

Human Rights Watch. 1997. *Routine Abuse, Routine Denial: Civil Rights and the Political Crisis in Bahrain.* New York: Human Rights Watch.

Ibrahim, Saad Eddin. 1995. "Liberalization and Democratization in the Arab World: An Overview." Pp. 29–57 in Rex Brynen, Bahgat Korany, and Paul Noble (eds.), *Political Liberalization and Democratization in the Arab World,* vol. 1: *Theoretical Perspectives.* Boulder: Lynne Rienner.

Khalidi, Rashid (ed.). 1991. *The Origins of Arab Nationalism.* New York: Columbia University Press.

Luciani, Giacomo (ed.). 1990. *The Arab State.* Berkeley: University of California Press.

Makiya, Kanan. 1993. *Cruelty and Silence: War, Tyranny, Uprising, and the Arab World.* New York: Norton.

Middle East Report. 2006. "Iran: Looking Forward." No. 241.

———. 2007. "The Shi'a in the Arab World." No. 242.

Nasr, Vali. 2006. *The Shia Revival: How Conflicts Within Islam Will Shape the Future.* New York: Norton.

Norton, Augustus Richard (ed.). 1995. *Civil Society in the Middle East.* Vol. 1. Leiden: E. J. Brill.

Peteet, Julie. 2007. "Unsettling Categories of Displacement." *Middle East Report,* no. 244:2–9.

Petraeus, David H. 2006. January–February. "Learning Counterinsurgency: Observations from Soldiering in Iraq." *Military Review,* pp. 2–12.

Rezaei, Ali. 2003. "Last Efforts of Iran's Reformists." *Middle East Report,* no. 226: 40–46.

Richards, Alan, and John Waterbury. 2007. *A Political Economy of the Middle East.* 3rd ed. Boulder: Westview Press.

Ricks, Thomas E. 2006. *Fiasco: The American Military Adventure in Iraq.* New York: Penguin Press.

Rivlin, Paul. 2009. *Arab Economies in the Twenty-first Century.* New York: Cambridge University Press.

Sadowski, Yahya. 1997. "The End of the Counterrevolution? The Politics of Economic Adjustment in Kuwait." *Middle East Report,* no. 204:7–11.

Schwedler, Jillian. 2006. *Faith in Moderation: Islamist Parties in Jordan and Yemen.* New York: Cambridge University Press.

Sela, Avraham. 1998. *The Decline of the Arab-Israeli Conflict: Middle East Politics and the Quest for Regional Order.* Albany: SUNY Press.

Sharp, Gene. 2010. *From Dictatorship to Democracy.* Boston: Albert Einstein Institute.

Stork, Joe. 1997. "Bahrain's Crisis Worsens." *Middle East Report,* no. 204:33–35.

Tétreault, Mary Ann. 2012. November 1. "Looking for Revolution in Kuwait." *Middle East Report Online.* www.merip.org.

Transparency International. 2012. "The 2012 Corruption Perceptions Index. http://cpi.transparency.org/.

Tibi, Bassam. 1997. *Arab Nationalism: Between Islam and the Nation-State.* 3rd ed. New York: St. Martin's Press.

Vela, Justin. 2012, June 13. "Exclusive: Arab States Arm Rebels as UN Talks of Syrian Civil War." *The Independent.* www.independent.co.uk.

Wilson, Frank L. 1996. *Concepts and Issues in Comparative Politics: An Introduction to Comparative Analysis.* Upper Saddle River, NJ: Prentice Hall.

Woodward, Bob. 2004. *Plan of Attack.* New York: Simon & Schuster.

——. 2006. *State of Denial: Bush at War, Part III.* New York: Simon & Schuster.

US Department of State. 2003. *World Military Expenditures and Arms Transfers, 1999–2000.* http://www.state.gov/t/avc/rls/rpt/wmeat/1999_2000/index.htm.

Yao, Souchou. 2002. *Confucian Capitalism: Discourse, Practice and the Myth of Chinese Enterprise.* New York: Routledge Curzon.

5

International Relations

Mary Ann Tétreault

What sovereignty means in the Middle East has been shaken by the Arab uprisings. Beginning in Tunisia with the self-immolation of a young fruit seller, popular mobilization against autocratic regimes swept countries across the region. The Arab uprisings had one trigger, but many causes. Like earlier movements for political opening, they were fueled by an expansion of information available to the general public. In the case of the Arab uprisings, organized dissidence grew in part from the spread of "new media" across the region (Janardhan, 2011; Lynch, 2006). The release of hundreds of thousands of documents by WikiLeaks, and their analysis and publication in *The Guardian, Der Spiegel,* and the *New York Times,* confirmed what citizens had long suspected about their leaders: that they were corrupt. The leaks also attested to the leaders' persistence in their positions, and how much was owed to external support for authoritarian regimes in a region widely regarded as an exception to democratization that had swept other world regions in the 1980s and 1990s (Posusney, 2005; Schlumberger, 2007). As information and comments percolated through social media like Twitter and Facebook, they brought activists and ordinary citizens into the streets and squares of Middle Eastern cities to protest government corruption, incompetence, and dishonesty (Amnesty International, 2011:xii), and jarred foreign observers concerned with the survival of their Middle Eastern alliance partners.

Deficiencies in governance are widespread in the Middle East. They are the main legacy of imperialism and the neocolonialism that funnels externally generated resources directly to autocratic rulers. Robert H. Jackson (1990) argues that the postcolonial international system was populated by mature states and quasi-states. The latter included most of the countries that had become nominally independent from their colonial masters by grace of the United Nations (UN) and its endorsement (and putative enforcement; see Weber, 1995) of the norm of negative sovereignty. Negative sovereignty consists in the externally guaranteed rights of sovereign states; that is, juridical sovereignty (Jackson, 1990:21). Yet although a quasi-state whose existence is a product of this international norm may be recognized as independent, in reality many of them lack state capacity and institutions capable of constraining and outlasting the individuals who occupy their offices (Jackson, 1990:22). Their citizens are denied the liberty, rights, and support that would enable them to engage in the political life of their nation, and the welfare and protection that their state should provide (Jackson, 1990:25). Unlike juridical statehood—a status under international law—state capacity measures positive sovereignty, the successful development of stable institutions and rules, political competence, and popular support (Migdal, 1988; Tilly, 1985). Robert H. Jackson calls quasi-states without positive sovereignty the equivalent of welfare cases, dependent on transfers from abroad to maintain themselves (1990:22). Libya under Muammar Qaddafi was perhaps the most extreme example, a state with virtually no institutions that survived on oil-financed security forces (Vandewalle, 1998).

Negative sovereignty is not always observed in fact but, compared to the order that defined status in most of the world prior to World War II, this norm truly inaugurated a new era in international relations. Earlier, nation-states were only one among several forms of political organization, few of which were sovereign in Jackson's (1990) sense. European governments and their agents—not only armies and navies, but also privateers and for-profit corporations such as the British East India and West India companies—freely pursued imperial ventures of various types, mostly outside Europe, and grew to be rich and powerful on the proceeds (Wolf, 1982). By the late nineteenth century, however, the "state ideal"—the desire to have a state of one's own—had spread across the globe. Opposition to imperialism became more common, and both local rulers (e.g., Anscombe, 1997) and popular movements of various kinds (e.g., Antonius, 1946) began to seek greater autonomy. European imperialists countered, justifying their continued control of foreign territories as fulfilling a "civilizing mission" that required them to bear the "white man's burden," which was to rule nations "unfit" to govern themselves (Jackson, 1990:71).

The desire to maintain great-power dominance of the Middle East ensured that the principle of "self-determination" touted by US president Woodrow Wilson as the model for world order following World War I would not be applied there. As discussed in Chapter 2, the Middle East was a strategic and economic crossroads linking Europe to Asia, on the sea and land routes of lucrative long-distance trade (Macris and Kelly, 2012). The discovery of oil in Persia by a British company strengthened Britain's determination to maintain economic access to the Gulf; the Suez Canal and Palestine lay on routes to India, the jewel in Britain's imperial crown. French imperial interests in the Middle East included dependencies in North Africa and France's long-standing patronage of the Christian community on Mount Lebanon. Both Britain and France desired privileged access to territories such as Iraq, suspected to be rich in petroleum reserves. The US government, with plenty of US investors' interests to protect, also wanted colonial domination of the Middle East to continue. US and British leaders were reluctant to apply the principle of self-determination to Palestine; both supported establishing a homeland for Jews in a land where the vast majority of the population was Arab (Christison, 2000).

Keeping the Ottoman Empire—the "sick man" of Europe—alive had been a concern of European foreign offices for decades. European leaders feared that if the Ottoman Empire were to collapse, their own countries would be drawn into a war to divide up its carcass. This picture changed after Britain and France became allies, their German rival was defeated in World War I, and revolution and the consequent preoccupation with internal consolidation that took Russia out of the "great game" (imperial competition with Britain in western Asia) altered the balance of power in Europe. The sick man was allowed to die because the wartime victors were confident that they could control the successor states without having to go to war to acquire them. The new states also were vulnerable to European insistence that some were simply too immature to be fully sovereign (Fromkin, 1989). Thus, Europeans decided that colonial possessions like Algeria, a French colony since 1830, and Libya, conquered by Italy in 1911, would remain colonies after the war. Protectorates and bonds, inexpensive special relationships that gave Britain control of the foreign policies of the small Gulf states in return for little from them, also remained in effect (Anscombe, 1997; Kelly, 2012). The League of Nations, forerunner of today's United Nations, granted mandates allowing Britain and France to control nominally independent states carved from the old Ottoman Empire, like Syria and Iraq. In consequence, leaders and populations throughout the Middle East felt cheated of their Wilsonian right to self-determination, and the achievement of negative sovereignty became a cherished goal of their political regimes. Unfortunately, the persistence of "traditional ideas on the privileges and vulnerability of states and a substantial amount of confusion between the national state apparatus and those who are manipulating it [resulted in] twenty-two . . . weak Arab states in a highly integrated world system" (Salamé, 1990:31).

The untidy situation produced in the aftermath of World War I shaped the foreign and domestic relations of Middle Eastern states thereafter. As shown in Chapters 2, 3, and 4, the formal boundaries of these states were themselves mostly products of postwar, great-power politics. Rather than conforming to local interests and traditions, territories and peoples were divided or combined to satisfy the interests of major powers and to weaken potential local challengers to their imperial domination. Large parts of Syria, the heart of the Arabs' hoped-for independent state, were sheared off by European imperialists or appropriated by ambitious locals. An independent Lebanon was carved from Syria to suit the French and their Maronite Christian protégés. In consequence, Syria became smaller, less viable economically, and consequently more dependent on France. Syria also lost ground against the founder of modern Turkey, Mustafa Kemal. Known after 1933 as Atatürk (Father of the Turks), he refused to accept the victorious powers as the sole arbiters of the boundaries defining the postwar Middle East. Taking to the battlefield, he extended the territory of Turkey through military conquest, adding a piece of Greater Syria to the area under his new government's control.

When the European mapmakers redrew the boundaries of Syria, they never considered the long-term consequences for Lebanon's integrity. The core of the new state, the community of Mount Lebanon, had evolved over 400 years under Ottoman rule as a politically pluralist, multicultural community. It incorporated substantial populations of Sunni and Shi'i Muslims and Druze along with the French-favored Maronite Christians, whose minority status in the new state increased their dependence on their French protectors. With French backing, the Maronites squeezed constitutional concessions from non-Christian groups to give Christians the lion's share of political authority in the new state. Even when their relative proportion in the Lebanese population declined, Maronites resisted allowing others to enjoy the same political rights as themselves. This undermined the legitimacy of the state and, beginning in 1958, led to recurrent civil war (Maktabi, 2000).

The fate of the Hashemite dynasty offers another example of initiatives by postwar mapmakers that sabotaged the sovereignty of Middle Eastern states. As detailed in Chapter 3, one reason why the British divided their Palestine mandate to create the Kingdom of Transjordan was to reward Abdullah ibn Hussein with a land of his own to rule. Faisal ibn Hussein, Abdullah's brother and the local leader most closely identified with the Arab Revolt, was proclaimed king of Syria in 1920. Postwar Syria was far from the Arab state that Faisal had dreamed of leading but, as things turned out, he did not get to lead it for long. A British protégé like his brother Abdullah, Faisal was ousted from Syria by France, the new mandatory power there. In 1921 Faisal became king of Iraq, a British Mandate.

Iraq presents one of the clearest examples of the perversity of boundary drawing and state building under the mandates. Iraq was assembled from large segments of what used to be three Ottoman districts: Baghdad, with its majority of Sunni Muslim Arabs; Basra, where the majority of the population is Shi'i Arab; and Mosul, where Iraqi oil was first discovered on the territory of primarily Sunni Muslim Kurds (Marr, 1985). Other minorities also lived in Iraq. Before the 1948 Arab-Israeli war, the world city with the largest Jewish population was Baghdad. Iraq's chronic problems with state building are rooted in its troubled history as a multicultural state governed by members of only one group (Allawi, 2007; Makiya, 1996).

After World War II, the international system was redefined. Before, only the most powerful states enjoyed negative sovereignty. With the establishment of the United Nations, negative sovereignty was declared a right of every state. Ghassan Salamé (1990) believes that this produced not only small, weak, and externally dependent regimes, but also states with a minimal capacity to mobilize enough support and loyalty of their citizens to govern without external resources. The ease of attracting those resources, especially by states with large deposits of oil and gas, allowed their governments to resist domestic pressures to share power while maintaining their reputations as enlightened rulers abroad (e.g., al-Nakib, 2011). Although citizen nationalists and governments alike tended to blame their countries' problems on Western imperialism, their governments depended on Western resources. Thus, around the world and especially in the Middle East, external intervention by major powers continued, often with the connivance of local rulers.

External intervention did bring some advantages to states with oil and gas reserves. These were discovered and developed by foreign companies, most based in Britain or the United States. Oil incomes at first were limited to royalties and fees, but they grew at astronomical rates following the oil revolution of the early 1970s. This revolution both pushed crude oil prices upward and transferred control of oil and gas reserves from foreign companies to national governments. A sizable proportion of this money was spent on arms (K. Dawisha, 1982–1983; Nitzan and Bichler, 2002), a pattern that reasserted itself with the return of high oil prices in the early twenty-first century, which generated sovereign wealth funds (SWF) that conferred investment autonomy on the richest exporters (Tétreault, 2012). It is no secret that having money gives governments and persons more autonomy. As foreign aid donors and arms buyers, wealthy Middle Eastern governments found they could exercise independent leverage abroad. Saudi Arabia's assistance to Islamist groups influenced those groups and other Arab states while, in Central Asia, Saudi money (along with US arms) nourished the most radical Islamist factions, including the Taliban and al-Qaeda (Coll, 2004; Rashid, 2001). Foreign investment is another source of leverage that rich oil-exporting governments can exploit (Tétreault, 1995, 2011; Tétreault, Wheeler, and Shepherd, forthcoming).

Chapter 8 shows how oil gave rulers more choices and greater leverage in foreign policy. Oil also insulated state-building elites from domestic demands for political participation. In consequence, development of the participatory institutions that form the bedrock of state capacity to preside over a self-sufficient society and economy was sidelined or derailed (e.g., al-Nakib 2011; Crystal, 1990; Gasiorowski, 1991; Tétreault, 2012; Vitalis, 2006; Zanoyan, 2002). In effect, hydrocarbons let oil-exporting regimes take the easy way out. They financed a strategy of economic development that offered ample room for corruption, but little support for a vibrant private sector (see Luke, 1983, 1985), and a strategy of political and social development based on co-opting disgruntled citizens rather than accommodating their demands for autonomous participation in national life (al-Nakib, 2011; al-Rasheed, 2007; Beblawi, 1990; Tétreault, 2000; Zanoyan, 2002). When these regimes did crack down on social activists, some dissidents used their years in prison and as voluntary and involuntary exiles to school themselves in their own versions of Islam, which they used to mount religious challenges to their governments and the external powers that supported them (al-Rasheed, 2007; Gerges, 2005). Fighting in Bosnia, Afghanistan, and later in Iraq, they developed organizational and military skills they could apply in their home countries and elsewhere in later life (Gerges, 2005; Matthiesen, 2011; Roy, 1994).

Local Challenges to State Sovereignty: Boundary Disputes

The arbitrary nature of state boundaries in the Middle East provided a focus for activists who wanted political integration to match the common religious, historical, and linguistic roots that they saw as uniting the region. Movements such as Arab nationalism and Islamism that transcend ethnic divisions, along with "historic missions" that transcend state boundaries—examples include defeating imperialism, liberating Palestine, reconstructing Eretz Yisrael, achieving Arab unity, and defending religious and cultural values (Salamé, 1994:87; A. Dawisha, 2003)—were used to justify territorial encroachment and intervention in the domestic affairs of Middle Eastern states by their ambitious neighbors.

Simple boundary disputes also plagued the region. In the Gulf, borders had been poorly defined by the colonial powers while a long history during which various empires, states, and tribes controlled oases, rivers, and ports at different times made claims that a piece of territory within the boundaries of one state "really" belonged to another plausible. In recent years, however, several disputed boundaries between Saudi Arabia and Oman, Yemen, and Qatar have been resolved. An interstate boundary was drawn to divide the former Neutral Zone, a jointly controlled territory established under the 1922 Treaty of Uqair to accommodate the migration of bedouin tribes between Saudi Arabia and Kuwait (Dickson, 1956). Oman and its other neighbors resolved most of their boundary disputes, but boundary quarrels continue to poison relations between Saudi Arabia and the United Arab Emirates (UAE). Since the Arab uprisings, however, the Gulf monarchies have muted their differences, preferring to focus their attention on domestic dissidents.

Perhaps the most notable of the relatively peaceful resolutions of border conflicts ended a long dispute between Qatar and Bahrain. Disputes over the Hawar Islands and Fasht al-Dibel rocks, both controlled by Bahrain but claimed by Qatar, and Zubarah, controlled by Qatar but claimed by Bahrain, persisted after decades of unsuccessful mediation. In 1991, Qatar petitioned the International Court of Justice (ICJ) in The Hague to rule on this matter. The ICJ gave its decision in March 2001, resolving the land dispute and also marking a maritime boundary between the two states through an area thought to contain oil and gas resources ("The Bahrain-Qatar Border Dispute," 2001). This dispute between Bahrain and Qatar had almost led to war in 1986, and both governments were relieved when what the ICJ had called the longest case in its history was finally settled (Gerner and Yilmaz, 2004).

Another long-standing boundary dispute with imperialist roots centers on the Western Sahara, a former Spanish colony located on the Atlantic coast of Africa that is rich in phosphates and thought to possess hydrocarbon reserves. Parts of this territory were claimed by Morocco and Mauritania, which sent armies to occupy it in 1975 when Spanish imperial authority was waning under the pressure of a national liberation movement that had evolved into an armed insurgency. Encroachment by neighboring Morocco and Mauritania forced thousands of Saharawis into exile in Algeria. There, they live in refugee camps that are "surprisingly well organized" and led by native administrators under the direction of a popular council with an elected president (Berke, 1997:3). The remaining insurgents forced Mauritania to relinquish its claims in 1979, but Morocco continues its occupation and insurgents continue to oppose it, although military activity is low level and sporadic. UN mediation efforts continue to be unsuccessful. Morocco refuses even to meet with representatives of the government-in-exile and a proposed referendum on the political future of the area has been delayed repeatedly.

The Western Sahara conflict aggravates relations between Morocco and its other neighbors: Algeria, which supports the government-in-exile, and Spain, which occupies two islands off the Moroccan coast. Morocco attempted to seize one of them, Parsley Island, in the summer of 2002, but pressure from the European Union (EU) forced Morocco to withdraw its troops. The tension created by more than a quarter-century of dispute over the Spanish Sahara destabilizes the entire western Mediterranean and, like the dispute between Bahrain and Qatar, shows the potential of conflicts over sovereignty to explode into war. Boundary conflicts between Iran and

Iraq, and Iraq and Kuwait, along with Israel's occupation and annexation of Arab territories, have led to full-scale wars. Some of these boundary conflicts continue, and are noted later in this chapter.

External Challenges:
The Middle East and the Great Powers

As discussed in Chapters 2, 3, and 4, most areas of the Middle East began the twentieth century as clients or dependencies of a European power. Even modern Turkey, the core of the old Ottoman Empire, had been an economic colony of its European creditors since the establishment of the Ottoman Debt Commission in 1881. Western ideologies were powerful in Turkey, and the Turkish state incorporated elements of what Atatürk saw as the greatest strengths of the West: modernization, secularization, and state-centered nationalism. His aim was to make Turkey an equal of the Great Powers, not a dependency of them. He pursued that goal with some success, wresting control of far more territory than the victors of World War I had intended to leave for the rump Turkish state that emerged from the shambles of empire.

North African communities were among the most eager to avoid or overthrow European rule. Examples of bitter and protracted anticolonial conflict include the bloody conquest of what is now Libya by the forces of Fascist Italy, backed by the Catholic hierarchy (Kramer, 2007:116), and the vicious eight-year war that ended 130 years of French control of Algeria. Both were exemplary in their brutality. European forces committed widespread terrorist violence and systematically tortured, executed, and assassinated thousands of civilians (Horne, 1977; Kramer, 2007; Morgan, 2006; Shatz, 2002). The French military had been disgraced by its "phony war" against Germany in 1940, and by its defeat at Dien Bien Phu, the 1954 battle that ended a nine-year attempt to crush the anticolonial movement in Vietnam. Chillingly depicted in Gillo Pontecorvo's 1966 film *The Battle of Algiers,* the conduct of what historian John Talbott (1980) called "the war without a name" brought France itself to the verge of civil war (Merom, 2003) while the philosopher of Algerian liberation, Franz Fanon, glorified revolutionary violence in his 1961 book *The Wretched of the Earth* as the only way to restore a culture with a degraded and degrading past. A loud echo of that far-from-purifying violence erupted across Algeria during the civil war that began in 1992. The uprising was ignited when the Algerian military, which effectively had controlled the country since liberation in 1962, canceled parliamentary elections that threatened to result in the victory of their Islamist rivals. The ensuing civil war has left its own legacy on the bodies of tens of thousands of tortured, executed, and assassinated Algerians.

As noted earlier, some Middle Eastern leaders quietly sought external intervention. Toward the end of the nineteenth century, Shaikh Mubarak, the emir of Kuwait (r. 1896–1915), actively angled for British protection.

He wanted to prevent his country from being attached to the Ottoman Empire by an energetic Turkish governor (Anscombe, 1997; al-Ebraheem, 1975), and also to gain British support for consolidating his own power and ensuring that his lineal descendants would rule Kuwait after his death (Rush, 1987). Abdul Aziz ibn Saud manipulated British officials to help him acquire more than half the territory of Kuwait in 1922 (Dickson, 1956). Until the conclusion of World War II, he used British and US gold to help him consolidate his conquests on the Arabian Peninsula and keep the leaders of subordinate tribes in his camp (I. Anderson, 1981). Other small Gulf principalities privately welcomed the suppression of piracy against their pearling fleets, and encroachments by neighboring rulers on the loyalty of their followers (Hightower, 2011). Nearly every Middle Eastern government was ready to welcome foreign-owned companies willing to pay for the right to prospect for oil. External intervention by the Great Powers or their agents was not always or uniformly condemned by Middle Eastern political leaders, although as Robert Vitalis (2006) recounts, Saudi nationalists often saw things differently.

Nationalists protested the grave burdens that imperialism imposed on their countries. Along with strategic interests such as protecting the route to India (Johnson, 2012), imperial powers used their colonies and dependencies to make themselves and their domestic economic clients rich (Wolf, 1982). Local economies were truncated by drawing national boundaries through areas and populations that were parts of larger trading and commercial markets. Colonies and economic dependencies were bled for the benefit of settlers and overseas investors. Oil companies took the lion's share of profits from their often wasteful exploitation of the region's petroleum reserves (e.g., Penrose, 1968; Rand, 1975; Tétreault, 1995). Foreign occupiers violated local customs with impunity, and mocked the religion, society, and culture of the populations they were exploiting (Ahmed, 1992; Lazreg, 1994; Tétreault, 1995). Zionist immigration into Palestine, which began decades before the Balfour Declaration of 1917 pledged British support for a Jewish homeland there, threatened communities and the livelihoods of the native population. All of these political, economic, and psychological burdens were aggravated by the imperialists' practice not only of playing social groups within countries against one another to enhance their political control (Migdal, 1988; al-Naqeeb, 1990), but also of pitting one country against others in situations such as negotiations for oil concessions to increase the colonizers' economic returns.

Dependency

Dependency is a relationship of economic inequality between a developing and a developed country (Caporaso, 1978). Creating dependency is a conscious aim of colonization and imperialism. During the nineteenth and twentieth centuries, imperialism enabled first Europe and then the United States to acquire preferential access to raw materials located in the Middle East. Governments signed exclusive contracts with British and US oil companies to develop local hydrocarbon industries. Oil companies purchased supplies and equipment from their home countries and imported most of their skilled workers (Mattheison, 2011; Vitalis, 2006). Oil development also distorted local economies. In oil-rich Hasa in Saudi Arabia, agriculture was destroyed to accommodate pipelines and pumping stations and supply water for oil operations (Jones, 2010; Munif, 1989). Most of the oil was sold overseas as a raw material that was processed and consumed outside of the countries where it had originated.

The way hydrocarbon reserves were developed and domestic economies of oil-exporting countries were constructed around oil production and sales tied the economies of these states to global markets and kept them economically and structurally dependent even after governments nationalized these industries in the early 1970s (Schreuder, 2009). The domestic economies of the wealthiest oil-exporting countries were organized to spend oil revenues rather than to produce goods and services to satisfy local needs and wants. Rivers of cash from oil sales, along with growing demand for foreign products from tanks and machine guns to cars and television programs, created consumption patterns that depended on imported goods (al-Nakib, 2011; Jones, 2010). Oil exporters expanded production capacity to ensure that they could continue to buy what they wanted from overseas. As global capacity expanded, some exporters were compelled to increase oil production, not only to justify their investment but also to support growing populations. But raising oil production glutted markets, pushed prices down, and encouraged even more production to earn the same level of income. This vicious circle came around again and again, but talk of structural reform never turned into action. When oil prices went up, incentives for exporting country governments to make fundamental changes to reduce dependency disappeared. Consequently, despite ups and downs in the oil market, the Middle East remains dependent on oil and gas sales as a primary source of government revenues.

Cliency

Cliency is a strategic relationship between a major power seeking a local base and a less powerful state whose assets are compatible with the needs of the major power (Gasiorowski, 1991; Tétreault, 1991). The client's stock in trade might be geographic location, port and basing facilities, and a regime willing to act internationally on behalf of the major power. In return, the major-power patron transfers arms, military training and equipment, and economic assistance to the less powerful client. Both sides gain from cliency but, unlike dependency, cliency offers the government of the smaller state proportionately more than it offers the larger partner. Indeed, as the client becomes embedded in the foreign policy strategies of its patron, the dependence of a patron on a client's strategic assets may grow at the same time that patron leverage against the client government declines. Meanwhile, the assets it receives from its patron can be used by a client government to protect itself against external and internal challenges. It can buy off foreign and domestic enemies and, if necessary, deploy patron-supplied and sometimes patron-delivered, force against them.

The Cold War increased the importance of cliency in relationships between Middle Eastern states and major outside powers. The superpowers sought economic gains from the effective exchange of hydrocarbons for arms (Nitzan and Bichler, 2002), but strategic concerns were primary. A large portion of foreign aid from the superpowers took the form of military transfers. Nearly all of it imposed obligations in the form of services required of Middle Eastern clients: diplomatic and military support and preferential access by the patron state and its agents to the client's domestic resources. Sometimes resources provided by patron states were used by rebellious military officers against weak and unpopular client governments. One example is the 1969 overthrow of King Idris in Libya. At other times, they were used by client governments against their own populations.

International politics changed during the Cold War and dependency relations changed as well. Competition increased in the market for Middle Eastern oil concessions, most markedly in Libya but also in Iran and the Arabian Peninsula states (Penrose, 1968). As detailed in Chapter 8, these changes helped to shift control of oil from international oil companies (IOCs) to host governments. Another apparent benefit of the Cold War was that imperialism was replaced by at least the rhetoric of negative sovereignty. The accepted convention, that all states were autonomous and could freely choose their own allies and partners, meant that the superpowers sometimes could be brought to bid for client allies, a situation that Egypt used to great advantage in financing its Aswan Dam project in the 1950s.

Too close an alliance with either superpower risked retaliation from disgruntled nationalists against overly compliant regimes. Strong leaders could carve out some autonomy from their Cold War patrons. In 1955, Egypt's Gamal Abdul Nasser, along with leaders of other developing countries, held a conference in Bandung, Indonesia, whose main product was the Non-Aligned Movement. Nonalignment was a declaration of independence from a permanent relationship to either superpower and was seen as a guarantee of the negative sovereignty of developing states. Yet despite declarations of nonalignment and promises of mutual support from other nominally nonaligned states, few countries in the Middle East were successful at finding a middle ground between the superpowers during the Cold War.

The end of the Cold War, and especially the end of the Gulf War (1990–1991), saw changes in cliency. Since the late 1960s, the United States had armed a few strong friends in the Middle East to protect its interests without direct US military intervention (Macris, 2012). Israel, Iran, and Saudi Arabia were recipients of arms and training, the latter two becoming the local embodiment of the Nixon Doctrine of President Richard M. Nixon, intended to reduce the near-term costs of projecting US power in the Gulf. Among the advantages to the United States was that Iran and Saudi Arabia were expected to purchase military equipment and services, reducing the average cost of weapons procurement for US forces and the balance-of-payments drain represented by oil imports. After the Iranian Revolution (1978–1980), the United States was forced to lean more heavily on its Arab allies, including small states like Bahrain where it had a naval base and Qatar where US military facilities were quietly built up out of sight of the local population (Holmes, 2010). Kuwait became an important forward base location after Saddam Hussein was expelled and Kuwaitis looked at the United States as the guarantor of the nation's physical integrity. Kuwait was key to US and British strategies during the Iraq War (2003–2010), when it supplied bases, fuel, and a range of support services to US troops. North Atlantic Treaty Organization (NATO) ally Turkey proved to be less reliable at the start of the Iraq War, when the parliament refused permission to the United States and its allies to launch their 2003 invasion of Iraq from Turkish soil. As discussed in Chapter 8, oil prices rose in the twenty-first century while Gulf SWF grew apace, contributing to the growing autonomy of the region's oil exporters.

Middle East Regionalism

Regionalism was a movement that began toward the end of World War II, attracting activists who hoped to build postwar institutions that would foster peaceful international relations. Regionalists thought that countries joined by proximity, culture, and common interests should form international organizations to work on specific goals like economic development and military security. The League of Arab States (or Arab League), founded in 1945, was among the first of these new organizations, but the Great Powers of World War II refused to accept the Arab League's "strong" definition of regionalism, which insisted that security be a matter wholly internal to participating states rather than subject to intervention by the larger world community (MacDonald, 1965:9–11). Even so, the Arab League was recognized by the United Nations and, at its inception, was hailed as a building block of the new postwar order.

Along with regional organizations like the Arab League, functional organizations such as the Organization of Petroleum Exporting Countries (OPEC) and the Organization of Arab Petroleum Exporting Countries (OAPEC) were established to advance the common economic interests of their members. OPEC is a multiregional organization; OAPEC is monoregional and monoethnic. An important goal of OPEC and OAPEC is consensus building, the development of joint positions based on shared interests sufficiently strong to keep members together even when they come under pressure.

The members of international organizations are states. Transnational movements like Arab nationalism and pan-Islamism undermine the authority of the state by promoting cross-border group identifications that states see as challenging their authority. Arab nationalism was feared by the region's monarchies, especially after Nasser and his colleagues overthrew Egypt's King Farouk in 1952. Popular adulation of Nasser stimulated antipopulist strategies by governments that, remarkably, included measures such as the Kuwaiti constitution that today are hailed as steps toward democracy (al-Nakib, 2011). States also sought to tame Islam by mobilizing and coordinating religious activism under state auspices. The Organization of the Islamic Conference (OIC, now the Organisation of Islamic Cooperation) was established in Rabat, Morocco, in 1969, another organization that is a creature of states that is intended to reinforce state authority.

Regional organizations support negative sovereignty. They spin a web of agreements and structures that are both interstate and limited in membership, insulating member states from some outside pressures, but exposing them to pressures from within. Theoretically, regionalism restricts negative sovereignty by assigning formal responsibility for particular policies to international organizations. But states crafting charters for these institutions incorporated rules requiring consensus to make decisions. This leaves authority in the hands of individual members who could veto policies they did not like. Sovereignty is saved, but at the expense of compromise and collective action.

Mobilizing a consensus on any issue gets harder as the membership or the issue slate of an organization grows. The Arab League got stuck at a low level of regional integration when it grew from a group of five closely neighboring states, four of which were strongly Arab nationalist (Egypt, Syria, Iraq, and Lebanon; the fifth founding member was Jordan), to a large organization with more than twenty members spread across two continents. The same problems afflict OPEC, whose five founding members (Venezuela, Iran, Iraq, Kuwait, and Saudi Arabia) had sufficient petroleum and financial resources to exercise market power collectively by limiting production. After adding small producers such as Gabon and Ecuador and economically desperate ones such as Nigeria and Indonesia, OPEC was unable to implement effective long-term strategies to regulate production. New members with different economic goals aggravated old quarrels within the group (Mikdashi, 1972). As OPEC grew, members devised informal conventions to free themselves from being bound by some collective decisions (Tétreault, 1981:42). OPEC was able to pursue a limited range of common interests, but it could not prevent individual members from pursuing independent interests even when their actions visibly harmed the common good or keep them in the organization when they decided they could do better on their own.

Well aware of how much organizational cohesion depends on close similarity among group members, the founders of the Gulf Cooperation Council (GCC, which includes Kuwait, Saudi Arabia, Qatar, Oman, Bahrain, and the UAE) decided to exclude Yemen. Formed in 1981, the GCC was intended to replace bilateral security arrangements with a regional security regime and also to promote economic integration among its members. Its founders decided that Yemen "did not share 'identical systems, identical internal and foreign policies, identical ideologies, identical aspirations and identical human, social, and political problems' [with] the Arab gulf littoral states" (Lawson, 1997:15). Iraq also was not invited to join the GCC because it was a politically incompatible state that, not incidentally, was a belligerent in the Iran-Iraq War (Peterson, 1988).

Commitment to compatible politics and ideologies as the foundation of the GCC was affirmed during the Arab uprisings. At its May 2011 meeting, the GCC considered expanding its membership to include the other two surviving Middle Eastern monarchies, Morocco and Jordan. Initially, this suggestion was met with a chorus of jokes about what this new GCC would stand for—perhaps the Global Counter-revolution Club. But the jokes did not conceal the fears of Gulf ruling families about the future of monarchy in a world where Facebook and Twitter can connect restive populations as effectively as religious ideologies or a transnational nationalism. The enlargement proposal was soon replaced by one for unification but, by the end of the year, it too was overtaken by regional crises presenting so many challenges and threats in every direction that, at its December 2012 GCC Summit, unification was tabled; it was postponed from consideration again at the May 2012 meeting (SUSRIS, 2012).

Although the relationship between Saudi Arabia and Bahrain approaches unification on several dimensions, other GCC members have been reluctant to risk absorption by their much larger neighbor. A Saudi bid in the mid-1980s to centralize police records and permit police forces of member states to cross the border into another member state in cases of hot pursuit was rejected by the Kuwaiti parliament. The status of this proposal seems to have strengthened at the end of 2012 because of the fears of the Kuwaiti emir that the Arab uprisings might be percolating there. A new parliament, chosen in the second unscheduled election of 2012, is likely to approve a GCC treaty incorporating these provisions.

Boundary issues simmer below the surface such as the one that popped up in 2009 when Saudi Arabia refused entry to UAE nationals carrying ID cards that the Saudis insisted featured an incorrect map of their territory ("Saudi and UAE Border in Dispute over ID Cards," 2009). Qatar's emir has devoted immense resources to building an array of independent international constituencies from governments to educational and cultural institutions supporting its survival as an independent state. The record of the GCC shows that, even in an institution where founding members perceive themselves as virtually identical, regional organizations in the Middle East must coexist with members' attachment to negative sovereignty.

The Middle East in the World

When Iraq invaded Kuwait in August 1990, a common refrain among Arabs was that such an event had never occurred before: "everybody knew" that Arab countries did not attack one another militarily. This was not true, however. Iraq had both threatened and invaded Kuwait several times before 1990: it had sent military forces to occupy part of northern Kuwait in the mid-1970s (Assiri, 1990) and had used "salami tactics" to acquire territory from Kuwait, periodically sending troops to the frontier to inch the border southward (Tétreault, 1995:123–124). Other inter-Arab conflicts also are forgotten. Egypt conducted extensive military operations in Yemen in the mid-1960s during its proxy war against Saudi Arabia, which also fought in Yemen, then and earlier. As noted earlier, Libya and Algeria oppose Morocco in the Western Sahara. The government of King Hussein mounted a strong military offensive against a semisovereign Palestinian enclave in Jordan during the Black September of 1970; Syria intervened militarily in Lebanon during the civil war and its military forces remained in Lebanon until 2005, when they were withdrawn at the request of the Lebanese government and the Arab League. Arabian Peninsula border clashes were common through most of the twentieth century, and boundary conflicts remain unresolved throughout the region.

While one could dispute the nature of the intervention that sent GCC troops into Bahrain in 2011 (discussed below), it was the Libyan war that introduced the most striking novelties in norms of Arab solidarity and negative sovereignty in the Middle East. The Arab uprisings surprised observers around the world and no more so than in the Middle East. Even more astonishing is that the first two uprisings, in Tunisia and Egypt, resulted in rapid initial success, ridding the country of leaders seen as corrupt and dictatorial. Surprise explains some of that success, but strategy and structure also were important. Tunisian and Egyptian demonstrators were committed to nonviolent opposition. Their restraint inhibited the usual repressive response to dissent by undermining the willingness of popular armies to fire on unarmed fellow citizens.

As demonstrations escalated in other Arab states, however, this inhibition did not operate. Sectarian staffing and direct military assistance from neighboring countries ensured that Sunni security forces in Bahrain would follow orders to fire on nonviolent (and even sleeping) demonstrators (Jones, 2011; Lynch, 2011). In Syria, a regime dominated by the Alawite minority fielded forces even more ruthless toward dissidents than those in Bahrain. Libya was defended by national forces organized along tribal lines and by foreign mercenaries working for pay who had no communal reason to identify with the activists (Heydemann, 2011). This allowed pro-Qaddafi forces to dominate the conflict, but only in the early months.

Violence characterized the demonstrations in Libya from their beginnings in mid-February 2011, and it came from both sides. In response to rapidly accumulating civilian casualties and a February 22 speech by Qaddafi urging his followers to fight to the last drop of his blood, the International Crisis Group (ICG), the leading early-warning nongovernmental organization (NGO) charged with monitoring global conflict, called for "immediate international steps . . . to stop atrocities in Libya." The ICG endorsed the suggestion that a no-fly zone be established to protect Libyan civilians from air assaults (ICG, 2011).

On February 26, the UN Security Council, operating under a new approach to sovereignty, adopted Resolution 1970 that condemned the violence against Libyan civilians, demanded that it be halted, and referred the case of Libya to the International Criminal Court (United Nations, 2011a). This novel doctrine, known as the responsibility to protect (R2P), marked a significant retreat from unconditional support for negative sovereignty. The first formal UN resolution on R2P, Resolution A/RES/63/308, was adopted by the General Assembly on September 14, 2009. Yet adoption by no means indicated a full acceptance either of the concept or any operations that might be authorized under its rubric (GCR2P, 2009). Several UN members expressed concern that R2P could be "manipulated by the powerful to justify intervention in weaker states, running counter to the principles of the Charter, especially the principle of non-intervention, enshrined in Article 2(4). Each critic evoked sovereignty as an absolute principle, not to be curtailed in any way" (GCR2P, 2009:2). As the situation inside Libya deteriorated further, however, calls for intervention grew louder and they came from surprising sources: not only individual Arab states like Qatar and Lebanon, but from the Arab League itself.

The debate on and passage of Security Council Resolutions 1970 and 1973 reflected international determination to apply pressure to get the Libyan regime to halt attacks on civilians and peaceful demonstrators. Libya's own representative to the United Nations praised Resolution 1970 as a token of moral support to the Libyan people and a signal that Qaddafi's regime should come to an end (United Nations, 2011a). Other Security Council members, Lebanon, and the Russian Federation "stressed the importance of affirming the sovereignty and territorial integrity of Libya [while] . . . (t)he Chinese representative said he had supported the resolution taking into account the special circumstances in Libya" (United Nations, 2011a). Resolution 1970 stopped short of armed intervention, which explains why it was supported unanimously by all fifteen members of the Security Council, including those who expressed concern about abridging Libyan sovereignty.

As might have been expected, Security Council support for Resolution 1973 authorizing armed intervention was not unanimous; the vote was ten in favor with five abstentions (Brazil, China, Germany, India, and the Russian Federation). Significantly, Lebanon, which had expressed concerns about violating Libya's sovereignty during the debate on Resolution 1970, voted yes on Resolution 1973, a result of the support of the Arab League and also of the inclusion in the text of the clause forbidding the occupation of even "one inch" of Libyan territory by foreign forces (United Nations, 2011b).

Resolution 1973 formalized what turned out to be a long, brutal, and messy effort to assist Libyan insurgents to overthrow Qaddafi's regime. The aftermath is marred by ineffective governance, violence, and competition among tribes, Islamist groups, and Qaddafi loyalists seeking power—and survival—in the new state (J. L. Anderson, 2011; Jawad, 2012). The long time that it took to end Qaddafi's hold on Libya also surprised naïve observers who did not expect to encounter so many difficulties in a country of only 4 million people where sectarianism was not an issue (Jawad, 2012; Lister, 2012).

Syria has many more people than Libya, and a larger and more powerful military. It borders several states engaged in domestic conflicts—Israel/Palestine, Lebanon, Iraq, and Iran—which have the potential to create a "new Congo" if Syria's war should spill very far over its borders. Like Iran, Turkey is a non-Arab neighbor. It harbors tens of thousands of Syrian refugees, which intensifies its interest in how and when the Syrian conflict will be resolved. Turkey also has been enmeshed in a long-running campaign to suppress the nationalist aspirations of its Kurdish population. Relations between Kurds and Turks improved enormously as a result of Turkey's efforts to meet the human rights requirements imposed by the EU on states applying for membership, a positive example of external intervention in a sea of mostly negative ones. Since major EU members have backed off from their earlier support of Turkish membership, however, there is no effective external political brake on a discreet resumption of suppression of Kurds. War in neighboring countries with Kurdish minorities could aggravate tensions in both places. The role of Kurds in another set of conflicts is elaborated on below, but here note that during the Iraq War (2003–2010), Turkey engaged in hot pursuit of Kurdish dissidents across its border with Iraq. The Syrian civil war heightens the danger of transborder incursions. In the autumn of 2012, Turkey began to fire back when Syrian artillery attacks on rebel forces penetrate its territory (Barnard and Saad, 2012).

The domestic conflicts triggered by the Arab uprisings add to the complexity of international relations in the Middle East. Governments expect support from their allies while those allies wonder whether they should be propping up regimes that have little popular support. Few countries outside the region relish another "Libya" under far worse conditions: no support from the United Nations or the neighbors for direct intervention (Chivers, 2012). But their apparent inaction in a brutalized Syria embitters dissidents who are unmoved by their fears that a wider war would ensue if other states became directly involved.

Bitterness is even more justified in the case of Bahrain where demonstrators attempted to ride the first wave of Arab uprisings to push for greater political rights and an end to sectarian discrimination. A large group of nonviolent demonstrators set up a local equivalent of Cairo's Tahrir Square at the Pearl Roundabout in Bahrain's capital, Manama, in February 2011. Despite a conciliatory statement from the emir, the police were sent in the middle of the night to arrest and beat sleeping demonstrators. Two were killed and many others wounded. Regime hard-liners, led by Khalifa bin Salman al-Khalifah, the king's seventy-five-year-old uncle, insisted that the demonstrators were all Shi'a and run by Iran, although the presence of Sunni demonstrators in the Pearl Roundabout was noted from the start. Even so, the sectarian "card" is powerful in Bahrain where Shi'a are a majority ruled by a Sunni government (Gengler, 2012). In addition to police repression, the demonstrators were attacked in state-run media. In early March, Bahraini security forces were joined by about 5,000 troops sent from Saudi Arabia and the UAE. By mid-March, the demonstrations were broken up and the government was back in firm control.

Yet repression continued long after the dissidents were crushed. The Pearl Roundabout was razed to the ground, and Shi'i mosques were destroyed. Hospitals were targeted as places where dissidents went for medical treatment, and nurses and doctors were arrested. The Medical Society and the Teachers Society were taken over by government authorities, along with the only independent local newspaper. Despite its denials, the government continued to imprison people convicted solely for participating in peaceful protests. On September 4, 2012, for example, a court of appeal upheld a military court's convictions of twenty-one protest leaders for exercising their right to freedom of expression, peaceful assembly, and association. An independent Commission of Inquiry made up of Bahrainis reported that many of those arrested were ill-treated to make them confess. Although the government said it would respond to the commission's policy recommendations by freeing prisoners who had been unjustly arrested and holding security forces accountable for their brutality, little has been done (Human Rights Watch, 2012).

Libya, Bahrain, and, increasingly, Syria have become arenas for what had formerly been unthinkable or denied: open intervention by Arab states in other Arab states. Iraqi sectarians are fighting with their fellow religionists in Syria, some of whom fought for them during the Iraq War (Ghazi and Arango, 2012). It is clear that resolution of these conflicts depends on the behavior of external agents, including neighboring governments. External intervention has usually spelled disaster in Middle Eastern wars. The erosion of the norm of negative sovereignty among the states in this region could draw additional participants to other axes of conflict in the region, including those in which non-Arabs are belligerents. This is because conflicts in the Middle East intersect with and amplify one another, especially when they attract involvement by one or more outside powers.

The Arab-Israeli conflict discussed in Chapter 6 is noteworthy for the contributions of outside powers to its genesis, conduct, and persistence. Here, we look at another arena where external intervention made an already lethal set of conflicts worse. The Kurds, like the Palestinians, are a nation without a state (McDowell, 1996). As detailed in Chapter 3, Kurds were promised an autonomous territory by the European powers under the Treaty of Sèvres following World War I. However, a large slice of Kurdistan, the Kirkuk area, was among the first oil-producing regions in the Middle East. Because of the oil, the British wanted Kirkuk attached to Iraq, one of their Mandates (Marr, 1985). Subsequently the territory of the Kurds, a non-Arab, non-Turkic people, was divided among five adjoining states: Iran, Iraq, Turkey, Syria, and the former Soviet Union (now Azerbaijan). Kurdish ethnic enclaves persist because high mountains separate communities, tribal leaders exercise strong authority over local populations, and, like Palestinians, internal disagreements among Kurds as well as tensions between Kurds and the governments of the affected states produce repeated conflicts.

Oil and separatist politics coincide in Iraq where one of the elements holding the Kurds together was their long insistence on local autonomy and rights to a share of Iraqi oil revenues. Iraqi Kurds engaged in repeated uprisings against the central government from the earliest years of the Iraqi state. During the 1930s and 1940s, Kurdish guerrillas led by Mullah Mustafa Barzani fought an intermittent civil war in Iraq. Iranian Kurds also refused to resign themselves to assimilation. During World War II, assisted by Soviet troops, Iranian Kurds established a short-lived independent republic called Mahabad. Despite rivalry among Kurdish tribal leaders, Kurds often assist one another in wars against the states. For example, Barzani led several thousand Iraqi Kurdish fighters into Iran to help defend Mahabad against Iranian troops.

Kurdish rebels in Iraq received periodic assistance from the Iranian government, and Iraqi and Iranian troops have fought one another in the Kurdish region during uprisings. During the early 1970s, Iraqi Kurdish rebels were aided both by Iran and, through Iran, by the United States. Negotiations between representatives of the Iraqi government and the Kurds produced compromises on many issues dividing the two sides. However, it was not until 1975, when the Iranian government and the United States agreed to halt military support of Iraqi Kurds in exchange for moving the boundary between Iraq and Iran, that this phase of the fighting ended (Ahmad, 1991).

During the Iran-Iraq War (1980–1988), Hussein treated the Kurdish region as a point of strategic vulnerability. Fighting took place not only between Iraq and Iran, but also between Iraqis and Kurds in both countries. In violation of international treaties, the Iraqi military used chemical weapons against Iranian troops and Iraqi Kurdish villages, including Halabja, and razed hundreds more Kurdish villages to the ground (Galbraith, 2006; Hilterman, 2004; Makiya, 1993). After the Gulf War decided the fate of Kuwait (1990–1991), Iraqi Kurds rose up against the government of Hussein, but brutal repression by Iraqi troops led to a massive outflow of refugees into Iran and Turkey. Britain, France, the Netherlands, and the United States created so-called safe havens for the Kurds, including a no-fly zone policed by British and US aircraft deployed from bases in Turkey, but no one created safe havens for Iraqi Shi'a, brutalized by Hussein and bombed by the United States and Britain in the name of keeping him in check.

Within the Kurds' safe haven, economic isolation and dependence on resources from outside brought Kurdish political factions into repeated conflict (Barkey, 1997). But under the protection of the no-fly umbrella, residents of the no-fly zone grew accustomed to their autonomy and what some touted as a model democracy for the region (see, e.g., Salih, 2002). Grateful to their protectors and fearful of Hussein, Kurds were strong supporters of US and UK intervention to topple Hussein's regime in the Iraq War (2003–2010), and their military arm, the Pesh Merga, fought side by side with the invaders against Hussein's forces.

After Hussein's defeat, the new Iraq's Kurdish minority submerged their differences to oppose centralization, which they feared would reduce their security and absorb the lion's share of revenues from exploitation of oil reserves under their land (Cole, 2011). Kurdish coherence contrasted with bitter conflicts among Shi'i factions and between the Shi'a and Sunni Arabs. They have been consistent opponents of a national oil law, preferring to let contracts themselves to exercise maximum control over where the income from concessions will go while maintaining their autonomy as Iraq consolidates under the increasing authoritarianism of a Shi'i regime.

Kathleen Cavanaugh

*The Kurdish region in Iraq now functions as a largely
autonomous entity. This Kurdish man relaxes in the afternoon sun.*

Religion often is seen as a determining factor in Middle East politics, but it
is unlikely that Sunni Kurds and Sunni Arabs, who still resent losing power
after Hussein was deposed, would be able to find sufficient common interests to join in challenging the current regime. It is even less likely that both
would join Shiʻi secularists, such as those associated with Iyyad al-Allawi,
to form a government with more internal balance than the current government in Iraq.

The Gulf Wars

Both the Israeli-Palestinian conflict and the Kurdish conflict intersect the
conflict between Iran and Iraq. Iran is not an Arab country and did not join
the Arab boycott against Israel mounted to protest its establishment and undermine its survival (Losman, 1972). Iran freely sold oil to Israel and increased oil production and its own income during anti-Israel Arab oil embargoes in 1967 and 1973, thereby undercutting the effectiveness of the
Arab "oil weapon" (Tétreault, 1981:43–44). Both Iran and Israel, aspiring

regional military powers, became US clients and partners during the Cold War. Their cliency relationships with the United States were enhanced under the Nixon Doctrine, which advocated greater US reliance on regional proxies to further its Cold War interests (Elon, 2002; Macris, 2012; Tétreault, 1985). Thus, it is not surprising that, during the Iran-Iraq War, the Ronald Reagan administration initiated illegal sales of weapons to Iran in exchange for money to aid the contras in Nicaragua through the agency of an Israeli intermediary (Draper, 1991).

Unlike Iran, Iraq was a prominent defender of the Palestinians, in part because Iraqi leaders wanted to lead the Arab nationalist movement. In 1967, Iraq led radical states in demanding an Arab oil embargo against Israel's allies in the Six Day War. The resulting income losses pushed three other Arab oil-exporting countries to establish OAPEC in January 1968 to block future Iraqi demands (Tétreault, 1981). Iraq fought beside Syria in the October 1973 war, despite the strong rivalry between these two Baathist regimes whose quarrels ranged from Euphrates River water rights to oil pipeline transit fees. Iraq's role as a champion of the Palestinian cause remained untarnished even when it refused to participate in the 1973–1974 oil embargo against Israel's allies (Tétreault, 1981). Before the Egyptian-Israeli peace treaty was signed in March 1979, Iraq led a drive at the Baghdad summit meeting of Arab states in November 1978 to retaliate against Egypt should it take that step (Ahmad, 1991).

Iraq's differences with Iran can be traced back through hundreds of years of rivalry between various Arab and Persian empires, but the modern roots of this conflict are another legacy of the imperialists responsible for shaping post–World War I territorial settlements. Territorial struggles also draw the Kurds into this conflict:

> The borders between the two countries, arranged for the most part by outsiders, have never been firmly accepted by either side. . . . Iraqi fear of Persian hegemony was, in their minds, based on gradual Iranian encroachment on "Arab" land, including the Arab territory of Khuzistan (formerly al-Muhammarah) in 1925, the incorporation of the waters around Khurramshahr in 1937, and the 1975 treaty that gave Iran half of the Shatt al-Arab. (Marr, 1985:291)

Successful maneuvering by Iran in the Iraqi-Kurdish dispute in the mid-1970s had moved the border between the two from the Iranian side of the Shatt al-Arab to the thalweg, an imaginary line down the middle of the waterway. Iran's victory reduced Iraq's access to the Gulf and increased its dependence on pipelines crossing Syria and Turkey to carry its oil to markets.

Following the successful 1978–1979 revolution in Iran, the leaders of Iran's revolutionary government stirred anti-Hussein sentiments among Iraqi Kurds in the north and made religious appeals to Iraqi Shiʻa in the south. In September 1980, Hussein invaded Iran, thinking he could take advantage of the domestic turmoil caused by internal struggles between Iran's clerics and other supporters of the revolution to control the postrevolutionary regime (Keddie, 1981; Moghissi, 1994). Hussein also wanted to end Iranian propaganda campaigns and border incursions. Iraqis expected a quick victory and a postwar settlement that would reverse decades of territorial gains by Iran. They were surprised at the resistance that they encountered and the lack of support from ethnic Arab citizens of Iran. The conflict bogged down into a war of attrition similar to the trench warfare that claimed so many casualties on the Western Front during World War I (Cordesman and Wagner 1990; Hiro, 1991).

The Iran-Iraq War had a significant oil dimension. As it ground on, Iran's far larger population base erased the strategic advantage that Iraq had seized by its surprise attack. Each side sought to devastate not simply the enemy's soldiers, but also the capacity of the enemy to wage war at all. Iraq persuaded wealthy Arab oil exporters to support its "Arab war" against Iran in spite of their membership in the new GCC. When Iran bombed Iraq's pipelines to cripple Iraq's capacity to earn oil revenues to buy more arms, crude production was earmarked by Kuwait and Saudi Arabia to be sold "on Iraq's account," keeping oil income flowing to Iraq anyway (Tétreault, 1993). The oil-rich Arab Gulf states also sent cash and arms. Kuwait imported war matériel destined for Iraq and even constructed a highway from Shuwaikh Port to the Iraqi border to carry it north more efficiently. When Iran retaliated by bombing Kuwaiti oil tankers, the Kuwaitis invited outside intervention by appealing to the Soviet Union, the United States, and other naval powers for protection, resulting in the reflagging of Kuwaiti ships to discourage Iranian attacks (Assiri, 1990). The United States also assisted Iraq with "intelligence, economic aid, helicopters, and licenses for exports that were crucial to [Hussein's] development of, among other things, the chemical weapons that he later used with great success to blunt Iranian counterattacks and to subdue the Kurds of northern Iraq" (Urquhart, 2002:16).

Perhaps the most important component of the oil war was the expansion of oil production by Saudi Arabia that began in 1985. This flood of oil raised money for the states financing the war, but it depressed oil prices worldwide to their lowest level (in constant dollars) since the 1960s. Arab Gulf exporters with excess production capacity could compensate to some degree for the loss of income from lower prices by increasing production. But Iran, already producing at full capacity and denied other sources of foreign exchange as the result of US sanctions, suffered a sharply reduced capacity to rearm. The oil war counterbalanced Iran's advantages in manpower, and helped to prevent an Iranian victory. It was not enough to allow Iraq to win the shooting war, which ended in a stalemate in 1988.

In the 1980s, young Iraqi women were trained to fight in the war against Iran.

By then, conditions in the belligerent countries were far from what they had been before the war. Despite the largesse of its Arab neighbors, Iraq was forced to borrow money from Western banks. By the end of the war, it owed $15 billion to nonconcessional lenders like banks (Tétreault, 1993: 96). Meanwhile, the Iraqi people, who had endured miserable conditions throughout the war, expected the peace to live up to all the promises their leader had made while it was going on (al-Khafaji, 2000). But Hussein could not satisfy both the banks and his population, especially given the depression in oil prices ensured by continued overproduction.

Tim Niblock (1982) sees a link between Iraqi conflicts with Iran and Iraqi assaults on Kuwait. He notes that Iran has repeatedly challenged Iraqi sovereignty and usually with success. Iraq's inability to win against Iran leads it to turn against Kuwait, which is much smaller and weaker but against which it has weak claims. Before 1990, every Iraqi challenge to Kuwait was rewarded with money, land, or leverage on the domestic and foreign policies of Kuwait (Assiri, 1990).

That things turned out so differently in 1990 reflects changes in the external environment that made intervention by a coalition of extraregional states against Iraq possible, although not inevitable. Indeed, some Kuwaiti aid and investment recipients supported Iraq. Jordan violated UN sanctions against Iraq by transporting military supplies off-loaded in the Gulf of Aqaba to the Iraqi border; Yemen supported the Iraqi position in most UN Security Council votes. Yet the majority of Arab governments lined up behind Kuwait. Whether, like the governments of other GCC states they fought in their own interests, or like Syria because they detested the Iraqi regime, or like Egypt because they were lured by the prospect of debt forgiveness and a new infusion of economic aid, many defied large and vocal segments of their own populations by that choice.

In the West, the differences between Kuwait and Iraq seemed clear. In the Middle East, the choice was far less obvious. Hussein was a prominent Arab nationalist. He was a loud proponent of the Palestinians. He benefited from vast and obvious differences in wealth between Kuwaiti tourists and the masses of impoverished citizens in Egypt, Morocco, and other far less wealthy countries. All that, and the association of the most prominent members of the anti-Iraq coalition with past imperialism and present dependency prompted many Arab citizens to support Iraq rather than Kuwait (Long, 2004). This was true not only for the common person in the "Arab street," but also for intellectuals like Moroccan sociologist Fatima Mernissi (1992). The diplomatic and economic isolation of Iraq following the liberation of Kuwait, despite Hussein's decision to set fire to Kuwaiti oil wells, repress with exemplary brutality a Shi'i intifada in the south (al-Shahristani, 1994; al-Khafaji, 1994), and crush a Kurdish uprising in the north (Hilterman, 2004), only increased widespread sympathy for Iraq throughout the Arab world.

Following the end of the Gulf War in 1991, Hussein played cat and mouse with UN inspection teams sent to monitor the dismantling of Iraq's chemical and biological weapons, often cheered from the sidelines by some Arab governments and most Arab populations. When the Iraqi government accused US nationals on the UN arms inspection teams of spying and then expelled them late in 1997, no Arab government, not even Kuwait, supported military retaliation against Iraq. In December 1998, all of the remaining UN inspectors were withdrawn by Richard Butler, the head of the inspections organization, the UN Special Commission. Six Arab governments, including Egypt and Syria, then reprimanded Iraq. The return of UN arms inspectors in December 2002 also evoked mixed reactions. On the one hand, despite energetic efforts the inspectors did not uncover a smoking gun; on the other hand, US insistence that weapons were there, coupled with the growing conviction that the administration would go to war whether weapons were found or not, raised concerns about the whole enterprise.

The George W. Bush administration had stated months before the resumption of inspections that it wanted to see "regime change" in Iraq, which it argued would begin a wave of democratization that would sweep across the region (Mann, 2004). The rationale for military attacks on countries whose regimes the United States wished to change was laid out in a redefined National Security Strategy of the United States of America, published on September 20, 2002. The inexorable march toward war with Iraq took place amid leader ambivalence and popular dissent (Fawn and Hinnebusch, 2006). Hussein's neighbors were not unhappy at the prospect of seeing him go, but they were uneasy about the ultimate aims of the United States and worried about domestic reaction to another US war on Iraq.

After US president George W. Bush declared victory in Iraq on May 1, 2003, Iran's external and internal security deteriorated. It was challenged by the intense interest of factions within the US government in taking what they viewed as a successful policy "on the road," perhaps to Tehran (Hersh, 2006). The rapid fall of Hussein's regime and the failure of the United States to plan for postconflict security arrangements resulted in a surge of lawlessness that soon became an armed insurgency against the occupying forces and anyone in Iraq who cooperated with them. The violent implosion of Iraq was hastened by ill-conceived policies such as excluding Baath Party members from jobs; disbanding the 300,000-strong Iraqi army; and the failure to sequester arms and weapons located in dumps all over the country and in the hands of the disbanded soldiers (Allawi, 2007; Chandrasekaran, 2006). Political changes were rushed to suit schedules in Washington, DC, rather than in Baghdad (Allawi, 2007).

The Kurds had the foresight to demand some institutional insulation from the rest of the country. After Iraqis adopted a new constitution in 2005, Shi'i victories in Iraqi elections reinforced Sunni perceptions that they were being unfairly excluded from power and soon Sunnis and Shi'a were fighting one another in cities and villages, especially in central Iraq. Disorder in the country made Iraq an incubator for terrorism imported from outside while Shi'i factions also vied with one another for primacy in the new central government that they dominated thanks to their electoral majorities. Some of these factions, notably the Dawa Party and groups associated with Muqtada al-Sadr, had ties to Iran, but the United States refused to work with Iran (or Syria) to stem the violence (Allawi, 2007).

When the weapons of mass destruction that served as the justification for invading Iraq could not be found, the George W. Bush administration raised the volume on its democratization rationale. This made autocratic governments across the region nervous and antagonistic (Neep, 2004; Recknagel, 2004). As US hostility toward Iran intensified, the Iranian government became more hostile to the United States and embarked on a very public effort to make enriched uranium, which it said was for electricity generation but which Israel, the United States, and now Europe interpret as a program to make nuclear weapons. Both Israel and the United States dislike the idea of an Iranian nuclear deterrent while even peaceful US programs to promote democracy in Iran have come under attack by Iranian officials who see them as attempts to foster a "velvet revolution" in Iran to overthrow the government. When the United States increased funding for "advancing human rights and freedom within Iran," including support for "civil-society groups—media, legal and human rights non-governmental organizations—both outside and inside Iran," they were called deliberate provocations and attempts to effect "regime change" (Azimi, 2007). In reaction, the Iranian government cracked down on dissidents, especially students and academics. In the spring of 2007, it arrested a number of persons who held dual citizenship in Iran and a Western country, including several Americans visiting elderly relatives in Iran. In July, two of the incarcerated Iranian Americans were shown on Iranian television "confessing" to having promoted contacts between Iranian and US citizens. Repression reached new heights during and after the Green Movement, which organized to protest government interference in the 2009 Iranian presidential election. As in the case of Syria in the Arab uprisings, videos and photographs of vicious retaliation against citizens by the Iranian government were ineffective in mobilizing an effective external effort to end government atrocities.

The reluctance of extraregional powers post-Libya to intervene militarily in the Middle East is understandable given the ambiguities of the outcome and the length of time it took to reach it. Powerful inhibitors include long-running conflicts, disagreements over the motives of interveners—not to mention the motives of those seeking their intervention—and the extent of territory and populations that would be affected by a larger internationalized war deploying deadlier weapons than local governments have at hand to use against their citizens. From this, we can see why Libya was an exception. Everyone hated Qaddafi, including his peers. Libya's military was not large and had to cover a huge territory, home of only about 4 million people. Sectarian conflict was absent while the prospect of genocide committed by a ruthless leader against the entire population goaded governments that had ignored the plights of Bosnians, Rwandans, and Sudanese. One of the major contributors to the Great Recession that began in 2008 was the belief held by bankers that their institutions were "too big to fail"; that is, that they could take enormous risks without penalty because their governments would always bail them out if they failed. A similar impression protects authoritarians that employ violence against their populations. They, with their likely allies, are too big for intervention because the outcome could be a general war in the region and perhaps beyond. With the exception of Israel, which has exerted major efforts to get the United States to back if not join it in a war against Iran to end Iran's nuclear program, few countries have the stomach to intervene militarily in the Middle East and even Israel would prefer that the United States take the lead when it comes to Iran.

Conclusion

The international relations of the Middle East are deeply influenced by legacies of imperialism and decades of external intervention whose perverse effects were to support repressive local regimes. The region is noted both for its authoritarian rulers and for their ineptitude in foreign policy, domestic policy—and sometimes both. This legacy has convinced leaders and populations alike that any attempts to change things for the better are vulnerable to the whims of manipulative neighbors. There is also lingering fear and distrust of the reigning great powers. Among the other lessons of Libya is that, despite the current economic malaise in the West, many Middle Eastern citizens still see "their" politics as a product of great-power manipulation.

Repeated efforts to create strong intraregional and extraregional alliances have failed so far to enable these countries to protect themselves. The Arab uprisings could change this situation, however. Boosted by election victories, Islamist parties in Egypt, Tunisia, Lebanon, and perhaps eventually in Libya and Syria are in the market for new alliances to cement their authority and further their programs (Agha and Malley, 2012). Each of these victorious parties has to deal with Islamist as well as secularist rivals. It is imperative for them to be seen as performing well if they hope to remain in power. The rise of Islamism, however fragmented, reintroduces a transnational dimension to interstate relations in the Middle East, one that could bring Islamist presidents and prime ministers to work more closely together—or increase their vulnerability by providing channels to direct resources to their political rivals. This makes alliances with Western partners, corporations as well as governments, attractive to leaders who can adopt a pragmatic approach. Consequently, it is too early to say that the end of formal imperialism actually put an end to outside interest in the Middle East and external intervention into its affairs.

Hydrocarbon resources attract other agents of intervention in the form of multinational banks and corporations. Often regarded as agents of their home governments, multinationals under globalization pursue foreign policies to suit their own interests, sometimes in accord with and sometimes against the stated positions of political leaders in their home or host countries. One example is pipeline politics. The rush of private investment in oil and gas development in Central Asia touched off controversy regarding the number and location of pipelines required to bring these new hydrocarbon supplies to market. For political reasons, the US government first advocated a new pipeline through Turkey and then, following the defeat of the Taliban, one through Afghanistan. For economic reasons, oil companies such as Chevron and Total preferred a plan that would put a pipeline through Iran.

Oil company executives, along with some academic observers, are among the most active advocates of reintegrating Iran into the international community. Their concerns are far broader than the simple issue of where to locate a pipeline. Investors have interests in the long-term stability of the region as a whole. Few knowledgeable observers believe that regional stability can be achieved if the war in Syria spreads or if Israel carries out its threats to bomb Iran. Economic and diplomatic interventions are seen as tools that should be applied by states and their surrogates to prevent violent outcomes.

Extraregional intervention in the Middle East by dominant countries, international organizations, and financial and economic actors was boosted by the defeat of Hussein and collapse of Iraq, by the ingathering of riches by regional oil exporters benefiting from demand from growing middle classes in South and East Asia, and by the concerns engendered by the Arab uprisings. Intervention does not have to be either one-sided or negative in its impact, but its complications cannot be ignored. Globalization promised to bring benefits from investment and economic development to many nations and, as SWF burgeoned, appeared to offer autonomous participation by Middle Eastern states and firms in the world economy. Yet strategic problems from other kinds of globalization—weapons proliferation and terrorism—along with well-documented human rights violations, remain to justify meddling by foreign governments and NGOs in the domestic politics and foreign policies of Middle Eastern states. The war on terrorism actually aggravates domestic and regional conflict. It suppresses concerns for human rights and civil liberties, causing external constraints on abusive governments and belligerent leaders to disappear. If strategic intervention were to be globalized through organizations like the United Nations, the experience in Libya shows that in the absence of capacity to remain on the ground to protect the transition to local governance, it is unrealistic to expect international intervention under the UN to be less destabilizing and more effective than military intervention by major powers.

Complicating all of these scenarios is the persistent incapacity of many Middle Eastern regimes to manage domestic conflicts peacefully. Higher oil prices reduced conflict arising from economic distress, but only in those states where populations shared in some of the wealth. Even there, oil income has had little impact on the rise of religiously based opposition groups. During the Cold War, some of these groups were viewed as foils against secular opposition groups and enjoyed the tacit and occasionally even the open protection of conservative governments (al-Mughni, 2000; Tétreault, 2000). Their domestic revolutionary potential was revealed in Iran and Afghanistan and understood by their home governments (e.g., al-Rasheed 2007), but their capacity to inflict damage outside the region was not fully appreciated until the September 11, 2001, attacks on the United States by Osama bin Laden's organization. Unfortunately, the war on terrorism has become a rationale for both internal crackdowns and external intervention in the Middle East. Vahan Zanoyan (2002) notes that the ability of Middle Eastern states to retain any significant autonomy depends critically on their ability to get their domestic houses in order. This includes taking regional approaches to strengthen their private sectors as a means of reducing dependency and opening their regimes to citizen participation.

The Arab uprisings scrambled the politics of political participation by increasing the insecurity of Middle Eastern regimes. Even Iran, which started off claiming to be the example that Tunisians, Egyptians, and others followed, is unnerved by persistence of dissidence in near neighbors such as Kuwait and even Bahrain where the government's behavior so closely mirrors its own. The Arab uprisings changed expectations about popular passivity and the predictability of the persistence of authoritarian regimes. However the uprisings turn out, they promise to change relations among the states of the Middle East and between them and the rest of the world.

Bibliography

Agha, Hussein, and Robert Malley. 2001. August 9. "Camp David: The Tragedy of Errors." *New York Review of Books*. www.nybooks.com.
————. 2012. November 8. "This Is Not a Revolution." *New York Review of Books*, pp. 71–73.
Ahmad, Ahmad Yousef. 1991. "The Dialectics of Domestic Environment and Role Performance: The Foreign Policy of Iraq." Pp. 186–215 in Bahgat Korany and Ali E. Hillal Dessouki (eds.), *The Foreign Policies of Arab States: The Challenge of Change*. 2nd ed. Boulder: Westview Press.
Ahmed, Leila. 1992. *Women and Gender in Islam*. New Haven: Yale University Press.
Allawi, Ali A. 2007. *The Occupation of Iraq: Winning the War, Losing the Peace*. New Haven: Yale University Press.
Amnesty International. 2011. *The State of the World's Human Rights*. London: Amnesty International.
Anderson, Irvine H. 1981. *Aramco, the United States, and Saudi Arabia: A Study of the Dynamics of Foreign Oil Policy, 1933–1950*. Princeton: Princeton University Press.
Anderson, Jon Lee. 2011. November 7. "King of Kings." *New Yorker*. www.new yorker.com.
Anscombe, Frederick F. 1997. *The Ottoman Gulf: The Creation of Kuwait, Saudi Arabia, and Qatar*. New York: Columbia University Press.
Antonius, George. 1946. *The Arab Awakening: The Story of the Arab National Movement*. New York: Simon and Schuster.
Assiri, Abdel Reda. 1990. *Kuwait's Foreign Policy: City-State in World Politics*. Boulder: Westview Press.
Azimi, Negar. 2007. June 24. "Hard Realities of Soft Power." *New York Times Magazine*. www.nytimes.com.
"The Bahrain-Qatar Border Dispute: The World Court Decision, Part 2." 2001. April 6. *The Estimate*. www.theestimate.com.
Barkey, Henri J. 1997. "Kurdish Geopolitics." *Current History* 96, no. 1 (January): 1–5.
Barnard, Anne, and Hwaida Saad. 2012. October 6. "Turkey Fires Back at Syria a Fourth Day in a Row." *New York Times*. www.nytimes.com.
Beblawi, Hazem. 1990. "The Rentier State in the Arab World." Pp. 85–98 in Giacomo Luciani (ed.), *The Arab State*. Berkeley: University of California Press.

Berke, Shari. 1997. "Sahara Dispute and Environment." Trade and Environment Database, Case no. 24. http://gurukul.ucc.american.edu.

Caporaso, James A. 1978. "Dependence, Dependency, and Power in the Global System: A Structural and Behavioral Analysis." *International Organization* 32, no. 1:13–43.

Chandrasekaran, Rajiv. 2006. *Imperial Life in the Emerald City: Inside Iraq's Green Zone.* New York: Alfred A. Knopf.

Chivers, C. J. 2012. October 6. "Rebels Say West's Inaction Is Pushing Syrians to Extremism." *New York Times,* pp. A4, A7.

Christison, Kathleen. 2000. *Perceptions of Palestine: Their Influence on US Middle East Policy.* Berkeley: University of California Press.

Cole, Juan R. I. 2011. "Shi'ite Parties and the Democratic Process in Iraq." Pp. 49–71 in Mary Ann Tétreault, Gwenn Okruhlik, and Andrzei Kapiszewski (eds.), *Political Change in the Arab Gulf States: Stuck in Transition.* Boulder: Lynne Rienner.

Coll, Steve. 2004. *Ghost Wars: The Secret History of the CIA, Afghanistan, and Bin Laden, from the Soviet Invasion to September 10, 2001.* New York: Penguin.

Cordesman, Anthony H., and Abraham R. Wagner. 1990. *The Lessons of Modern War,* vol. 2: *The Iran-Iraq War.* Boulder: Westview Press.

Crystal, Jill. 1990. *Oil and Politics in the Gulf: Rulers and Merchants in Kuwait and Qatar.* Cambridge: Cambridge University Press.

Dawisha, Adeed. 2003. *Arab Nationalism in the Twentieth Century: From Triumph to Despair.* Princeton: Princeton University Press.

Dawisha, K. 1982–1983. "The USSR in the Middle East: Superpower in Eclipse? *Foreign Affairs* 61, no. 2:438–452.

Dickson, H. R. P. 1956. *Kuwait and Her Neighbours.* London: Allen & Unwin.

Draper, Theodore. 1991. *A Very Thin Line: The Iran-Contra Affairs.* New York: Touchstone Books.

al-Ebraheem, Hassan Ali. 1975. *Kuwait: A Political Study.* Kuwait City: Kuwait University.

Elon, Amos. 2002. May 23. "No Exit." *New York Review of Books,* pp. 15–16, 18, 20.

———. 2003. May 29. "An Unsentimental Education." *New York Review of Books,* pp. 4, 6–7.

Fawn, Rick, and Raymond Hinnebusch (eds.). 2006. *The Iraq War: Causes and Consequences.* Boulder: Lynne Rienner.

Fromkin, David. 1989. *A Peace to End All Peace: The Fall of the Ottoman Empire and the Creation of the Modern Middle East.* New York: Avon Books.

Galbraith, Peter W. 2006. *The End of Iraq: How American Incompetence Created a War Without End.* New York: Simon & Schuster.

Gasiorowski, Mark J. 1991. *US Foreign Policy and the Shah: Building a Client State in Iran.* Ithaca: Cornell University Press.

GCR2P (Global Centre for the Responsibility to Protect). 2009. September. *GCR2P Summary of Statements on Adoption of Resolution RES A/63/L80 Rev 1.* New York: GCR2P.

Gengler, Justin. 2012. January 17. "Bahrain's Sunni Awakening." *Middle East Report Online.* www.merip.org.

Gerges, Fawaz A. 2005. *The Far Enemy: Why Jihad Went Global.* New York: Cambridge University Press.

Gerner, Deborah J., and Ömür Yilmaz. 2004. *A Question of Sovereignty: Bahrain, Qatar, and the International Court of Justice.* Pew Case Studies in International Affairs. Washington, DC: Institute for the Study of Diplomacy, Georgetown University.

Ghazi, Yasir, and Tim Arango. 2012. October 28. "Iraqi Sects Join Battle in Syria on Both Sides." *New York Times,* New England Edition, pp. 1, 10.

Hersh, Seymour M. 2006. November 27. "The Next Act." *New Yorker,* pp. 94, 96, 98, 101–104, 106–107.

Heydemann, Steven. 2011. February 25. "Steven Heydemann on Libya." Washington, DC: United States Institute of Peace. www.usip.org.

Hightower, Victoria Penziner. 2011. "In the Time Before Oil: A History and Heritage of Pearling in the United Arab Emirates." PhD diss. Tallahassee: Florida State University.

Hilterman, Joost. 2004. "Outsiders as Enablers: Consequences and Lessons from International Silence on Iraq's Use of Chemical Weapons During the Iran-Iraq War." Pp. 151–166 in Lawrence G. Potter and Gary G. Sick (eds.), *Iran, Iraq, and the Legacies of War.* New York: Palgrave Macmillan.

Hiro, Dilip. 1991. *The Longest War: The Iran-Iraq Military Conflict.* New York: Routledge.

Holmes, Amy Austin. 2010. "The Political Economy of Protection: Democratization and the American Presence in Kuwait, Qatar, and Bahrain." Unpublished paper, American University of Cairo.

Horne, Alistar. 1977. *A Savage War of Peace: Algeria 1954–1962.* New York: Viking.

Human Rights Watch. 2012. September 19. "Bahrain: Act on UN Human Rights Commitments." Press release. www.hrw.org.

ICG (International Crisis Group). 2011. February 22. "Immediate International Steps Needed to Stop Atrocities in Libya." Brussels: ICG. www.crisisgroup .org.

Jackson, Robert H. 1990. *Quasi-States: Sovereignty, International Relations and the Third World.* Cambridge: Cambridge University Press.

Janardhan, N. 2011. *Boom and Gloom: The Spirit of Possibility in the 21st Century Gulf.* Reading, UK: Ithaca Press.

Jawad, Rana. 2012. March 15. "Syria and Libya: Two Paths to Freedom." BBC. www.bbc.co.uk.

Johnson, Robert. 2012. "The Great Game and Power Projection." Pp. 31–48 in Jeffrey R. Macris and Saul Kelly (eds.), *Imperial Crossroads: The Great Powers and the Persian Gulf.* Annapolis: Naval Institute Press.

Jones, Toby. 2010. "Saudi Alchemy: Water into Oil, Oil into Water." *Middle East Report,* no. 254:24–29.

———. 2011. June 16. "Democracy Now! Interview with Toby Jones on Saudi Arabia's Role in Bahrain and Yemen." *Jadaliyya.* www.jadaliyya.com.

Keddie, Nikki R. 1981. *Roots of Revolution: An Interpretive History of Modern Iran.* New Haven: Yale University Press.

Kelly, Saul. 2012. "The Gamekeeper Versus the Mercenary Spirit: The Pax Britannica in the Gulf." Pp. 49–59 in Jeffrey R. Macris and Saul Kelly (eds.), *Imperial Crossroads: The Great Powers and the Persian Gulf.* Annapolis: Naval Institute Press.

al-Khafaji, Isam. 1994. "State Terror and the Degradation of Politics." Pp. 20–31 in Fran Hazelton (ed.), *Iraq Since the Gulf War: Prospects for Democracy.* London: Zed Books.

———. 2000. "War as a Vehicle for the Rise and Demise of a State-Controlled Society: The Case of Ba'thist Iraq." Pp. 258–291 in Steven Heydemann (ed.),

War, Institutions, and Social Change in the Middle East. Berkeley: University of California Press.

Kramer, Alan. 2007. *Dynamic of Destruction: Culture and Mass Killing in the First World War*. Oxford: Oxford University Press.

Lawson, Fred H. 1997. "Dialectical Integration in the Gulf Co-Operation Council." Occasional Paper No. 10. Abu Dhabi: Emirates Center for Strategic Studies and Research.

Lazreg, Marnia. 1994. *The Eloquence of Silence: Algerian Women in Question*. New York: Routledge.

Lister, Tim. 2012. February 8. "No Libya Play for the West in Syria." CNN. www .cnn.com.

Long, Jerry M. 2004. *Saddam's War of Words: Politics, Religion, and the Iraqi Invasion of Kuwait*. Austin: University of Texas Press.

Losman, Donald L. 1972. "The Arab Boycott of Israel." *International Journal of Middle East Studies* 3, no. 2:99–115.

Luke, Timothy W. 1983. "Dependent Development and the Arab OPEC States." *Journal of Politics* 45, no. 4:979–1003.

———. 1985. "Dependent Development and the OPEC States: State Formation in Saudi Arabia and Iran Under the International Energy Regime." *Studies in Comparative International Development* 20, no. 1:31–54.

Lynch, Marc. 2011. March 16. "Bahrain Brings Back the Sectarianism." http://lynch.foreignpolicy.com/posts/2011.03.16/bahrain_brings_back_the _sectarianism.

MacDonald, Robert W. 1965. *The League of Arab States: A Study in the Dynamics of Regional Organization*. Princeton: Princeton University Press.

Macris, Jeffrey R. 2012. "Why Didn't America Replace the British in the Persian Gulf?" Pp. 61–74 in Jeffrey R. Macris and Saul Kelly (eds.), *Imperial Crossroads: The Great Powers and the Persian Gulf*. Annapolis: Naval Institute Press.

Macris, Jeffrey R., and Saul Kelly (eds.). 2012. *Imperial Crossroads: The Great Powers and the Persian Gulf*. Annapolis: Naval Institute Press.

Makiya, Kanan. 1993. *Cruelty and Silence: War, Tyranny, Uprising, and the Arab World*. New York: Norton.

———. 1996. October 17. "The Politics of Betrayal." *New York Review of Books*, pp. 8–12.

Maktabi, Rania. 2000. "State Formation and Citizenship in Lebanon: The Politics of Inclusion and Exclusion in a Sectarian State." Pp. 146–178 in Nils A. Butenschøn, Uri Davis, and Manuel Hassassian (eds.), *Citizenship and the State in the Middle East: Approaches and Applications*. Syracuse: Syracuse University Press.

Mann, James. 2004. *Rise of the Vulcans: The History of the Bush War Cabinet*. New York: Viking.

Marr, Phebe. 1985. *The Modern History of Iraq*. Boulder: Westview Press.

Matthiesen, Toby. 2011. "The Shia of Saudi Arabia: Identity Politics, Sectarianism and the Saudi State." PhD diss. London: School of Oriental and African Studies.

McDowell, David. 1996. *A Modern History of the Kurds*. London: I. B. Tauris.

Mernissi, Fatima. 1992. *Islam and Democracy: Fear of the Modern World*. Trans. Mary Jo Lakeland. Reading, MA: Addison-Wesley.

Merom, Gil. 2003. *How Democracies Lose Small Wars: State, Society, and the Failures of France in Algeria, Israel in Lebanon, and the United States in Vietnam*. New York: Cambridge University Press.

Migdal, Joel S. 1988. *Strong Societies and Weak States: State-Society Relations and State Capabilities in the Third World*. Princeton: Princeton University Press.

Mikdashi, Zuhayr. 1972. *The Community of Oil Exporting Countries*. Ithaca: Cornell University Press.

Moghissi, Haideh. 1994. *Populism and Feminism in Iran*. New York: St. Martin's Press.

Morgan, Ted. 2006. *My Battle of Algiers: A Memoir*. New York: Collins.

al-Mughni, Haya. 2000. "Women's Movements and the Autonomy of Civil Society in Kuwait." Pp. 170–187 in Robin L. Teske and Mary Ann Tétreault (eds.), *Conscious Acts and the Politics of Social Change*. Columbia: University of South Carolina Press.

Munif, Abdulrahman. 1989. *Cities of Salt*. New York: Vintage International.

al-Nakib, Farah. 2011. "Kuwait City: Urbanisation, the Built Environment, and the Urban Experience Before and After Oil (1716–1986)." PhD diss. School of Oriental and African Studies, London.

al-Naqeeb, Khaldoun Hasan. 1990. *Society and State in the Gulf and Arab Peninsula: A Different Perspective*. Trans. L. M. Kenny. London: Routledge.

Neep, Daniel. 2004. "Dilemmas of Democratization in the Middle East: The 'Forward Strategy of Freedom.'" *Middle East Policy* 11, no. 3:73–84.

Niblock, Tim. 1982. "Iraqi Policies Towards the Arab States of the Gulf, 1958–1981." Pp. 125–149 in Tim Niblock (ed.), *Iraq: The Contemporary State*. New York: St. Martin's Press.

Nitzan, Jonathan, and Shimshon Bichler. 2002. *The Global Political Economy of Israel*. London: Pluto Press.

Penrose, Edith T. 1968. *The Large International Firm in Developing Countries: The International Petroleum Industry*. Cambridge: MIT Press.

Peterson, Erik. 1988. *The Gulf Cooperation Council*. Boulder: Westview Press.

Posusney, Marsha Pripstein. 2005. "The Middle East's Democracy Deficit in Comparative Perspective." Pp. 1–20 in Marsha Pripstein Posusney and Michele Penner Angrist (eds.), *Authoritarianism in the Middle East: Regimes and Resistence*. Boulder: Lynne Rienner.

Rand, Christopher T. 1975. *Making Democracy Safe for Oil*. Boston: Little, Brown.

al-Rasheed, Madawi. 2007. *Contesting the Saudi State: Islamic Voices from a New Generation*. Cambridge: Cambridge University Press.

Rashid, Ahmad. 2001. *Taliban: Militant Islam, Oil, and Fundamentalism in Central Asia*. New Haven: Yale University Press.

Recknagel, Charles. 2004, March 23. "U.S.: Washington's 'Greater Middle East Initiative' Stumbles Amid Charges It Imposes Change." Radio Free Europe. www .rferl.org/featuresarticle/2004/03/aa4668e1-6bc1-46dc-9a0d-e62d8657857d .html.

Roy, Olivier. 1994. *The Failure of Political Islam*. Trans. Carol Volk. London: I. B. Tauris.

Rush, Alan. 1987. *Al-Sabah: History and Genealogy of Kuwait's Ruling Family, 1752–1987*. London: Ithaca Press.

Salamé, Ghassan. 1990. "'Strong' and 'Weak' States: A Qualified Return to the Muqaddimah." Pp. 29–64 in Giacomo Luciani (ed.), *The Arab State*. Austin: University of Texas Press.

——— (ed.). 1994. *Democracy Without Democrats? The Renewal of Politics in the Muslim World*. London: I. B. Tauris.

Salih, Barham. 2002. December 9. "A Kurdish Model for Iraq." *Washington Post*, p. A23.

"Saudi and UAE Border in Dispute over ID Cards." 2009. August 23. Reuters.

Schlumberger, Oliver. 2007. "Arab Authoritarianism: Debating the Dynamics and Durability of Nondemocratic Regimes." Pp. 1–20 in Oliver Schlumberger (ed.), *Debating Arab Authoritarianism: Dynamics and Durability in Nondemocratic Regimes.* Stanford: Stanford University Press.

Schreuder, Yda. 2009. *The Corporate Greenhouse: Climate Change Policy in a Globalizing World.* London: Zed Books.

al-Shahristani, Hussein. 1994. "Suppression and Survival of Iraqi Shi'is." Pp. 134–140 in Fran Hazelton (ed.), *Iraq Since the Gulf War: Prospects for Democracy.* London: Zed Books.

Shatz, Adam. 2002. November 21. "The Torture of Algiers." *New York Review of Books,* pp. 53–57.

SUSRIS (Saudi-US Relations Information Service). 2012. July 26. "Toward a Gulf 'Single Entity': A Conversation with Jane Kinninmont." www.susris.com.

Talbott, John. 1980. *The War Without a Name: France in Algeria, 1954–1962.* New York: Alfred A. Knopf.

Tétreault, Mary Ann. 1981. *The Organization of Arab Petroleum Exporting Countries: History, Policies, and Prospects.* Westport, CT: Greenwood Press.

———. 1985. *Revolution in the World Petroleum Market.* Westport, CT: Quorum Books.

———. 1991. "Autonomy, Necessity, and the Small State: Ruling Kuwait in the Twentieth Century." *International Organization* 45, no. 4:565–591.

———. 1993. "Independence, Sovereignty, and Vested Glory: Oil and Politics in the Second Gulf War." *Orient* 34, no. 1:87–103.

———. 1995. *The Kuwait Petroleum Corporation and the Economics of the New World Order.* Westport, CT: Quorum Books.

———. 2000. *Stories of Democracy: Politics and Society in Contemporary Kuwait.* New York: Columbia University Press.

———. 2011. "Gulf Arab States' Investment of Oil Revenues." Pp. 9–21 in Matteo Legrenzi and Bessma Momani (eds.), *Shifting Geo-Economic Power of the Gulf: Oil, Finance and Institutions.* Surrey, UK: Ashgate.

———. 2012. "Stuff Is Not Enough: Resources and Governance in the Middle East." Pp. 33–49 in Abbas Kadhim (ed.), *Governance in the Middle East and North Africa.* New York: Routledge.

Tétreault, Mary Ann, Deborah Wheeler, and Benjamin Shepherd. Forthcoming. "Win-Win Versus Lose-Lose: Investments in Foreign Agriculture as a Food Security Strategy for the Arab Gulf States."

Tilly, Charles. 1985. "War Making and State Making as Organized Crime." Pp. 169–191 in Peter B. Evans, Dietrich Rueschemeyer, and Theda Skocpol (eds.), *Bringing the State Back In.* New York: Cambridge University Press.

United Nations. 2011a. February 26. "In Swift, Decisive Action, Security Council Imposes Tough Measures on Libyan Regime, Adopting Resolution 1970 in Wake of Crackdown on Protesters." Press release and resolution text. www.un.org/News/Press/docs/2011/sc10187.doc.htm.

———. 2011b. March 17. "Security Council Approves 'No-Fly Zone' over Libya, Authorizing 'All Necessary Measures' to Protect Civilians, by Vote of 10 in Favour with 5 Abstentions." Press release and resolution text. www.un.org/News/Press/docs/2011/sc10200.doc.htm.

Urquhart, Brian. 2002. December 19. "The Prospect of War." *New York Review of Books,* pp. 16, 18, 20, 22.

Vandewalle, Dirk. 1998. *Libya Since Independence.* Ithaca: Cornell University Press.

Vitalis, Robert. 2006. *America's Kingdom: Mythmaking on the Saudi Oil Frontier.* Palo Alto: Stanford University Press.

6

The Israeli-Palestinian Conflict

Simona Sharoni and
Mohammed Abu-Nimer

The Arab-Israeli conflict, and especially its Israeli-Palestinian dimension, has been at the heart of Middle Eastern politics in the twentieth century. Indeed, the Israeli-Palestinian conflict provides a unique opportunity to examine a host of concepts important to understanding Middle Eastern politics and world politics more generally. These concepts include national identity and self-determination, security dilemmas, the role of religion, the increasing importance of nonstate actors, the relative impotence of international law and international organizations such as the United Nations (UN) in dealing with complicated conflicts, globalization and economic interdependence, and forms of violent and nonviolent conflict resolution. Given the theoretical and political significance of these issues, it is not surprising that the Israeli-Palestinian conflict is among the most researched topics across academic disciplines as well as in applied settings; it also receives regular and prominent coverage in the media. Yet despite the growing body of literature and media accounts of the conflict, many still view it either in a simplistic, one-dimensional manner or as distant and too complex to be grasped by ordinary people.

In this chapter we provide a framework for understanding the Israeli-Palestinian conflict and the prospects for its resolution. The analysis is interdisciplinary in scope and, uniquely, coauthored by two conflict resolution scholars: a Jewish Israeli and a Palestinian who holds Israeli citizenship. Our academic expertise notwithstanding, both of us have been actively involved for the past three decades in attempts to bring about a just and lasting solution to the conflict.

All too often, media accounts and academic scholarship on the Israeli-Palestinian conflict have fallen into a trap of false symmetry. Typically, the conflict has been presented as an intractable struggle between two national movements with competing claims over the same territory. Such an interpretation obscures the asymmetrical power relations between Israeli Jews and Palestinians, both in the past and in the present. For example, it is seldom recognized that the creation of the State of Israel in 1948, which affirmed the national aspirations of the Jews, came at the expense of Palestinians, whose desire for self-determination and territorial sovereignty remains largely unfulfilled (see K. Nakhleh and Zureik, 1980; Said, 1980; I. Abu-Lughod, 1982; Quigley, 1990; Aruri, 1995; Pappe, 2001). We choose to stress this point from the start not to glorify one party or vilify the other. Rather, we do so because we believe that a successful resolution of this conflict depends to a great extent on the recognition of these structured inequalities and the ability to devise a framework to transform these power relations.

Toward this end, we draw both on conflict resolution literature and on our own life experiences and familiarity with the region to illustrate the complexity of this conflict and highlight possible venues for its resolution. As with any other conflict, a comprehensive analysis should begin with a careful examination of the parties involved and of the historical turning points that marked its escalation and deescalation. History in general and histories of protracted conflicts in particular are never simple or objective and always reflect particular political positions. Thus, our analysis begins with a description of the parties to the conflict to provide a context for understanding their contending interpretations of history. After an overview of central turning points and crucial dynamics throughout the history of the conflict, we examine the core issues and points of contention. Finally, the chapter offers a framework to examine past and present attempts to resolve the conflict and identify the conditions and processes that we deem essential to a just and lasting resolution.

The Parties: Two Peoples— Palestinians and Israeli Jews

The Israeli-Palestinian conflict has shaped the lives of at least three generations of Israelis and Palestinians. The Arab-Israeli conflict, particularly its Israeli-Palestinian dimension, has played a central role not only in the daily lives of people throughout the Middle East but also in the lives of Palestinians and Jews living outside Israel and the Occupied Territories, many of whom see their existence as inseparable from political developments in the region (Kelman, 1982; Segal, 1989; Heller and Nusseibeh, 1991; Rothman, 1992; Gerner, 1994; Tessler, 1994; B. Haddad, 2012). Many scholarly and media accounts, however, tend to overlook this fact, presupposing the existence of two cohesive and unified parties locked into a conflict. Little or no attention is devoted to the composition of the parties themselves; that is, to differences not only between, but also within, the Palestinian and Israeli Jewish collectivities.

To come to terms with the Israeli-Palestinian conflict requires a more complex analysis of the parties involved. Such an analysis ought to approach the parties as diverse and often fragmented communities and must take into account how the parties define themselves and how they are viewed by others. It is important to note, however, that the meanings assigned to particular notions of identity and community change over time. Thus, a careful examination of Palestinian and Israeli Jewish collectivities should underscore the changes in their composition, self-image, and perceptions of and interactions with one another (Kimmerling and Migdal, 1993; Sharoni, 1995b; Kimmerling, 2010; C. Suleiman, 2011).

Indeed, the Israeli-Palestinian conflict has played a central role in shaping the collective identities of Jews and Palestinians, for the most part in direct opposition to one another, and until recently each reflected denial of the legitimacy of the other party's identity claims (Kelman, 1982; Moses, 1990; Volkan, 1990; Kimmerling, 2010; C. Suleiman, 2011). The terms *Palestinians* and *Israelis,* which are currently used to describe the conflict in both media and scholarly accounts, were once in themselves a topic of contention. In fact, until the mid-1970s many Jews in Israel and elsewhere as well as numerous politicians, scholars, and media analysts worldwide did not use the term *Palestinians,* thus failing to acknowledge Palestinians' rights to self-determination and territorial sovereignty (Hajjar and Beinin, 1990; Friel and Falk, 2004; Dunsky, 2008). The term *Palestinians* has been integrated into the mainstream discourse on the conflict only since the 1980s; it has been used almost exclusively (including in Israel) in both scholarly and popular references to the conflict. A similar trend has occurred in recent years, following the signing of the Oslo Accords and the establishment of the Palestinian National Authority (PNA), with the term *Palestine* beginning to replace other formulations such as *the territories* and *the West Bank and Gaza Strip* (see Usher, 1995a; M. Suleiman, 1995; C. Suleiman, 2011).

The extensive use of the term *Israelis* is also relatively new, dating to the establishment of the State of Israel on May 15, 1948, when the collective reference to *Jews* was replaced by the term *Israelis.* Although large segments of the international community immediately adopted the term, until the 1990s the Arab countries and a handful of sympathizers with the Palestinian cause, including several national liberation movements, avoided the use of the term *Israelis,* using instead such terms as *Jews* or *Zionists.*

The prevalent use of the terms *Israelis* and *Palestinians* underscores the view that the Israeli-Palestinian conflict is first and foremost an intractable conflict between two national movements that claim the same piece of land. In addition, the gradual acceptance and normalization of these terms signals more than a mere semantic shift; it points to a growing recognition of the legitimacy of both parties' identity claims and opens up space for a possible reformulation of these claims in ways that are not mutually exclusive (Fernea and Hocking, 1992).

Palestinians

The term *Palestinians* refers to the Arabs—Christian, Muslim, and Druze—who have lived in Palestine for centuries. The number of Palestinians worldwide is estimated at more than 5 million, and they are usually divided into three major subgroups: Palestinians who live in the West Bank and Gaza Strip, those who live inside Israel's pre-1967 borders and hold Israeli citizenship, and those who live in the diaspora. The Palestinian diaspora is a direct result of the creation of the State of Israel, which resulted in the destruction of Palestinian Arab society, dispersing hundreds of thousands of Palestinians to lives in exile or as refugees. Almost 70 percent of the inhabitants of the Gaza Strip and 15 percent of the inhabitants of the West Bank have lived in refugee camps since 1948 (Said et al., 1990; Yahya, 1991).

The experience of occupation and displacement fueled a national liberation struggle, which was led and represented by the Palestine Liberation Organization (PLO). Since its establishment in 1964, the PLO played a central role in the politicization of Palestinian society and in the consolidation of a collective Palestinian identity (Cobban, 1984; Nassar, 1991). The creation of the PLO with the support of the Arab League marked a move by Palestinians toward independence from the Arab regimes. The PLO served as the umbrella organization for different political factions with varying ideological orientations and operative strategies. The major factions included Fatah, the largest group, headed by Yasser Arafat; the Popular Front for the Liberation of Palestine (PFLP); the Democratic Front for the Liberation of Palestine (DFLP); and the Palestine Communist Party (PCP). The differences between these political factions notwithstanding, Palestinians and many within the international community viewed the PLO as the sole legitimate representative of the Palestinian people (Makovsky, 1996; Chamberlin, 2012).

A careful analysis of Palestinian collectivity ought to pay attention to the social, economic, and religious makeup of the society as well as to political differences. For Palestinians in the West Bank and Gaza Strip and in Israel, the place of residence often reflects their socioeconomic status. Working-class Palestinians in the West Bank and Gaza Strip—many of whom worked until recently in Israel—reside in refugee camps and in villages. The villages are also home to peasants whereas the elites and the petit bourgeois class, which includes merchants, traders, and professionals, can often be found in the urban centers (Hiltermann, 1990; Taraki, 2006).

Another crucial social sphere that is affected by social class is education. The educational experience of Palestinians varies, depending on the geographical location as well as on the historical and political context. For example, during the first Palestinian uprising, known as the intifada, which began in 1987, Palestinians' access to education in the West Bank and Gaza Strip was restricted due to the widespread closure of educational institutions by the Israeli military and the arrest, imprisonment, or expulsion of professors and students (al-Haq, 1988:419–434; Nasser, Berlin, and Wong, 2011). It is seldom acknowledged that, despite these difficult circumstances, Palestinians have the highest per capita rate of university graduation in the Arab world and one of the highest worldwide (Said et al., 1990).

Another fact that is often overlooked is that not all Palestinians are Muslims; Palestinian Christians live as a minority in both the West Bank and Israel (J. Abu-Lughod, 1987). Nevertheless, due to specific historical and political challenges that have confronted Palestinians, religious differences within Palestinian society have by and large been set aside as Palestinians have sought unity under the banner of national liberation and self-determination. In recent years, however, political Islam has come to play a more prominent role within Palestinian society and politics (Taraki, 1989; Legrain, 1990; Usher, 1995a, 1995b). The early months of the first Palestinian intifada saw the emergence of the Islamic Resistance Movement (which is better known by its acronym, Hamas) in the West Bank and Gaza Strip. By the close of the 1980s, Hamas became part of the Palestinian political scene, regularly polling second only to Arafat's Fatah movement in professional and student elections across the West Bank and especially in the Gaza Strip. Since the signing of the Oslo Accords in September 1993, Hamas has established itself as the single largest political opposition group in Palestinian society (Usher, 1995b; Milton-Edwards, 1999; Rougier, 2007).

The redeployment of Israeli troops in some parts of the West Bank and Gaza Strip and the establishment of the PNA inevitably brought change to Palestinian society and politics. In the middle to late 1990s, Palestinians achieved limited self-rule, held general elections, and began to establish social and political institutions such as security services, a legal system, a Palestinian supreme court, and a house of representatives called the Palestinian Council. These accomplishments, however, were merely symbolic and short lived. Most of the institutions that were established failed to bring about Palestinian self-determination or to advance the struggle to establish an autonomous Palestinian state (Usher, 1995a; Rabbani, 1996; Guyatt, 1998; Parsons, 2005).

The Al-Aqsa Intifada, which erupted in September 2001, was ignited by the failure of the Oslo agreements and other negotiated agreements that failed to usher in a plan that would end the Israeli occupation of the West Bank and Gaza. Known as the second intifada, it underscored the same message that antioccupation activists in Israel and Palestine put forth during the first intifada: that an end to the illegal Israeli occupation is a necessary condition for a just and lasting peace in the region. However, unlike the bottom-up popular character of the first uprising, the Al-Aqsa Intifada has resembled more a guerrilla war.

The mainstream global media were quick to represent the escalation in violence in the region, focusing attention on such desperate acts of violence as suicide bombings carried out by Palestinians. There was little to no analysis of the fact that Palestinians who condone the use of armed struggle do so because of their deep disappointment with the failure of both Israeli society and the international community to grasp the message of the first intifada, which was mostly nonviolent in both principle and practice. Also missing from the dominant media representations of the second intifada was analysis of the systemic repression stemming from the Israeli military occupation, including home demolishing, checkpoints, targeted killings, and an economic crisis (Friel and Falk, 2004).

Most of the autonomous Palestinian institutions were severely undermined, if not completely destroyed, by the Israeli military between 2001 and 2003 with the excuse of crushing the Al-Aqsa Intifada (Jones and Pedahzur, 2005). Indeed, the delegitimization of Palestinian leadership has reached new highs following the landslide victory of Hamas in the January 2006 election (Tamimi, 2006; Gunning, 2008). Within days, Israel, the United States, the European Union (EU), and several European countries cut off their aid to the Palestinians, claiming that the Islamist political party rejects Israel's right to exist. Independent analysts, on the other hand, concluded after a careful examination of Palestinian voting patterns, that Hamas's victory should not be interpreted as a sign of the Islamization of Palestine. Rather, it is a vote of no confidence in the political status quo and a vote of support for the one party that continues to openly resist the Israeli occupation (T. Haddad, 2006; Murray, 2006).

The failure of the political diplomacy to bring about a just and lasting resolution to the conflict, coupled with the deterioration of living conditions in Palestine in general and in the Gaza Strip, has led to an unprecedented fragmentation of Palestinian society. This fragmentation has escalated periodically into open street fighting between Hamas and Fatah (Mishal and Sela, 2006). The majority of Palestinians have condemned the fighting and urged the political factions to set their differences aside and adhere to a platform of national unity designed to end the occupation and advance the Palestinians' struggle for self-determination (Perlman, 2003).

The devastation inflicted on Palestinians by the massive Israeli invasions of and attacks on Gaza in December 2008 and November 2012 have further complicated the Palestinian political landscape (Levy, 2010). At the same time, the international community, including its mainstream media, responded to the urgent calls for support and solidarity from Palestinians in Gaza and around the world. In addition to ongoing humanitarian and solidarity visits from internationals, two particular initiatives have strengthened the Palestinians' position and quest for peace with justice. The first initiative is known as the Boycott, Divestment, and Sanctions movement (BDS), and the second involves the UN General Assembly vote on November 29, 2012, by a more than two-thirds majority to recognize the state of Palestine.

Israelis

The term *Israelis,* which has been in use only since the establishment of the state in 1948, invokes biblical references to the people of Israel and to the ancient Israelites. Yet scholars have pointed out numerous inconsistencies in the theses that suggest that the Jews who presently reside in Israel are the descendants of the ancient Israelites (see Evron, 1995; Shahak, 1995). Most scholarly and media accounts of the conflict use the term *Israelis* because they assume a natural overlap between the state and its citizens. However, this usage is highly misleading because one-sixth of Israel's population consists of Palestinians who hold Israeli citizenship (Rekass, 1989; Rouhana, 1989; Smooha, 1989, 1992). The terms *Israeli Jews* or *Jews who live in Israel,* which is used in this chapter, more accurately describe this party to the conflict.

Peaceful demonstrations against the Israeli occupation are common throughout Israel and the West Bank and Gaza.

Israeli Jewish society identifies itself as a Zionist society, morally, politically, and technically. The moral aspect of this identification is grounded in the presupposition that Jews can never hope to achieve equality of rights as religious or cultural minorities in Gentile societies. The political aspect of this identification has been predicated on two correlative elements: (1) the mobilization of Jews throughout the world to immigrate to Palestine; and (2) the establishment of a Jewish state in Palestine, namely the State of Israel, and the mobilization of moral and material support from Jews and non-Jews worldwide for the continued existence of Israel as a Jewish state. Finally, Israel is a Zionist society technically in that its legal structure and the routine of its everyday life are determined in every domain by the distinction between Jews and non-Jews (Davis, 1986:176–177).

Divisions exist, however, not only between Jews and non-Jews but also within the Israeli Jewish population, which comprises more than 80 percent of Israel's overall population (Reich, 1985). Israeli Jewish society is quite heterogeneous, composed of immigrants from numerous countries and reflecting a variety of ethnic and linguistic groups; religious preferences; and cultural, historical, and political backgrounds. The two main ethnic groupings are the Ashkenazi Jews, who originated mostly in Europe and North America, and the Mizrachim, whose origins can be traced mainly to North Africa and the Middle East. The term *Mizrachim* (Orientals in Hebrew) is gradually replacing other terms, such as *Sephardim,* previously used to refer to this segment of Israel's population (Shohat, 1988; Swirski, 1989). Another term that has been in use recently in reference to this group is *Arab Jews,* a term that highlights the sociocultural similarities between Jews from the Middle East and North Africa and their fellow Arabs. The Israeli establishment sought to suppress these similarities, using the Arab-Israeli conflict as an excuse (Alcalay, 1993), and the same excuse was used to downplay the disparities in power and privilege between Ashkenazi and Mizrachi Jews. These disparities have remained largely unaddressed as the Israeli establishment utilized the salience of the Israeli-Palestinian conflict to establish unity in the face of the enemy and to construct a strong sense of national identity (Sharoni, 1995a). The centrality of the conflict has also shaped the Israeli political system and the leading political parties.

Following the January 2013 elections, there are twelve parties (some of which comprise several smaller parties) represented in the nineteenth Israeli parliament, the Knesset. Historically, the two principal political parties in Israel have been Labor and Likud. The Labor Party, which is predominantly Ashkenazi and secular, controlled Israeli politics between 1948 and 1977. Its original ideology has undergone significant transformations in recent years as it has attempted to reconcile the tensions between Zionism, socialism, and democratic practices (Kimmerling, 1983; Shapira, 1992). Over the years, the party's positions and policies on the Israeli-Palestinian conflict have been mixed. Officially, the party supports a "land for peace" solution and, therefore, it is generally perceived to be more moderate and willing to compromise than Likud. At the same time, the Labor Party encouraged the construction of settlements in the West Bank and Gaza Strip after 1967, was tough in dealing with the first intifada, and for many years opposed the establishment of an independent Palestinian state alongside Israel. More recently, however, the Labor Party, and especially Shimon Peres and Yitzhak Rabin, were credited with making a significant step toward peace with the signing of the Oslo Accords.

The Likud Party, which came to power for the first time in 1977, is more conservative economically and religiously than Labor and enjoys more support among Mizrachi and working-class Jews. The party has traditionally taken a more hard-line stance on the Arab-Israeli conflict in general and the Palestinian issue in particular. Its original platform claimed Jewish sovereignty over all territories occupied by Israel in 1967, with the exception of the Sinai, which was returned to Egypt following the signing of the Camp David Accords in 1979 (Lesch and Tessler, 1989; Saunders, 1985). Likud and Labor have alternated in power since 1984, with the Likud Party headed by Benjamin Netanyahu defeating Labor in the May 1996 elections. Although Likud initially opposed the Oslo Accords and the subsequent agreements and vowed to derail their implementation, its position was somewhat modified due to both internal and international pressure. Nevertheless, the policies of the Netanyahu government led to a major stalemate in the negotiations between Israel and the Palestinians, one of many factors that resulted in early elections in May 1999, with the new Labor leader, Ehud Barak, replacing Netanyahu as prime minister.

But Barak's tenure was short lived. He lost the 2000 elections to Ariel Sharon, the Likud candidate, after the outbreak of the Al-Aqsa Intifada. The massive propaganda about the far-reaching concessions that Barak had supposedly offered, and the Palestinians rejected, contributed a great deal to Sharon's victory (Hiro, 1999; Thomas, 1999; Reinhart, 2002). Despite Sharon's failure to deliver the security that he promised Israelis in his election platform and the collapse of his coalition government in late 2002, he was reelected in January 2003 by a landslide with the Labor Party suffering the most significant loss in its history. But analysts argue that Sharon's reelection does not represent an unwillingness on the part of Israelis to reach a negotiated solution with the Palestinians. Rather, it calls into question the Israeli political system, which fails to represent the majority of Israelis (Reinhart, 2002).

The March 2006 elections changed the Israeli political scene dramatically. As a result a new party, Kadima (forward in English), is leading the Israeli parliament. It was the first time that a third party positioned itself as a dominant force on the Israeli political landscape.

The establishment of Kadima and its victory in the 2006 elections further complicates the analysis of the Israeli political landscape. Kadima was formed by former Israeli prime minister Sharon after he left the right-wing Likud Party in November 2005. During the public relations campaign surrounding the establishment of the new party, Sharon claimed that Kadima would grant him the freedom to carry out his policy of a unilateral disengagement plan—removing Israeli settlements from Palestinian territory and fixing Israel's borders with a prospective Palestinian state. Nevertheless, quite a different scenario unfolded in the aftermath of the elections.

First, Sharon himself was not able to stand for election after suffering a major stroke in December 2005 and was replaced by his deputy in the new party and the acting prime minister Ehud Olmert. Second, the original promise of Kadima to remove settlements and move toward the establishment of a a Palestinian state was forgotten as Kadima formed a coalition government with the explicitly racist party, Israel Beiteinu (Hebrew for "Israel is our home"). This relatively new party, which pushed past Likud to become one of Israel's major political parties, has focused its campaign on one key issue: ethnically cleansing Israel of the remainder of the indigenous Palestinian population (Barghouti, 2006; Levy, 2006; Makdisi, 2006). Accordingly, far from the promise to lead Israel back to the negotiation table, the coalition government that was established as a result of the 2006 elections represents a step in the opposite direction.

Despite the plurality of political views and perspectives on the Israeli-Palestinian conflict and the prospects for its resolution, most opinion polls were correct in predicting a decisive win for the right-wing party, Likud-Beiteinu, led by Netanyahu. Given the January 2013 election results it is highly unlikely that the Israeli government would reengage in peace initiatives, without considerable pressure, both from its citizens, and from outside forces.

The History and Dynamics of the Conflict

The conventional view among conflict resolution scholars and diplomats in the West is that dwelling on the history of conflicts in general and on the Israeli-Palestinian conflict in particular is counterproductive, mainly because the parties' interpretations of history often appear irreconcilable. At the same time, history has played a central role in shaping people's collective identities, perceptions of one another, and general attitudes toward the conflict and the prospects for its resolution. According to this view, if history is ignored, it would be extremely difficult to establish the framework and conditions for a just and lasting peace. Thus, the question is not whether to deal with history, but rather how to approach history so that its examination contributes to both the analysis of the conflict and the exploration of new venues for its resolution. Toward this end, we review some of the history of the conflict presented in Chapter 3, identify a number of significant turning points in that history, and examine their contributions to the escalation or deescalation of the conflict. In this discussion, particular attention is given to the differences and similarities in Palestinians' and Israelis' perceptions of these events.

Modern Zionism and the Partition of Palestine

The first turning point of the conflict involves the emergence of Zionism and the beginning of Jewish immigration to and settlement in Palestine in the 1880s. The Zionist movement emerged in the late nineteenth century in Europe in response to the rise of European nationalism and anti-Semitism. During and after the Holocaust, which increased the flow of Jewish immigrants to Palestine, the Zionist movement gained significant international recognition and support.

There is no single definition for the term *Zionism*. As with many other contested terms, the meanings and practices associated with Zionism depend on the particular standpoint of the person or group defining it. Although there are different strands of Zionism (socialist or nonsocialist, religious or secular), for most Jews, Zionism is a movement for Jewish national self-determination designed to restore their right to live in the land of their ancestors (Herzberg, 1962). Palestinians and many others, however, view Zionism as an exclusive ideology that underlies the settler-colonial movement responsible for the occupation of Palestine and the dispossession and exploitation of its indigenous population (Said, 1980; Abdo, 1992; Zunes, 1994).

The divergent interpretations of this turning point by Palestinians and Jews lie not only in their differing views of Zionism both as an ideology and as a political project, but also in their different perspectives regarding the origins of the conflict. According to prevalent Jewish interpretations, the conflict is centuries old, and Zionism was an attempt to ensure the return of Jews to the land of Israel, Eretz Yisrael, which God promised to Abraham and his descendants (Sachar, 1964; Parkes, 1964; Grayzel, 1968; Tessler, 1994). According to Palestinian interpretations, the Israeli-Palestinian conflict is a modern phenomenon whose origins lie not in the Bible, but rather in Zionist ideology and its implementation in Palestine through policies that are reminiscent of other settler-colonial projects around the world (Khalidi, 1971; Muslih, 1992; Kimmerling and Migdal, 1993; Lustick, 1993; Finkelstein, 1995; Greenstein, 1995).

Many conventional accounts of the conflict overlook the fact that Palestine was not "a land without people for the people without a land," as the Zionist slogan proclaimed; it had an existing indigenous population that sought independence first from the Ottoman rulers and later from the British (Khalidi, 1971). Thus, Jewish immigration to Palestine precipitated a century-old clash between two national movements struggling for self-determination and territorial sovereignty. From the start, Palestinians were placed in a disadvantageous position. According to Palestinian historians, the root cause of the Palestinians' disadvantage lies in two political decisions made in Europe. The first decision was made in 1897 by the World Zionist Organization, which met in Basel, Switzerland, and resolved to establish a Jewish state in Palestine. The second decision, known as the Balfour Declaration, was made by the British in 1917, undermining the rights of the indigenous Palestinian population and promising to support the establishment of a Jewish national home in Palestine (Muslih, 1992).

Given this context, the collision between Zionism and Palestinian nationalism was almost inevitable and escalated into violent confrontations in 1920 in Jerusalem, in 1921 in Tel Aviv–Jaffa and the surrounding areas, and in 1929 in Jerusalem and Hebron. One of the most dramatic escalations of the conflict occurred during the Arab Revolt, which lasted from 1936 to 1939. This revolt was the longest-running Palestinian protest against Jewish national aspirations in Palestine prior to the establishment of the State of Israel. This mostly grassroots movement involved violent as well as nonviolent dimensions such as strikes, nonpayment of taxes, and other forms of civil disobedience (Khalidi, 1971; Hirst, 1984).

The first period of the revolt ended at the request of the newly formed Arab Higher Committee for Palestine (AHC), which urged Palestinians to wait for the outcome of deliberations by the Palestine Royal Commission, known as the Peel Commission, which was set up by Britain to investigate the situation. The revolt's second stage was sparked by the Peel Commission's report recommending the partition of Palestine into two states in order to accommodate the competing claims of Palestinians and Jews, which resulted in further escalation of the situation with Zionist, Palestinian, and British forces fighting for control. Given the fierce resistance to the plan among both Palestinians and Jews, Britain was eventually forced to abandon the 1937 partition plan.

Nevertheless, partition plans continued to surface; these became particularly popular and gained international legitimacy in the aftermath of World War II and the Holocaust, which resulted in the near destruction of the Jewish people in Europe, as well as Gypsies, homosexuals, disabled persons, and others deemed "undesirable" by the Nazis. The best-known is the 1947 United Nations partition plan, also known as Resolution 181, which called for the creation of a Jewish state and an Arab state in Palestine (see Map 6.1). The plan, which indicated that the British Mandate over the area was to end on May 15, 1948, "gave the new Jewish state 57 percent of Palestine, including the fertile coastal region." Palestinians viewed this proposal as fundamentally flawed and unjust since "at the time Jews represented only about 33 percent of the population and owned only 7 percent of the

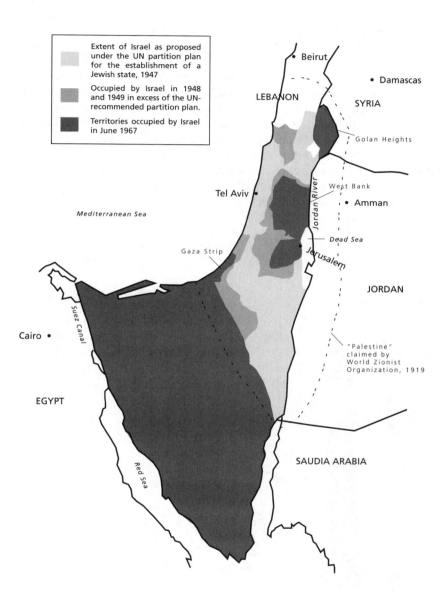

Map 6.1 Israel/Palestine, Showing the 1947 Partition Plan, 1948 Boundaries, and Borders After the 1967 War

land." Indeed, UN estimates suggest that the division of territory spelled out in the 1947 partition plan would have given the Jewish state economic revenues three times as great as those of the Palestinian state. On November 29, 1947, the General Assembly voted in favor of this particular plan (Gerner, 1994:43).

The Zionist response to Resolution 181 was to endorse it with reservations, insisting that the Jewish homeland be distinctively Jewish rather than religiously and ethnically pluralistic. At the same time, Zionist leaders did not abandon the conviction that eventually all of Palestine should come under Jewish control. From the Palestinian perspective, the UN partition plan was an illegal and illegitimate attempt to divide Palestine. Moreover, Palestinians feared that the establishment of two states would result in the expulsion of Palestinians who lived in areas that fell within the designated territory of the Jewish state. But contrary to common representations of this event that tend to portray Palestinians as rejectionists unwilling to compromise, the Arab leadership in and outside of Palestine did not simply reject the partition plan; it endorsed the alternative proposal of the UN Special Committee on Palestine, which called for a single, unified state in Palestine

Anne Paq/activestills.org

A Palestinian man holds a large "key" as part of a demonstration on the anniversary of al-Nakbah (catastrophe) when the Palestinians were forced from their lands. Because many refugees left all their belongings but took a key in the expectation of returning home, the key is a prominent symbol at such demonstrations.

that would be democratic and secular and grant equal rights to all its citizens (see Flapan, 1987; Finkelstein, 1995).

The UN vote on partition sparked an unprecedented wave of violence, which escalated into a full-fledged war following the establishment of the State of Israel on May 14, 1948. The differences in the interpretations of history by Palestinians and Jews have been most evident in the ways in which they refer to this war. Jews refer to it as a war of independence, marking the fulfillment of their national aspirations with the establishment of the State of Israel. For Palestinians, however, the 1948 war (known as al-Nakbah, which means "the catastrophe") meant disaster and destruction. In the course of the war, the Palestinian community was virtually destroyed. Approximately 780,000 Palestinians became refugees as a direct result of Israel's establishment. Some Palestinians fled, others were driven out by force, and 418 Arab villages were destroyed or depopulated (Morris, 1988, 1990). The war ended with the establishment of Israel on roughly 77 percent of the total area of Palestine. The remaining 23 percent was divided between Jordan, which gained control over the West Bank (including East Jerusalem), and Egypt, which took upon itself the administration of the Gaza Strip (Muslih, 1992).

International Conflicts

In most literature on the conflict, the years since the establishment of the State of Israel are often divided into three periods: May 1948 to June 1967; June 1967 to December 1987; and December 1987 to the present. During the first period, Palestinians were in a state of shock and despair. The difficult circumstances and the lack of political leadership and economic resources forced them into a state of dependency on neighboring Arab states. As a result, until 1967, with the exception of the establishment of the PLO in 1964, Palestinian nationalism was for the most part muted; resistance to Israel was expressed primarily by Arab leaders residing outside Palestine. Meanwhile, on the other side of the Israeli-Palestinian divide, Israeli Jews worked to build a Western-style Jewish state in the middle of the Arab world. Consequently, the Palestinians who remained in Israel after the 1948 war were viewed as a problem for the evolving Jewish state. They were placed under military rule until 1966 and subjected to a slew of discriminatory regulations under the pretext of Israel's "national security" (Gerner, 1994:47, 57–58; Lustick, 1980; Zureik, 1979).

The June 1967 war, also referred to as the Six Day War, is one of the most significant turning points in the history of the conflict. It dramatically changed the map of the Middle East, resulting in Israel's occupation of the West Bank and Gaza Strip, the Sinai, and the Golan Heights. Contrary to conventional Israeli interpretations, however, which have insisted that

Israel occupied these territories in a war of self-defense, ample evidence illustrates that Israel initiated the war under the pretext of a "preemptive attack" (Zilka, 1992). At the conclusion of the war, Israel's conquest appeared to be just temporary. In fact, on June 19, 1967, the Israeli cabinet voted unanimously to give back the Sinai to Egypt and the Golan Heights to Syria in return for demilitarization and peace. With regard to Jordan, Israel demanded border adjustments, citing security reasons, but the status of Jerusalem was considered nonnegotiable; the city was unified and declared an indivisible part of Israel (Zilka, 1992:33). However, despite Resolution 242, which was unanimously adopted on November 22, 1967, and called for Israeli withdrawal from the territories occupied during the war, Israel objected to a complete withdrawal and refused to withdraw from any territory before a peace treaty was signed. Syria rejected the resolution altogether, and Egypt and Jordan refused to sign a peace treaty prior to Israel's withdrawal.

Israel's victory in the Six Day War and its conquest of the remaining 23 percent of Palestine left Egypt, Syria, and Jordan shocked and humiliated and turned Palestinians' hopes to a deep sense of despair. Those Palestinians who were not forced to flee (many for the second time) and become refugees in the surrounding Arab countries were subjected to harsh military laws imposed by Israel. In addition, large amounts of land were confiscated to build Jewish settlements in the West Bank and Gaza Strip, which Israeli officials started referring to by the biblical names of Judea and Samaria. Jewish settlement construction in the Occupied Territories began within six months and had massive government support.

The 1973 war, which Israelis often refer to as the Yom-Kippur War, represents yet another significant turning point in the history of the Israeli-Palestinian conflict, marking the last war between Israel and an allied Arab force. The war began on October 6, 1973, with a coordinated attack launched by Egypt and Syria. But after a massive airlift of advanced military equipment from the United States, Israel was able to turn things around. On October 24, at the conclusion of the war, Israel had recaptured most of the Sinai territory from which it was forced to retreat and solidified its hold over the Golan Heights. This military victory notwithstanding, the 1973 war was politically costly for Israelis; it ended the collective sense of euphoria created in the aftermath of the 1967 war and shattered the illusion of military invincibility, clearing the way for a more realistic and critical assessment of Israeli society and politics and especially of the Arab-Israeli conflict. For Palestinians, the 1973 war marked yet another chapter in their growing disillusionment with the ability of Arab states to lead the struggle over Palestine.

As a result of the 1967 war and especially in the aftermath of the 1973 war, Palestinians sought their independent representation through the national resistance movement led by the PLO. Arafat's election as chairperson of the organization in 1969 represented an important milestone in the Palestinians' struggle for self-determination, and international recognition of the PLO as the sole representative of the Palestinian people. By 1974, Palestinians were able to alert the international community to the plight of their people; achieve independent representation in many international bodies, including the UN and its related organizations; and gain recognition on the world stage. Yet throughout this period, Israel refused to recognize Palestinians' existence and right of self-determination (Kimmerling and Migdal, 1993:209–239).

The civil war in Jordan in 1970, which was characterized by daily violent confrontations between Palestinians and the Jordanian regime, was a major setback in the Palestinian efforts to strengthen the national movement outside Palestine. The months of buildup escalated into eleven days of bloodshed, often referred to as Black September, which resulted in the killing of thousands of Palestinians and Jordanians, spoiled the relationship between the Palestinian leadership and the Jordanian regime, and destroyed the political and military infrastructure established by the PLO in Jordan (Tessler, 1994:460–462). Following these events, the PLO began building its bases in Lebanon. Meanwhile, the Palestinian resistance movement in the territories was growing. Its strength and organization were reflected in the results of the first municipal elections in the West Bank in 1976. But when Likud came to power in 1977, Israel moved against these elected mayors and the newly elected municipal councils, appointing instead people who were considered more "moderate" and easy to control (Gerner, 1994:91).

Contrary to the gloomy predictions of many analysts, the unexpected victory of the right-wing Likud Party in the 1977 elections resulted in a temporary deescalation of the Arab-Israeli conflict. A few months after Likud came to power, Egyptian president Anwar Sadat surprised the Israeli government and public, as well as the Arab world and the international community, when he became the first Arab head of state to visit Jerusalem. Another event that both reflected and contributed to the deescalation of the conflict was the emergence of a distinct peace movement in Israel: Peace Now. The group, founded in 1978 by reserve officers and soldiers, argued that the Israeli government was not doing enough to bring about peace with Egypt (Bar-On, 1985; Wolfsfeld, 1988). Although Peace Now could not take much credit for this development, the Israeli and Egyptian governments began direct negotiations that year, and in 1979 Israel signed a formal peace treaty with Egypt, often referred to as the Camp David Accords.

The Camp David Accords have been viewed as significant in the history of the Israeli-Palestinian conflict because of the problematic manner in which they addressed the Palestinian dimension of the Arab-Israeli conflict and because they enabled the United States to establish itself as a major

peace broker in the region and thus increased its sphere of power and influence. The accords contained two documents; the one titled "A Framework
for Peace in the Middle East" attempted to address the Palestinian problem.
With its vague formulation regarding the nature of Palestinian autonomy
and its failure to recognize the PLO as the official representative of the
Palestinian people and thus as a party to the negotiations, the document
provoked strong negative reactions from the Palestinians (Lesch and Tessler, 1989).

It soon became clear that the government of Menachem Begin had no
intention of allowing the Camp David Accords to lead to an Israeli withdrawal from the West Bank and Gaza Strip. To the contrary, in the 1980s Israel pursued its plan to lay the foundation for the permanent retention of the
Occupied Territories. The government expanded settlement construction,
applied Israeli laws to Jews residing in these areas, and took additional
steps in such areas as transportation, communication, and economic activity to link the West Bank and Gaza more closely to Israel and to blur the
1967 border, often referred to as "the Green Line" (Tessler, 1994:519–521).
For Palestinians, this period has been characterized by harsh economic conditions and growing dependency on Israel, a shortage of adequate housing,
a crisis in education and deteriorating school facilities, and many other
problems that have become more acute as a result of the Israeli occupation
(E. Nakhleh, 1980; Tamari, 1980).

Its reservations regarding the Camp David Accords notwithstanding,
during this period the PLO began to signal its readiness for a political settlement. Israel refused to acknowledge, let alone act on, the softening in the
PLO's public statements and political agenda; instead, it took actions to remove the remaining elected Palestinian leaders in the West Bank and Gaza
Strip and to set up instead the Village Leagues, whose Arab members were
appointed by Israel and thus lacked credibility among Palestinians. These
actions prompted fierce resistance by Palestinians, resulting in serious
clashes between Palestinians and Israeli soldiers in March, April, and May
1982. Another significant event during this period was the emergence of the
popular committees, including women's groups and labor unions, across the
West Bank and Gaza Strip. These local committees were affiliated with the
various factions of the PLO and established to address the service needs of
the Palestinian community.

The Israeli invasion of Lebanon in 1982 marked a serious escalation of
the Israeli-Palestinian conflict. The Israeli government's decision to inflict
damage on the PLO's political and military bases in Lebanon stemmed directly from the insistence of most members of the Israeli government at the
time that the PLO was the source of unrest and trouble in the West Bank
and Gaza Strip. Nevertheless, the Israeli government's previous attempt, in
1978, to destroy the PLO's headquarters and bases in Lebanon not only

failed, but triggered the escalation of Israeli-Palestinian hostilities across the Israeli-Lebanese border and heightened tensions between Israel and the Arab states (Gerner, 1994:124–128; Tessler, 1994:568–599). In June 1982, Israeli troops invaded Lebanon for the second time, instigating what became the most controversial war in Israel's history.

The officially stated Israeli goals were to move Palestinian fighters out of range of northern Galilee and to eliminate the PLO's political and military infrastructure in Lebanon. Yet Israeli troops proceeded into Lebanon beyond the twenty-five miles initially announced, encircling and bombing Beirut in an effort to force the evacuation of Arafat and the PLO (Schiff and Ya'ari, 1984). Israel agreed to stop the bombing only after the completion of the PLO's evacuation in late August 1982.

The cease-fire did not last long. In mid-September 1982, following the assassination of Beshir Gemayel, the newly elected Lebanese president, Israeli troops returned to Beirut, occupying the entire city and sealing off the Sabra and Shatila refugee camps, home to many Palestinians and poor Lebanese. These actions precipitated one of the most tragic events in the history of the conflict: the Sabra and Shatila massacre. The massacre was carried out by Lebanese Maronite Christians, who were known for their hatred of Palestinians, with Israeli knowledge and according to some accounts even tacit approval. Forty hours later, when the camps were finally unsealed, the body count reached 700–800 people, according to Israeli estimates, the majority of whom were civilians, including many women and children. Contending accounts indicated that the number of people murdered was perhaps as high as 1,500 or 2,000 (Schiff and Ya'ari, 1984; Tessler, 1994:590–599).

The Israeli invasion of Lebanon reinvigorated existing Israeli peace groups such as Peace Now and the Committee for Solidarity with Birzeit University (which decided to rename itself the Committee Against the War in Lebanon). In addition, the invasion triggered the emergence of new protest groups such as Parents Against Silence, Women Against the Invasion of Lebanon, and Yesh Gvul (literally, "There is a limit") (Kaminer, 1996; Sharoni, 1995a:106–109). Questioning the legitimacy and morality of the war, Yesh Gvul called on Israeli soldiers to refuse to serve in Lebanon. Not only did hundreds of soldiers sign petitions declaring that they were prepared to take this course of action, but also a significant number of soldiers were sent to jail for their "refusal to carry out an order" (Kaminer, 1996:36–38).

For the first time in Israel's history, Israeli citizens not only questioned their government's policies, but also took to the streets to voice their discontent. From the beginning of the invasion, a flurry of protest activities included vigils and demonstrations in the streets and on university campuses, antiwar petitions, and letters to the editors. The first national demonstration against the war on June 26, 1982, drew approximately 20,000 Israelis who demanded the immediate withdrawal of their country's army from Lebanon. A few months later, in response to the Sabra and Shatila massacre, Israel witnessed its largest demonstration ever; according to Peace Now and media reports, about 400,000 people participated. Political protest intensified following the publication of the report by the Kahan Commission, a special inquiry commission set up to investigate Israeli involvement in the Sabra and Shatila massacre (Kaminer, 1996:34–36). The commission's report and the public debates it triggered, coupled with the widespread anti-war demonstrations (which lasted until the partial Israeli withdrawal from Lebanon in 1985), signaled a gradual erosion of the Israeli consensus regarding issues of peace and security.

For Palestinians, the defeat of the PLO in Lebanon resulted in internal fragmentation and disputes among the different PLO factions as well as among the Arab countries that supported them. At the same time, the internal Palestinian leadership had been growing and organizing against the Israeli occupation. In fact, the destruction of the PLO infrastructure in Lebanon contributed to the emergence of a more organized grassroots, autonomous resistance movement in the West Bank and Gaza. This resistance movement gained prominence on the world's stage with the outbreak of the first intifada in December 1987.

The 1987 Palestinian Uprising

The popular uprising was precipitated on December 8, 1987, "when an Israeli army tank transporter collided with a line of cars filled with Palestinian workers waiting at the military checkpoint at the north end of the Gaza Strip" (Gerner, 1994:97). The accident left four Palestinians dead and seven seriously injured, and rumors began to spread that the collision was not an accident but rather a deliberate act carried out by Israel in retaliation for the killing of an Israeli salesperson in Gaza a few days earlier. The funerals of the dead turned into a massive demonstration; Palestinians continued to protest the following day, and the demonstrations and resistance rapidly spread from the Gaza Strip to East Jerusalem and the rest of the West Bank. Although the accident is often viewed as the catalyst for the uprising, analysts agree that the conditions under which Palestinians lived resembled a pressure cooker and, thus, an explosion was imminent (Nassar and Heacock, 1991). The literal meaning of the Arabic word *intifada* is "shaking off." For Palestinians, this word has symbolized not only their determination to shake off the Israeli occupation, but also their disillusionment with external forces—the UN, the United States, and the Arab states and Arab League—and their resolve to take matters into their own hands. Palestinian mobilization was unprecedented not only in scope and magnitude, but in organization as well. People who took part in the mostly nonviolent actions that characterized the first intifada—from street demonstrations, tax resistance, and commercial strikes to the establishment of agricultural cooperatives and alternative education centers—were extremely disciplined and came from various socioeconomic backgrounds, political affiliations, and all walks of life. Within weeks, the focus of the conflict and the world's attention turned to scores of Palestinians in the West Bank and Gaza Strip, led by an indigenous leadership (the Unified National Leadership of the Uprising) who demanded the withdrawal of the Israeli military from their occupied land and a just and lasting solution to the conflict (Nassar and Heacock, 1991; Gerner, 1990; Brynen, 1991; Hunter, 1991). The grassroots-led, popular uprising also caught by surprise the PLO leadership, which was based mostly in Tunisia (Aburish, 1998).

On the other side of the Israeli-Palestinian divide, the Israeli government, which the first intifada had caught by surprise, was trying with great difficulty to formulate a response to the uprising and at the same time launch a public relations campaign designed to redeem Israel's image worldwide. Indeed, the first intifada marked a significant shift in power relations between Israel and the Palestinians. Although in strategic terms the advantage still lay with the Israeli side, Palestinians had the moral high ground. For the first time in the history of the conflict, the David versus Goliath analogy was used in scholarly analyses and media reports, describing Israel as Goliath, the mighty aggressor, and the Palestinians as David, the underdog who is determined to win against all odds because his cause is just (Lockman and Beinin, 1989; Schiff, 1990; Perez, 1990).

But Palestinians were well aware that in order to fulfill their aspirations for self-determination, they needed to establish their own social, political, and economic infrastructure, a project prevented by the Israeli occupation. Toward this end, Palestinians established five principal popular committees to deal with agriculture, education, food storage, health care, and security. These committees, which operated both nationally and locally, soon became the most practical mechanism for political mobilization and for the preservation of the community. For many Palestinians, the committees represented the infrastructure of the future Palestinian state, or at least transient democratic institutions designed to govern the community during the first intifada. Palestinian women were actively involved in the establishment and operation of all the popular committees, which resembled the women's committees that had been active in the West Bank and Gaza Strip for more than a decade (Jad, 1990; Hiltermann, 1991; Sharoni, 1995a:72–73).

During the first two years of the first intifada, the general atmosphere within the Palestinian community was extremely positive. The sense of purpose and self-reliance, coupled with the ability to forge unity within and mobilize international support for the Palestinian cause, empowered Palestinians and filled many with pride and hope that a diplomatic solution was in sight. Indeed, analysts agree that the first intifada enabled Palestinians to renounce the armed struggle, recognize Israel's right to exist, and resolve to establish a Palestinian state in the West Bank and Gaza Strip alongside Israel (Tessler, 1994:717–725). This dramatic transformation became evident in November 1988, when Arafat formally and publicly endorsed the two-state solution and proclaimed the independent state of Palestine in the West Bank and Gaza Strip.

For the most part, the Israeli government ignored the significance of the 1988 declaration, and efforts to achieve a political solution foundered. Instead, the Israeli government and military continued to respond to the uprising with repression and intransigence. As happened during the 1982 invasion of Lebanon, the government's actions were met with growing public criticism and protest. Although the main currents in the Israeli peace camp had already acknowledged the destructive effects of the occupation on Israeli society long before the first intifada began, the uprising was a watershed for political mobilization on the Israeli left. Women and groups who were previously involved in solidarity work with Palestinians led the struggle, which centered around one or more of the following messages: end the occupation, negotiate peace with the PLO, and create two states for two peoples (Kaminer, 1996:41–48). Although the peace movement was fairly successful in mobilizing public opinion, its efforts fell short of changing the Israeli government's policies. By late 1990 the Israeli-Palestinian conflict had settled into a grim war of attrition as the world's attention was diverted to the crisis in the Gulf (Hajjar and Beinin, 1990; Gerner, 1991).

Palestinians and Israeli Jews in the 1990s

The Gulf crisis, which began on August 2, 1990, with the Iraqi invasion of Kuwait and escalated into a war in January 1991, represents another turning point in the history of the conflict (Bennis and Moushabeck, 1991; Sifry and Cerf, 1991; Hiro, 1992). Contrary to the common view among scholars and media analysts that Palestinians made a poor political choice by siding with Saddam Hussein, the Palestinian position was far more complex (Andoni, 1991). Throughout the crisis, the official Palestinian position underscored two principles: denunciation of the Iraqi occupation and opposition to a military solution to resolve the crisis (Ashrawi, 1991:191). But like many other societies, Palestinian society is not monolithic; there were Palestinians who expressed sympathy with Hussein for standing up to the Gulf states, the United States, and the West more generally and especially to Israel. Nevertheless, regardless of their view on the Gulf crisis, Palestinians criticized the explicit double standard of the international community that utilized the UN and appeals to international law to demand Iraq's immediate withdrawal from Kuwait, but failed to apply the same measures to the Israeli occupation of the West Bank and Gaza Strip (Ashrawi, 1991: 192–195).

The Gulf crisis and war contributed to the escalation of tension between Israeli Jews and Palestinians. When the US-led air attacks on Iraq began, Israel imposed a twenty-four-hour curfew on Palestinians in the West Bank and Gaza Strip, which lasted a full month and a half. Iraq responded to the air attack with largely ineffective, but frightening, Scud missile attacks on Saudi Arabia and Israel. Although only two Israelis died directly as a result of those attacks, the country was in a state of panic, and thousands of Israelis fled from the urban areas to the countryside to avoid a possible missile attack. Israelis' sense of helplessness was compounded by the fact that they were asked not to retaliate against Iraq because the United States feared that an Israeli attack might break the already fragile coalition (Schiff, 1990). At the same time, on the other side of the Israeli-Palestinian divide, 1.5 million Palestinians were under total curfew, many on the verge of starvation, with no warning sirens against Scuds and no gas masks to protect them against the possibility of an airborne chemical attack (Strum, 1992:59–78; Sharoni, 1995a:82–83).

In addition to its effects on Israel and on Israeli-Palestinian relations, the Gulf War had grave implications for Palestinians both in the West Bank and Gaza Strip and in the Gulf. The long curfew caused great economic hardship, which intensified when Palestinians who had worked in Israel before the war discovered that their employers had replaced them with recent Jewish immigrants. Palestinians in the Occupied Territories were also affected by the fate of relatives who had been working and living in the Gulf. Close to 400,000 Palestinians living in Kuwait lost their livelihoods and were forced once again to flee and look for refuge elsewhere. Since most of these people had been supporting family members in the West Bank and Gaza Strip, their unexpected displacement translated into a direct loss of income for many families. Moreover, external contributions from the Gulf states to the PLO and to Palestinian institutions, such as hospitals, schools and universities, and social welfare organizations, stopped almost instantly (Andoni, 1991).

In the aftermath of the Gulf War, the Arab-Israeli conflict was back on the agenda of US Middle East policy. In October 1991, after months of intense and systematic shuttle diplomacy efforts carried out by US secretary of state James Baker, an international peace conference was convened in Madrid, under joint sponsorship of the United States and the Soviet Union (Gerner, 1992). The conference's participants included Egyptian, Syrian, Lebanese, and Israeli delegations, and a joint Jordanian-Palestinian delegation because the Israeli government refused to accept an independent Palestinian delegation led by the PLO. These peace talks continued throughout

1992 and the first half of 1993 in Washington, DC, and elsewhere on two parallel tracks: bilateral and multilateral. Despite the fact that no agreements were reached during that period and that by mid-1993 negotiations on the Israeli-Palestinian track had reached a total stalemate, some analysts contend that the very fact that Palestinian and Israeli Jewish officials were engaged in face-to-face negotiations was a major step forward in Israeli-Palestinian relations (Tessler, 1994:748–750).

The victory of the Labor Party in the 1992 Israeli elections triggered for many the hope for progress in the peace process. Another encouraging sign in this direction was the new government's introduction of a bill removing the ban on unauthorized meetings with members of the PLO. These developments notwithstanding, the situation in the West Bank and Gaza Strip continued to be tense, escalating into occasional violent clashes. Then in late August 1993, the world learned that secret negotiations between Israeli government officials and official representatives of the PLO had been taking place in Norway for many months. The announcement that the two parties had signed a joint Declaration of Principles (also known as the Oslo Accords) was both surprising and encouraging. Soon thereafter the world witnessed PLO president Arafat and Israeli prime minister Rabin shaking hands after signing the Oslo Accords at the White House in Washington, DC.

On July 1, 1994, after twenty-seven years in exile, Arafat set foot on Palestinian soil, greeted by hundreds of thousands of Palestinians. Soon thereafter he formed the Palestinian National Authority, and the first democratic Palestinian elections were held in January 1996. Initially, the Oslo Accords enjoyed public support on both sides of the Israeli-Palestinian divide. Ordinary people, fed up with the cycle of violence that characterized the conflict, were eager to reap the benefits of peace promised to them by their leaders. But as negotiations dragged on and living conditions failed to improve, support for the agreement, and the peace process in general, declined. Moreover, the stalemate in the process and the failure of the leadership on both sides to keep the public informed about the dynamics and points of contention, coupled with the lack of improvement in Palestinians' living conditions, precipitated a new wave of violence.

The atmosphere of crisis strengthened the opposition to the Oslo Accords and exposed internal divisions and conflicts within both Palestinian and Israeli societies. These divisions, which became clearer following the signing of the Oslo Accords, involve questions of identity and community and contending views not only about the boundaries between Israel and Palestine and the relationship between them but also about the social and political character of each society. The sharp political divisions within Israeli society became evident in November 1995 following the assassination of Rabin by a fellow Jew who opposed Rabin's notion of peace.

But contrary to common perceptions, the Oslo Accords were not a peace treaty. Rather, they constituted an agenda for negotiations covering a five-year interim period, which was expected to lead to a permanent settlement based on UN Security Council Resolutions 242 and 338. The accords called for a transitional period during which Israel would gradually withdraw its troops from major Palestinian centers in the Occupied Territories, beginning with Gaza and Jericho (Aruri, 1995; Usher, 1995a). In May 1994, nearly five months behind schedule, following the signing of the Cairo agreement that was designed to ratify the Oslo Accords, the Israeli military began its redeployment as the Palestinian police began to move into the newly autonomous areas.

At the end of the 1990s, the Palestinians had full autonomy in 27 percent of the Occupied Territories (Area A; 6.6 percent of the territory of historical Palestine). In the West Bank, this translated into 3 percent of the total surface area, whereas in Gaza the PNA controlled 60 percent of the territory. In the West Bank villages (Area B), however, the PNA had only civil and police powers; Israel remained responsible for "internal security," the meaning of which was open to interpretation (see Map 6.2). Furthermore, because the towns and villages are mostly noncontiguous and Israel remained in command of the road network connecting them, all movement of goods and persons into and out of these enclaves as well as between them could be interdicted at will (Rabbani, 1996:4).

Further complicating the already delayed implementation of the Oslo Accords was the unexpected victory of the Likud Party, led by Netanyahu, in Israel's May 1996 elections. Netanyahu argued, and many analysts agreed, that his policies of settlement expansion and the "judaization" of East Jerusalem merely followed those set by earlier Labor governments. Nevertheless, the blunt and uncompromising manner in which Netanyahu carried out these policies resulted in a serious escalation of tensions between Israelis and Palestinians and a serious setback in, if not total collapse of, the peace process. The main disputes have revolved around two central issues: Jewish settlements and Jerusalem. Both of these issues, along with the questions of Palestinian refugees and final borders, were not addressed in the Oslo Accords but rather left to be discussed during final status negotiations, which were originally set to begin in September 1998 but had not started when the five-year Oslo transition period ended in May 1999.

The Al-Aqsa Intifada

The Al-Aqsa Intifada started on September 28, 2000, following a provocative visit by Likud leader Sharon, accompanied by hundreds of soldiers, to the Haram al-Sharif (Dome of the Rock) in Jerusalem, one of the holiest Muslim sites. Unlike the first intifada, which was by and large an unarmed

200

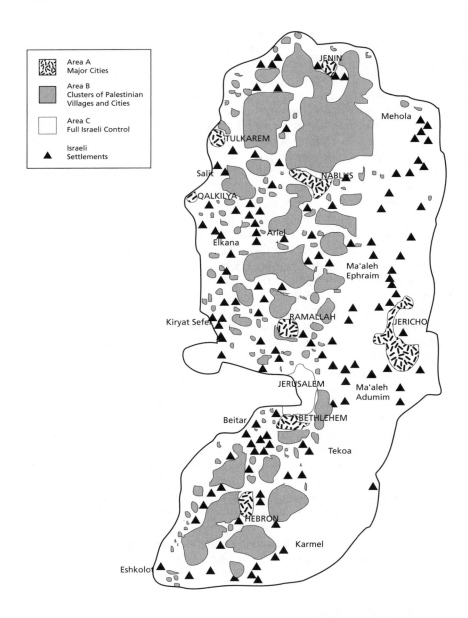

Map 6.2 The Oslo Accords: Areas A, B, and C Within the West Bank

popular revolt, Palestinian armed men led the Al-Aqsa Intifada right from the start. The Israeli military tried to suppress the movement with massive force. More than 7,000 Palestinians were reported injured in the first five weeks of the uprising, with many suffering injuries in the head and upper body (Reinhart, 2002). In addition to further restrict the free movement of Palestinians between the West Bank and the Gaza Strip and within towns and villages in the West Bank, the Israeli military gradually but systematically invaded areas that had been handed over to the Palestinian Authority (PA) as stipulated in the Oslo Accords. Moreover, Sharon started a political assassination campaign, targeting key leaders and activists of all Palestinian factions.

Palestinian militants responded with intensified shootings directed at Israeli settlements, especially around Jerusalem, and a growing number of suicide bombings targeted at Israeli cities and towns. Israeli forces and policymakers utilized these attacks as a pretext to launch massive retaliation operations into densely populated Palestinian areas in the West Bank and Gaza. The uneven nature of this violent confrontation is reflected in an ever-increasing death toll; as of September 2003, at least 2,468 Palestinians and 870 Israelis had been killed in this second intifada, a ratio of three Palestinians for each Israeli.

The terrorist attacks against the United States on September 11, 2001, had grave implications for the already deteriorating situation in the West Bank and Gaza Strip. Despite the fact that Palestinian leadership has continuously and unequivocally denounced the attacks and offered to help the United States in its efforts against terrorism, the coordination and cooperation between the US and Israeli governments have strengthened. Backed by the US administration, Sharon declared that Arafat was irrelevant, and that there would be no negotiation until he was removed or replaced by another leader. To materialize this objective, the Israeli army twice besieged Arafat's compound and destroyed it, leaving him with a single building and isolated from the international community.

Various leaders around the world criticized Israel's systematic humiliation of Arafat. Nevertheless, by June 2002, Arafat and the Palestinian leadership more generally were isolated and in serious crisis. The PA had lost all its security forces and its ability not only to control, but also to move from town to town. In addition, the economic situation reached an all-time low with unprecedented unemployment rates and the utter collapse of all economic development plans (Taraki, 2006). This crisis has contributed to the rising influence and support for Hamas and Islamic Jihad ideology in the Palestinian streets as well as for secular militant groups (Mansour, 2002; Abu-Nimer, 2003).

The November 2012 UN vote in support of Palestinian statehood was more than a symbolic gesture in support of Palestinians. The fact that most members supported the motion, despite attempts by Israel and the United States to block it, underscores the legitimacy of Palestinians' quest for self-determination and an independent state they can call home.

One Land, Two Peoples:
Central Issues and Points of Contention

As the previous section illustrates, the dynamics of the conflict, the range of solutions, the role of outside actors, and the political positions of both Palestinians and Jews have dramatically changed throughout the course of the conflict. At the same time, the central issues underlying the conflict have not been dramatically transformed. One such set of issues involves the competing claims of two national movements for the same piece of land.

The Israeli-Palestinian conflict has served as both the catalyst and the touchstone for the consolidation of particular notions of the national "imagined community" for Palestinians and for Israeli Jews. For Palestinians, the imagined community came to be seen as a future sovereign Palestinian state. Apart from differences concerning the territorial boundaries and the political and social character of their future state, there is a broad consensus among Palestinians that the principles of national self-determination and territorial sovereignty are inseparable and crucial to the survival of the Palestinian people. A consensus around the same principles has served as the basis for the Israeli Jewish imagined community. Although Jews realized their dream and established a Jewish state, this has come at the expense of Palestinians, whose desire to fuse national self-determination with territorial sovereignty remains unfulfilled. This turn of events has in many ways formed the basis for the present conflict.

The principles of national self-determination and territorial sovereignty underlie the early conflicts between Zionist settlers and the indigenous Palestinian population. The dynamics and intensity of the Israeli-Palestinian conflict and its significant military component over the years have contributed to the escalation of the conflict and reinforced sharp distinctions between "us" and "them." The establishment of the State of Israel further exposed the differences between Palestinian and Israeli nationalisms: first, the difference between institutionalized state nationalism and the nationalism of a liberation movement; and, second, the disparities in power relations between an occupying state and a population struggling to rid itself of that state's rule.

The emerging Jewish state has placed a special emphasis on its national security. For Palestinians, however, national liberation has emerged as the most important focus of their collective identity, especially following the Israeli occupation of the West Bank and Gaza Strip in 1967 and the emergence of the PLO as a vehicle of national aspirations. Within Israeli Jewish society, the constant invocation of Israel's security concerns has helped reinforce an overt and covert militarization of people's lives. But for Palestinians, the centrality of the conflict has manifested itself in the privileging of national liberation not only as the primary ideology of struggle against Israeli occupation, but also as the principal discourse that shapes certain ideas and ways of thinking about Palestinian identity and community.

National security and national liberation doctrines are similar in that they view the potency and unity of the nation as superior to issues raised by private citizens and various social groups within that nation. As a result of the primary emphases on national security and national liberation, different social and economic problems within both communities have been put on the back burners until the Israeli-Palestinian conflict is resolved. Nevertheless, the differences between Israeli Jewish and Palestinian nationalism, which are often overlooked, are far greater than the similarities. They involve fundamental differences in the history and social context of the two national movements and, most particularly, striking disparities of power and privilege between the two communities.

In order to formulate a solution to this long-standing conflict that would be acceptable to both Palestinians and Jews, one should first identify the central issues for each party. During this process, it is important to pay attention to the changes that occurred in the parties' framing of issues over the years as well as to similarities and differences in the parties' perceptions of central issues. The following is a preliminary list of some of the issues that analysts view as central to a just and lasting resolution of the conflict:

- Fixed, agreed-on borders between Israel and its neighbors.
- The assurance of mutual security for all states and peoples in the region.
- The status of Jerusalem.
- Jewish settlements in the West Bank and Gaza Strip.
- Compensation for Palestinians who were forced to leave their homes and property as a direct result of the Israeli-Palestinian conflict.
- The political, civil, and national status of Palestinians who live in Israel and hold Israeli citizenship.
- The economic viability of Israel, Palestine, and the other states in the region and the economic relations among them.
- The allocation of resources such as water among the states of the region.
- The role of the international community in peacekeeping, peacemaking, and peacebuilding.

These points are not listed in any particular order. In fact, if Palestinians and Israeli Jews were asked to prioritize them, they would most likely come up with very different lists. Moreover, many of these issues are interrelated, and some have been addressed at least partially within the framework of the Oslo Accords. Other issues, however, such as settlements, final borders, the fate of Palestinian refugees, and the status of Jerusalem, have been identified as topics to be discussed during final status negotiations.

On these particular issues, it is interesting to note the differences between the official Israeli and Palestinian positions. For Palestinians, these are the main issues presently underlying the Israeli-Palestinian conflict. Concerned (for good reason) that the process would break down before these issues could be discussed, Palestinians wanted to place these issues on the agenda from the start. Israel, however, preferred to defer the discussion of these important issues primarily because the resolution of any one of them would have been impossible without an Israeli concession. Although the decision to delay the discussion of these critical issues was presented to the parties as a compromise, a careful study of the Israeli position reveals that Israel, the more powerful party in the negotiations, was able to impose its will on the Palestinians with the help of a third party that wanted to keep the peace process on track.

These same issues and power dynamics continued to haunt the Israeli-Palestinian negotiators in their last round of direct negotiation in Camp David II. With the intensive and direct intervention of President Bill Clinton, who was in his last few months in office and under pressure to deliver a major political gain to seal his presidency and long involvement in the Israeli-Palestinian peace process, Barak offered the PA control over 95 percent of Palestinians in the West Bank and Gaza Strip. Palestinians rejected the offer, arguing that the proposed settlement would prevent the creation of a viable Palestinian state due to the lack of territorial contiguity and the fact that the West Bank was to be divided into three main sections by Israeli highways designed to connect Jewish settlements. For its part, Israel did not fully accept the terms put forth in the Clinton plan, although Arafat's reservations and rejection of Barak's offer overshadowed Israel's own numerous objections.

Another bone of contention involved the question of Palestinian refugees. According to Palestinian negotiators, the number of 1948 refugees who would be allowed to return was too low; Palestinian negotiators asked for 500,000 while the Israeli negotiators offered 25,000. Moreover, Barak's proposal did not grant sovereignty on the Haram al-Sharif area. Regardless of the details of the Camp David offer, as of mid-2003 it was clear that the same issues that had been postponed by the Oslo Accords in 1993 remained unresolved. Such an outcome is not surprising given that, by the time Arafat and Barak arrived at Camp David, the level of trust among Palestinian and Israeli leaders and their faith in reaching an agreement was far lower that the euphoria of the historical breakthrough in Oslo in 1993.

(Barak and Arafat did not meet face-to-face during any of the Camp David sessions.)

Regardless of when the next phase of negotiation occurs, there is little hope that these two populations will reach any sustainable and just resolution without addressing the root causes of the conflict. Among the most critical issues that must be addressed are the physical and psychological insecurity of Palestinians and Israelis, the indiscriminate killing of Israeli and Palestinian civilians, the lack of viable Palestinian statehood, the right of return for refugees, the economic deterioration (a 60 percent to 70 percent unemployment rate was estimated in Gaza during the second intifada), the massive collective punishment through curfews and closures, and the continued expansion of settlements.

Another point to keep in mind in examining changes that occurred in the parties' positions over time involves the question of political representation. More specifically, the changes occurred mostly in Israel's position, and they center mainly on Israel's willingness to finally accept the PLO as the legitimate representative of the Palestinian people. The negotiations that led to the signing of the Camp David Accords in 1978 did not treat the Palestinians as an autonomous party, nor did they acknowledge the PLO as their sole representative. At the time, many elected officials in Israel publicly denied the existence of a Palestinian people. This situation changed dramatically with the outbreak of the 1987 intifada. Yet until the summer of 1993, the Israeli government refused to negotiate with the PLO. This policy was particularly evident in the period preceding the Madrid Conference in 1992, when the Israeli government vetoed certain Palestinian delegates because of their suspected affiliation with the PLO. Moreover, the Israelis refused to accept an independent Palestinian delegation and insisted on a joint Jordanian-Palestinian delegation instead. According to many analysts, the Oslo Accords were signed because Israeli officials who took part in the secret meetings with PLO officials realized that, if Israel were serious about peace, it would have to negotiate directly with the PLO. Ironically, twenty years after Oslo, Israelis and Palestinians remained embroiled in a debate over who should participate in the negotiation process.

In the early stages of the second intifada in 2000, the Israeli government (backed by the United States) declared that it would not negotiate with the Palestinian leadership as long as Arafat was heading the PA. As a result, the Palestinians came under enormous international pressure to make amendments to their political system and introduce the position of a prime minister. The Palestinian leadership maintained that Sharon was not a serious partner for negotiation and had no political offer or agenda for resolution except the declaration that he would accept a Palestinian state on 42 percent of the territories. However, his policy on the ground was contrary to any intention to reach a peaceful resolution. Nevertheless, several Palestinian leaders, such as Mahmoud Abbas and Ahmad Qura'i, met with Sharon on various occasions during 2003. At the same time, Palestinian opposition groups and nongovernmental organizations (NGOs) continued to call for political and economic reforms and refused to accept Arafat's removal as Sharon's condition for negotiation.

The Road Map initiative was developed by the Quartet—the EU, UN, United States, and Russian Federation—to promote a resumption of negotiations, the implementation of a cease-fire, and reformation of the Palestinian political system (including the removal of Arafat from direct day-to-day governance) in a way that would be politically palatable to both parties. Under European and US influence, Arafat appointed Abbas, one of the architects of Oslo, to a newly created prime minister post in early 2003. After less than a year Abbas resigned, indicating that the unclear division of authority made his position untenable. These pressures have intensified significantly following the victory of Hamas in the 2006 elections.

In spite of completing these political revisions, the Palestinians continue to live under full Israeli reoccupation of the territories and without functioning authority. Israeli forces have now reoccupied the majority of the areas that they handed to the PA under the various terms of the Oslo Accords, including large parts of the Gaza Strip. The social welfare, health, education, and other basic needs of larger segments of Palestinian society services are in a state of crisis. This crisis, which fuels resistance, must be addressed in order to deescalate the present conflict (Taraki, 2006).

Finally, once the parties agree on a preliminary agenda and on who will be involved in the negotiations, they must address a set of important procedural issues: when, where, and for how long negotiations will take place; whether the process requires a third party to mediate issues; and, if so, who that party should be. Before the parties meet at the negotiation tables, delegates must study the issues, prepare position papers, and review past attempts to resolve the conflict. A careful analysis of past and present conflict resolution attempts, their success (or failure), and the ways in which they were perceived in both communities may inspire new thinking and creative ideas for the resolution of the conflict.

The Rocky Road to Peace: Past and Present Attempts to Resolve the Conflict

Since the turn of the twenty-first century, numerous attempts at resolution have been carried out separately and jointly by Palestinians, Jews, and various members of the international community. The following is a partial list of some of the major scenarios that have been proposed by various actors over the years:

- Two states for two people: a Palestinian state alongside Israel, in the West Bank and Gaza Strip.
- Greater Israel: a Jewish state that would annex the West Bank and Gaza Strip and "transfer" the Palestinian population to Jordan and other Arab countries.
- Greater Palestine: a Palestinian state on all the territory of historical Palestine, with no Israeli Jews except those whose families lived in Palestine before 1948.
- Greater Israel: a Jewish state in all the territory of historical Palestine with Palestinians as citizens.
- Greater Palestine: a Palestinian state in all the territory of historical Palestine with Israeli Jews as citizens.
- A partial autonomy, more or less according to the terms described in the Oslo Accords: Palestine controls the civic affairs and internal security in its cities and villages, and Israel administers external security and controls the land and natural resources.
- Return to the pre-Oslo situation: Israel continues to control the territories.
- A binational state on the land of Palestine/Israel.

It is important to distinguish between those attempts that have addressed primarily the needs and aspirations of one party to the conflict (Jews or Palestinians) and those that have sought to take into account the needs, aspirations, and preferred solutions of both Palestinians and Jews. According to some analysts, to come to terms with the contending resolution perspectives on the Israeli-Palestinian conflict, it may be useful to place them along a continuum bounded by the terms *exclusivist* on one end and *accommodationist* on the other (Vitalis, 1992:290). This continuum clearly reflects the dominant view, according to which the conflict stems from competing claims of two peoples to the exclusive right of national self-determination and sovereignty rights on the same piece of land. According to this view, the single-state solutions—whether Jewish or Palestinian—are exclusivist in nature since they undermine the other party's vision and claims.

There is a tendency, especially among scholars writing about resolution of the conflict, to view the transition from exclusivist scenarios to accommodationist ones as a combination of historical progression and rational choice. Thus, the Zionist state-building project in Palestine, which led to the establishment of the Jewish state in 1948 by completely undermining the existence of the indigenous Arab population, is often compared with the attempts in the 1950s and 1960s of Palestinians supported by Arab leaders to liberate their homeland.

According to this interpretation, with time and the impact of particular political developments, since both Israeli Jews and Palestinians concluded that their vision of an exclusive homeland was not likely to lead to peace, they gradually began to explore accommodationist scenarios. These scenarios reflected some willingness to compromise and acknowledge, although with many reservations, the other party's national aspirations and right to the land. This acknowledgment, which is particularly evident in such proposals as the two-state solution and the binational state, is praised in the literature as a "win-win solution" and presented as the best scenario for a peaceful resolution of the conflict (Kelman, 1982; Vitalis, 1992). However, such scenarios overlook the grave power differentials between Palestinians and the State of Israel, which are crucial to the understanding of the transition from exclusivist to accommodationist visions within both communities.

Another common continuum of analysis is that between violent and nonviolent attempts to resolve the conflict. Like the exclusivist-accommodationist categorization, this continuum has been inspired by a combination of rational choice theories with some historical analysis. Accordingly, over time, most Palestinians and Israeli Jews came to the conclusion that the conflict could not be resolved through military might and that diplomacy might be a better venue. Yet in most media accounts of the conflict, there has been a tendency to present Palestinians as more prone to violence and more reluctant to accept diplomatic solutions. This tendency also manifests itself in differential treatment of violence carried out by Palestinians, which is usually referred to as "terrorist attacks," whereas violence carried out by the State of Israel is said to be done in the name of "national security."

The debate over the use of suicide bombing campaigns carried out by Hamas and Islamic Jihad during the second intifada and the excessive use of the military and targeted assassinations by Israeli security forces further illustrates the impact of such differences in power relations. Many Palestinian leaders, including Arafat, have consistently criticized the use of suicide bombing. Those Palestinians who do not denounce the use of this tactic have consistently argued that the cycle of violence stems from the occupation itself. Furthermore, systematic research on the use of suicide bombing suggests a link between the Israeli leader's policies and the suicide bombings. More specifically, some argue that Sharon's policies have significantly contributed, as a matter of course and in some cases deliberately, to the persistence of suicide bombings (Niva, 2003).

As critical scholarship on terrorism has underscored, rather than blaming the underdog in a conflict for resorting to violent means, we must examine the conditions under which certain groups see no other alternative but violence to achieve their goal. By pursuing this line of thinking, we do not condone violence, but instead look beneath the surface for its root causes in an attempt to propose a more comprehensive and long-lasting solution (see Rubenstein, 1987). Thus, in the context of the Israeli-Palestinian conflict, as the PLO achieved legitimacy on the world stage and especially after it was recognized by Israel and the United States as the official representative of the Palestinian people, it appears to have gradually and willfully moved away from military struggle to pursue diplomatic means for the resolution of the conflict.

It is important to note that neither Palestinian nor Israeli collectivities are homogeneous; both communities have individuals and groups who still refuse to move away from exclusivist and militant solutions to the conflict. From a conflict resolution perspective, characterizing these people as simply "enemies of peace" and therefore suppressing their activities would be a mistake. Rather, we must examine the impetus behind the behavior of these individuals and groups and their contending solutions to the conflict.

What could further complicate the dynamics of the conflict and the prospects for its resolution is the role of outside parties, with their own agendas and definitions of peace. The United States has a long and complex history of vested economic and political involvement in the Middle East. Most US administrations agree that a resolution of the Israeli-Palestinian conflict is crucial to achieving a comprehensive peace in the Middle East. Peace is viewed as synonymous with stability, which is necessary for continued US hegemony in the region. To further this end, the United States has assumed the role of referee and principal negotiator.

Yet despite its self-portrayal and peacemaking initiatives, the United States hardly fits the role of an impartial third party. In fact, some analysts have argued that, in the Middle East as in many other parts of the world, the United States has acted more as a cobelligerent than as a peacemaker. This has been the case especially after September 11, 2001 (Abu-Nimer, 2003). As Israel's chief ally and protector, the United States was simply unable to discharge its self-assigned mission as a catalyst for peace; the tensions between such roles as mediator and those of Israel's chief diplomatic backer, bankroller, and military supplier have surfaced quite often (Aruri, 1995: 19–21). Moreover, due to the largely unchallenged US insistence that it is the only party that can act as a mediator between Palestinians and Israeli Jews, the services of other potential third parties have been ignored or relegated to backstage initiatives. Even in the Quartet, the United States remains the overwhelmingly dominant player. This trend has resulted in the marginalization of the United Nations as a potential peacemaker and in the abandonment of the once popular idea of convening a UN-sponsored international peace conference (Bennis, 1996:211–232).

When discussing past and present attempts to resolve the conflict, most media accounts, like much of scholarly literature on the conflict, tend to focus on the activities of elected officials, thus overlooking attempts by citizens on both sides of the political divide to bring about a peaceful resolution to the conflict. Some scholars have distinguished between peace-from-above and peace-from-below, or top-down and bottom-up conflict resolution attempts (Falk, 1994:189; Sharoni, 1996). In the context of the Israeli-Palestinian conflict, top-down conflict resolution takes place primarily around negotiation tables, usually outside the region, and is often characterized by attempts to apply generic, universal models of conflict resolution. Bottom-up peace initiatives, however, tend to emerge from the inside, from within Palestinian and Israeli societies and struggles. According to those who emphasize bottom-up solutions, social movements, protest, and grassroots activism are viewed as crucial venues for peacemaking and conflict resolution (Sharoni, 1996).

Indeed, long before the much-celebrated handshake between Arafat and Rabin, Palestinians and Israelis at the grassroots level had launched both separate and collaborative initiatives designed to bring about a just and lasting solution to the conflict. Despite their absence from the negotiation table, Palestinian and Israeli Jewish women have played a significant role in the struggle to end the Israeli occupation of the West Bank and Gaza Strip (Hiltermann, 1991; Strum, 1992; Sharoni, 1995a; Emmett, 1996). Other examples of conflict resolution initiatives at the grassroots level include such groups as Israeli-Palestinian Physicians for Human Rights,

Israeli peace activists like Uri Avnery of Gush Shalom play an important, but often ignored, role in promoting strategies for conflict resolution.

which provides medical attention and services to Palestinians in need, and joint educational projects and dialogue groups designed to counter stereotypes and fear and establish conditions for coexistence between Palestinians and Israeli Jews (Abu-Nimer, 1993; Hurwitz, 1992; Fernea and Hocking, 1992; Rosenwasser, 1992; Kaminer, 1996).

Such activities even continued during the second intifada, although on a much smaller scale than during the first uprising. The majority of the Israeli peace groups associated with the Zionist left and center stopped their joint activities and peace protests with the intensified Israeli campaign in the West Bank and Gaza Strip and with the suicide bombings inside Israel. Besieged by Sharon's policy and the suicide bombings, only a few groups, such as Taayush, Rabbis for Human Rights, the Israeli Committee Against House Demolitions, and certain local women's initiatives, remained active. On the Palestinian side, in response to the lack of condemnation of the Israeli military campaign against the PA, most of the NGOs responded to direct instructions from the PA in November 2000 and suspended all contacts with their Israeli counterparts. However, the PA and the NGOs resumed their cooperation and joint work in the late summer of 2001. In early 2003, the Israeli peace movement and joint Israeli-Palestinian cooperation for peace began to increase again. More demonstrations and protests were staged in Israeli cities and towns and Israeli-Palestinian meetings again occurred, both inside and outside the Middle East (Abu-Nimer, 2003).

The emergence of the BDS movement and the rise in international solidarity with Palestinians have reignited grassroots peace initiatives in Israel and in Palestine. For Palestinian activists, the BDS movement opened up space for new modes of organizing, diverse coalitions, and campaigns, including some featuring constituencies and messages that have been previously relegated to the margins of the political scene in the region. An interesting example of this new mode of organizing can be found in the establishment and work of Palestinian Queers for BDS (PQBDS), which was launched in response to the Palestinian civil society call for Boycott, Divestment, and Sanctions against Israel. In June 2010, PQBDS issued a call to queer activists around the world, explicitly articulating connections between their oppression as members of the Gay Lesbian Bisexual Transgender (GLBT) community and as Palestinians. Highlighting the proud history of the queer movement worldwide, which has joined numerous global sociopolitical struggles against manifestations of oppression, imperialism, injustice, and discrimination around the world, PQBDS urged GLBT activists around the world to address the connections between their oppression as a sexual minority and the oppression of Palestinians (Sharoni, 2012).

In Israel, the Coalition of Women for Peace (CWP), an umbrella organization of several women's peace groups, responded to the Palestinian call for Boycott, Divestment, and Sanctions by initiating a unique research project under the title: "Who Profits from the Occupation?" Starting with the premise that alongside various political, religious, and national interests, the Israeli occupation of the West Bank, Gaza, and Golan Heights is also fueled by corporate interests, the project works to expose companies and corporations that profit from the occupation (Sharoni, 2012).

These initiatives clearly demonstrate that the expertise for resolving conflicts peacefully does not reside solely with official government personnel or procedures. Rather, citizens and groups from a variety of backgrounds and with a variety of skills can play an important role in peacemaking and conflict resolution processes. Moreover, there is a growing realization among conflict resolution experts and ordinary citizens alike that formal, government-to-government official interactions between instructed representatives of sovereign nations are not sufficient to secure international cooperation or resolve deep-rooted conflicts. Even if the parties to the conflict sign a peace agreement, its successful implementation depends on the support of grassroots constituencies on both sides of the political divide (Sharoni, 1996). In fact, one of the major shortcomings of the Oslo Accords was in the failure of both Palestinian and Israeli Jewish officials to draw on the experience and expertise of peace and community activists on both sides of the Israeli-Palestinian divide. This rupture in the relationship between official and unofficial peacemakers may have its roots in different definitions of peace that inform the groups' practices and affect their relations with one another.

One more way to examine various peace and conflict resolution initiatives is by focusing on the definition of peace that informs them. One of the most popular distinctions in the field of peace and conflict resolution studies is that between negative peace and positive peace (Barash, 1991:529–590). *Negative peace* is defined merely as the absence of war or direct violence whereas *positive peace* requires the eradication of all forms of violence, including structural violence, and a transformation of society grounded in the principles of equality, social justice, and nonviolence. In the case of the Israeli-Palestinian conflict, it seems that official representatives of the two collectivities viewed peace mostly as the absence of war and direct violence (negative peace) whereas grassroots activists within both communities envisioned peace as a transformative process grounded in the presence of justice (positive peace). The advantage of this distinction is that it enables us to come to terms with competing sets of values, experiences, and political discourses that inform various definitions of peace.

For example, peace has been defined and envisioned differently by Israeli Jews and Palestinians both before and after the signing of the Oslo Accords. Peace for Jews has primarily meant peace with security, although since the signing of the Oslo Accords, this formulation has been used interchangeably with terms such as *peace and stability* and *peace and prosperity.*

For Palestinians, however, references to peace have almost always been accompanied by invocation of such terms as *justice, equality, liberation,* and *self-determination* (Sharoni, 1995b:400–401). The significant differences between them notwithstanding, these definitions are not mutually exclusive, but rather interdependent. Both the two-state solution and the binational state option can accommodate these contending visions of peace.

The main challenge, however, is not only for each collectivity to recognize the validity of the other party's vision. Because of the asymmetrical nature of the conflict, the fulfillment of these interdependent visions appears to depend on the willingness of the stronger party to the conflict, the Israeli government, to take the first step and recognize the Palestinians' right of self-determination. To win the support of its electorate for such an act, the Israeli government must introduce it not as a unilateral concession, but rather as an essential step toward long-lasting peace in the region. In accepting the two-state solution and recognizing Israel's right to exist, Palestinians have demonstrated their realization that the fulfillment of their national aspirations depends on Israel's sense of security. It is imperative now that Israeli Jews understand and publicly acknowledge that their quest for security, stability, and prosperity will not materialize as long as Palestinians' quest for justice, equality, and national self-determination remains unfulfilled.

Conclusion

In the 1990s, the Palestinian leadership and the Israeli government moved away from exclusivist military solutions to the conflict to more accommodationist diplomatic ones; however, this shift did not last. The two national collectivities continue to hold very different definitions of peace, informed to a great extent by the power disparities between them that the Oslo Accords failed to address. This asymmetry in power relations has been reinforced by the failure of past and present conflict resolution attempts to successfully address the two central issues at the heart of the Palestinians' struggle—national self-determination and territorial sovereignty. Most Palestinians feel that they have already made a serious concession by giving up the dream to reclaim historical Palestine and instead accepting the two-state formula; that is, a Palestinian state in the West Bank and Gaza Strip, alongside Israel.

The implementation of the two-state solution, however, depends on a complete Israeli withdrawal from the territories that it occupied in 1967 in violation of international law. So far, the Israeli government has refused to comply and return to the pre-1967 borders. The Oslo Accords offered a temporary cover-up of the situation by highlighting Israel's willingness to negotiate directly with the PLO and grant Palestinians limited autonomy to govern their internal affairs.

With the total collapse of the Oslo Accords, Israel remains in control of most of the contested land, and Jewish settlements continue to expand. As a result, Palestinians across the West Bank and Gaza Strip, who have seen little improvement in their daily lives since the signing of the Oslo Accords in 1993, are growing more and more impatient. Under the pretext of safeguarding its national security, the Israeli government has continued to engage in assassination of Palestinian leaders and unprovoked attacks on centers of Palestinian population. The building of the omnipresent separation wall is the latest chapter in Israel's unilateral actions.[1] Israel has continued to use its national security, which has been narrowly defined and in zero-sum terms, as a precondition for peace. In doing so, it has failed to recognize that Israelis will not be secure until Palestinians fulfill their national aspirations through a political solution they deem just (Carter, 2006).

Rather than subsume alternative visions of what peace might look like under the narrow formulations of those presently in power, we ought to treat more seriously the divergent positions of the people—Palestinians and Israeli Jews—whose lives have been entangled in the conflict. Such voices and perspectives often point out that the Israeli-Palestinian conflict is more than simply an intractable territorial dispute between two national collectivities; it also involves contending visions concerning the resolution of the conflict and the future of the Middle East that have been the subject of

Palestinians line up to cross through the separation wall to reach Jerusalem during Ramadan.

heated political debates and contestations within both Palestinian and Israeli Jewish communities.

Finally, as citizens of the Middle East and as conflict resolution scholars, we would like to voice our skepticism regarding conflict resolution initiatives carried out by such interested third parties as the United States or a myriad of conflict resolution experts. Far from being neutral or impartial facilitators, these outside parties, whose intentions are sometimes noble, tend to marginalize or altogether ignore the hopes and fears of ordinary people in the region while imposing their own conflict resolution frameworks and visions of peace. In contrast, we believe that Palestinians and Israeli Jews, if not their present leaders, hold the key to a just and lasting resolution of the conflict. The role of Middle Eastern scholars and conflict resolution experts, or the international community more generally, is not to bring peace to the Middle East, but rather to empower and support those people in the region who have long been involved in the elusive search for peace.

The growing number of international initiatives in solidarity with Palestinians has empowered local activists and movements like Palestinian Queers for BDS and the Coalition of Women for Peace to launch creative campaigns to transform the conflict. Rooted in an understanding of multiple and intersecting oppressions as the basis for cross-community and transnational solidarity, these campaigns provide a coherent discourse, and a more radical platform for action. Indeed, the BDS movement has provided nonstate actors in Palestine, Israel, and worldwide with a clear vision and manifold opportunities to mobilize the international community to confront Israeli apartheid. However, it appears highly unlikely that Israel would join the efforts to bring about a just and lasting resolution of the conflict without pressure from such powerful states and entities like the United States, the European Union, and the United Nations.

Note

1. While Israel describes the intrusive barrier as a fence, the structure is a massive wall in all but a few sparsely populated areas. For the Palestinians, who have had their communities divided or isolated and their land seized for construction of the wall, the structure might more aptly be described as an apartheid wall.

Bibliography

Abdo, Nahla. 1992. "Racism, Zionism, and the Palestinian Working Class, 1920–1947." *Studies in Political Economy* 37, no. 2:59–93.

Abu-Lughod, Ibrahim (ed.). 1982. *Palestinian Rights: Affirmation and Denial*. Wilmette, IL: Medina Press.

Abu-Lughod, Janet. 1987. "The Demographic Transformation of Palestine." Pp. 139–164 in Ibrahim Abu-Lughod (ed.), *The Transformation of Palestine*. Evanston: Northwestern University Press.

Abu-Nimer, Mohammed. 1993. "Conflict Resolution Between Arabs and Jews in Israel: A Study of Six Intervention Models." PhD diss. Fairfax, VA: George Mason University.

———. 2003. "September 11 and Palestinian Reaction: No Win." Pp. 135–151 in Rashied Omar (ed.), *Multiple Voices: Opportunities and Challenges for Islamic Peacebuilding After September 11*. Notre Dame: Notre Dame University Press.

Aburish, Said. 1998. *Arafat: From Defender to Dictator*. New York: Bloomsbury.

Alcalay, Ammiel. 1993. *After Jews and Arabs: Remaking Levantine Culture*. Minneapolis: University of Minnesota Press.

Andoni, Lamis. 1991. "The PLO at the Crossroads." *Journal of Palestine Studies* 81, no. 2:54–65.

Aruri, Naseer. 1995. *The Obstruction of Peace: The US, Israel, and the Palestinians*. Monroe, ME: Common Courage Press.

Ashrawi, Hanan Mikhail. 1991. "The Other Occupation: The Palestinian Response." Pp. 191–198 in Phyllis Bennis and Michel Moushabeck (eds.), *Beyond the Storm: A Gulf Crisis Reader*. Brooklyn: Olive Branch Press.

Barash, David. 1991. *Introduction to Peace Studies*. Belmont, CA: Wadsworth.

Barghouti, Omar. 2006. "The Israeli Elections." *Z Magazine*. www.zmag.org.

Bar-On, Mordechi. 1985. *Peace Now: The Portrait of a Movement*. In Hebrew. Tel Aviv: Hakibbutz Hameuchad.

Baroud, Ramzy. 2006. *The Second Palestinian Intifada: A Chronicle of a People's Struggle*. London: Pluto.

Bennis, Phyllis. 1996. *Calling the Shots: How Washington Dominates Today's UN*. Brooklyn: Olive Branch Press.

Bennis, Phyllis, and Michel Moushabeck (eds.). 1991. *Beyond the Storm: A Gulf Crisis Reader*. Brooklyn: Olive Branch Press.

Brynen, Rex (ed.). 1991. *Echoes of the Intifada: Regional Repercussions of the Palestinian-Israeli Conflict*. Boulder: Westview Press.

Carter, Jimmy. 2006. *Palestine: Peace Not Apartheid*. New York: Simon & Schuster.

Chamberlin, Thomas. 2012. *The Global Offensive: The United States, the Palestine Liberation and the Making of the Post–Cold War Order*. Oxford: Oxford University Press.

Cobban, Helena. 1984. *The Palestinian Liberation Organization: People, Power, and Politics*. Cambridge: Cambridge University Press.

Davis, Ury. 1986. "Israel's Zionist Society: Consequences for Internal Opposition and the Necessity for External Intervention." Pp. 176–201 in Ejaz Eaford (ed.), *Judaism or Zionism: What Difference for the Middle East?* London: Zed Books.

Dunsky, Marda. 2008. *Pens and Swords: How the American Mainstream Media Report the Israeli-Palestinian Conflict*. New York: Columbia University Press.

Emmett, Ayala. 1996. *Our Sisters' Promised Land: Women, Politics, and Israeli-Palestinian Coexistence*. Ann Arbor: University of Michigan Press.

Evron, Boas. 1995. *Jewish State or Israeli Nation?* Bloomington: Indiana University Press.

Falk, Richard. 1994. "World Order Conceptions and the Peace Process in the Middle East." Pp. 189–196 in Elise Boulding (ed.), *Building Peace in the Middle East: Challenges for States and Civil Society*. Boulder: Lynne Rienner.

Fernea, Elizabeth Warnock, and Mary Evelyn Hocking (eds.). 1992. *The Struggle for Peace: Israelis and Palestinians*. Austin: University of Texas Press.

Finkelstein, Norman. 1995. *Image and Reality of the Israel-Palestine Conflict*. London: Verso.

Flapan, Simha. 1987. *The Birth of Israel: Myths and Realities*. New York: Pantheon Books.

Friel, Howard, and Richard Falk. 2004. *The Record of the Paper: How the New York Times Misreports US Foreign Policy*. London: Verso.

Gerner, Deborah J. 1990. "Evolution of the Palestinian Uprising." *International Journal of Group Tensions* 20, no. 3:233–265.

———. 1991. "Palestinians, Israelis, and the *Intifada*: The Third Year and Beyond." *Arab Studies Quarterly* 13, no. 3–4:19–60.

———. 1992. "The Arab-Israeli Conflict." Pp. 361–382 in Peter J. Schraeder (ed.), *Intervention in the 1990s: US Foreign Policy in the Third World*. Boulder: Lynne Rienner.

———. 1994. *One Land, Two Peoples: The Conflict over Palestine*. 2nd ed. Boulder: Westview Press.

Grayzel, Solomon. 1968. *A History of the Jews*. New York: New American Library.

Greenstein, Ran. 1995. *Genealogies of Conflict: Class, Identity, and State in Palestine/Israel and South Africa*. Hanover, NH: Wesleyan University Press.

Gunning, Jeroen. 2008. *Hamas in Politics: Democracy, Religion, Violence*. New York: Columbia University Press.

Guyatt, Nicholas. 1998. *The Absence of Peace: Understanding the Israeli-Palestinian Conflict*. London: Zed Books.

Haddad, Bassam (ed.). 2012. *The Dawn of the Arab Spring: End of an Old Order?* London: Pluto Press.

Haddad, Toufic. 2006. January 31. "The Hamas Victory: Green Dawn, Red Dusk?" *Electronic Intifada*. http://electronicintifada.net/v2/article4434.shtml.

Hajjar, Lisa, and Joel Beinin. 1990. *Palestine and Israel: A Primer*. Washington, DC: Middle East Research and Information Project.

Al-Haq. 1988. "Repression of Education." Pp. 419–448 in Al-Haq (ed.), *Punishing a Nation: Human Rights Violations During the Palestinian Uprising*. Ramallah, West Bank: Al-Haq.

Heller, Mark, and Sari Nusseibeh. 1991. *No Trumpets, No Drums: A Two-State Settlement of the Israeli-Palestinian Conflict*. New York: Hill & Wang.

Herzberg, Arthur (ed.). 1962. *The Zionist Idea: A Historical Analysis and Reader*. New York: Doubleday.

Hiltermann, Joost. 1990. "Work in Action: The Role of the Working Class in the Uprising." Pp. 143–158 in Jamal Nassar and Roger Heacock (eds.), *Intifada: Palestine at the Crossroads*. New York: Praeger.

———. 1991. *Behind the Intifada: Labor and Women's Movements in the Occupied Territories*. Princeton: Princeton University Press.

Hiro, Dilip. 1992. *Desert Shield to Desert Storm: The Second Gulf War*. London: HarperCollins.

———. 1999. *Sharing the Promised Land: A Tale of Israelis and Palestinians*. Brooklyn: Olive Branch Press.

Hirst, David. 1984. *The Gun and the Olive Branch: The Roots of Violence in the Middle East*. 2nd ed. London: Faber & Faber.

Hunter, Robert. 1991. *The Palestinian Uprising*. Berkeley: University of California Press.

Hurwitz, Deena (ed.). 1992. *Walking the Red Line: Israelis in Search of Justice for Palestine*. Philadelphia: New Society.

Jad, Islah. 1990. "From Salons to the Popular Committees: Palestinian Women 1919–1989." Pp. 125–142 in Jamal Nassar and Roger Heacock (eds.), *Intifada: Palestine at the Crossroads*. New York: Praeger.

Jones, Clive, and Ami Pedahzur (eds.). 2005. *Between Terrorism and Civil War: The Al-Aqsa Intifada*. New York: Routledge.

Kaminer, Reuven. 1996. *The Politics of Protest: The Israeli Peace Movement and the Intifada*. Sussex: Academic Press.

Kelman, Herbert C. 1982. "Creating the Conditions for Israeli-Palestinian Negotiations." *Journal of Conflict Resolution* 26, no. 1 (January):39–75.

Khalidi, Walid. 1971. *From Haven to Conquest: Readings in Zionism and the Palestine Problem Until 1948*. Beirut: Institute for Palestine Studies.

Kimmerling, Baruch. 1983. *Zionism and Territory: The Socio-Territorial Dimensions of Zionist Politics*. Berkeley: University of California Press.

———. 2010. *Clash of Identities: Explorations in Israeli and Palestinian Societies*. New York: Columbia University Press.

Kimmerling, Baruch, and Joel Migdal. 1993. *Palestinians: The Making of a People*. New York: Macmillan.

Legrain, Jean-François. 1990. "The Islamic Movement and the Intifada." Pp. 175–189 in Jamal Nassar and Roger Heacock (eds.), *Intifada: Palestine at the Crossroads*. New York: Praeger.

Lesch, Ann M., and Mark Tessler (eds.). 1989. *Israel, Egypt, and the Palestinians: From Camp David to the Intifada*. Bloomington: Indiana University Press.

Levy, Gideon. 2006. March 26. "One Racist Nation." *Haaretz*. http://rense.com.

———. 2010. *The Punishment of Gaza*. London: Verso.

Lockman, Zachary, and Joel Beinin (eds.). 1989. *Intifada: The Palestinian Uprising Against Israeli Occupation*. Boston: South End Press.

Lustick, Ian. 1980. *Arabs in the Jewish State: Israel's Control of a National Minority*. Austin: University of Texas Press.

———. 1993. *Unsettled States, Disputed Lands: Britain and Ireland, France and Algeria, Israel and the West Bank and Gaza*. Ithaca: Cornell University Press.

Makdisi, Saree. 2006. March 31. "3 Views of the Israeli Election: The Real Winner in Israel." *San Francisco Chronicle*. www.sfgate.com.

Makovsky, David. 1996. *Making Peace With the PLO: The Rabin Government's Road to the Oslo Accord*. Washington, DC: Washington Institute for Near East Policy.

Mansour, Camille. 2002. "The Impact of 11 September on the Israeli-Palestinian Conflict." *Journal of Palestine Studies* 31, no. 2:5–18.

Milton-Edwards, Beverley. 1999. *Islamic Politics in Palestine*. New York: I. B. Tauris.

Mishal, Sahul, and Avraham Sela. 2006. *The Palestinian Hamas: Vision, Violence, and Coexistence*. New York: Columbia University Press.

Morris, Benny. 1988. *The Birth of the Palestinian Refugee Problem, 1947–1949*. Cambridge: Cambridge University Press.

———. 1990. *1948 and After: Israel and the Palestinians*. Oxford: Oxford University Press.

Moses, Rafael. 1990. "Self, Self-View, and Identity." Pp. 47–55 in *The Psychodynamics of International Relationships*. Vol. 1. Lexington, MA: Lexington Books.

Murray, Eoin. 2006. January 26. "Palestinian Elections: Forcing the West to Awake to the Voices of the People." *Live from Palestine*. http://electronicintifada.net.

Muslih, Muhammad. 1992. "History of the Israeli-Palestinian Conflict." Pp. 62–79 in Elizabeth Warnock Fernea and Mary Evelyn Hocking (eds.), *The Struggle for Peace: Israelis and Palestinians*. Austin: University of Texas Press.

Nakhleh, Emile (ed.). 1980. *A Palestinian Agenda for the West Bank and Gaza*. Washington, DC: American Enterprise Institute.

Nakhleh, Khalil, and Elia Zureik (eds.). 1980. *The Sociology of the Palestinians.* New York: St. Martin's Press.

Nassar, Jamal R. 1991. *The Palestine Liberation Organization: From Armed Struggle to the Declaration of Independence.* New York: Praeger.

Nassar, Jamal, and Roger Heacock (eds.). 1991. *Intifada: Palestine at the Crossroads.* New York: Praeger.

Nasser, Ilham, Lawrence N. Berlin, and Shelley Wong (eds.). 2011. *Examining Education, Media, and Dialogue Under Occupation: The Case of Palestine and Israel.* London: Multilingual Matters.

Niva, Steve. 2003. February 27–March 5, 2003. "A Predictable Cycle of Violence." *Al-Ahram Weekly,* no. 627. http://weekly.ahram.org.eg.

Pappe, Ilan. 2001. *The Making of the Arab-Israeli Conflict 1847–1951.* New York: I. B. Tauris.

Parkes, James. 1964. *A History of the Jewish People.* Baltimore: Penguin Books.

Parsons, Nigel. 2005. *The Politics of the Palestinian Authority: From Oslo to Al-Aqsa.* New York: Routledge.

Perez, Don. 1990. *Intifada: The Palestinian Uprising.* Boulder: Westview Press.

Perlman, Wendy (ed.). 2003. *Occupied Voices: Stories of Everyday Life from the Second Intifada.* New York: Thunder's Mouth Press; Nation Books.

Quigley, John. 1990. *Palestine and Israel: A Challenge to Justice.* Durham: Duke University Press.

Rabbani, Mouin. 1996. "Palestinian Authority, Israeli Rule: From Transitional to Permanent Arrangement." *Middle East Report,* no. 201 (October–December): 2–6, 22.

Reich, Bernard. 1985. *Israel: Land of Tradition and Conflict.* Boulder: Westview Press.

Reinhart, Tanya. 2002. *Israel/Palestine: How to End the War of 1948.* New York: Seven Stories Press.

Rekass, Elie. 1989. "The Israeli Arabs and the Arabs of the West Bank and Gaza: Political Affinity and National Solidarity." *Asian and African Studies* 23, nos. 2–3:119–154.

Rosenwasser, Penny. 1992. *Voices from a "Promised Land": Palestinian and Israeli Peace Activists Speak Their Hearts.* Willimantic, CT: Curbstone Press.

Rothman, Jay. 1992. *From Conflict to Cooperation: Resolving Ethnic Conflict and Regional Conflict.* Newbury Park, CA: Sage.

Rougier, Bernard. 2007. *Everyday Jihad: The Rise of Militant Islam Among Palestinians in Lebanon.* Cambridge: Harvard University Press.

Rouhana, Nadim. 1989. "The Political Transformation of the Palestinians in Israel: From Acquiescence to Challenge." *Journal of Palestine Studies* 79, no. 3:38–59.

Roy, Sara. 2010. March 1. "Gaza: Treading on Shards," *The Nation.* http://www.the nation.com.

Rubenstein, Richard. 1987. *Alchemists of Revolution: Terrorism in the Modern World.* New York: Basic Books.

Sachar, Abram Leon. 1964. *A History of the Jews.* New York: Alfred A. Knopf.

Said, Edward. 1980. *The Question of Palestine.* New York: Vintage Books.

Said, Edward, Ibrahim Abu-Lughod, Janet Abu-Lughod, Muhammad Hallaj, and Elia Zureik. 1990. *A Profile of the Palestinian People.* Chicago: Palestine Human Rights Campaign.

Saunders, Harold. 1985. *The Other Walls: The Politics of the Arab-Israeli Peace Process.* Washington, DC: American Enterprise Institute for Public Policy Research.

Segal, Jerome. 1989. *Creating the Palestinian State: A Strategy for Peace*. Chicago: Lawrence Hill Books.

Schiff, Ze'ev. 1990. *Intifada: The Palestinian Uprising—Israel's Third Front*. New York: Simon & Schuster.

Schiff, Ze'ev, and Ehud Ya'ari. 1984. *Israel's Lebanon War*. New York: Simon & Schuster.

Shahak, Israel. 1995. *Jewish History, Jewish Religion: The Weight of Three Thousand Years*. London: Pluto Press.

Shapira, Anita. 1992. *Land and Power: The Zionist Resort to Force, 1881–1948*. New York: Oxford University Press.

Sharoni, Simona. 1995a. *Gender and the Israeli-Palestinian Conflict: The Politics of Women's Resistance*. Syracuse: Syracuse University Press.

———. 1995b. "Peace as Identity Crisis." *Peace Review* 7, nos. 3–4:399–407.

———. 1996. "Conflict Resolution and Peacemaking from the Bottom Up: The Roles of Social Movements and People's Diplomacy." Paper prepared for the fourth seminar of the International University of People's Institutions for Peace, August, Rovereto, Italy.

———. 2012. "Gender and Conflict Transformation in Israel/Palestine." *Journal of International Women's Studies* 13, no. 4:113–128.

Shohat, Ella. 1988. "Sephardim in Israel: Zionism from the Standpoint of Its Jewish Victims." *Social Text* 19, no. 10:1–35.

Sifry, Micah, and Christopher Cerf (eds.). 1991. *The Gulf War Reader*. New York: Times Books; Random House.

Smooha, Sammy. 1989. *Arabs and Jews in Israel*, vol. 1: *Conflicting and Shared Attitudes in a Divided Society*. Boulder: Westview Press.

———. 1992. *Arabs and Jews in Israel*, vol. 2: *Change and Continuity in Mutual Tolerance*. Boulder: Westview Press.

Strum, Philippa. 1992. *The Women Are Marching: The Second Sex and the Palestinian Revolution*. New York: Lawrence Hill Books.

Suleiman, Camelia. 2011. *Language and Identity in the Israeli-Palestinian Conflict: The Politics of Self-Perception in the Middle East*. New York: I. B. Tauris.

Suleiman, Michael (ed.). 1995. *US Policy in Palestine: From Wilson to Clinton*. Normal, IL: Arab-American University Graduates Press.

Swirski, Shlomo. 1989. *Israel: The Oriental Majority*. London: Zed Books.

Tamari, Salim. 1980. "The Palestinians in the West Bank and Gaza Strip: The Sociology of Dependency." Pp. 84–111 in Khalil Nakhleh and Elia Zureik (eds.), *The Sociology of the Palestinians*. New York: St. Martin's Press.

Tamimi, Azzam. 2006. *Hamas: A History from Within*. New York: Interlink Books.

Taraki, Lisa. 1989. "The Islamic Resistance Movement in the Palestinian Uprising." Pp. 171–177 in Zachary Lockman and Joel Beinin (eds.), *Intifada: The Palestinian Uprising Against Israeli Occupation*. Boston: South End Press; Middle East Research and Information Project.

——— (ed.). 2006. *Living Palestine: Family, Survival, Resistance, and Mobility Under Occupation*. Syracuse: Syracuse University Press.

Tessler, Mark. 1994. *A History of the Israeli-Palestinian Conflict*. Bloomington: Indiana University Press.

Thomas, Baylis. 1999. *How Israel Was Won: A Concise History of the Arab-Israeli Conflict*. Lanham, MD: Lexington Books.

Usher, Graham. 1995a. *Palestine in Crisis: The Struggle for Peace and Political Independence After Oslo*. East Haven, CT: Pluto Press in association with the Transnational Institute and the Middle East Research and Information Project.

————. 1995b. "What Kind of Nation? The Rise of Hamas in the Occupied Territories." *Race and Class* 37, no. 2:65–80.

Vitalis, Robert. 1992. "The Palestinian-Israeli Conflict: Options and Scenarios for Peace." Pp. 285–313 in Elizabeth Warnock Fernea and Evelyn Hocking (eds.), *The Struggle for Peace: Israelis and Palestinians*. Austin: University of Texas Press.

Volkan, Vamik. 1990. "An Overview of Psychological Concepts Pertinent to Interethnic and/or International Relationships." Pp. 31–46 in Vamik D. Volkan, Demetrios A. Julius, and Joseph V. Montville (eds.), *The Psychodynamics of International Relationships*. Vol. 1. Lexington, MA: Lexington Books.

Wolfsfeld, Gadi. 1988. *The Politics of Provocation: Participation in Protest in Israel*. Albany: SUNY Press.

Yahya, Adil. 1991. "The Role of the Refugee Camps." Pp. 91–106 in Jamal Nassar and Roger Heacock (eds.), *Intifada: Palestine at the Crossroads*. New York: Praeger.

Zilka, Avraham. 1992. "History of the Israeli-Palestinian Conflict." Pp. 7–61 in Elizabeth Warnock Fernea and Mary Evelyn Hocking (eds.), *The Struggle for Peace: Israelis and Palestinians*. Austin: University of Texas Press.

Zunes, Steve. 1994. "Zionism, Anti-Semitism, and Imperialism." *Peace Review* 6, no. 1:41–49.

Zureik, Elia. 1979. *The Palestinians in Israel: A Study in Internal Colonialism*. London: Routledge & Kegan Paul.

7

The Economies of the Middle East

Agnieszka Paczynska

The Middle East has been at the crossroads of international trade for centuries. As early as the second century BCE, the Silk Route connected Europe, the Mediterranean, Central Asia, and China and carried silk, spices, silver, textiles, and other commodities. By the eighteenth century, however, as Europe's trade grew, the Middle East became largely peripheral to the global trading system, although it continued to export silk, wools, coffee, and cereals. In the twentieth century, the Middle East and North Africa were once again geopolitically important due to having the world's largest petroleum reserves.

By the end of the twentieth century, as world trade and capital movements grew at unprecedented rates and new forms of production increased global economic interdependence, the Middle East nevertheless remained poorly integrated into these new trading, investment, and production networks. And despite the wealth generated by oil exports and a long history of foreign economic assistance, many of the region's peoples remained impoverished.

In fact, one of the striking features of the region is the stark contrast between socioeconomic classes within and among countries. The Middle East is among the most inequitable regions of the world. It is home to societies with some of the highest per capita incomes as well as some of the world's lowest (Table 7.1). It is home to the shiny new skyscrapers of the Gulf petrostates and to the crowded alleys of the Gaza Strip, the refugee camps around Khartoum, and the violent streets of Baghdad. In this chapter I explore the evolution of the region's economies along these different trajectories and examines the particular role that conflict has played in generating such disparities.

Table 7.1 Indicators of Development, 2011

Country	Rank	Life Expectancy at Birth	Mean Years of Schooling[a]	GNI/Capita (in constant PPP$)	HDI Score[b]
Algeria	96	73.1	7.0	7,658	0.698
Bahrain	42	75.1	9.4	28,169	0.806
Comoros	163	61.1	2.8	1,079	0.433
Djibouti	165	57.9	3.8	2,335	0.430
Egypt	113	73.2	6.4	5,269	0.644
Iran	88	73.0	7.3	10,164	0.707
Iraq	132	69.0	5.6	3,177	0.573
Israel	17	81.6	11.9	33,357	0.888
Jordan	95	73.4	8.6	5,300	0.698
Kuwait	63	74.6	6.1	47,926	0.760
Lebanon	71	72.6	7.9	13,076	0.739
Libya	64	74.8	7.3	12,637	0.760
Mauritania	159	58.6	3.7	1,859	0.453
Morocco	130	72.2	4.4	4,196	0.582
Occupied Territories	114	72.2	8.0	2,656	0.641
Oman	89	73.0	5.5	22,841	0.705
Qatar	37	78.4	7.3	107,721	0.831
Saudi Arabia	56	73.9	7.8	23,274	0.770
Somalia	n.a.	51.2	n.a	n.a	n.a.
Sudan	169	61.5	3.1	1,894	0.408
Syria	119	75.9	5.7	4,243	0.632
Tunisia	94	74.5	6.5	7,281	0.698
Turkey	92	74.0	6.5	12,246	0.699
United Arab Emirates	30	76.5	9.3	59,993	0.846
Yemen	154	65.5	2.5	2,213	0.462

Source: Data from UNDP, *Human Development Report 2011: Sustainability and Equity: A Better Future for All* (New York: UNDP, 2012).

Notes: a. Mean years of schooling is the average number of years of education received by people aged twenty-five years and older, converted from education attainment levels using official durations of each level.

b. The Human Development Index (HDI) was created to provide a more accurate picture of development levels than was possible when using only gross domestic product (GDP) per capita. HDI includes such measures as access to education and health services, life expectancy, child mortality rates, and access to potable water.

n.a. indicates data not available. PPP is purchasing power parity. GNI is gross national income.

Middle East Economies Before World War II

Trading patterns in the Middle East and North Africa changed significantly beginning in the eighteenth century as the Ottoman Empire, which controlled these areas, weakened. In the sixteenth century, the empire exported to Europe wheat and luxury goods such as silk and carpets. By the seventeenth century, it was also exporting cattle, wool, hides, cotton, and tobacco as well as olive oil, dried fruit, and angora. In the eighteenth century, cotton, maize, and tobacco exports grew significantly as did exports of semi-processed goods, particularly textiles. The empire imported about three to four times more than it exported to Europe. During this time, the Ottomans also actively traded with Asian countries, importing pharmaceuticals, perfumes, precious stones, spices, indigo, and cloth. They also imported dyes, sugar, and coffee from European colonies in the Americas. However, it was the internal trade within the empire that was most important both to its economic prosperity and to its political cohesion (Panzac, 1992).

The end of the Napoleonic Wars in 1815 fundamentally changed the political orientation of European powers. While during the wars they focused on continental conflicts, now their competition for domination became externalized as they sought to spread their influence internationally. Changes in manufacturing and organization of production increased Europe's need for raw materials and pushed European states and in particular Britain and France, but also Belgium, Switzerland, and Germany to look for new export markets for their products. The technological revolution in the first part of the nineteenth century introduced railways and steamships, which allowed, for the first time, the profitable shipment of bulk goods. Trade was further facilitated by the development of international money markets (Issawi, 1995).

During this period, cash crops expanded. Egypt specialized in cotton exports, Lebanon in silk, Tunisia in olive oil and phosphates, Palestine in oranges, and Algeria in wine. Europe on the other hand exported manufactured products as well as tea, coffee, and sugar to the region. As European interests in the region increased, maintaining access to these markets became vitally important. Under pressure from European powers, commercial laws were enacted by Middle Eastern states that allowed European merchants to travel and trade freely in the region and to have commercial disputes resolved in special tribunals instead of in Islamic courts. In November 1869 the Suez Canal, linking the Mediterranean and Red seas, opened to commercial traffic. It inaugurated new trade routes between Europe and Asia that were especially important to the British Empire (Hourani, 1991).

In response to European penetration of the region, local rulers sought to modernize their states and gain control over imports and exports. As a consequence, the foreign debt of many Middle Eastern and North African Ottoman provinces grew, resulting in ever greater reliance on Europe and a gradual loss of independence. By 1875 the Ottoman government was no longer able to meet its debt obligations, and in 1881 foreign creditors established the Public Debt Administration. Between 1830 and 1911, Europe took over financial control of the governments of Algeria, Egypt, Tunisia, and Morocco when these countries began struggling to repay their large foreign debts. In 1911, Italy invaded Libya. This was the era of "new imperialism," when Europe established colonies in the Middle East and North Africa and sub-Saharan Africa (Hourani, 1991). Despite this European penetration of the region, between 1820 and 1913 the Middle East's share in global trade fell from 3.0 percent to 1.5 percent (Issawi, 1995).

Following World War I, as the Ottoman Empire crumbled, European powers expanded their control over the Middle East. Britain gained control over Iraq, Palestine, and Transjordan while France took control of Syria and

Lebanon. This allowed Britain and France to maintain open markets for their manufactured goods such as textiles and machinery and gave them access to important raw materials for industrial production and, increasingly, oil. It also provided them with a field for investments, particularly in mining and agriculture.

Oil was discovered in Iran in 1908 and its extraction began in 1914. In the 1920s it was discovered in Iraq and Bahrain, and during the next decade in Saudi Arabia and Kuwait. As a consequence of these discoveries, colonial powers intensified their interest in the region. For the first few decades of oil extraction, British, French, Dutch, and US companies controlled the production process. As discussed in Chapter 8, eventually states in oil-producing countries came to own the oil production facilities. The growing importance of oil fundamentally changed the economic profiles of some states and the trading profile of the region.

Economic Development Following World War II

The presence of oil in the region has had a profound impact on both oil-producing countries and those lacking petroleum resources. Equally important to understanding the dynamics of economic development in the Middle East are its climate, demographic characteristics, geopolitical location, and conflict dynamics. The region's limited rainfall and arid soils make unirrigated agriculture difficult (Richards and Waterbury, 1990:52). Its rapidly growing population puts tremendous pressure on public services and labor markets. The involvement of great powers and the funds funneled to purchase weapons has contributed to regional arms races that have drained resources from the civilian economy. And the persistence of conflicts both between and within states has undermined economic development in a number of countries.

As detailed in Chapters 3, 4, and 5, the political map of the region changed significantly following the end of World War II. When the colonial empires disintegrated, new independent states emerged in the Middle East and North Africa. With the exception of the small Persian Gulf states, which remained under British control until the 1970s, most gained independence by the 1960s. And in 1948, Israel was established as a Jewish homeland. The United States emerged as the dominant international actor in the region and for decades contested the Soviet Union for influence. Economic policies also changed and emphasized developing national industrial capacity and social development. In many countries large segments of the economy were brought directly under state control.

At the end of World War II, as the European colonial empires ceded direct political control of the region's states to local elites, the Middle East seemed poised to become one of the wealthier and more developed areas of the world. Egypt's level of development was no different from that of

Greece; Algeria's economic prosperity was closely tied with that of France; and, as part of the Truman Doctrine, Turkey was the beneficiary of a large US aid package (Henry and Springborg, 2001:2).

The future of Iraq and Iran seemed even more promising thanks to the large oil deposits in the two countries. As the course of this chapter shows, these high expectations have been largely dashed. Israel can boast a techno-logically advanced and diversified economy. Turkey has also experienced significant improvement in its level of economic development, especially in the past two decades, making accession negotiations with the European Union (EU) possible. Other countries, however, have experienced very different patterns of development. Unexpectedly, it is the Gulf states that have seen the most spectacular economic expansion thanks to oil discoveries. But those countries that seemed to hold most promise at the end of World War II have seen their economies stumble.

In many of the region's states following independence the new political elites sought to launch economic development projects to make their countries less dependent on former colonial empires and ensure that the deep social inequalities that characterized the region, which were seen by nationalists as a direct consequence of colonial exploitation, would become a thing of the past. The new political coalitions that became dominant in many states incorporated previously excluded social strata; for instance, peasants and labor. In order to maintain these groups' political support and to fulfill the objective of raising income levels of the poorest segments of society, the new regimes expanded the provision of services such as health care, education, and consumer subsidies (Waldner, 1999).

At the same time, economic policies shifted significantly. The new regimes implemented land reforms aimed at both undercutting the power of the old agrarian elites as well as providing greater access to and control over land to peasants. Most states also placed a new emphasis on promoting industrialization, which was seen as the backbone of economic development. As in many other developing countries, states in the Middle East initiated import substitution industrialization (ISI) policies, which aimed at developing local industries to reduce dependence on exports and promote local development. In order to shield these infant industries from international competition and allow them time to develop, countries relied on protective tariffs. With expanding industrial employment opportunities, the previously largely agrarian societies became increasingly urban.

Regardless of the prevailing political ideology, most state elites during the 1960s were dubious about the private sector's ability to launch an economic development project since across "the region it was assumed that the private sector could not be relied upon to undertake this kind of resource mobilization and planning . . . and too concerned with short term profits" (Richards and Waterbury, 1990:189).

Some states that espoused a socialist ideology, like Algeria, Egypt, and Tunisia, went further in redistributing wealth and were more hostile to foreign capital and the local private sector. In these countries, the state became directly involved in economic planning as well as in production. During the 1960s, the number of state-owned enterprises expanded significantly, providing the local markets with new consumer goods and ensuring employment possibilities to the growing labor force. However, even in countries that placed more faith in market mechanisms, such as Jordan and Morocco, the state became more involved in both production and in provision of welfare services. Because state control over the economy expanded so significantly, private sector businesses also became highly dependent on state contracts and state subsidies (Bellin, 2002).

Initially, the results of this new approach to economic development were encouraging. Literacy levels improved, urbanization rates accelerated, and access to health care expanded. In countries where the agricultural sector had once dominated, industrial production and services came to play a more significant role (Table 7.2).

By the late 1960s to early 1970s, however, economic problems emerged. Living standards first stagnated and then began to deteriorate. Public sector enterprises were plagued by inefficiencies, production bottlenecks, and bloated employment rolls (Waterbury, 1993). State bureaucracies expanded, making interactions with public administration more cumbersome. A number of countries that had promoted socialist principles, in particular Tunisia

Table 7.2 Contributions of Agriculture and Industry to GDP (percentage)

Country	1958		1968		1978	
	Agriculture	Industry	Agriculture	Industry	Agriculture	Industry
Algeria	25	20	n.a.	n.a.	7	49
Egypt	33	24	25	24	24	27
Iran	32	30	22	34	9	46
Iraq	20	50	15	43	7	67
Israel	12	32	8	34	4	23
Jordan	18	14	15	21	6	21
Lebanon	n.a.	n.a.	11	21	9	21
Libya	n.a.	n.a.	4	65	2	68
Morocco	35	26	32	29	18	33
Saudi Arabia	n.a.	n.a.	6	62	1	79
Sudan	59	12	39	15	36	14
Tunisia	n.a.	n.a.	18	21	16	27
Turkey	30	28	25	27	17	37

Source: Elias Tuma, "The Economies of the Middle East," in Deborah J. Gerner and Jillian Schwedler (eds.), *Understanding the Contemporary Middle East*, 2nd ed. (Boulder: Lynne Rienner, 2004), p. 230.

Note: n.a. indicates data not available. GDP is gross domestic product.

and Egypt, began to abandon them. Egyptian president Anwar Sadat, for instance, initiated a policy of infitah (economic liberalization) in 1974, which sought to reorient economic policies toward a greater reliance on domestic and foreign private investment. Nonetheless, even where private investment was encouraged, the state continued to dominate the economy and public sector employment expanded.

In the early 1980s, much of the developing world began to experience deep economic problems and struggled with mounting foreign debts. The crisis came to a head in 1982 when Mexico announced that it was suspending its debt repayments. Most developing countries turned to the International Monetary Fund (IMF) and the World Bank for assistance in dealing with the macroeconomic and financial crises and began implementing structural adjustment reforms to address underlying weaknesses in their economies. Although most countries in the Middle East tinkered with economic reforms during the 1980s and sought to reduce the state's role in economic planning and production, these attempts were generally half-hearted and did not result in significant transformation of the region's economies.

A number of reasons account for this lack of progress in implementing economic reform. As in other regions, the initiation of structural reforms was politically difficult. Social groups that had benefited from the prevailing economic arrangements resisted reforms. These groups included elites, who through connections to regime insiders were able to secure profitable contracts, and organized labor, which benefited from access to public sector jobs with higher salaries and more benefits and job security than available in the private sector. The riots that erupted in Egypt in 1977 when President Sadat attempted to cut subsidies on consumer goods were a stark reminder of the political costs that reforming leaders were likely to incur.

At the same time, leaders in the Middle East faced less pressure to reform than their counterparts in other regions. Most important, the oil-producing countries provided direct aid to other states in the region and workers from resource-poor countries migrated to the Gulf, thus relieving pressure on local labor markets and sending remittances back home. The region's strategic importance to the two superpowers, the United States and the Soviet Union, also ensured large amounts of aid and assistance to their client states.

The United States has been the most important source of economic aid, but since the Camp David Accords of 1978, the overwhelming majority of this assistance has been channeled to Egypt and Israel. This pattern has not changed after the resignation of President Hosni Mubarak in February 2011, although levels of assistance to Egypt have become more contentious among US lawmakers. Before its disintegration, the Soviet Union was also an important source of foreign aid. Most of its aid went to Egypt, Syria, South Yemen, and Iraq. Europe and China and, more recently, Turkey have also provided assistance, albeit at lower levels. In other words, the availability of oil and strategic rents made reforming economies a less urgent task in the Middle East than in many other parts of the developing world.

Labor Migration and Remittances

Labor migration and workers' remittances have played a key role in economic dynamics in the region. In fact, the Middle East has the highest ratios of migrants to the total population in the world (Baldwin-Edwards, 2005). The Middle East and, particularly, the Gulf states are a major destination for migrant labor. In 2010 the International Organization for Migration estimated that the region was host to 26.5 million international migrants (IOM, 2010). The region also serves as a transit area for migrants from other areas, especially sub-Saharan Africa, who are looking to migrate to Europe. Although exact figures of migrants are hard to pin down, most analysts agree that the data collected by the United Nations (UN) underestimates their total numbers (Table 7.3).

For a number of countries in the region, especially Turkey and the Maghreb, workers' remittances have been crucial. Morocco, for instance, has encouraged migration out of the country in order to maintain unemployment at politically acceptable levels. At the beginning of the twenty-first century, approximately 2.3 million Moroccans, or about 10.0 percent of the total population, lived abroad, sending back $3.3 billion in remittances, which accounted for 9.7 percent of gross domestic product (GDP) (Baldwin-Edwards, 2005:4).

For decades, migrants' primary destination has been the Gulf region. However, the composition of foreign labor in the oil-producing states has changed over time. Prior to 1974, the overwhelming majority of migrants came from other Arab countries. In the 1970s and early 1980s during the

Table 7.3 Estimated Migrants in Selected Host Countries, 2010 (in thousands and as a percentage of total population)

Country	N	Percentage
Qatar	1,305	86.5
United Arab Emirates	3,293	70.0
Kuwait	2,098	68.8
Bahrain	315	39.1
Israel	2,940	40.4
Oman	826	28.4
Saudi Arabia	7,289	27.8
Libya	682	10.4

Source: United Nations, *International Migration Report 2009: A Global Assessment* (New York: UN Department of Economic and Social Affairs, 2011).

first oil boom, the Gulf states, with huge financial windfalls but small, young, and poorly educated populations, sought to attract skilled workers from the United States and Europe as well as from the Middle East in order to fulfill their ambitious development plans (Table 7.4). Resource-poor countries in the region, on the other hand, were eager to export workers since their own labor markets were unable to meet the demands of an expanding population. They also saw in the remittances an important source of foreign exchange. The number of Arab migrants soared. Egyptians, Yemenis, and Palestinians in particular relocated to the Gulf during this period.

For workers, migration to the Gulf was attractive. The salaries that prevailed there were much higher than in resource-poor states. Unskilled workers could earn almost thirty times more in Saudi Arabia than they could in rural Egypt. Skilled workers also could anticipate their incomes to triple (Richards and Waterbury, 1990:377). Citizens of Gulf states on the other hand, who were the beneficiaries of generous welfare programs set up by governments following the rise in oil prices, were often reluctant to take on many of the available jobs.

Migration to the Gulf thus reduced pressures on the labor market in the resource-poor states in the Middle East. In a number of countries with large migrant worker populations, especially Egypt, Jordan, and Yemen, the departure of large numbers of laborers created new employment opportunities for less skilled workers and new entrants in their home countries. Simultaneously, as workers moved from rural to urban areas lured by new job opportunities, agricultural wages increased at unprecedented rates. In addition, the remittances that migrant workers sent back to their home countries stimulated local consumption. The remittances were also, although to a lesser extent, invested in real estate and land, and to set up small businesses. Remittances proved to be an important source of foreign exchange used to finance imports (Richards and Waterbury, 1990:388–389).

Table 7.4 Official Remittances in Selected Countries During the First Oil Boom (US$ millions)

	1973	1976	1979	1982
Egypt	123.0	842.0	2,269.0	2,481.0
Jordan	55.4	401.8	509.0	932.9
Morocco	211.0	499.0	891.0	840.0
Sudan	6.3	36.8	115.7	107.1
Tunisia	91.0	128.0	271.0	361.0

Source: International Fund for Agricultural Development, *Sending Money Home: Worldwide Remittances Flows to Developing Countries* (Rome: International Fund for Agricultural Development, 2007).

The exact volume of remittances is difficult to estimate. Government figures reflect only those remittances that have come through official banking channels. However, in the majority of the developing world, including the Middle East, most of the money that migrants send back home is sent through informal channels. For example, one study conducted in the mid-1980s estimated that official figures captured only 13 percent of remittances that workers were sending back to Sudan. If correct, this meant that, rather than the $249 million that was officially recorded, more than $1.9 billion was coming annually into that country (Choucri, 1986:702).

In the Middle East like in other parts of the developing world, informal channels of transferring money are an effective mechanism for people with low incomes who "may be outside the read of the formal financial sector and who transfer relatively small sums that are often subject to prohibitively high minimum charges at conventional institutions" (Buencamino and Gorbunov, 2002:1). These informal channels operate, often openly, parallel to the official banking sector. Today, there are two large systems in operation worldwide: the *hawala*, which originated in South Asia, and the *fech'ien*, which originated in China. The *hawala* system, in which money is transferred through a network of brokers, is widely used in the Middle East as well as in parts of Africa and Asia. Money transferred through informal channels likely amounts to anywhere from $100 billion to $300 billion annually (Buencamino and Gorbunov, 2002:2). By one estimate in 2010, more than $35 billion was remitted to the Middle East annually (World Bank, 2012b). Other estimates put the number even higher (Table 7.5). Remittance

Table 7.5 Official Remittances, 2010

	US$ millions	Percentage of GDP
Algeria	2,120	1.6
Egypt	7,656	5.7
Iran	1,115	0.4
Iraq	389	0.6
Jordan	3,434	21.8
Lebanon	5,769	23.4
Libya	16	0.0
Morocco	6,730	9.2
Palestinian Authority	598	11.0
Sudan	1,769	3.2
Syria	824	2.2
Tunisia	1,716	4.9
Yemen	1,322	6.1

Source: International Fund for Agricultural Development, *Sending Money Home: Worldwide Remittances Flows to Developing Countries* (Rome: International Fund for Agricultural Development, 2007).

Note: GDP is gross domestic product.

flows were negatively affected by the eruption of the global financial crisis in 2007, declining by as much as 20 percent in some of the region's countries in 2008. They did not begin to recover until 2011, when their volume rose for the first time since the crisis began. However, this recovery was slower than in other parts of the world because of the unrest related to the Arab uprisings. While remittance flows to South Asia increased by 10.1 percent and to East Asia and Pacific by 7.6 percent for example, they grew by only 2.6 percent in the Middle East (World Bank, 2012b). On the other hand, migrant employment in the Gulf countries after declining in 2010 was once again growing by 2011 thanks to the rise in oil prices and renewed spending in the region on various economic and infrastructure development projects. Need for migrant labor rose. In 2011, for example, the number of Bangladeshi migrant workers in the Gulf countries increased by 37 percent (World Bank, 2012b).

During the latter part of the 1970s, the numbers of Arab migrants in the Gulf began to decline while the numbers of those coming from Asia, especially India, Pakistan, and Sri Lanka, increased. Governments in the Gulf states came to prefer non-Arab migrants, who they saw as less politically troublesome and less likely to stay permanently. Moreover, when the major construction projects funded by the first oil boom were completed, demand for unskilled workers who tended to come from Arab countries eased.

After oil prices fell in 1982, workers were increasingly recruited from Asia rather than the Middle East. During this period, more women began migrating to the Gulf area, especially from the Philippines, Bangladesh, and Sri Lanka, to work primarily as domestic workers. As shown later on in this chapter, the rise in oil prices during the first decade of the twenty-first century once again promoted an explosion of development projects in the Gulf, generating an unprecedented construction boom that again increased the demand for foreign workers in the Gulf Cooperation Council (GCC) states. During the global financial crisis the demand dipped, rebounding in 2010 as oil prices surged.

Foreign workers have also been migrating in increasing numbers to Israel. Initially, after the 1967 war, Palestinians from the Occupied Territories began working in Israel, primarily as day laborers. By 1986, they composed about 7 percent of the labor force (Baldwin-Edwards, 2005). After the first Palestinian intifada in 1987, Israel began recruiting foreign workers. This trend accelerated in the 1990s. By 2003 foreign workers, primarily from Romania, Thailand, and the Philippines, made up more than 13 percent of the labor force. They were employed in agriculture, nursing, and domestic services as well as construction. There were also illegal immigrants, mostly from West Africa, South America, and Eastern Europe, who worked in housekeeping, childcare, and the food services industry (Baldwin-Edwards, 2005).

Although labor migration had a number of positive ripple effects in the sending countries, it also had a number of negative consequences. Two, in particular, proved significant for the sending countries' economies. The first was the brain drain that accompanied labor migration. Many skilled workers and professionals left their countries in search of better employment opportunities, initially in the Gulf and then toward the end of the twentieth century, increasingly in Western Europe and the United States. This meant that businesses in the sending countries faced a shortage of personnel with appropriate expertise. By the late 1990s, this problem became especially acute in a number of Maghreb countries and, especially, in Morocco. There is anecdotal evidence, however, that the economic crisis that Western Europe and the United States have been experiencing since 2007 and the optimism generated by the 2011 popular uprisings are beginning to reverse this trend with more entrepreneurs and highly skilled and educated professionals returning to home countries.

The second negative consequence of labor migration has been the large-scale return of migrants during economic downturns and in moments of political turmoil. In those circumstances, not only do returning workers flood local labor markets, thus contributing to the rise of unemployment rates, but their return also means a decrease in the value of remittances that are a critical source of sending countries' foreign exchange (Yousef, 2005). The difficulties that can be generated by the return of migrant laborers to their home countries were brought to stark relief during the 1991 Gulf War when 800,000 Yemeni workers were expelled from GCC states, primarily, Saudi Arabia; 700,000 Egyptians went home from Iraq, Kuwait, and Jordan; and 200,000 Jordanians and 150,000 Palestinians returned from working in the Gulf. This sudden influx of workers put tremendous strain on their home labor markets (Baldwin-Edwards, 2005:5). In 2011, the crisis in Libya led to a mass departure of migrant labor from that country. Since February 2011, more than 300,000 Egyptians, 60,000 Tunisians, and 40,000 African workers have returned home (African Development Bank, 2012).

Economic Crises and Structural Adjustment

In the 1980s, most countries in the Middle East and North Africa experienced deep economic crises. In response, they turned to the IMF and the World Bank for financial assistance. These organizations, however, were willing to offer assistance only if far-reaching structural adjustment programs were implemented. The international financial institutions (IFIs) subscribed to the increasingly dominant neoliberal analysis that identified state involvement in the economy as the primary reason that much of the developing world, including the Middle East, faced such profound economic difficulties in the 1980s.

Structural adjustment programs, therefore, emphasized limiting that involvement and allowing the unencumbered functioning of markets. Often dubbed the Washington Consensus, structural adjustment policies had a number of common features. They emphasized reducing public expenditures, liberalizing the trade regimes, encouraging foreign direct investment (FDI), and privatizing state-owned enterprises (Williamson, 1990).

These economic changes and the belt-tightening measures, including the slashing of consumer subsidies, meant that the relationship between the state and society had to be fundamentally renegotiated. The state would no longer provide employment or subsidies, and market forces would now determine the allocation of resources in the economy. It did not take long for those negatively affected by the changes to make their opposition to the new economic policies heard. Across the region, bread riots erupted: Egypt in January 1977, Morocco in January 1984, Tunisia in January 1984, Sudan in March 1985, Algeria in October 1988, and Jordan in April 1989.

Most states in the Middle East agreed that reforming their economies was essential if growth was to resume and if the region's states were to become more competitive in the increasingly globalized world economy. However, for years, their record of reform implementation had been decidedly mixed. Although most have succeeded in stabilizing their macroeconomic situation, structural and institutional reforms proved to be more difficult to implement and often remained largely on the drawing boards for years.

During the initial phase of structural adjustment reforms in the late 1980s and in the 1990s, the progress of institutional reforms was slow as governments concentrated their efforts primarily on privatizing public sector enterprises and cutting government expenditures (Alissa, 2007). By the beginning of the twenty-first century, both international financial institutions as well as Middle East governments came to recognize that sustained economic growth was unlikely without significant reforms of institutions indispensable to the functioning of a market economy. As issues of good governance took center stage, the region's governments increasingly began to focus on reforming the judiciary, corporate governance, and tax codes, among others.

As happened during the first wave of economic reforms in the late 1970s and in the 1980s, during this second phase of implementing structural adjustment policies, growing social inequalities and high unemployment levels have contributed to rising social tensions. Although the largest demonstrations have focused on expressing solidarity with the Palestinians, protesting the US-led invasion of Iraq, and demanding political accountability and democracy, others focused more explicitly on economic issues have occurred as well; for example, in August 1996, Jordanians protested the lifting of wheat subsidies (Andoni and Schwedler, 1996). Egypt has also experienced three waves of massive labor unrest. The first was in the late 1990s when over 170 workers' protests took place (Paczynska, 2006). The second, even larger wave of workers' strikes and demonstrations, occurred in 2006 and 2007 (Beinin and el-Hamalawy, 2007). The third wave occurred during the January 2011 uprising against the Mubarak regime and continued following his ouster as economic crisis intensified.

Although a number of countries have achieved impressive growth rates, economic recovery has not benefited all social strata. On the contrary, one of the characteristics of this economic recovery has been the anemic job growth. The Middle East continues to have the highest unemployment rates in the world, hovering around 12 percent between 1998 and 2008 (World Bank, 2012a). However, there is great variation among countries' unemployment rates; in 2011, in Qatar it was 0.3 percent while in the West Bank and Gaza it was 23.7 percent and in Iraq and Yemen around 15.0 percent (ILO, 2011). Unemployment has been an especially acute problem among better-educated young people. Youth unemployment in the region was above 25.0 percent and even higher among young women, reaching on average 31.5 percent in 2011 (ILO, 2012). Many of the available jobs offered low pay, poor working conditions, few if any benefits, and no secure contracts. Those rates increased further as a result of the global financial crisis. Although fertility rates in the region have fallen significantly since the 1950s, from 6.9 children per woman to 2.7 per woman in 2010, creating a sufficient number of jobs for young people entering the workforce annually remains a challenge for many countries. In Egypt, for instance, about 1 million young people enter the workforce on an annual basis (Manpower Group, 2012:30). These difficult economic conditions, combined with anger over social inequalities, growing poverty, and widespread corruption, contributed to the eruption of popular uprisings in the region in late 2010.

Despite renewed efforts on the part of many Middle Eastern governments to attract FDI, the results have been mixed. Although capital flows to the region have grown, the region continues to lag behind other developing countries. FDI flows to Egypt grew for a number of years, reaching $10 billion in 2006, as did inflows into Sudan. In the former investments poured primarily into projects that were not related to oil, whereas in the latter most of the new investments were channeled toward developing the petroleum industry. However, political developments in both countries have impacted these flows. Foreign investment to Egypt slowed in the wake of the January 2011 revolution as political uncertainty about the country's future deepened; it recovered only in the fourth quarter of 2012, although still not reaching the prerevolution levels. An exception has been Chinese investments in Egypt, which have continued to grow. Also in January 2011, South Sudan voted in a referendum to become an independent country. As a result,

Sudan's oil revenues plummeted by 75 percent, GDP growth slowed significantly (African Economic Outlook, 2012), and continued conflict in the border regions of the two countries has discouraged private investors. An exception is an increase in Saudi Arabian investment in Sudan's agricultural sector.

Additionally, a number of large-scale privatization projects in the early years of the twenty-first century, such as the telecommunications companies' sale in Jordan and Turkey, encouraged the entry of foreign investors into the region. For a number of years, FDI to the Gulf countries and Turkey had grown, reaching $60 billion in 2006, a 44 percent increase over the previous year. In particular, while oil prices remained high, FDI in the hydrocarbons industries increased. At the same time, efforts by the Gulf petroleum producers to begin diversifying their economies brought new foreign investments into the manufacturing sector. In response to the high oil prices, a number of Gulf countries, especially Kuwait, also began to invest abroad. However, the global financial crisis and regional unrest in 2011 had negative impact on investment flows. In GCC countries, many of the ambitious construction projects started during the oil boom were scrapped and FDI inflows declined for three straight years to $49 billion in 2011 (UNCTAD, 2012a).

Table 7.6 GDP Growth in the Middle East (percentage)

	2007	2008	2009	2010	2011
Resource-poor/labor-abundant					
Egypt	7.1	7.2	4.7	5.1	1.8
Jordan	8.2	7.2	5.5	2.3	2.5
Lebanon	7.5	9.3	8.5	7.0	1.5
Morocco	2.7	5.6	4.9	3.7	4.3
Tunisia	6.3	4.5	3.1	3.1	−0.8
Resource-rich/labor-abundant					
Algeria	3.0	2.4	2.4	3.3	2.5
Iran	6.4	0.6	3.9	5.9	2.0
Syria	5.7	4.5	5.9	3.4	n.a.
Yemen	3.3	3.6	3.9	7.7	−10.5
Resource-rich/labor-importing					
Bahrain	8.4	6.3	3.1	4.5	1.8
Kuwait	4.5	5.0	−5.2	3.4	8.2
Libya	7.5	5.4	−0.1	2.5	−61.0
Oman	5.3	12.9	1.1	4.0	5.5
Qatar	18.0	17.7	12.0	16.6	18.8
Saudi Arabia	2.0	4.2	0.1	4.6	6.8
United Arab Emirates	6.5	5.3	−3.3	0.9	4.9

Source: International Monetary Fund, *Regional Outlook Update* (April) (Washington, DC: International Monetary Fund, 2012), p. 10.

Note: n.a. indicates data not available. GDP is gross domestic product.

Table 7.7 Size of the Informal Economy as a Percentage of GDP

Country	2000	2003	2007
Algeria	34.1	35.8	37.1
Egypt	35.1	34.8	37.0
Iran	18.9	19.6	20.5
Israel	21.9	21.2	23.0
Jordan	19.4	20.1	21.7
Kuwait	20.1	20.9	n.a.
Lebanon	34.1	35.0	36.2
Libya	35.1	35.3	39.6
Morocco	36.4	37.8	39.8
Oman	18.9	19.4	n.a.
Saudi Arabia	18.4	18.5	20.0
Syria	19.3	19.3	20.1
Tunisia	38.4	39.4	41.4
Turkey	32.1	32.4	35.2
United Arab Emirates	26.4	26.5	n.a.
Yemen	27.4	27.7	28.0

Source: Data from Friedrich Schneider, Andreas Buehn, and Claudio E. Montenegro, "Shadow Economies All over the World: New Estimates for 162 Countries from 1999 to 2007," World Bank Working Paper No. 5356 (Washington, DC: World Bank, July 2010), pp. 45–47.

Note: n.a. indicates data not available. GDP is gross domestic product.

One consequence of structural adjustment programs has been the expansion of the already large informal sector of the economy sometimes also referred to as the *shadow economy*. Economic growth that does not generate sufficient employment opportunities or improved income distribution does not reduce the size of the informal sector. In much of the developing world, including the Middle East, structural adjustment policies and the cutbacks in public sector employment were not accompanied by a sufficient expansion of the private sector to compensate for the job losses. Often business regulations have discouraged the formal private sector from investing in labor-intensive production, focusing instead on establishing capital-intensive manufacturing, which is unable to absorb sufficient numbers of job seekers. Furthermore, the reduction of many consumer subsidies meant that low-income families had to find new means of supplementing their formal incomes. As one study estimates, in 2004 "non-agricultural employment share of the informal workforce" was 78 percent in Africa, 57 percent in Latin America and the Caribbean, and 45 percent to 85 percent in Asia (Becker, 2004:8). In the Middle East, the informal sector accounts for close to 40 percent of GDP in some cases and over 20 percent in nearly all countries in the region. Most of activities performed within the informal economy are legal, although they are performed outside of the formal business, tax, and labor regulations. Informal production tends to be small scale and labor intensive, offers lower wages than does the formal sector, and provides no social security coverage.

Trade

Although petroleum products dominate the region's exports, other goods and services are also produced and sold by the region's countries. Egypt's exports, while dominated by petroleum, are more diversified than that of the Gulf countries. It also exports textiles, clothing, and to a lesser extent steel, chemicals and fertilizers, and food products. Europe and the United States have been Egypt's important trading partners. Thanks to the Qualifying Industrial Zone (QIZ) protocol, in which Egypt began participating in 2005, companies located in these zones have gained access to the US market free of tariffs and nontariff barriers if the products contain inputs produced in Israel. In the second decade of the twenty-first century, Egypt's trade with China grew significantly. Jordanian and Moroccan exports have been highly dependent on potash. Since the late 1980s, however, both have expanded manufacturing exports. Like Egypt, Jordan has also gained duty-free access to the US market for products that contain inputs made in Israel through the QIZ protocol of 1996.

Since 1998, ten such zones have been designated in Egypt and thirteen in Jordan. As a result, Jordanian and Egyptian exports to the United States have grown significantly. Jordanian exports increased from $31 million in 1999 to $6.7 billion in 2011 while Egyptian exports grew from about $1.3 billion in 2004 to over $2.7 billion in 2012. The existence of QIZ meant that the ending of the Multifiber Agreement in 2005 had a less dramatic impact on Egypt's textile exports. The Multifiber Agreement gave Egyptian, Moroccan, and Tunisian textile exports privileged access to European markets. Tunisia and especially Morocco, on the other hand, have been hit hard by the agreement's expiration, especially since it coincided with the slowdown of European economies (World Bank, 2006:18–19).

Prior to the eruption of civil war in 2011, Syria, in addition to cotton and textiles, had been exporting fruits and vegetables, meat and live animals, petroleum products, and machinery. Sanctions imposed on Syria by the EU and the United States in February 2012 have, however, prohibited a number of Syrian exports. Tunisia's exports are dominated by agricultural commodities, phosphate and iron, as well as textiles and light manufacturing. Lebanon, since the end of its devastating civil war in 1990, has concentrated on rebuilding its financial services sector and the tourist industry. It exports agricultural products, prepared foodstuffs, textiles, and machinery. In most states that are not oil dependent, imports exceed exports, leading to an adverse balance of trade. Israel has the most diversified exports, which include agricultural commodities, chemicals, telecommunications and equipment, weapons, and precious stones. Countries across the region, however, have seen their exports decline as a result of the global financial crisis and, particularly, the crisis in the eurozone.

Regional trade in the Middle East and North Africa has been small. Establishing trading relationships has been difficult because most states in the region produce similar commodities in competition with one another. Since the late 1980s, however, as most countries of the region began to implement economic reforms and open their markets to international competition, there has been a renewed effort to improve regional economic cooperation and establish new trading relationships with countries outside the region. In addition to the GCC, the Arab Maghreb Union was created in 1989 by Algeria, Libya, Mauritania, Morocco, and Tunisia. The Agadir trade agreement signed in 2004 by Egypt, Tunisia, Morocco, and Jordan is expected to increase the volume of trade between these four countries. In 2007 Egypt's free trade agreement with Turkey went into effect, and that same year Egypt and Russia signed an agreement that established the Russian Industrial Zone in Egypt. Trade between China and Egypt has also grown significantly, reaching $8.8 billion in 2011, up 40 percent since 2008. In 2005, the Greater Arab Free Trade Area (GAFTA) was established. This project, initiated at the Arab League summit in Amman in 1997, aims

Egypt's once thriving textile industry has taken a large hit with the increase of cheaper cloth imported from places like China and India. This dress market in Cairo is full of garments made in China.

to create an Arab economic bloc that will allow the region to more effectively compete internationally and, through the removal of tariffs and non-tariff barriers, to encourage intraregional trade in manufactured goods.

The goal of the Euro-Mediterranean Free Trade Area is to remove trade and investment barriers between the EU and its neighbors in the southern Mediterranean and to eventually create a free-trade zone. By 2012 Euro-Mediterranean Association Agreements have been implemented with all partners except Libya and Syria. Eventually this free-trade area will cover the EU, the European Free Trade Association (EFTA), the EU customs unions with third states, the EU candidate states, and partners in the Barcelona process to establish the free-trade area. Finally, a new US plan proposed in 2003 is expected to expand economic ties with the region through trade and investment framework agreements, bilateral investment treaties, and free-trade agreements. To date, the United States has signed free-trade agreements with Israel (1985), Jordan (2000), Morocco (2005), Bahrain (2006), and Oman (2006). Talks between the United States and Oman concluded in 2005 and are ongoing with the United Arab Emirates (UAE). As of 2012 Israel, Jordan, Morocco, Bahrain, Egypt, Tunisia, Oman, Kuwait, the UAE, Qatar, Saudi Arabia, and Turkey were members of the World Trade Organization (WTO). Lebanon, Algeria, Yemen, Libya, Iraq, and Iran were negotiating for full membership. Prior to the eruption of the civil war, Syria also expressed an interest in joining the organization.

Although the volume of trade has increased, the Arab world continues to play a minor role in global trade, accounting in 2011 for only 5.4 percent of world exports and 5.3 percent of world imports. Oil accounted for 90 percent of exports from the region. (See Tables 7.8 and 7.9.)

Oil producers are primarily members of the GCC: Bahrain, Kuwait, Oman, Qatar, Saudi Arabia, and the UAE as well as Yemen, Libya, Egypt, and Algeria. Historically an important oil producer, Iraq since the 2003 US invasion has struggled to increase production, which has been hampered by the precarious security situation and lack of investment in the sector resulting from years of sanctions and war. Although in recent years the oil-producing countries have sought to diversify their economies, they remain highly dependent on oil exports. In 2012 in Iran, Kuwait, and Saudi Arabia, oil accounted for 90 percent or more of the countries' exports, and in Algeria for 98 percent. Most oil exporters also sell natural gas on the world markets.

Since 2000, trading partners of the Gulf states have changed substantially. Most significant, the importance of the United States has declined. Most of the Gulf countries have expanded trade with China, Japan, South Korea, Taiwan, and India, and more recently with Indonesia, Thailand, Malaysia, Singapore, the Philippines, and Vietnam. While thirty years ago 85 percent of the GCC's trade was with Organisation for Economic Cooperation and Development (OECD) countries, by 2009 emerging market countries accounted for 45 percent. Since 1980, trade with emerging market

Table 7.8 Middle East Exports by Destination (percentage)

| Country | Year | Developed Economies | | | Developing Economies | | | | |
		Europe	United States	Japan	Africa	Latin America	East/South Asia	Western Asia	Other[a]
Algeria	1990	70.2	19.2	0.9	2.5	2.1	0.6	1.7	2.8
	2000	63.8	15.7	0.1	1.4	8.2	0.8	6.3	3.7
	2011	53.1	20.6	0.3	3.3	5.8	7.0	3.6	6.3
Egypt	1990	43.3	8.6	2.7	3.7	0.0	6.9	8.2	26.6
	2000	48.0	12.8	2.0	4.1	0.9	9.7	11.2	11.3
	2011	32.2	5.2	1.2	3.7	1.3	14.4	26.0	6.0
Iran	1990	50.0	1.5	20.7	—	4.4	10.9	3.1	9.4
	2000	26.8	0.6	18.1	6.0	0.2	30.0	4.2	14.1
	2011	18.1	0.0	10.8	3.5	0.1	53.3	12.6	1.6
Israel	1990	39.5	28.8	7.3	1.3	2.6	8.6	0.7	11.2
	2000	30.2	36.8	2.6	1.5	2.8	15.2	1.5	9.4
	2011	29.8	33.2	1.5	2.2	3.9	21.0	3.4	5.0
Jordan	1990	4.1	0.6	2.1	8.1	0.1	40.3	40.9	3.8
	2000	4.0	4.9	1.0	8.7	0.4	32.9	39.0	9.1
	2011	5.0	13.2	0.7	7.3	0.4	23.5	38.9	11.0
Kuwait	1990	23.5	6.8	18.6	1.8	1.9	29.2	6.0	12.2
	2000	13.9	14.4	24.1	1.0	0.5	42.8	2.7	0.6
	2011	5.7	8.4	13.7	3.9	0.4	63.0	3.8	1.1
Morocco	1990	62.8	1.8	3.6	6.2	1.3	7.3	4.9	12.1
	2000	73.2	3.4	3.8	3.7	1.8	6.3	2.1	5.7
	2011	61.2	4.8	0.7	7.1	6.8	14.0	3.1	2.3
Saudi Arabia	1990	18.4	24.0	19.0	4.0	3.3	19.1	9.4	2.8
	2000	17.9	17.4	17.3	5.5	1.5	31.8	6.8	1.8
	2011	10.8	13.5	14.0	4.3	1.2	48.1	6.8	1.3
Sudan	1990	39.0	2.8	6.0	7.1	0.0	24.9	10.5	9.7
	2000	10.5	0.1	17.2	2.8	0.7	58.4	9.5	0.8
	2011	1.7	0.1	15.3	2.0	0.2	67.6	10.0	3.1
Syria	1990	42.4	0.9	0.1	2.8	0.0	0.5	18.6	34.7
	2000	62.7	3.0	0.3	2.7	0.1	1.7	24.2	5.3
	2011	29.8	2.8	1.3	6.5	0.4	2.5	55.1	1.6
Tunisia	1990	77.7	0.9	0.3	9.5	0.9	4.1	3.5	3.1
	2000	79.4	0.7	0.2	8.3	1.1	3.4	2.5	4.4
	2011	74.9	2.0	0.9	1.4	1.0	4.0	2.7	13.1
Turkey	1990	59.0	7.2	1.8	5.6	0.3	7.7	8.7	9.7
	2000	55.5	11.3	0.5	4.9	1.0	3.7	4.8	18.3
	2011	48.5	3.4	0.2	7.7	1.8	7.7	13.9	16.8
United Arab Emirates	1990	9.5	4.0	37.7	2.7	0.5	25.2	5.0	15.4
	2000	5.2	2.2	33.0	3.8	0.2	32.7	7.0	15.9
	2011	5.0	1.0	17.2	4.3	0.3	60.3	9.0	2.9

Sources: UNCTAD, *Handbook of Statistics 2006–2007* (New York: UNCTAD, 2006); UNCTAD, *Handbook of Statistics 2012* (New York: UNCTAD, 2012a).
Note: a. Other indicates other developed economies and transitional economies.

countries has risen by 11 percent annually (Economic Intelligence Unit, 2011). Trade between China and the GCC in 2011 rose more than 40 percent to reach $133 billion. India-GCC trade has tripled in volume since 2007, reaching $130 billion in 2012. China and India, among others, have also been investing more heavily in the region.

Table 7.9 Middle East Imports by Origin (percentage)

		Developed Economies			Developing Economies				
Country	Year	Europe	United States	Japan	Africa	Latin America	East/South Asia	Western Asia	Other[a]
Algeria	1990	67.6	11.6	4.6	1.8	2.6	1.4	2.5	7.9
	2000	59.8	11.6	3.0	2.1	2.9	6.3	4.5	9.8
	2011	53.4	4.6	2.3	3.6	8.9	18.7	5.7	2.8
Egypt	1990	48.7	14.0	3.7	1.4	2.9	8.6	2.9	17.8
	2000	39.3	16.9	3.7	1.6	3.1	14.6	6.9	13.9
	2011	30.9	10.7	2.2	3.0	6.7	20.3	16.3	9.9
Iran	1990	53.1	0.3	10.3	—	3.7	8.0	9.7	14.9
	2000	40.4	0.7	4.8	1.5	6.7	17.2	10.5	18.2
	2011	17.2	0.3	2.0	0.3	3.1	33.5	37.0	6.6
Israel	1990	61.3	17.8	3.6	1.8	1.1	3.3	0.2	10.9
	2000	48.0	18.1	3.2	1.0	0.9	10.8	1.7	16.3
	2011	43.2	18.1	3.7	1.2	2.0	24.1	3.9	3.8
Jordan	1990	34.5	17.5	3.2	3.0	0.5	9.1	26.9	5.3
	2000	32.8	9.9	3.9	1.9	2.7	14.5	23.9	10.4
	2011	21.5	5.9	2.0	4.9	2.8	20.5	35.8	6.6
Kuwait	1990	37.9	10.9	11.4	0.1	1.0	14.1	2.5	22.1
	2000	34.2	12.1	8.7	1.4	1.5	20.3	18.1	3.7
	2011	21.6	12.4	6.2	1.7	2.0	31.2	20.7	4.2
Morocco	1990	52.8	5.5	1.6	6.6	2.3	3.2	10.4	17.6
	2000	58.4	5.6	1.7	4.6	3.2	8.7	10.4	7.4
	2011	48.2	8.6	0.9	5.4	4.5	11.4	13.5	7.5
Saudi Arabia	1990	43.5	16.7	15.3	2.3	1.6	13.1	4.6	2.9
	2000	33.3	19.2	10.4	1.4	2.4	11.7	5.0	16.6
	2011	30.1	12.1	5.7	2.5	3.9	33.0	8.9	3.8
Sudan	1990	42.8	3.6	3.9	16.2	0.1	9.5	19.5	4.4
	2000	33.2	1.3	2.3	5.6	1.5	31.1	18.2	6.8
	2011	16.3	0.9	3.4	8.3	2.3	38.7	25.1	5.0
Syria	1990	48.8	10.8	3.3	2.7	2.9	4.3	11.9	15.3
	2000	36.6	4.3	2.4	2.1	2.2	17.4	8.5	26.5
	2011	22.3	2.2	1.3	6.2	4.1	25.2	27.3	11.4
Tunisia	1990	68.0	4.9	1.6	5.4	2.5	4.4	3.8	9.4
	2000	72.4	4.6	2.0	6.5	1.6	4.7	3.6	4.6
	2011	65.4	2.5	0.4	8.0	2.3	9.6	5.2	6.6
Turkey	1990	47.5	9.9	4.8	5.8	2.4	7.9	10.1	11.6
	2000	52.4	7.2	3.0	5.0	1.2	10.2	3.3	17.7
	2011	40.3	6.7	1.8	2.8	2.2	23.9	2.2	20.1
United Arab Emirates	1990	34.9	9.1	14.2	0.5	1.0	24.8	8.6	6.9
	2000	38.8	7.9	9.6	1.0	0.7	30.9	6.9	4.2
	2011	23.1	8.2	3.8	2.5	1.5	49.5	8.3	3.1

Sources: UNCTAD, *Handbook of Statistics 2006–2007* (New York: UNCTAD, 2006); UNCTAD, *Handbook of Statistics 2012* (New York: UNCTAD, 2012a).

Note: a. Other indicates other developed economies and transitional economies.

Since 1993 China has become a net importer of oil, with most of it coming from the Middle East. It is interested in securing oil deliveries and promoting its own oil service products. At the same time, various refineries, port development projects, and oil tank farms in China are being funded and built by Dubai, Kuwait, and Saudi Arabia. In July 2004 China and the

GCC began negotiations on a China-GCC free-trade zone. India and the GCC expect to sign a free-trade agreement in 2013.

The New Oil Boom

By mid-2008 oil prices reached record levels, hitting $139 per barrel for the first time, and the oil economies of the Gulf region experienced unprecedented growth rates. Unlike in previous periods of buoyant prices, the GCC states tried to be more careful about how they spent the windfall and focused on "building up liquidity through external reserves, oil stabilization funds, and paying down debt" (World Bank, 2006:10). They also sought to diversify their economies to ensure continued economic growth once oil reserves are depleted.

As discussed in Chapter 8, the high price of oil has spurred an unprecedented construction boom in the Gulf states that fundamentally transformed that region. The additional oil rents also allowed them to bolster their status as the regional finance, business, and tourist hub (World Bank, 2006). In order to realize these ambitions, huge development projects were commissioned by the governments that transformed the Gulf coastline through reclamation projects and the construction of whole new cities, which their developers envisioned would eventually accommodate hundreds of thousands of permanent residents and millions of tourists annually. Among the largest of these were King Abdullah City in Saudi Arabia priced at $26 billion, Blue City in Oman at $15 billion, and the Lusail development in Qatar at $5 billion (Property World Middle East, 2005). Dubai, however, was leading the construction boom with an estimated $200 billion worth of projects. The largest among these were the $9.5 billion theme park and World Palm Islands developments, which were anticipated to increase the UAE beachfront by over 160 percent. Dubai also constructed the world's tallest building, the Burj Khalifa skyscraper. This half-mile-tall building officially opened in January 2010. Additionally, Dubai was developing free-trade zones, located mostly in desert areas to attract cutting-edge companies. Others in the Gulf, in particular Qatar and Saudi Arabia, were also establishing free-trade zones to attract high-tech companies from abroad.

The boom in the Gulf, however, exacerbated social tensions, leading to especially serious confrontations in Dubai, where foreign workers rebelled against working conditions. Similar protests occurred in Kuwait, Saudi Arabia, Qatar, Bahrain, and Oman. In Dubai, workers destroyed cars and construction equipment and broke windows in office buildings. In Kuwait, Bangladeshi workers stormed their own embassy to protest working conditions ("Bangladeshi Workers Storm Kuwait Embassy," 2005). In most of these states, an overwhelming majority of laborers working in the private sector, sometimes as high as 98 percent, were noncitizen migrant workers who came primarily from Asia. These workers enjoyed little legal protection, and reports of substandard housing, lack of potable water and sanitary facilities, hazardous work sites, and nonpayment of wages were common. Consequently, during the oil boom years, labor unrest was frequent although vastly underreported.

The same high oil prices that allowed the GCC states to experience high rates of economic growth presented severe challenges to the resource-poor states in the Middle East. During the previous era of high oil prices, these resource-poor states also experienced economic expansion thanks to a number of mechanisms that allowed wealth generated in the Gulf to trickle through the rest of the region. Most important, the GCC states funneled financial aid to their resource-poor neighbors, and workers from the resource-poor states found employment in the Gulf countries, thus allowing them to send significant remittances back home. This time, these sources of funding were greatly diminished. The high oil import bills put severe strains on the budgets of the resource-poor countries. These strains were further exacerbated by the rise of global food commodity prices, which according to the IMF had increased 56 percent between January 2007 and January 2008.

The Global Financial Crisis and the Arab Uprisings
The rise in food and fuel prices was followed by the deepening of the global financial crisis, which put strains on both resource-poor and resource-rich countries in the region. What initially looked like a subprime mortgage loan crisis in the United States rapidly spread to other world regions. In 2009, the crisis had deepened and the global economy shrunk by 2.2 percent according to the UN. Although growth picked up the following years to 4.3 percent, in 2011 it declined again to 2.7 percent (United Nations, 2011a). Like other areas, the Middle East was also affected by the global financial crisis although its impact differed among the region's countries. For some like Iran, Iraq, Syria, Lebanon, and Jordan, the initial impact of the crisis was relatively small because of the low level of global integration of these countries' financial sectors. Countries with more globally integrated financial sectors were affected more severely. In Egypt, for instance, stock market indices declined by just under 70 percent between March 2008 and March 2009 (United Nations, 2009). At the same time, what was a commodity price boom turned into a bust. The economic expansion in the GCC fueled by the high oil prices came to a halt. In 2009, oil prices began to dip below $40 per barrel. GDP plummeted, banks experienced significant liquidity problems, and the real estate bubble burst. Housing prices declined by 52 percent in Dubai, 35 percent in Qatar, and 62 percent in Kuwait (Salah, 2010). In the Gulf states, with the exception of Bahrain, which

experienced significant clashes between the regime and the opposition in 2011, growth resumed as oil prices began to rise again in 2011, reaching on average $112 per barrel in 2012.

For resource-poor countries of the region, the rise in oil prices, the already high unemployment levels, and the declining remittances and investment flows put more pressure on local economies. At the same time, the popular uprisings against regimes that many countries in the region began to experience in late 2010 affected economic conditions; however, the impact was greater in states that experienced upheavals than in those that saw few popular demonstrations. Because the uprisings unfolded at a time when the world economy and especially the eurozone was struggling with the effects of the global financial crisis, the economic impact of the popular uprisings was magnified. The economies most affected by the uprisings were those of Libya, Syria, Egypt, Tunisia, Yemen, and Bahrain. According to the IMF (2012a), GDP losses in these six countries in 2011 alone were about $20.56 billion while the Council of Arab Economic Unity (2012) put the losses of Libya, Syria, Egypt, Tunisia, and Yemen at close to $100 billion due to declining exports and loss of production, investment, and tourism. As a result of the combined effects of the global economic slowdown and political uncertainty, personal incomes in region stagnated or even contracted and unemployment levels reached 18 percent and hit youth especially hard.

Although a number of economic indicators suggest that economic recovery has begun in a number of countries, the process is likely to be gradual. For instance, although the tourist sector in Egypt saw a significant growth during the first quarter of 2012, with a 35 percent increase in tourists from Europe and 45 percent from the Middle East, the overall levels were still 25 percent lower than in 2010 (Business Monitor International, 2012). The conflict between President Mohammad Mursi and the opposition that intensified in late 2012, however, contributed to political uncertainty and negatively affected the tourist sector.

Conflict and Regional Economies

The region has been highly conflict prone. Its geopolitical location has led to intervention in local political dynamics by foreign powers. During the Cold War, the United States and the Soviet Union funneled military aid to the region, helping to fuel arms races. The establishment of the State of Israel in 1948 was followed by a number of wars with its Arab neighbors in 1956, 1967, 1973, and Israeli invasions of Lebanon in 1982 and 2006. Additionally, a protracted and bloody conflict has been ongoing between Israel and the Palestinians, a conflict that has continued despite the signing of the Oslo Accords in 1993. Other recent conflicts that have erupted in the region include the 1980–1988 Iran-Iraq War; the 1990 Iraqi invasion of Kuwait, and the US-led intervention that followed; the 2003–2010 US-led invasion of Iraq; the civil wars in Sudan, Lebanon, Yemen, Somalia, Algeria, Libya, and Syria; and the conflict between Morocco, Mauritania, and the Polisario independence movement over Western Sahara. All of these conflicts have had a profound impact on the economies of the states involved in these clashes and often have reverberated through the economies of states not directly engaged in them.

One of the consequences of the high levels of conflict in the region, coupled with the involvement of outside powers, has been an extremely high level of militarization of the Middle East. Yahya M. Sadowski estimates that in the 1980s the Middle East was the world's largest arms market, importing at least $154 billion worth of weapons (1993:1), siphoning money that could have been used for economic development. The militarization of the region has thus affected the development prospects of all states involved in the arms races. Conflict has had an even more profound impact on states that have experienced long-term conflict and violence—in particular Lebanon, Sudan, the Gaza Strip and West Bank, Iraq, Yemen, and Algeria, and more recently Libya and Syria.

Algeria and Yemen sought to address challenges stemming from civil conflicts while implementing structural adjustment programs. Both attempted to undertake reconciliation and reconstruction and to implement reforms aimed at reducing the role of the state in the economy. In the case of Yemen, the conflict once again intensified in 2011, setting back economic reconstruction and reform efforts.

Yemen has experienced conflict since the unification of North and South Yemen in May 1990. Four years of negotiations over new political arrangements collapsed, leading to the eruption of a civil war in May 1994. Although the fighting was over within a couple of months, other conflicts have simmered since then, which have made the launch of an economic development program difficult. In particular, clashes between the central government in Sana'a and the Houthi group in the Saada governorate in the northern part of Yemen have caused serious damage to infrastructure in that part of the country. Over time, as the International Crisis Group points out, "conflict has become self-perpetuating, giving rise to a war economy," in which drug smuggling, people trafficking, and gunrunning have become lucrative economic activities (International Crisis Group, 2009:ii). Despite government pledges to finance reconstruction, the slow pace of structural reform implementation, low growth rates, and high inflation and unemployment have contributed to social tension and to repeated popular protests, especially in the southern part of the country (World Bank Group Sana'a Office, 2007:1–2). Among the most difficult development challenges that remain are depletion of the country's oil resources and water scarcity. In January 2011, Yemen experienced a wave of popular demonstrations protesting high unemployment and political repression and demanding the resignation of President Ali Abdallah Salih. Although he finally resigned from office nine months after the protests began, the fundamental economic challenges have remained unresolved. By 2012, unemployment had reached 35 percent and over 45 percent of the population lived below the poverty line and struggled with inflation that reached 20 percent (World Food Program, 2012:7).

Between 1992 and 1998, Algeria experienced what was essentially a civil war that killed at least 100,000 people according to official figures, although other sources put the figure even higher (International Crisis Group, 2001). The conflict erupted after the cancellation of parliamentary elections that the Islamic Salvation Front was poised to win. Although in 1999 it appeared that the conflict was over, violence continued to plague the country as did popular dissatisfaction with the regime. In December 2007 two bombs exploded in Algiers, one close to the Constitutional Court and the other next to the UN headquarters, casting doubt on the ability of the Algerian government to ensure long-term stability. In 2011, however, as neighboring Tunisia witnessed the resignation of President Zine Abidine Ben Ali, Algeria remained relatively calm. Although a number of antiregime protests took place, they were relatively small and dissipated quickly. Here, the government benefited from the rising oil prices that allowed it to increase spending on food subsidies and provide pay increases to civil servants and interest-free loans to young entrepreneurs (Achy, 2012).

The hydrocarbon industry has continued to attract FDI. The main reason that the sector has remained largely immune to the political turmoil is its location far from the main urban centers in the Saharan desert. However, although the hydrocarbon industry has maintained its production levels and accounts for 97 percent of Algeria's foreign export earnings, the rest of the economy has felt the aftershocks of the civil war (International Crisis Group, 2001). Public and private investment in other sectors of the economy have remained stagnant for years. Because the oil sector produces few jobs, unemployment levels have remained high especially among the young.

For many years, although Algeria's structural reforms have focused on reducing the role of the state in the economy through privatization of the public sector and institutional reforms, the high levels of violence have had a deep and negative impact on employment generation—a challenge unique to countries experiencing violent conflict during the transition from a planned to a market economy (Kpadar, 2007). Although Algeria has sought to diversify its economy by launching a $60 billion, five-year development program in 2005 with the goal of making the country less dependent on the fluctuations in the petroleum markets, the results have not been encouraging. The petroleum industry continues to dominate the economy, accounting for 35 percent of GDP and 95 percent of exports in 2011.

Before civil war erupted in 1975, Lebanon with its free-market, liberal economy was the banking center of the Middle East. In the years before the eruption of the civil war, it enjoyed steady growth rates and rising per capita incomes. Tourism, transit trade, services, and workers' remittances were all important sources of foreign exchange. However, this growth was highly uneven and socioeconomic disparities were deep. The civil war that lasted from 1975 to 1989 devastated the country. Although the exact numbers are not known, it is estimated that as a result of the initial year of civil war (1975–1976), 600,000 to 900,000 people fled the country. Even though some began returning after the cessation of hostilities and the beginning of the postwar reconstruction program, the reoccurring violence, most recently in 2006 and 2007, has reversed this inward flow.

At least 100,000 people were killed during the sixteen years of fighting. Along with its human toll, the civil war destroyed infrastructure, especially in Beirut. Industrial production declined and the tourist sector was essentially destroyed. The conflict contributed to high inflation rates, massive capital flight, and persistent fiscal and monetary instability, and it destroyed state institutions indispensable to the management of public policies. As the state disintegrated, rival militias established parallel institutions for tax collection, administration, and production and frequently operated their own ports, airports, and goods and services (Adwan, 2004).

The Taif Accords were signed at the end of the civil conflict and the beginning of the reconstruction effort. The top priorities were the rebuilding of the devastated city of Beirut and the reconstruction of southern Lebanon, Mount Lebanon, and public institutions and infrastructure. The results of these efforts, however, were mixed. The process quickly became mired in accusations of corruption, nepotism, mismanagement, and waste. Furthermore, the presence of the Syrian army on Lebanese territory as well as a large number of Syrian migrant workers further complicated and politicized the reconstruction effort. Nonetheless, the government made significant progress in rebuilding the country's infrastructure. The Beirut city center revitalization, spearheaded by Rafiq al-Hariri, a billionaire businessman and later Lebanon's prime minister, was especially successful. Al-Hariri's assassination in February 2005, however, underscored how volatile the political situation in Lebanon continued to be. The overall reconstruction effort has been expensive, resulting in $52 billion debt or 130 percent of GDP.

Nonetheless, by the time Syrian troops departed in April 2005, the Lebanese economy was growing at a healthy rate, and the tourist, trade, and banking sectors were again the principal agents of growth. Once again, however, conflict and violence brought the economy to a standstill when, in the summer of 2006, the Israeli army clashed with Hizbullah militia in a month-long conflict. The Israeli air raids in response to Hizbullah's capture of Israeli soldiers caused widespread damage of the Lebanese infrastructure, roads, bridges, air- and seaports, and housing stocks. The tourist sector, one of the most important sources of income, was once again devastated as were agricultural and industrial production. The conflict also caused extensive environmental damage, and the direct and indirect costs of this round of conflict are estimated at between $10 billion and $15 billion (UNEP, 2007a).

The conflict that erupted in Syria between the regime of President Bashar al-Assad and the opposition in 2011 began to spill over into neighboring Lebanon, Turkey, and Jordan by 2012. Inspired by the Tunisian and Egyptian revolutions of 2011, what initially started as a wave of popular protests against economic hardships and political repression transformed over the following months into a full-scale civil war. By the end of 2011, at least 40,000 Syrians had perished and 3,000 Syrians a day were fleeing the country (UNHCR, 2012a). The United Nations High Commissioner for Refugees (UNHCR) estimates that more than 450,000 people fled the fighting, with 100,000 Syrians living as refugees in Lebanon, 125,000 in Jordan, close to 124,000 in Turkey, over 55,000 in Iraq, and about 10,000 in various North African countries. According to the UNHCR, by the end of 2012, an estimated 700,000 Syrians had become refugees and 2.5 million were internally displaced. The impact of the civil war had a devastating effect on the Syrian economy, with huge damage to the country's infrastructure, economic production, and cultural and historical treasures (UNHCR, 2012a). The Syrian government estimates economic losses due to conflict were $34 billion by the end of 2012 while the Syrian opposition puts the figure at closer to $100 billion ("Civil War Leaves Syrian Economy, Cities in Ruin," 2012). The final costs will become apparent only when the fighting stops. The conflict also is affecting neighboring economies. For instance, the influx of refugees is straining the Lebanese government, which lacks the resources to provide refugees with necessary assistance.

The civil war in Libya likewise had tremendous economic costs both for Libya as well as neighboring countries. As noted earlier, hundreds of thousands of migrant workers fled the country as the fighting between the Muammar Qaddafi regime and the rebel forces intensified. In all more than 900,000 people, including 600,000 Libyans, left Libya and 200,000 became internally displaced (UNHCR, 2012b). The conflict had an immediate and negative impact on neighboring Tunisia, reducing its economic growth by 0.4 percent in 2011. The IMF estimates that during the year of conflict, the Libyan economy shrunk by about 60 percent. Crude oil production essentially ceased, industrial production declined by 50 percent, and much of the country's infrastructure was destroyed. The reconstruction processes are estimated to cost between $200 billion and $480 billion over the next ten years (Business Monitor International, 2012).

Another country whose economic development has been deeply shaped by conflict is Sudan. Since achieving independence from Britain in 1956, Sudan has experienced internal conflict almost continuously, with the exception of a fragile peace that held between 1972 and 1983. As a result of the civil war, more than 5 million Sudanese have been displaced and agricultural production has been brought to nearly a standstill in large parts of the country. Although a peace agreement was signed between the Sudanese government and the Sudan People's Liberation Army in January 2005, ostensibly ending the conflict between the northern and southern parts of the country, the long-simmering tensions in the Darfur region in the western areas of Sudan erupted in a new civil war in 2003.

Although the economy grew at a fast rate in the mid-2000s, primarily due to an expanding oil industry and agricultural sector, this growth came to a halt in the aftermath of the January 2011 referendum when South Sudan voted to become an independent country. South Sudan became an independent country in July 2011 and, for the next few months, the conflict between the two countries intensified over border demarcation and sharing of oil profits, with fighting breaking out in the border regions where vast oil reserves are located. Although in September 2012 an agreement was reached between the two countries on border security and oil production and transit, by December 2012 tensions were on the rise again. As a result, Sudan's GDP contracted by 0.2 percent in 2011 and 0.4 percent in 2012. South Sudan fared better in 2011 because of high oil prices. However, because oil from the landlocked country needs to transit through Sudan, the closure of pipelines in 2012 deprived the government of close to 100 percent of its income. In addition, the decades of conflict have meant that the Sudanese economy still faces a number of challenges. Among these are land degradation and deforestation, which together with climate change pose a challenge to ensuring long-term food security and sustainable development (UNEP, 2007b:6). These environmental issues have also contributed to the persistence of tension and violence in Sudan through competition over land and other natural resources such as oil and gas reserves, timber, and water.

Conflict has also had a devastating effect on the Palestinian and Iraqi economies. Ironically, since the signing of the Oslo Accords between Israel and the Palestinian Authority in 1994, the economic situation in the Palestinian Territories has deteriorated significantly and the fragmentation of the Palestinian Territories has increased. Israel constructed checkpoints, barriers, and settler roads within the Gaza Strip and the West Bank, and expanded the building of settlements in the West Bank; Sara Roy (2006) estimates that, since 1994, these have cost the Palestinian economy 5 percent annually. A key reason for this economic deterioration has been the Israeli policy of closure, which bars Palestinian workers from entering Israel as day laborers and stops regular trade flow across the border. Because of the economic integration of the Israeli and Palestinian economies that followed the 1967 war, the closures have caused massive disruption of the Palestinian economy, leading to extremely high unemployment and poverty rates.

Since the beginning of the second intifada in 2000, economic conditions in the Palestinian Territories have deteriorated further and territorial fragmentation has intensified. In 2004 for instance, more than 700 Israeli checkpoints divided the Palestinian Territories and an estimated 60 percent of Palestinians were living below the poverty line (UNDP, 2005). The extensive demolition of Palestinian houses, office buildings, and factories, and the bulldozing of cultivated farm areas by the Israeli army have significantly disrupted social and economic life in the Palestinian Territories. In 2012 for example, 40 percent of the West Bank land, 82 percent of groundwater, and over two-thirds of grazing land were no longer accessible to the Palestinians with a devastating impact on the economy (UNCTAD, 2012b).

The economic situation in the Gaza Strip deteriorated even further following the Israeli disengagement in August 2005. The Gaza Strip Economic Development Strategy designed by the Palestinian Authority at that time sought to launch a sustainable economic development program in the area. However, the goals of the strategy remain unfulfilled, and Gaza is experiencing an "acute and debilitating decline marked by unprecedented levels of poverty, unemployment, loss of trade, and social deterioration especially with regard to delivery of health and educational services" (Roy, 2006:1).

The situation has been especially dire since the Hamas victory in the Legislative Council elections in 2006. Following the formation of the Hamas-led government, aid from international donors was suspended and Israel began withholding Palestinian tax revenue, leading to a severe fiscal crisis in the Palestinian Territories. The restrictions on trade mean that exports

Olives and olive oil have been an important part of local and regional economies as well as a source of identity and pride. Here, a Palestinian man picks over a harvest.

from Gaza were below 2 percent of their value prior to 2007 (UNCTAD, 2012b). By one estimate, the costs of the Israeli restrictions were $6.9 billion in 2010 or 85 percent of the total Palestinian GDP (International Federation for Human Rights, 2012:10).

Tax withholdings affect both the Hamas-controlled Gaza Strip and the government of President Mahmoud Abbas in the West Bank. In 2012, for example, Israel withheld Palestinian tax revenues in response to the successful campaign in the United Nations to upgrade the status of Palestine at the organization. The transfers are normally used by the Palestinian Authority to pay its civil servants and security forces. In Gaza, the economic situation deteriorated even further after the eight-day Israeli attack on the territory in 2012. Economic losses resulting from the attack are estimated at around $300 million by the Palestinian Chamber of Commerce (Al Wehaidy, 2013:3).

The uncertainty generated by the closures, furthermore, has made the private sector extremely reluctant to invest, thus adding to the economic contraction. As a result of the economic crisis, unemployment in Gaza and the West Bank has hovered around 30 percent in 2012, although among young people it is estimated to be closer to 47 percent (IMF, 2012). In addition to the almost complete suspension of trade, the agricultural and industrial sectors have been devastated, public investment in infrastructure has nearly ceased, and large amounts of capital have fled abroad. Consequently, the economy increasingly is relying on foreign aid, borrowing, and workers' remittances (World Bank, 2007).

Iraq's economic development also has been profoundly affected by conflict. First came the Iran-Iraq War, which began in 1980, followed by the 1991 Gulf War when an international coalition led by the United States ousted Iraq from Kuwait. Next, came a period of economic sanctions imposed by the United Nations, followed by the 2003 US-led Iraq War. The cumulative effects of these years of war and sanctions have reduced what in 1980 had been a middle-income country with abundant natural resources, a well-developed infrastructure, a highly educated workforce, and a widely admired health care system to a poor, violence-plagued country. In 1980, the per capita income was around $3,600, with oil dominating exports, an expanding public sector, and a large agricultural sector (World Bank, 2007). After an economically draining conflict with Iran when Iraq's oil exports plummeted, Iraq's infrastructure was devastated by allied bombing in 1991, followed by years of UN sanctions that contributed to the gradual contraction of the public sector and the expansion of the private informal sector. At the same time, Iraq's foreign debt increased at a brisk rate, reaching $80 billion by 1988 and by 2003 hovering around $130 billion (Pan, 2003). Shortly before 2003, one report estimates that "industry has ceased to exist and unemployment may be as high as 50 percent. The agricultural sector is in complete disarray, leaving more than 60 percent of the population to rely on the UN Oil for Food program [for basic needs]. About 40 percent of the nation's children are suffering from malnutrition" (Parker and Moore, 2007:7).

The Iraq War did not lead to the turnaround of the economy that was anticipated once hostilities ceased. The initial period following the invasion witnessed the large-scale looting and destruction not just of infrastructure, but also of documents from various ministries. The de-Baathification of public administration ordered by the Coalition Provisional Authority further depleted experienced civil servant ranks. Following the dismantling of the old state structures, however, the US-led coalition found it difficult to create new administrative institutions and to restore basic infrastructure (UNDP, 2004). One of the main assumptions that the coalition made following the invasion was that the private sector would help jump-start the Iraqi economy. Without security, however, bringing in investors has proven to be difficult. The only part of the economy that has expanded since the invasion is the informal economy. Indeed as one recent study found, "militias supporting or opposing the Iraqi government—not the government itself—control import supply chains and, indeed, regulate whole sectors of the Iraqi economy" (Parker and Moore, 2007:6).

Furthermore, the long periods of conflict and sanctions have affected the availability of skilled workers in Iraq. During the past three decades, public infrastructure and education has deteriorated; literacy levels among women, for example, have plummeted from 75 percent in 1987 to 25 percent by 2007. As a consequence of inflation, food shortages, and insecurity, people came to rely on the informal market and on smuggling of goods across international borders for survival. One study estimates that the informal sector accounted for 65 percent of Iraqi GDP by 2005 (Looney, 2006:999).

Additionally, because of the continuing violence, large numbers of Iraqis, many of whom are highly educated professionals, have fled the country. The UN estimates that the violence in Iraq has displaced more than 4.4 million Iraqis or about 15 percent of the population. Some 2.2 million of them have become internally displaced while 2.2 million have fled the country to Syria and Jordan as well as Iran, Egypt, Lebanon, Yemen, and Turkey. By 2007, the continuing violence was forcing an average of 60,000 people a month to leave their homes. The growing number of Iraqi refugees is exporting economic problems from Iraq to neighboring countries and, in particular, to Jordan and Syria (UNHCR, 2008). In the early months after the invasion, many of those fleeing the violence were members of the middle class and skilled professionals. As the conflict dragged on, those seeking to escape the conflict had fewer assets from which to draw for sustaining themselves in exile. Numbers of Iraqi refugees have swelled in urban areas of neighboring countries and put pressure on the Syrian and Jordanian economies, straining their infrastructure and adding to political tensions (Peteet, 2007).

Toward the end of the first decade of the twenty-first century, the security situation in Iraq began to improve, and in 2011 the United States withdrew its forces from the country. Foreign investment rose and the energy, construction, and retail sectors grew. Economic growth has been facilitated by the high price of oil, which still accounts for 90 percent of government revenue. However, the economy remains fragile and unemployment continues to be a problem, especially among young people.

Conclusion

The Middle East has entered the twenty-first century as a region that has undergone profound transformations given that most states gained independence following World War II. Yet the trajectory of these changes has been different from the one that was anticipated in the 1950s. The countries that seemed to hold the most promise in terms of achieving high levels of economic development, in particular Iraq and Lebanon, have seen their economies devastated by long-simmering conflicts. Prior to the eruption of popular uprisings in 2010, Egypt, Syria, and Algeria struggled as a result of years of ineffective state economic planning. On the other hand, the countries of the Gulf, many of which were little more than sleepy fishing outposts in the middle of the past century, have become extremely wealthy states thanks to some of the largest oil deposits in the world.

What have not changed, however, are the deep social inequalities that continue to plague the region. Despite impressive gains in providing education and health care to their citizens, many Middle Eastern societies continue to rank low on the UN Human Development Index (UNDP, 2012). Furthermore, although the arms races that were fueled by the Cold War between the United States and the Soviet Union are over, the militarization of the region has not been reduced. Continuing and new conflicts within the region have had a profoundly negative impact on economic development in numerous countries. The challenges that the region's economies thus face in the twenty-first century are many. In addition to launching sustainable development programs that can address the poverty and inequality that plague the region and resolving economically, socially, and politically ruinous conflicts and rebuilding destroyed societies, the region also faces the challenge of diversifying its economies to make them relevant and competitive in the new global economy.

Bibliography

Achy, Lehcen. 2012. May 31. "Can Algeria Avoid the Arab Spring?" Washington, DC: Carnegie Endowment for International Peace.

Adwan, Charles. 2004. December 1. "Corruption in Reconstruction: The Cost of National Consensus in Post-War Lebanon." Washington, DC: Center for International Private Enterprise.

Africa Development Bank. 2012. *North Africa Quarterly Analytical,* no. 1. Tunis: Africa Development Bank Group.

Africa Development Bank Group. 2012. *Africa Economic Outlook 2012: Promoting Youth Employment.* Tunis: Africa Development Bank Group.

Alissa, Sufyan. 2007. "The Political Economy of Reform in Egypt: Understanding the Role of Institutions." Carnegie Papers no. 5. Washington, DC: Carnegie Endowment for International Peace.

Al Wehaidy, Reham. 2013. "Palestinian National Plan 2011–2013—Current Priorities, Challenges and Opportunities." United Nations Seminar on the Assistance to the Palestinian People. Rome: Food and Agriculture Organization of the United Nations, February 28.

Andoni, Lamis, and Jillian Schwedler. 1996. "Bread Riots in Jordan." *Middle East Report,* no. 201:40–42.

Baldwin-Edwards, Martin. 2005. January. "Migration in the Middle East and Mediterranean." Athens: Mediterranean Migration Observatory, Panteion University.

"Bangladeshi Workers Storm Kuwait Embassy." 2005. April 24. British Broadcasting Corporation. http://news.bbc.co.uk/.

Becker, Kristina Flodman. 2004. *The Informal Sector.* Stockholm: Swedish International Development Cooperation Agency.

Beinin, Joel, and Hossam el-Hamalawy. 2007. May 9. "Strikes in Egypt Spread from Centers of Gravity." *Middle East Report Online.* www.merip.org.

Bellin, Eva R. 2002. *Stalled Democracy: Capital, Labor, and the Paradox of State-Sponsored Development.* Ithaca: Cornell University Press.

Buencamino, Leonides, and Sergei Gorbunov. 2002. "Informal Money Transfer Systems: Opportunities and Challenges for Development Finance." DESA (Department of Economic and Social Affaris) Discussion Paper no. 26. New York: United Nations.

Business Monitor International. 2012. *Libya Infrastructure Report 2012.* Dublin: Research and Markets.

Choucri, Nzali. 1986. "The Hidden Economy: A New View of Remittances in the Arab World." *World Development* 14, no. 6:697–712.

"Civil War Leaves Syrian Economy, Cities in Ruin." 2012. October 9. Associated Press. http://bigstory.ap.org.

Council of Arab Economic Unity. 2012. *The Arab World on the Eve of the "Arab Spring."* Geneva: Arab-Swiss Chamber of Commerce and Industry.

Economic Intelligence Unit. 2011. *GCC Trade and Investment Flows: The Emerging Market Surge.* London: Economic Intelligence Unit.

Henry, Clement M., and Robert Springborg. 2001. *Globalization and the Politics of Development in the Middle East.* Cambridge: Cambridge University Press.

Hourani, Albert. 1991. *History of the Arab Peoples.* Cambridge: Harvard University Press.

IFAD (International Fund for Agricultural Development). 2007. *Sending Money Home: Worldwide Remittances Flows to Developing Countries.* Rome: International Fund for Agricultural Development.

ILO (International Labour Organization). 2011. May. "Statistical Update on Arab States and Territories and North African Countries." ILO Department of Statistics. http://laborsta.ilo.org.

———. 2012. *Global Employment Trends 2012: Preventing a Deeper Jobs Crisis.* Geneva: ILO.

IMF (International Monetary Fund). 2012a. December. "Political Risk Index—Asia: Risk in the World's Most Dynamic Region." *Political Monitor*.

———. 2012b. *Regional Outlook Update* (April). Washington, DC: IMF.

International Crisis Group. 2001. October 26. *Algeria's Economy: The Vicious Cycle of Oil and Violence*. Africa Report no. 36. Brussels: International Crisis Group.

———. 2009. May 27. *Yemen: Defusing the Saada Timebomb. Middle East Report*, no. 86:3–7.

International Federation for Human Rights. 2012. December. *Trading Away Peace: How Europe Helps Support Illegal Israeli Settlements*. Paris: International Federation for Human Rights.

IOM (International Organization for Migration). 2010. *Migration Report: The Future of Migration: Building Capacities for Change*. Geneva: International Organization for Migration.

Issawi, Charles. 1995. *The Middle East Economy: Decline and Recovery*. Princeton, NJ: Markus Wiener.

Kpadar, Knagni. 2007. August. "Why Has Unemployment in Algeria Been Higher than in MENA and Transition Countries?" IMF Working Paper no. 07/210. Washington, DC: International Monetary Fund.

Looney, Robert. 2006. "Economic Consequences of Conflict: The Rise of Iraq's Informal Economy." *Journal of Economic Issues* 40, no. 4:991–1007.

Manpower Group. 2012. "Youth Unemployment: Challenge and Solutions: What Business Can Do." Milwaukee: Manpower Group.

Paczynska, Agnieszka. 2006. "Globalization, Structural Adjustment, and Pressure to Conform: Contesting Labor Law Reform in Egypt." *New Political Science* 28, no. 1:45–64.

Pan, Esther. 2003. December 31. "Iraq: The Regime's Debt." New York: Council on Foreign Relations.

Panzac, Daniel. 1992 "International and Domestic Maritime Trade in the Ottoman Empire During the Eighteenth Century." *International Journal of Middle East Studies* 24, no. 2:189–206.

Parker, Christopher, and Pete W. Moore. 2007. "The War Economy of Iraq." *Middle East Report*, no. 243:6–15.

Peteet, Julie. 2007. "Unsettling the Categories of Displacement." *Middle East Report*, no. 244:2–9.

Property World Middle East. 2005. December 21. "Qatari Diar Launches Qatar's Single Biggest Development." www.ameinfo.com.

Richards, Alan, and John Waterbury. 1990. *A Political Economy of the Middle East: State, Class, and Economic Development*. Boulder: Westview Press.

Roy, Sara. 2006. October 4. "The Economy of Gaza." Boston: Women's International League for Peace and Freedom. http://wilpf.org.

Sadowski, Yahya M. 1993. *Scuds or Butter? The Political Economy of Arms Control in the Middle East*. Washington, DC: Brookings Institution.

Salah, Isam. 2010. "The Effects of the Financial Crisis on the Middle East." *Global Business Law Review* 1, no. 99:99–108.

Santi, Emanuele, Saoussen Ben Romdhane, and Mohamed Safouane Ben Aïssa. 2012. *North Africa Quarterly Analytical, Africa Development Bank*, no. 1:1–16.

Schneider, Friedrich, Andreas Buehn, and Claudio E. Montenegro. 2010. July. "Shadow Economies All over the World: New Estimates for 162 Countries from 1999 to 2007." World Bank Working Paper no. 5356. Washington, DC: World Bank.

Sufyan, Alissa. 2007. May. "The Challenge of Economic Reform in the Arab World: Toward More Productive Economies." Carnegie Papers no. 1. Washington, DC: Carnegie Endowment for International Peace.

Tuma, Elias. 2004. "The Economies of the Middle East." In Deborah J. Gerner and Jillian Schwedler (eds.), *Understanding the Contemporary Middle East*. 2nd ed. Boulder: Lynne Rienner.

UNCTAD (United Nations Conference on Trade and Development). 2006. *Handbook of Statistics 2006–2007*. New York: UNCTAD.

———. 2012a. *Handbook of Statistics 2012*. New York: UNCTAD.

———. 2012b. *Report on UNCTAD Assistance to the Palestinian People: Developments in the Economy of Occupied Palestinian Territory (July)*. New York: UNCTAD.

UNDP (United Nations Development Programme). 2005. *Arab Human Development Report: Toward Freedoms in the Arab World*. New York: UNDP.

———. 2012. *Human Development Report 2011: Sustainability and Equity: A Better Future for All*. New York: UNDP.

UNEP (United Nations Environment Programme). 2007a. *Lebanon: Post-Conflict Environmental Assessment*. Geneva: UNEP.

———. 2007b. *Sudan: Post-Conflict Environmental Assessment*. Geneva: UNEP.

UNHCR (United Nations High Commissioner for Refugees). 2008. "Iraq Situation." Geneva: UNHCR.

———. 2012a. March 12. *Refugees Daily*. Geneva: UNHCR.

———. 2012b. July 8. *Refugees Daily*. Geneva: UNHCR.

United Nations. 2009. *The Global Economic and Financial Crisis: Regional Impacts, Responses and Solutions*. New York: United Nations.

———. 2011a. *The Global Economic Crisis: Causes and Transmission*. New York: United Nations.

———. 2011b. *International Migration Report 2009: A Global Assessment*. New York: UN Department of Economic and Social Affairs.

UNRWA (United Nations Relief and Works Agency for Palestinian Refugees in the Near East). 2007. June 30. "UNRWA Emergency Appeal Progress Report, January–June 2007." UNRWA.

Waldner, David. 1999. *State Building and Late Development*. Ithaca: Cornell University Press.

Waterbury, John. 1993. *Exposed to Innumerable Delusions: Public Enterprise and State Power in Egypt, India, Mexico and Turkey*. New York: Cambridge University Press.

Williamson, John (ed.). 1990. *Latin American Adjustment: How Much Has Happened?* Washington, DC: Institute for International Economics.

World Bank. 2006. *Economic Development and Prospects 2006: Financial Markets in a New Age of Oil*. Washington, DC: World Bank.

———. 2007. September 24. "Two Years After London: Restarting Palestinian Economic Recovery." Economic Monitoring Report to the Ad Hoc Liaison Committee. Washington, DC: World Bank.

———. 2012a. September 23. *Fiscal Crisis, Economic Prospects: The Imperative for Economic Cohesion in the Palestinian Territories*. Washington, DC: World Bank.

———. 2012b. *Migration and Remittances Factbook 2011*. Washington, DC: World Bank.

World Bank Group Sana'a Office. 2007. *Yemen Economic Update (Fall)*. Sana'a: World Bank Group.

World Food Program. 2012. *The State of Food Security and Nutrition in Yemen: Comprehensive Food Security Survey*. Rome: World Food Program.

Yousef, Tarik. 2005. February. "The Changing Role of Labor Migration in the Arab World." Working Paper Series. Washington, DC: Georgetown University, Edmund A. Walsh School of Foreign Service. http://ssrn.com/abstract=793804.

8

The Political Economy of Middle Eastern Oil

Mary Ann Tétreault

Oil is the commodity most people associate with the Middle East. That is where the largest proven petroleum reserves in the world are located, along with huge deposits of natural gas. Oil and gas drew major-power intervention and investment into the region, leading to conflict as well as cooperation among international oil companies (IOCs), the home governments of the countries where the IOCs were headquartered, and the host governments of the countries where they did their work. During the century of their exploitation, Middle East hydrocarbon resources mediated a number of power transitions among contenders seeking control of the oil market. This chapter looks at changing patterns of conflict and cooperation among actors engaged in the exploration, development, transport, processing, and sale of hydrocarbons and their products.

To oil-exporting countries, hydrocarbons are both a blessing and a curse. The blessing is easy enough to understand: massive earnings of hard currency and plenty of fuel for a wide range of development strategies. Among the curses was oil's allure to imperialists, even though oil exploitation imposed fewer social disruptions than other forms of colonial exploitation. Oil production is geographically localized; its technology and capital intensity isolate it from the rest of a national economy. Except in the local areas where oil operations are conducted, normal life continues pretty much as before, unlike the effects of a shift from subsistence agriculture to cash crops (Munif, 1989; Vitalis, 2007).

Yet oil money was profoundly destabilizing because it changed the balance of power between state and society in oil-exporting countries. It gave local rulers effective tools for suppressing popular institutions and movements, and allowed them to ignore or thwart traditional checks on their

259

While the mechanisms behind oil pricing can be complex, the impact is felt around the globe. These gasoline prices are from January 2013 in New York City.

authority because it made governments so much more powerful than any other social force (Gasiorowski, 1991; Vitalis, 2007).

The *rentier state* is theorized as a polity that relies for significant state income on external sources, allowing it to escape demands for popular participation in politics and constitutional limits on the regime (e.g., Beblawi, 1990). Rulers with resources that do not derive from collecting taxes are thought to garner support from citizens or subjects by allocating resources to rather than extracting resources from them (Luciani, 1990). Particularly with regard to income generated from assets like oil, the exploitation of which is geographically confined, earnings from such enclave industries create little in the way of forward and backward economic linkages. As a result, they retard social changes with the potential to shift norms and expectations, and economic changes that reduce direct citizen dependence on the state (Ross, 2001). Rentier income allows these states to nurture traditional political forms, such as tribes, to keep populations divided and dependent on their rulers (Crystal, 1994; but see also Tétreault and al-Ghanim, 2012). Thus, it should not be surprising that oil money decreased legitimate political participation in the Middle East (Crystal, 1990; Tétreault, 2000).

Industry Structure
Structure is an important characteristic of power. Location and concentration as well as legal, physical, and political constraints limit what any actor,

no matter how intelligent or lucky, can do. The oil industry is intrinsically global. Crude production and most customers for products are located in different countries (Penrose, 1968). This made oil an engine of globalization from the industry's earliest days (Sampson, 1975). Oil's importance in the evolution of the modern Middle East helps explain why the region is hyperglobalized, a nexus of world investment and trade where size, market access, and financial resources are key components of high performance.

Complexity and global reach present many points of political and economic leverage where an actor, such as a firm or a country, can exert significant control. One source of hydrocarbon leverage is production (Blair, 1976). Whoever possesses mineral rights controls access to them. As in most countries and nearly all the US states, mineral rights belong to the state in Middle Eastern nations. When oil was first developed there, oil companies had to negotiate with local governments for exploration and production rights.

Before World War II, Middle Eastern governments competed for oil company investment in a market where the largest companies were more afraid of having too much oil, which would cause prices to fall, than not having enough. In the 1920s, the companies agreed among themselves to limit production, fix prices, and reduce competition in product markets. In 1928, the three largest IOCs, Jersey Standard (ExxonMobil), Royal Dutch Shell, and Anglo-Iranian/British Petroleum (BP),[1] along with a few smaller partners, signed the Red Line Agreement pledging that none would explore for oil or develop new production capacity anywhere in the former Ottoman Empire unless every partner consented. Countries inside the Red Line had difficulty attracting investment in oil exploration because the big Red Line IOCs feared oversupply and falling prices. Iraq suffered the most because Red Line companies owned all of the oil rights there (Anderson, 1981; Sampson, 1975).

Middle Eastern oil exporters were often at a disadvantage in bargaining because most dealt with only one operating company (e.g., Chisholm, 1975). Although many operating companies were joint ventures (partnerships), host countries found themselves sitting across from a single operator on the other side of the bargaining table. Oil was first developed in Kuwait by the Kuwait Oil Company (KOC), a partnership between Gulf Oil and BP. Even though both put capital in and took profits from Kuwait's oil, all of their business in Kuwait was conducted by a single entity, KOC. IOCs, however, participated in multiple operating companies worldwide. They had plenty of opportunities to coordinate production, set prices, and collude on which would seek new contracts.

Kuwait's freedom to choose which IOCs would own its operating company was limited by the British government, whose treaties with Kuwait gave Britain the final authority over Kuwait's foreign policy. The British would not permit the Kuwaitis to contract with a non-British company, though the emir successfully held out until they agreed to approve a company that had at least one non-British partner (Chisholm, 1975). Once the concession was granted, Kuwait's autonomy was reduced further. The terms of its contract with KOC gave the company exclusive rights for ninety-nine years to find and produce oil over Kuwait's entire land area. If the Kuwaiti government were to violate this contract by seeking better terms from another IOC during the ninety-nine years, that IOC could be sued by BP and Gulf Oil, and home-country courts likely would decide in their favor. An even greater threat was the possibility of political intervention by a home government—in Kuwait's case, Britain and the United States—should Kuwait try to remove KOC from its privileged position.

In 1951 the Iranian government, under Prime Minister Mohammad Mossadeq, nationalized Iran's oil. Iran's operating company was unusual in the Middle East because a single IOC (BP) owned all of it. When BP's holdings were nationalized, the company obtained court orders enjoining other IOCs from buying oil from the Iranian government. Afraid of the example that a successful nationalization might set for other Middle Eastern oil-exporting hosts of US and British IOCs, the British and US governments worked to destabilize and eventually to overthrow the Mossadeq regime. The restoration of the shah of Iran in 1953 following a brief period of ouster also reinstated IOCs as managers of the nationalized Iranian oil company. Instead of restoring BP to its former position as sole owner, however, the Iranian government sought a "Kuwait solution." The shah invited non-British participation in the National Iranian Oil Company (NIOC). When the NIOC was reorganized, US companies and the French National Oil Company (CFP) were given 60 percent of the shares, and BP was left with only 40 percent (Sampson, 1975).

The one company–one country pattern of concessions throughout much of the Middle East made it easy to balance global supply and demand by regulating production there because the largest IOCs, whose production holdings stretched across the globe, operated in multiple Middle Eastern concessions. Once they had decided what total supply should be, the companies could regulate production by increasing or decreasing offtake in countries whose governments could not easily retaliate against them. The one company–one country pattern did not hold in Libya, whose oil was discovered and developed much later than that of most of the Gulf countries (Rand, 1975). As long as most exporting countries had little leverage over their operators, however, the companies' cartel was difficult to overthrow.

Governments and IOCs in developed countries wanted to regulate oil production to protect their domestic industries and their foreign investments. Regulations were even applied in the United States where the antitrust tradition was strong, but not so strong as to counter either the threat of business failure in the 1930s or the Cold War politics of the period following World War II (Prindle, 1981). Indeed, oil policy during the Cold

War found IOCs and their home governments cooperating closely for their mutual benefit. The companies preached an ethic of oil statesmanship to justify their interference in politics and markets and to explain why they were entitled to their home government's assistance. The governments, in turn, expanded their use of oil companies as foreign policy surrogates in relations with host governments. By the end of World War II, foreign oil was widely regarded as an important ingredient of national power and one of the most lucrative businesses in the world (Penrose, 1968).

The System Unravels

Economic theory tells us that when firms make huge profits, new competitors will enter the industry, eventually reducing profits for all. This is what happened in the international oil industry. The success of even imperfect cartel arrangements made oil hugely profitable, and IOCs were among the world's largest and richest firms. Competition came from brand new companies, companies that formerly had operated only in their own home countries, and from state-owned firms. These new competitors offered potential oil-exporting countries more money and better terms, including attractive prices for offshore rights in countries whose onshore operators had not thought to ask for them in their original contracts. This willingness to write contracts highly favorable to host countries encouraged Middle Eastern governments to ask all their operating companies to liberalize contract terms.

Even the largest IOCs had to compete for new contracts, but some agreed to sweeten the terms of ongoing contracts to maintain good relations with their hosts. Others had to be asked to relinquish territory they were not developing so that the host governments could sell the rights to someone else. Both increased the costs of doing business, reducing company profits. Taxes also squeezed profits. Shortly after the end of World War II, the Venezuelan government threatened to nationalize foreign oil operations unless the companies agreed to split their profits on Venezuelan oil fifty-fifty with the government. Mindful of Mexico's nationalization in 1938, companies operating in Venezuela agreed. Soon after, Middle Eastern governments began demanding the same terms. This was the trigger of the conflict between BP and Mossadeq's Iran in the early 1950s.

In 1950, US tax law was "reinterpreted" to allow Arabian American Oil Company (ARAMCO) to deduct taxes paid to Saudi Arabia from their US taxes. This foreign tax credit soon became available to every US firm operating abroad. British law did not let BP pass a similar proportion of its foreign taxes along to taxpayers in Britain, causing the community of interests among the IOCs to diverge (Kaufman, 1977). Other pressure on the oil companies came from the Soviet Union. US Cold War policies restricted Soviet trade with the West, forcing it to rely increasingly on commodity (gold and oil) sales to earn foreign exchange. Under Nikita Khrushchev, total Soviet oil production doubled in the five years following Stalin's death in 1953.

Perhaps the last straw for the IOCs was the 1959 decision of the US government to impose a limit—a quota—on the amount of oil that they could import into the United States. The US market was the largest in the world and doubly lucrative because the high cost of domestically produced oil gave sellers of lower-cost foreign oil a larger profit margin. But US oil companies that operated entirely at home were politically strong in the postwar era. These domestic producers, citing national security and scaring Americans about the prospect of becoming dependent on foreign oil imports, demanded protection against cheap imported oil. In 1959, what had started as a voluntary program in 1954 became law (Vietor, 1984).

The IOCs could see which way the wind was blowing in their markets and shifted their strategy for propping up declining profits. In the early 1950s they had developed the "posted price system" to help host governments estimate their anticipated oil revenues more easily. The companies posted or published prices so that host governments could use them to calculate the amount of taxes the companies would be paying even though little oil was actually traded at the posted price. When posted prices were first introduced, company profits on foreign operations were high and small deviations in the real prices at which crude oil traded were insignificant. Stable posted prices quickly became an accepted industry norm. Host country governments did not pay much attention to posted prices either, lobbying instead for profit sharing and improved concession terms to increase their shares of oil profits (Penrose, 1968).

But as costs and competition increased, the operators began to look at posted prices as a source of higher profits. In February 1959, after consulting with one another (but not their hosts), the companies lowered posted prices—and, thereby, the taxes they owed to host governments. An immediate outcry arose, and the host governments decided to coordinate their own actions. Such a strategy was difficult, however, because host countries competed for investment and production. Also, their national industries were started at different times by different firms with different cost structures. The Venezuelan industry was organized in many independent segments instead of the uncompetitive one company–one country pattern common in the Middle East while the age of Venezuela's industry made it more expensive to produce oil there.

When the IOCs, oblivious to all but their own desires and conflicts, lowered posted prices again in August 1960, five oil-exporting governments on two continents tried again to salvage their economic interests. These five—Venezuela, Saudi Arabia, Iran, Iraq, and Kuwait—formed the Organization of Petroleum Exporting Countries (OPEC) in September 1960 (Mikdashi, 1972).

OPEC's aims from the very beginning included helping host governments gain autonomy and greater control over their oil. Progress was incremental during OPEC's first ten years and was complicated by adding new members. Competition among members remained a constant problem, one that was aggravated by political divisions between conservative, monarchical states like Saudi Arabia and postrevolutionary radical states like Iraq (Dawisha, 2003). There also were political differences between Arab and non-Arab states, economic differences between large and small exporters, and a conflict over whether oil was an economic or a strategic good. One of the last centered on the Arab *oil weapon,* production (and, therefore, income) cuts by Arab oil producers intended to force political concessions from countries supporting Israel.

The oil weapon was ineffective when it was used in conjunction with the Arab-Israeli wars of 1948, 1956, and 1967. Arab oil production cuts were offset by higher production from other producers—including other members of OPEC—and by IOCs, which redistributed supplies internationally. Until 1967, short and unevenly administered attempts to use the oil weapon had little impact on policy toward Israel. The 1967 oil embargo did move France away from Israel toward closer relations with Arab governments. This is because, following the loss of Algeria, France had fewer assured sources of petroleum. France also distrusted US leadership of the Western alliance, and was wary of sacrificing good relations with Arab oil suppliers for the benefit of a US client (Israel) with no oil.

The IOCs thought the 1967 Arab oil embargo was a nonevent. They continued to be obsessed by fears of oversupply despite structural changes in the world oil market brought about by war and a booming world economy that shifted the balance of power between IOCs and host governments. The 1967 war closed the Suez Canal, creating an effective tanker shortage for oil shipments to Europe from the Gulf because tankers had to travel the far longer distance around Africa to reach the Mediterranean. The IOCs did not take precautions against a possible supply cut by exporters on the Mediterranean. Most saw the narrowing supply-demand gap as beneficial to their interests and were skeptical that the global oil market could be disrupted by political pressure since so little disruption had resulted during attempts to apply such pressure in the past (Vernon, 1976).

The IOCs also were unconcerned by rising demand for oil worldwide, and by falling oil production in the United States. US oil production peaked in 1970 even as US demand continued to rise and additional supply for ever growing US consumption had to be made up from foreign sources. Another effect of the shift in the US energy balance was that, as actual US production approached total production capacity, excess capacity under direct US control shrank. Should the oil weapon be used again, there would be no way to increase production from the United States, a tactic that had minimized the impact of the oil crises of 1956 and 1967.

The Politics in Oil's Political Economy

In September 1969, a revolution in Libya replaced a pro-Western king with a militantly anti-US colonel determined to increase Libya's oil income. Muammar Qaddafi isolated two of Libya's more than forty operators, demanding that they increase payments to the Libyan government or else be shut down. Occidental Petroleum had no other sources of oil in the Eastern Hemisphere. It did have contracts with European buyers imposing heavy financial penalties should it fail to deliver. It soon gave in. Qaddafi then moved to apply the same technique to other operators until they all agreed to the higher price. Qaddafi's success made the shah of Iran jealous, and in 1971 he demanded higher prices for the Gulf oil-producing countries too.

The IOCs wanted to negotiate simultaneously with Libya and the Gulf producers to prevent being picked off one at a time in Tehran as they had been in Tripoli, but the cliency relationship between the United States and Iran prevented US companies from getting the government support they needed to make this happen. The United States could not apply pressure on Iran without making concessions to the shah or risking his strategic cooperation in the future. As the oil companies feared, alternating demands between Tehran and Tripoli led to a short volley of negotiations between Libya and the Gulf. The oil revolution was under way: oil-exporting countries were commanding ever higher prices for their oil in spite of long-term contracts specifying much lower prices.

Negotiations were speeded along by deterioration in the US economy causing the US government to devalue the dollar in 1971 and again in 1973. Because the dollars received by oil exporters were declining in value, they wanted more dollars to compensate for the lost purchasing power. Negotiations after the second devaluation were still in progress in the fall of 1973, when other events snowballed the price issue into the larger question of who would control OPEC oil (Tétreault, 1985).

US companies also were in trouble at home. Domestic oil supplies in the highly regulated US market were falling behind demand while quota restrictions on oil imports triggered spot shortages and price increases. These market disruptions prompted congressional hearings and widespread public criticism of the oil companies well before the "oil shock." The supply situation became so dire that oil import quotas were ended in April 1973. The energy crisis, which is remembered as the result of the use of the oil weapon in the October 1973 war, had in reality begun months—if not years—earlier.

The October 1973 decision by Arab oil exporters to try the oil weapon once again was signaled throughout 1972–1973. Arab governments promised openly and repeatedly to use the oil weapon against the United States if a Middle East settlement conforming to United Nations (UN) Security Council Resolution 242, which required Israeli withdrawal from the Occupied

Territories, was not achieved. Saudi Arabian officials went so far as to call in representatives of all four ARAMCO operating company partners to deliver a message. They said that another war between Israel and Arab governments was imminent and that, when it came, Arab oil would be cut off to Israel's supporters. One partner, Mobil, took the warning so seriously that it bought an ad on the *New York Times* op-ed page to urge a settlement of the Arab-Israeli conflict. The other partners relied on private channels to communicate their message (Tétreault, 1985).

By the summer of 1973, the exposure of criminal behavior in congressional hearings into the Watergate scandal were absorbing most of the attention of the White House. But President Richard Nixon's domestic problems were not the only forces inhibiting direct US involvement in a Middle Eastern settlement. Foreign policy problems loomed as well. The Nixon Doctrine was a strategy based on US reliance on a few chosen client regimes, built up by foreign aid and arms transfers, that would pursue US interests throughout the world without requiring direct intervention by the United States (Petersen, 2012). This was the philosophy behind the Vietnamization of the Vietnam War, and the arming of Israel, Iran, and eventually Saudi Arabia in the Middle East. US dependence on its Middle East clients meant that the United States could not force Israel to accept UN Resolution 242 in 1972 and 1973 any more than it could force the shah of Iran to accept joint negotiations with the oil companies in 1971 (Petersen, 2012; Tétreault, 1985).

When war came in October 1973, Arab governments waited for some sign that the United States would respond to their concerns. Finally, on October 17, at the request of the Arab League, the Organization of Arab Petroleum Exporting Countries (OAPEC), a group that included the Arab members of OPEC along with Bahrain, Egypt, and Syria, imposed an oil embargo against Israel's allies (Tétreault, 1981). Crafted to be more effective than the earlier embargoes had been, the 1973–1974 embargo was intended to be both extensive and discriminating. OAPEC aimed to keep Arab oil from enemies of the Arab states while, at the same time, allowing Arab oil to flow to friendly nations.

Some aspects were successful. Total supplies of oil to the world market were cut, creating local shortages and higher prices in most oil-importing countries. Another success was in altering perceptions of Arab governments that had previously been dismissed as weak and ineffective. But despite the care taken in drawing up the embargo provisions, its spirit was systematically violated, preventing the targeting plan from working. As in previous applications of the oil weapon, oil supplies were exchanged between and within IOCs. Arab oil that could not be sent to the United States or the Netherlands was swapped for unrestricted supplies from non-Arab sources. All importing countries experienced about the same level of shortages whether they supported the Arab states or Israel. The failure of targeting meant that, although the embargo did succeed in inflicting hardship on the friends of Israel, it also inflicted hardship on the friends of the Arabs.

The most lasting effect of the embargo was to consolidate the oil price revolution. Bids for spot or individual cargoes of crude oil reached high levels. OPEC's price hawks, countries like Libya, Iraq, and Iran, insisted that OPEC members stop negotiating with the IOCs and set their own prices much higher. Others, like Saudi Arabia, supported setting an OPEC price, but opposed the size of the price increase advocated by the price hawks because they did not want to reduce future demand. The two groups fought during OPEC's December 1973 meeting and eventually compromised on a price between the two extremes. This price, $11.65 per barrel, was four times higher than the average price of OPEC crude just a year earlier.

The Oil Revolution

The oil revolution was not just a price revolution. Even more important, it marked a change in the ownership of oil. Prior to 1973, IOCs controlled the oil of most OPEC members. These companies decided how much oil to produce, what to pay for it, and how much to invest in the host's national industry. Although oil companies and host governments did bargain over prices and production levels, the companies had the last word.

Several oil-exporting countries had nationalized their oil industries prior to the oil revolution, but nationalization did not mean that control of oil would pass to the host government. Iran had nationalized its oil in 1951, but the restoration of the shah also restored IOC control of Iran's oil. Nationalizations by Iraq and Libya were more effective in transferring control of domestic industries to host governments. As other countries nationalized their industries or took over ownership more gradually through participation, decisionmaking power passed from IOCs to oil ministries of host governments. This transfer of authority also took place in Iran.

The IOCs were criticized for being nothing more than "tax collectors for OPEC" rather than independent actors in the international oil market (Adelman, 1972–1973). They did not use their structural or political assets to challenge OPEC head-on. Most IOCs probably were rooting for the host governments to succeed in keeping prices high. High prices made for vastly higher profits while the nationalizations at first neither cut off nor reduced the revenues of most oil companies operating in the Middle East (Nitzan and Bichler, 2002). Many IOCs made enough money to invest in high-cost exploration and development outside of OPEC, including in the expensive United States. They bought other oil companies and invested in companies producing coal and nuclear energy. Some bought firms in industries totally unrelated to energy. One even tried to buy a circus.

State-owned national oil companies took over IOC operations. Some host countries already had state firms and others created them expressly to take charge of newly nationalized industries. This shift in corporate ownership led to a restructuring of the industry as a whole. Now that OPEC set crude oil prices, IOCs stopped using profits from oil production to subsidize other operations. In the past, they would set the transfer prices at which oil was sold between subsidiaries of the same company to show high profits on crude sales and low profits on refining and on sales of products. Because tax rates were lower in producing countries than in consuming countries, they could save money on taxes if it looked as though they were earning most of their profits from producing oil overseas rather than from refining and marketing oil in the United States, Europe, or Japan.

After the oil revolution, the price of crude oil became a real cost and not just a strategy for tax evasion. Without production from now-nationalized holdings, other IOC operations had to earn real—and not just paper—profits. Obsolescent equipment was replaced and the downstream phases of the industry—refining and marketing—were rationalized wherever possible. Where these operations could not be made profitable for their owners, they were sold. Gasoline stations were snapped up by national oil companies of OPEC countries eager to have their own marketing outlets in oil-importing countries. Some had to take less attractive operations, like obsolete refineries, as part of these packages (Tétreault, 1995).

Another effect of the new OPEC price structure was that production anywhere in the world earned its owners *windfall profits,* the difference between the marginal cost of what they produced and the much higher prices at which oil now was sold. Increasing production in the United States and elsewhere outside OPEC became an IOC priority, even though US regulations limited the windfall profits companies could reap and host governments began to charge higher royalties and fees for oil produced in their countries (Tétreault, 1985).

Higher oil prices also depressed demand. By 1978, inflation had erased most of the value of the 1973–1974 price increases. Consumers believed that they were paying more for oil because the nominal prices of products like gasoline and heating oil stayed about the same. But because real prices (corrected for inflation) had actually fallen, consumption, which had dropped in 1974 and 1975, soon began to rise. When oil prices shot up again during the Iranian Revolution, consumption had reached about the same level that it was in January 1973 before the oil embargo.

Oil Politics in the Middle East

Higher oil prices and greater autonomy for oil-producing countries did not take oil out of Middle Eastern politics. On the contrary, OPEC's new power in the international industry increased its appeal as an arena for pursuing political goals. Ongoing ethnic, religious, and territorial disagreements between Iran and Arab Gulf nations aggravated conflicts over oil prices, but no single cause motivated conflicts within OPEC. For example, Arab states (chiefly Libya, Algeria, and even Iraq) occasionally joined Iran to press for oil price increases, and Saudi Arabia and its allies among the smaller Gulf states opposed them. Thus, the Arab-Iranian conflict often cut across other ongoing regional conflicts such as the "Arab civil war" between traditional and revolutionary regimes (Skeet, 1988).

The Iranian Revolution (1978–1979) aggravated conflicts within OPEC over oil prices and organization leadership. Ayatollah Ruhollah Khomeini's revolutionary government saw raising oil prices as a way to attack the United States while increasing Iran's national income and foreign exchange reserves. Iranian price militancy was effective in raising oil prices as long as the panic set off by Iran's revolution continued. Throughout 1979, Iran and other OPEC price hawks imposed extravagant price increases that also pulled up the prices of more moderate OPEC members. When prices weakened in 1980, Iran also proved to be an aggressive price-cutter in the battle over shrinking markets, despite its denials.

Iran's aggressive nationalism in oil marketing was matched by its aggressive nationalism in regional politics. Iran hoped to export its revolution to other Islamic states, and OPEC meetings soon became places for revolutionary exhortation and guerrilla tactics. Iraq was a favorite Iranian target because of its large Shi'i population, its convenient location on the western border of Iran, and a history of enmity between the two countries. As recounted in Chapter 5, rivalries over oil and oil revenues added to other axes of conflict between these two old enemies.

Iraq's oil power, long obscured by oil company limits on expansion of supply capacity inside the Red Line, promised to overtake Iran's. Iraqi development policies were more successful than those of Iran. Iraq's growing economic and political strength made its new leader, Saddam Hussein, confident that he could overturn the 1975 settlement with Iran of the long-running border dispute between the two countries. In September 1980, Iraq attacked Iran, setting off a long, brutal war marked by high casualties among civilians and soldiers on both sides (Cordesman and Wagner, 1991; Potter and Sick, 2004; see also Chapter 5).

The effect of the war on OPEC was also devastating. Meetings turned into shouting matches. With OPEC facing competition from new production in Britain and Norway, and the Soviet Union dumping large quantities of crude oil into West European markets, the Iran-Iraq War impeded efforts to coordinate production and maintain a united OPEC front. Even the day-to-day operations of OPEC were affected when neither Iran nor Iraq would accept a secretary-general from the other country and the organization had to be run for several years by the assistant secretary-general, Fadhel al-Chalabi—an Iraqi.

Oil Politics and the Price Bust

The most serious effect of the Iran-Iraq War for oil exporters was that it prevented OPEC members from cooperating to limit the effects of outside assaults on the price structure. At that time, there were three main threats to oil prices in addition to price-cutting by OPEC members themselves. First, just as in 1973–1974, the new round of price increases depressed consumer demand; second, these high prices also prompted oil companies to expand supplies, especially supplies originating outside of OPEC; third, the cash-strapped Soviet Union became an aggressive crude seller in dollar-denominated markets. These developments marginalized OPEC as the dominant world supplier of crude oil and slashed OPEC government revenues.[2]

When the IOCs looked carefully at the supply situation, they found that oil exploration and development begun in response to the oil price increases of the early 1970s had started to pay off within a few years. New oil came to the market from the North Sea, non-OPEC developing countries, and the continental United States. The Soviet Union was so attracted by the new high prices that it reneged on contracts to sell oil to its clients in Eastern Europe (Jentleson, 1986) so that it could sell it at or close to OPEC prices in Western markets. Refiners bought crude oil first from these sources and only afterward from OPEC. By 1979, OPEC production had recovered to 1973 levels, 31 million barrels per day. In 1980 this dropped to 27 million barrels per day, and by 1983 it had plummeted to 17.6 million barrels per day.

Extra crude supplies came from unexpected sources. One was inventories. After the 1973–1974 oil embargo, developed countries came together to form a kind of countercartel, the International Energy Agency (IEA). The IEA required each member to maintain a ninety-day supply of oil in a strategic reserve to be used in case of oil supply interruptions. If the amount of oil available to any member were to fall below 7 percent of requirements, it could apply to the IEA and draw supplies from its own and other members' strategic stocks. These stocks were too low to be useful during the 1979 crisis; at the same time, the crisis encouraged importers and companies to buy more stocks, contributing to the upward pressure on prices. Afterward, many found that the combination of falling consumer demand and the massive buildup of stocks resulting from their frantic purchases in 1979 and 1980 left them with much more oil than they needed to meet IEA requirements.

In 1983 and again in 1985, large quantities of excess stocks were dumped onto the market, pushing prices downward. In 1983, OPEC so feared the loss of customers, revenues, and control over the market that, for the first time, it lowered the price of its *marker crude,* the reference crude against which the prices of crudes of different quality were set, by $5 per barrel. It also made mandatory a production regulation scheme it had adopted as a voluntary measure to restrict production the year before. The intention was to punish price-cutters inside and outside OPEC by reducing their oil incomes, and to halt or reverse the drop in oil demand by reducing prices. Neither plan succeeded, in part because of the independent effect of exchange rate fluctuations.

US monetary policy from 1981 through most of 1985 affected exchange rates by keeping the value of the dollar, the currency for which virtually all crude oil was sold, high. Dollars acquired through oil sales could be traded for pounds, yen, marks, francs, and other hard currencies, maintaining the purchasing power of oil sellers even after prices were cut. Although both price-cutters and price-defenders in OPEC complained about the oil price reduction, few actually suffered from it unless they also had to pay off loans or make purchases in dollars.

Consumers outside the United States experienced the reverse. Higher prices for the dollars needed to buy oil meant that oil prices in local currencies remained constant or actually rose after the OPEC price cut. These higher real prices erased any price incentive that nondollar consumers might have had to buy more oil. Although US consumers, whose dollar economy enjoyed the full effects of the price reduction, did react as OPEC had hoped, their contribution to world demand for crude oil was not enough to solve OPEC's problems because of the ineffectiveness of its production controls.

OPEC's inability to control production contributed to global oversupply. The production control regulations that it adopted for its members were complicated and full of loopholes. For example, heavy crudes and condensates—liquids precipitated from natural gas—were not counted as oil production. During the Iran-Iraq War, the cutoff of Iraq's pipelines by Iranian bombing led to extra production by Kuwait and Saudi Arabia "on Iraq's account," but the amounts produced tended to be more than Iraq's share and they were not cut back when exports from Iraq resumed. The depressed global economy encouraged barter and other countertrade arrangements outside normal oil sales channels, making it hard for OPEC accountants to find out which country was exporting how much oil and to whom. Several OPEC members cheated outright by producing oil over their allotted quotas while non–OPEC members continued to enjoy a free ride on the OPEC price structure.

The main responsibility for holding OPEC production to the ceiling set by the group as a whole belonged to Saudi Arabia, the swing producer. Saudi Arabia also was a primary target of Iranian political pressure, and the combination of declining oil production and continuing threats from Iran pushed the Saudis to push back. After months of warning, the Saudis "turned up the faucet" on their oil production in October 1985. A price that was wobbly but holding at about $25 per barrel at the end of 1985 became $12 per barrel and not holding six months later. The consequent drop in oil income was painful for every oil producer. In January 1986, officials of the Mexican government visited other oil-exporting countries in an attempt to stem the fall in oil prices, but it was as though a plug had been pulled out of a full bathtub: the whole OPEC price structure just slid down the drain.[3]

Prices rose a little over the next few years. Seldom reaching OPEC's new target of $18 per barrel, they continued to be exquisitely vulnerable to destabilizing events and rumors of events. Persistent depressed demand coupled with low per barrel prices affected every OPEC country. Budgets contracted and even *low absorbers,* those countries whose populations were small compared to their incomes, had to make painful financial adjustments, including foreign borrowing. Adjustment coincided with fiscal strains on Arab Gulf exporters from war loans and payments to Iraq during the Iran-Iraq War, and further reductions in income when Gulf shipping became a target during the tanker war phase of that conflict (al-Assiri, 1990).

The end of the war in 1988 did not bring relief to economies and civil societies anywhere in OPEC. Oil demand and prices remained depressed while domestic populations grew restive, even in relatively wealthy Kuwait. There, citizen protests against the continued suspension of the parliament and constitutionally protected civil liberties, imposed in July 1986 in response to internal and external threats arising from the war (Boghardt, 2006), became widespread in 1989. High prices and a depressed local economy contributed to criticism of the regime's economic policies and to charges of corruption. The government felt pressed to satisfy the population's economic demands so as to mute the political demands that it was even less happy to deal with. That year, Kuwait's oil production consistently exceeded its OPEC quota. And Kuwait was not alone. Other Gulf exporters, most notably the United Arab Emirates (UAE) and Saudi Arabia, also produced over their quotas.

Overproduction by OPEC members contributed to depressed world oil prices. But Kuwait faced special risks in taking this route. Its boundary with Iraq had been contested since the 1930s, and years of diplomatic efforts and billions of dollars in loans and grants had not been enough to persuade Iraq to drop its claims to Kuwait. Continuing to produce at levels above its OPEC quota made Kuwait vulnerable to Iraqi retaliation.

Iraq's economic problems included huge war debts to foreign banks as well as to Kuwait and other Arab governments. It was convenient for Iraqi president Hussein to blame Kuwait for Iraq's problems. He clothed his invasion of Kuwait as an "oil war," a war to remove Kuwait's oil weapons, which he said were overproduction and theft of Iraqi oil produced along the disputed boundary. But just as many other conflicts in the Middle East concern much more than oil, so did this one. Hussein's problems required a quick infusion of cash. His diplomatic probes during the six months prior to the invasion convinced him that no power capable of stopping him would intervene if he were to invade Kuwait and take what he needed. He expected that victory in Kuwait would be quick and easy rather than the disaster that his attack on Iran a decade earlier had turned into. Instead, Hussein's 1990 invasion of Kuwait was reversed seven months later by a multilateral force led by the United States (Freedman and Karsh, 1993; Smith, 1992; Tétreault, 1993).

The Iraqi invasion began the Gulf War (1991) and introduced new oil weapons into world politics. One was cited by President George H. W. Bush when he said that the United States had to fight to keep Middle Eastern oil from being controlled by Hussein. From Bush's perspective, the war was intended to preserve an oil market where oil-exporting countries participate individually rather than under the hegemony of a regional military power. For Hussein, one objective of the war was to create such a hegemony under his leadership.

Other new oil weapons were ecological. Hussein promised to release Kuwaiti oil into the Gulf and to destroy Kuwait's production, processing, and export facilities if Iraq were attacked either at home or in Kuwait. These threats became real when the US-led coalition drove Iraq out of Kuwait and departing Iraqi soldiers set fire to Kuwait's oil fields. This demonstrates once again the strategic inferiority of oil weapons to deter undesired behavior when the stakes include the survival of a nation or its current regime.

The Iraq War: A New Oil Regime?

The end of the Gulf War left world oil markets in a state of uncertainty. Officially, Iraq was kept out of the market by a boycott until 1996 when the UN's oil-for-food program finally went into effect. This gave the UN authority to sell Iraqi oil and spend the proceeds on humanitarian assistance to the Iraqi population. It also allowed the UN to sequester 30 percent of these proceeds to pay reparations to those making claims against Iraq for the war damages that it had inflicted.

Both before and after the oil-for-food program began operating, however, illicit Iraqi oil flowed into neighboring countries and was smuggled by ship to buyers farther away. The money from this illegal trade sustained the Iraqi regime through the long years of economic sanctions imposed by the victors of the Gulf War. The primary burden of the sanctions fell on the Iraqi population in the form of food and medicine shortages, and periodic bombing by the United States and Great Britain in retaliation for Hussein's activities.

In 2002 the United States and Britain spearheaded a new attack on Iraq, first in the UN, where the arms inspection regime imposed after the Gulf War and suspended in 1998 was reinstated and strengthened. The inspectors reported frequently during the few months in which they were permitted to work that they had found no weapons of mass destruction (WMD), either nuclear, biological, or chemical, in Iraq (Blix, 2004). Despite those reports, in March 2003, the United States, Britain, and Australia launched a military invasion. The Iraq War differed from both of its predecessors. Rather being than a result of Iraqi aggression, it marked the first time that a new US strategic doctrine, published in September 2002, was implemented. This doctrine asserted a US right to mount preemptive attacks against countries accused by the US government of aiding or harboring terrorists or amassing WMD. It included as a goal the acquisition of "bases and stations within and beyond Western Europe and northeast Asia" for future US-force projections (US Department of State, 2002:6, 15, 29). The fallout from the Iraq War had several major effects on world oil markets, not all of which were anticipated.

The expectations of US policymakers were that the war would be over quickly, leading to massive investment by IOCs in development and infrastructure, and a flood of Iraqi oil onto world markets that would pay for postwar reconstruction (Allawi, 2007; Packer, 2005). This did not happen, the result of faulty military strategy (Ricks, 2006), the George W. Bush administration's disdain for postconflict recommendations from planners (e.g., Crane and Terrill, 2003), and a shocking lack of intellectual resilience that prevented needed adjustment to realities on the ground (Chandrasekaran, 2006; Packer, 2005). Thanks to the lack of security anywhere in the country, what the US president called a victory rapidly devolved into insurgency and continued warfare, and eventually into organized crime (Moore, 2012). With the exception of the Kurdish region, which had been protected from Hussein's army by US forces since mid-1991 and had maintained its hard-won political and social coherence even after Hussein had been deposed, much of the rest of the country was devastated and vulnerable to predation (Allawi, 2007; Moore, 2012; Packer, 2005). In spite of expectations that Iraq's domestic oil production could be restored quickly, postwar Iraq remained a net energy importer a decade later (Allawi, 2007:256, 360; Ratcliffe, 2012). Electricity generation in 2012 was still below the level it had been under Hussein. The average Iraqi household received power for fewer than eight hours per day, a figure that looks better than it is in reality because it includes homes in the Kurdish area, a semiautonomous region where citizens have access to electricity twenty-four hours per day (Ratcliffe, 2012). During the first years of the US occupation, pipelines suffered terrorist attacks while the theft of crude and products along the entire domestic supply chain was brisk and kept domestic supplies below demand

(Institute for War and Peace Reporting, 2007; Moore, 2012). The IOCs did not rush in either, despite the efforts of Paul Bremer, the US viceroy in Iraq, to guarantee that they would have the first crack at Iraqi oil (Allawi, 2007:256–257). Bremer's plans for a national oil law came to nothing, and the moment passed when accommodation across the social and political forces jockeying for power in post-Hussein Iraq might have been possible. Even by 2013, the national government remained unable to reach agreement on an oil law that would establish nationally set and enforced ground rules for oil investment. Part of the reason undoubtedly lies in the huge amount of money that the organized theft of Iraqi oil funnels to political parties and religious groups in Iraq and business interests, mostly in the emirates (Moore, 2012). Meanwhile, in 2007, the US Department of State gave a green light to US oil companies to enter into contract negotiations with the local government in the Kurdish area. Divergence between the economies of Kurdistan and the rest of Iraq adds to the antagonism that keeps this conflict simmering (Van Heuvelen, 2012a).

IOC access to Iraqi oil is regarded by some analysts as one of several motivations for the US invasion of Iraq, attested to in the growing pile of books about the George. W. Bush administration written or told by Washington insiders (the earliest such revelation can be found in Suskind, 2004; another appears in Greenspan, 2007). A majority of Iraqis—76 percent—polled in April 2006 said that the US desire to control Iraqi oil was the most important reason for the invasion (University of Michigan, 2006). And in 2011, nearly half the Iraqi population said that the United States was the country that had benefited most from the war (Zogby Research Services, 2011).

Yet if IOC control of oil was a reason for the US-led invasion, it is a goal whose pursuit endangers other aims, most notably a democratic, stable postwar Iraq. The criminality characterizing a significant segment of Iraq's oil industry is far from democratic while the growing autonomy of Iraqi Kurdistan enabled by IOC investment and income from oil exports undermines stability. The ability to attract oil investment independent of Baghdad strengthens the Kurds' desires to chart their own course and gives them the financial capacity to try.

The lack of a national oil law justifies to some the decisions by Kurdish officials to develop their oil fields on their own. But northern Iraq is not the only territory attracting IOC attention. Southern Iraq also is an oil-rich region as can be recalled from the conflict over oil production along the boundary between Iraq and Kuwait. Now that Iraq is coming into its own as an oil producer, this ambiguous situation has produced multiple contracts that correspond to different interpretations of Iraqi law depending on whether the regional Kurdish government or the national government in Baghdad is the host partner (Van Heuvelen, 2012b).

Unfortunately, postwar oil development strengthens both sides in the conflict over which entity will decide on and direct future oil investment in Iraq. The rapid expansion of oil production and improvements in infrastructure in southern Iraq also boosted oil income. Theoretically, rising income and control of potentially giant fields in the south empowers the national government and its backers. Yet the continued standoff on a national oil law means that contracts signed with Kurdistan can (and do) offer substantially better terms than contracts signed with Baghdad. The largest and most powerful IOCs like ExxonMobil and China's Sinopec thus have an incentive to invest in the Kurdish area regardless of Baghdad's objections, even at the risk of losing claims to potentially lucrative fields in the south whose ultimate payout is likely to take longer, making them more vulnerable to Iraq's corrupt and unstable politics.

The balance of power between host and IOC is one prize in the conflict between Baghdad and ExxonMobil over whether or not the IOC can write contracts directly with the Kurds and continue to hold on to its position in a giant field in Basra. The balance seems to favor the IOC since Baghdad has yet to carry through on its promise to kick ExxonMobil out of Basra for signing with Kurdistan. Kurdish independence is another potential prize (LeVine, 2012), one that is likely to come at a high cost, and not only to Iraq. Some observers see the willingness of powerful IOCs to engage in what Baghdad calls "illegal" dealings with Kurdistan as creating conditions likely to lead to a showdown over the issue of Kurdish independence (Van Heuvelen, 2012b), a possibility that past experience predicts could touch off a conflict with the potential to spread beyond Iraq's borders.

Oil, Climate Change, and World Order

A civil war in Iraq would reduce supplies to international markets at the same time that sanctions on Iran are squeezing the amount of Iranian oil available to foreign buyers. There are huge loopholes in the international sanctions imposed on Iran to force the government to halt what the West perceives as a drive to develop nuclear weapons and Iran insists is an attempt to diversify domestic energy sources to leave more hydrocarbons available for export. Even under the sanctions, Iran has managed to sell hydrocarbons, if at a huge discount, to customers like India and China (Vakhshouri, 2012).

A related issue affecting all the major oil exporters is that domestic oil and gas consumption is skyrocketing, thanks to industrialization, growing populations, and government subsidies that underwrite a massive waste of energy by consumers (Krane, 2012). Whatever the impact on global energy markets, to shift fuel to domestic markets will reduce government income and provide a new round of real-time empirical tests of the rentier state thesis (Hunter, 1986; Tétreault, 2012).

The unsettled nature of today's oil market was roiled even further by a 2012 report from the International Energy Agency predicting a return to global oil power for the United States:

> The recent rebound in US oil and gas production, driven by upstream technologies that are unlocking light tight oil and shale gas resources, is spurring economic activity—with less expensive gas and electricity prices giving industry a competitive edge—and steadily changing the role of North America in global energy trade. By around 2020, the United States is projected to become the largest global oil producer (overtaking Saudi Arabia until the mid-2020s) and starts to see the impact of new fuel-efficiency measures in transport. The result is a continued fall in US oil imports, to the extent that North America becomes a net oil exporter around 2030. This accelerates the switch in direction of international oil trade towards Asia, putting a focus on the security of the strategic routes that bring Middle East oil to Asian markets. The United States, which currently imports around 20% of its total energy needs, becomes all but self-sufficient in net terms.

The revival of the United States as a major hydrocarbon producer changes the global balance of oil and strategic power profoundly. It frees up production for new consumers in Asia, reducing the pressure on prices from rising demand that set up the oil price revolution in the early 1970s. In doing so, it elevates the strategic value of Pacific transit routes, giving a boost to China's strategic ambitions that could be ameliorated but probably not erased by its dependence on imports of oil and gas to fuel its own growing economy. Even leaving aside the issue of Taiwan, US allies in East Asia, such as Japan and South Korea, are likely to want a more visible US presence in the Pacific to ensure the security of their supply lines, a challenge to Chinese ambitions that could affect the global balance of power.

Rising US energy production would also have a direct impact on the Middle East by restoring the United States as an oil power rivaling Saudi Arabia and the region's rising oil power, Iraq. These two Arabian Peninsula neighbors are already preparing for a clash over which will bear the cost of production cuts if a supply surplus should cause oil prices to fall to unacceptable levels (Bakr and Mackey, 2012). US production would increase the downward pressure on prices and, as in the past, also could undercut future applications of Arab oil power to pursue a peace settlement between Israel and Palestine.

Perhaps the most disturbing result of a reincarnation of US oil power globally is the harmful impact of the technology used to exploit unconventional US oil and gas resources on freshwater supplies and especially on greenhouse gas emissions (Fischetti, 2012). Called *fracking,* this technology

A traditional dhow passes an oil tanker in the Bahraini port.

is associated with the generation of "fugitive" methane, a much more problematic greenhouse gas than carbon dioxide because it absorbs more solar energy and remains in the environment for a longer time. The United States has refused to participate in global regimes to limit greenhouse gas emissions, freeing it from external restraints on its own behavior but also negating any diplomatic leverage it might have had over the rapidly rising levels of greenhouse gases coming from China and India (Schreuder, 2009). The power of the IOCs in US politics amplifies these problems in the form of generous government subsidies to already hugely profitable IOCs. Their economic and political clout greases the transplantation of their trademark polluting energy systems to developing countries despite the availability of cleaner technologies whose other effects include the transfer of power over energy supplies and transmissions from IOCs to decentralized producers (Schreuder, 2009).

It might seem paradoxical but the major oil producers, which have been staunchly negative with regard to reducing foreign consumption of fossil fuels, now find that their interests are shifting. Because of the rising domestic demand for fuels noted earlier, several are seeking development of alternative energy sources such as Iran's nuclear power bid, which is being watched not only as a threatening strategic move but also as an attractive economic one.

Because of the boost in oil prices touched off by the 2003 invasion of Iraq, oil-exporting countries have money to invest in new technologies that would leave them more oil and gas to use at home. Even better, long-range strategic investments could enable them to leave more hydrocarbons in the ground to use over a longer period and in higher value-added industries than mere oil and gas production. Industries that use oil and natural gas as raw materials offer opportunities for technology transfer and skilled employment. This outcome, of course, depends on the foresight and business acumen of producing countries, but opportunities are there and competent policymakers are taking advantage of them (Henni, 2012).

That such a radical change in producer strategy is even conceivable is a result of the growth in sovereign wealth funds (SWF), the cash balances accruing to exporters able to amass trade surpluses. In 1976, Kuwait established the Reserve Fund for Future Generations (RFFG). Intended to serve as a source of externally generated income in the postoil future, it receives 10 percent of Kuwait's annual oil revenues. Since then, other states enjoying large export surpluses (including China, an energy importer) also have set up SWF as repositories for their investment assets. When Kuwait pioneered the RFFG, most of its investments were in safe assets such as US Treasury securities. Virtually all of today's SWF have been transformed from passive accumulators of low-return securities issued by Western governments to aggressive direct and portfolio investors in a wide range of assets.

Oil influences exporters' investment policies quite broadly because it is both a source and a target of investment capital. Hydrocarbon income allows them to devote significant resources to projects projected to reduce their dependence on income from exported oil and gas (Aissaoui, 2009; Morse, 2009). They have grown accustomed to analyzing complex trends in global trade and financial markets (including their effects on oil prices) as they seek new ways to invest hydrocarbon windfalls to generate supplementary income streams (e.g., Krane, 2009). One way is by investing in alternative forms of energy.

Oil and Money in the Middle East

This chapter began by saying that oil is a blessing for countries that have it. One of the chief blessings of oil comes from its easy convertibility into foreign exchange. The higher oil prices that resulted first from the oil revolution, then from the revolution in Iran, and more recently from a bouquet of complex changes in energy markets raised the earnings streaming into oil-exporting countries to flood levels. Yet as we all know, floods, whatever their other qualities, are also disasters. This flood was no exception; it too brought good news and bad news.

The good news was that a huge amount of money was suddenly available to oil-exporting countries for economic development and national defense, and to provide for the economic and social welfare of their people. The bad news was that the increases came too fast and did not last. Income over the medium and long term was neither steady nor predictable. In 1973, economists worried that rising oil prices would cause an economic depression in oil-importing countries. They also predicted that higher oil incomes would be virtually unusable by most oil-exporting countries, especially the Arab states along the Gulf with their small populations and large revenues. Both worries were overstated. The unusable dollars that so concerned these economists turned out to be a chimera. Nicknamed "petrodollars," the cash balances of oil-exporting countries first went into the international banking system where they were recycled as loans, and more recently into pools of money available for a wide range of investments worldwide (Tétreault, 2011). Too many of them were siphoned off by political leaders and criminals for their private enrichment.

The flood of money was a mixed blessing to the domestic economies of oil-exporting states. It aggravated domestic inflation rates and boosted demand for imports—the so-called Dutch disease. Oil exporters quickly learned to spend their money as fast as it came in so that, by the time of the second round of price increases in 1979–1980, many had started to amass their own foreign debt. As discussed in Chapter 4, arms purchases were an especially perverse outcome of the oil price increases of the 1970s (Nitzan and Bichler, 2002), and they also followed the oil price rises after 2003 (Tétreault, 2012). The diversion of excessive amounts of oil revenue to military purchases took resources from domestic economies, added to the arsenals of regional belligerents, and financed all three Gulf wars.

Some states, like Kuwait, the UAE, and Bahrain, made notable efforts to redistribute oil revenues across their populations through direct transfers and by subsidizing housing, utilities, education, and medical care. Some capital redistribution was effected through real estate transfers. Yet as the Arab uprisings made authoritarian rulers tremble from Morocco to Iran, oil revenues are going to support the security forces charged with repressing nonviolent demands for political liberalization, including a Gulf Cooperation Council (GCC) military contingent sent to Bahrain in 2012 to free up domestic forces engaged in brutal retaliation against demonstrators there.

Other domestic effects of high oil prices include subsidized and pampered native populations in many Gulf states who lost interest in low-status jobs that required the importation of guest workers to make local economies function (Tétreault, 2012). The economy and ecology of Saudi Arabia was damaged by government assistance such as occurred when it provided unlimited fossil water to support wheat production. Countries exporting labor to the rich oil exporters often found their domestic economies and societies as radically altered as those of their richer neighbors by the roller-coaster economy and the sometimes cross-pressuring influence of radical preachers of consumerism (Chalcraft, 2010; Chaudhry, 1997). The oil-rich states of the Middle East are often criticized for their "wasteful" development projects, yet most have done no worse than their oil-poor peers whose economic decisions are overseen by foreign bankers and officials of patron governments.

Oil money also increased the foreign policy autonomy of oil-exporting countries. They found it less necessary than before to bind themselves as clients to an extraregional patron state in exchange for economic or military assistance. The relative weakness of Middle Eastern states implies a continued dependency on external support but, spurred by the Arab Spring, such support is coming increasingly from within the region rather than outside it. Although new, oil-enabled external influences remain important ("China Targets 9 Countries," 2007; Huus, 2006), they are not the only sources of strategic support to national governments and dissident movements in the Middle East. Not only were GCC troops sent to support the government of Bahrain, but the Libyan revolutionaries discussed in Chapter 4 also received financial and military assistance from Qatar along with support from North Atlantic Treaty Organization (NATO) forces. Syrian dissidents have received more help from neighboring countries than from those outside the region.

Conclusion

Oil gave a number of Middle Eastern countries the economic independence to try development strategies and forge political bonds foreclosed to poorer states. It also offered a substitute for conventional (i.e., military) attributes of power, forcing other nations to reexamine their own foreign policies in the light of long-term economic interests. Thus, it helped to erode the post–World War II dominance of the superpowers by providing incentives and resources for their Middle Eastern alliance partners, clients, and dependencies to act more autonomously.

Oil instilled a false sense of power and economic security in the minds of policymakers in oil-exporting states. Few used the fat years following the first two enormous oil price hikes to prepare for the lean years that came after. Sovereign wealth funds make the diversification of oil revenue investment possible, but they have not solved the rentier state dilemma that still causes nervous authoritarians to reach for their checkbooks when they are challenged by restive populations instead of using their nation's common resources together with citizen partners to work for a common future (Tétreault, 2012).

Consequently, despite oil's opportunities, its exploitation has exacted high social, political, and economic costs. Uncertain as to the shape of the new regional order that will rise on the debris generated by interstate wars and violent responses to popular demands for human rights and political participation, we can only speculate as to whether oil has been a blessing or a curse to Middle Eastern nations and their peoples. A similar analysis of the energy politics of other regions is likely to reveal equally ambiguous effects and equally uncertain prognoses for the futures of oil exporters and importers alike.

Notes

1. To reduce the confusion that might arise from the frequent name changes of the various oil companies operating in the Middle East, these companies are referred to by their contemporary names rather than by whatever names they might have been called at the time of the particular events discussed.

2. Except where noted, material in this section comes from Tétreault (1985).

3. I have written elsewhere (1993) about the effect of the price collapse on the two combatants in the Gulf War (1991). Low oil prices were felt disproportionately by Iran, which did not have neighbors sending it financial and military assistance. In an interesting way, the price collapse of the mid-1980s acted as another kind of oil weapon.

Bibliography

Adelman, M. A. 1972–1973. "Is the Oil Shortage Real? Oil Companies as OPEC Tax Collectors." *Foreign Policy,* no. 9:69–107.

Aissaoui, Ali. 2009. "The Shrinking MENA Energy Investment Outlook." *Oxford Energy Forum,* no. 77:7–9.

Allawi, Ali A. 2007. *The Occupation of Iraq: Winning the War, Losing the Peace.* New Haven: Yale University Press.

Anderson, Irvine H. 1981. *ARAMCO, the United States, and Saudi Arabia: A Study of the Dynamics of Foreign Oil Policy, 1933–1950.* Princeton: Princeton University Press.

Al-Assiri, Abdul-Reda. 1990. *Kuwait's Foreign Policy: City-State in World Politics.* Boulder: Westview Press.

Bakr, Amena, and Peg Mackey. 2012. December 12. "UPDATE 5—Iraq, Saudi on OPEC Collision Course over Next Oil Curb." Reuters. www.reuters.com.

Beblawi, Hazem. 1990. "The Rentier State in the Arab World." Pp. 85–98 in Giacomo Luciani (ed.), *The Arab State.* Berkeley: University of California Press.

Blair, John. 1976. *The Control of Oil.* New York: Pantheon.

Blix, Hans. 2004. *Disarming Iraq.* New York: Pantheon.

Boghardt, Lori Plotkin. 2006. *Kuwait Amid War, Peace and Revolution.* London: Palgrave Macmillan.

Chalcraft, John. 2010. October. "Monarchy, Migration and Hegemony in the Arabian Peninsula." Occasional Paper No. 12. London: Kuwait Programme in Globalisation and Governance.

Chandrasekaran, Rajiv. 2006. *Imperial Life in the Emerald City: Inside Iraq's Green Zone.* New York: Alfred A. Knopf.

Chaudhry, Kirin Aziz. 1997. *The Price of Wealth: Economies and Institutions in the Middle East.* Ithaca: Cornell University Press.

"China Targets 9 Countries for Oil Investment." 2007. March 1. *International Herald Tribune.*

Chisholm, Archibald H. T. 1975. *The First Kuwait Oil Concession Agreement: A Record of the Negotiations, 1911–1934*. London: Frank Cass.

Cordesman, Anthony H., and Abraham R. Wagner. 1991. *The Lessons of Modern War*, vol. 2: *The Iran-Iraq War*. Boulder: Westview Press.

Crane, Conrad C., and W. Andrew Terrill. 2003. *Reconstructing Iraq: Insights, Challenges, and Missions for Military Forces in a Post-Conflict Scenario*. Carlisle, PA: US Army War College, Strategic Studies Institute.

Crystal, Jill. 1990. *Oil and Politics in the Gulf: Rulers and Merchants in Kuwait and Qatar*. Cambridge: Cambridge University Press.

———. 1994. "Authoritarianism and Its Adversaries in the Arab World." *World Politics* 46, no. 2:262–289.

Dawisha, Adeed. 2003. *Arab Nationalism in the Twentieth Century: From Triumph to Despair*. Princeton: Princeton University Press.

Fischetti, Mark. 2012. January 20. "Fracking Would Emit Large Quantities of Greenhouse Gases." *Scientific American*. www.scientificamerican.com.

Freedman, Lawrence, and Efraim Karsh. 1993. *The Gulf Conflict, 1990–1991: Diplomacy and War in the New World Order*. Princeton: Princeton University Press.

Gasiorowski, Mark J. 1991. *US Foreign Policy and the Shah: Building a Client State in Iran*. Ithaca: Cornell University Press.

Greenspan, Alan. 2007. *The Age of Turbulence: Adventures in a New World*. New York: Penguin.

Henni, Abdelghani. 2012. June 27. "Analysis: Kuwait's Costly K-Dow Misadventure." *Arabian Oil and Gas.com*. www.arabianoilandgas.com.

Hunter, Shireen T. 1986. "The Gulf Economic Crisis and Its Social and Political Consequences." *Middle East Journal* 40, no. 4:593–613.

Huus, Kari. 2006. May 4. "In China's Oil Quest, No Deal Is Too Unsavory." MSNBC. www.msnbc.msn.com.

Institute for War and Peace Reporting. 2007. September 10. "Special Report: Oil and Corruption in Iraq." Iraq Crisis Report No. 232. Washington, DC: Institute for War and Peace Reporting.

International Energy Agency. 2012. *World Energy Outlook 2012: Executive Summary*. Paris: International Energy Agency. www.iea.org.

Jentleson, Bruce W. 1986. *Pipeline Politics: The Complex Political Economy of East-West Energy Trade*. Ithaca: Cornell University Press.

Kaufman, Burton J. 1977. "Mideast Multinational Oil, U.S. Foreign Policy, and Antitrust: The 1950s." *The Journal of American History* 63, no. 4:937–959.

Krane, Jim. 2009. *City of Gold: Dubai and the Dream of Capitalism*. New York: St. Martin's Press.

———. 2012. November. "Stability Versus Sustainability: Energy Policy in the Gulf Monarchies." Paper presented at the meeting of the Middle East Studies Association, Denver.

Lando, Ben. 2007a. October 10. "Kurds Talk Contracts with Big Oil: It's Now or Never." *Alternet*. www.alternet.org.

———. 2007b. October 12. "Analysis: Hunt, State Talked on Iraq Oil." United Press International. http://warisacrime.org.

LeVine, Steve. 2012. August 1. "Will Oil Companies Provide Kurdistan Its De Facto Statehood?" *Foreign Policy*. http://oilandglory.foreignpolicy.com/

Luciani, Giacomo. 1990. "Allocation vs. Production States: A Theoretical Framework." Pp. 65–84 in Giacomo Luciani (ed.), *The Arab State*. Berkeley: University of California Press.

Mikdashi, Zuhayr. 1972. *The Community of Oil Exporting Countries.* Ithaca: Cornell University Press.

Moore, Pete. 2012. "Making Big Money on Iraq." *Middle East Report,* no. 252. www.merip.org.

Morse, Edward L. 2009. "The Impact of Low Oil Prices on Investments." *Oxford Energy Forum,* no. 77:3–5.

Munif, Abdulrahman. 1989. *Cities of Salt.* New York: Vintage.

Nitzan, Jonathan, and Shimshon Bichler. 2002. *The Global Political Economy of Israel.* London: Pluto Press.

Packer, George. 2005. *The Assassin's Gate: America in Iraq.* New York: Farrar, Straus & Giroux.

Penrose, Edith. 1968. *The Large International Firm in Developing Countries: The International Petroleum Industry.* Cambridge: MIT Press.

Petersen, Tore T. 2012. "Richard Nixon, Great Britain, and the Anglo-American Strategy of Turning the Persian Gulf into an Allied Lake." Pp. 75–89 in Jeffrey R. Macris and Saul Kelly (eds.), *Imperial Crossroads: The Great Powers and the Persian Gulf.* Annapolis: Naval Institute Press.

Potter, Lawrence G., and Gary G. Sick (eds.). 2004. *Iran, Iraq, and the Legacies of War.* New York: Palgrave Macmillan.

Prindle, David S. 1981. *Petroleum Politics and the Texas Railroad Commission.* Austin: University of Texas Press.

Ratcliffe, Verity. 2012. "Power Generation a Top Priority in Iraq." *MEED Supplement.* www.meed.com.

Rand, Christopher T. 1975. *Making Democracy Safe for Oil.* Boston: Little, Brown.

Ricks, Thomas E. 2006. *Fiasco: The American Military Adventure in Iraq.* New York: Penguin.

Ross, Michael L. 2001. "Does Oil Hinder Democracy?" *World Politics* 53, no. 2: 325–361.

Sampson, Anthony. 1975. *The Seven Sisters: The Great Oil Companies and the World They Shaped.* New York: Viking.

Schreuder, Yda. 2009. *The Corporate Greenhouse: Climate Change Policy in a Globalizing World.* London: Zed Books.

Skeet, Ian. 1988. *OPEC: Twenty-five Years of Prices and Politics.* New York: Cambridge University Press.

Smith, Jean Edward. 1992. *George Bush's War.* New York: Holt.

Suskind, Ron. 2004. *The Price of Loyalty: George W. Bush, the White House, and the Education of Paul O'Neill.* New York: Simon & Schuster.

Tétreault, Mary Ann. 1981. *The Organization of Arab Petroleum Exporting Countries: History, Policies, and Prospects.* Westport, CT: Greenwood Press.

———. 1985. *Revolution in the World Petroleum Market.* Westport, CT: Quorum Books.

———. 1993. "Independence, Sovereignty, and Vested Glory: Oil and Politics in the Second Gulf War." *Orient* 34, no. 1:87–103.

———. 1995. *The Kuwait Petroleum Corporation and the Economics of the New World Order.* Westport, CT: Quorum Books.

———. 2000. *Stories of Democracy: Politics and Society in Contemporary Kuwait.* New York: Columbia University Press.

———. 2011. "Gulf Arab States' Investment of Oil Revenues." Pp. 9–21 in Matteo Legrenzi and Bessma Momani (eds.), *Shifting Geo-Economic Power of the Gulf: Oil, Finance and Institutions.* Surrey: Ashgate.

————. 2012. "Stuff Is Not Enough: Resources and Governance in the Middle East." Pp. 33–49 in Abbas Kadhim (ed.), *Governance in the Middle East and North Africa*. New York: Routledge.

Tétreault, Mary Ann, and Mohammed al-Ghanim. 2012. July. "Transitions in Authoritarianism: Political Reform in the Arab Gulf States Reconsidered." Paper presented at the Exeter Gulf Studies Conference. Exeter.

University of Michigan. 2006. "Iraqi Attitudes: Survey Documents Big Changes." Press release. http://ns.umich.edu.

US Department of State. 2002. September. "The National Security Strategy of the United States of America." www.state.gov.

Vakhshouri, Sara. 2012. February 27. "The Coalition Against Iranian Oil: Winners and Losers." *Huffington Post*. www.huffingtonpost.com.

Van Heuvelen, Ben. 2012a. May 8. "As Iraqi Oil Industry Booms, Power, Profit and Problems." *Washington Post*.

————. 2012b. December 18. "In Iraq, Exxon Oil Deal Foments Talk of Civil War." *Washington Post*. http://articles.washingtonpost.com.

Vernon, Raymond (ed.). 1976. *The Oil Crisis*. New York: Norton.

Vietor, Richard H. K. 1984. *Energy Policy in America Since 1945: A Study of Business-Government Relations*. New York: Cambridge University Press.

Vitalis, Robert. 2007. *America's Kingdom: Mythmaking on the Saudi Oil Frontier*. Stanford: Stanford University Press.

Zogby Research Services. 2011. November. "Iraq, the War, Its Consequences, and the Future." Paper prepared for the Sir Bani Yas Forum. Abu Dhabi. http://aai.3cdn.net.

9

Population Growth, Urbanization, and the Challenges of Unemployment

Valentine M. Moghadam

The Middle East has experienced rapid rates of urbanization and population growth over the past several decades. Although countries are at different levels of urbanization, the region as a whole has a majority of its population living in urban areas. Until relatively recently, population growth rates in the Middle East–North Africa (MENA) region were among the highest in the world, second only to those in sub-Saharan Africa. More recently, fertility rates have been falling, especially among young, educated women in urban areas. Yet the population is expected to swell to 576 million by 2025—more than double the current size. Given the aridity of much of the region, these growing numbers will place increasing demands on water and agricultural land, and currently strained urban services will need to be vastly expanded and improved.

Rapid urbanization and rapid population growth have transformed the structure of the labor force. In many countries, the population has shifted from one engaged predominantly in rural and agrarian production systems to one involved in various types of urban industrial and service-oriented economic activities. Moreover, because of previously high fertility rates, the age structure of the labor force is skewed toward the group younger than age twenty-five, which demographers call the "youth bulge."[1] Meanwhile, due to both economic and demographic factors, urban labor markets have been unable to absorb the growing labor force. This has resulted in the expansion of the urban informal sector, income inequalities, urban poverty, and rates of unemployment that are among the highest in the world. In particular, youth and female unemployment rates are exceedingly high. These factors, among others, were behind the mass urban protests that brought down the governments in Tunisia and Egypt in early 2011 and triggered Morocco's Movement 20 Février.

In this chapter I examine the interrelated processes of urbanization, population growth, employment challenges, and poverty in the Middle East and North Africa. For ease of exposition, each is examined separately, even though the issues are linked. Furthermore, to reflect differences in population and labor force size as well as income levels, I frequently refer to the region in terms of two sets of countries: the small, oil-rich states that belong to the Gulf Cooperation Council (GCC), encompassing Bahrain, Kuwait, Oman, Qatar, Saudi Arabia, and the United Arab Emirates (UAE); and the larger and more diversified countries (Algeria, Egypt, Iran, Iraq, Israel, Jordan, Lebanon, Libya, Morocco, Syria, Tunisia, Turkey, and Yemen). To the extent possible, the West Bank and Gaza Strip are included in my analysis.

Urbanization

The urban population of the region has been growing rapidly since 1950. Its share of the total population grew from 24 percent in 1950 to 57 percent in 1990 (Omran and Roudi, 1993:21), and to about 73 percent in 2010. The most rapid growth in urbanization occurred in the oil-exporting countries; the population doubled between 1960 and 1980 in Saudi Arabia, Oman, Libya, and the UAE, and between 1950 and 1985 in Iran and Iraq (Assaad, 1995:21). Among countries that are not already highly urbanized, the slowest rate of urbanization was in Egypt, whose urban share increased from 32 percent in 1950 to 43 percent in 2001 and has remained stable since then. The three largest countries in the region—Iran, Turkey, and especially Egypt—have extensive land with relatively large rural populations that constitute a pool of future rural-to-urban migrants; this is also true of Morocco, Syria, and Iraq. Yemen is the least-urbanized country in the region whereas Kuwait, Qatar, and Bahrain are virtually city-states. Within the UAE, the urban growth of Dubai has been especially noticeable. Table 9.1 illustrates the varying levels of urbanization across the region. It should be noted that, along with Latin America, the MENA region has the highest level of urbanization in the developing world.

Urbanization is a key aspect of social change and of economic development. It entails the implementation of policies leading to the growth of cities and rural-to-urban migration. The latter is typically fueled by both push and pull factors: the push of population pressure on natural resources and the lack of economic opportunity in the rural areas, and the pull of perceived economic opportunity and a better lifestyle in the large cities (Omran and Roudi, 1993:21). The continuing growth of cities and of rural-to-urban migration is often exacerbated by the urban bias of government policies and development strategies, which leads to underdevelopment of

Table 9.1 Population and Urbanization in the MENA Region

Country	Total Population (millions)		Percentage Urban		
	1950	2010	1950	1980	2010
Algeria	8.75	35.5	22.2	43.5	72.0
Bahrain	0.116	1.26	64.4	86.1	88.6
Egypt	21.5	81.1	31.9	43.9	43.4
Iran	17.414	74.0	27.5	49.7	68.9
Iraq	5.72	31.7	35.1	65.5	66.5
Israel	1.26	7.42	71.0	88.6	91.8
Jordan	0.449	6.19	37.0	59.9	82.5
Kuwait	0.152	2.74	61.5	94.8	98.2
Lebanon	1.44	4.23	32.0	73.7	87.1
Libya	1.03	6.36	19.5	70.1	77.6
Morocco	8.95	32.0	26.2	41.2	56.7
Oman	0.456	2.8	8.6	47.6	73.2
Qatar	0.025	1.76	79.2	89.4	98.7
Saudi Arabia	3.12	27.5	21.0	65.9	82.1
Syria	3.54	20.4	30.6	46.7	55.7
Tunisia	3.53	10.5	32.3	50.6	66.1
Turkey	21.5	72.8	24.8	43.8	70.5
United Arab Emirates	0.07	7.51	54.5	80.7	84.0
West Bank and Gaza	0.932	4.04	37.3	62.4	74.1
Yemen	4.32	24.0	5.8	16.5	31.7

Source: United Nations, *World Urbanization Prospects, 2011 Revision* (New York: United Nations, March 2012). http://esa.un.org/unup/pdf/WUP2011_Highlights.pdf.

rural areas, greater investment in urban infrastructure, and income and education gaps between rural and urban citizens.

International migration can also play a part in urbanization. In the case of Israel, immigration by Jews from other countries has contributed to the growth of Tel Aviv and West Jerusalem. And in the case of the small, oil-rich GCC countries, labor migration from other Arab countries contributed to the rapid rates of urbanization, especially during the 1970s and 1980s. In more recent decades, the majority of labor migrants to the Gulf countries has come from South Asia. Comprising anywhere from 50 percent (Saudi Arabia) to 90 percent (Qatar) of the labor force (Baldwin-Edwards, 2011), they provide the manpower for the construction boom that has accelerated urban growth in the GCC countries.

Between 1950 and 1980, there was tremendous growth of the large cities in the region, including Tehran, Cairo, Istanbul, and Baghdad, as a result of high fertility rates and rural-to-urban migration. In 1950, only four cities had a population exceeding 1 million; by 1970, there were nine (Assaad, 1995:22). By 1990, the number of such cities had exceeded twenty and, ten years later, some twenty-five cities had a population of over 1 million.

Megacities such as Cairo, Istanbul, and Tehran saw the growth of their populations during the 1980s, but so did a second tier of cities such as Alexandria, Isfahan, Mashhad, Riyadh, Ankara, and Adana (see Table 9.2). Some of the megacities, especially Cairo, have extremely high population densities, severe shortages of housing and services, and lack of regulation of construction and urban development. Indeed, the economies of the cities cannot absorb their large urban populations, which leads to unemployment, underemployment, and poverty among urban populations. Other problems include a shortage of clean drinking water, the growth of slums or shantytowns, polluted air, inadequate waste disposal systems, and rundown public transportation systems

Table 9.2 Cities in the MENA Region with Populations over 1 Million, 2010

Country	City	Population (millions)
Algeria	Algiers	2.9
Egypt	Cairo	11.0
	Alexandria	4.4
Iran	Tehran	7.2
	Mashhad	2.7
	Isfahan	1.7
	Karaj	1.6
	Tabriz	1.5
	Shiraz	1.3
	Ahvaz	1.1
Iraq	Baghdad	5.9
	Mosul	1.5
Israel	Tel Aviv	3.3
Jordan	Amman	1.2
Kuwait	Kuwait City	2.3
Lebanon	Beirut	2.0
Libya	Tripoli	1.1
Morocco	Casablanca	3.0
	Rabat	1.8
	Fes	1.1
Saudi Arabia	Riyadh	5.2
	Jeddah	3.5
	Mecca	1.5
	Medina	1.1
Syria	Aleppo	3.1
	Damascus	2.6
	Homs	1.3
Turkey	Istanbul	10.9
	Ankara	4.1
	Izmir	2.8
	Bursa	1.7
	Adana	1.4
United Arab Emirates	Dubai	1.8
Yemen	Sana'a	2.3

Source: United Nations, *World Urbanization Prospects, 2011 Revision* (New York: United Nations, March 2012). http://esa.un.org/unup/pdf/WUP2011_Highlights.pdf.

View of downtown Cairo and the Nile River.

used primarily by low-income residents. Sexual harassment on the streets is a by-product of urbanization; widespread in Tehran in the 1960s and 1970s, it has assumed serious proportions in contemporary Cairo.

Population Growth

According to theories of epidemiological and demographic transitions, a population's fertility and mortality will decline from high to low levels as a result of economic and social development. The decline in mortality usually precedes the decline in fertility. This transition occurred in European countries during the nineteenth century and in the developing world during the twentieth century. In the latter part of the twentieth century, the countries of the Middle East and North Africa were differentially situated along the transition continuum and were characterized by varying levels and combinations of mortality and fertility.

The Middle East and North Africa saw a population explosion in the 1950s, a result of high fertility and declines in the crude death rate, although infant mortality rates were still high. In the 1960s the region had the world's highest fertility rate among developing regions, but after 1970 fertility began to fall, leaving sub-Saharan Africa with the world's highest fertility rates. The MENA region's annual population growth reached a peak of 3 percent around 1980 while the growth rate for the world as a whole reached its peak of 2 percent annually more than a decade earlier (Roudi, 2001).

For the region as a whole, the total fertility rate (average number of births per woman) decreased from 7.0 children per woman in the period 1950–1975 to 4.8 in 1990. The fertility rate declined further to about 3.6 in 2001 and fell steadily during the decade, especially among urban educated women (see ILO, 2012:47). By 2010, and as seen in Table 9.3, the total fertility rate hovered at around the replacement level in Iran, Kuwait, Lebanon, Tunisia, Turkey, and the UAE. Fertility rates were highest in Iraq, Jordan, Palestine (West Bank and Gaza), Saudi Arabia, Syria, and Yemen. The fertility decline in the region is associated with effective family planning campaigns and increases in women's education. Indeed, whereas in 1980, average years of schooling for women in most MENA

Table 9.3 Fertility Rates and Related Sociodemographic Features in the MENA Region

Country	Total Fertility Rate[a] (percentage)		Tertiary Enrollments, Female, 2003–2010[b] (percentages)	Age at First Marriage, 2010[c]		Contraceptive Prevalence in Women, 2005–2009[d] (percentages)
	1990–1995	2005–2010		Male	Female	
Algeria	4.1	2.4	37	33	29	61
Bahrain	3.4	2.7	28	30	26	62
Egypt	3.9	2.9	31	—	23	60
Iran	4.0	1.8	43	26	24	79
Iraq	5.8	4.9	12	28	25	50
Israel	2.9	2.9	71	29	26	—
Jordan	5.1	3.3	41	29	25	59
Kuwait	3.2	2.3	31	30	25	52
Lebanon	3.0	1.9	59	31	27	58
Libya	4.1	2.7	57	32	29	45
Morocco	3.7	2.4	12	31	26	63
Oman	6.3	2.5	29	26	22	32
Qatar	4.1	2.4	26	28	26	43
Saudi Arabia	5.4	3.0	39	27	25	24
Syria	4.9	3.1	12	29	25	58
Tunisia	3.1	2.0	41	30	27	60
Turkey	2.9	2.2	40	—	23	73
United Arab Emirates	3.9	1.9	39	26	23	28
West Bank and Gaza	6.5	4.7	42	27	23	50
Yemen	7.7	5.5	6	25	22	28

Sources: a. Data on fertility from *Human Development Report 2010: The Real Wealth of Nations—Pathways to Human Development* (Houndsmills, UK, and New York: Palgrave Macmillan), http://hdr.undp.org.

b. Data on tertiary enrollment from United Nations, "Statistics and Indicators on Women and Men," table 4d, http://unstats.un.org/unsd/demographic/products/indwm/default.htm.

c. Data on mean age at marriage from United Nations, "Statistics and Indicators on Women and Men," table 3b, http://unstats.un.org/unsd/demographic/products/indwm/tab2b.htm.

d. Data on contraceptive prevalence from United Nations, "Statistics and Indicators on Women and Men," table 2d, http://unstats.un.org/unsd/demographic/products/indwm/default.htm.

Note: — indicates data not available.

countries was well below the international norms (with Jordan being a clear exception), by 2010 the MENA region as a whole had caught up with international averages. In 2012, the average years of schooling for the region was about 9 years (roughly the same as Mexico), albeit with variations, from 2.4 years in Yemen to 10 years in the UAE (Barro and Lee, 2013). Increased educational attainment, among other factors, has contributed to the rising age at first marriage, which also significantly affects fertility rates (see Table 9.3).

The infant mortality rate, which was as high as 200 per 1,000 live births in 1955, began to decline in 1960, and by 1990 it had reached about 70 per 1,000 live births (Assaad, 1995). Eight years later it was down to 45 per 1,000 live births—higher than Latin America, the Caribbean, eastern Asia, Europe, and Central Asia, but lower than southern Asia and sub-Saharan Africa (see World Bank, 2000:table 2.18, 108). For some countries, the changes in infant, child, and maternal mortality occurred rapidly and dramatically. For example, in 1960, Tunisia had an infant mortality rate of 159, and its mortality rate among children younger than five years old was 255. In the 1980s these declined to 58 and 83, respectively. By 2000 the rate of infant mortality had dropped to just 30, and in 2009 it was 21.[2] Iran similarly saw impressive achievements in the health of children as well as of mothers during the 1990s. Indeed, maternal mortality rates have dropped throughout the region, though they remain highest in Yemen, the poorest and most rural of the MENA countries. According to *Arab Human Development Report 2009* (UNDP, 2009a), maternal mortality is highest in Yemen and Morocco, with rates of 430 and 240 per 100,000 live births, respectively (see also ILO, 2012:47). Life expectancy varies; the regional average for Arab states (this does not include Israel, Iran, or Turkey) rose from fifty-two years in the early 1970s to sixty-seven years in the early 2000s. It is highest in the Gulf states (seventy-five years) and Israel (seventy-four years) and lowest in Yemen (sixty years).[3]

Iran and Turkey have had some volatility in their demographic transitions. Turkey was the earliest to begin its transition, in the 1950s, only to experience a kind of baby boom in the early 1970s. Iran's total fertility rate declined during the 1970s, but increased during the 1980s following the Iranian Revolution. The dramatic population growth rate of the 1980s is attributed to the pronatalist policies of the new Islamic regime, which banned contraceptives and encouraged marriage and family formation (Moghadam, 2003:chap. 6). But it may also be a result of rural fertility behavior, which was slow to decline during the 1970s. After the reversal of the pronatalist policy following the results of the 1986 census and the introduction of an aggressive family planning campaign after 1988, there was a dramatic change from the fertility and population growth trends of the 1980s. In the mid-1990s, fertility declined again. Today, Iranian women, especially in the largest cities, have a fertility rate that is estimated to be between 1.8 and 2.0.

In most countries, fertility rates are considerably higher in rural areas than urban areas, as was confirmed by Demographic and Health Surveys (DHS). In Morocco, Tunisia, and Turkey, fertility declined faster in urban than in rural areas, suggesting the effect that urbanization and its corre-lates—mainly, female education, employment opportunities, delayed mar-riage, and access to contraceptives and family planning information—have had in those countries. But in Turkey and Tunisia and to a lesser degree in Morocco and Iran, fertility declines are being registered in rural areas as well, partly due to the availability of contraception.

Like the World Fertility Surveys of the late 1970s and early 1980s, the more recent DHS research confirmed the link between the mother's educa-tion and total fertility rate: the higher the educational attainment, the fewer the number of children.[4] In Jordan in 2000, for example, women with no formal education had an average fertility rate of 6.9 children whereas the figure for those with a secondary or higher education was 4.1 per woman. The average fertility rate subsequently declined to 3.3 children (see Table 9.3), but this figure is high relative to the educational attainment of Jordan-ian women. Jordan is unique in its relatively high fertility rate among edu-cated women; this may be a function of the low labor force participation of women—23 percent in 2010 (ILO, 2012:table A1, 130).

MENA countries have exhibited a variety of population policies and concerns. *Population policy* is understood to be an intention to improve the overall well-being of the nation's citizens. Definitions of *well-being* vary and are certainly debatable, as are prescriptions of how to reach objectives. In the 1990s, countries that were concerned about the rate of population growth (e.g., Iran and Egypt) faced the dual goal of improving health facil-ities on the one hand, thus reducing natal and infant mortality, and of de-creasing the birthrate on the other hand. Other countries seek to reduce mortality rates and improve the population's health, but do not actively seek to reduce birthrates (e.g., Israel and Saudi Arabia). At the level of state policymaking, the approach to population growth ranges from pronatalist to laissez-faire to pro–family planning. In several of the countries—notably Iran, Lebanon, Tunisia, and Turkey—the combined effects of socioeco-nomic development, women's educational attainment, and state-sponsored family planning programs have produced the lowest fertility rates of the re-gion. Indeed, the average of about 2.5 children per woman in these MENA countries today is even lower than the fertility rate of many Latin American countries.

Yet decades of high birthrates have helped to keep the population of Middle Eastern countries young. According to *Arab Human Development Report 2009* (UNDP, 2009a), some 35 percent of the Arab region's popula-tion in 2005 was aged fifteen years and younger and 60 percent was under age twenty-five, whereas only 4 percent was aged sixty-five years and older.[5]

There are of course variations across the region. In 2005 the share of the population younger than age fifteen ranged from 19.8 percent in the UAE to greater than 45 percent in Yemen and the West Bank and Gaza. Similarly, in Iran in 2009, some 70 percent of the population was younger than age thirty-five. The existence of a large population of young people has economic and political implications. Young people tend to suffer from high rates of unemployment and may engage in social protests either for jobs, housing, and income or for cultural change and freedoms; young men also may constitute a recruiting base for Islamist movements or radical campaigns. The youth bulge in the region may have reached its peak (ILO, 2012:47), but countries with young populations exhibit a high dependency ratio and small tax base, a situation exacerbated by the low labor force participation of women in nonagricultural and modern occupations.

Labor Force Growth and Employment Challenges

The height of the region's oil-based economic development during the 1970s saw considerable intraregional labor migration, which was characterized by a massive outflow of surplus labor from countries such as Egypt, Jordan, Tunisia, Yemen, and Lebanon, as well as the West Bank, to capital-rich and labor-poor GCC countries and to Libya and Iraq. Non-Arab workers, including Koreans, Filipinos, Sri Lankans, and Yugoslavs, who were attracted by the high wages offered in the capital-rich countries, were also brought in. In 1975, foreign labor constituted 47 percent of the labor force in the Gulf countries, and by 1990 the figure had increased to 68 percent. In Kuwait in 1990, fully 86 percent of the workforce was foreign (ESCWA, 1993). Remittances from nationals working abroad became especially important to the economies of Egypt, Jordan, and Yemen.

Jordan was unique among Arab countries in being a labor-exporting country that also imported labor. It exported skilled workers and educated professionals to the rich Gulf states, but it also imported unskilled and low-wage workers for construction, domestic services, and some public services that Jordanian nationals would not perform such as waiting tables, cleaning buildings, and cleaning streets. Most of the imported Arab labor was Egyptian (Moghadam, 1998b:chap. 6). Most domestic workers were (and remain) from the Philippines, with a smaller proportion from Sri Lanka. A distinctive result has been the underutilization of Jordanian women, who in the absence of labor force attachment tend to have 3.3 to 3.5 children per woman, as discussed above.

The labor migration patterns of North Africans and Turks have been different. Their preferred destination has been Europe, notably Germany for Turks and France for Algerians, Moroccans, and Tunisians (although Tunisians also went to Libya). Furthermore, labor migration began earlier, during the 1950s and 1960s, in response to European guest worker programs. In the 1970s, European countries began to reduce the influx of guest workers, although the number of Turks in Germany continued to grow through a combination of natural increase, family reunification, and illegal immigration (OECD, 1992; Omran and Roudi, 1993:24). North African emigrants continued to head to Europe in the 1980s and, since the 1990s, the migration streams have included women on their own.

The heyday of intra-Arab labor migration came to an end in the early 1990s. (In oil-rich Iran, the revolution of 1978–1979, along with the change in development strategy adopted by the new Islamic regime, put an end to the influx of skilled and professional labor from abroad.) Political and economic instabilities reduced intraregional labor flows, affecting mainly Jordanian, Palestinian, and Yemeni workers laboring in Kuwait and Saudi Arabia. The expulsion of the expatriate workers was a punishment for their countries' stance on the 1991 Gulf War, revealing the facade of Arab unity. At the same time, Kuwait and Saudi Arabia rewarded Egypt for its position against Iraq and in favor of the war by replacing expelled Jordanians, Palestinians, and Yemenis with Egyptian workers. Still, a large number of Egyptians left the Gulf and returned to Egypt as a result of the Gulf War. The United Nations (UN) Economic and Social Commission for West Asia (ESCWA, 1995) estimated the total number of returnees at 2 million people. Most returnees were nationals of Yemen (732,000), Egypt (700,000), and Jordan (300,000, including Palestinians). The return of expatriates was a mixed experience; in some cases returnees contributed to a boom in the construction industry and in small businesses (especially in Jordan), but in other cases returnees experienced unemployment, slow absorption into the local labor market, or poverty. Poverty became especially acute for Yemenis who were largely unskilled workers unable to find employment at home.

The expulsion of Arab workers, along with the rapid urbanization and modernization of the oil-rich Gulf states, led to an influx of migrant labor from South Asia. In the GCC countries, the public sector is reserved almost exclusively for nationals, and predominantly for men, although Kuwaiti women make up nearly half of their country's government workforce. Public sector employment in Kuwait, Saudi Arabia, and Qatar is on the order of 72 percent to 88 percent of the total employed native population. The private sector is almost entirely comprised of migrant or immigrant labor. Under the *kafala* (sponsorship system), households or firms may import or hire what is meant to be a flexible stock of temporary foreign labor, but which in reality is more permanent (Baldwin-Edwards, 2011; see also Shah, 2005, 2007). In the twenty-first century, there have been significant declines in the immigrant proportions of the labor force in Kuwait, Saudi Arabia, and the UAE. But Qatar and Bahrain have seen massive increases in the ratio—from 87 percent to 94 percent for Qatar, and from 63 percent to

76 percent for Bahrain over the past decade (Baldwin-Edwards, 2011:8). Such a reliance on migrant labor is considered to be unsustainable and suggestive of either underutilization of the native population or education–labor market mismatch.

In the large and diversified MENA economies, migrant labor is almost nonexistent. (Exceptions are Lebanon and Jordan, with their importation of nannies.) Urbanization has altered the geoeconomic landscape, though roughly one-third of the total population may continue to depend on agriculture for its livelihood in a number of countries. The proportion of the labor force in agriculture varies: in 2009–2010 it was about 40 percent in Morocco, 32 percent in Egypt, 21 percent in Iran, 24 percent in Turkey, and 15 percent in Syria, and as low as 2 percent in Israel and the small Gulf states.[6] In Jordan, the share of agriculture in total employment declined from 42 percent in the 1960s to less than 7 percent in the early 1990s (Shaban, Assaad, and al-Qudsi, 1995:71), and then to just 2 percent in 2010, according to the World Bank's *World Development Indicators*.[7] Economic modernization altered the sectoral distribution of the labor force, with a growing proportion of workers now involved in services and, to a lesser degree, in industry. In the nonoil and mixed-oil economies, development strategies from the 1960s to 1980s included protection and promotion of the manufacturing sector, leading to increases in (mostly male) employment in industry. In general, though, the manufacturing sector has not fared as well, partly due to the reliance on wealth generated from oil exports, while the services sector has been expanding and thriving throughout the region. The expanding services sector has helped the growth of the female labor force, even though female labor has remained a relatively small percentage of the total salaried workforce.

Labor force statistics in the region are not always exact, and women's economic activity outside the formal and modern sector has tended to be underestimated, but most of the measured female labor force is found in the services sector, largely in professional fields (teaching and health care and, to a lesser degree, public administration). This is especially the case in the highly urbanized GCC countries (which, as noted, rely on nonnationals for construction work and domestic service, some occupations in the retail and hotels sector, and some higher-level professional jobs). While Kuwaiti, Emirati, Saudi, Qatari, and Omani women are found across the professions, less prestigious or "culturally inappropriate" service work is performed by imported female labor. The involvement of women in industry is negligible, except in Oman.

Elsewhere, the available evidence suggests that a large part of the female economically active population in many of the countries, such as Egypt, Iran, Iraq, Syria, and Turkey, remains rooted in agriculture. Turkey is somewhat anomalous, in that it is the most modern and industrial of the countries in the region and yet the one where women are most likely to be found in agriculture, although the proportion has been declining in recent years. Throughout the region, most of the salaried female workforce is found in the public sector where their shares are between 30 percent and 45 percent. But because of their absence from the private sector, the female share of the total salaried workforce is small in most cases, at under 20 percent (see e.g., Livani, 2007:4). Clearly, salaried work is a male domain in the region—a reality that has not changed despite the impressive advances in women's educational attainment, lower fertility rates, and rising age at first marriage. What is more, women's unemployment rates are high, as are the unemployment rates of young people in general. This is true of the GCC countries as well as the larger MENA countries.

Rising Unemployment

By the mid-1990s, the demographic transition characterized by high fertility, rural-to-urban migration, and changes in the pattern of intraregional labor migration had led to rapid growth of the labor force. In a situation of economic stagnation, this resulted in high rates of unemployment, especially in urban areas.

The unemployment situation was a shock particularly to the educated population, which had come to expect guaranteed jobs in the public sector. During the 1960s and 1970s, state-sponsored economic development resulted in an expansion of public sector employment. For example, Egypt had a policy of guaranteeing public sector jobs to graduates of vocational secondary schools and universities. Morocco had a similar scheme, albeit one that provided temporary employment to graduates. As a result of these policies, some countries, such as Egypt, Jordan, and Algeria, employed more than 50 percent of the labor force in the public sector. A majority of the workforce in the GCC countries was also employed in the public sector.

As a result of the recessionary conditions experienced in the region in the mid-1980s, structural adjustment policy prescriptions to contract the public sector wage bill, and the adoption of neoliberal policies of liberalization and privatization, governments slowed down public sector hiring and encouraged the growth of the private sector, entrepreneurship, and flexible labor markets.[8] Initially, due to political and social concerns, MENA governments preferred the strategy of wage deterioration or encouragement of early retirement rather than outright layoffs, although denationalization of previously state-owned enterprises and restructuring in the private sector did result in worker layoffs in Tunisia, Morocco, and Turkey. For the most part, however, the unemployed population has consisted of first-time job seekers; that is, graduates of high schools and colleges, male and female alike, who are seeking jobs out of economic need.

The contraction of public sector employment and declines in government social spending led to the deterioration of real wages, which in turn made household incomes fall substantially in many countries (Karshenas, 1997). For example, the real wage rate in Jordan increased by 45 percent over the period 1975–1987, but by 1990 it had declined to roughly its value in 1975 (Shaban, Assaad, and al-Qudsi, 1995:74). The drop in real wages was not, however, accompanied by an increase in job creation or the demand for labor or by a decrease in the unemployment rates. This suggests that the problem in the labor market was not high wages (as in the past), but a lack of competitiveness and productivity and inefficient utilization of human resources. It also suggests the underdevelopment of the private sector in the region and its inability to absorb the growing labor force.

Until recently, when the worldwide recession and problems in the euro-zone led to soaring unemployment in southern Europe, youth unemployment rates in the Middle East and North Africa were the highest of any region, and exceptionally high for women of all ages. Even the GCC countries, which historically had low rates of unemployment and in fact imported labor to meet demand, now came to face increasing joblessness among their native populations. Unemployment is often difficult to measure in developing countries. Most of the countries in the Middle East have only recently started to count those who are either unsuccessfully seeking jobs for the first time (as with high school and college graduates) or who have lost jobs due to enterprise restructuring (a far smaller proportion). Measured unemployment is usually urban, although countries are now increasingly including the rural areas in their enumeration; thus, some countries now disaggregate unemployment by urban or rural area as well as by gender.

Urban unemployment rates began increasing in the 1980s and reached highs of 10 percent to 18 percent in Algeria, Tunisia, Egypt, Jordan, Iran, Turkey, and Yemen. According to ESCWA (1995), the rates were as high as 30 percent in Yemen, the West Bank, and Gaza. As mentioned, unemployment is age specific, with much of it consisting of new entrants to the workforce in the age groups of fifteen to nineteen years old and twenty to twenty-four years old. Joblessness varies by educational attainment, but in some countries college graduates experience high rates of unemployment. In the early 1990s, unemployment rates among high school graduates were between 17 percent and 29 percent in Algeria, Egypt, Jordan, Morocco, and Tunisia; college graduates showed unemployment rates of 15 percent and 23 percent in Egypt and Morocco, respectively; and among workers with primary education or less, unemployment rates were 17 percent to 27 percent in Algeria, Morocco, and Tunisia (ILO, 1999; CAWTAR, 2001).

In the 1990s, female unemployment rates soared to highs of 25 percent, indicating a growing supply of job-seeking women, in contrast to an earlier pattern of "housewife-ization." (The average rate of female labor force

With unemployment soaring across the region, even low-level jobs are sought after. Here a man transports bread by bicycle amid traffic in Cairo.

participation in the MENA region only increased from 22 percent in 1980–1985 to about 28 percent in 2005–2010.) This was so despite the advances in women's educational attainment. The trend seemed to be one of higher unemployment accompanying greater literacy and schooling. In almost all countries, female unemployment rates were considerably higher than male rates. As such, they were disproportionately high, given that women's labor force participation rates and employment shares are so much smaller than those of men. What is more, women college graduates exhibited higher rates of unemployment than their male counterparts.

Table 9.4 provides data on unemployment for women and men, as well as total youth unemployment rates. It illustrates the prevalence of joblessness among women, and especially among young women. Women's high unemployment rates appear to be a function of both women's preferences for public sector jobs, which are not available, and the private sector's exclusion of women, typically due to maternity leave requirements under labor law. In the 1990s, women's unemployment rates ranged from 20 percent to 34 percent in all countries except Iraq, Lebanon, Syria, and Yemen. Iranian women's high rate of unemployment in 1991 was almost halved by 1996, and this may be because more women began starting their own businesses and nongovernmental organizations (NGOs) and entering universities. In the present decade Iranian women's unemployment rate has been 16 percent to 17 percent, but still far higher than the 9 percent rate for men and

Table 9.4 Unemployment Rates in the MENA Region, 2010 (percentage)

Country	Unemployment Rates by Gender		Youth Unemployment by Gender	
	Female	Male	Female	Male
Algeria	20.0	10.0	34	18
Bahrain	20.0	2.0	33	26
Egypt	20.0	6.0	46	18
Iran	17.0	9.0	34	20
Iraq	30.0	16.0	69	35
Israel	7.0	7.0	11	12
Jordan	22.0	10.0	46	23
Kuwait	−2.0	−2.0	13	11
Lebanon	10.0	−8.0	23	23
Libya	−13.0	−6.0	30	17
Morocco	9.0	9.0	15	17
Oman	−15.0	−6.0	30	17
Qatar	3.0	0.2	4	0.7
Saudi Arabia	16.0	4.0	54	23
Syria	23.0	6.0	41	15
Tunisia	16.0	14.0	29	32
Turkey	13.0	11.0	21	17
United Arab Emirates	14.0	2.0	25	9
West Bank and Gaza	19.0	26.0	41	36
Yemen	24.0	11.5	45	22

Sources: International Labour Organization, *Rethinking Economic Growth: Toward Productive and Inclusive Arab Societies* (Beirut: ILO, Regional Office for the Arab States, 2012), figure 2.7, p. 51, for unemployment data; figure 2.10, p. 53, for youth unemployment data. Data on Iran, Israel, and Turkey from World Bank, *World Development Indicators 2011* (Washington, DC: World Bank), http://data.worldbank.org/indicator.

disproportionately high given women's far lower participation rate; unemployment among young women remains extraordinarily high. In the 1990s, Yemen seemed to depart from the regional norm of high rates of female unemployment, and this may have reflected the effects of returning male migrant workers as well as low rates of female labor force participation (Yemen Ministry of Planning and Development, 1998). In the new century, however, the combination of educational attainment and economic need propelled more Yemeni women to the labor force, though without much success in an untoward economic environment; hence, the high rates of female unemployment in Yemen. The available evidence is clear: the feminization of unemployment is a defining feature of urban labor markets in the Middle East and North Africa.

The almost total absence of unemployment insurance in Arab countries has been quite striking given that the region has had some of the highest unemployment levels in the world for at least three decades. The main exceptions have been Algeria, Tunisia, Egypt, and Bahrain, largely systems that combine both contributory and noncontributory elements;

Jordan introduced a similar scheme in 2011. The schemes typically cover insiders, but even so, less than half of those in government and the formal economy who have contributed enough to qualify have received coverage. Tunisia's unemployment scheme, covered by social insurance, was limited to formal sector workers only. It had a coverage rate of 37 percent of the economically active population, but in 2008 only 3 percent of the unemployed (13,000 people) received benefits (ILO, 2011). According to a recent ILO report, the unemployment benefits that have been introduced "fail to meet the two objectives of typical unemployment protection schemes, that is, insurance against the risk of workers losing their jobs or social assistance based on an income test" (ILO, 2012:87).

How do the unemployed—those who expect jobs in the formal sector, but do not find them—fare in countries where unemployment insurance is not in place or is not available to new entrants? For some time, North Africans migrated to Europe—France, Belgium, Spain, and the Netherlands—in search of a livelihood. Many established legal residence and raised families there, but others seeking an income traveled without papers. In recent years, however, the European authorities have clamped down on illegal migration while the global economic crisis of 2008 and growing unemployment in Europe has restricted the availability of jobs. Back in the MENA region, some job seekers—especially, men—appear to have gravitated to the urban informal sector, which by all accounts has grown tremendously in the region. Informal sector workers may include taxi drivers, construction workers, domestic workers, workers in souks and bazaars (the traditional markets in the Middle East), hairdressers, barbers, seamstresses, tailors, workers in or owners of small industrial or artisan workshops, hawkers of sundry goods, and repairmen. Also included are home-based female pieceworkers such as women in Turkey, Syria, and Jordan who are engaged in sewing and embroidery for a contractor or subcontractor. There is also higher-end informal work, under-the-table activities and transactions including tutoring, consulting, catering, personal training, and jewelry making. The nature and function of the informal sector has been much debated; although it serves to absorb the labor force and to provide goods and services at lower cost, it is also unregulated and untaxed, leading to poor labor standards and income (such as the wealth of many merchants) that is not redistributed. The informal sector both contributes to and is a reflection of income inequality in the society.

Poverty and Inequality

Poverty and inequality are measured by household income and consumption and by quality-of-life indicators. Conventional studies distinguish between "absolute poverty" and "relative poverty," and they establish an income-based "poverty line" against which households are measured. International organizations also establish poverty lines, which may range from $1.25 a day to $2 a day; a Gini coefficient measures income inequality. In an alternative conceptualization, the definition of *poverty* is broadened to include measures of "capabilities" or "human development" such as literacy, life expectancy, and access to clean water. This better captures gender differences while also recognizing the multidimensionality of poverty. Studies show considerable improvement over time in standards of living in the Middle East and North Africa, as measured by such social indicators as life expectancy, infant mortality, maternal mortality, access to safe water, adequate sanitation facilities, rising age of first marriage, fertility rates, literacy, and school enrollments as well as by wage rates and household incomes. However, gender gaps exist and, given the income levels of many countries in the region, the social indicators should be better. Moreover, although levels of absolute poverty have been decreasing in some parts of the region, poverty has actually been increasing in other parts (most notably and visibly in Iraq since the 2003 US-led invasion) while inequalities have been widening everywhere. This is partly a function of high population growth, but the creation of new poverty groups in urban areas has also been caused by economic recession, rising prices, deteriorating wages, unemployment, and inadequate investments in health care, education, and social welfare (UNDP, 2009a, 2011; ILO, 2012).

Even though poverty is not as severe in the Middle East as in some other regions (UNDP, 2002b, 2009a), its persistence or increase has been a source of concern. The number of poor people in the Middle East and North Africa increased from an estimated 60 million in 1985 to 73 million in 1990, or from 30.6 percent to 33.1 percent of the total population (World Bank, 1993:5; ESCWA, 1993:121; see also ESCWA, 1995). Poverty assessments prepared by the World Bank, which were derived from surveys of living standards undertaken within various countries, revealed growing poverty in Egypt and Jordan and the emergence of urban working poor in Tunisia and Morocco (see e.g., World Bank 1991, 1994, 1995). According to official statistics, 23 percent of the population in Egypt in 1991 and 18 percent of the population in Jordan in 1993 was considered to be living under the poverty line. Most believe that the poverty incidence could be as high as 30 percent in both countries (Moghadam, 1998a, 1998b). In both countries poverty was largely rural, and the rural poor were small landholders and tenants, landless agricultural workers, and pastoralists (ESCWA, 1993:6). In Egypt the urban poor included the unemployed and female-headed households (Fergany, 1994). In all countries, because of gender differences in literacy, educational attainment, employment, and income, women are especially vulnerable to poverty during periods of economic difficulty or in the event of divorce, abandonment, or widowhood.

In Lebanon, the main factors behind the increase in the incidence of poverty recorded in the 1990s were the civil war and misguided economic policies, including tax write-offs for large firms engaged in the country's reconstruction and the absence of any property taxes (see, e.g., ESCWA 1995, 1997). In 1996, about 1 million Lebanese (28 percent of the population) lived below the poverty line, and some 75 percent of the poor were urban dwellers. The country's unemployment rate was 15 percent in 1996, compared with 8.1 percent of the workforce in 1975, before the country's long civil war began. Throughout the 1990s, studies commissoned by ESCWA identified the absence of government social spending and the maldistribution of wealth as the main factors behind the rise in nutritional deficiencies, lack of sanitation in poor areas, and the lowering of teaching and health standards. Unlike other countries in the region, Lebanon has always had a minimal state, with social provisioning largely relegated to faith-based charities.

For some countries, poverty and lack of progress in human development have resulted from high military expenditures. In Iraq, Oman, Saudi Arabia, Syria, and Yemen, military expenditures in 1990 far exceeded expenditures on education and health care (see UNDP, 1996:table 19). In 2000, military expenditures in Saudi Arabia amounted to 11.6 percent of gross domestic product (GDP); in Jordan, the figure was 9.5 percent. Even Turkey committed nearly 5 percent of GDP toward military expenditures, compared with 2.2 percent of GDP for education and 3.3 percent for health care (UNDP, 2002a:table 17). Iran and Libya spent less than most MENA countries on the military sector—on the order of 1 percent to 2 percent of GDP—while Israel spent about 7 percent. From 2000 to 2010, military spending as a percentage of GDP remained high in Oman and Saudi Arabia (10 percent); in those countries and in the UAE, military expenditures were considerably higher than health and education spending across all years. In Yemen, military expenditure as a percentage of GDP was higher than health expenditure in some years (2000–2004), and in other years (2006–2008) only slightly less; in Syria, it was consistently higher. In some countries, therefore, there was a trade-off between national security and human security and between military development and social development.[9]

In the case of Iraq, of course, war and economic sanctions have exacerbated the situation of the poor and created new poverty-stricken groups. The destruction of Iraq's infrastructure by US-led coalition bombings in January 1991 (see Drèze and Gazdar, 1992) and again in March–April 2003, the shortage of medical supplies and foodstuffs caused by the long sanctions regime, and the collapse of public services following the 2003 invasion have completely transformed a country that was once urbanized, mechanized, and prosperous. Yet the ongoing problems of security, and perhaps the new relationship with the United States, have resulted in fully 5.1 percent of GDP spent on the military.

Because of different poverty measurements, as well as changes in a country's economic or fiscal health, figures might differ across years as well as across datasets. Data from the *Arab Human Development Report 2009* (UNDP, 2009a) show that some 19 percent of Moroccans and 23 percent of Algerians were living below the nationally determined poverty line while 14 percent of Moroccans and 15 percent of Algerians lived on less than $2 per day. The UNDP's *Human Development Report 2010* and *Human Development Report 2013* show somewhat different figures, as seen in Table 9.5. Though it is true that poverty is not as severe in the MENA region as it is in South Asia and sub-Saharan Africa, it is also true that the region has made slow progress in reducing poverty (UNDP, 2011:24). What the data also show is the extent of income inequality, as measured by the Gini coefficient. Is it any wonder, then, that the region erupted in mass protests in 2011?

According to some observers, income inequalities have been widening (El-Ghonemy, 1998; Richards and Waterbury, 1996; Bibi and Nabli, 2010). This is said to be the result of the economic policies of structural adjustment and trade and price liberalization as well as the old policies of high

Table 9.5 Poverty and Inequality in the MENA Region

Country	Population Below Income Poverty Line 2002–2011/12 (percentage)		Gini Income Coefficient, 2000–2010[a]
	PPP $1.25 a Day	National Poverty Line	
Algeria	—	—	35.3
Egypt	1.7	22.0	30.8
Iran	> 2	—	38.3
Iraq	2.8	22.9	—
Israel	—	—	39.2
Jordan	0.1	13.3	35.4
Lebanon	—	—	—
Morocco	2.5	9.0	40.9
Palestine	0.0	21.9	35.5
Qatar	—	—	41.1
Saudi Arabia	—	—	33.0
Syria	1.7	—	35.8
Tunisia	1.4	3.8	41.4
Turkey	0.2	18.1	39.0
Yemen	17.5	—	37.7

Sources: UNDP, *Human Development Report 2010* (New York: UNDP), table 5; *Human Development Report 2013* (New York: UNDP), table 5 (poverty estimates are based on surveys conducted in 2002 and beyond); and *Human Development Report 2013* (New York: UNDP), table 3, for Gini income coefficient data.

Notes: a. Gini income coefficient measures income distribution or consumption among individuals or households; the higher the figure, the higher the income inequality.

PPP = purchase power parity

— indicates data not available.

military spending and inadequate taxation. The share of working poor in the total employed population of the Arab region was 22 percent in 2011, down from 31 percent in 1991. This share is larger than in East Asia, Latin America and the Caribbean, and the countries of Central and Eastern Europe and the former Soviet Union (ILO, 2012:figure 3.1, 64). MENA countries are on average more equal in terms of income than middle-income countries, but not low- or high-income countries. The average Gini coefficient for MENA is close to 40, compared to 43.6 for middle-income countries and 36 for the high-income group (Salehi-Isfahani, 2010). To put this in perspective, Sweden and Finland have low rates of inequality (25 and 27, respectively) while Brazil has a high Gini coefficient (54). The US level of income inequality, at nearly 41, is also considered high.

Beyond poverty rates and income inequality, human development indicators show progress in some areas, but reversals or stagnation in others, largely the result of privatization and lower public spending in education, health care, and social welfare. The available evidence indicates serious gaps in Iraq, Morocco, Yemen, and rural areas in Egypt, and the deterioration of the quality of public education in most countries. In some countries, therefore, some of the Millennium Development Goals (MDGs) are not expected to be achieved by 2015, and rural populations will continue to lag behind. According to the UN's *Millennium Development Goals Report 2010,* disparities in educational outcomes and attainments align with gender, income, and locality; in particular, education and its completion are elusive for poor, rural, and female populations (United Nations, 2010). Some 60 percent of children not enrolled in school in Arab countries are girls, with higher ratios in Egypt, Iraq, Yemen, and Syria. Indeed, the average years of education of a rural Egyptian girl are four, considerably below the national average of ten (United Nations, 2010). World Bank survey data show that in Morocco, less than 1 percent of poor and of rural children make it to Grade 9 versus 60 percent and 43 percent for rich or urban children, respectively (cited in UNESCO, 2011).

Most countries are on target toward achieving full completion rates of the primary grades, except for Iraq, Morocco, and Yemen. However, the Arab region performs less well in terms of completing secondary education, and displays significant rates of repeaters. Despite some progress since the 1990s, in 2007 the percentage of repeaters in the primary grades for Arab states stood at 5.6 percent, above the rate of 3.3 percent for middle-income countries (United Nations, 2010). Moreover, family out-of-pocket expenditures on education, connected to the expansion of private schools and private tutoring as a way of compensating for poor public schooling or to ensure admission into university, has exacerbated or created a new source of inequality.

The good news is that some countries—the GCC countries, Iran, Jordan, and Lebanon—show high ratios of female participation in postsecondary education and, in those and other countries, most college students are

Many governments of the Middle East have a cabinet position dedicated to youth and sports in an effort to provide recreation and discipline to the underprivileged. Here, teenagers play basketball in a government recreation center in le Kef, Tunisia.

women. But postsecondary education remains out of reach for most of the region's large population of young people. What is more, a college degree does not necessarily lead to salaried employment, as was noted above (see also ILO, 2012).

All the MENA countries have public health care systems, but these do not adequately cover the entire population, neglecting in particular rural areas and poorer income groups. Estimates are that public health covers 30 percent to 40 percent of the population, with much lower coverage in Egypt, Morocco, and Yemen. Furthermore, the systems are fragmented because financing and risk management are split between the public funds and public agencies involved (twenty-nine in the Egyptian case), leading to considerable inefficiencies and distortions (FEMISE, 2009; UNDP, 2009a: chap. 7; Salehi-Isfahani, 2010; ILO, 2012). A notable exception is the GCC countries, whose citizens enjoy universal health care coverage of relatively good quality.

High-quality medical care is not universally provided, with the notable exceptions of Tunisia, Turkey, Iran, and the GCC countries. Elsewhere, access to primary health care facilities is typically restricted to public sector employees and related to social insurance contributions. According to the *Millennium Development Goals Report 2010* (United Nations, 2010), maternity mortality rates in rural areas are sometimes more than five times greater than those in the capital cities. Health outcomes are also differentiated by income groups, so that poorer income groups display indicators that are much worse than the national averages. Hence, child mortality rates are 2.6 times higher for the poorest income quintiles in Egypt while infant mortality is three times higher (El-Laithy, 2011; UN 2012).

Public health systems have had to contend with shrinking or stagnant resource availability, although they have had to serve a larger population (FEMISE, 2009; UNDP, 2009a; Salehi-Isfahani, 2010; ILO, 2012). Public spending on health care as a share of GDP in the non-GCC countries is well below the international norms, with the exception of Jordan. What is more, the introduction of user fees and cost recovery in many services has added the squeeze on the very poor. According to Djauad Salehi-Isfahani (2010), with longer waiting times and less availability, users have increasingly had to turn to the less affordable private sector. Except for Turkey and Algeria, non-GCC countries, including Tunisia and Libya, have some of the highest ratios of out-of-pocket health spending in the world, and certainly much higher than average norms for their per capita income levels. Consequently, the lower income quintiles of the population are faced with high health expenditures, worsening their vulnerability and poverty (see, e.g., El-Laithy, Abu-Ismail, and Hamdan, 2008, on Lebanon).

As a result of the slow withdrawal of the state from social protection, civil society actors and faith-based groups have come to constitute a large share of social service providers. While there has been much research on this phenomenon (e.g., Clark, 2004; Jawad, 2009), empirical studies are lacking on quality, long-term impact on poverty, and contribution to social outcomes.

In sum, there have been notable achievements in literacy, educational attainment, and life expectancy since the 1960s, but the region's human development indicators should be more robust than they are. In the countries with relatively good human development indicators—such as Turkey, Lebanon, and Iran—inequalities or relative poverty are quite pronounced and have been growing. The persistence of destitution, or absolute poverty, mainly in rural areas, is a problem in such low-income countries as Egypt, Yemen, and Morocco, and the Gaza Strip. In the wake of its own version of the Arab Spring, however, Morocco set about launching a new national health services program, benefiting 8.5 million poor Moroccans and financed by a surtax of 1 percent on private companies' earnings (Ottaway, 2012). Although urbanization has brought about access to health care, safe water, and sanitation for residents in most of the countries, some countries continue to have difficulties in the provision of such urban services. Other countries experience distinct rural-urban disparities.

For access to services, urban living is certainly superior to rural living, but population growth and reductions in government social spending have been straining the quality and quantity of urban services. These pressures are not conveyed by the statistics, but are best discerned by visits to and stays in the nonelite sections of the cities of the Middle East and North Africa where overcrowding, rundown and inadequate public transportation, streets in disrepair, polluted air, high noise levels, slums, and lack of building codes are only some of the many problems that low-income urban dwellers endure.

Conclusion

This chapter has surveyed trends in population growth, urbanization, labor force growth, rising unemployment, poverty, and inequality. These social and demographic trends have implications for household well-being, individual capabilities, and political stability, and may be considered underlying factors in the mass social protests in Iran in June 2009 and in Arab countries in 2011. Urbanization holds promise for people—including a wider range of options, activities, and services—but unchecked population growth has created enormous pressures on urban services. High fertility rates have resulted in the emergence of a large population of young people who are seeking, but not finding, jobs. The combination of population growth, economic liberalization, and reduced or misguided government spending has increased inequality while rising unemployment and political conflicts have exacerbated or caused poverty and deprivation. Poverty and inequality are social phenomena, reflecting a class structure and skewed distribution of income, wealth, and opportunities, but gender inequality renders women more vulnerable than men to poverty.

For at least a generation, the countries of the Middle East and North Africa have been faced with a number of social and demographic challenges that require concerted action involving governments, NGOs, citizen groups, and international organizations. The uprisings of 2011 imparted some urgency to the matter, but most governments have tended to institute stopgap, ad hoc measures rather than engage in a deliberative process of building consensus for a new social development strategy. Identifying problems and solutions call for short-term, medium-term, and long-term perspectives informed by both developmental imperatives and the social rights of citizens. Public-private partnerships that create internships, apprenticeships, and cooperative education, along with programs that encourage participation in the creative arts, could be one way of mitigating youth unemployment and, indeed, of rewarding creativity as well as enhancing employability. Other needed policies and steps include measures to improve women's access to jobs as a way of enhancing productivity, expanding the tax base, and raising household incomes while also expanding women's capabilities; investments in the physical and social infrastructure to upgrade urban services as well as create employment; reforming the legal and regulatory framework to raise labor and environmental standards as well as to improve the system of taxation; and community development programs that involve high school and college graduates, as a way of mitigating youth unemployment, alleviating urban poverty, and instilling social solidarity. The absence of such policies may have contributed to mass social discontent and the protests that led to the downfall of governments in Tunisia and Egypt. It remains to be seen whether the new governments will enact such measures toward citizen rights and well-being.

Notes

1. On the youth bulge, see Assaad and Roudi-Fahimi (2007) and Fargues (2008).

2. Data are from UNDP (2011a:table 9, 159).

3. Data are from World Bank (2000:table 2.18, 108), and UNDP (2009a); Israeli data from UNDP (2009b:table N, 199).

4. The Demographic and Health Surveys were carried out by Macro International, with funding from the US Agency for International Development. Final reports and other publications for the countries surveyed may be found on the DHS website, www.measuredhs.com. See also, *World Fertility Survey: Major Findings and Implications* (Voorburg, Netherlands: International Statistical Institute, 1984).

5. Data are from UNDP (2009a:table 4, 232). Although the older population is still a fraction of the younger population, it is expected to grow in line with lowered fertility rates. Care for older people is already a matter of social concern in Lebanon, although it remains largely the responsibility of women in the family (Sugita, Esim, and Omeira, 2009).

6. World Bank, *World Development Indicators, Employment in Agriculture (% of Total Employment)*, http://data.worldbank.org/indicator/SL.AGR.EMPL.ZS.

7. Ibid.

8. The extensive literature on liberalization and privatization in the Middle East and North Africa includes Harik and Sullivan (1992), Niblock and Murphy (1993), Karshenas (1997), Richards and Waterbury (1996), and Moghadam (1998b). See also ERF (1996, 1998); and the various *Arab Human Development Reports* for a critique of the economic reforms undertaken by Arab states. For a contrasting view, see World Bank (1993).

9. To put these figures in some perspective, the United States (which is the highest spender in the world) spends about 5 percent of its GDP, or 18 percent of the federal government budget, on the military. The data on military expenditures come from the online databases of the Swedish International Peace Research Institute, www.sipri.org/databases, and the World Bank, *World Development Indicators*, http://data.worldbank.org.

Bibliography

Assaad, Ragui. 1995. January. *Urbanization and Demographic Structure in the Middle East and North Africa with a Focus on Women and Children.* Regional Papers no. 40. New York: Population Council.

Assaad, Ragui, and Farzaneh Roudi-Fahimi. 2007. *Youth in the Middle East and North Africa: Demographic Opportunity or Challenge?* Washington, DC: Population Reference Bureau. www.prb.org/pdf07/youthinmena.pdf.

Baldwin-Edwards, Martin. 2011. March. *Labour Immigration and Labour Markets in the GCC Countries: National Patterns and Trends.* Research Paper no. 15. London: Kuwait Programme on Development, Governance and Globalisation in the Gulf States, London School of Economics Global Governance Center.

Barro, Robert, and Jong-Wha Lee. 2013. April. *Barro-Lee Educational Attainment Dataset: Educational Attainment for Population Aged 15 and Over, MENA.* www.barrolee.com/data/yrsch.htm.

Bibi, S., and M. Nabli. 2010. *Equity and Inequality in the Arab Region.* ERF Policy Research Report no. 33. Cairo: ERF.

CAWTAR (Center for Arab Women Training and Research). 2001. *Globalization and Gender: Economic Participation of Arab Women.* Tunis: CAWTAR.

Chaaban, J. 2010. *Job Creation in the Arab Economies: Navigating Through Difficult Waters.* Arab Human Development Reports Research Paper Series no. 3. New York: UNDP.

Clark, Janine A. 2004. *Islam, Charity, and Activism: Middle Class Networks and Social Welfare in Egypt, Jordan and Yemen.* Bloomington: Indiana University Press.

Drèze, Jean, and Haris Gazdar. 1992. "Hunger and Poverty in Iraq." *World Development* 20, no. 7:921–945.

ERF (Economic Research Forum). 1996. *Economic Trends in the MENA Region.* Cairo: ERF.

———. 1998. *Economic Trends in the MENA Region.* Cairo: ERF.

ESCWA (Economic and Social Commission for West Asia). 1993. January 19. *A Conceptual and Methodological Framework for Poverty Alleviation in the ESCWA Region.* New York: United Nations.

———. 1995. *Survey of Economic and Social Developments in the ESCWA Region, 1994.* New York: United Nations.

———. 1997. February. *Survey of Economic Development in the ESCWA Region, 1996.* New York: United Nations.

Fargues, Philippe. 2008. *Emerging Demographic Patterns Across the Mediterranean and Their Implications for Migration Through 2030.* Washington, DC: Migration Policy Institute.

FEMISE (Forum Euroméditerranéen de Sciences Économiques). 2009. *FEMISE Report on the EuroMediterranean Partnership: Mediterranean Partner Countries Facing the Crisis.* Marseilles: FEMISE.

Fergany, Nader. 1994. *Urban Women, Work and Poverty Alleviation in Egypt.* Pilot study sponsored by the International Labour Organization and the United Nations Development Programme. Cairo: Al-Mishkat Research Institute.

El-Ghonemy, M. Riad. 1998. *Affluence and Poverty in the Middle East.* London: Routledge.

Harik, Ilya, and Denis Sullivan (eds.). 1992. *Privatization and Liberalization in the Middle East.* Bloomington: Indiana University Press.

ILO (International Labour Organization). 1999. *World Labour Report, 1999.* Geneva: ILO.

———. 2011. "Statistical Update on Arab States and Territories and North African Countries." Geneva: ILO, Department of Statistics.

———. 2012. *Rethinking Economic Growth: Towards Productive and Inclusive Arab Societies.* Geneva: International Labour Organization, in cooperation with the UNDP Regional Bureau for Arab States.

Jawad, Rana. 2009. *Religion and Social Welfare in the Middle East: A Lebanese Perspective.* Bristol, UK: Policy Press.

Karshenas, Massoud. 1997. "Macroeconomic Policy, Structural Change, and Employment in the Middle East and North Africa." Pp. 320–396 in Azizur Rahman Khan and M. Muqtada (eds.), *Overcoming Unemployment*. London: Macmillan.

El-Laithy, Heba. 2011. September 8–9. "Levels of Provision of Social Security in ESCWA Countries." Paper prepared for the Expert Group Meeting on Social Security in Western Asia: Accessibility and Sustainability. Beirut: ESCWA.

El-Laithy, Heba, K. Abu-Ismail, and K. Hamdan. 2008. *Poverty, Growth and Income Distribution in Lebanon*. Country Study no. 13. Brasilia: International Poverty Centre, UNDP. http://www.ipc-undp.org/pub/IPCCountryStudy13.pdf.

Livani, Talajeh. 2007. *Middle East and North Africa: Gender Overview*. Washington DC: World Bank.

Moghadam, Valentine M. 1998a. "The Feminization of Poverty in International Perspective," *Brown Journal of World Affairs* 5, no. 2:225–248.

———. 1998b. *Women, Work, and Economic Reform in the Middle East and North Africa*. Boulder: Lynne Rienner.

———. 2003. *Modernizing Women: Gender and Social Change in the Middle East*. 2nd ed. Boulder: Lynne Rienner.

Niblock, Tim, and Emma Murphy (eds.). 1993. *Economic and Political Liberalization in the Middle East*. London: Academic Press.

OECD (Organisation for Economic Co-operation and Development). 1992. *Trends in International Migration*. Paris: OECD.

Omran, Abdel R., and Farzaneh Roudi. 1993. "The Middle East Population Puzzle." *Population Bulletin* 48, no. 1:1–40.

Ottaway, David. 2012. August. "Morocco's Islamists: In Power Without Power." *Viewpoints* No. 5. Washington, DC: Woodrow Wilson Center, Middle East Program.

Richards, Alan, and John Waterbury. 1996. *A Political Economy of the Middle East*. 2nd ed. Boulder: Westview Press.

Roudi, Farzaneh. 2001. October. "Population Trends and Challenges in the Middle East and North Africa." Washington, DC: Population Reference Bureau Policy Brief. www.prb.org/pdf/PoptrendsMiddleEast.pdf.

Salehi-Isfahani, Djavad. 2010. *Human Development in the Middle East and North Africa*. Human Development Reports Research Paper no. 2010/26. New York: UNDP.

Shaban, Radwan A., Ragui Assaad, and Sulayman S. al-Qudsi. 1995. "The Challenge of Unemployment in the Arab Region." *International Labour Review* 134, no. 1:65–81.

Shah, Nasra. 2005. "Restrictive Labor Immigration Policies in the Oil-Rich Gulf Countries: Implications for Sending Asian Countries." Paper prepared for the 25th annual IUSSP International Population conference, Tours, France, July 18–25. http://iussp2005.princeton.edu/papers/50842.

———. 2007. "Migration to Kuwait: Trends, Patterns and Policies." Paper prepared for the conference on Migration and Refugees Movement in the Middle East and North Africa, The American University in Cairo, Egypt, October 23–25. www.aucegypt.edu/GAPP/cmrs/Documents/Nasra_Shah.pdf.

Sugita, Seiko, Simel Esim, and Mansour Omeira. 2009. March. "Caring Is Work: Meeting Social Care Needs in Lebanon." Paper prepared for the Mediterranean Research Meeting, Montecatini Termé, Italy.

UNDP (United Nations Development Programme). 1996. New York: Oxford University Press.

———. 2002a. *Arab Human Development Report 2002*. New York: UNDP.

———. 2002b. *Human Development Report 2002: Deepening Democracy in a Fragmented World*. New York: Oxford University Press.

————. 2009a. *Arab Human Development Report 2009.* New York: UNDP.

————. 2009b. *Human Development Report 2009.* New York: UNDP.

————. 2011. *Arab Development Challenges Report 2011: Toward the Developmental State in the Arab Region.* Cairo: Regional Centre for the Arab States.

UNESCO (United Nations Educational, Scientific, and Cultural Organization). 2011. *UNESCO Institute of Statistics Fact Sheet (June)*, no. 12. Paris: UNESCO. United Nations.

United Nations. 2000. *The World's Women, 2000: Trends and Statistics.* New York: United Nations.

————. 2010. *The Millennium Development Goals Report 2010.* New York: United Nations.

————. 2012. January 5. *Report: Expert Group Meeting on Social Security in Western Asia: Accessibility and Sustainability.* New York: UN Economic and Social Council.

World Bank. 1991. *Egypt: Alleviating Poverty During Structural Adjustment.* Washington, DC: World Bank.

————. 1993. *Implementing the World Bank's Strategy to Reduce Poverty: Progress and Challenges.* Washington, DC: World Bank.

————. 1994. *Morocco: Poverty, Adjustment, and Growth.* Vols. 1–2. Washington, DC: World Bank.

————. 1995. August. *Republic of Tunisia: Poverty Alleviation: Preserving Progress While Preparing for the Future.* Washington, DC: World Bank.

————. 2000–2006. "Key Development Data and Statistics." Washington, DC: World Bank.

————. 2013. *World Development Indicators.* Washington, DC: World Bank. http://data.worldbank.org.

Yemen Ministry of Planning and Development. 1998. *Yemen Human Development Report 1998.* Sana'a: Yemen Ministry of Planning and Development.

10

Kinship, Class, and Ethnicity

Laurie King-Irani

Scarcely a day passes without dramatic news bulletins about conflict and violence in the Middle East. Over the past decade, this region has come to register in the consciousness of most Americans as an area of chronic volatility and dangerous divisiveness, much of which, it is assumed, arises from "essential" ethnic or religious antagonisms. The mainstream media's depictions of such conflicts as being rooted in ancient tribal or sectarian animosities might lead casual observers to conclude that political tensions in this large and diverse region are simply inevitable—encoded in the very genetic makeup or the cultural programming of various Middle Eastern populations. The perceived salience of collective, as opposed to individual, bases of political representation, legal categorization, and public participation underpins assumptions that conflicts in this region are tribal, deeply rooted, essential, and thus inevitable. Middle Eastern peoples are frequently depicted as warlike, troubled, violent, and barbaric. Invocations of ancient history are common in the mainstream media's tendency to speak of conflict in "the Holy Land," a term that resonates with compelling cultural images rather than reflecting contemporary political realities. Similarly, Israeli prime minister Benjamin Netanyahu frequently reminds Cable News Network (CNN) audiences that "this is a dangerous neighborhood of the world; we can't deal with things here the way you would in the West!"[1]

The weight of history and entrenched collective stereotypes hang heavy over Israel/Palestine, Lebanon, and Iraq. Yet as historian Ussama Makdisi (2000) notes in his incisive study of the roots of Lebanon's protracted conflict, sectarianism is not an ancient and deeply rooted identity system. Rather, it first appeared as a thoroughly modern response to jarring internal

315

and external changes in the mid-nineteenth-century Ottoman Empire. Sectarianism, like ethnicity, is about contests for power in uncertain settings. It is not genetically transmitted, an ineluctable set of traits, or a communally rooted phenomenon. This chapter attempts to deconstruct popular notions of the "tribal," "ethnic," and "sectarian" by using contemporary anthropological thinking about formal and informal politics and the textures of everyday life in the Middle East.

Collective identities based on sectarian identity influence political representation, action, and social organization in Israel, Iran, and Turkey as well as in Arab countries. Indeed, it is no exaggeration to state that both Lebanon and Israel are living remnants of the Ottoman *millet* system, discussed below. Citizenship—as juridical category, social institution, bundles of rights and duties, and lived practice—differs in Israel and Lebanon from most Western nation-states in that citizens' jural relationships to the state, as well as their political agency, are mediated through ascribed membership in hierarchically ranked ethnoconfessional sects. That means that one's rights to attain particular offices, own or sell land, or receive state benefits, to give just a few examples, are contingent on whether one is a Jew or a non-Jew in Israel, or whether one is a Maronite, Sunni, Shi'a, Druze, or any one of the eighteen officially recognized ethnoconfessional sects in Lebanon, a country unique in being composed solely of minorities. In both Lebanon and Israel, personal status issues (i.e., all matters related to marriage, divorce, child custody, inheritance, and burial) are overseen not by the state, but by various religious courts and the clergy. Hence, in Lebanon and Israel alike, civil marriage between individuals of different ethnoconfessional communities is not permitted.

How and why has the Middle East come to be associated with political crises and violent hatreds? How have state-making practices and processes over the past century shaped the emergence of new forms of identity and the experience of political violence and social dislocation? As discussed in Chapters 2, 3, 4, and 5, the region went from empire to mandates to colonies to refugeedom to states to United Nations (UN) membership in less than a half-century. Because identities, actions, and ideologies unfold within state-administered frameworks, the state and its assumed monopoly on the use of coercive force—no less than the way various state agencies, actors, and institutions are key to shaping and channeling agency and memory—are crucial components to understanding kinship, ethnicity, and social class in the Middle East.

The lack of a state structure for Palestinians and the weakness of the state in postwar Lebanon and Iraq, for example, render accountability and agency, and thus conflict resolution, problematic. How should people react to violations of rights and conflict over resources: as Palestinians, Iraqis, or Lebanese, or as Sunnis, Shi'a, Jews, or Christians? As citizens, or as members of an extended patrimonial line? All of these questions have their institutional and procedural correlatives. Should people choose tribal reconciliation, family intervention, nongovernmental organizations, or courtroom justice? Personal vengeance or public compensation? For many Palestinians, whether refugees or those living in the West Bank and Gaza, that lack of a viable overarching administrative-legal-judicial structure (given the ongoing Israeli occupation and the deficiencies and weaknesses of the Palestinian Authority) makes it especially difficult to resolve problems at the local or regional level. Palestinians under occupation face special problems not encountered elsewhere, but Lebanese and Iraqis also live under weak states. A weak judicial branch in particular fails, to provide any mechanisms through which individuals or groups can attain justice and apportion resources.

No country of the modern Middle East has a homogeneous population. State borders rarely coincide with geographic, riparian (river), or linguistic/religious/ethnic boundaries. Despite the newness of the nation-state as an administrative entity or ideological concept, informal institutions of great historical depth, traditional cultural practices, art forms, cuisines, languages, and social practices continue to structure daily life. This is true even as people live increasingly urban lives, participate in modern world markets and media, and adopt and enjoy the latest transportation, communication, and education technologies. In contrast to popular—and mistaken—notions about ethnicity and ethnic conflict in the contemporary Middle East, this chapter examines the emergence, mobilization, consolidation, and institutionalization of the region's ethnic identities not as indices of unchanging biological predispositions or cultural "essences," but rather as humanly shaped and strategic responses to specific environmental, geographical, historical, political, and economic realities. Changing configurations of ethnic identity and the dynamics of majority-minority relations in the various states in this region offer valuable lessons in the contingent and political—and, therefore, constructed and strategic—nature of ethnicity in the contemporary Middle East.

To understand the genesis, nature, and trajectory of Middle Eastern ethnic phenomena, we must first survey the region's ecological, historical, geographical, and administrative contexts. In other words, we must investigate the politics of identity. The formation of ethnic groups in the Middle East, as well as the dynamics of collaboration and competition among such groups and between these groups and the states in which they are situated, arises from ever changing balances of power and shifting frameworks of decisionmaking and resource distribution at the local, national, regional, and international levels. Since ancient times, and indeed up until the present moment, the region has been a key prize for various world powers, from the ancient Roman and Persian empires, to the European colonial powers of the nineteenth and early twentieth centuries, and ultimately to the multinational corporations and high-tech Western armies of the present era.

Given its marked strategic importance, the Middle East and its people are no strangers to the intrigues and interventions of local, regional, and global politics. As can be seen in some of the following case studies, the most harrowing episodes of interethnic conflict in the Middle East have occurred when all three dimensions of competition for political power and economic resources—global, regional, and local—have coincided, as they did in Lebanon during its long and bloody civil war, which was also a regional war fought out on Lebanese soil, and in Iraq where the nation's marginalized Shi'i and Kurdish communities rose up in a bloody, but ultimately futile, challenge to the ruling Sunni Baathist regime of Saddam Hussein in 1991.

Key Concepts

In this chapter I employ an anthropological perspective on kinship, ethnicity, and social class in the contemporary Middle East in order to illustrate the contexts and processes of daily interaction for peoples of the region. Kinship and ethnicity are examined here not as monolithic, unchanging facts, but rather, as social constructs, adaptive strategies, political resources, and emotionally charged symbolic expressions of belonging. An anthropological approach to any society views human social behavior through the twin lenses of modes of organization (social, economic, and political) and frames of meaning (values, beliefs, ideologies, affect, and worldviews). Kinship and ethnicity are simultaneously modes of organization and frames of meaning.

Although the concept of social class seems, at first glance, to be related to economic phenomena, ethnographic field research quickly reveals that collective political goals, the maintenance of key social relationships, and strategic invocations of identity and morality all shape individuals' class status and life chances in ways that purely statistical data could never reveal. The sociocultural dimensions of class in the Middle East become particularly clear when we examine informal social networks and an associated, recurrent type of relationship of unequal interdependence found throughout the region: the patron-client tie (Denoeux, 1993; Roniger and Ayata, 1994; Singerman, 1995; Gilsenan, 1996).

Since Middle Eastern societies are hierarchically organized, culturally and ethnically plural, and rooted in highly literate and ancient urban cultures, kinship, ethnicity, and social class cannot be examined as isolated phenomena. In the simpler, smaller-scale societies that anthropologists commonly studied in the early twentieth century, kinship was often the primary mode of organization structuring the domains of politics, economics, law, morality, and religion. Like ethnicity and religion, kinship intertwines and interacts dynamically with many other, often competing modes of organization and frames of meaning in the large-scale, centrally administered, and rapidly urbanizing societies of the region. Formal institutions and legal codes transcending family, faith, and tribe sometimes harmonize with, and sometimes contradict, the frames of meaning and modes of belonging provided by primary identity categories. New organizational and expressive forms, ranging from politicized Islam to hip-hop youth culture—which sometimes overlap—are emerging in the cities of the Middle East (and among the Middle Eastern diaspora in European and North American cities) in response to globalized markets and media (McMurray, 2002).

Yet even in the rapidly changing nation-states and burgeoning cities of the contemporary Middle East, kinship as a symbolically rich and morally compelling system of meanings and values retains considerable power to galvanize ideologies, shape perceptions, and guide actions in the realm of politics, commerce, and administration. Symbols of shared blood and belonging help to structure the social and legal classifications that are so crucial for the establishment of large-scale state institutions and organizations (Herzfeld, 1997). Kinship imagery and symbolism have been instrumental in the construction of conceptions of citizenship and national identity in newly formed and externally imposed nation-states lacking broad-based legitimacy (Shryock, 1997; Wedeen, 1999; Joseph, 2000).

Symbols associated with family and blood ties are often used to express issues of rights and power on the local and global stage. In my own research in Nazareth, the largest Arab Palestinian city in Israel, I noted that the sentiments and values associated with close family relations, particularly the nurturing mother-child bond and the egalitarian brother-sister tie, served as models of proper political behavior for the city's communist-dominated political coalition. Similarly, the community's conception of its relation to the state as a nonassimilating minority group (i.e., non-Jews in a Jewish state) frequently employed metaphors of foster parenting and stepparent-stepchild relationships to emphasize an unnatural and stilted relationship devoid of strong affective ties of nurturance and belonging. The importance of kinship as a cultural system of meanings was also implicit in another term that Communist Party members frequently used to describe Palestinian citizens in Israel: *aytaam* (orphans), particularly following the collapse of the Soviet Union (King-Irani, 2001).

An anthropological approach to the prevailing modes of organization and frames of meaning structuring everyday life in the Middle East leads us to ask critical questions about Western assumptions, rooted in liberal political traditions, concerning the dividing lines between the individual and the group, the formal and the informal, and the public and the private. Divisions that seem natural in one society may make no sense in another.

Anthropologically informed inquiries go to the very heart of contentious issues of identity, rights, and power that now occupy center stage in Western
political and media discussions about the Middle East, and can even illumi-
nate the interactions and connections between the Middle East and the West
in ways that may surprise us (Pitcher, 1998; Jean-Klein, 2000; Antoun,
2000; Mamdani, 2002; McMurray, 2002).

The Historical Context of the Environment

Kinship and ethnicity are employed as adaptive strategies to environmental
challenges. As modes of organization and identification, they help to define
individual and collective rights and duties and allocate resources necessary
for survival, whether in rural or urban contexts. As discussed in Chapter 4,
for centuries the most common modes of subsistence in the Middle East
were agriculture and horticulture, pastoral nomadism, commerce, and
small-scale industry and resource extraction. Although popular stereotypes
of the landscapes and peoples of the region usually feature the camels,
tents, and caravans distinctive of a nomadic lifestyle, it has been the region's urban settings and institutions that have played a decisive role in
shaping the cultures, traditions, and values of the Middle East. After all, it
was in the fertile river valleys of the Nile and the Tigris and Euphrates that
some of the earliest cities and urban civilizations first emerged, thanks to
irrigation and intensive agricultural practices.

The peoples of the Middle East have not been strangers to harsh and
uncertain environments, whether natural, economic, or political. Inhabiting
an ecological zone characterized primarily by semiaridity, steep valleys,
rugged mountains, widely separated riparian systems, unpredictable rainfall, and poor soils—as detailed in Chapter 2—Middle Eastern communities
were often compelled to combine a variety of modes of subsistence such as
pastoral nomadism, small-scale agriculture, commerce, hunting, and fishing
in order to make a living. The resulting mixed economies linked urban, nomadic, and agricultural communities in interdependent (and, at times, unequal) relationships of reciprocity, redistribution, and market exchange. The
lack of large-scale, widespread, and permanent agricultural modes of subsistence rendered the formation of large-scale, enduring, and clearly defined corporate institutions difficult. Social, economic, and administrative
structures tended to have shifting borders and negotiable boundaries. Up
until the nineteenth century, the region saw a lack of large-scale, long-term,
economic integration and the corresponding lack of an enduring, centralized administrative integration of large areas into clearly bounded corporate
structures. As a result, local and regional coalitions centering on cities,
sects, and families were common modes of organizing political and economic life.

Groups dwelling in this arid and semiarid region elaborated distinctive cultural patterns and sociopolitical institutions that served to minimize the hardships and uncertainties arising from the conditions of their natural environment. Today, as in the past, the peoples of the Middle East remain justly famous for their loyal attachment to their families, distinctive rituals of hospitality and conflict mediation, and effective and flexible kin-based collectivities, such as the lineage and the tribe, which until quite recently performed most of the social, economic, and political functions of rural communities in the absence of centralized state governments (Khoury and Kostiner, 1990; Tapper, 1990).

With the emergence of clearly bounded nation-states in the nineteenth and twentieth centuries, tribal confederations and other modes of social organization did not go away even as they saw some of their power over political and economic matters diminish. The vast majority of nomadic peoples have been sedentarized—settled into villages and cities where they earn a modest living as farmers, skilled and unskilled laborers, or professionals—but everyday life in the modern Middle East continues to revolve around family membership to a far greater extent that in most Western societies. Despite the fact that the state bureaucracies of most countries in the region are well entrenched and heavily subsidized, few states have succeeded in distributing resources equitably, administering justice fairly, protecting and advancing the interests of the majority of the people, and thereby winning popular support for their rule. The Arab uprisings that spread across much of the region in 2011 are testament to the illegitimacy of many regimes in the eyes of the people. Even today, most states in the Middle East serve narrow elite interests rather than the common good (Sharabi, 1990; Barakat, 1993; al-Khafaji, 1995).

Even since the Arab uprisings, the majority of the region's population does not participate in the economic and political decisionmaking processes that greatly influence their lives and the lives of their children. The peoples of the Middle East instead place their trust in those they know well and with whom they share similar interests, goals, and characteristics: their relatives, neighbors, friends, and members of their own ethnic, religious, and linguistic groups (Sayigh, 1981; Singerman, 1995).

Indeed, the states in the region have never fully claimed the same kind or degree of support, loyalty, and legitimacy that kin and patron-client networks continue to claim (Zubaida, 1994; Denoeux, 1993; Ayubi, 2001; Joseph, 2000). For example, in many states individuals' interactions with state bodies and governmental bureaucracies take place primarily through patron-client relationships (interdependent, but unequal, relationships based on an ideology of mutual benefit that reaffirms and reproduces institutionalized hierarchies) mediated by ties of kinship (actual or fictive), political party membership, or ethnic and sectarian affiliation (Cunningham and

Sarayrah, 1993). In most Middle Eastern societies, governmental ministries primarily serve those who have connections and contacts (*wasta* in Arabic, *protektzia* in Hebrew). Those who participate in informal networks of inter-locking patron-client relationships can traverse physical and social space through their links to individuals and groups on the other side of class, po-litical, and ethnic dividing lines in order to pursue their interests and goals (Denoeux, 1993; Singerman, 1995). Citizenship, an identity category that derives its significance from the jural, formalized relationship of each indi-vidual to the nation-state, often carries much less emotional, moral, legal, and political weight in the Middle East than do identity categories rooted in ideologies of mutual assistance, moral duty, and group solidarity (i.e., kin-ship, ethnicity, and religion).

Understanding why citizens of Middle Eastern nation-states cling to subnational primary affiliations (i.e., family, ethnicity, and religion) helps us understand the causes of intrastate turmoil and interstate hostilities in an ethnographically sound manner. Discovering how Middle Eastern peoples strategically invoke and manipulate kin ties, ethnic affiliations, and patron-client relationships gives us a new appreciation of the creative and effective means through which individuals and groups survive and thrive in a chal-lenging socioeconomic environment while preparing for future contingen-cies. To analyze the interrelationship of kinship, ethnicity, and social class formation in the context of the contemporary Middle East, let us first re-view some key anthropological viewpoints on these important modes of or-ganization and frames of meaning.

Kinship

At first glance, it would seem self-evident that kinship is a naturally occur-ring phenomenon rather than a cultural construct. After all, every living person has or has had kin (relatives), linked to him or her through blood and probably also through marriage. Common sense tells us that biological relationships are a human universal; even babies conceived in vitro have bi-ological parents, regardless of whether or not they have ever met them. The anthropologist's goal is interpretive rather than explanatory, aiming to deci-pher the meanings of the underlying concepts, attitudes, and values that guide people's choices and interactions. These meanings are not visible; they must be inferred from carefully observed behavior over time. Whereas a geneticist examines deoxyribonucleic acid (DNA) to determine biological kinship, an anthropologist attends simultaneously to the biological as well as to the cultural, economic, moral, and political dimensions of kin ties. Hence, an anthropologist investigating the kinship system of a particular community will be less concerned with discovering the actual, empirically verifiable genetic links between individuals than with ascertaining how individuals in this community conceive of kinship connections and the extent to which these cultural conceptions influence behaviors among individuals who consider themselves kin.

For example, not all human societies interpret and value biological connections in precisely the same way. In societies characterized by bilateral kinship systems, such as found in many parts of North America, individuals recognize and value equally their links to relatives on both their mother's and father's sides of the family. Children of their mother's siblings (maternal cousins) occupy the same social category and moral status as children of their father's siblings (paternal cousins). A particular set of cultural expectations and values guides interactions between cousins in North America (D. Schneider, 1968). Cousins are people we enjoy seeing; we feel a connection to them that is stronger than friendship, but not as complicated or demanding as the tie between siblings. Most people in North America would never contemplate marrying a first cousin; in some US states, such a marriage would even be illegal.

In the Middle East, however, people often do marry their first cousins; in some communities, the union of a man and his father's brother's daughter (FBD; *bint 'amm* in Arabic) is still considered to be the preferred marriage choice (Murphy and Kasdan, 1959; Abu-Lughod, 1986). Maternal and paternal cousins are also distinct categories in the Middle East. An individual behaves differently toward his female paternal cousin than he does toward his female maternal cousin, and the tone of his relationship to a male paternal cousin is likely to be more formal, reserved, and subdued whereas mutual affection and joking usually characterize his relationship with a male maternal cousin. To understand the reasons for differential treatment of maternal and paternal kin and marriage preferences in the Middle East, we must examine the observed patterns of kinship relations as a system; in this case, one that is patrilineal.

Anthropologists researching Middle Eastern societies as widely separated as Morocco and Iran have identified several key characteristics of kinship in the region. Middle Eastern kinship systems are patrilineal (determining membership, defining rights, and allocating resources based on blood ties through fathers, sons, brothers, and uncles), extended, patriarchal, hierarchical, and often endogamous (Murphy and Kasdan, 1959; H. Geertz, 1979; Abu-Lughod, 1986; Barakat, 1993; Joseph, 1994). Within the family, authority and respect are accorded to men and older family members of both sexes who, occupying the top positions in the family hierarchy, wield more power, prestige, and rights than female family members and children of either sex.

The Middle Eastern family is not an egalitarian structure, although considerable variation exists across the region and particularly across class lines. Most commonly, men's and women's roles are considered to be complementary and integrative—not equal. Men are the primary decision-makers and breadwinners, and they usually control material resources. Women, however, have always exercised more power within the family behind the scenes than is immediately apparent (Abu-Lughod, 1986; H. Geertz, 1979; Friedl, 1991; Bahloul, 1992; Peteet, 1991; Sayigh, 1994; Mundy, 1995; Singerman, 1995; Kapchan, 1996; Jean-Klein, 2000; Joseph, 2000). Traditionally, a man's overarching responsibility has been to lead, protect, and provide for his family completely. A woman's primary role has been to make a comfortable home, oversee all aspects of the private, domestic sphere, and bear and nurture children.

As discussed in Chapter 11, however, gender roles in the Middle East, as in the rest of the world, are diverse and are also undergoing changes as a result of increased education, urbanization, new economic configurations, and employment of women. Nonetheless, Middle Eastern men and women largely continue to place a high value not on their own personal achievements, but rather on their family affiliations in general and on their roles as generators of new families in particular. In other words, men's and women's roles as parents are more valued than virtually any other role they can fulfill. Young people in most Middle Eastern societies are not considered to be truly adults until they have completed the rites of passage of marriage and parenthood. Westerners visiting Middle Eastern societies are invariably asked about their marital status, and women who are unmarried or married and not yet mothers after the age of twenty-five find themselves repeatedly explaining their unusual single or childless state to their concerned Middle Eastern hosts (Fernea, 1969; Singerman, 1995).

An oft-noted characteristic of Middle Eastern kinship systems is the practice of *endogamous marriage,* or marriage between men and women belonging to the same kinship group. As previously mentioned, a preferred form of marriage in the Middle East has traditionally been that between a man and his FBD. Because Middle Eastern kinship systems are *patrilineal* (i.e., based on ties of agnation and descent traced through paternal relatives), a man and his FBD are always members of the same lineage. In anthropological terminology, cousins in this category of relationship to each other are known as *parallel cousins.* The daughters of a man's mother's brother usually do not belong to his patrilineage; anthropologists refer to this category of cousins as *cross-cousins.*

Marriages can and do take place between both categories of cousins in the Middle East, and many scholars have noted that endogamy refers more to a preference than an actual practice. For instance, the Lebanese anthropologist Fuad Khuri (1970), conducting research among Muslim residents of Beirut in the late 1960s, discovered that only 11 percent of marriages in his sample were endogamous (FBD) marriages. My research among Palestinian citizens of Israel in Nazareth in 1992–1993 indicated that less than

Unmarried couples can meet easily and publicly in all but the most conservative parts of the Middle East. Here, a couple shares laughs in Cairo.

10 percent of a sample of 341 households consisted of spouses who were parallel cousins (King-Irani, 2001).

Given the prevalence of labor migration and rapidly increasing urbanization in the region as discussed in Chapter 9, extended families of grandparents, parents, brothers, sisters, cousins, aunts, and uncles living under the same roof and sharing the same resources are less and less common. In the major cities of the Middle East, where the bulk of the region's population now lives, anthropologists have discovered that unions between members of the same neighborhood, sect, ethnic group, and social class compose the overwhelming majority of marriages. Hence, a form of sociocultural, if not familial, endogamy continues to persist in the region because families prefer that their sons and daughters marry individuals whose social backgrounds and kinship networks are well known to them (al-Akhras, 1976; Singerman, 1995).

Endogamous marriage patterns, which are practiced by few cultures outside the Middle East, stem not from exotic cultural beliefs, a peculiar mentality, or unquestioned obedience to ancient traditions, but rather from a desire to enhance and strengthen the group's internal solidarity and external boundaries. *Endogamy* is a strategy for retaining individuals' loyalty and commitment, as well as their wealth (whether in the form of bridewealth, productive property, or inheritances), within the family circle, widely defined. Such desires and strategies are indices of a long historical experience of economic scarcity, harsh environmental conditions, political uncertainty, and pronounced competition for limited resources in this vast, semiarid zone. The interplay of these ecological, political, and economic factors has at times engendered an atmosphere of unpredictability and mistrust in Middle Eastern societies (J. Schneider, 1971; Meeker, 1979).

In examining the patrilineal nature of Middle Eastern kinship systems, we must look beyond the domain of the nuclear family's domestic concerns to the public realm of the community's political and economic interests, which are greatly affected and conditioned by the natural and human environments. As one anthropologist notes, "kinship is the dominant mode of forming the larger groupings central to social and political life in pre-industrial societies. Kinship provides solutions to ecological and organizational challenges in space and time" (Keesing, 1975:8).

The choice of the patrilineage as the key sociopolitical mode of organization in the Middle East was not arbitrary since "unilineal descent groups [whether matrilineal or patrilineal] were a crucial development in the evolution of tribal societies. They provided an adaptive solution in different ecological settings to the problem of maintaining political order and defining rights to land and other resources across the generations" (Keesing, 1975:24). Nomadic, agricultural, and urban communities all evidenced patrilineal modes of organization and frames of meaning. Kinship was an idiom, a language, for expressing and negotiating economic and political relationships and assigning groups their roles within regional administrative arrangements. The lives of nomads, farmers, and city dwellers were always in actual or potential contact, and their respective interests were occasionally in conflict (Ibn Khaldun, 1967; Nelson, 1973; Khoury and Kostiner, 1990).

In the absence of a strong, centralized governmental administration, well-armed, roving bedouin tribes (i.e., coalitions of patrilineages claiming descent from a common, distant ancestor) could easily sweep into poorly defended agricultural settlements and take goods, crops, livestock, and other forms of wealth by force. Some nomadic tribes coalesced into powerful federations capable of extracting payments of tribute (in effect, protection rackets) from sedentary villagers over a wide area. In some cases, wealthy urban elites formed alliances with leaders of bedouin tribal federations in an effort to extract maximum economic resources from the land and people in the countryside, thus controlling the political dynamics of an entire region (Khoury and Kostiner, 1990; Barakat, 1993).

The patrilineal descent groups found throughout Middle Eastern society had their genesis thousands of years ago as an adaptive response to the interrelated ecological and political conditions of the region (J. Schneider, 1971; Meeker, 1979). *Pastoral nomadism,* previously a key component of the region's mixed economy, is a strenuous mode of subsistence that both demands and frustrates cooperative, interdependent social relations. Pastoral nomadism requires the careful and timely coordination of different activities by different people. If the needs of the herds and flocks are not met, they and the human community dependent on them for its livelihood can easily perish. Members of nomadic groups are thus willing to pitch in for the common good and extend themselves magnanimously if the situation demands brave and generous behavior. But in this arid ecological zone, people also had to be selfish and calculating at times in order to survive. This fact "places heavy burdens on interpersonal relations, for everyone must think first of his immediate household's interests and needs and resist undue claims for assistance from kinsmen and friends" (J. Schneider, 1971: 5). Among pastoral nomads, the immediate need for water may well outweigh compelling claims of blood ties.

The natural environment in which pastoral nomads live is clearly harsh and uncertain. The social environment is also threatening since it is highly competitive. It is thus imperative for all pastoral nomadic peoples to institute

> organizational solutions to the compelling ecological problem of regulating access of humans and animals to natural resources. . . . Migratory groups cannot establish rights to land on a permanent basis, or fence it off against incursions. Raiding and animal theft are therefore endemic. . . . The determination of boundary lines is subject to continual human intervention; the definition of the group is problematic as well: social boundaries are difficult to maintain, and internal loyalties are questionable. . . . Individuals and groups are at once . . . vulnerable and opportunistic. (J. Schneider, 1971:24)

Depending on the need or the task at hand, nomadic peoples could employ patrilineal ideologies and rhetoric in order to mobilize groups ranging from a person's immediate male kin (brothers, father, grandfather, sons, uncles, and cousins) to a huge tribal federation numbering thousands of individuals representing many different patrilineages related through a distant founding (or apical) ancestor. Yet since the natural environment could not support a large number of nomads and their animals living at the same place for any significant length of time, Middle Eastern patrilineages never developed into the sustained, enduring, clearly bounded unilineal descent groups found in more temperate and fertile ecological zones. Rather than becoming corporations, Middle Eastern kin groups were most often shifting coalitions that could be forged and broken according to the relevant context and prevailing interests. Anthropologists term this process *segmentation,* and many social scientists characterize Middle Eastern societies as segmentary because of the prevalence of many similar yet differentiated components (e.g., families, lineages, guilds, ethnic groups, or sects) that can coalesce to cooperate or fragment to fight.

Pastoral nomadism as a primary mode of subsistence is now rare in the Middle East. A lifestyle that requires constant movement does not mesh with the needs and requirements of nation-states demarcated by well-defended, impassable borders. Pastoral modes of subsistence continue, but the rapid and dramatic urbanization and proletarianization of the region's population eclipse them. In some states, such as Israel, the government has actively sought to settle nomadic groups into permanent locations, thereby freeing up open land for development or state use. Yet the values and practices of tribally based groupings continue to be important to Middle Eastern culture, society, and politics, as evidenced by oral and written literature, everyday morality, and the phenomenon of fictive kinship ties that link friends, colleagues, neighbors, and business partners through relationships that have the emotional closeness and moral implications of actual blood relations.

Kinship, as an idiom of identity and social organization no less than as a basis of affiliation, protection, and cooperative action, continues to be important in the Middle East today. One's identity as a member of a kin group entitles him or her to rights and services, just as it entails making considerable sacrifices for the sake of the group. These practices are openly reflected in many of the region's ruling regimes. For instance, the kingdom of Saudi Arabia is often called the House of Saud in recognition of its roots in a particular kinship grouping. Syria and Iraq were long run by tightly knit, patrilineal coalitions of brothers and cousins; indeed, the Iraqi government under Hussein was known, in diplomatic circles, as the Tikriti regime after the name of the Sunni Muslim village in north central Iraq from which Hussein and his family hailed. It is instructive to note that Syria's Bashar al-Assad is a member of a religious minority group in his own country. Sunni Muslims are the majority community in Syria, where al-Assad's Alawite community holds the decisive reins of power. Emerging as part of the Arab uprisings, Syria's civil war can be understood not only as an uprising of a people against a repressive regime, but of a majority Sunni population against a minority Alawite regime (and its Druze allies). In Iraq, a majority population of Shi'a lived under the rule of Hussein, a Sunni, for more than two decades. These two leaders' rise to the top posts in their countries in spite of their minority status speaks volumes about the strength and efficacy of kin ties and networks in Middle Eastern societies and polities.

As a strategy for survival, the patrilineal kinship system has certainly proved flexible and effective over many centuries under a variety of social, economic, and political conditions in the Middle East. What began as an adaptive response to ecological and social limitations gradually became a valued institution embodying a rich cultural complex of expectations, attitudes, values, beliefs, rituals, and behaviors. Indeed, kinship systems function in a many different ways, but to most they remain a valued part of the region's civilizational heritage.

Not all anthropological studies of kinship in the Middle East center on the politics of patrilineal competition, however. Since the late 1970s, a growing number of ethnographies of Middle Eastern communities have taken women's lives, domesticity, reproduction, and sexuality as their point of departure (H. Geertz, 1979; Abu-Lughod, 1986; Inhorn, 2003; Mundy, 1995; Joseph, 1994; Peteet, 1991; Singerman, 1995; Kahn, 2000; Kanaaneh, 2002). The majority of these ethnographies have been written by women, and most are influenced by feminist and postmodern theories emphasizing the contentiousness of power relations, the mutability of identity, and the social construction of gender (i.e., sexual differences, culturally defined). By including the perspectives and voices of women in ethnographic depictions of daily life in Middle Eastern societies, these ethnographers have highlighted important questions about how power is conceptualized and deployed in the most intimate spaces of everyday life. A recurring theme in these works centers on strategies of resistance to hierarchical power arrangements and the elaboration of counternarratives that challenge and occasionally subvert dominant narratives that legitimate the patriarchal status quo (Abu-Lughod, 1986; Layoun, 1999).

Gender-oriented kinship studies have enriched an understanding of the symbolic and interactive processes that produce and reproduce the structures and categories of everyday life while showing how and where changes and contradictions emerge by tracing these developments through the experience, choices, and negotiations of individuals' interactions. Gendered studies of kinship and family also highlight the affective and moral frames of meaning, in addition to the economic and political modes of organization, associated with kinship. As such, these studies show the interrelationship of men's and women's worlds and lives, no less than the connections and interrelationships between the intimate domain of the household and the public domain of governance and resource distribution (Singerman, 1995).

Let us now examine another adaptive strategy of contemporary Middle Eastern societies, which like kinship centers on the individual's identification and affiliation with extensive and potentially far-reaching networks. Through these connections, one can construct meaningful moral boundaries while obtaining access to power, protection, and resources in a highly competitive socioeconomic and political environment.

Ethnicity

It is easy to assume that ethnic differences are essentially racial differences, and thus are determined largely by biological criteria such as hair, skin and eye color, height, and physique, and only further distinguished by such characteristics as language, cultural patterns, and religious faith. Scholars examining the phenomenon of ethnicity, however, note that it is a strategic, more so than a genetic, phenomenon (R. Cohen, 1978; Royce, 1982; Anderson, 1993; Eller and Coughlan, 1993). *Ethnic identity,* whether referring to subjective criteria (an individual's awareness of and feelings about his or her membership in a particular ethnic category) or objective criteria (others' categorization of an individual on the basis of physical or cultural characteristics), cannot exist in a homogeneous society in which everyone shares the same cultural, religious, class, and linguistic background. Ethnicity and ethnic identity are oppositional and relational phenomena par excellence; they emerge only in societies where different types of people from a wide variety of backgrounds are recognized. Due to migration from rural to urban areas and the impact of enhanced communications and transportation systems, individuals and groups from a wide variety of cultural, linguistic, socioeconomic, and religious backgrounds are increasingly brought into contact.

Ethnicity, with its affective, symbolic, and political dimensions, has been a key topic of anthropological inquiry for decades. Urban anthropologists have tended to approach ethnic groups as "subcultures" (Hannerz, 1980), and the past forty-five years have witnessed a gradual shift from primordialist theories of ethnicity, which view ethnic identity as inborn, innate, and ascribed (C. Geertz, 1973; Fishman, 1980), to constructivist, utilitarian, and circumstantialist theories (Barth, 1969; A. Cohen, 1974; Royce, 1982), which view ethnicity as rooted in political processes and as constructed, strategic, and even achieved identity categories. The latter theoretical approach holds that ethnic identity is not a state of being, or a noun, but rather a verb (identifying with an ethnic group) that can be viewed from the bottom up or the top down. Bottom-up identification processes are evident in resistance movements and coalition building. Top-down identification processes are visible in state policies and legislation defining the boundaries between, and hierarchies among, groups characterized by particular cultural, linguistic, and religious characteristics.

In the rapidly growing cities of the Middle East, various ethnic groups interact and compete with one another in new and sometimes alienating sociopolitical contexts characterized by economic scarcity and uneven development. The recognition of ethnic differences thus also implies the recognition of economic and political differences. Depending on administrative frameworks of governance and the economic status of the groups involved, individuals' growing awareness of relative and absolute economic differences can lead to conflict, competition, and opposition organized along ethnic lines. As anthropologist Ronald Cohen notes, "Ethnicity is . . . one of the many outcomes of group interaction in which there is differential power between dominant and minority groups. From this perspective, ethnicity is an aspect of stratification, rather than a problem on its own" (1978:386).

The categorization of individuals or groups according to their ethnic identity and membership is a salient feature of most contemporary societies.

Crucial are not cultural, religious, or linguistic differences per se, but rather the structured arrangement of relationships between the different groups, the administrative and economic frameworks in which these various groups are encapsulated. What creates tension or harmony is not the supposedly essential cultural attributes or traditional customs of various groups, but rather the institutionalized structure of relationships between them and groups' perceptions of those relationships. Are they egalitarian or hierarchical? Symmetrical or asymmetrical? Are differences codified in law, as discussed in Chapter 12, such that identity becomes determinative of one's rights, duties, and life chances, as is the situation for many ethnic and religious minority groups in the Middle East? If so, conflicts are likely to result.

One of the greatest challenges facing sociologists and anthropologists conducting research on societies of the non-Western developing world lies in identifying the dividing lines (if any) between ethnic groups, kinship groups, and socioeconomic classes (Barakat, 1993). Ethnicity in the Middle East presents many definitional and methodological challenges for researchers since ethnic groups often behave like kin-based tribal groupings, especially in the way they mobilize their members by invoking a shared identity in some contexts while segmenting into competing groups in other contexts. At the same time, ethnic differences often correspond closely to socioeconomic distinctions.

For instance, in Israeli society, Western-oriented Ashkenazi Jews, although numerically the minority community, are the dominant class in terms of wealth and control of the state's decisionmaking bodies in comparison with the more numerous Mizrachi (or Sephardic) Jews who come from Arab countries and whose cultural attitudes and practices have long been looked down on by Ashkenazi Jews. Prior to the convulsions of the Lebanese civil war (1975–1990), the wealthy power brokers and owners of factories, banks, and businesses in Lebanon were usually Maronite Christians whereas the poorer, less powerful, agricultural communities in Lebanon tended to be populated by Shi'i Muslims.

There are, of course, exceptions to these correlations between class, ethnicity, and kinship. Only sustained and fine-grained research can elucidate the dynamic interrelationships of kinship, class, and ethnicity in the contemporary Middle East. Most social scientists consider ethnic political organizations and activities key phenomena of the modern world. Some scholars forecast the further solidification and entrenchment of ethnic and cultural identities as competition and conflict over limited goods increase throughout the world (Huntington, 1996). These recent predictions of social unrest and political violence between different cultural groups stand in stark contrast to the expectations of an earlier generation of academics and policymakers who, in the post–World War II era, expressed confidence that the universal adoption of a modernizing, liberal, secular, and technologically advanced culture and social system would facilitate homogenization and harmonization between different peoples within and between states. What these optimistic observers left out of their social equations were cultural dissonance, alienation, relative and absolute economic deprivation, unequal distribution of resources, and differences in the types and amounts of power available to various ethnic groups in any given society. It is not the differences in cultural practices, religious beliefs, or linguistic characteristics that cause friction between members of opposing ethnic communities. Rather, "inequality, not ethnicity, is the basis of social stratification" and thus conflict (R. Cohen, 1978:400).

If Middle Eastern kin-based institutions like patrilineages and tribes were the primary adaptive responses to the ecological challenges and socioeconomic problems of intense competition over scarce resources in a harsh natural environment, then the ethnic group is the chief survival strategy of the politically marginalized individual in the harsh social and economic environments of the contemporary Middle East. Torn loose from the familiar moorings of village, home, and family as a result of poverty or war; struggling to make a decent living in crowded, impoverished, and poorly serviced cities; and underrepresented by or underprovided for by a concerned government, the average individual in the contemporary Middle East is likely to feel lost, lonely, alienated, and powerless. If unable to find kin or people from his or her region to provide guidance, mutual assistance, and support, an uprooted individual will most likely turn to other individuals and groups with whom he or she shares some common background characteristics, values, orientations, and goals. Hence, we see the development of the ethnoreligious group, which performs some of the same functions as the tribe but is neither based entirely on blood relationships nor as clearly bounded in terms of its membership as is the tribe. An organized and mobilized ethnic group or religious sect may serve the economic, social, and political needs of its members far better than the state apparatus of many Middle Eastern countries.

At the beginning of the twentieth century, city dwellers accounted for less than 10 percent of the total population of the Middle East. As described in Chapter 9, urbanization has increased dramatically in recent decades, and studies by the UN predict that urban populations will reach 80 percent of the total for the Middle East within the next decade. Thus, the current trend of relying on family and ethnoreligious ties to survive in Middle Eastern cities is likely to continue. Ronald Cohen succinctly describes how comforting and empowering an ethnic reference group and support network can be to such displaced young people:

> If alienation is a malfunction of modern society, then ethnicity is an antidote. . . . Ethnicity provides a fundamental and multifaceted link to a

category of others that very little else can do in modern society. . . . In a multiethnic society in which a plurality of groups, ethnic and non-ethnic, vie for scarce rewards, stressing individual human rights leads ultimately to unequal treatment. . . . Individuals are fated to obtain more rewards because of their group identities. Organized ethnic groups can fight for equal rights. (1978:401–402)

In other words, an ethnic group is not simply a racial unit or a cultural unit, but also a political unit. Ethnic groups are interest groups; they are structured to serve the various needs of affiliated members while competing with other interest groups for the limited resources to be obtained within the framework of the modern state. The group that can mobilize the greatest numbers of supporters and patrons, deliver the highest number of voters during elections, forge the strongest links with powerful groups within or without the society, and devise the most compelling and convincing arguments to advance its rights to resources, political posts, or economic redress will take the lion's share of the services, governmental posts, protection, and wealth that can be extracted from the state. Indeed, a well-organized and ambitious ethnic or religious group can even take complete control of the entire state apparatus, as did the Alawites of Syria and the Sunnis of Iraq in the early 1970s.

The Historical Context of Identity Categories

Ethnic groups and officially recognized ethnoreligious identity categories predate the creation of the region's nation-states. Prior to the advent of the nation-state system in the Middle East and even before the colonial era, most of the peoples of the region (with the exception of those living in Morocco and Iran) lived under Ottoman rule in the sociopolitical framework of a vast, decentralized empire. Day-to-day matters of administration and basic governance were in the hands of local political elites chosen by the Ottoman leadership, as well as the local clergy. As an empire, the Ottoman system was organized not according to ethnic or national principles and categories, but according to religious distinctions. Individuals living in the Ottoman Empire did not identify themselves as Ottomans, Turks, Arabs, or Kurds, but rather as Muslims, Christians, Jews, or Druze. Within this system of organization, Muslims were in the majority, both in terms of absolute numbers and in terms of privilege, rank, status, and opportunities. Christians and Jews were formally recognized as religious minorities.

As discussed in Chapter 12, Islam considers Christians and Jews to be "Peoples of the Book," categorized as *dhimmi* communities (literally meaning "on the conscience" of the larger and more powerful Muslim community). They are supposed to be protected from harm or persecution by the majority Muslim community in return for their acceptance of a subordinate status, payment of a *jizyah* (special tax), and abstention from any public display of their religious practices such as processions and liturgical ceremonies. Under Ottoman rule, as long as the non-Muslim communities obeyed Ottoman laws and paid their taxes, they were supposed to be left unmolested to conduct their lives alongside the Muslim community. *Dhimmi* communities were under the jurisdiction of Islamic courts in criminal cases and some property disputes, but obeyed the jurisdiction of their own community's religious laws and precepts concerning any issues related to religious and family matters. As non-Muslims, Christians, Druze, and Jews were not subject to the rulings of sharia in matters of personal status such as marriage, divorce, inheritance, and other family issues. Instead, Christian sects and Druze and Jewish communities sought guidance, mediation, and rulings from their own religious hierarchy, the leaders of which had the power to make binding judicial decisions in the domain of family law and to represent their religious communities in official dealings with the Ottoman authorities. As detailed in Chapter 3, this system of legally recognized non-Muslim communal autonomy was known as the *millet* system (meaning people or community in Turkish).

As this brief historical overview indicates, the Middle East has always been culturally heterogeneous. During the Ottoman era, the rugged mountainous areas of the eastern Mediterranean became a refuge for a variety of Christian and Islamic religious sects and splinter groups seeking to escape persecution by orthodox religious authorities. Dwelling high atop these mountains, minority groups such as the Maronites, Druze, Shi'a, and Alawites could pursue their religious traditions free of interference from either Christian or Muslim authorities. The plural nature of Middle Eastern urban areas is inscribed in the very towers, walls, and gates that marked off the various named quarters of traditional urban settlements, such as the Muslim Quarter, Armenian Quarter, Jewish Quarter, Orthodox Quarter, as are found in such ancient cities as Jerusalem, Cairo, Damascus, Istanbul, Sana'a, and Baghdad. A division of labor among these distinct communities paralleled the spatial separation of different religious and ethnic groups in the traditional Middle Eastern city.

Christians, Muslims, and Jews occupied different professional categories in the Ottoman social and economic structure. The traditional city's division of labor was usually characterized by accommodation, complementarity, and integration rather than by competition and conflict. Muslims held positions in religious courts and schools as well as in the military and in local governmental administration, and non-Muslims served primarily as doctors, merchants, advisers, artisans, and religious and legal specialists for their own sectarian communities. The Ottoman division of labor is recorded to this day in the names of many Christian families from Lebanon, Palestine, and Syria, which designate the professional and artisan roles that their ancestors played in Ottoman society: *sabbagh* (dyer), hakim (doctor), *khab-baz* (baker), *banna* (builder), *sayigh* (goldsmith), *hayek* (weaver), *najjar* (carpenter), *khoury* (priest), and shammas (sexton).

The cultural and religious heterogeneity of the Middle East did not result from rapid urbanization or the establishment of nation-states in the twentieth century, nor is it a by-product of colonialism (although colonial powers certainly employed tactics based on a policy of divide and rule to consolidate their control of local political systems). Different ethnic and religious groups have been living side by side in the great cities of the Middle East for centuries, sometimes in conflict but more often than not in harmony. What is new in the ethnic and religious configuration of the contemporary Middle East is the encapsulating social, political, and economic framework in which different groups live, work, and struggle. The relatively recent political processes that led to the region's incorporation into the global economy and then to the establishment of nation-states have altered the traditional balance of power and the system of accommodation that had prevailed during the Ottoman era (Makdisi, 2000). Although the Ottoman Empire was hardly a model of economic efficiency or social justice, it nonetheless encouraged a relatively stable and viable form of accommodation and cooperation among the region's diverse ethnic and religious groupings.

To understand how the various ethnic and religious communities of the Middle East became embroiled in conflicts that are continuing, we must now examine the historical processes of social class formation, which exacerbated competition and thus engendered conflicts between the different ethnic communities of the region.

Social Class

Unlike the identity categories of kinship and ethnicity, social class is not based on biological or cultural criteria, but rather on economic and political differences. Like ethnic groups, social classes are structural phenomena: a social class cannot exist except in relation to other social classes since the idea of a class entails a hierarchical arrangement of groups based on differences of wealth, power, and control over resources. A society whose members all share the same resources equally, own wealth in common, participate fully in all decisionmaking, and have equal rights and duties in relation to one another would be a classless society. The distinguishing criteria of any social class structure are inequalities of wealth and differential access to resources and means of economic production. Thus, class distinctions entail relationships of dominance and subordination between different competing groups, each of which continually strives to improve its relative position or, having attained a position of relative advantage, struggles to retain it.

According to social historian Philip Khoury, the social class structure of the Middle East was relatively simple and stable until the middle of the nineteenth century. Just 150 years ago, the Middle East began to be integrated into the capitalist world system. Consequently, new social classes gradually emerged as a result of changing modes of economic production and new forms of ownership and control of resources (Khoury, 1983). The most significant economic change during the nineteenth century was the advent of new forms of landownership. Following a series of military and economic defeats at the hands of rising European powers, the Ottoman leadership decided to institute a number of administrative reforms in an effort to improve and strengthen the Ottoman system by imitating European societies and governments.

Chief among these reforms were new land laws that encouraged private rather than communal ownership of productive property. Muslim and non-Muslim elites favored by the Ottoman rulers benefited from these reforms by taking control of formerly communal properties on which they planted cash crops such as tobacco in place of subsistence crops. This agricultural regime served the interests of international markets rather than the needs of the local populace. At the same time, merchants (often Christians and Jews) in cities such as Beirut, Damascus, Acre, Cairo, Alexandria, and Ladhakia began to earn a considerable profit as middlemen overseeing trade between European producers of goods and newly wealthy Middle Eastern consumers of fine furnishings, clothing, household equipment, and medicines. This shift from local to foreign markets for consumer goods had a debilitating effect on local artisans and manufacturers who, along with peasants displaced from agricultural lands by private landownership, high taxation, and wars, became members of a new social class formation: the urban proletariat. This period marked the advent of a sharply pyramidal class structure characterized by the political and economic domination of a large mass of impoverished people by a handful of extremely wealthy landowning families.

Although markets and modes of production have changed dramatically since the mid–nineteenth century, the social and economic class structure of the Middle East is still profoundly pyramidal. Despite the omnipresent stereotype of the superrich Arab oil shaikh, the vast majority of people in the region live at or below the poverty line, and only a handful of people own and control considerable wealth derived from the oil industry, its subsidiaries, and the consumption habits of the oil-producing elite. Economic activity in the region as a whole consists of consumption more than production, and the exchange of goods and services between countries of the region is limited, resulting in poor regional economic integration and heightened dependency on Western goods and services (World Bank, 1996).

As discussed in Chapter 7, close examination of the economies of the region reveals a glaring absence of industry and manufacturing in most countries, with the exception of oil-related industries in the Gulf region, computer and military industries in Israel, and a variety of industrial activities in Turkey. Textile and cotton production Egypt, an important export during the twentieth century, has been in decline as land is converted to more profitable outputs such as cattle and sheep for meat, which are disproportionately consumed by the upper classes and tourists. By and large, the countries of the region consume much more than they produce. Agriculture is underdeveloped in Lebanon and Syria, countries that could technically produce significant amounts of agricultural goods; hence, most foodstuffs are imported and therefore too expensive for the average family to afford on a daily basis (World Bank, 1996).

As a result of the poor performance of the oil sector in the 1980s, countries throughout the region felt the effects of falling oil prices in the form of decreasing remittance payments sent back to countries such as Syria, Lebanon, Egypt, Yemen, and Jordan by migrant workers in the Gulf, particularly after the Gulf War of 1991. Even before the fall in oil prices, poverty in the region was already pronounced: in 1980, approximately 44 percent of the population in Morocco and Egypt was living below the poverty line (Barakat, 1993); the situation has improved little since then. During the past two decades, the Arab world has seen a

> progressive decline, or perhaps near elimination, of subsistence production, massive occupational shifts from agrarian to service . . . activities; a massive exodus of surplus rural labor to urban conglomerations [while at the same time witnessing] the rise of a new Arab bourgeoisie, a class of contractors, middlemen, brokers, agents of foreign corporations, and wheeler-dealers . . . typically engaged in nonproductive work. (Farsoun and Zacharia, 1995:273)

In the narrow space between the upper class (those few who possess and control great wealth) and the lower class (the millions of impoverished former peasants who are constantly streaming into the crowded urban areas of the region), we find the only productive sector of Middle Eastern society: a relatively small middle class composed primarily of small-scale commercial enterprises, self-employed merchants, repairmen, artisans, teachers, some white-collar professionals, and government employees. The members of this weak and vulnerable socioeconomic formation have discovered that remaining middle class requires a concerted family effort. Hence, the patrilineal kinship group that emerged as a strategic adaptation so long ago is once again the basic productive unit among much of the urban middle classes in the modern Middle East. As Samih K. Farsoun notes, "rent income, small business income, and income from wages and other labor have emerged as key sources for an increasing number of multiple income families. . . . Most of these petty economic activities are traditional in style of

organization and in the social relations of work, i.e., patriarchal and patronage" (1988:224).

Kinship, Class, and Ethnicity in Context:
Strategies or Straitjackets?

Negatively affected by social and political transformations and economic
restructuring at the local, regional, and international levels, particularly in
the post–Cold War era, individuals in the Middle East have turned to their
nuclear and extended families for support and mutual assistance. They have
reactivated and emphasized traditional family structures, kinship networks,
affiliations to ethnoreligious groups, and ties of patronage even as they
have embraced the latest developments of modern technology such as cel-
lular telephones and the Internet.

Halim Barakat reflects that it is difficult for observers to interpret socioeconomic developments in the region because "the contemporary Arab
economic order is a peculiar cluster of different modes of production, all
operating at once, which renders it simultaneously semi-feudal, semi-
socialist, and semi-capitalist" (1993:77). The side-by-side existence of patrilineages and multinational corporations, rationalized bureaucracies and
religious brotherhoods, modern nation-states and tribal federations, and traditional practices and cosmopolitan attitudes illuminates the challenges of
nation-state formation and national integration in the contemporary Middle
East. It also reveals the degree to which the peoples of the region have
compensated for the weaknesses of nation-states by adapting and revitaliz-
ing traditional sociocultural modes of survival.

Perhaps it is not too far-fetched to argue that extensive networks of
overlapping kin- and ethnic-based patron-client relationships linking those
in the government with those outside of it constitute the actual glue that
holds the Middle Eastern nation-state together. Although patron-client relations "play an important role in facilitating the distribution of goods and
services among the population and harnessing popular support behind leaders" (Khoury and Kostiner, 1990:18), ties of patronage are essentially
asymmetrical: the perpetuation of these relationships also perpetuates and
reinforces unequal power structures in the starkly stratified societies of the
contemporary Middle East. Patron-client ties ensure that people are kept in
their place: the rich and powerful maintain their dominant positions, from
which they have the advantage of becoming even more rich and powerful,
and the less fortunate are kept in their subordinate position of dependency,
remaining powerless over the decisionmaking processes and larger forces
that shape their lives.

Taking a broader view of the Middle East in a global context and examining the structures and processes through which the region is encapsulated

at the international level, it appears that the vertical integration of society, polity, and economies through patron-client relations at the local and national levels has clear echoes and similarities in the asymmetrical patterns of integration between the Middle East and the global economy. Many countries in this region are clients of the world's current superpower: the United States. A holistic and contextualized anthropological approach demands that we view kinship, ethnicity, social class, and nation-states in the Middle East within all relevant contexts, including that of the global political economy. In so doing, we quickly discover that many of the Middle East's problems are not internally generated or self-inflicted. Critiquing the 2002 UN *Arab Human Development Report* on the social and economic state of the Middle East and North Africa, historian Mark Levine notes the absence of a contextualized, culturally sensitive analysis in the report's findings:

> [The] report [does not] consider the strategic yet marginalized (or better, strategically marginalized) position of the Middle East and North Africa in the larger world political economy. Such lacunae allow the authors to avoid grappling with the cycle of Arab petrodollars for Western arms, the disproportionate and generally increasing military budgets of Arab governments, or the disastrous impact of US and European agricultural subsidies (which flood markets with under-priced Western products that force local farmers out of business) that are crucial to the region's perpetual economic dependence on the West. (2002)

The foreign aid policies of powerful states, no less than the decisions and dictates of the World Bank and the International Monetary Fund, serve to replicate relations of dependence between the most populous states of the Middle East and the West while consolidating mutually supportive ties between the regimes of the region and Western suppliers of military and economic aid packages (Pfeifer, 1999). This is not a recipe for national and regional integration, nor does it strengthen the institutions of civil society and civic participation at the grassroots level. Also, a public that has fragmented into separate, segmentary groups of kinsmen and coreligionists is facilitating its own control, exploitation, co-optation, and manipulation by repressive state governments. A divided population is much easier to rule, as the colonial powers so deftly proved.

The institutionalization—and essentialization—of ethnic and religious identities for legal and administrative purposes, seen most clearly in states such as Lebanon and Israel, is a double-edged sword. Although official recognition of cultural heritage and religious laws may provide answers to individuals' psychological needs and communal organizational problems, institutionalized identities can also trap individuals in the vise of inflexible collective categories not of their own choice or making, thus limiting their personal options and opportunities while preventing the development of a more inclusive sense of overarching national loyalty and identity. The most extreme example of the triumph of the ethnic group over both the individual citizen and the overarching state is that of Lebanon, a state composed entirely of seventeen officially recognized ethnoconfessional groups, membership in which defines Lebanese individuals' rights and duties in the context of the state. Reflecting on the tragedy of Lebanon, Lebanese sociologist Samir Khalaf notes that "the very factors that account for much of the viability, resourcefulness, and integration of the Lebanese are also the factors that are responsible for the erosion of civic ties and national loyalties. . . . In short, the factors that enable at the micro and communal level disable at the macro and national level. This is, indeed, Lebanon's predicament" (1986:14).

Or, in the words of Ziad Rahbani, the bard of the Lebanese civil war whose captivating music and ironic lyrics allowed the Lebanese to look at themselves with jaundiced but compassionate eyes: *yaa zaman at-ta'ifiyya! ta'ifiyya, ta'ifiyya/kheli eidek 'alal-howia; shidd 'alaiha qad ma fiik!* ("Oh, these are confessional times, such confessional times!/So best keep your hand on your identity [card]; and grasp it for all that you are worth!"). The song refers both to the wartime retreat into primary identities and the horrifying practice of political murders perpetrated by militiamen who routinely killed civilians on the basis of their religious confession, which is recorded on every Lebanese citizen's identity card.

The problems of the contemporary Middle East are not cultural ones centered on the resilience of traditional practices and primary identity categories in a modern world. Rather, the region's political and economic problems stem primarily from the weaknesses and deficiencies of an imposed nation-state system that is not meeting people's basic needs, and from regional hostilities rooted in historical injustices and shortsighted policies initiated by Western powers during the colonial period and replicated in today's globalized, neocolonial era, characterized by a form of economic integration that is neither egalitarian nor sustainable.

Conclusion

My goal in this chapter has been to analyze and interpret kinship, ethnicity, and social class in the contemporary Middle East by showing how sociocultural phenomena are related to ecological, economic, psychological, administrative, and political realities and how they interact with and shape one another. Social, political, and cultural behaviors in the Middle East have historically been affected by the limitations of a harsh natural environment in which economic scarcity and pronounced political competition were constants whereas sustained relationships of mutual trust and permanent, broad-based, sociopolitical formations were not. Furthermore, the region underwent rapid economic and political changes in the nineteenth century, encapsulating the Middle East in a Western-dominated political and economic order that permanently altered traditional class structures and produced sharp socioeconomic inequalities, which were then exacerbated by colonialism and the imposition of arbitrarily defined nation-states. The resulting conundrums and inequalities remain unresolved to this day.

Lacking meaningful representation by or assistance from most nation-states of the region, many Middle Eastern peoples continue to rely on localized identity categories and organizational structures to navigate their place in the challenging world that confronts them. Although they have succeeded in this effort, it has not been without costs and consequences. In the long run, resorting to kinship, ethnicity, and patron-client ties could have a negative effect on societies that may soon be forced to reconcile their segmented and fragmentary nature with increasing political and economic pressures for integration, coordination, and cooperation in the globalizing economy.

There is much room for optimism, however. The peoples of the Middle East are talented survivors possessing an exceptionally rich and resilient cultural heritage that can be adapted to serve them in all political, economic, and temporal environments.

Note

1. Jerrold Kessel notes that "right-wing Prime Minister Benjamin Netanyahu has convinced at least half his countrymen that the Middle East is still 'a very bad neighborhood'—a place where suspicion and deep-rooted security concerns are again the dominant sentiments. Peace lags far behind security in the double-barreled promise on which Netanyahu came to power two years ago" (1998).

Bibliography

Abu-Lughod, Lila. 1986. *Veiled Sentiments*. Berkeley: University of California Press.
al-Akhras, Muhammad Safouh. 1976. *The Structure of the Arab Family*. Damascus: Ministry of Culture.
Anderson, Benedict. 1993. *Imagined Communities*. London: Verso.
Antoun, Richard. 2000. "Civil Society, Tribal Process, and Change in Jordan: An Anthropological View." *International Journal of Middle East Studies* 32, no. 4 (November):441–463.
Ayubi, Nazih. 2001. *Overstating the Arab State*. London: I. B. Tauris.
Bahloul, Joelle. 1992. *The Architecture of Memory: A Jewish-Muslim Household in Colonial Algeria, 1937–1962*. Cambridge: Cambridge University Press.
Barakat, Halim. 1993. *The Arab World: Society, Culture, and State*. Berkeley: University of California Press.
Barth, Frederik. 1969. *Ethnic Groups and Boundaries*. Boston: Little, Brown.

Cohen, Abner. 1974. *Two-Dimensional Man: An Essay on the Anthropology of Symbolism and Power in Complex Societies*. Berkeley: University of California Press.

Cohen, Ronald. 1978. "Ethnicity: Problem and Focus in Anthropology." *Annual Review of Anthropology* 7:379–403.

Cunningham, Robert B., and Yasin K. Sarayrah. 1993. *Wasta: The Hidden Force in Middle Eastern Society*. Westport, CT: Praeger.

Denoeux, Guilain. 1993. *Urban Unrest in the Middle East: A Comparative Study of Informal Networks in Egypt, Iran, and Lebanon*. Albany: SUNY Press.

Eller, Jack, and Reed Coughlan. 1993. "The Poverty of Primordialism: The Demystification of Ethnic Attachments." *Ethnic and Racial Studies* 16, no. 2:183–202.

Farsoun, Samih K. 1988. "Class Structure and Social Change in the Arab World." Pp. 221–238 in Hisham Sharabi (ed.), *The Next Arab Decade: Alternative Futures*. Boulder: Westview Press.

Farsoun, Samih K., and Christina Zacharia. 1995. "Class, Economic Change, and Political Liberalization in the Arab World." Pp. 261–282 in Rex Brynen, Bahgat Korany, and Paul Noble (eds.), *Political Liberalization and Democratization in the Arab World*, vol. 1: *Theoretical Perspectives*. Boulder: Lynne Rienner.

Fernea, Elizabeth Warnock. 1969. *Guests of the Sheikh*. New York: Doubleday.

Fishman, Joshua. 1980. "Social Theory and Ethnography." Pp. 84–97 in Peter Sugar (ed.), *Ethnic Diversity and Conflict in Eastern Europe*. Santa Barbara, CA: ABC-CLIO.

Friedl, Erik. 1991. *Women of Deh Koh*. New York: Penguin.

Geertz, Clifford. 1973. *The Interpretation of Cultures*. New York: Basic Books. (Orig. pub. 1969.)

Geertz, Hildred. 1979. "The Meaning of Family Ties." Pp. 315–391 in Clifford Geertz, Hildred Geertz, and Lawrence Rosen (eds.), *Meaning and Order in Moroccan Society*. New York: Cambridge University Press.

Gilsenan, Michael. 1996. *Lords of the Lebanese Marshes: Violence and Narrative in an Arab Society*. Berkeley: University of California Press.

Hannerz, Ulf. 1980. *Exploring the City: Inquiries Towards an Urban Anthropology*. New York: Columbia University Press.

Herzfeld, Michael. 1997. "The Dangers of Metaphor: From Troubled Waters to Boiling Blood in Europe." Pp. 74–88 in Michael Herzfeld (ed.), *Cultural Intimacy: Social Poetics in the Nation State*. London: Routledge.

Huntington, Samuel. 1996. *The Clash of Civilizations and the Remaking of World Order*. New York: Simon & Schuster.

Ibn Khaldun. 1967. *The Muqaddimah: An Introduction to History*. Trans. Franz Rosenthal. Princeton: Princeton University Press.

Inhorn, Marcia. 2003. *Local Babies, Global Science: Gender, Religion, and In Vitro Fertilization in Egypt*. London: Routledge.

Jean-Klein, Iris. 2000. "Mothercraft, Statecraft, and Subjectivity in the Palestinian Intifada." *American Ethnologist* 27, no. 1 (February):100–127.

Joseph, Su'ad. 1994. "Brother-Sister Relationships: Connectivity, Love, and Power in the Reproduction of Patriarchy in Lebanon." *American Ethnologist* 21, no. 1:31–54.

———. 2000. *Intimate Selving in Arab Families: Gender, Self, and Identity*. Syracuse: Syracuse University Press.

Kahn, Susan Martha. 2000. *Reproducing Jews: A Cultural Account of Assisted Conception in Israel*. Durham: Duke University Press.

Kanaaneh, Rhoda Ann. 2002. *Birthing the Nation: Strategies of Palestinian Women in Israel*. Berkeley: University of California Press.

Kapchan, Deborah. 1996. *Gender on the Market: Moroccan Women and the Revoicing of Tradition*. Philadelphia: University of Pennsylvania Press.

Keesing, Roger. 1975. *Kin Groups and Social Structure*. New York: Holt, Rinehart & Winston.

Kessel, Jerrold. 1998. "Stalled Peace Process Casts Pall on Celebration." CNN. www.cnn.com/SPECIALS/1998/israel/kessel.essay.

al-Khafaji, Isam. 1995. "Beyond the Ultranationalist State." *Middle East Report,* no. 187–188:34–39.

Khalaf, Samir. 1986. *Lebanon's Predicament*. New York: Columbia University Press.

Khoury, Philip. 1983. *Urban Notables and Arab Nationalism: The Politics of Damascus, 1860–1920*. Cambridge: Cambridge University Press.

Khoury, Philip, and Joseph Kostiner (eds.). 1990. *Tribes and State Formation in the Middle East*. Berkeley: University of California Press.

Khuri, Fuad. 1970. "Parallel Cousin Marriage Reconsidered: A Middle Eastern Practice That Nullifies the Effects of Marriage on the Intensity of Family Relationships." *Man* 5:596–618.

King-Irani, Laurie. 2001. "Maneuvering in Narrow Spaces: An Analysis of Emergent Identity, Subjectivity, and Political Institutions Among Palestinian Citizens of Israel." PhD diss. Indiana University, Bloomington.

Layoun, Mary. 1999. "A Guest at the Wedding: Honor, Memory, and (National) Desire in Michel Khleife's Wedding in Galilee." Pp. 92–110 in Caren Kaplan, Normal Alarcon, and Minoo Moallem (eds.), *Between Woman and Nation: Nationalisms, Translational Feminisms, and the State*. Durham: Duke University Press.

Levine, Mark. 2002. July 26. "The UN Arab Human Development Report: A Critique." *Middle East Report Online*. www.merip.org.

Makdisi, Ussama. 2000. *The Culture of Sectarianism: Community, History, and Violence in Nineteenth-Century Ottoman Lebanon*. Berkeley: University of California Press.

Mamdani, Mahmood. 2002. "Good Muslim, Bad Muslim: A Political Perspective on Culture and Terrorism." *American Anthropologist* 104, no. 3 (September): 766–775.

McMurray, David. 2002. *In and Out of Morocco*. Minneapolis: University of Minnesota Press.

Meeker, Michael. 1979. *Literature and Violence in North Arabia*. Cambridge: Cambridge University Press.

Mundy, Martha. 1995. *Domestic Government: Kinship, Community, and Polity in North Yemen*. London: I. B. Tauris.

Murphy, Robert, and Leonard Kasdan. 1959. "The Structure of Parallel Cousin Marriage." *American Anthropologist* 61, no. 1 (February):17–29.

Nelson, Cynthia (ed.). 1973. *The Desert and the Sown: Nomads in the Wider Society*. Berkeley: Institute for International Studies, University of California.

Peteet, Julie M. 1991. *Gender in Crisis: Women and the Palestinian Resistance Movement*. New York: Columbia University Press.

Pfeifer, Karen. 1999. "How Tunisia, Morocco, Jordan, and Even Egypt Became IMF 'Success Stories' in the 1990s." *Middle East Report,* no. 210:24–30.

Pitcher, Linda. 1998. "'The Divine Impatience': Ritual, Narrative, and Symbolization in the Practice of Martyrdom in Palestine." *Medical Anthropology Quarterly* 12, no. 1:8–30.

Roniger, Luis, and Ayse Gunes Ayata (eds.). 1994. *Democracy, Clientelism, and Civil Society*. Boulder: Lynne Rienner.

Royce, Anya Peterson. 1982. *Ethnicity: Strategies of Diversity*. Bloomington: Indiana University Press.

Sayigh, Rosemary. 1981. "Roles and Functions of Arab Women: A Reappraisal." *Arab Studies Quarterly* 3, no. 3:258–274.

———. 1994. *Too Many Enemies: The Palestinian Experience in Lebanon*. London: Zed Books.

Schneider, David M. 1968. *American Kinship: A Cultural Account*. Englewood Cliffs, NJ: Prentice Hall.

Schneider, Jane. 1971. "Of Vigilance and Virgins: Honor, Shame, and Access to Resources in Mediterranean Societies." *Ethnology* 10, no. 1 (January):1–24.

Sharabi, Hisham (ed.). 1990. *Theory, Politics, and the Arab World: Critical Responses*. London: Routledge.

Shryock, Andrew. 1997. *Nationalism and the Genealogical Imagination: Oral History and Textual Authority in Jordan*. Berkeley: University of California Press.

Singerman, Diane. 1995. *Avenues of Participation: Family, Politics, and Networks in Urban Quarters of Cairo*. Princeton: Princeton University Press.

Tapper, Richard. 1990. "Anthropologists, Historians, and Tribespeople on Tribe and State Formation in the Middle East." Pp. 48–73 in Philip Khoury and Joseph Kostiner (eds.), *Tribes and State Formation in the Middle East*. Berkeley: University of California Press.

Wedeen, Lisa. 1999. *Ambiguities of Domination: Politics, Rhetoric, and Symbols in Contemporary Syria*. Chicago: University of Chicago Press.

World Bank. 1996. *Middle East and North Africa*. Washington, DC: World Bank.

Zubaida, Sami. 1994. "National, Communal and Global Dimensions in Middle Eastern Food Cultures." Pp. 33–48 in S. Zubaida and R. Tapper (eds.), *Culinary Cultures of the Middle East*. Berkeley: University of California Press.

11

The Role of Women

Lisa Pollard

To study the role of women in the modern Middle East, one must first become familiar with the political, social, cultural, and economic systems in which Middle Eastern men and women circulate and through which the activities of both sexes acquire meaning. This means approaching the subject of Middle Eastern women in the same way one approaches the study of women in any society: by considering the various roles women play in those cultures, by becoming acquainted with the diverse activities and institutions in which women participate, by learning the history of those institutions, and by analyzing categories associated with women. Classifications like "mother," "wife," "worker," and "professional" are social constructs that have developed and changed over the course of the modern era.

At the same time, however, to study modern Middle Eastern women we must also reckon with our own culture. The West has a lengthy history of attributing all kinds of bizarre and denigrating characteristics to the Middle East. The misperception of Islamic societies has been particularly true with regard to women. Western societies have long reduced Middle Eastern women only to customs such as veiling, seclusion, and polygamy, and viewed those customs as stand-ins for the Middle East in general. The result has been a conflation of the Middle East with frequently limited understandings of women's roles and traditions. When we come to study women in the modern Middle East, we therefore have to navigate between understanding the practices and the circumstances of the women who inhabit the region while grappling with our misconceptions about them.

The task of separating the real from the imaginary is further complicated by the fact that, particularly in the modern era, Middle Easterners themselves also have used constructions of women and their customs to define and advance certain agendas. Intellectuals and politicians in the Middle East have responded to Orientalist discourses about them by advancing the idea that women and their behaviors symbolize the essence and aspirations of their nations. State builders, for example, have used idealized images of women to herald reform programs, and to demonstrate their states' departures from tradition. Similarly, debates about women have been mobilized by reformers and intellectuals in order to construct nationalisms and ethnicities, and to promote and institutionalize both secular and religious agendas. Polemicists and revolutionaries have, in turn, used discussions about women to applaud or to contest state agendas. The constructed, idealized images of women that result from such state-building projects and the debates that surround them frequently fail to represent women's real contributions to the societies in which they live or to advance women's aspirations.

Because both modern Middle Eastern women and the students and scholars who study them must constantly steer between fantastical and symbolic constructions of idealized womanhood, and between prescriptive behavior for women and women's actual aspirations and activities, this chapter presents an overview of women in the modern Middle East through a discussion of the fantastic, the symbolic, and the real. Beginning briefly with the late nineteenth century, the chapter illustrates how Europeans linked misconceptions about the intimate lives of women in the Ottoman Empire and Qajar Persia at the same time as European geopolitical interests in those regions began to intensify. Those frequently fantastical perceptions of women were therefore linked to territorial interests in the European imagination and often were used to justify colonialist incursions. The response of Ottoman and Qajar subjects to such discourse, which were spread through student missions to Europe and through the advance of Western education in Ottoman and Qajar territories, became a period of intense debate, culminating in a series of reforms directed at women. Thus, in this chapter, I examine the "woman question" debates that erupted in the region at the turn of the twentieth century to illustrate how the reform programs and nationalist movements that emerged from them also involved heightened attention to women, once again linking territory to women and their behavior. The discussion then turns to the ways in which debates and discussions about women have been transformed by politicians and ideologues into state-building and antistate platforms, illustrating the central role that defining and determining women's behavior has been to shaping modern Middle Eastern nation-states. In the final section of the chapter, I turn to women, not as constructs, but as subjects, demonstrating the many ways in which women's agendas for themselves contradict and challenge state agendas. Through an examination of women's contributions to nationalist movements, women's lengthy struggle for political rights and for legal reforms, women's outreach to fellow citizens who fall outside the state's reach, and women's role as revolutionaries, we see how the idealized behavior produced by "woman question" debates does not always match the needs and goals of real women.

I do not pretend to discuss in this chapter all Middle Eastern women in the many contexts in which they live. Rather, I use episodes in the histories of Turkey, Egypt, Iraq, and Iran to illustrate the centrality of women and of debates about them to the modern Middle East, and to discuss women's actual experiences. The goal not only is to illustrate the tensions between the constructed women who appear in debates and the real women who seek various forms of emancipation for themselves, but also to underscore the idea that examining women as symbols, as objects of fantasy and debate, and as historical actors with agendas of their own is essential to understanding the topic broadly defined as "the role of women" in the modern Middle East.

The Middle East and the Woman Question

While Muslim women had long been of interest to Europeans who traveled through the Islamic world, in the modern era Western travel writers increasingly came to use women as tropes for defining differences among the territories that made up the Islamic empires and for defining the differences between Western and Islamic civilizations. During the Enlightenment, over the course of which European imperial interests began to challenge the Islamic empires, male and female travelers from Europe increasingly used women as a means of describing the territories that made up what we now call the Middle East. Writing from the Levant in the eighteenth century, for example, Lady Mary Wortley Montagu used descriptions of female bodies and of women's fashion to note differences between herself and Ottoman women and to denote territorial boundaries within Ottoman territories (Van Renen, 2011). As the Enlightenment's comportment literature increasingly encouraged elite European women to be exemplars of domestic practices, Muslim women of the harem emerged in European travel accounts as negative models against which to measure European feminine virtues (Kahf, 1999). (European writers compared harem women's alleged licentious behavior, for example, with monogamy and chastity.) Over the course of the nineteenth century, as European geopolitical interests in the Middle East intensified, so too did the Western appetite for harem literature. In that literature, harem women increasingly served as stand-ins for Middle Eastern women in general (Ahmed, 1995:150).

By the late nineteenth century, Europeans conflated harem women with the very territory through which they traveled. Both male and female travelers therefore made it their goal to get inside of harems so that they could demonstrate that they knew a territory intimately (Melman, 1995; Pollard, 2005). European women might well have had access to harem space, by virtue of their sex. The majority of late-Victorian travel writers were men, however, and the likelihood that they made actual entrances into harem space is rare. Their lack of real knowledge about the harem notwithstanding, travel writers claimed to present the Middle East to readers via allegedly accurate accounts of Muslim women's traditions. European writers used the so-called inmates of the Ottoman sultans' harems to exemplify Oriental despotism, to illustrate differences between an emerging West and a declining Ottoman Empire, and to justify military intervention when necessary (Ishom-Verhareen, 2006).

In the case of Egypt, for example, as the opening of the Suez Canal in 1869 made British access to India easier, and as raw materials continued to feed British industry, travelers, entrepreneurs, and scientists arrived in Egypt in greater numbers. In their accounts of Egypt, the territory was frequently conflated with women's habits and domestic customs (Pollard, 2005). By that same period, Montesquieu's *Persian Letters* had popularized the idea that the harem was a ubiquitous institution, and the sequestered, deprived, and often depraved woman became a common trope through which European writers depicted Persia (Ishom-Verhareen, 2006). Similarly, a travel guide for visiting Ottoman territories, including Mesopotamia, introduced the idea that travelers could not claim to know the region without a visit to a harem. By the 1870s, travel guides encouraged women to make female friends during their travels: only an invitation to visit harem space would assure them thorough knowledge of the region (Melman, 1995:76).

Two main conclusions about women emerged from this body of literature. The first was that Islam required women to live in sequestration, indolence, and depravity. Western writers imagined that so-called harem inmates were forced into polygamy and encouraged to lounge endlessly, gossip, drink tea, and smoke hashish—all at the expense of attention to their children. A second conclusion was that such idle and childish harem women ruined men and made them incapable of running their countries.

In the case of Egypt, for example, Europeans saw the ruling elite as both foolish and cruel despots, raised as they were by harem women and spoiled by the practice of polygamy. Europeans claimed that Khedive Isma'il (r. 1863–1879) had a penchant for capriciously murdering his ministers, a habit he allegedly picked up from his mother, herself a harem inmate (Pollard, 2005:90). The khedive's mother was allegedly so consumed by sexual desire that she sent for young men each evening, had her way with them in the confines of the harem, and disposed of their headless bodies in the Nile each following morning (Boyle, 1965). Stories about Isma'il's harem roots distracted European readers from the khedive's successes in developing his country, and served to illustrate how backward a leader the Egyptian ruler was.

Sometimes the conclusions that Victorian-era travel writers reached about Middle Eastern women had long-lasting consequences. When the British occupied Egypt in 1882, they pointed to the harem and its practices as legitimizations for an unpopular invasion. Occupied Egypt's first consul general, Lord Cromer (r. 1883–1907), confessed that he had relied on travel literature in order to assess the Egyptian ruling class and, therefore, to shape his administrative practices (Pollard, 2005:88). The argument of Cromer and his contemporaries was fairly simple: depraved habits and customs like the use of harem space had led Egypt to ruin. If Egyptian governing institutions were to be reformed, then the first step had to be saving women from their degraded state. For Cromer and a generation of men and women who, in both official and unofficial capacities made reforming the Middle East their rallying cry, the condition of women and the region's alleged shortcomings had become conflated.

In response to such discourse, and in order to inaugurate changes in their own societies, intellectuals throughout the Ottoman Empire and Persia similarly displayed an intense focus on women and their behavior. In each region discussions about women were instrumental in shaping emerging nationalisms, and the woman question was a powerful vehicle through which budding nationalists defined their past, critiqued their present, and offered suggestions about the future. Whereas women had historically been symbolic of familial genealogies and of political alliances, by the turn of the twentieth century they had come to embody the aspirations and agendas of reform programs and emerging nationalist agendas (Pierce, 1993; Ishom-Verhareen, 2006).

In Persia, for example, some reform-minded intellectuals critiqued the Qajar dynasty (1785–1925) by equating the position of women with the dynasty's governing practices. Such reformers sought to rescue "traditional women" from corrupt Qajar culture, which, critics argued, manifested itself in poverty, superstition, and ignorance. Mirza 'Abd al-Hosayn Khan Kermani, for example, referred to Persian women as "the living dead" (Amin, 2003:27). Kermani sought to bring those women back to life through a reform of local marriage and domestic practices, which he saw has having been corrupted by the Qajars' Ottoman roots as well as by the Arabs' centuries-long influence on Persian culture. In several of his *Hundred Sermons* (*Sad Khatabah*), Kermani argued that reform of Qajar practices would eradicate outside influences and result in a purer Persian culture. Women would act as purifying agents, Kermani argued, by transmitting this renewed Persian culture to their children (Afary, 1996; Amin, 2003).

In Egypt, after the 1882 British occupation, an increasingly active (and quickly burgeoning) press took up the discussion of topics related to women as a means of responding to British critiques of Egyptian society. The most famous of this group was the lawyer and intellectual Qasim Amin. His many journal articles and his two published books, *Tahrir al-Mar'a* (The Liberation of Women, 1899) and *al-Mar'a al-Jadida* (The New Woman, 1901), inaugurated a series of discussions that harnessed women's position in Egyptian society to the secular nationalist project. Amin argued that the condition of Egypt's largely sequestered and frequently uneducated elite class of women represented Egypt's relatively backward stage of development, and suggested that Egypt would neither modernize nor be free of the British until women were liberated from traditional customs such as veiling and seclusion. His texts defined Egypt as a territory and as a historical subject through accounts of women's customs and behavior. The best known of Amin's critics, economist and businessman Mohammed Tala'at Harb, encouraged more traditional forms of education and dress. Harb urged Egyptian women to emulate women from the time of the Prophet Muhammad, indicating that it was Egypt's Islamic past that was most appropriate for solving the dilemmas of the present.

In Anatolia in the years surrounding the Young Turk Revolution of 1908, reformers and revolutionaries of both secular and traditional orientations similarly used women as tropes for outlining their platforms. Sociologist and political reformer Ziya Gökalp, whose ideas would later influence independent Turkey's first ruler Mustafa Kemal Atatürk (r. 1923–1938), argued that modernization was not uniquely a Western phenomenon. Gökalp saw women as repositories of the Turkish past. By examining women's roles in that past, he argued, reformers could find roots of democracy and feminism and use them to modernize Turkish society. Gökalp contended that, unless Islam and the West could be made compatible with traditions, they should be rejected as models for the new Turkish woman (Fleming, 1998). Gökalp's brand of Turkish feminism involved recapturing the ancient strength of Turkish women and promoting that power in all spheres, including warfare (White, 2003).

Reformers linked debates about women to reforms, many of them educational, that had been taking place across the region over the course of the nineteenth and early twentieth centuries. Local reformers attached women's education to the modernization of their societies. From Istanbul to Tehran, girls' schools opened their doors between 1873 and 1918. Teacher training colleges and some university courses were opened to women. European and US Christian missionary schools also promoted the modernization of the region through the education of women. Classroom lessons mirrored debates among intellectuals: transforming women into literate, savvy wives and mothers was an essential part of political and economic reform (Russell, 2004).

A crucial by-product of these reforms and debates, in the regions discussed above and in other parts of the Ottoman Empire, was the idea that emerging nations embodied the qualities of reformed women. Male cartoonists in the Ottoman, Egyptian, and Persian press, for example, used satirical depictions of "old" and "new" women to depict the dilemmas of social change, and to illustrate the many forms that new nations might take. In the period immediately after the Young Turk Revolution, for example, the female image of "Türkiye" embodied an emerging Turkishness that was neither ultra-Westernized nor, by contrast, hesitant to modernize along Western lines. While Türkiye took many forms, her beauty and grace confronted the aggression of other nations, and she embodied honor and virtue (Brummett, 1998). "Lady Egypt" was similarly represented in ongoing debates about Egypt's nature. She was often arrayed in clothing representing Egypt's Pharaonic past; on other occasions, cartoonists portrayed her in traditional attire. Sometimes she wore a mixture of European and traditional fashion. Like Türkiye, she embodied the nation's assets and protected the emerging nation from European aggression (Baron, 2005; Pollard, 2005). Nations depicted as women were rallying symbols for the aspirations of a growing number of nationalists who linked allegedly feminine virtues with emerging national projects.

Often these female representations of the nation reified the contributions of Ottoman, Egyptian, and Persian women as wives and mothers to the national cause. In 1907, during the Constitutional Revolution, an image of "mother Iran" was shown protecting the infant majles (parliament) from its enemies.[1] In Istanbul, the *nesli cedid* (new generation) was announced by a young mother contributing to the nation by rocking a cradle. In it, a baby soldier—neither male nor female—sports a fez and carries a rifle.[2] During the 1919 Egyptian revolution, "lady Egypt" was depicted breastfeeding the newly organized Bank of Egypt, a project which—according to the cartoonist—was certain to succeed because it was nurtured through the breast milk of mother Egypt.[3] In each case, the success of the nation rested on maternalism.

Like the harem inmate of the nineteenth-century European imagination, these women were not real. Rather, they represented the fears and ambitions of male intellectuals and politicians who sought to transform the nature of local rule and to respond to European imperialism. While women certainly benefited from the educational projects that accompanied state reform, women's aspirations for themselves were not necessarily depicted in these new woman debates or in symbolic, gendered-feminine representations of the nation. Nonetheless, as debates about women became incorporated into state-building projects, women whose objectives were different from those of male nationalists would frequently find themselves in conflict not only with men but with the symbolic "ladies" whom male reformers had constructed to represent them.

Building the Nation Through Women

Debates about the relationship between women and the success of the nation were translated by politicians into state-building platforms in the decades following World War I. New woman debates became the pillars of the Westernization and modernization platforms of Atatürk and Reza Shah Pahlavi (r. 1926–1941) as both men steered their newly created nations away from the traditions and institutions of the dynasties that preceded them. Both the president of Turkey and the shah of Iran translated the reforms and debates from earlier decades about women's role in society, past and present, into governing strategies..

On the one hand, such state platforms for women were pragmatic. In both Turkey and Iran, the state inaugurated increased educational opportunities for women, continuing Ottoman and Qajar modernization platforms. While an earlier generation of reforms had been aimed only at the elite classes, in 1924 Atatürk made education universal and compulsory. Over the course of the 1930s, women had access to higher education and received degrees in medicine, engineering, and law. The result was the proliferation of female professionals by the end of the 1940s. By 1928, Iranian girls were similarly encouraged to attend new state-run primary and secondary schools. In 1934 the state opened a number of teacher training colleges, and encouraged women's enrollment in them. After a 1934 visit to Turkey, the shah began further implementation of primary and secondary schools for girls nationwide. In 1935, he established Iran's Women's Center through which the state continued to promote educational reform. That same year, the University of Tehran opened its doors to women and men. By 1936, women were visible among the ranks of Iran's burgeoning civil service.

On the other hand Turkey and Iran's state platforms were symbolic of state agendas and were not necessarily aimed at improving women's lives. As both Atatürk and Reza Shah worked to cultivate Turkish and Iranian nationalisms, for example, and to marginalize or to lessen the role of Islam in their countries, they waged powerful campaigns against those traditions that they deemed reminiscent of the Islamic past. Fashion was a tool through which both Atatürk and Reza Shah manufactured secular Turkish and Iranian identity. Men in both societies were subjected to propaganda campaigns and laws against the wearing of the fez, turbans, and other forms of traditional headgear. Turkish and Iranian women were encouraged to abandon veiling or forbidden to wear it. Atatürk pointed to his wife Latife Uşakligil as a model of Westernization; she was unveiled in public appearances and in photographs, posing both alone and with her husband (who favored top hats and fedoras). Reza Shah issued legal injunctions against veiling in 1936. As it had been at the turn of the twentieth century, the veil in republican Turkey and Iran symbolized the nature and potential of the nation. Unveiled women in both countries symbolized a dramatic rupture from the past. In neither country were women consulted about their preferences (Paidar, 1995).

Still other reforms mixed pragmatism with symbolism. As a means of lessening the power and prestige of the religious establishment and to give Turkey a further patina of Westernization, for example, Atatürk replaced sharia with Western civil codes. His 1926 adoption of the Swiss Legal Code for matters pertaining to the family gave women greater access to divorce and to custody of their children. At the same time, the code cemented the husband as head of household and reduced women's rights with regard to inheritance. Reza Shah similarly introduced the Marriage Law of 1931, requiring marriages to be registered with the state, outlining specific conditions for divorce, and raising the minimum age of marriage to fifteen for women and eighteen for men. In both countries, the state encouraged women to be informed wives and mothers, and to make domestic activities their primary concern (Keddie, 2007; Paidar, 1995). While women benefited from state reforms in both Turkey and Iran, it is important to emphasize that both nations' top-down reforms were aimed less at representing women's interests than they were at transforming the nation along the lines of Atatürk's and Reza Shah's visions.

Women were similarly useful vehicles for advancing the cause of secular Arabism and pan-Arabism in places like Syria, Egypt, and Iraq. In the late 1940s, the coauthors of Baathist ideology Michel Alfaq and Salah al-Din al-Bitar dedicated the Baath Party to eradicating backward thinking about women, suggesting that to do so would liberate Arabs from the feudalism and tribalism from which the party sought to distance its followers. Baathist socialism included the development of practical programs designed to allow women to participate in public life, to work toward their own liberation, and to free Arab society from the vestiges of Western imperialism (Rassam, 1992:91). In 1950s Egypt, fellow pan-Arabist Gamal Abdul Nasser (r. 1956–1970) articulated his own vision of the new woman. Like the Baathists, who are discussed in greater detail in Chapter 4, Nasser used women-focused agendas to distance his socialist agendas from the governing strategies of an earlier generation of elite politicians. He also used the woman question to articulate a secular Arab identity. Nasser's vision of society required a double duty of women: they were to serve the nation through their roles as wives and mothers while remaining highly visible as workers and symbols of the state's industrial progress (Bier, 2011).

When pan-Arabist ideology was transformed into governing platforms in places like Iraq and Egypt, the result was state-mandated agendas for women. Arab socialist forms of state feminism became national causes. The Egyptian Constitution of 1956 and the National Charter of 1962 formally recognized women as citizens, and Nasser used reforms directed at women as evidence of his commitment to achieving freedom, unity, and socialism in Egypt. The Nasser regime gave women the right to vote and to run for political office in 1956, and extended education and health care services to an increasingly large number of Egyptians. By 1957, Egypt had its first female parliamentarian, Rawya Attiya. Similarly, the regime granted women the right and the duty to work and passed laws protecting female workers by granting them maternity leave. Nasser's 1964 laws regarding guaranteed employment for university graduates also increased the number of women in the workforce. But suffrage and promises of employment did not necessarily translate into women's freedom to define themselves outside the boundaries of Nasser's vision of Arab socialism. The same year that Nasser granted women the right to vote, for example, he forced Egypt's active women's movement to limit itself strictly to social issues, effectively placing the state in the position of shaping women's movements. At the same time, Nasser resisted the reform of Egypt's personal status laws, furthering women's inequality within the conjugal family unit (Hatem, 1992).

In Iraq, the brief rule of Abd al-Karim Qasim (r. 1958–1963) witnessed a view of secular Arabism that was similar to Nasser's. In addition to promoting education, Qasim implemented the progressive Personal Status Code in 1959: the code granted women equal inheritance rights, worked against polygamy and unilateral divorce, and made women's consent to marriage a necessity. As the Baath consolidated its control of Iraq after 1963, the state granted women full citizenship rights and promised them full political participation as members of the party. Iraqi Baathist officials considered marriage to be a national duty, and the new state therefore encouraged and facilitated marriage through continued education and health care reforms for women. In the economic realm, the state pursued attitudes and strategies comparable to Nasser's, promoting women's work outside the home and equipping them to do so effectively. The Baath's commitment to women's education quickly bore fruit: by 1976 women were roughly 39 percent of educational field workers, 31 percent of physicians, 25 percent of laboratory technicians, 15 percent of accountants, 11 percent of factory workers, 4 percent of engineers, and held 3 percent of high government posts (Rassam, 1992:92). The 1973 oil boom prompted the state to continue pumping resources into women's education and vocational training and to elevate the female worker to the same symbolic status she enjoyed in Nasser's Egypt (al-Ali, 2012:97). For many women, the first decade of Baath Party rule was a golden age: economic reform and expansion, women-friendly laws, a flourishing middle class (al-Ali, 2007:112–113). Iraqis of that era pointed to women and their accomplishments as symbolic of the ideologies that shaped Iraq after its independence from the British: Iraqi nationalism, pan-Arabism, and democratic political pluralism. Men encouraged women to participate in an open political arena as philanthropists, political activists, and demonstrators (al-Ali, 2007).

The state continued to advance women's education and participation in the labor force, It also co-opted many women's associations, however, into a Baath Party apparatus called the General Federation of Iraqi Women. Party officials used the federation to supervise women's behavior (al-Ali, 2007:136–137). After the foundation of the General Federation, Iraqi women continued to be active, taking on illiteracy campaigns, volunteer activities, and vocational and industrial training. The state's issuance of Law 39 in 1972, however, signaled that women's individual interests were not at the forefront of the General Federation's mission. Rather the law listed the Arab nation's struggles against imperialism, Zionism, and backwardness as the federation's main goals, effectively subordinating women's interests in favor of Baathist agendas (Farouk-Sluglett, 1993).

However much Iraqi women resented this increased state role in their private and public lives, their dissent tended to be buffered over the 1970s by a flourishing, oil-driven economy from which many women benefited (al-Ali, 2007:127–131). After taking power, Saddam Hussein (r. 1979–2003) claimed that women were half of society, and he accordingly encouraged women's education and participation in an economy that was increasingly buoyed by oil. As part of Hussein's "new Iraqi woman" discourse, women's salaries went up and state assistance for working mothers increased. Iraqi men were fined if they failed to allow women to participate in education and labor. For Iraq the 1970s was thus a decade of contradictions between women's repression and advancements (al-Ali, 2007:131–137).

In Iran, Mohammad Reza Shah (r. 1941–1979) accelerated his father's pattern of linking women's emancipation with modernizing agendas. In the early years of his reign, the country's diverse array of political parties had branches for women. Women's organizations proliferated; they worked with political parties and with the state to advance women's education and integration into the workforce. In 1951 and 1952, under the brief administration of Prime Minister Mohammad Mossadeq, women participated in municipal elections. The shah extended women's right to political participation as part of his White Revolution, which he commenced in 1963, giving Iranian women the right to vote and to run for office. Six women were elected to Iran's majles that year; the shah appointed a female minister in 1965. His family protection acts of 1967 and 1975 raised minimum ages of marriage (to eighteen for women and twenty for men in 1975), secularized marriage and divorce registration, expanded women's rights within marriage and the family, and limited men's privileges with regard to polygamy. The years between 1963 and 1979 witnessed rapid modernization, funded—as in Iraq—by oil revenue. The shah channeled state revenues into education at all levels and the number of female workers and professionals increased dramatically. Labor laws, passed in 1974, made the workplace safer for women and allowed breaks for nursing mothers. Abortion was made legal in Iran in 1977 (Paidar, 1995).

As in Hussein's Iraq, however, seemingly progressive laws were coupled with increased state supervision of women. From 1953, after a coup removed Mossadeq from office and, as the shah subsequently began curtailing political and press freedoms in Iran, he also began placing women's activities under state control. Between 1956 and 1966, he established the High Council of Women in order to bring women's activities under the state's supervision. The council oversaw the charitable organizations that would henceforth be women's sole domain, and strengthened the state's control over the legal and educational domains. In 1966 the council was replaced by the Women's Organization of Iran (WOI), which, while continuing to contribute to women's education, was also a bureaucratic apparatus (by 1977, it had 400 branches and 70,000 members) through which the state supervised women's activities (Paidar, 1995:150). The WOI continued to promote many of the policies that had been central to Iran's earlier state feminism, suggesting that although professional women were crucial to promoting both shahs' visions of modernity, their primary responsibility was to home and family.

As had been the case under his father's tenure, Mohammad Reza Shah's reforms mainly helped the middle and upper classes. As the shah increasingly cracked down on Iranians' political freedoms, even the women whose lives were ostensibly improved by state-driven reforms became hostile opponents of the state. By the end of the 1970s, Iranian women found themselves in a situation similar to that of women in Iraq, where state advancements for women were coupled with harsh repressions.

In Egypt in the 1970s and 1980s, Anwar Sadat (r. 1970–1981) made women's issues high profile, championing platforms pertaining to women both as a means of sustaining the projects undertaken by Nasser and of differentiating his regime from that of his predecessor. The president's wife, Jehan Sadat, was also an advocate of women's issues, including literacy and economic self-sufficiency. President Sadat promulgated a constitution guaranteeing a balance between women's private and public roles and duties. He set up a quota system whereby women would be guaranteed seats in Egypt's legislature. On June 20, 1979, he issued a presidential decree, which added 30 seats for women in parliament and allocated 10–20 percent of seats to women on government councils nationwide. That year, 9 percent of 390 elected members of parliament were women (Sullivan, 1986:43). Also in 1979, Sadat revised Egypt's personal status laws (known as "Jehan's laws" because of his wife's role in promoting them) giving women greater divorce and custody rights. Sadat continued Nasser's commitment to education.

Sadat departed from Nasser's economic agenda by privatizing national industries and by opening Egypt to increased foreign trade. Sadat also opened Egypt to development by the West and by the oil-rich nations of the Gulf. The result was a rise in employment opportunities for women, including the new services industries that accompanied increased tourism in Egypt. According to government estimates, the number of working women doubled between 1978 and 1980 (Sullivan, 1986:179).

Sadat's administration also produced a host of conditions that would bring women back into the spotlight as objects of heated debate. The flooding of the public realm with professional women, the increased crowding in urban areas, the increasingly high cost of living, and an emerging cultural conservatism combined to bring traditional forms of dress back in vogue. As the hijab became increasingly popular, debates about idealized womanhood intensified, among both women and men. Sadat's self-promotion as a pious person, with his subsequent reinclusion of Islamists into acceptable public discourse and increased attempts to appease their determination to include Islam in politics, elevated the woman question to a position reminiscent of the early twentieth century. Egyptians were once again divided over the relationship between women's behavior, women's access to the public sphere, and the state of the body politic.

That division continued through the regime of Hosni Mubarak (r. 1981–2011), whose policies both resembled and departed from Sadat's. Mubarak's educational and health policies perpetuated the idea from the turn of the twentieth century that women contributed best to society as wives and mothers. Mubarak continued to promote the family ideal that had its roots in the early twentieth century: in 1985, for example, he attempted to repeal Sadat's reforms of the Personal Status Laws as a gesture toward those who saw those reforms as departing from Islamic tradition. It would not be until 2000 that Egyptian women could divorce without their husband's permission (Cuno, 2008:196). Mubarak made the protection of the female body high profile after Egypt hosted the 1994 International Conference on Population and Development. When international attention was subsequently drawn to women's issues in Egypt, including the practice of female genital cutting, Mubarak made gestures toward abolishing the practice and improving women's access to education and health care. As discussed in Chapter 7, his continuation of Sadat's neoliberal economic policies intensified the gap between the rich and the poor, increasing illiteracy and unemployment and rendering such gestures insufficient and ineffective. At the same time, however, Mubarak allowed for the reemergence of organized women's movements, ending Nasser and Sadat's practices of limiting and supervising them (Badran, 2009:132).

Over the course of the 1970s in Iran, Mohammad Reza Shah's increased crackdown on human and political rights created fertile soil for the cultivation of a woman question debate that was far from the secularizing discourse of the Pahlavi dynasty. Followers of the exiled Ayatollah Ruhollah Khomeini, a powerful voice of opposition to the shah, rekindled debates that were also reminiscent of discussions and debates from earlier in the century, equating the secular Iranian state's failures in part with women's

Images like this of women fully covered in Qom, Iran,
dominate many Western understandings of women in the Middle East.

departure from their proper domestic roles. As the revolution progressed, women were once again symbolic of Iran's break from its past; this time, from a secular past. The Islamic Republic that emerged from the Iranian Revolution of 1979 saw resurgence of traditional forms of dress and the ideological linking of women's dress to the potential of the new forms of government. The new regime reversed several of the Pahlavis' policies toward women, particularly the Family Protection Law of 1967. The new government also closed family planning centers and, while continuing to support women's education, applied quotas for female university applicants in a wide range of scientific and professional fields. (In each case, the state later revised its actions in response to women's reactions against restrictions of their rights.) Women retained the right to vote and to be elected to public office, but the new constitution of 1981 reinstated sharia law, defined the family as central to the state, and allowed the state to define the family. Motherhood reemerged as Iranian women's primary responsibility; new dress codes, including required veiling, would protect mothers. The legal age for marriage was set at thirteen years old for girls and fifteen years old for boys. For some, such state-mandated reforms were a dramatic betrayal after a revolution in which women often took active roles (Esfandiari, 1997). Said one Iranian woman: "Of the Revolutionary triad 'Independence, Freedom, Islamic Republic,' all we got was the Islamic Republic" (Esfandiari, 1997:54).

The state's use of women to define its agendas in the years following the revolution represented a continuation of earlier debates and presaged a pattern whereby the state defined its agendas by promoting some women's agendas and curtailing others. A lengthy war with Iraq (1980–1988), for example, required women to work in realms the regime had previously defined as "masculine," leading to the relaxation, if not the transformation, of labor and educational policies. Similarly, following Khomeini's death in 1989, an overpopulation crisis required the state to rethink its earlier stance against family planning (Esfandiari, 1997). That same year, in a move that seemed to promote women's rights, Iran's parliament passed a limited divorce reform bill requiring court permission for divorce (Keddie, 2007: 114). In each case, women's fortunes were linked to the promotion of the state's needs and agendas.

Over the course of the 1990s, which were liberal in comparison to the Khomeini era, woman question debates reemerged as the press served once again as an arena for debates about reform in the Islamic Republic. During the presidency of Mohammad Khatami (r. 1997–2005), 60 percent of the student body in Iran's universities was female (Esfandiari, 2012). The 2000 return to power of politicians who prefer Khomeini-era laws and norms, however, has again witnessed crackdowns on women's dress, behavior, and circulation in public spaces. Mahmood Ahmadinejad (r. 2005–) has used his tenure as Iran's president to promote reforms reminiscent of the immediate postrevolutionary era. He has campaigned against birth control, promoted the lowering of Iran's already early legal marriage ages for both sexes, endorsed a family protection bill that removed men's need for their wives' consent to polygamy, and twice introduced quotas against women in Iran's universities (particularly in the medical and scientific fields).

In Hussein's Iraq, years of wars and sanctions resulted in apparent about-faces in the state's gender ideology. As the result of the Iran-Iraq War and the Gulf War (1991) and subsequent United Nations (UN) sanctions, state discourse shifted away from one that favored women's participation in the workforce to one of more conservative and traditional roles for women (al-Radi, 1998). Hussein's state promoted a discourse in which women were expected to resign their jobs, return home, and allow men to take over scarce jobs. The housewife replaced the working woman as Hussein's state-sponsored icon (al-Ali, 2007:188–189). The state became more conservative, pointing to Islamic tradition rather than secular values as a means of solving Iraq's crises. Hussein became obsessed, for example, with the idea that Iraqi women had given up their morals in favor of prostitution, and he acted aggressively to repress women's sexuality. Dress codes consequently became stricter. Men began demanding that women wear the abaya, equating women's dress with Iraq's many years of crisis (al-Ali, 2007:200–201).

In the aftermath of the US invasion and occupation of 2003, the sectarian- and ethnic-based groups that still struggle to gain control of the Iraqi body politic employ women, and women's behavior, as symbols of their agendas. Women continue to be used by Islamists and others as a means of articulating anti-Baath, anti-Western, and anti-imperialist agendas (al-Ali and Pratt, 2009:13). As a means of claiming control of the political arena and of defining Iraq to their liking, Islamist militias, both Sunni and Shi'i, have used dress codes, gender segregation, and *fatawa* (legal opinions) against women who would leave their homes (al-Ali, 2007:240–242).

In Turkey, Kemalist single-party rule gave way to political pluralism in the years following World War II. Nonetheless, Atatürk's vision of republican motherhood continued to define state agendas for women through the end of the 1950s (Z. Arat, 1998:13). (Indeed, the goal of the 1960 military coup was the preservation of Kemalism.) From 1961 to 1983, as multiparty political life flourished in Turkey (albeit punctuated by two subsequent military interventions), parties of various orientations politicized women by recruiting them to expand their base of support. While those parties frequently had women's auxiliaries, they rarely promoted women's issues, addressing allegedly more pressing problems such as Turkey's population increase, rapid urbanization, and outward migration (Z. Arat, 1998:17–18). Constitutions written in 1961 and 1982 expanded civil and social liberties, but left Kemalist-era family codes favoring men as head of household in place. In the area of education, however, devotion to the Kemalist commitment to women appeared to have waned: by 1975, only 48 percent of Turkish women were literate compared to 75 percent of men (Cleveland, 2004:282).

From the early 1980s, those in Turkey who continue to champion Kemalism have been joined by other political orientations, including those who support an increased role of Islam in the political realm. As discussed in Chapter 12, the electoral victory of the Motherland Party in the 1983 elections brought a coalition of Islamic revivalists and secularists to power. Since the election of the Justice and Development Party (AKP) in 2002, and under the leadership of Prime Minister Recep Tayyip Erdoğan (r. 2003–), moderate Islam has joined both secular voices and more radical religious orientations, each possessing agendas for women. In 2001, the Turkish Grand National Assembly (TGNA) amended the 1926 Turkish Civil Code, redressing inequalities in marriage and divorce and raising the minimum age for marriage to eighteen years old for both sexes. While the amendment resulted in part from activism from within Turkey, the TGNA's decision to address gender inequality, particularly the 1926 clause that made men the head of household, came as the result of Turkey's desire to join the European Union (EU). The dictates of the EU related to Turkey's ascension, specifically full promotion of liberal democracy and human rights, ultimately helped women. The TGNA issued the amendment despite the objections of Islamists who came to power the following year (Y. Arat, 2010).

Secularists and Islamists in Turkey regularly square off over the continued application of Atatürk-era bans on wearing the hijab (headscarf) in the public sector, now extended to include universities. Contemporary debates about veiling are reminiscent of those from an earlier era. Women and their dress have again emerged as potent symbols in discussions about whether or not Turkey belongs in the Western or the Islamic world, about the role of secularism in Turkey, and about the place of Islam in Turkish society. Those debates are not about women's rights.

In each of the above examples, women appear both as symbols of backwardness and success, as objects of reform, as emblems of ethnicities, and as tokens in state-building projects and revolutionary movements. While political reforms have brought women increasingly into the public realm as educated professionals and enfranchised citizens, women are at the mercy of state agendas that promote or revoke women's access to that realm at the expense of their interests and needs. Studying women in these capacities reveals the crucial discursive role that women have played in the shaping of the modern Middle East, but does not provide a full picture of women's histories or experiences. That picture can only be completed by examining women as subjects—both in step with national agendas and working against them.

Middle Eastern Women
Beyond the Woman Question

Telling the story of women in the modern Middle East without the woman question reveals a different picture of women's experiences. This is not to argue that women have not contributed to woman question debates, or that they have not supported or participated in state reform movements. Rather, it is to suggest that women have joined in activities that have escaped the attention of Orientalists, challenged state agendas, and promoted the interests of women as real individuals instead of symbolic constructs. Women's movements therefore appear, at times, to be in harmony with state agendas—promoting women's literacy and health, for example. Women's movements have also defined a set of agendas that have challenged the state, served state-like functions, and fallen outside of the state's grasp.

To return briefly to the nineteenth century: had Western travelers been in search of similarities between themselves and residents of the Middle East, and had they relied less on fantasy, they might well have seen that parts of the Ottoman Empire and Persia had begun to resemble Europe. While Europeans were fixated on the harem and despotism, for example, Istanbul, Cairo, and Tehran had been undergoing modernization and reform processes across the nineteenth century. The Ottoman sultans, the Ottoman-Egyptian viceroy Mehmet Ali (r. 1805–1848) and his descendants, and the Qajar shahs inaugurated reforms of their respective infrastructures, militaries, bureaucracies, and educational systems. Among the products of those reforms were subjects who clamored for the kinds of governing institutions that, Europeans argued, differentiated the West from other parts of the world: movements in favor of constitutional reform in Istanbul and Cairo in 1876 and 1882, respectively, and a revolution in favor of constitutionalism in Persia between 1906 and 1911. Polygamy was on the wane among the elite classes and the number of large harems had therefore declined. Although Westerners did not recognize it in their travels to the region, reformers were already using the press and the classroom to encourage and cultivate companionate marriage, writing and teaching about the same kinds of topics that appeared in Victorian and Edwardian newspapers and textbooks.

As for the harem, it continued to exist and to function but looked little like the harems of the Western imagination. While elite women throughout the region were, in fact, largely limited to harem space through the early decades of the twentieth century, they were hardly idle inmates. They were increasingly literate, versed in local and European languages as state attention to girls' education, the presence of missionary schools, and the availability of female European tutors increased in parts of the region. Harem women were often economically powerful: as members of the landed class, some were property holders who used the tax revenue from their landholdings to fund charitable projects of substantial reach and reputation. Elite women ran their households, making decisions about menus and budgets and the hiring and firing of servants. In a word, while the harem made up many elite women's worlds, it was not a place of idleness, nudity, and depravity. Harem women's reality was much like that of elite women of the Victorian era in which the household was the woman's world, and in which women's authority was largely unchallenged when it came to household matters (Marsot, 1978; Fay, 2012).

Far from being silent prisoners, elite women made their own contributions to the flurry of publications about women at the end of the nineteenth century. In Egypt, Syrian immigrant Maryam Nahhas Nawfal published the first female-authored biographical dictionary about women in 1879, *The Fine Woman's Exhibition of Biographies of Famous Women.* The book, like those that followed it by other female authors, provided object lessons in morals and behavior, taking the woman question debate out of the realm of the abstract, and providing concrete examples of real women (Booth, 2001). In Anatolia, Fatima Aliye wrote *Muslim Women* in 1891, using her pen to challenge conservative defenses of polygamy. In 1908 Halit Hamit wrote *Feminism and Islam, of Complete Equality for the World of Womanhood,* in which she argued for women's suffrage and women's right to run for public office. *The Vices of Men,* published circa 1900 in Iran by Bibi Astarabadi, championed companionate marriage and argued that men's vices would decrease in proportion to their marital happiness (Keddie,

2007). Such texts responded to emerging woman question debates among men but, at the same time, suggested that women were not merely objects of debate. Rather, female authors provided models, topics, and interpretations that readers could apply to their own lives.

From the late nineteenth century, a nascent women's press added to the number of female authors addressing polemics by discussing topics such as the domestic sciences, history, and literature and advancing the cause of women's education. In Anatolia, the first women's journal *Terraki* (Progress) was established in 1868. In Egypt, *al-Fatah* (The Young Woman) was first published in 1879. In Iran, *Danesh* (Knowledge) appeared in 1910. Journals like these provided women with an arena in which to write, and to add their voices to the debates that preoccupied men of the era, as women took up the topics of veiling and polygamy and offered their own interpretations of the roots of such traditions. While women also used the press to champion nationalism and to suggest—as had men—that reformed households would form the bedrock of new nations, their discussions of home life were as informative as they were symbolic, providing women with the opportunity to increase their knowledge as educated subjects and individual consumers in addition to promoting nationalist causes (Russell, 2004).

Skills acquired in the harem allowed elite women in Anatolia, Egypt, and Persia at the turn of the twentieth century to fund and run charitable organizations, aimed at providing women of the lower economic classes with literacy, vocational skills, and medical care (Marsot, 1978). Zeynab Anis founded the Society for Compassion for Children in Cairo in 1908, and directed the group in its fund-raising activities. In Tehran, sixty female activists joined efforts to establish the Anjoman (Council) of the Ladies of the Homeland. Among the group's concerns were adult education and the support of orphanages. In the era leading up to World War I, a dozen women's organizations were founded in Anatolia. During that war, writer and activist Halide Edip Adivar used one such group to promote the reform and reorganization of mosque schools for the poor.

Women's organizations also promoted the interests of their memberships. The Iranian Women's Freedom Society, founded in 1906, concerned itself with the inferior position of women in Iran. In Istanbul in 1908, Halide Edip opened an organization in support of women's suffrage and linked the association to British suffragettes and to a local prosuffrage men's group, the Society for the Defense of Women's Rights. That same year, Fatima Rashid opened the Society for the Advancement of Women in Cairo in order to promote the recognition of women's rights in Islam (Baron, 1994).

While male intellectuals of the period encouraged women to contribute to nationalism from the home, women in the early decades of the twentieth century took to the streets in demonstrations in support of constitutionalism and in nationalist uprisings against foreign occupation. Women in these demonstrations acted not as symbolic constructs of domesticity and motherhood, but rather as determined subjects. During Iran's 1906–1911 Constitutional Revolution, women repeated a role that they had played a decade earlier when they participated in the 1891 revolt against a British monopoly on tobacco in their country. Between 1906 and 1911, Iranian women organized and facilitated strikes and boycotts of foreign goods, formed human barriers to keep state troops away from male demonstrators, and contributed funds to help open a national bank (Afary, 1996). The Anjoman of the Ladies of the Homeland led boycotts against foreign companies and their commodities; in 1907, members of the group visited men's teahouses to encourage patrons not to use imported sugar in their tea (Afary, 1996).

In 1919, Egyptian women of all classes joined in the organized boycotts and demonstrations against continued British presence. The 1919 Revolution resulted in a semi-independent Egyptian nation. Peasant women burned fields and engaged in other acts of sabotage designed to make Egypt ungovernable. Urban women boycotted British goods and took to the streets in protest of Great Britain. During the revolution, elite women formed the Wafdist Women's Central Committee (WWCC) to support the Wafd Party. The members of the WWCC used their substantial organizational skills to raise money, and organize and participate in demonstrations. Later, when the Wafd Party's requests for inclusion in the post–World War I peace conferences led to their exile from Egypt, women acted as their stand-ins. The WWCC served in a similar capacity once the Wafd was allowed to negotiate Egypt's partial independence in Paris. Women of all classes were therefore a substantial presence in the revolution, risking their lives and challenging social conventions in order to secure Egypt's independence.

In 1919, elite Ottoman women participated in the successful efforts of nationalists to drive foreign troops out of Anatolia. Mustafa Kemal (later known as Atatürk) encouraged women to join the military and women of all classes did so, volunteering as nurses and factory workers. Elite women joined with Halide Edip to form the Anatolian Women's Organization for Patriotic Defense, the branches of which extended all over Anatolia and helped to mobilize women's efforts. After the establishment of independent Turkey, Edip translated her wartime experiences into involvement in Atatürk's campaigns to promote his vision of Turkish identity (D'Amico and Beckman, 1995).

In Iraq in 1920, women participated in uprisings against the establishment of the British Mandate, helping to support the independence movement in both urban and rural areas. Women's support was headed by Na'ima Sultan Hamuda, wife of the patriarch of a powerful local family. In addition to participating in street demonstrations in Baghdad, she and other elite women contributed to the uprising by donating their money and jewelry

(Efrati, 2004). They also sought political interventions through Gertrude Bell who, as Britain's Oriental secretary, played an intermediary role between Iraqis and the British. In the countryside, women carried weapons and accompanied male combatants.

Women's commitment to and participation in revolutions and independence movements set several important precedents in the modern Middle East. The most immediate was the translation of women's experiences in rebellions into effective, well-organized women's movements. Over the course of the twentieth century, those women's organizations both supported and challenged nation-states and national causes, promoting the interests of women as individual citizens—workers, wives, and mothers—rather than as symbols of national agendas. Women's movements often supported causes that were similar to state feminisms (e.g., education, health care, and employment). Women's efforts have also challenged state agendas by promoting causes that fell outside of the state's definition of "feminist." Women's movements have also challenged the state by aiding women who fall outside of the state's reach; and by insisting on suffrage, varying forms of gender equality, and legal reforms.

The 1920s were a crucial stage in the establishment of women's movements. In Egypt, the elite women who had been prominent in the 1919 Revolution as members of the WWCC established the Egyptian Feminist Union (EFU). Hoda Sha'rawi, Nabawiyya Musa, and Ceza Nabarawi organized and mobilized other elite women to promote and provide women's education and health care, and to campaign for suffrage and for women's legal equality. In Iraq, the wives of several prominent intellectuals and political leaders formed the Women's Awakening Club. Like their Egyptian counterparts, members of the club promoted women's rights to education and enfranchisement.

In both countries, independence struggles allowed women legitimate access to the public realm where their efforts were linked to the national cause. Women were shut out of politics in both countries after independence, however. Therefore, women's organizations focused their attention on providing services that the emerging Iraqi and Egyptian states often failed to make available to all citizens. By providing education, health care, and vocational training, women effectively performed state-like functions. While women's activities in both countries would later be eclipsed by regimes advancing platforms for women, the efforts of organized women's movements were nonetheless successful in tipping the state's hands in the direction of greater reforms for women. In Egypt, Doriyya Shafik worked both to include the working and middle classes in the growing women's movement and to confront the state in favor of enfranchising women. The increasingly confrontational efforts of Shafik and her fellow Daughters of the Nile organization members ultimately pushed Nasser to extend suffrage to women (Nelson, 1996). In Iraq, Naziha al-Dulaymi and the large Iraqi Women's League led a tireless campaign for Iraqi women's legal rights. That campaign bore fruit in Qasim's reform of Iraq's Personal Status Code in 1959 (al-Ali, 2012:95–96).

Since the 1980s Egypt has witnessed the emergence of women's movements of various orientations, including ever-widening circles of women who argue for Islamic forms of feminism. While women's movements with religious orientations square off against secularists over definitions of feminism and over the nature of women's rights, they each draw on a common legacy of providing services for urban and rural women who were increasingly impoverished by the neoliberal economic policies of the Sadat and Mubarak eras. Women's movements have been joined by local civil society organizations, labor and professional organizations, and international NGOs to continue to push for gender parity (however they choose to define it) and to provide services and training for the needy. In the years since the 1995 Beijing Declaration and Platform of Action for Women's Rights and Participation and the UN's subsequent release of its Gender and Development Index and Gender Empowerment Measure, women in Egypt and elsewhere have had units of measure to help them articulate their demands and gauge their successes (Arenfeldt and al-Hassan-Golley, 2012:20–21).

Turkish women used their experiences in political parties over the 1960s and 1970s to form women's organizations in the 1980s, seeking to

Protesting violence against women.

translate the gratitude of their mothers' generations to the Kemalist emancipation into liberation movements of their own design. Women also drew on the experiences of feminists from the 1920s, such as Nizihe Muhittin whose Turkish Women's Union was ultimately shut down by Kemalist state feminism. The 1980s feminist movements, like other civil society organizations that flourished over the course of that decade, established democratic models for the promotion of gender equality and women's increased access to the public sphere (Tekeli, 1995). Over the 1980s, secular feminists were persistent in their assertions that women's rights are more important than state definitions of women's realms and that women are individuals outside of the family unit. In 1986, for example, women from Istanbul and Ankara united to petition the government to comply fully with the UN Convention on the Elimination of All Forms of Discrimination Against Women (CADAW), which it had first promoted in 1979. Women's periodicals flourished over the course of the 1980s, and universities opened centers for women's studies. In 1990, the Turkish prime ministry established a department specifically designed to improve the rights and status of women. In 2001, the efforts of women's organizations joined with pressure from outside Turkey to influence the TGNA in favor of amending the 1926 Legal Code. Indeed, the slogan of many women's organizations in that campaign was: "Democracy in the Family means Democracy in Society" (Y. Arat, 2010:241).

The secular Turkish feminists of the 1980s have been joined in recent decades by an emerging Islamic feminism movement and by women supporting Kurdish nationalism, both of which raised concerns about the limited interests of secular feminism. Beginning in the mid-1990s, Kurdish women established feminist organizations that provide services and support networks. The women who promote Islamic feminism are typically educated university graduates, whose activism has revived turn-of-the-twentieth-century debates about the nature of modernity and modernization, the role of religion in politics, the place of women in the home, and the importance of veiling. They have produced feminist readings of the Quran, and have worked against the use of Quranic verses to discriminate against women. The *tesettür* (new veiling) that is practiced by many of these women is viewed as a challenge to Turkish secularism. For the women who practice it, veiling is a kind of self-modernizing process in which they use their own terms, and not the state's, to define modernity (Iyasoğlu, 1998). Kurdish feminists point to two forms of exploitation: patriarchy within the Kurdish movement and Kemalist ideology, neither of which promote their rights as Kurdish women (Diner and Toktaş, 2010:48). While religious, secularist, and Kurdish feminisms are not always in lockstep with one another over their goals, they are united in support of women's right to work and to women's independent activity.

In Iran in the 1960s, the WOI was still under state supervision. But a new generation of feminists had taken leadership roles in the organization and used its apparatus to push for reforms for women, especially legal equality. The group lobbied the government, provided services for women of all classes (including literacy classes and vocational training), and expanded the organization's base among the working and lower classes. The organization's centers provided family planning and day care. The group organized talks, radio programs, and seminars designed to promote the extension of women's rights and legal protections. The WOI presented the government with a National Plan of Action in 1978, representing women's demands for total equality (Esfandiari, 1997:32–34).

While women's movements emerged during the Iranian Revolution, they were forced to cease operations during the militarist atmosphere of the Iran-Iraq War. In the 1990s, the women's magazine *Zanan,* founded by the self-identified Muslim feminist Shahla Sherkat, served as an arena in which Iranian women could articulate various feminist agendas. The government shut down the magazine in 2008. Because the Islamic Republic's constitution created laws that subordinated and discriminated against women, the legal field has been an important avenue for women's rights, and lawyers of both sexes have worked to reestablish gender equality. Women have established nongovernmental organizations (NGOs) to continue advocating for women's rights, often framed in the context of civil or human rights. The 2003 Nobel Peace Prize winner Sherin Ebadi, for example, founded the Society for Protecting the Rights of the Child in 1994 and the Center for Defenders of Human Rights in 2001. Ebadi has been joined by a host of other lawyers who work for Iranian women's rights within a global, human rights framework (Tohidi, 2010:380–381). Outside of the legal field, NGOs have been a vital arena through which women have maintained a presence in the public realm, often providing services reminiscent of earlier stages of Iranian feminism. The cultural arts, particularly film and literature, have also been important vehicles for maintaining the visibility of feminist agendas.

While the General Federation of Iraqi Women was part of the Baath Party, women nonetheless used the organization to lobby the state for further reforms such as continued changes to Iraq's Personal Status Laws. The General Federation also collaborated with the state in providing education and vocational training to women in both urban and rural settings (Joseph, 1991). Semiautonomy in Iraq's Kurdistan allowed Kurdish women to establish civil society associations and to be active in politics. In the early 1990s, Kurdish women established the Independent Women's Organization, which took up campaigns against domestic violence and honor killings (al-Ali, 2012:99–102).

After the US invasion in 2003, women's organizations in central and southern Iraq worked together to provide the functions of a state: health care, education, housing, vocational training, social services, and humanitarian relief. The Organization of Women's Freedom in Iraq has taken a lead role in mobilizing against attempts by various political parties to replace Iraq's secular Personal Status Laws with laws dictated by religion. The organization has also worked to keep religion out of Iraq's political realm. Women's groups have worked to exert their influence over the shape of Iraq's constitution, demanding, and achieving, quotas for women in parliament. Activist Shanez Rashid said: "We had an equal share of pain and we need an equal share of peace" (al-Ali and Pratt, 2009:126). Kurdish women's organizations providing services and advocacy have proliferated since 2003 (al-Ali, 2012). The country's descent into chaos has made women's access to the public realm increasingly difficult. Lawlessness and violence against women persists, particularly against those women who seek a place for themselves in the public realm (al-Ali, 2012:103–106).

A second precedent set by women's participation in early-twentieth-century nationalist movements and uprisings has been women's use of the public realm to confront and resist the state. In the 1930s and 1940s, Egyptian women joined in demonstrations against the monarchy, and against the lingering presence of British troops in their country. On the eve of the July revolution of 1952, such participation took the form of street skirmishes against British troops in the Suez Canal Zone. In the 1970s, women were active participants in demonstrations against Sadat's policies, both for women and for the nation in general. Physician and activist Nawwal al-Sa'adawi challenged patriarchal systems and the Sadat administration's inattention to women's health issues with her work on the physical and psychological problems facing women in their families and in the public realm. As discussed in Chapter 13, her prolific writings attempted to address women's sexuality and challenged patriarchal systems and beliefs. Ultimately, her outspokenness on these issues led to her dismissal as Egypt's director of public health. Nonetheless, she succeeded in raising awareness of women's sexuality and of the damages caused by practices such as female genital cutting. Appearing in 1985 the Committee for the Defense of the Rights of Women and the Family succeeded, in limited measure, in challenging Mubarak's temporary rescinding of Sadat's reformed Personal Status Laws (Badran, 2009).

Women were active participants in labor strikes and street demonstrations against the Mubarak regime in the years leading up to the January 25th Revolution of 2011. Asmaa Mahfouz posted the video blog that helped mobilize participation in initial demonstrations, and hundreds of thousands of unnamed women from across Egypt's spectrum of political orientations and social classes took to the streets. Samira Ibrahim squared off against the Supreme Council of Armed Forces (SCAF), then in control of Egypt's body politic, over the military's use of virginity tests on the women it arrested during the uprisings. In the months following Mubarak's resignation, women were critical in organizing the strikes that pressured the SCAF to allow for elections and to oversee Egypt's full transition to democratic rule. The small number of seats (8 of 508 or 2 percent) that women took in the new parliament has led observers both in and outside of Egypt to draw parallels between Egyptian women's experience in 2011 and that of 1919. Current president Mohammad Mursi's decision to appoint Cairo University professor of political science Pakinam al-Sharkawi as one of his four aides nonetheless attests to women's crucial role in the uprising. Women have worked consistently to ensure that the committees currently drafting Egypt's new constitution protect women's rights outside of the conjugal family unit (Doss, 2012).

In Iran, movements against the shah brought women back into activism and rebellion. By the late 1960s and early 1970s the shah's reforms had certainly improved the lives of women across classes, providing educational and economic opportunities to many, bringing women into high-ranking political positions, and producing a vast array of female professionals. For many women, the shah's reforms were therefore tolerable. For many others, male and female, professional advancement without political freedom became increasingly unbearable. In the mid-1960s two clandestine opposition

Anne PaqActivestills.org

Women across the Middle East participate in political demonstrations, including in the highly conservative states of Iran and Saudi Arabia. Here, young Palestinian women protest in honor of the death of Mustafa Tamimi.

currents emerged in Iran, both of which attracted women: Marxists, including the Iranian People's Fedayeen Guerrillas (OPIFG), and the People's Mojahedin Organization of Iran (PMOI). The PMOI espoused the egalitarian treatment of women within Islam and therefore was appealing to a variety of women. When both groups began their armed resistance to the shah in the late 1960s, women defied social conventions in order to continue their participation. Women frequently played a support role, providing logistical and financial assistance. When the shah's secret police arrested OPIFG and PMOI leaders, women staged nationwide demonstrations in protest. As 1978 brought increased demonstrations against the shah, women joined men in the streets. Women also organized and participated in strikes, distributed leaflets, and helped build barricades (Paidar, 1995). Regardless of their political background, the women who participated in the demonstrations leading up to the shah's abdication and to the establishment of the Islamic Republic in 1979 certainly believed that regime change would bring them increased political rights. While the OPIFG, PMOI, and Khomeini were silent or vague about the role of women's issues in the revolution, women seized the opportunity to expand their freedoms (Esfandiari, 1997:38).

Since the 1990s the women who are visible in all arenas of Iranian life have been working to end gender inequality, often through active rebellion. In 1997, for example, thousands of women stormed Tehran's soccer stadium in celebration of the national team's qualification for the 1998 World Cup and in protest of sex segregation. Women's continued practice of breaking into stadiums led to the brief overturning of the ban against women entering stadiums in 2006. In July 1998, women participated in the massive uprisings that began at Tehran University and spread to Iran's major cities, first in protest against state censorship of reformist periodicals and, later, against state brutality. Women took an active role in support of Green Movement candidate and former prime minister (r. 1981–1989) Mir-Hussein Mousavi Khameneh in the June 2009 elections. In the lead-up to the elections, Mousavi's wife, Zahra Rahnavard, gave public speeches in favor of gender equality and coalitions of feminists pressed for his election. Women participated in the demonstrations following Ahmadinejad's contested victory. Neda Agha-Soltan, the twenty-six-year-old demonstrator who was shot and killed during the demonstrations, became a worldwide icon of the Iranians' ongoing struggle for democracy.

In Iraq, Kurdish women have participated in the Kurdish national movement, serving both as support crew to the Pesh Mergas (fighters) and as fighters themselves (al-Ali, 2012:101). In Turkey many Kurdish women have joined the Kurdistan Workers Party (PKK), which has been fighting the Turkish state an autonomous Kurdistan and for increased cultural and political rights since 1984. In Istanbul in 1987, the first street demonstration since the 1980 coup was organized by women to protest domestic violence (Tekeli, 1995:14). Turkish women regularly demonstrate against the ban against the hijab and in protest of government indifference to violence against women. In the summer of 2012, women took to the streets to protest the AKP's move to ban abortions.

Women have also used clothing as a means of challenging state agendas and protesting debates waged both by secularists and Islamists about the relationship between women's attire and the body politic. In the 1920s and 1930s, the elite women at the helm of women's movements removed their veils in nations like Egypt and Iraq, where there were no state-mandated laws regarding veiling, to signal a break from traditions such as the harem. For such women unveiling also meant a departure from the discourses that had defined them as wives and mothers of new nations and heralded their contributions as citizens. More recently women have used clothing to resist secular Western notions of modernity, and have chosen new forms of veiling as a means of advancing a modernity defined by Islamic rather than Western traditions. Turkish women who practice *tesettür*, for example, are like their counterparts in Egypt who veil or who take part in the growing piety movement, signaling forms of women's empowerment that fall outside of Western definitions of feminism (Göle, 1996). Since 2010, Iran's morality police have once again cracked down on what they deem "bad hijab": women using uncovered hair and makeup as a means of flouting the Islamic Republic's mandated veiling policies (Naghibi, 1999). In Egypt, young veiled women also have begun "downveiling," using less concealing and less conservative forms of dress to contest attempts by the political elite to control their behavior (Herrera, 2012). In each case, women use clothing as a means of contesting state-driven political agendas and defining their own subjectivities.

Conclusion

Over the course of more than a century, women's roles in the Middle East have been defined by imagination, debate, symbolism, state reforms, and women's efforts and activism. Women have been used by men and women seeking to shape new societies and define place, ethnicity, nation, and modernity. Reformers have used women's roles as housewives, mothers, and workers to embody the aspirations of emerging nations. Women's behavior, dress, and professional horizons have been shaped and circumscribed by male politicians seeking to define new states, and to advance those states' interests. As such, women have frequently been stand-ins for the political arenas where they have struggled to be participants. The efforts of several generations of female activists—writers, doctors, professionals, organizers—have frequently advanced state goals. Those women's efforts have also worked against state definitions of women's "place" and women's "position," however, and have succeeded in carving out alternatives to state agendas. Indeed, over the twentieth century the Egyptian, Turkish, Iranian, and Iraqi states produced classes of women who both promoted state platforms for women and contested those platforms for themselves and others.

As a result of reform and activism, women in modern Turkey, Iran, Iraq, and Egypt continue to defy the Western imagination. The George W. Bush administration (r. 2001–2009), for example, linked the 2003 invasion of Iraq with rescuing Iraqi women, whom he referred to as "women of cover" (al-Ali and Pratt, 2009). Americans who watched events in Iraq unfold in the media came to equate Iraqi women with the abaya of the post-2003 era and remained largely ignorant of those women's contributions to the postinvasion social and political order. While Western media rightfully report the Iranian state's recent curtailing of women's rights, they fail to portray women's achievements in education, political participation, social mobilization, human rights activism, and the cultural arts. During the 2011 revolution in Egypt, the West applauded what Egyptians already knew: that women had been active participants in revolts and uprisings for almost a century. Western audiences, while comfortable with arguments about the rights of Turkish women not to veil, are surprised to learn that women make arguments in favor of veiling as well, claiming the right to self-definition both at home and in the public realm.

Women have been active participants in all of the Arab uprisings.
These Tunisian women are celebrating on the occasion of
Tunisia's first free elections in the fall of 2011.

Understanding the role of women at this nexus of symbolism, state building, and activism helps students and scholars to understand the multiplicity of ways that women have contributed to the modern Middle East. Each aspect of the woman question covered in this chapter offers avenues for understanding Middle Eastern women as objects of intrigue, targets of state reform, and champions of women's rights and subjectivities. In each case, women have played an integral role in the development of what we think of as the modern Middle East.

Notes

1. *Mulla Naser al-Din,* March 31, 1907 (cited in Afary, 1996:illustrations insert).
2. *Kalem,* May 5, 1910 (cited in Brummett, 1998:36–37).
3. *Al-Lata'if al-Musawwara,* August 2, 1920 (cited in Pollard, 2005:191).

Bibliography

Afary, Janet. 1996. *The Iranian Constitutional Revolution, 1906–1911.* New York: Columbia University Press.
Ahmed, Leila. 1995. *Women, Gender and Islam: Historical Roots of a Modern Debate.* New Haven: Yale University Press.
al-Ali, Nadje Sadig. 2007. *Iraqi Women: Untold Stories from 1948 to the Present.* London: Zed Books.
———. 2012. "The Iraqi Women's Movement: Past and Contemporary Perspectives." Pp. 93–110 in Pernille Arenfeldt and Nawar al-Hassan-Golley (eds.), *Mapping Arab Women's Movements: A Century of Transformation from Within.* Cairo: American University of Cairo Press.
al-Ali, Nadje Sadig, and Nicola Pratt. 2009. *What Kind of Liberation: Women and the Occupation of Iraq.* Berkeley: University of California Press.
Amin, Camron Michael. 2003. *The Making of the Modern Iranian Woman: Gender, State Policy and Popular Culture, 1865–1946.* Gainesville: University Press of Florida.
Arat, Yesim. 2010. "Women's Rights and Islam in Turkish Politics: The Civil Code." *Middle East Journal* 64, no. 2:235–251.
Arat, Zehra F. 1998. "Introduction: Politics of Representation and Identity." Pp. 1–36 in Zehra F. Arat (ed.), *Deconstructing Images of "The Turkish Woman."* New York: St. Martin's Press.
Arenfeldt, Pernille, and Nawar al-Hassan-Golley (eds). 2012. *Mapping Arab Women's Movements.* Cairo: American University of Cairo Press.
Badran, Margot. 2009. *Feminism in Islam: Secular and Religious Convergences.* Oxford: One World Press.
Baron, Beth. 1994. *The Woman's Awakening in Egypt: Culture, Society and the Press.* New Haven: Yale University Press.
———. 2005. *Egypt as a Woman: Nationalism, Gender and Politics.* Berkeley: University of California Press.
Bier, Laura. 2011. *Revolutionary Womanhood: Feminists, Modernity and the State in Nasser's Egypt.* Stanford: Stanford University Press.
Booth, Marilyn. 2001. *May Her Likes Be Multiplied: Biography and Gender Politics in Egypt.* Berkeley: University of California Press.

Boyle, Clara Asch. 1965. *Boyle of Cairo: A Diplomatist's Adventures in the Middle East.* London: Titus Wilson & Son.

Brummett, Palmira. 1998. "New Woman and Old Nag: Images of Women in the Ottoman Cartoon Space." Pp. 13–58 in Fatma Müge Göçek (ed.), *Political Cartoons in the Middle East.* Princeton: Marcus Wiener.

Cleveland, William. 2004. *A History of the Modern Middle East.* 3rd ed. Boulder: Westview Press.

Cuno, Kenneth. 2008. "Divorce and the Fate of the Family in Modern Egypt." Pp. 196–216 in Kathryn M. Yount and Hoda Rashad (eds.), *Family in the Middle East: Ideational Change in Egypt, Iran and Tunisia.* London: Routledge Press.

D'Amico, Francine, and Peter R. Beckman. 1995. *Women in World Politics: An Introduction.* Westport, CT: Bergin and Garvey.

Diner, Cagla, and Şhule Toktaş. 2010. "Waves of Feminism in Turkey: Kemalist, Islamist and Kurdish Women's Movements in an Era of Globalization." *Journal of Balkan and Near East Studies* 12, no. 1:41–57.

Doss, Leyla. 2012. October 5. "Constitution Draft Raises Concerns About Women's Rights." *Egypt Independent,* p. 1.

Efrati, Nora. 2004. "The Other Awakening in Iraq: The Women's Movement in the First Half of the Twentieth Century." *British Journal of Middle East Studies* 31, no. 2:153–173.

Esfandiari, Haleh. 1997. *Reconstructed Lives: Women and Iran's Islamic Revolution.* Baltimore: Johns Hopkins Press.

———. 2012. "Iran Curtails Female Education." In Robyn Wright (ed.), *The Iran Primer.* Washington, DC: United States Institute of Peace. http://iranprimer.usip.org.

Farouk-Sluglett, Marion. 1993. "Liberation or Repression: Pan-Arab Nationalism and the Women's Movement in Iraq." Pp. 52–72 in Derek Hopwood, Habib Ishow, and Thomas Kosinowski (eds.), *Iraq: Power and Society.* Oxford: Ithaca Press.

Fay, Mary Ann. 2012. *Unveiling the Harem: Eite Women and the Paradox of Secular Exclusion in Eighteenth Century Cairo.* New York: Syracuse University Press.

Fleming, Katherine. 1998. "Women as Preservers of the Past." Pp. 127–138 in Zehra F. Arat (ed.), *Deconstructing Images of the Turkish Woman.* New York: St. Martin's Press.

Göle, Nilüfer. 1996. *The Forbidden Modern: Civilization and Veiling.* Ann Arbor: University of Michigan Press.

Hatem, Mervat. 1992. "Economic and Political Liberation in Egypt and the Demise of State Feminism." *International Journal of Middle East Studies* 24, no. 2:231–251.

Heath, Jennifer. 2008. *The Veil: Women Writers on Its History, Lore and Politics.* Berkeley: University of California Press.

Herrera, Linda. 2012. "Downveiling: Gender and the Contest over Culture in Cairo." Pp. 265–271 in Jeannie Sowers and Chris Toensing (eds.), *The Journey to Tahrir: Revolution, Protest and Social Change in Egypt.* London: Virgo Press.

Ishom-Verhareen, Christine. 2006. "Royal French Women in the Ottoman Sultans' Harem: The Political Use of Fabricated Accounts from the Sixteenth Through the 21st Century." *Journal of World History* 17, no. 2:159–196.

Iyasoğlu, Aynur. 1998. "Islamist Women in Turkey: Their Identity and Self-Image." Pp. 241–262 in Zehra F. Arat (ed.), *Deconstructing Images of "The Turkish Woman."* New York: St. Martin's Press.

Joseph, Suad. 1991. "Elite Strategies for State Building: Women, Family, Religion and the State in Iraq and Lebanon." Pp. 176–200 in Denise Kandiyoti (ed.), *Women, Islam and the State*. Philadelphia: Temple University Press.

Kahf, Mohja. 1999. *Western Representations of Muslim Women: From Termagant to Odalisque*. Austin: University of Texas Press.

Keddie, Nikki R. 2007. *Women in the Middle East: Past and Present*. Princeton: Princeton University Press.

Marsot, Afaf. 1978. "The Revolutionary Gentlewoman." Pp. 261–276 in Louis Beck and Nikki Keddie (eds.), *Women in the Muslim World*. Cambridge: Harvard University Press.

Melman, Billie. 1995. *Women's Orients: English Women and the Middle East, 1718–1918: Sexuality, Religion and Work*. Ann Arbor: University of Michigan Press.

Naghibi, Nima. 1999. "Bad Feminist or Bad *Hejabi*? Moving Outside the *Hejab* Debate." *Interventions: International Journal of Postcolonial Studies* 1, no. 4:555–571.

Nelson, Cynthia. 1996. *Doria Shafik, Egyptian Feminist: A Woman Apart*. Gainesville: University Press of Florida.

Paidar, Parvin. 1995. *Women and the Political Process in Twentieth-Century Iran*. Cambridge: Cambridge University Press.

Pierce, Leslie. 1993. The Imperial Harem. New York: Oxford University Press.

Pollard, Lisa. 2005. *Nurturing the Nation: The Family Politics of Modernizing, Colonizing and Liberating Egypt, 1805–1923*. Berkeley: University of California Press.

al-Radi, Nuha. 1998. *Baghdad Diaries: A Woman's Account of War and Exile*. New York: Vintage Press.

Rassam, Amal. 1992. "Revolution with the Revolution? Women and the State in Iraq." Pp. 88–99 in Tim Niblock (ed.), *Iraq: The Contemporary State*. London: St. Martin's Press.

Russell, Mona L. 2004. *Creating the New Egyptian Woman: Consumerism, Education and National Identity*. New York: Palgrave Press.

Sullivan, Earl L. 1986. *Women in Egyptian Public Life*. Syracuse: Syracuse University Press.

Tekeli, Sirin. 1995. *Women in Modern Turkish Society: A Reader*. London: Zed Books.

Tohidi, Nayreh. 2010. "The Women's Movement and Feminism in Iran: A Global Perspective." Pp. 375–414 in Amrita Basu (ed.), *Women's Movements in the Global Era: The Power of Local Feminisms*. Boulder: Westview Press.

Van Renen, Denys. 2011. "Montagu's Letters from the Levant: Contesting the Borders of European Selfhood." *Journal for Early Modern Cultural Studies* 11, no. 2:19–34.

White, Jenny B. 2003. "State Feminism, Modernization and the Turkish Republican Woman." *National Women's Studies Association Journal* 15, no. 3:145–159.

12

Religion and Politics in the Middle East

Jillian Schwedler

The Middle East is home to the three major monotheistic religions—Judaism, Christianity, and Islam—and several minor ones. Much of the politics of the region, from the Arab-Israeli conflict to the Iranian Revolution to the emergence of extremist groups such as al-Qaeda, has been viewed by those inside and outside of the region as driven by religious conflict. Yet the politics of the region have never been exclusively about religion, even when religious rhetoric and symbolism have been invoked. In some of the Arab uprisings, such as in Tunisia, Egypt, Yemen, and Libya, religion seemed to be almost irrelevant as Muslims of diverse sects protested together, sometimes alongside atheists and Christians. In Syria, religious sectarianism appeared to play a larger role. In Bahrain, the regime sought to portray the uprising as sectarian—Shiʻa seeking to topple a Sunni regime—ignoring the reality that many protesters were also Sunni. Even when religion is invoked in the region's politics, we should take pause to examine whether what is happening is really about religion.

Politics at its heart is about power, and political actors of every ilk bring their own understandings of the causes of injustice and the appropriate means for political change. In the Middle East, many of these visions are explicitly religious in orientation. However, Western countries have also seen a resurgence of political debate around religion, from its appropriate place in national politics to the growing number of religious revivalist movements. In this regard, the politics of the Middle East is not necessarily any more about religion than are politics in Western countries. Furthermore, the role of religion is not only about the use of religious symbolism in political conflicts or the ways in which regimes and their challengers claim legitimacy based on religious authority. Religion is also a central part of daily

life in every Middle Eastern country, informing the ways in which most ordinary citizens understand politics as well as their own place in the world.

In this chapter I provide a brief background to the major religions in
the Middle East and the resurgence of politicized religion, from the establishment of the Jewish state of Israel to the popular revolution in Iran that
led to the creation of an Islamic state there. Next, I focus on the two main
categories of politicized religious activism, both of which believe that religious communities must conform more closely to their religious values.
The first group, moderate religious activists, make up the vast majority of
politicized religious groups and engage in formal political processes to realize gradual political, social, and economic reforms; the second group, religious extremists, seek to rapidly overthrow the existing political order,
through the use of violence if necessary. Though far fewer in number, extremists have left their mark on regional as well as global politics. Finally, I
examine the role of religious groups during and after the Arab uprisings,
exploring possible trajectories as long-time opposition groups find themselves holding powerful and elected government offices.

The Historical Role of Religion in the Middle East

The Middle East is the birthplace of the world's three Abrahamic religions:
Judaism, Christianity, and Islam. Arthur Goldschmidt examines the emergence of these religions and the conflicts between them in greater detail in
Chapter 3. I provide in this chapter an overview of each and then focus on
contemporary issues of religion and politics, including the role and experiences of the followers of minority religious communities.

Judaism

The first of the three great monotheistic religions is Judaism, which is more
than 4,000 years old. According to Hebrew tradition, Moses led the Jewish
people, with God's guidance, out of their slavery in Egypt and brought them
to the Holy Land to establish a kingdom of God (around 1450–1250 BCE).
Christians and Muslims share this vision of Judaism's origins, as each recognizes its faith as part of the same religious lineage (Judaism to Christianity
to Islam) and believes in the same God. God revealed to Moses the first five
books of the Hebrew Bible, called the Torah, which together with the Talmud (a secondary text that includes interpretations of Jewish law, the ha-
lakha, and the Torah) is the basic source of religious principles for the Jewish faith. As a people, Jews might best be described as a religious-racial
community, one that carefully guards its communal identity (Cavendish,
1980:133–170) and emphasizes marriage and procreation from within the
community more than conversion (although conversion is possible).

In 70 CE, Jews were forced out of Jerusalem and Judea by the Romans who also destroyed the Second Temple, which had been built on the site of Solomon's Temple (the First Temple). Exiled Jews settled in many directions and maintained a strong identity not only of a single community, but also of one that would one day reunite. In the Diaspora, they maintained their religious practices and rituals, sustaining their identity through close-knit communities. In Europe they lived under (largely) Christian persecution for the next 2,000 years, although they enjoyed some degree of tolerance in parts of the Muslim world, even flourishing as a religious community during the Islamic age in Spain (Cavendish, 1980:165).

In the late nineteenth and early twentieth centuries, increased violence and discrimination against Jews in Europe led to the emergence of a Jewish nationalist movement—Zionism—that aimed to establish a Jewish homeland and possibly even a Jewish state on the lands of historic Israel. Thousands of Zionists emigrated to Palestine over the next fifty years, sometimes living in peace with the indigenous Christian and Muslim Palestinians, and sometimes clashing, particularly over the control of land. Chapters 3, 4, 5, and 6 examine these events in greater detail. The Jewish State of Israel was formally established in 1948.

Many of the first Zionists were secular and even Marxist in orientation, viewing Judaism as an identity and Zionism as a means for this religious-racial community to live on the land to which they felt strong historical connections. This perspective continues to characterize the political left in Israel today, which views the Israeli state more as a protector of the Jewish community rather than as a strictly religious state. On the religious right, Zionism is viewed as an effort to realize God's intention that the Jewish people should establish a kingdom of God on that specific land. For them, the State of Israel is a religious state, one whose role is not only to protect the community but also to ensure that its Jewish citizens adhere closely to the Torah and Talmud in all aspects of life.

Today, Judaism has some 14 million adherents worldwide. In the contemporary Middle East, most Jews live in Israel, although small communities remain in Iran, Iraq, Syria, Yemen, Tunisia, and Morocco. The Jewish population in the United States is larger than that of Israel by about a million.

Christianity

Christianity is the largest religion in the world, with 2.3 billion followers. It finds its roots in the teachings of Jesus of Nazareth, a Jew whose later followers came to believe he was also the Messiah and the son of God. Jesus was born in Bethlehem and crucified by the Romans in Jerusalem some thirty-two years later. Christianity initially spread through the Mediterranean, but today has large communities of followers on every continent.

Like Judaism, Christianity has an intimate history with politics. Jews (and, thus, early Christians) were exiled from Jerusalem in 70 CE by the Romans, migrating primarily to lands along the eastern Mediterranean, though often remaining under the repressive authority of Roman administrators. Christianity spread rapidly over the next 300 years, gradually gaining acceptance, as demonstrated by Constantine I's declaration of Christianity as an officially tolerated religion in 333 CE; by 380, the edict of Theodosius I declared Christianity the official religion of the Roman Empire. Christianity continued to thrive in Europe following the Islamic conquest of the Middle East beginning in the seventh century, though Christian communities remained active throughout the Muslim world. By the twelfth century, Christianity was deeply intertwined with European politics through the papacy. Under Pope Innocent III (pope from 1198 to 1216), the papacy controlled vast territories and exercised extraordinary social control—for example, over familial practices, marriage, education, and the legitimacy of political leaders. The power of the papacy declined over the next decades as kings, emperors, and the papacy struggled over power and authority. The relationship of Christian authority to European regimes changed forever with the Protestant Reformation (1500–1650), though the numbers of faithful themselves continued to grow.

The period before the Reformation also marked the concerted efforts of European leaders to shape Middle East politics in the name of religion. The Crusades were not a single campaign, but nine major European military invasions into the region from the eleventh to thirteenth centuries. In 1096, Christian armies responded to Pope Urban II's call to reestablish a kingdom of God in the Holy Land. Their early successes were followed by numerous defeats. Following the 1099 capture of Jerusalem, the invading army formally pardoned those who surrendered, then continued to massacre all remaining Muslim survivors, including women and children (Runciman, 1992). They converted al-Aqsa Mosque and the Dome of the Rock, the third holiest site in Islam (both built on the Haram al-Sharif/Temple Mount, also the historic site of the First and Second Jewish temples), into churches. Saladin recaptured Jerusalem in 1187, and a subsequent putsch by Richard the Lion-Hearted of England to recapture the city did not even reach the city walls. The last Crusader stronghold in the Holy Land, in Acre, fell to Muslim control in 1291.

Foreign Christian intervention in the Middle East returned in great strength during the European colonial period. In addition to direct political intervention by the governments of the predominantly Christian countries of Britain and France, colonialism brought Christian missionaries, with the strongest presence in lands closest to the Mediterranean. As detailed in Chapters 3, 4, and 5, Britain and France divided much of the region into new political units, often installing regimes sympathetic to colonial rule.

Krak des Chevaliers, a Crusader castle in Syria, was damaged in the civil war that began in March 2011 as part of the Arab uprisings. This photo was taken prior to that time.

Christian missionaries, enjoying the support of the colonial power and their emissaries in the region, opened schools, publishing houses, and hospitals, and proselytized Muslims at every opportunity. As John Esposito argues, given this historical connection of Christianity and colonialism, it is not surprising that many independence struggles against colonial powers in the Middle East were fought in the name of religion (1999). Outside of the region, Christians were among the strongest supporters of the creation of the State of Israel; revivalist Christian movements continue to support Israel today as well as advocate for the rights of Christian minorities throughout the region.

Today, Christians make up significant populations in Lebanon and the West Bank and Gaza, and have smaller communities in Iran, Iraq, Jordan, Syria, and Egypt. These include Copts, Maronites, Greek Orthodox, Greek Catholic, Armenians, and Chaldean Catholics. The number of Christians (and, particularly, Catholics) in the Middle East has significantly increased in recent decades as a result of the presence of large numbers of foreign workers, including laborers and domestic workers.

Islam

The third of the Abrahamic faiths is Islam, founded in the early seventh century when Muhammad of Mecca (570–632 CE) received the last revelations of God (in 610 CE) via the angel Gabriel. Muhammad was ordered to spread a simple message: that there is only one God (in Arabic, Allah), and no other god is worthy of worship. This message was the same as that revealed to Abraham, Moses, and Jesus, among other prophets, except that Muhammad was to be the final prophet, delivering God's last set of instructions to humankind. A follower of the Islamic faith is called a *Muslim,* meaning one who submits (to the will of God).

From the outset, Islam gained followers not only for the simplicity and clarity of its message, but because it declared—in contrast to centuries of Christian political domination in Europe—that individual believers (Muslims) had no intermediaries between themselves and God. Following Muhammad's hijra (emigration) from Mecca in 622 CE, the first Muslims recaptured Mecca against much stronger armies, a success that facilitated the first of many large-scale conversions to Islam by demonstrating that God was on Muhammad's side. Jews and Christians were declared to be protected *dhimmi* (religious communities) and were (at least officially) not to be targets of conversion, though voluntary conversion was welcome. In practice, of course, Jews and Christians often experienced discrimination, but at times they prospered under Muslim rulers' relatively more tolerant environment (particularly for Jews) as compared to Europe. Because literacy is so central to Islam, Muslim leaders supported the creation of numerous centers of higher education—one of the oldest universities in the world is Al-Azhar University in Cairo, still a major center of Sunni learning. Early Muslim scholars were also responsible for preserving the classic texts and histories of the Greek and Roman periods, and for reintroducing them to Europe during the Middle Ages.

There are several divisions within the larger Muslim *umma* (global community), though Muslims view these differences with varying degrees of importance. The most significant divide came early in Islam's history when, following the death of Muhammad, there emerged a dispute over authority within the community. The majority view—what has come to be called the orthodox view by that virtue alone—was that authority should be shared and that a new leader, to the extent one is needed, should be selected from among the community. The followers of this view are called Sunni Muslims. The alternative view is that authority should have passed to a direct blood descendant of Muhammad, and to his nephew, Ali, in particular. These followers or partisans of Ali are the Shi'a, sometimes called Shiites. Shi'a are today located throughout the Middle East but have significant communities (and sometimes majorities) in Iraq, Bahrain, Saudi Arabia, Lebanon, Yemen, Syria, Turkey, and Iran.

For all Muslims the basic text of Islam is the Quran (*recitation*) and, unlike the Hebrew and Christian bibles, it is believed to be the literal word of God as conveyed to Muhammad through the angel Gabriel. The Quran and the Sunna—the hadith (sayings and doings) of the Prophet Muhammad—together provide all the guidance a Muslim needs in life. The Quran and the Sunna together form the basis of sharia. *Sharia,* meaning the path or the road, is conventionally translated into English as *Islamic law,* but is more akin to a set of guiding principles derived from the Quran and the Sunna. Within Sunni Islam, there are four main schools of interpreting sharia. Individual Muslims may choose to follow any school they find most compelling, but a central tenet of Islam is that individual believers must make their own choices, drawing guidance from scholars who study sharia, but ultimately being responsible for making their own decision. Islamic scholars of sharia (the ulama) are often asked by followers to issue a fatwa (opinion) on a particular topic. Many have personal followings, but their opinions and interpretations are never binding on either their followers or indeed Muslims anywhere. A Muslim must listen to the reasoned and educated opinions of others and then make one's own choice.

The Islamic conquest spread quickly throughout the Arab world and beyond; by the sixteenth century, three great empires were Islamic: the Turkic Ottoman (which dominated the Arab world), the Safavid in Iran, and the Mogul on the Indian subcontinent. While Muslim rulers gradually lost control of the far reaches of these empires—Muslim Andalusia in southern Spain was lost in 1492—the Islamic faith is today the world's fastest-growing religion, with its 1.65 billion adherents.

The Experiences of Religious Minorities

Muslims make up a majority of the population in all of the countries of the Middle East except for Israel, so all of the Christian communities (and all the Jewish ones outside of Israel) are minorities in a numerical sense. How minority religious communities are treated varies considerably in practice. Most Arab Jews emigrated from Iraq, Iran, Syria, Yemen, Morocco, and Tunisia to Israel in the decades before and after 1948. Jews of Arab or African origin—called Sephardim or, more recently, Mizrachim, meaning "Orientals"—have often experienced discrimination within Israel (Shohat, 1988). The tiny Jewish communities that remain in Iran, Iraq, Yemen, Morocco, Tunisia, and Syria are tolerated, often in a manner similar to Christian communities.

Islam formally protects all Abrahamic communities, and Jews and Christians are protected under sharia: they are permitted to practice their faith and are not subject to proselytizing. In Iran, the elected national assembly even provides for representation of religious minorities: 5 seats (of 290) include 1 for Jews, 1 for Zoroastrians, 1 for Chaldean and Assyrian Catholics, and 2 for Armenian Christians. Jordan's parliament reserves 12 seats (of 150) for religious minorities: 9 for Christians (who make up some

5–7 percent of the population) and 3 for minority Muslim communities (2 for Circassians and 1 for Chechans). In Egypt, Coptic Christians make up some 10 percent of the population.

Although sharia clearly mandates the protection of Jewish and Christian communities, in practice they are frequently the subject of discrimination and even outright attacks. In Egypt, Islamist extremists operating illegal organizations have targeted Coptic Christians and their communities, attacking their churches and businesses.

Lebanon presents a more unique situation, as various Christian sects made up half of the population as recently as the mid–twentieth century. The bloody fifteen-year civil war, which formally ended in 1989 with the signing of the Taif Accords, saw internecine fighting as religious and ethnic communities formed their own militias under the leadership of warlords. The war was characterized by at least as much intra-Christian violence as Christian-Muslim violence (but, interestingly, no incidence of Sunni-Shi'i violence). The agreement that formally ended the fighting provided for a parliament with seats equally divided between Christians and Muslims, even though by that time Muslims were estimated to make up as much as two-thirds of the population. The 128-seat sectarian parliament provides a given number of seats dedicated to each religious sect: Sunnis (27 seats), Shi'a (27 seats), Alawites (2 seats), and Druze (8 seats) on the Muslim side; and Maronites (34 seats), Armenians (6 seats), Greek Orthodox (14 seats), Greek Catholic (6 seats), and other Christians (4 seats) (Norton and Schwedler, 1994:52). Sectarian conflict continues in Lebanon, though it is not always clear to what extent the fighting has to do with religious differences and to

A mural of Jesus in Beirut.

what extent it reflects power struggles between leaders who happen to belong to different religious and ethnic communities.

Sudan is another country long marked by bloody conflict between a sizable Christian community in the south and the Arab and Muslim government of the north. Between 1990 and 2005, more than 2 million Sudanese were killed in the civil war, which was formally ended by truce in 2005. The south then enjoyed autonomous rule until it finally achieved independence in 2011 following a referendum that gained 98.8 percent of the vote. The majority of the population in South Sudan is Christian, along with 18 percent Muslims and numerous smaller communities of traditional indigenous religions.

Christians and Jews are not the only minority religions in the Middle East. Iran is ethnically diverse but predominantly Muslim, though it provides formal protection and representation for Jews and Christians as well as Zoroastrians, a small community that believes in the sanctity of all aspects of the natural world. Followers of the Bahai faith, by comparison, have been subject to extreme persecution. The faith was founded by Baha'ullah in nineteenth-century Persia (Iran) and emphasizes the unity of mankind. Because its followers—who today number some 6 million worldwide—view Baha'ullah as the latest (but not final) messenger of the Abrahamic faiths, they are viewed as heretical by Muslims who view Muhammad as the last of the prophets.

Indeed, many divides among Muslims effectively create minority religious communities, particularly sects that are considered heretical. Another minority Muslim community is the Druze, based primarily in Lebanon, Syria, Jordan, and Israel, which numbers fewer than a million followers worldwide. Their beliefs developed as an offshoot of the Ismaili Shi'a, but theologically draw on neo-Platonic philosophies and non-Abrahamic traditions. The Alawites are another minority Shi'i sect, numbering some 3 million, who (like the Druze) are considered heretical even by most Shi'a; in Syria, Alawites have held power for some forty years, though they frame their rule around Baathism's mix of socialism and Islam and not around their particular Alawi beliefs. Currently, their rule is being challenged in the civil war that began in 2011 as part of the Arab uprisings. In Saddam Hussein's Iraq, Shi'a constituted a clear majority but were excluded from power; since 2003 they have made steady gains in power, though they remain somewhat divided. In Bahrain, the majority Shi'i population gained political representation when the state became a constitutional monarchy in 2002, though they remain subject to ongoing repression by the ruling al-Khalifah family, which is Sunni. The Shi'i majority was a significant force in the Pearl Revolution in Bahrain that also began as part of the Arab uprisings, but Sunni citizens were also significant participants. The Bahraini regime has portrayed the uprising as sectarian rather than political, gaining support from Saudi Arabia and other Sunni Gulf states to violently repress the uprising. As of this writing, the Bahraini protests have diminished but have not been entirely crushed.

Religion and States

Most countries in the Middle East could be defined as religious in the sense of defining a formal place for religion. What this means in practice, however, varies dramatically from formal religious states (Saudi Arabia, Israel, and Iran) that prioritize the full application of religious law in all political, social, and economic matters, to the more nominally religious states, whether the ruling elite claim authority based on direct descent from the bloodline of the Prophet Muhammad such as Jordan, Morocco, Saudi Arabia, Bahrain, and Kuwait, or whether the constitution provides a formal status for Islam as the official religion and the president to be a Muslim such as Egypt, Yemen, Syria, prewar Iraq, Libya, Algeria, Oman, and Tunisia.

Many regimes in the Middle East claim their legitimacy at least in part based on religion. We think of Saudi Arabia, postrevolutionary Iran, Mauritania, and Sudan as Islamic states, and Israel as a Jewish state, but religion is actually written into the constitutions of most states in the Middle East. This is an important indicator of the centrality of religious values in the region, though it says little about the relationship of religion and politics in practice. Many of the challengers to the existing authoritarian regimes criticize the political elite for not living up to their claims to be guided by the values of their religion.

The Jewish Israeli State and the Symbolism of Jerusalem

In the late nineteenth century, Jewish activist Theodor Herzl (1860–1904) led the Zionist movement in its quest to establish a Jewish homeland. Zionism spread among Jews throughout Europe, particularly after the first Zionist conference was held in 1897. When the Ottoman Empire was dismantled after World War I, Britain gained control of most of Palestine and was convinced by European Zionists to draw up the Balfour Declaration. This 1917 document, which was accepted by the League of Nations, called for the establishment of a Jewish state in Palestine. Hundreds of thousands of Jews migrated to Palestine, largely from Europe but also from Arab countries. The UN passed a resolution in 1947 that divided Palestine and called for the creation of the State of Israel. In the months before May 15, 1948, when the British Mandate over Palestine was set to expire, Zionists and Arabs in Palestine fought a bloody civil war that drove many Palestinians into exile. Israel declared independence on May 15, forming a modern nation-state with an overtly religious identity.

The question of Israel as a Jewish state cannot be divorced from struggles over the sovereignty of Jerusalem, a city not only claimed by both Israelis and Palestinians as their capital, but by all three Abrahamic religions as historically and symbolically central to their faiths. The status of the city is contested under international law, and the Israeli claim of Jerusalem as its capital is not recognized by most nations. For Jews, the Mishnah (a second-century compendium of Jewish laws) states that the Western Wall is the site of continuous divine presence (*scechina*) (Breger, 1996). This area was the site of King Solomon's Temple and the Second Temple, the latter of which was destroyed in 70 CE by the Romans. The annual Passover ceremonies conclude each year with Jews worldwide reiterating the prophetic idea that Jewish exiles will eventually return to the ancestral land: "Next Year in Jerusalem."

With the establishment of Israel in 1948, Jerusalem was divided, with the Jewish quarters under Israeli control and the eastern quarters (including the Western Wall and the site of the Haram al-Sharif/Temple Mount) under Jordanian control. Israelis and Jews worldwide celebrated the reunification of the city when Israel recaptured the eastern quarters in the 1967 Six Day War.

For Christians, too, Jerusalem is a city of tremendous symbolic significance. Christianity originated in Jerusalem, where Jesus preached, died, and was resurrected. The central goal of the Crusades was the recovery of Jerusalem by Christian armies in order to establish a (Christian) kingdom of God there. Millions of Christians make pilgrimages to holy sites in Jerusalem each year as well as to other holy sites in the West Bank (notably Bethlehem and Nazareth) and Jordan (notably the baptismal site on the East Bank of the Jordan River).

Jerusalem is the third holiest place in Islam, after Mecca and Medina (in present-day Saudi Arabia). The Prophet Muhammad is believed to have ascended to heaven, the *miraj haqq,* from the site of the rock on the Haram al-Sharif where Abraham was willing to sacrifice his son Isaac to God.

A young Orthodox Jew praying at the Western Wall in Jerusalem.

(Jews built the First and Second temples on the site for the same reason, where early Jewish priests practiced sacrifices to God.) Muslims also believe that the end of time will begin in Jerusalem. The loss of Jerusalem from Muslim control to Jewish control in the twentieth century is viewed by many Muslims as a dire warning from God to renew and deepen their faith. Indeed, many Islamic revival groups view the success of foreign powers in colonizing and dominating Muslims' lands as a result of the widespread loss of faith among Muslims. Only by returning to the fundamental teachings of their faith, they argue, can Muslim peoples ever hope to gain dignity and control over their destinies.

The establishment of a Jewish state has thus been monumental not only for being the first popularly driven attempt to create a modern religious nation-state in the region, but also because that success has come at great symbolic and material loss for the followers of other faiths, most notably Muslim and Christian Palestinians.

Strongly Islamic States

Israel was not the first religious state created in the modern Middle East. Putting aside centuries-old dynasties that claim authority to rule based on religious legitimacy, the Middle East has four states established in the twentieth century as religious: Saudi Arabia, Mauritania, Iran, and Sudan. Strongly religious states not only claim their legitimacy to rule on religious grounds, but also give religious leaders high levels of power and the authority to exercise control over governance. What this means in practice, as we shall see, varies dramatically.

The Kingdom of Saudi Arabia was established by the House of Saud in 1932 as an Islamic state. Although perhaps a marriage of convenience, the Saudi monarchy was formed through an alliance with a conservative Islamic revival movement, Wahhabism, which called for a return to the letter of the Quran. King Abdul Aziz ibn Saud had in fact swept to power with the support of bedouin and Islamic extremists, whose fearlessness and commitment to an Islamic vision led them to conquer village after village. Indeed, these early extremists, called the Muslim Brethen (no connection to the Muslim Brotherhood discussed below), were more zealous than Ibn Saud in terms of religion and the desire for political conquest. In 1929 Ibn Saud was forced to fight his own forces of Muslim Brethren in order to stop their continued conquest into lands controlled by the British. Despite Saudi Arabia's highly conservative brand of Islam, the United States has forged a close relation with the state since the 1940s (Vitalis, 2007).

The Iranian Revolution of 1978–1979 is conventionally understood as Islamic in character because of its symbolism and rhetoric. However, the

Islamic Republic was not fully established until more than a year after the fall of the shah in 1979: clerics initially vied with nationalists for control of the new state, with the former only gradually gaining dominance and implementing a strict interpretation and application of Islamic principles. But for more than a millennium, Iran (formerly Persia) had been under Islamic rule of one sort or another. Even in the twentieth century, the 1906 Constitutional Revolution had brought a new constitution that provided the clerical establishment a formal role in overseeing matters of state. That constitution was never fully realized in practice, but it formalized a relationship between the political elite (at that time, the Qajar dynasty) and the religious establishment that ceded decisions and power on religious matters to the latter. Unlike the Safavid dynasty before it, the Qajars did not claim authority to rule based on religious legitimacy, so their rule marked the separation of religious and political authority that was formalized in the 1906 Constitution. When Reza Khan seized control in 1921 and established the Pahlavi dynasty in 1926, the clerical establishment was marginalized but Islam remained the official state religion.

The 1979 revolution that brought down the regime of Mohammad Reza Pahlavi was realized only through a broad alliance of bazaar merchants, clerical elites, nationalists, intellectuals, feminists, students, and laborers, among others. But it took more than a year before the clerics, under the leadership of Ayatollah Ruhollah Khomeini, emerged triumphant against the nationalists and established the Islamic Republic of Iran. Clerics were given their full authority provided in the 1906 Constitution, wherein the Council of Guardians passes judgment on all political matters by declaring whether or not policies are in line with sharia. The Council of Guardians uses its power to exert extreme control over political, social, and economic matters, for example, by determining which candidates may stand for elections, what sorts of foreign investment are permissible, how citizens may dress, and even whether they may use contraceptives.

One of the stated goals of the early Islamic Republic was to export the revolution: to encourage and indeed support Muslims in other countries to rise up against their regimes and establish Islamic states in their wake. This objective was an overwhelming failure, although the impact of this policy (which was largely pushed to the back burner following the death of Khomeini in 1989) continues to be felt in terms of the support Iran provides to a few Islamist groups, notably Hizbullah in Lebanon. One country that did become Islamic in the wake of the Iranian Revolution was Sudan. Then-president Jaafar Nimeiri declared Sudan to be an Islamic state in 1983 and called for the full implementation of sharia (Voll, 1991). As already noted, largely Christian South Sudan gained full independence in 2011, but is not officially a religious state.

A mosque in Esphahan, Iran.

Nominally Islamic States

Most states in the Middle East accord some formal status to religion, often stipulating Islam as the official religion. Turkey is the notable exception: when Mustafa Kemal (later Atatürk) established the modern state of Turkey in 1923, he advocated a program of forced secularism, dismantling religious courts, abolishing the caliphate, and outlawing religious dress. Most states in the region, however, embrace an Islamic identity. The monarchies and emirs of Jordan, Morocco, Kuwait, Bahrain, Oman, and the United Arab Emirates, like Saudi Arabia, all claim authority to rule based in part on their descent from the bloodline of the Prophet Muhammad's family. Jordan's King Hussein also called himself keeper of Islam's two holy places in Jerusalem (the Dome of the Rock and al-Aqsa Mosque, both on the Haram al-Sharif), a title that proved embarrassing when Jordan lost control of East Jerusalem to Israel in the 1967 Six Day War (Katz, 2004). The king of Morocco uses the title "Commander of the Faithful."

Many republics, too—such as Egypt, Yemen, Tunisia, Algeria, Syria, and Iraq—established Islam as the official state religion and sharia as a source of law and legislation. What this meant in practice varied considerably even prior to the Arab uprisings. Certainly the president must be a Muslim, and it is not unusual on high Muslim holidays or during times of domestic or regional turmoil to see television broadcasts of the president and other state officials prominently praying. During the Gulf War of 1990–1991, Hussein added the words "God is Great" to the Iraqi flag: although his religious credentials were thin, he perhaps thought that the phrase might win him greater support from other Muslim countries.

In Egypt, the office of mufti is filled by a prominent cleric from Al-Azhar University; his job is to provide a stamp of approval (or rejection) on state policies attesting to their adherence to sharia. Unlike Iran's Council of Guardians, this office is largely symbolic; nevertheless, the need for the regime of Hosni Mubarak to at least appear to conform to sharia underlined the power of Islamic symbolism in sustaining the state's authority to rule. As Egypt transitions into a post-Mubarak era, it remains unclear whether the mufti will remain as a rubber stamp position or will gain more power— if the position is retained at all. The ulama from Al-Azhar University continue to function as a conservative (but not extremist) force in Egypt; they control the religious courts and provide imams (prayer leaders) to each of the country's tens of thousands of mosques. Religious parties explicitly outlawed under Mubarak were legalized after the revolution. As shown below, the long-established but formerly illegal Muslim Brotherhood has emerged in the post-Mubarak era as a powerful political party, although it faces challenges from even more conservative Islamist groups that entered the political scene after the revolution.

Overall, the vast majority of states in the Middle East accord some official status to religion. Some regimes use religion to expand the perceived legitimacy of their rule while others maintain an official status for religion out of popular pressure. In the early 1970s, for example, Syrian president Hafez al-Assad tried to remove from the constitution the condition that the president be Muslim, but abandoned the aim due to societal pressure. Since the Arab uprisings, the role of Islam in the new regimes and constitutions has been a hotly debated issue and is likely to continue to be as a range of religious and nonreligious political actors struggle over what the new political institutions will look like.

Religious Activism

The contemporary Middle East has seen an expansion of religious revivalist groups, in part inspired by anticolonial struggles and the desire for cultural authenticity. Indigenous Jewish and Islamic revivalist movements have had the greatest impact, although Jewish and Christian movements based outside the Middle East have had their share of influence on the region. Much of the Arab world remained under Ottoman control by the late nineteenth century, although the farther reaches of the empire were gradually gaining local autonomy. For many parts of the Middle East, the spread of European colonialism meant the exchange of one foreign occupier (Ottoman Turks) for another. The lack of Arab autonomy was viewed as extremely humiliating, and it was in this context that a diverse range of independence movements

emerged. Two of the dominant narratives were Arab nationalism and Islamic revivalism; both offered means of imagining alternative political
arrangements in which Arabs would regain dignity through control of their
own destinies. Islamic revivalism took many forms, but a common theme
was that Muslim peoples had diverged too far from their faith, and a return
to the core values of their religion would restore the rightful dignity to the
community—along with political, social, and economic control of their
lives. Jewish religious revivalism took several forms, but was consistently
framed in relation to Zionism and the need to establish (and later defend)
the State of Israel.

In the broadest terms, religious revivalist movements seek to reform or
replace existing political structures and social practices with those viewed
as more in line with core religious values. The means by which this envisioned change is to be realized, however, varies considerably, from the political violence of extremist groups to the reformist measures of groups and
political parties who seek to enact change gradually, either by working
within the existing political structures or from below, through education
and socialization programs. All of these revivalist groups, whether Jewish,
Christian, or Islamic, are sometimes called *fundamentalist.* The term *fundamentalist* is not very illuminating, however, as it could be appropriately applied to any individual or group that seeks to return to the fundamental
teachings of one's faith. In practice, the term *fundamentalist* might be accurately applied to groups as diverse as Amish communities in the United
States, the Protestant Christians of Europe from whence the term came, and
al-Qaeda. With regard to the Middle East, the term *Islamic fundamentalism*
is not only applied to extremist groups such as al-Qaeda but also to groups
like the Muslim Brotherhood that seek peaceful reform and accept the authority of the existing regimes. Instead, in this chapter, two terms are used
to describe different trends within revivalist movements in the Middle East:
moderate religious activism, characterized by efforts to achieve gradual,
nonviolent reform by working within the existing political systems; and *religious extremism,* characterized by efforts to bring rapid change, often
through the use of political violence against regimes and sometimes civilians. In practice, the extremist moderate dichotomy does not imply that
moderate groups do not seek profound change in the long run: they may
strive for the full implementation of religious law in all areas of life, but reject the use of violence as a means to achieve it. At the same time, moder-
ates may hold views that others feel are extremist—for example, some
protodemocratic Islamic groups hold highly conservative views concerning
the appropriate role of women. In terms of understanding the diverse political roles of religious revivalist movements in the Middle East, however,
the categories of religious extremism and moderate religious activism provide better means of understanding trends than does the term *fundamentalism*

because they emphasize key differences in how these groups work to realize their religious agendas.

Moderate Religious Activism

Even prior to the Arab uprisings, most religious political activism in the Middle East was moderate rather than extremist. In fact, the region is flush with religious revivalist groups from all the Abrahamic faiths that advocate gradual reform, organize political parties (and strive for legal status), and cooperate with groups of divergent ideological orientation. In much of the region, for example, Islamic groups routinely cooperate with communists, socialists, liberals, Christians, and nationalists—practices that were largely unimaginable even fifteen years ago. Indeed, the range of religious activism is so diverse that this chapter could not hope to mention every group or examine every dimension of religion and politics. Instead, it illustrates the major trends and the broad trajectories that will characterize the next decade.

All Muslims view Islam as a whole way of life. Some believe that as long as one adheres to the spirit and values of the Quran and the hadith, a wide range of political systems, from socialism to liberal democracy to monarchy, are acceptable. Others believe in more radical political change and have a strict view of the appropriate application of sharia.

Many Islamist revival movements emerged in the Middle East and Pakistan, but one of the most important was the Muslim Brotherhood, founded in Egypt in 1928 by Hassan al-Banna. Al-Banna (1905–1949) was a school teacher who advocated a return to Islam's core values through reading and study groups and by working within existing political structures. The group was an early advocate of literacy programs for men as well as women, as it believes that truly Islamic society requires that all Muslims are able to read the Quran. Politically, the Muslim Brotherhood was alternately tolerated and targeted by the monarchies of the kings Fuad and Farouk. After a decade of confrontations with King Farouk's regime, al-Banna was assassinated by the police in 1949 with the full knowledge of the prime minister. The Muslim Brotherhood supported Gamal Abdul Nasser and the Free Officers Movement that overthrew the monarchy in 1952. When Nasser sought to consolidate his power, however, he viewed the Muslim Brotherhood as a primary threat and outlawed the organization in 1954, after accusing its members of attempting to assassinate him. From that period until Nasser's death in 1970, thousands of its members were jailed and many were executed (Mitchell, 1969).

The Muslim Brotherhood organization spread outside of Egypt as early as the 1930s. Branches were formed in Jordan, Syria, Yemen, Tunisia, Palestine, and Sudan, among other places; they were formally independent but retained close relations with the mother organization in Egypt, particularly during al-Banna's lifetime. The experience of the Muslim Brotherhood in Jordan contrasts starkly with that of Egypt. The Muslim Brotherhood gained its first followers in Jordan in the late 1930s, but the organization was not formalized until 1946, just after Jordan gained independence from Britain. From the beginning, the group had close relations with the monarchy: King Abdullah I inaugurated the group's headquarters in downtown Amman in 1946. For decades, the Muslim Brotherhood had a symbiotic relationship with the regime, supporting the monarchy against the various communist and socialist groups that challenged the regime in the 1950s and 1960s.

Although all branches of the Muslim Brotherhood have since 1948 placed the full liberation of Muslim Palestine among their primary objectives, the experiences of the group in Jordan are instructive. During the period 1948–1967, when Jordan ruled (and had formally annexed) the West Bank, including a portion of Jerusalem, the Jordanian and West Bank branches of the Muslim Brotherhood functioned together (Boulby, 1999). After Jordan lost control of the West Bank in the 1967 Six Day War, Palestinian militant groups—mostly leftists—began launching attacks and raids from bases in Jordan, on the East Bank of the Jordan River. King Abdullah sought to shut down these activities, culminating in months of bloody conflict in the summer and fall of 1970. What is significant about this period is that although the Muslim Brotherhood embraced the goal of liberating Palestine, in these events it sided with the monarchy against Palestinian militants. Muslim Brotherhood leaders in Jordan went on to hold prominent government positions as high as the cabinet level (Schwedler, 2006).

The Muslim Brotherhood branches in Egypt and Jordan had almost opposite experiences during the 1950s and 1960s. In both countries, the group advocated gradual reform by working within existing political structures: in Egypt by working with the republican regime and in Jordan with the monarchy. But while Nasser outlawed the group and imprisoned its members, King Hussein found in the Muslim Brotherhood ready allies against the threat from leftists and nationalists who were the real radicals of the period. Perhaps not surprisingly, many Jordanian leftists sought refuge in Egypt during this period while many Egyptian Muslim Brotherhood members fled to Jordan.

Following Nasser's death in 1970—and following his ignominious defeat during the 1967 Six Day War—new Egyptian president Anwar Sadat sought a changed relationship with the Muslim Brotherhood. Sadat had forged a friendship with al-Banna in the late 1930s, and he believed that the repression of the group was neither politically expedient nor morally defensible. While he undertook a period of economic opening, discussed in detail in Chapter 7, he also sought to improve relations with the Muslim Brotherhood and released hundreds of their numbers from prison. Since then, the group has sought to realize its reform agenda by working within the system: fielding candidates for the People's Assembly, opening health care clinics and schools, and participating actively in professional associations and labor unions (Wickham, 2002; Brown, 2012b). After Sadat's assassination by Islamic extremists in 1980, President Mubarak repeatedly refused to grant the Muslim Brotherhood formal legal status, despite the group's condemnation of Islamic militants in Egypt.

In Jordan, the Muslim Brotherhood has had legal status as a social organization since 1946, but this renders it ineligible to also register as a political party. With King Hussein's call for full elections in 1989—the assembly had been suspended in 1967—the group fielded candidates and, together with a handful of independent Islamists, won 40 percent of the assembly. In the early 1990s, it held five cabinet posts, though it was largely unsuccessful (and unpopular) for its efforts to implement reforms such as a ban on alcohol and a prohibition against fathers watching their daughters (and, thus, viewing other young girls) compete in athletic events. Nevertheless, the group remained committed to working within the political system and, when political parties were legalized in 1992, many of its prominent members joined forces with independent Islamists to form the Islamic Action Front (IAF). The IAF, now dominated by the Muslim Brotherhood, competes regularly in local and national elections and has forged strong relations with other opposition parties, including nationalists, communists, socialists, and liberals.

In Yemen, the Muslim Brotherhood has participated in elections as a segment of the legal Yemeni Congregation for Reform, or Islah party, since 1993. Though Muslim Brotherhood members are sometimes at odds with other trends within the Islah party, they strongly support pluralist politics and held numerous cabinet positions in the mid-1990s as a result of the party's success at the polls and its alliance with the ruling party, the General Popular Congress (GPC). With the defeat of the Yemeni Socialist Party during the 1994 civil war, the Islah party saw a decline in its political influence, as the ruling GPC of President Ali Abdullah Salih dominated the political field much the way the National Democratic Party did in Egypt. The Islah party has been a strong partner in the Joint Meetings Party (JMP), a bloc of secular as well as religious opposition parties, which emerged in the early 2000s. The JMP has played a formal role in Yemen's transition since the 2011 uprising, although as a part of the formal opposition it remains distant from much of the popular opposition mobilization on the street. Tuwakkal Karman, 2011 Nobel Peace Prize winner, was herself an Islah member who had been elected to that party's primary governing body, the Shura Council.

The experiences of the Muslim Brotherhood in Jordan, Yemen, and Egypt are in many ways typical of other Islamist groups—and not only branches of the Muslim Brotherhood—that seek to realize their reforms gradually and by working within the existing political systems. Some of these parties are outlawed (e.g., al-Nahda in Tunisia prior to the 2011 revolution), some function but do not have legal status (e.g., the Muslim Brotherood in Egypt prior to the 2011 revolution), and some are legal political parties (e.g., the Islah party in Yemen, Hizbullah in Lebanon, and the IAF in Jordan). Kuwait has multiple Islamist groups that hold seats in its parliament, and Islamist groups are active in parliamentary politics in Iraq, Turkey, Algeria, Sudan, and Morocco.

In addition to formal participation in elected national assemblies and local elections, moderate Islamic activist groups are also known for their provision of social services, particularly where state services are nowhere to be found. Hizbullah provided significant services in southern Lebanon during the civil war and after. Most moderate Islamist groups are engaged in literacy programs and schools, although the curriculum is carefully controlled. Some scholars have questioned the depth and effectiveness of these social programs, arguing that they are championed for public relations purposes but in practice are far less effective. One study shows that Muslim Brotherhood–run health clinics in Cairo are seldom staffed by a medical doctor (Clark, 2003). Nevertheless, these moderate Islamic activists constitute the majority of Islamic revivalist movements.

Religious Extremism

Extremist religious groups garner the most headlines even though they make up a small proportion of Islamic revivalist groups, and the impact of their activities can be profound. Extremists tend to emerge out of the most repressive contexts and aim to achieve political change not through gradual reform, but by directly attacking those in power. Their targets include foreign agents—foreign-owned businesses and tourists as well as troops and diplomats—and local regimes they believe to be illegitimate. The latter includes those imposed by colonial and imperial powers, such as Israel, as well as those regimes deemed to have abandoned Islamic values and teachings.

Of the thousands of Muslim Brotherhood members imprisoned in Egypt during the 1950s and 1960s, one was Sayyid Qutb (1906–1966), whose experiences of repression led him to abandon al-Banna's commitment to working with existing Muslim governments to realize change. In his *Milestones* (2007), he argues that Muslims are not, in fact, obligated to accept the legitimacy of the leadership of Muslim rulers—a common interpretation of sharia—if those leaders are not ruling in accord with Islam. Emancipation of Muslim communities must come through movement, he argues, rather than through works (teaching) alone. This position was radical because it justified attacking and overthrowing Muslim regimes. Qutb was executed in 1966 along with two others for allegedly plotting against

Nasser's regime; many view these charges as a set-up. The impact of his teachings and his death have been profound.

Qutb inspired the emergence of extremist groups throughout the Muslim world. Among the Muslim Brotherhood members that Sadat released from prison were a number of followers of Qutb who formed small groups that advocated the violent overthrow of the regime. These included the Islamic Group (Gama'a Islamiyyah) and Islamic Jihad (Jihad al-Islami). In 1981, Islamic Jihad member Khalid Islambuli assassinated Sadat, hoping that his death would spark an Islamic revolution in Egypt and the Arab world, following the one in Iran just two years earlier. No popular uprising emerged, however, and Islambuli and his co-conspirators were arrested. Islambuli was executed, but a number of others were exiled, including several who found refuge in Afghanistan and later joined al-Qaeda. In Egypt, the Islamic Group and Islamic Jihad regrouped and mounted a series of violent acts throughout the country, culminating in the 1997 massacre in the Valley of the Kings, which claimed the lives of four Egyptians and fifty-eight foreign tourists (along with six responsible for the attack). Jihad leaders already imprisoned at the time dissociated themselves from that attack, condemning it and formally disbanding their organization. Egypt has experienced little extremism since then, though the potential for a revival of religious extremism remains considerable as long as Egypt remains a repressive, nondemocratic state.

Egypt is not the only country to suffer from domestic Islamic extremism. Algeria experienced a virtual civil war by and among Islamist groups in the 1990s, but notably that bloodshed began after the Islamic Salvation Front (FIS) won parliamentary elections that the military quickly annulled. Yemen has seen violence by extremists against tourists and missionaries as well as against the holy shrines of minority Muslim groups and a former brewery in the south. Beginning in the 1970s, extremists from North Yemen assassinated hundreds of socialists from South Yemen; even after unification in the 1990s, attacks against socialists continued, particularly as the 1993 elections approached. Although these attacks subsided somewhat during the remainder of the 1990s, in 2002 the prominent socialist leader Jar Allah Umar was assassinated: he was shot point-blank as he left the stage after addressing an assembly of the Islamist Islah party's general membership.

Islamic extremism is not confined to domestic attacks; indeed, the acts of violence that have gained the most attention internationally are those that target Israel, US troops in the Middle East, and, of course, the attacks of September 11, 2001, on the Pentagon and World Trade Center in the United States. Palestinian militants have launched attacks on Israel since the 1960s, but it was not until the formation of Hamas in 1987 during the first intifada that Palestinian Islamic groups began using political violence. Hizbullah has also launched numerous attacks on Israeli troops and Israeli soil. Hamas and Hizbullah differ from many other militant Islamist groups, however, in that their attacks are aimed at ousting what they view as foreign troops illegally occupying their land. Both groups have participated in their own governments peacefully, campaigning in elections and winning free and fair elections.

Islamic extremists justify their use of violence as jihad, a legitimate use of force necessary to defend one's faith against threats. Conventional wisdom in the West holds that holy war is specific to Islam in the contemporary period, although it was famously waged by Christians during the Crusades. However, the idea of holy war also emerged early in Judaism and continues to have a strong influence in political affairs. All three Abrahamic religions view struggles to defend their religion as not only legitimate but required. In the Hebrew Bible, God (Yahweh) was always on the side of those who fought the enemies of Zion (Esposito, 1998). Muslims view the success of the Prophet Muhammad's early political campaigns in a similar light. Jews waged war against the Canaanites to gain control of the land they believe God had intended for them. Zionists view the capture of land from Arabs in 1947 and 1948 as akin to these early holy wars (Armstrong, 1991:7–12).

Many Islamist groups do invoke the concept of jihad as a justification for their political projects, particularly the use of overt force or political violence. Al-Qaeda is the most famous and active transnational extremist group, one that justifies attacking foreigners and civilians as responsible for the conditions that oppress Muslim peoples worldwide. While the activities of al-Qaeda represent an escalation of Islamic extremism in the scale of its tactics and the boundlessness of its targets, the movement has never enjoyed popular support within the Arab or Muslim world. Indeed, following the September 11 attacks, dozens of Muslim countries immediately expressed condolences to the citizens of the United States, and many Muslim communities organized candlelight vigils in neighborhoods and mosques in remembrance of the victims. While the extremism of groups like al-Qaeda is abhorrent in its targeting of innocents, it is crucial to remember that such fringe organizations are not the norm.

Islamist Groups Since the Arab Uprisings

The Arab uprisings that began in Tunisia in late 2010 have changed the equation for many Islamist groups by creating opportunities for meaningful participation in governing institutions (Wright, 2012). In Tunisia, the an-Nahda movement, while not a central player in the protests themselves, was quick to refashion itself with the return of its leader, Rachid Ghanouchi, who for decades had been exiled to London. A moderate revivalist group, an-Nahda had long espoused support for a democratic and liberal political system, but like all opposition had been outlawed by Zine Abidine Ben Ali. In Tunisia's first free elections for its Constituent Assembly (parliament) in October 2011, an-Nahda won 37 percent of the seats, the largest bloc, and party member Hamadi Jebali was appointed Tunisia's first postrevolution prime minister.

In Egypt, the Muslim Brotherhood was long the most important nongovernmental group in the country, able to mobilize thousands for (largely) peaceful protests against the regime's policies and the dominance of the National Democratic Party in national politics. Under Mubarak's regime it remained an illegal organization, although it frequently fielded "independent" candidates for the People's Assembly as well as in local elections. After years of winning few seats, during the 2005 elections it won eightyseven seats (nearly 19 percent of the assembly). During Egypt's January 25 Revolution in 2011, the Muslim Brotherhood did not emerge as a significant actor until the protests had reached revolutionary levels. In fact, the group had first instructed its followers to not join the protests at all. With Mubarak's resignation and the ensuing struggles over what the new Egypt would look like politically, the Muslim Brotherhood emerged as a major player (Brown, 2012a). This is not surprising given the group's decadeslong presence in communities and its institutional resources. It formed the Freedom and Justice Party (FJP) and won 47.2 percent of the seats in parliamentary elections held between November 2011 and January 2012. Although the group had previously declared that it would not field a candidate for president, it revised its position and in June 2012 Muslim Brotherhood member Mohammad Mursi won Egypt's first free presidential election.

Thus, in two states that saw regime change through popular uprisings, Islamist movements won the largest blocs in freely elected national assemblies and assumed the highest governing office (prime minister in Tunisia and president in Egypt). These events mark a sea change in the region. While moderate Islamists had gradually worked their way into power in Turkey, here were two cases in which old regimes had been replaced by Islamist revivalists through democratic elections. Other political parties also won seats and, in Tunisia in particular, an-Nahda worked with two center left parties to share the three highest offices (with the prime minister, the speaker of parliament, and president); Egypt's FJP has not sought to build a coalition with other, non-Islamist parties.

The success of Islamist parties after the uprisings is not surprising. In addition to possessing established constituencies, these groups presented stark alternatives to the corrupt regimes of Ben Ali and Mubarak. Islamists are often seen as highly moral and, owing to years suffering under severe state repression, unconnected to the old regime. The coming years will tell whether these new parties will adhere to their commitments to uphold democratic rule. In the meantime, they face the challenge of rebuilding crumbling economies and must contend with other strong political forces vying for power, such as Egypt's Supreme Council for the Armed Forces (SCAF), that have their own agendas and priorities for reform.

In addition to these moderate revivalist Islamists, Tunisia and Egypt have seen Salafi groups emerge onto the political scene since the uprisings. The term *Salafi* is a broad category of Islamist revivalists who seek to adhere closely to the practices and beliefs of the earliest Muslims, or *salaf* (ancestors or predecessors). Salafi groups exist across the region and are not a united or cohesive movement. In many states, such as Jordan, Salafi groups have long been quiescent: they constrain their activities largely to Islamic study and take no position on the legitimacy of the ruling regime. (Recently, a more jihadi Salifi movement has begun to attract a small following.) Following the uprisings in Tunisia and Egypt, however, some Salafi groups (but not others) altered this position and formed formal political parties to contest elections. In Tunisia, Salafi have openly criticized an-Nahda for cooperating with secular groups and for not moving to quickly implement sharia. In Egypt, the Salafi an-Nour party won 27.8 percent of the parliamentary votes in the November 2011–January 2012 contest. Since most of these groups have engaged with existing regimes even less than groups like the Muslim Brotherhood, they are perceived by many as entirely pure and uncorrupt. The future role of Salafi on the formal political scene will likely continue to range from formal political engagement to quiescence.

Conclusion

Religion plays a central role in Middle East politics, in part because political struggles have for centuries been understood as religious conflicts (e.g., the Crusades; colonialism's connection to Christian proselytizing; Western support for Israel; targeting of Muslims in the war on terror) and in part because of the intimate ties of the three Abrahamic faiths to the region. In this chapter I have sought to outline the major religions in the Middle East and the diverse ways in which states as well as opposition movements invoke religion in their political activities and view regional and global developments through religious lenses. The great diversity of religious experiences and practices are a core feature of the region, from whether minority religious communities enjoy inclusion or repression, to the ways in which states accept or reject religious political parties, to the diverse means of invoking religious symbols and rhetoric in expressions of dissent. Religion will undoubtedly continue to be a central component of politics in the Middle East for decades to come. But as some recent trends of inclusion and tolerance illustrate, that situation need not necessarily entail violence and contention.

Bibliography

Armstrong, Karen. 1991. *Holy War: The Crusades and the Impact on Today's World*. New York: Doubleday.

Boulby, Marion. 1999. *The Muslim Brotherhood and the Kings of Jordan, 1945–1993*. Atlanta: Scholar's Press.

Breger, Marshall. 1996. "Religion and Politics in Jerusalem." *Journal of International Affairs* 50, no. 1:91–118.

Brown, Nathan. 2012a. *When Victory Becomes an Option: Egypt's Muslim Brotherhood Confronts Success*. Washington, DC: Carnegie Endowment for International Peace. http://carnegieendowment.org.

———. 2012b. *When Victory Is Not an Option: Islamist Movements in Arab Politics*. Ithaca: Cornell University Press.

Cavendish, Richard. 1980. *The Great Religions*. New York: Arco Press.

Clark, Janine Astrid. 2003. *Faith Networks, Charity, and the Middle Class: Islamist Services in Egypt, Jordan, and Yemen*. Bloomington: Indiana University Press.

Esposito, John L. 1998. *Islam and Politics*. 4th ed. Syracuse: Syracuse University Press.

———. 1999. *The Islamic Threat: Myth or Reality?* 3rd ed. New York: Oxford University Press.

Katz, Kimberly. 2004. *Holy Places and National Spaces: Jerusalem Under Jordanian Control*. Austin: University of Texas Press.

Mitchell, Richard P. 1969. *The Society of the Muslim Brothers*. Oxford: Oxford University Press.

Norton, Augustus Richard, and Jillian Schwedler. 1994. "Swiss Soldiers, Ta'if Clocks, and Early Elections: Toward a Happy Ending?" Pp. 45–65 in Deirdre Collins (ed.), *Peace for Lebanon? From War to Reconstruction*. Boulder: Lynne Rienner.

Qutb, Seyyid. 2007. *Milestones*. Beirut: Dar al-Ilm.

Runciman, Steven. 1992. *The First Crusade*. Abridged ed. New York: Cambridge University Press.

Schwedler, Jillian. 2006. *Faith in Moderation: Islamist Parties in Jordan and Yemen*. New York: Cambridge University Press.

Shohat, Ella. 1988. "Sephardim in Israel: Zionism from the Standpoint of Its Jewish Victims." *Social Text* 19, no. 10:1–35.

Vitalis, Robert. 2007. *America's Kingdom: Mythmaking on the Saudi Oil Frontier*. Stanford: Stanford University Press.

Voll, John (ed.). 1991. *Sudan: State and Society in Crisis*. Bloomington: Indiana University Press.

Wickham, Carrie Rosefsky. 2002. *Mobilizing Islam: Religion, Activism, and Political Change in Egypt*. New York: Columbia University Press.

Wright, Robin. 2012. *The Islamists Are Coming*. Washington, DC: Woodrow Wilson Center Press. http://theislamistsarecoming.wilsoncenter.org.

13

Middle Eastern Literature

miriam cooke

In this chapter I discuss the emergence of literature in the Middle East as a new art form. European modernity hit the countries of the Middle East hard. Everything formerly accepted as normative came under question, and nothing more so than literature. Traditional notions of what literature was and what function it should fulfill in the life of the individual and society changed. No longer the repository for all knowledge, *adab* (literature) branched out into the various genres of drama, short story, novel, and a radically new conception of poetry.

It is not possible to understand the role of literature in the Middle East without first glancing at its history and, above all, its evolution during the first half of the twentieth century. Although Middle Eastern literatures have become privileged sites for recording and engaging with sociopolitical tensions and conflicts, this was not always the case. In the medieval and early modern periods, Middle Eastern literatures had been the preserve of the elite, providing them with literary frames in which they might elaborate an already familiar tradition and demonstrate formal skills and erudition. Popular literature such as *A Thousand and One Nights* also relied on the already known. Social commentary was generally downplayed.

European Colonialism and Its Discontents

The arrival in the late eighteenth and nineteenth centuries of the French and British colonial expeditions, with their technological, cultural, and intellectual institutions, forced a new look at society and culture. Contact with European modernity cast Islamic cultures in a poor contrastive light. Egyptians

403

in particular, because they were the first to experience French colonialism, became concerned to learn about Western culture and science.

Under such Ottoman governors as Muhammad Ali Pasha and his son Ibrahim Pasha, groups of male scholars traveled to Western Europe, particularly to France, to study scientific texts and to translate them into Arabic. Because of the enormity of the task, these scientific missions might stay in Europe for months on end. When they were not squirreled away in the libraries or archives, they were in the theaters watching plays by French playwrights like Jean-Baptiste Molière or in their rooms reading short stories in French by such writers as Guy de Maupassant or the Russian Anton Chekhov in French translation. The genre that was the newest and most intriguing was the novel, and these men returned with translations of European masterpieces by Honoré de Balzac, Gustave Flaubert, Leo Tolstoy, and Ivan Turgenev, to mention only a few.

Some of these intellectuals believed that the writing and function of literature in the Middle East had to change to accommodate the new realities in their lives. They knew, however, that those who were unfamiliar with the new genres of short story, novel, and play, and modern poetry might resist their introduction. The apparent focus of European fiction writers on entertainment at the expense of traditional education, or on sociopolitical critique rather than literariness, was greeted by some with the skepticism reserved for the introduction of anything new anywhere. Like the reactionary defenders of the Western canon, who in the 1980s announced the end of civilization as we know it if marginalized literatures were to replace some of the time-tested writings of dead white men, the conservative elites of the region warned of civilizational decline, even extinction. Some feared that the great classical literatures of the Arabs, Persians, and Turks might not survive the invasion into literature of the trivia of the modern world. Literary practitioners would surely lose their storehouse of classical knowledge if they did not continually tap into it, repeat it, and thus "renew" it. They would lose their verbal agility if they turned from the eloquent description of great events in history to the banality of the world around them. Others saw in the dialogue between their own cultural traditions and those of others the possibility of reimagining national identity within a common modernity.

Whether they were closed or open to the outside world, Middle Eastern intellectuals considered the question of language to be vital in the process of modernization. Some interrogated the boundary between the high-culture languages and the vernaculars while others considered the implications of importing foreign words. In Iran, historian Mohamad Tavakoli-Targhi explains, the key was to

> disassociate from the Islamic past and to project a "pure" national origin. Arabic words that had been part of the language for half a millennium

were purged, and "authentic" Persian terms were forged, and neologisms and lexicography were constituted as endeavors for "national reawakening." . . . The invention of an idealized past was contemporaneous with the restyling of language, which was achieved in a dialogic relationship with Iran's Arab-, European-, and (the often ignored) Indian-Other. . . . The Persian language was reconstituted as the essential component of Iranian national identity. (1990:77, 86).

Language reform "was not an aftereffect of the constitutional revolutions in Iran and the Ottoman Empire but a prelude to them. Purists constituted language as the essential component of the national identity" (Tavakoli-Targhi, 1990:91). History could not be reconceived without a radical transformation of the language and its grammar.

In the case of Turkish and Arabic, the linguistic situation was more extreme because of the distance between the written and the spoken languages. Indeed, in both cases there had emerged a kind of bilingualism. The written language of the Turks was so different from the spoken that it was even named differently: it was called Ottoman Turkish. Written in the Arabic script and filled with Persian and Arabic vocabulary—as much as 75 percent—this Ottoman Turkish had to be learned as an entirely distinct language with its own rules of grammar (Halman, 1982:36). The Westernization campaign of Mustafa Kemal (1881–1938, known as Atatürk after 1933), which attempted to erase Islamic elements in the language and introduced the Latin alphabet, put an end to the "bilingual" situation that had pertained in Turkey for centuries. Paradoxically, the poetry of the mystic Yunus Emre (d. ca. 1321), written before the Turks' importation of a foreign lexicon (partly as a result of their embracing Islam), is more accessible to Turks schooled in the post-Atatürk era than the literature they learned from their grandparents.

There has been no comparable revolution in the Arab world, and so the split between the classical and colloquial Arabic languages persists. The codification of the spoken language is still tentative because the Arabic of the Quran retains its place of honor as the literary medium of expression. Conservative Arab intellectuals feared that the use of colloquial expressions in literature, particularly since there was no consensus over the codification of the colloquial, might herald the demise of the scriptural language. To accept the many colloquial languages would create a Tower of Babel in which multiple, mutually incomprehensible local literatures would vie for a small spot on the grand stage of what had once been a unified literary tradition. The answer has been to create a modern standard Arabic used by the media and understood from the Atlantic Ocean to the Gulf.

Anxieties about language were compounded by the forcible introduction of colonial languages. Indeed, French had become the lingua franca among Middle Eastern intellectuals, even in countries like Turkey that had not experienced the European *mission civilisatrice* (civilizing mission). The positive aspect of linguistic colonialism was the opening up of European literature to Middle Eastern readers. French, English, and Russian writers of the day, including Gustave Flaubert and Guy de Maupassant, Charles Dickens, and Percy Bysshe Shelley, as well as Anton Pavlovich Chekhov, Ivan Sergeyevich Turgenev, and Leo Tolstoy in French translation, all provided models of how to represent current crises and concerns. Translations of nineteenth-century European literature into the languages of the Middle East were followed by literary experimentation. The Syrian-Lebanese Jurji Zaydan (1861–1914), for instance, wrote a series of historical novels and even a short autobiographical piece about his education during a time of major upheaval, having recognized in his experiences those of others.

Cultural Ferment at the Turn of the Twentieth Century

The literary hub of the Arab Middle East in the early twentieth century was Egypt. Intellectuals censored at home moved to Cairo. Literary salons convened men and sometimes even women to discuss the latest developments in politics and literature. At a time when most middle- and upper-class women were confined to their homes, these gatherings of intellectuals were almost the only places where women could appear with men. Literary schools in Egypt, such as the Diwan School, the New School, and the Apollo School (none of which included women among their numbers), encouraged the production of new kinds of writing that were then often published in their own journals and newspapers. These debates and their publication produced a new space, that of the public sphere. Discussions about national identity and the new roles women and men were expected to play in the future nation became matters concerning everyone and were no longer restricted to a small community of scholars, often religious scholars. In the process, new conceptions of literary criticism appeared.

The new critics' insistence on the centrality of the imagination in works of art and the need for the work to interact with and hopefully to change society influenced a new generation of critics and writers. The notion that criticism should not be descriptive, but rather investigative led to some radical critical writing. Taha Husayn (1889–1973), the Egyptian author of dozens of books, including novels, works of philosophy, and his own autobiography, titled *The Days* (1929), led the charge. In 1926 he published *On Pre-Islamic Poetry,* which calls into question the dating of some of this poetry. The book provoked a scandal because this poetry said to have been composed before the time of the Prophet Muhammad was considered to be the paragon of literary expression and, with the Quran, it was cherished as the perfect classical Arabic language that the Prophet spoke.

To cast doubt on its dating was to unsettle other certainties connected to the founding moment of Islam. New literary critical tools were opening up new ways of approaching old texts and, above all, they were revolutionizing literary production.

Simultaneous with this literary activity in Egypt, two revolutions broke out in Turkey and Iran. Young Turks and Iranians brought up on Enlightenment ideals rebelled against autocratic, self-indulgent rule by the last rulers of the Ottoman and Qajar empires. Between 1919 and 1922, Atatürk waged his war of independence against the British, French, Italians, and Greeks. The expulsion of these foreigners was followed by a series of revolutions that continued beyond the 1923 founding of the Turkish republic. Upon assuming national leadership, Atatürk abolished the Ottoman caliphate in 1924 and then implemented his secularization program. He introduced a new Europeanized dress code and declared illegal the wearing of Islamic dress such as the veil. As mentioned above, most traumatic for traditional litterateurs, in 1929 he replaced the Arabic-based Ottoman script with the Latin alphabet. Yakup Kadri Karaosmanoglu (1889–1974) is the writer who best encapsulates the mood of the times, which Talat Sait Halman describes as being marked by "the disintegration of Ottoman society, ferocious political enmities, and the immoral lives of religious sects, as well as the conflicts between urban intellectuals and poverty-stricken peasants" (1982:29). Karaosmanoglu presented the challenges facing cultural revolutionaries in his book *The Outsider*. It tells the paradigmatic story of an alienated bureaucrat in a rural outpost where the farmers remain indifferent to the cultural and nationalist revolution.

In 1905, Iran was rocked by its Constitutional Revolution. Nationalists confronted the British and local feudal landlords, demanded a constitution that would vouchsafe them democracy and justice, and eventually agreed on a compromise. The period was rich with new kinds of writing, most of it referred to as *pishru* (progressive). These liberal and often socialist writings depict the turmoil of the period and react against the social irrelevance of the Qajar writers. After his coup in 1921, Mohammad Reza Shah became absolute monarch of Iran. He introduced strict censorship and centralized control, but he also concerned himself with the position of women. In 1936, perhaps in response to Atatürk's recent prohibition on the wearing of the veil, the shah enforced unveiling. While some see this measure as helpful to women, others recognize in it yet another violence done to women in the name of progress. To force a woman to unveil if she is not ready to reveal her face is tantamount to asking her to strip publicly. Many writers have dealt with the topic.

Such legislation against veiling should be seen against the background of late-nineteenth-century debates about feminism that were going on throughout the Middle East and beyond. Claims on behalf of women's education were entering the public sphere. Research by feminist scholars both in the Middle East and elsewhere has revealed that it was women themselves who were the first to raise the issue of women's absence in decisionmaking positions at the national or local levels. Yet it was not until the men took up the "woman question" that it became a matter for common concern.

In 1899, the Egyptian reformer Qasim Amin (1865–1908) published his controversial book *The Liberation of Women,* in which he called for women's education, unveiling, and greater participation in the life of the nation. His emphasis on women as the gauge of a society's progress reflects James Mill's reference in 1817 to India's barbarity being demonstrated by the fact that "women were in a state of abject slavery." As employee of the East India Company, Mill clearly felt himself authorized to make such pronouncements. The Western, colonial origin of these ideas was not lost on the Middle Eastern intelligentsia.

It was not only in his native Egypt, but also throughout the Middle East that Amin's treatise was influential. In 1900, *The Liberation of Women* was partially translated into Persian. Its publication in Iran did not launch the kind of debate about the rights and roles of women that it had in Egypt because it fell on fallow ground (Najmabadi, 1998:100–104). In 1921, Mohammed Ali Jamalzadeh (1896–1997) brought out his first collection of stories, titled *Once upon a Time.* The collection is as famous for its introduction, which explains the new function of literature as a mirror for the times, as it is for its satirical descriptions of Shi'i scholars and sympathetic portrayals of the lives of ordinary women and men (Daragahi, 1984:104–123). The following year, Morteza Moshfeq Kazemi published his two-volume work *Horrible Teheran,* which takes up the cause of women by describing the numerous abuses they routinely suffer.

Atatürk may not have been directly influenced by the Middle Eastern debates surrounding the woman question, but his fascination with the West, where feminists were beginning to attract attention, had predisposed him to advocate women's rights. After coming to power, he gave them the vote. One of the women he supported was Halide Edip Adivar (1884–1964), an ardent revolutionary who was pictured during the occupation of Istanbul preceding the war of independence lecturing crowds of men even while veiled. Journalist, feminist activist, literary critic, and novelist, her 1926 autobiography describes her adventures with the nationalists, which included the experience of cross-dressing so as to be able to fight in the army with the Young Turks. Her best-known work is *The Clown and His Daughter,* which appeared first in English in 1935 and a year later in Turkish. Novels during this early Republican period became a tool in the fashioning of the new nation-state.

During this same period, the European Zionist movement was becoming active and some Jews emigrated from Europe to settle the land of Palestine.

Zionism at that time was primarily a socialist ideology owing more to Russian-inspired communism than to Judaism. As such, it looked much like the *missions civilisatrices* that the French and the British had been dispatching to the Middle East since the eighteenth century. These alarming developments in the region gave rise to fledgling Islam-inspired reform movements. Their members warned against unthinking Westernization and urged the relevance of Islam in the process of modernization.

The Short Story as a Literary Pioneer

First the short story and later the novel provided frames within which intellectuals could address the problems of their age. The short story, with its Middle Eastern precedents in folk literature such as *A Thousand and One Nights,* developed most rapidly as a local genre. It was well suited to the needs of writers with urgent sociopolitical messages. Quickly written and published often in literary magazines and newspapers, the short story became an important vehicle for socially engaged intellectuals.

Arabic Stories

It was in Egypt that the Arabic short story first took hold, and therefore its history there can be considered to be exemplary. Lawyers like Yahya Haqqi (1905–1991) and Tawfiq al-Hakim (1898–1987), who is better known for his drama, turned some of their cases into stories that became part of a general debate about modernization. Haqqi's "The First Lesson," published in 1926, is an example of naturalist criticism of the new that was often symbolized by the train. Preparing for his first day in school, the son of the station master of a remote milk train stop watches the Nubian station guard, a deeply spiritual man and his only friend, slip off the platform and roll under the wheels of the train. The tragedy does not disrupt the day's assignment: to write an essay on the advantages of the train. Twenty-seven years later, Haqqi returned to the theme of the destructiveness of the railway in his indictment of the 1952 Free Officers Movement. *Good Morning!* is a novel, the only one Haqqi wrote, that contrasts the fullness of life in a village before the introduction of the train with the pain and suffering they experience after the station is built.

Engineers and doctors also turned their professional experiences into the stuff of fiction. They made the lives of the urban and rural poor available and sometimes important for their mostly middle-class readers. Engineer Mahmud Tahir Lashin (1894–1954) wrote several stories about his professional visits to government offices, popular cafes, and villages. His 1929 story "Talk of the Village," which has been described as marking the maturation of the Arabic short story (Hafez, 1992:274), confronts an urban intellectual with the reality of the romanticized village. This is no utopia for women who may have to pay food bills with their bodies.

The most diverse and complex of early Arabic short story writers was Yusuf Idris (1927–1991). A doctor who had spent years practicing medicine before he turned to story writing, he brought his experience in the clinic to his creative work. His first collection of short stories, *The Cheapest Nights* (1954), deals with the customs and diseases of the peasants. The title story is a manifesto for family planning. After having searched in vain for affordable entertainment, a villager comes home to produce another mouth to feed! In "The Dregs of the City," Idris turns to the city to present a middle-class man preying on his servant, her theft of his watch, his humiliating recovery of the watch, and her consequent ejection to walk the streets as a prostitute. The storyline is not new; what is different and moving is the narration of inevitable destruction. In his many other collections of stories, as in his novels and plays, Idris examines the lives of his compatriots, dissecting those elements that lead people to destroy each other.

Several Arab women chose the short story. In 1929, Egyptian Suhayr Qalamawi published a collection of short stories titled *Grandmother's Tales*. The figure of the "grandmother" became popular as women sought models of feminine strength and stability in a patriarchal past. The piety of the grandmother was ambivalently presented: it could be a sign of blind faith and superstition or a trace of a time when there was security from outside forces threatening one's belief system.

Many women have followed in Qalamawi's steps, claiming that the short story suits a life in which domestic preoccupations prevent concentration on a protracted plot. Syrian Ulfat Idilbi (1912–2007) did not begin publishing until the early 1950s but she, too, dwelt on the problems women confront in a conservative society poised on the edge of change. Another Syrian, Ghada al-Samman (b. 1942), wrote a collection of stories under the title *Your Eyes Are My Destiny* (1961), in which she explored the possibilities for women in a male-dominated world.

One of the most famous—and notorious—short stories is "Spaceship of Tenderness to the Moon" (1964) by Lebanese Layla Baalbaki (b. 1936). An early morning moment in the life of a couple reveals their erotic love for each other and their conflict over the desire for a baby. A trial was held to assess whether or not the story was pornographic. Baalbaki was acquitted, but the controversy has entered the annals of twentieth-century Middle Eastern literature.

In most of these women's writings, the heroine is defeated by the struggle against patriarchy. Whether she gives in to a man or abandons him, the final decision brings no satisfaction. A single woman cannot successfully rebel when society is not ready to incorporate her into its fabric.

Iranian Stories

At the end of the nineteenth century, encyclopedist Ali Akbar Dehkhoda introduced the short story to Iranian readers with the publication of some satirical articles. However, it was Jamalzadeh who turned this journalistic precedent into a local literary genre with his 1921 introduction to *Once upon a Time*, described as "a manifesto for modernist Persian prose writing" (Moayyad, 1991:31). The stories in the collection provided Iranian intellectuals with a model of how to integrate this new genre into the repertoire of a transformed national literature.

The first Iranian to succeed in writing a fully developed short story in an accessible language was Sadeq Hedayat (1903–1951). Born into the Iranian nobility, he was educated in Paris where he was attracted to surrealism. His early work described Iran's great past whereas his later writings, which were influenced by European writers and particularly by Franz Kafka, were as dark and despairing as his life. He committed suicide in 1951. Hedayat wrote novels, critical essays, plays, and short stories that portrayed with sympathy the life of the destitute in Iran's cities. He also used colloquial expressions, but his goal was more political than artistic: literature needed to participate in the fight against tradition and religious customs, as the nation became part of the modern world. During the 1930s and 1940s, he published three collections, including *The Stray Dog* (1942). Through the eyes of a dog, Hedayat told a story of rejection and alienation. The animal protagonist derives from a strong tradition of animal fables.

In 1947, with the appearance of *Fire Quenched*, Simin Daneshvar (1921–2012) became the first woman in Iran to publish a collection of short stories. Farzaneh Milani praises her protagonists who are not simply victims of an overbearing patriarchy, but rather active human beings struggling to give meaning to their lives. In the later work of women like Shahrnush Parsipur (b. 1946) and Goli Taraqqi (b. 1939), Milani recognizes Daneshvar's focus on the disappointments inherent in mostly middle-class relationships in transitional societies, where individualism is in tension with traditional values (Milani, 1992:199).

Sadiq Chubak (1916–1998) and social critic Jalal Al-e Ahmad (1923–1969) elaborated what Hedayat began. It was Chubak who first experimented artistically with the use of the colloquial in formal writing. In *The Puppet Show* (1945), he strove to render the rhythm of the spoken language and not merely to include vernacular vocabulary for political effect. Like others, he was committed to describing and thus changing the situation of women.

The son of a Muslim Shi'i cleric, Al-e Ahmad focused on political oppression and, in the early stages of his writing career, on religious hypocrisy. He has been most closely associated with the notion of "Westoxification," the title of a book he wrote in 1962, which was used as a slogan against the shah in the 1960s. For Al-e Ahmad, as for many of his contemporaries, the greatest danger was the cultural, economic, and political subordination of countries like Iran to the West. As Tavakoli-Targhi said in an interview in 1999, Al-e Ahmad "envisaged an alternative modernity informed by Islam. This work became important for Ayatollah Ruhollah Khomeini and other Iranian religious scholars who viewed Islam as the foundation of Iranian cultural independence." This book may be seen as an early warning of the growing conservatism and anti-West sentiments that led to the Iranian Revolution of 1978.

During the 1960s, many new short fiction writers appeared, most notably Gholam Hosayn Saedi (1935–1985). A psychiatrist practicing in Tehran, he applied his clinical experience to thirty volumes of stories, plays, essays, and ethnographies. Like Al-e Ahmad, he was severe in his criticism of the Westernization of Iranian society. Yet once the Islamic government was in power, he did not hesitate to criticize it. His 1984 play *Othello in the Wonderland* was performed in Paris where Saedi ran less risk for his mocking portrayal of the system's obsession with covering women's bodies.

The Iranian Revolution produced a new generation of writers, many of whom are women. Critics like Heshmat Moayyad praise these writers, whether they called for the overthrow of the monarchy or not, for their brave stand against corruption. However, many chose exile.

Turkey's Storytellers

One of the earliest Turkish writers of short stories was Sait Faik Aziz Abasiyanik (1906–1954). Like his counterparts in the rest of the Middle East, Abasiyanik was interested in daily life both within and outside the cities. The most prolific and admired short story writer in Turkey, as well as in Iran, where many of his works were translated into Persian, was Aziz Nesin (1915–1995) who has been called the twentieth-century Nasreddin Hoca, a witty, eloquent folk hero. Nesin wrote dozens of books, including *Elephant Hamdi* and *Madmen on the Loose*. In "House on the Border," a Kafkaesque story about a tenant, the six thieves who prey on him, and their final forced collaboration to fight injustice, he takes on the repressive government apparatus. Nesin's involvement in the translation and publication of the controversial novel *Satanic Verses* by Salman Rushdie (b. 1947) almost cost him his life. He is one of the few Middle Eastern writers who made a living from his writings; most others have had to rely on income from other professions such as journalism to allow them to write fiction. After his death, his family established the Nesin Foundation, which supports literary activity as well as social projects.

Francophone Novels in North Africa

In the countries of North Africa that the French colonized in the nineteenth century (Algeria in 1830 and Tunisia in 1881), the first novelistic attempts appeared in French at the beginning of the twentieth century. In Tunisia, Jewish intellectuals like Jacques Victor Levi first used the novel to chronicle their daily lives. They described a multicultural society in which Arabs, Berbers, Italians, Maltese, Africans, Muslims, and Jews had lived together easily until the arrival of the colonizers. It was then that racial and religious differences began to matter. Novelists evoked the two worlds of the medina (old Arab city) and the *ville nouvelle* (new city) that accommodated the French and the constant border crossings between them. The hammam (Turkish bath) became the emblematic site of local authenticity and segregation.

In 1953, three years before Tunisia was to gain its independence, Albert Memmi (b. 1920) published his semiautobiographical novel. Written two years before *The Colonizer and the Colonized,* his classical study of colonial relations, *Pillar of Salt* provides a case study of the dehumanizing effects of colonial desire both on the subject as well as on the object of domination. The colonizer wants the colonized to forget who he is and to want to emulate him. The colonizer encourages the colonized to persist in the mimicry until they have almost perfected their performance; at that point the unbridgeable gap between them is revealed and the hope to identify with the masters is shattered. He fosters that desire until it nears fulfillment and then he reveals the hope to have been always empty. Benillouche, son of a working-class family granted permission to study at a lycee, swings between his multiple and overlapping identities, at once loving and hating who he is but also the person he is becoming. This is more than self-criticism; it is refusal of self. The hero's highly conflicted relations with his father anticipate the novels of the Moroccans Driss Chraïbi (1926–2007) and Tahar Benjelloun (b. 1944) in the 1960s and 1970s, which dwell on the rule of the father, transparent symbol for the patriarchal past, and the need to end it.

During the 1980s, Benjelloun wrote the two-volume novel *Sand Child* and *Sacred Night* that won him the Prix Goncourt, the prestigious French literary prize that until then had been awarded almost exclusively to French citizens. The novel tells the story of a father's refusal to accept the fact that his eighth child is yet another girl. This time he will have a son, and he turns the infant Fatima into Ahmed and produces a freak. This postmodern novel about gender construction in an Islamic patriarchy caused a scandal in Morocco. Benjelloun was accused of pandering to French voyeuristic desire for the exotic and the perverted. Some dismissed the Prix Goncourt as Benjelloun's reward for cultural betrayal.

In Algeria and Egypt, it was women who pioneered the francophone novel.[1] In the 1940s, Assia Débèche wrote about middle-class women's experiences of biculturalism: they were educated to expect opportunities for choice in love and life, but their realities often turned out to be quite different. Francophone Lebanese Egyptian Andrée Chedid (1920-2011) explored the same problem two years after the success of the Free Officers Movement. *From Sleep Unbound* (1954) was praised, if not warmly, for its bleak depiction of the fate of a woman in a rural Coptic setting where any attempt, however slight, to improve a black destiny was greeted with shock and redoubled rejection. In the story, Samya's murder of her foul husband is as much activism as a paralyzed woman in such a context could be expected to exercise.

The Arabic Novel

The novel in Arabic developed a little later than the francophone novel. It was too long and too epic a form to suit the purposes of the early social and cultural reformers. More than the short story, the novel seemed an unfamiliar genre, developed as it had been for the needs and interests of the European bourgeoisie of the eighteenth and nineteenth centuries. Above all, publication was an issue. The new Arabic printing presses were given over primarily to newspapers and journals, which became the most effective outlets for works of fiction. Even today some writers continue to serialize their novels and autobiographies in these publications, which often retain the services of creative writers as though they were journalists.[2] This form of publication lends itself to the cliffhanger style familiar to European readers of nineteenth-century sociorealist fiction.

In Egypt, it was 1988 Nobel laureate Naguib Mahfouz (1911–2005) who first brought this longer genre to maturity. After publishing a few short stories in the 1930s, he turned to the longer literary format. His novels from the late 1940s on provide a window on the evolving sociopolitical situation of Egypt and Egyptians in the world system.

In the 1940s, Mahfouz published two novels that revolve around events supposed to have happened during the times of the Pharaohs, focusing on the expulsion of invaders by ancient Egyptians. The allegorical nature of these works is transparent. This was a period of self-searching in Egypt, when local failure to act effectively in an international context was compensated for by recourse to past greatness. This turn to a past predating the seventh-century arrival of the Peninsula Arabs became a reflex in other Middle Eastern countries whose intellectuals were struggling with a crisis of identity. In Turkey, for example, just after Atatürk's death in 1938, novelist Kemal Tahir (1910–1973) wrote *Mother State,* about the Ottoman Empire in the thirteenth and fourteenth centuries when it was at the height of its power.

Egyptian Nobel laureate Naguib Mahfouz is best known for the sociorealist style of his novels, many of which have been translated into English.

Mahfouz pioneered sociorealism along with Turkish short story writer Sabhattin Ali (1907–1948) and novelist Orhan Kemal (1914–1970). *Midaq Alley* (1947), the first of Mahfouz's novels to be translated into English, reflects the concerns of other Middle Eastern writers who turned city neighborhoods into rich microcosms of their countries. The setting here is World War II Cairo, and British global dominion is quickly fading. This intricate novel was followed by Mahfouz's trilogy *Palace Walk, Palace of Desire,* and *Sugar Street* (1956–1957), which many claim won him the Nobel Prize. Although he wrote the trilogy during the Free Officers Movement in 1952, he did not publish it until several years later. The saga of the 'Abd al-Jawads, an upper-middle-class family, it parallels events of the first half of the twentieth century. The lives of three generations mirror the crises through which Egyptians were passing from World War I through independence. But once again, history provides a disguise for current concerns. Mahfouz draws the reader into the inner sanctum of a traditional home where women and men interact in a way invisible to the outsider. Readers are privileged to share the first moment of disobedience perpetrated by a usually submissive wife. There is a penalty to be paid, but the die has been cast. Her children, who witnessed their mother's unwonted daring, become politically engaged. Their different avenues of activism, Muslim Brother as opposed to communist, often produce internal clashes, but kinship ties do finally survive the stresses.

In 1959 Mahfouz published *Children of Gebelawi,* a novel that tells the story of the Abrahamic faiths and their adherents through the lives of individual members of the Gebelawi family. This book was banned in several Muslim countries for its negative portrayal of the Prophet. But Muhammad is not the only one subjected to moral scrutiny; all the great prophets of monotheism, culminating with Arafa, the prophet of science, spiritual skepticism, and alienation are far from perfect. It was this book that earned Mahfouz a 1994 knife attack by a zealous Muslim fundamentalist. Mahfouz pursued this existentialist theme throughout the 1960s, depicting hopeless characters in search of some little meaning to give to their lives.

The Six Day War of 1967 produced an intellectual crisis in the Arab world to which Mahfouz reacted strongly, in terms of both content and form. Many readers and critics regretted the loss of the linear narrative line of his first novels, as his writing of the 1970s fragmented into the staccato of alarm and surreal confusion. In the 1980s, Mahfouz changed his style and themes again. This time he turned to the classics and wrote modern versions. He produced his own take on *A Thousand and One Nights* and also a travel narrative written in response to the famous travelogue of fourteenth-century Moroccan traveler Ibn Battutah, which Mahfouz titled *The Journey of Ibn Fattouma* (1983) in recognition of the influence.

The novel has provided many writers with the frame appropriate to contain nostalgic reflections on a world that has passed. *Fragments of Memory* by Syrian writer Hanna Mina (b. 1924) tells the tale of a village before the onslaught of foreign values. Unlike most Arab novelists who place their stories in the city or in the village, Saudi exile Abd al-Rahman Munif (1933–2004) situated his novels in the desert. His magnum opus is a five-volume novel titled *Cities of Salt,* which he published throughout the 1980s. Having begun his career as a petroleum economist, he was familiar with the impact of oil on the economies and lives of people living in oil-rich states. The quintet traces the transformation in the environment as well as in the consciousness of the local inhabitants after the discovery of black gold. The reader witnesses the growing brutalization of the bedouin as they recognize that in this new world of competition and profit, there is more to be gained by individual enterprise than in tribal solidarity. This book displeased his Saudi government, which deprived him of citizenship.

The Iranian Novel

The Iranian novel, of which the three-volume collection *Travel Diary of Ebrahim Beg* (1890s) is said to be the first, appeared before the Arabic novel. Iranian writers, more than the Arabs, tended to work in both short story and novel genres. This was true for Hedayat, Chubak, Al-e Ahmad, and Daneshvar.

One of the best-known Iranian novels is Hedayat's *Blind Owl*, which was written by 1930 but not published until 1937 in India and 1941 in Iran, after Reza Shah abdicated and censorship was lifted. It is a book of highly introspective notes that Hedayat wrote "for my shadow." He describes a husband tortured by his relations with a wife who gives herself easily to her many lovers, but not at all to him. He becomes an opium addict, a misfit, a murderer, and a madman. The despair in this novel foreshadowed Hedayat's suicide in 1951.

Chubak wrote several novels that have been praised for their keen attention to detail. In 1963 he published his first novel, *Tongsir*, to great acclaim. It tells the story of an exploited man who takes revenge on those who try to defraud him. At about the same time, both Al-e Ahmad and his wife, Simin Daneshvar, were actively and publicly engaged in the literary scene where left-wing intellectuals struggled to resist the shah's attempts to organize and co-opt cultural production. Al-e Ahmad's novel *The School Principal* (1958), written five years after the end of the regime of Mohammad Mosaddeq, criticizes the Iranian system of education in place at the time; its publication was a politico-literary event. As had been the case with the short story, Daneshvar was the first woman in Iran to publish a novel. *A Persian Requiem* (1969) takes place in British-occupied Shiraz toward the end of World War II. Neighbors and kin are at each other's throats, tribal leaders have revolted against the government, and Zari is at home trying to maintain order. She is contrasted to a woman who writes, despite the prohibition on women's literary voices, and who struggles to hold on to her autonomy but is consequently committed to a psychiatric hospital. As can be read in women's writings everywhere, this madness is not a clinical disorder but rather society's disciplining of a woman's rebellion. The novel was a best seller and was translated into several languages (Milani, 1992:59–61, 183).

The Turkish Novel

In 1922, Yakup Kadri Karaosmanoğlu published *Sufi Sheikh of Light*. Advocating a Turkist idealism, the novel ridicules Sufi brotherhoods that the Kemalist government would soon outlaw. According to Erdag Goknar, this "politicization of Islamic symbols and everyday ritual practice marks this period of literary production . . . the novel argues for the drastic measures witnessed in the Republican cultural revolution. Here, as with previous novels, women, their freedom and contribution to social life, are the gauges of modernity" (2008:485–486). Almost three decades later, Ahmet Hamdi Tanpınar (1901–1962) examined the transition between Ottoman and Turkist states in his nostalgic *A Mind at Peace* (1949).

Two novelists in Turkey have earned international acclaim: Yashar Kemal (b. 1923) and Orhan Pamuk (b. 1948). Kemal pioneered the "village novel." Best known is his quartet titled *Memed, My Hawk,* translated into almost thirty languages, which revolves around the ultimately unsuccessful resistance of peasants against their landlords. Halman describes his work as "one of the truly stirring achievements in the history of Turkish literature" (1982:30).

The first work of 2006 Nobel laureate Orhan Pamuk was a family saga titled *Jevdet Bey and His Sons* (1979) and, much like Mahfouz's trilogy, it follows the fortunes of three generations whose lives span most of the twentieth century. In his 1985 *White Castle,* Pamuk chronicles the uncertain process of exchange and transformation that links and separates two strangers. Set against the background of the 1683 Ottoman defeat in Vienna, the novel follows the intertwinement of the narrator, an unnamed Venetian scholar who has been captured and delivered into slavery, and his master Hoja, a Turk in the court of the child sultan Mehmet IV. From the moment that the Christian lays eyes on his Muslim master, he is alarmed by their physical similarity. Slave of a man who looks uncannily like him, he resists all conversion attempts, even at the risk of losing his life. Narrating themselves to each other they absorb new details, and in the process begin to lose control of their own narratives. With time, they become uncertain about where some of the facts fit into their lives. The imbrication of their memories creates crises of identity as they lose confidence in their past. After living together for twenty years, Hoja begins "repeating that I was he and he was I" while the Venetian declares himself to be "Hoja's very self ... it seemed for a moment that what paced, agonized, inside this room was not Hoja, but my own youth. The person I once had been had left me and was gone." The novel ends with the appearance of "Him"—with a capital H—after one of them (it is not clear who) returns to Venice and the other (whoever he may be) stays and longs for the time of struggle when each knew who he was and engaged with the other as other. The mysterious "He" is not God, but a third entity that is the product of their differences and retains their separation. So reciprocal has their learning become that, in the end, neither knows who has taught the other what; the exchange has been complete, but neither has been reduced or assimilated or converted to the other. It is not possible to say that one has influenced the other, but it is possible to say that their exchange has been so productive that it has generated something new. "He" is both of them and neither, but rather a new creature.

The Ottoman theme recurs in *My Name Is Red* (1998), "a complex and fragmented work that redefined the flat, two-dimensionality of the Ottoman miniature painting as a living, vital, aesthetic model pertinent to the present-day" (Goknar, 2008:497). *Snow* (2002) revolves around the hijab controversy that has pitted secular nationalists against Islamists. The novel explores the implications of the prohibition for Turkish girls to cover, their brave insistence on its moral and religious necessity, and their consequent suicides in remote Kars.

Istanbul: Memories and the City (2003), Pamuk's controversial, tell-all autobiography, separates and brings together two eras: the early modern cosmopolitanism of the Ottoman Empire and the Westernization project of the Turkish republic. Between memoir and encyclopedia, *Istanbul* elegizes his city. Filtering his vision of the city through the engravings, writings, and photographs of eighteenth- and nineteenth-century European travelers and their turn-of-the-century Turkish admirers, including Tanpinar, Pamuk creates a contemporary Istanbul that is still caught in that historical moment, still dynamically processing the cultural convergence between East and West. Pamuk was not present during that hinge moment when the two cultures were embracing, but his four writers were witnesses to that moment of transition, of break but also of creation. Pamuk's oeuvre that dwells on the intersection of the Ottoman past and the Republican present has garnered him both fans and foes.

The Israeli Novel

Unlike all other Middle Eastern literatures, which draw on deep historical pasts, Israeli literature is just sixty years old. The first Israeli novel, Moshe Shamir's (1921–2004) *Beneath the Sun,* appeared two years after the establishment of the state in 1948. It is a highly political work that draws the profile of the new Israeli, the *sabra,* a term used to refer to those who are born on the land of Israel. The sabras are entirely enmeshed in the new nation's history and environment, but can fall prey to unfriendly neighbors (Yudkin, 1984:42–47). A frequently translated Israeli novelist is Amos Oz (b. 1939). After beginning his writing career with short stories, he turned to the novel. His work has been described as heavy with threat. This is particularly the case with his best-known novel, *My Michael* (1968). The heroine is obsessed by her conflicted feelings of fear and desire for the Arab twins she has known since childhood. Oz's body of work plays on borders, both real and symbolic. This is significant in a country that, from the start, has been uncertain about its geographical limits. Oz has situated many of his writings in the experience of the kibbutz, the communes in which many Israeli socialists lived (Yudkin, 1984:135–143, 168).

Particularly in the post-1967 period, some Palestinians within Israel wrote in Hebrew. Anton Shammas (b. 1950) wrote *Arabesques,* an autobiographical novel that has been hailed by some as a masterpiece of Hebrew prose. Yet despite the critical acclaim, the novel has not been fully accepted as part of the canon of Hebrew literature. Shammas has retrospectively described this work as his challenge to the Israeli claim that the Palestinians living under Israeli rule could be integrated as Israeli citizens. No matter how assimilated they tried to become in Israeli society, no matter how excellent the Palestinians' command of Hebrew, they could never become Israeli citizens in the full sense of the word.

Shammas was long in conversation with A. B. Yehoshua (b. 1936), who is considered to be one of Israel's most important fiction writers and social critics. His fiction unveils the Arab in the Jew. From "Facing the Forest" (1962) to his first novel *The Lover* (1977), he points to the dreaded other that is always there lying in wait for the opportunity to reveal itself. The derelict intellectual of the short story, keeping watch lest a fire destroy the forest planted to hide the traces of a Palestinian village destroyed in 1948, foreshadows the hero of the novel who recognizes his dead son in a Palestinian boy who comes to his garage in search of work. The figure of the Arab lies at the core of Israeli identity. Whether Palestinian or Mizrachi Jew, the Arab disturbs the unmarked Europeanness of Israeli identity. The more it is repressed the more violent its ultimate eruption into consciousness.

The presence of Palestinians and Arab Jews in Israel has become an increasingly important political issue. Two popular uprisings by Palestinians living in the Occupied Territories have hardened official Israeli resolve against accommodation and, thus, rendered peace a distant prospect. In 2004, the Iraqi-Israeli Sasson Somekh (b.1933) published his autobiography *Baghdad Yesterday*. Without sentimentality, he recalls his childhood and youth in one of the world's most ancient cities. At the age of seventeen years old, Somekh moved to Israel where he later became professor of Arabic literature in Tel Aviv University. Readers are taken back to a time when Jews lived side by side with Muslims and Christians and, although they were aware of some cultural differences, they were not stigmatized by them. Like the Tunisian Albert Memmi, Somekh narrates the challenges faced by Jews in Arab countries who lived in the interstices between local and colonial systems that both privileged them as Jews and emphasized their outsider status.

Drama: Grafting the New onto the Old

As with the other genres coming in from Europe, Middle Eastern intellectuals sought to find indigenous precedents for the theater. Some Arabs invoked the *maqama,* a tenth-century lyrical art form that told the story of an eloquent rascal who manages to deceive all, particularly a wealthy patron. Others cited the shadow play, which had its origin in the Turkish *karagoz.* Like the *maqama*, the *karagoz* is a comedy that revolves around the adventures of the uneducated but smart *karagoz.* Although the *karagoz* does deal with daily life and the struggles of the oppressed, its inherent frivolity and unchanging characters and plots resisted the serious intent of early Middle Eastern dramaturges. According to Halman, other popular performances common in Turkey include "peasant plays, pageants, rites, processions, mock fights, festival acts . . . and *Ortaoyunu* (Turkish *commedia dell'arte*)" (1976:14).

Like the novel and the short story, modern drama was introduced into the Middle East through translations. Major plays by William Shakespeare, Jean-Baptiste Molière, and Anton Chekhov were adapted for the Arab stage. Particularly in the torn, nostalgic works of Chekhov that described the passing of an age and the uncertainty of the future, Middle Easterners could recognize their own dilemmas. The theater appealed to a much wider section of the public because it did not rely on literacy. It provided a context within which writers could experiment with the introduction of colloquialisms, which were anathema to the writers of prose and poetry who feared the loss of the purity of their languages. With time, successful implementation of the colloquial in conversations between illiterate characters that were often offset by the high classical language of the educated provided models for fiction writers.

In 1873, the Turk Namik Kemal (ca. 1840–1888) staged his play *Fatherland,* which was enthusiastically greeted by audiences and censured by the government of Sultan Abdulaziz. Halman claims that this play marked the beginning of "the political significance of literature in Turkish life." Atatürk saw in drama an important aspect of Westernization that he exploited by establishing the City Theater of Istanbul in 1927. Writers in other genres like Yashar Kemal, Nazim Hikmet Ran, Orhan Kemal, and Aziz Nesin experimented in theatrical writing. Much of the dramatic writings of the 1960s are "village dramas," which marked the first significant move away from Western influence (Halman, 1976:13, 37, 41–47).

The name that stands out above all others in the field of Arab drama is that of the Egyptian Tawfiq al-Hakim who wrote his first plays in the early 1920s. Unlike many of his contemporaries, al-Hakim was not supportive of the burgeoning feminist movement. While others were writing of the injustices women were facing, he criticized the "new woman" who heralded moral chaos. After three years spent studying law in Paris, al-Hakim returned to Cairo in 1928. At this point, he turned to philosophical playwriting and his treatment of women mellowed, as in *Shahrazad* (1934). This change may be due to his experiences with women in Paris, about which he wrote in his autobiography.

In 1960, al-Hakim joined other writers who were criticizing the new regime, brought into power by the Free Officers Movement, when he published *The Sultan's Dilemma.* The sultan is a slave whose owner, the previous sultan, had died before manumitting him. He must gain his freedom and can only do so by being bought and then freed by his next owner. He is bought in auction by a woman who has heard of his dictatorial ways, but discovers that he is gentle. She gives him his freedom once he has learned its real meaning. In 1964, Yusuf Idris published *Farfoors,* a play that relied on the *karagoz* genre as well as on Sufi rituals. He wanted to prove that drama was not new to Arabic literature and that traditional forms could hold the new politically charged content.

In the late 1960s, students throughout the Arab world turned to the theater to stage their sociopolitical grievances. In Syria, a group of students founded the Thorn Theater Company, which produced skits and plays of surprising daring. The screen of comedy and fiction allowed actors to convey political messages that would elsewhere be deemed sedition. Government officials and censors allowed this dangerous practice to continue, recognizing that the people needed an outlet for their frustration and anger with a repressive regime. Along with other forms of cultural production but more visibly, the theater also helped to fashion a facade of democracy for the Baath state.

Writers schooled in the Thorn Theater have continued to write on the razor's edge between dissidence and martyrdom. Some, like Sa'dallah Wannus (1941–1997) and Mamduh 'Adwan (1941–2004), stayed with the stage. Wannus's first play, *An Evening's Entertainment for the Fifth of June,* came out in 1967 shortly after the Six Day War, and it has been described as the richest literary reaction to the terrible defeat. In it Wannus criticized, even if allegorically, the current Baathist regime. First in 1977 with *The King Is the King* and then fifteen years later with *Historical Miniatures,* he revealed the oppressive strategies of dictatorial rule. In the more recent play, he used the relationship between fourteenth-century Mongol tyrant Tamerlane and North African historian Ibn Khaldun to criticize intellectuals for their complicity with a corrupt system. 'Adwan's play *The Ghoul* (1996) focuses on the cruelty of the last Ottoman governor to be sent to Syria. The nightmares that torment his sleep might be those of any dictator. His warning at the end of the play that, if the tyrannical system is not crushed, it will recur has proven to be prophetic with the rise of Bashar al-Assad. The 2011–2013 mass revolt of the Syrians against the regime seems to respond to Adwan's call to the people not to cut off the hand of the jailor, but to destroy the prison.

Other graduates of the Thorn Theater, like Durayd Lahham, have moved from the stage to television or the cinema. Paradoxically, the film industry has become the most radical of all cultural producers: exclusively controlled by the Ministry of Culture, it is engaged in stringent criticism of the government. What are the political position and ultimate fate of filmmakers like Muhammad Mallas who are in the pay of the government but whose films, on the rare occasions when they are shown, leave their audiences breathless at their critical audacity? This is what should be called commissioned criticism because it serves to make the government look open-minded and democratic when it so wishes (cooke, 2007).

Poetry and the Hold of the Desert

Of all genres, the most resistant to change was poetry. The new emphasis on personal expression and free style was regarded almost as heresy. Throughout the Middle East, poetry has been and continues to be the most highly prized literary art. In the pre-Islamic period, politics and poetry had been intermeshed, and tribal leaders were expected to be accomplished poets. Islamic rulers generally continued to value the art of poetry and patronized it generously. Wherever it was composed, whether in Arabic, Turkish, or Persian, classical poetry retained elements of its origins in the desert. There were familiar tropes, images, meters, and form. Any changes had to be carefully introduced lest the innovation be considered a sign of incompetence. More formulaic even than prose literature, classical poetry did not allow for the expression of individual emotion.

The first attempts to make poetry more responsive to contemporary concerns began modestly in the mid–nineteenth century. Neoclassical poets like Turkish writer Yahya Kemal Beyatli (1884–1958) and Egyptians Mahmud Sami al-Barudi (1839–1904) and Ahmad Shawqi (1868–1932) were to give new life to classical motifs and language, with only slight modification in content. In general, they were formal conservatives (Somekh, 1992:40–41). The first substantive reform of poetry came from such poets as the Turk Ahmet Hasim (1885–1933), the Syrian Khalil Mutran (1872–1949),

Syrian poet Nizar Kabbani lived from 1923 until 1998.
The poem is "No. 43" from One Hundred Love Letters.

the Tunisian Abu al-Qasim al-Shabbi (1909–1934), and the Iranian Nima Yushij (1895–1959) who all had been inspired by such French and English Symbolists and Romantics as Charles-Pierre Baudelaire and Alphonse-Marie-Louis de Prat de Lamartine, William Wordsworth, and Percy Bysshe Shelley. Their experiments with meter, form, and language transformed poetry in the Middle East.

A revolution was in the making, but opposition to free verse remained strong. In Turkey, the Marxist Nazim Hikmet Ran (1902–1963) was the first to be recognized for his free verse. Halman relates how, in 1921, Atatürk had urged the already famous poet to "write poems with a purpose" (1982:25). He did, but he had to pay for his "obedience." His outright condemnations of social and political injustices as well as his poetic calls for revolution gained such a wide following that he was made to bear responsibility for political unrest. During the late 1930s, just before Atatürk's death, he was imprisoned on the trumped-up charge of conspiracy to overthrow the regime, and his writings were banned. On his release, Ran fled to Moscow where he is buried alongside such great Russian writers as Fyodor Dostoyevsky. He is the most widely translated Turkish poet. His poems "Some Advice to Those Who Will Serve Time in Prison" and "Awakening" were written for those who had to undergo what he did, but who were not as strong:

> I mean it's not that you can't pass
> 10 or 15 years inside,
> and more even—
> you can,
> as long as the jewel
> in the left side of your chest doesn't lose its luster.

In the Arab world and in Iran, it was women who brought to fruition what male poets had long been trying to achieve. The Iraqi Nazik al-Mala'ika (1923–2007) finally succeeded in introducing free verse into modern Arabic poetry. In 1949, she published her anthology of free verse, *Ashes and Shrapnel.* Although others before her had experimented with this new poetic form, they had had little success; critics accused them of incompetence rather than welcoming the innovation. Her work paved the way for others like Syrian Nobel nominee Adonis (Ali Ahmad Said, b. 1930) and Iraqi poet Badr Shakir al-Sayyab (1926–1964). Both of these writers gained prominence through their adoption of mythic themes of resurrection, particularly in connection with the plight of the Palestinians. In 1968, Adonis published his pathbreaking work *The Stage and the Mirrors,* which introduces a new poetic lexicon, rhythm, structure, and sensibility. His work is highly philosophical, filled with symbols, allegories, and mythical allusions.

He claims that poetry should appeal to the mind, not to the emotions, and because this new poetry is a political weapon, it must be subtly wielded.

The political nature of Arabic poetry and the repressiveness of several of the regimes within which these poets function has compelled some to write obliquely, surreally, and anonymously. Arab women, particularly in more traditional countries like those of the Arabian Peninsula, have often chosen abstract symbolism to articulate emotions otherwise considered taboo. This new poetry by women like Kuwaiti princess Su'ad Mubarak al-Sabah was at first censured, even when not quite understood, because it came from the pen of a woman. In the late 1990s, however, this kind of poetry began to find a new, international audience. In March 1997 and in places as far-flung from the United Arab Emirates as Vietnam and North Carolina, newspapers carried the story of the publication of a new anthology titled *The Female Poets of the Emirates*.

In Iran, two women poets rose to prominence. Forugh Farrokhzad (1935–1967) and Simin Behbahani (b. 1927) both rebelled against poetic norms. Behbahani's first collection of poetry, *Broken String*, came out in 1951. Whereas Behbahani's rebellion took the form of neotraditionalism (Milani, 1992:235–239), Farrokhzad's method involved rejection. In 1955, she published what some considered to be a "scandalously frank" anthology titled *Captive*. But she is best known for her collection *Another Birth*, which was published in 1964. Like al-Mala'ika, she breaks with formal convention as she describes the oppressive life of a Middle Eastern woman. The personal and the political fuse in a single poetic vision.

Independence and Postcolonial Struggles

As previous chapters have illustrated, the second half of the twentieth century witnessed cycles of violence throughout the Middle East. There were liberation struggles followed by socialist activism followed by breakdown of law and order and widespread depression and disappointment. After independence, many wanted to reconstruct their countries and to fashion a local, "authentic" identity. Conflict and violence are so much a part of the history of the Middle East that no consideration of its literature can afford to ignore them.

Writers were concerned to play a role in the new societies that came with independence from colonial rule. Acting as conscience of the people, they set out to "revolutionize the revolution." In 1946 the Iran-Soviet Society sponsored the first congress of Iranian writers, during which the centrality of ideology to literature was announced. Seven years later, in Lebanon, the first editorial of the influential monthly periodical *Al-Shi'r* declared that all forms of writing must henceforth be politically engaged. The time of art for art's sake had passed, to be replaced by a revolutionary ethic in all creative activities.

Paying the Price

This emphasis on political commitment in literature appeared at a time when the Middle East was in the throes of revolutions and wars of liberation. Literature was to make an intervention in the political realm, to praise and promote the social good, and to criticize the retrograde. Wars of liberation from colonial rule were clearly good, but some conflicts were not so easily judged as good or bad. This was the case with the Egyptian Free Officers Movement of 1952. It was clearly good in that it brought back Egyptian rule after what some argued was a hiatus of millennia; namely, since the Pharaohs. Others soon felt misgivings about the autocratic nature of the *nouveau regime* (new regime).

As mentioned above, Haqqi's 1954 novel *Good Morning!* openly criticized Gamal Abdul Nasser and his new regime. In the same year, another lawyer, 'Abd al-Rahman al-Sharqawi (1920–1987), published *Egyptian Earth,* which filmmaker Yusuf Shahin turned into a film titled *The Land.* It examines the impact of the revolution on the lives of the fellahin and shows the oppressiveness of the centralized authority structure that the Free Officers put in place. Again, the plot revolves around the introduction of a symbol of modernization, in this case a road, into a village that has kept aloof from the corruption of city life. The fact that the longed-for revolution had brought only misery to the people was difficult for many to accept.

In the Middle East, writers have a moral authority scarcely imaginable in the West. They are expected to stand up for their convictions and to lead public opinion. Their boldness may earn them prison sentences, but that is as it should be. For the prisoner of conscience, the intellectual who has done time, this experience is a badge of honor. Many prisoners of conscience in the Middle East have written of their incarceration.

Iranian writer Buzurg Alavi (1904–1997), who had become involved in the Marxist Tudeh Party, was imprisoned in 1937. During his four years "inside," he wrote two books: *Scrap Papers from Prison* and *Fifty-Three Men.* These stories about his experiences reveal the intense emotions of the prisoners but also their determination: "I gained in spirit in the prison and became better equipped for the struggle" (quoted in Sajida Alvi, 1984:283). Along the same lines, Egyptian writer Adonis (Ali Ahmad Said, b. 1930) wrote *The Eye with an Iron Lid* (1982), an intricate tale of his thirteen years behind bars first under the British and then under Nasser. His former partner, Nawal El Saadawi (b. 1931), also recorded her prison months under Anwar Sadat in *Memoirs from the Women's Prison* (1983). As mentioned above, Turkey's premier poet, Nazim Hikmet Ran, wrote extensively about his years inside. The fact that these intellectuals have had such experiences, and that they then publish them, gives them a moral authority that others may never achieve.

The Algerian War of Independence (1954–1962)

Tunisia and Morocco gained their independence from the French in 1956, but the Algerians, who had begun their anticolonial war in 1954, did not succeed until 1962. The war produced libraries of novels, short stories, and poetry, and even today it haunts the imagination of cultural producers, including filmmakers. Most recently, *Joseph and the Legend of the Seventh Sleeper* (1995) made the rounds of the Arab film festivals. It tells the story of a prisoner of war who escapes to find his companions. He discovers that they, like the Quranic sleepers in the cave, perished in a cave with their dog. He buries his erstwhile companions and then is himself killed by traitors. The theme of the betrayal of the revolution was common in the 1990s as intellectuals found themselves under attack by religious extremists.

But in the 1950s and early 1960s, hope was high. Everyone was expected to write about the war. Women like Assia Djebar (b. 1936), whose 1957 *The Thirst* narrated women's doomed thirst for independence, were criticized by the male literary establishment for obsession with individual problems at a time when the nation needed its citizens to unite. Later novels by Djebar, including *Children of the New World* (1962) and *Naive Larks* (1967), describe women's mobilization without any sense of its significance for them in a postbellum society.

In contrast, male writers were writing with dread about women's growing power and influence in a society at war. One of the best-known novels of the war is *Nedjma* (1956), by Kateb Yacine (1929–1996). The critics have interpreted this story of a mysterious beauty, the four suitors to whom she is related, her legendary father, and her French mother, to be an allegory for Algeria. I have argued instead that it narrates men's growing anxieties as they watch the emergence of the new Algerian woman out of the ashes of the war (cooke, 1997:chap. 3). This thesis is more forcefully brought out in Mohamed Dib's surreal novel *Who Remembers the Sea* (1962) where the narrator loses his mind as he loses control over his wife, a guerrilla fighter. For those writers like Malek Haddad (1927–1987) who left Algeria during the war, the dread of the woman soldier is intense. It is not so surprising, then, that when the war was over, the women were quickly returned to their homes.

The story of women's disempowerment in the aftermath of the war is well known; in fact, Arab women elsewhere refer to it as the "Algerian lesson." This lesson taught others that they must not allow society to forget women's contributions during a time of crisis and need. In the 1980s, Djebar started to bring out her quartet, which she has described as autobiographical. Each volume presents a radical revision of Algerian colonial history as seen through the eyes of women. In the second volume, *Fantasia: An Algerian Cavalcade* (1985), she links the stories of unknown nineteenth-century women resisters, omitted in the official histories and chronicles, with those of living women who had been active and then silenced during the war and with her own story.

Djebar's quartet forms part of a national critique on the part of revolutionary women who have recognized, perhaps too late, the dangers of silence. The war of liberation was not a revolution, they claim, because its outcome did not change the material and social conditions for half the population. As long as discrimination against women continues, the expulsion of the French cannot be considered to have been a national success. During the 1990s and 2000s, the Islamic fundamentalist attacks on intellectuals, and particularly women, may be seen as the next phase of a war that was not resolved in the early 1960s.

The Question of Palestine

Immediately after the departure of the British in 1948, Palestinians wrestled with their new loss of independence. Although most Palestinian intellectuals left in 1948, a few, like poet Mahmud Darwish (1942–2008), did stay behind what came to be called the Green Line. Darwish's family left in the first exodus and then soon stole back in. They returned after the period for registering Palestinians had passed, and so the poet's writings dwell on the lack of identity papers. His poem "Identity Card" (1965) became emblematic of the Palestinian condition.

After 1967, the Palestinians who found themselves under Israeli rule in the Gaza Strip and the West Bank began to understand why it was that those who had stayed on their land inside the Israeli borders in 1948 were not necessarily complicit, but rather might be regarded as nationalists. The importance of staying, whatever the cost, became a nationalist virtue. The founder of the binational Israeli Communist Party, Emile Habibi (1921–1996), won both the Jerusalem Prize for Literature awarded by the Palestine Liberation Organization and the Israel Prize for his 1974 *The Secret Life of Saeed, the Ill-Fated Pessoptimist: A Palestinian Who Became a Citizen of Israel*. It tells the picaresque tale of a hapless Palestinian stumbling through life and people in Israel.

Two years later, from Nablus inside the Occupied Territories, Sahar Khalifa (b. 1941) published the first of her three novels on the experience of occupation by Israeli forces. From *Wild Thorns* (1976) to *Bab al-Saha* (1990), Khalifa paints the canvas of resistance. Her heroines demonstrate how women's ways of fighting are more effective than those of the men. Mothers who give their sons and daughters stones to throw at soldiers confuse the rules of war. Are these women and their offspring civilians or militants? Can they be shot? Or must they be tolerated, their stones deflected? This ambiguity disappeared in the later stage when the women's individual acts of resistance—like the mythical Hydra, when one of its heads is cut off, two will appear in its stead—were turned into a unified strategy for revolutionary action. The militarization of local oppositions was named the intifada (uprising). It is arguable that this transformation of individual Palestinian actions into a single movement empowered the Israelis to crush the popular uprising (cooke, 1997:chap. 4).

The War in Lebanon (1975–1990)

Even before civil war broke out in Lebanon in the spring of 1975, some were sensing its inevitability. This was again true before the Israeli invasion in June 1982. Both al-Samman and Etel Adnan (b. 1925) wrote works that were filled with the dread of anticipation. *Beirut 75* (1974), by al-Samman, uncannily predicts the civil war as the novel collapses into a series of nightmares. Five years later at the height of the war, she returned to the nightmare format. *Beirut Nightmares* (1979) takes readers into the maelstrom of the fall of 1976 hotels battle, which pitted opposing militias against each other for weeks. Many have read in Adnan's novel *Arab Apocalypse* (1980) a premonition of the Israeli invasion of 1982. The staccato poetry interrupted with symbols and figures lies splattered on the page like shrapnel exploding out of a bomb, like blood spurting out of a wound.

As happened in Iran after the Iranian Revolution, chaos in Lebanon produced literature, much of it by women (Lewis and Yazdanfar, 1996:xix–xxi). The Beirut Decentrists, a school of women writing in Beirut during the war, wrote into the space of violence a script for a transformed society that would include all its members and treat them with justice (cooke, 1988). But during the civil war, they did more than that. These women writers blamed the men for creating the terrible conditions that threatened to destroy the country. Hanan al-Shaykh's (b. 1945) novel *The Story of Zahra* (1980) traces the growth in consciousness of a woman who had been a social misfit. As the war rages, she comes to see a role for herself, and she fights in her own limited but intense way to do something to end at least part of the madness. Emily Nasrallah (b. 1931) wrote prolifically on the devastating effects of the war on women's lives. Her three collections of war stories capture moments of horror and loss that other genres could not quite encompass.

The Iran-Iraq War, the Gulf War, and the Iraq War

While the war in Lebanon was at its height, farther to the east the 1979 Iranian Revolution ousted the shah from the Peacock Throne. Saddam Hussein, the new leader of Iraq, tried to take advantage of what he had mistakenly assumed to be total disarray in neighboring Iran. The Iran-Iraq War that he launched in late 1980 as a blitzkrieg persisted for eight bloody years. Like many dictators, Hussein had an ambivalent relationship with the intellectual elite of his country. He needed them, and therefore he feared them.

Throughout the war, he coerced the writers and artists who could not or did not choose to leave to glorify the war in ink and paint. Aliya Talib, for example, published her daring criticisms of an autocratic regime in the succinctness of quirky tales. The Ministry of Culture established literary series and organized festivals designed to serve the purposes of the war. Many did as they were told. Some did not. Under the watchful eye of the censor, some writers managed to articulate criticism of a war they were paid to praise. Using allegory and a surreal style, they published writings that evoked the harrowing experiences through which Iraqis were forced to pass (cooke, 1997:chap. 5). Ironically, the Iranian government was doing exactly the same as its enemy; namely, sponsoring books of praise for the war.

The Iraqi invasion of Kuwait on August 2, 1990, and the Gulf War that several Western and Arab countries under the leadership of US president George H. W. Bush launched against Iraq on January 17, 1991, produced Kuwaiti and Iraqi journals, novels, and short stories. In *Black Barricades* (1994), Kuwait's leading woman writer, Layla al-'Uthman (b. 1945), collects stories she wrote during the eight-month occupation of the capital city. The tone is one of confusion, which aptly reflects the mood of the Kuwaitis as well as of the Iraqis. The destitute, illiterate men wreaking havoc in the palaces of the Kuwaiti oil magnates may not know why they are there beyond the looting, but they do know that they do not wish to return to the tyranny of their home country.

Inside Iraq itself, several wrote against the brutality of the allied forces and, particularly, the US pilots who seemed to consider their Iraqi targets no more human than characters in a Nintendo game. The Ministry of Culture continued its publication of war stories. One of Iraq's leading women poets, Dunya Mikha'il (b. 1965), brought out her *Journal of a Wave Outside the Sea* in 1995. Far from glorifying the war as might be expected from such a government-sponsored text, this poem depicts extreme alienation in a continuing reign of terror.

In March 2003, a year and a half after the September 11, 2001, attacks on the World Trade Center in New York and the Pentagon in Washington, DC, the US military launched the Iraq War. The pretext was Iraq's alleged complicity in the September 11 attacks and the goal was to eliminate the weapons of mass destruction that until today have not been found. After toppling Hussein, the US forces stayed another eight years. Sectarian violence spun out of control. Young bloggers were the first to inform the world about life in Iraq under US occupation. Two have achieved renown: Salampax and Riverbend. Both of them have published books of their blogs; indeed, this melding of blog and literary text has become a trend in contemporary Arabic literature. Riverbend's *Baghdad Burning: Girl Blog from Baghdad* (2005) can be read as a chronicle of the coming to literary awareness of a woman who war imprisoned in her home and gave her time to reflect on her circumstances. The early, hurried jottings of moments of panic give way to careful crafting of her emotions and reflections. In 2007, Sinan Antoon published his *I'jam: An Iraqi Rhapsody,* an imagined prison memoir that recollects the anxiety and fears that have ruled Iraqis' lives since the Iran-Iraq War.

Emigration and Exile

There are many reasons for leaving the country of one's birth. Some, such as education and work opportunities, are voluntary; others, such as political oppression and intolerable violence, are involuntary. The travels of a young man, his head filled with dreams, to Europe; his apprenticeship for a period; and his disappointed return to his native land for education and the shock of return form a topos shaping many Middle Eastern works of fiction during the first part of the twentieth century. Egyptian writer Yahya Haqqi wrote the emblematic text of this "travel and return transformed" genre. *The Lamp of Umm Hashim* (1946) follows Isma'il from Cairo to London and then back to Cairo after seven years of training as an ophthalmologist. It is only after experiencing a religious epiphany that he is able to resolve the tension between traditional and Western medicine. The novella was hailed as an Islamic model of how to become a Western-style scientist while nonetheless remaining a righteous Muslim.

Twenty years later, the Sudanese al-Tayyib Salih (1928–2009) developed this theme, although without the religious angle, in *Season of Migration to the North* (1966). This novel reverses the nineteenth-century colonialist's move from the metropole to the colony; Mustafa Sa'id goes north (to England) to learn, but also to exact revenge on behalf of his oppressed people. The story of Mustafa Sa'id has often been compared to that of Othello; it has also been called the answer to Joseph Conrad's novel *Heart of Darkness* as well as to Frantz Fanon's depiction of the impotence of the black man facing the white woman (Fanon, 1967).

Many Middle Eastern intellectuals have chosen to leave their native lands because they can no longer live there. Sometimes the reasons are economic, sometimes political. For over a century, the Lebanese and Egyptians have left for Europe and the Americas and more recently the Turks for Germany, in search of prosperity unavailable in the eastern and southern Mediterranean. Citizens of repressive regimes, like the former Iraqi regime of Hussein, the Syrian Baathist government, and the Islamic Republic of Iran, have fled so as to find a place where they might breathe and speak freely. Many Middle Eastern intellectuals have congregated in Paris, London, and New York where they have founded publishing houses and launched newspapers and magazines.

Emily Nasrallah has examined the question of emigration from a Lebanese perspective. *September Birds* (1962), a novel about a village whose vitality was being drained as the young people were lured away to the capital and to the glittering West, was supposed to have a sequel about the return of the migratory birds. The war in Lebanon forced her and others like her to understand that there was to be no return, either because they were too comfortable in their new homes or because they had failed and were ashamed not to have realized the dream. In 1994 she published *Sleeping Embers,* a novel that seemed to bring closure to the question of emigration. Those who left should not come back because, when they do, they dredge up stories that disturb people's tranquility.

The twentieth century was the century of mass migration, and so the story of the stateless person has come to symbolize the dilemma of globalization: to be nowhere at home. The various political upheavals in the Middle East have caused many to leave their homes without hope of return. Ghassan Kanafani (1936–1972) was one such refugee who went to Beirut. His 1963 novel *Men in the Sun,* which was adapted into a film titled *The Dupes,* explores the possible outcome of the choice to leave one's home and to seek asylum in Arab countries. Three men entrust themselves to a Palestinian guide who has promised to drive them across the desert separating Iraq and Kuwait. When they have almost made it, the driver is delayed at a border post. The men, hidden in the truck's empty water tank, suffocate in the heat.

Palestinian writer Ghassan Kanafani,
who was murdered in a car bomb explosion
in Beirut in 1972.

Jabra Ibrahim Jabra (1919–1995), who left Palestine for Iraq, has written several novels, all of which delve into the lives of dispersed Palestinians. *In Search of Walid Mas'ud* (1978) brings together those who have chosen to write about their situation with others who have decided to fight to change it. They debate the most appropriate means to defend a cause.

After the Iranian Revolution and then during the punishing Iran-Iraq War (1980–1988), many Iranians fled the country. They are now scattered all over Europe and North America where some are writing in the languages of their new countries, but many continue to write in Persian. The latter include Mahshid Amirshahi (b. 1940), with her books *At Home* (1986) and *Away from Home* (1998), and Goli Taraqqi, who lives in Paris. In 1992, Taraqqi published *Scattered Memories,* a collection of stories about the pains of exile. Like Nasrallah, she reveals the impoverished lives of those who had emigrated. Taraqqi reminds readers that exile means leaving the physical home where there is privacy and autonomy, but it also entails humiliation since it forces dependence on others. Shahrnush Parsipur, an acclaimed feminist writer whose 1989 book *Women Without Men* was banned by the Islamic Republic, is now in California, where she wrote *Tea Ceremony in the Presence of the Wolf* (1993). This collection of short stories elaborates on the sense of terrible loss and the condemnation to perpetual wandering that mark the experience of exile.

Those who write in exile often feel farther from home than the miles that mark that distance. Like the Algerians who left during the war of independence they feel, perhaps, that they should be fighting side by side with those intellectuals who have chosen to stay regardless of the cost. Yet in a world where borders are increasingly porous and where migration is a necessary part of many people's lives, a new kind of cultural nationalism is emerging that allows those who are living far from their land of birth or ancestry to retain very real ties of identity. Literary associations in the Middle East are slowly recognizing that their writers may not live in the country that they claim as their nation. Turkish novelist Habib Bektas (b. 1951) is a good example. Since 1972, he has been living and writing in Germany. In 1997, his book *The Smell of the Shadow* won the Turkish Inkilab Kitabevi Press annual prize; it was the first time this coveted prize had been awarded to a nonresident Turk. Bektas explained that his Turkishness did not consist in residence in Turkey, but in language: he lives in Turkish. This adoption of the language as nation is a strategy that many writers in exile invoke.

The Muslim State

The Iranian Revolution had been simmering long before it boiled over. Mention has already been made of Al-e Ahmad and Daneshvar, whose writings during the late 1960s seemed to be calling for reform of a society that was too much given over to the delights of the West. There is a pronounced Islamic tone in what they write. Two years before the revolution, Parsipur wrote *The Heat of the Year Zero*. The heroine's description of suffocation in the overwhelming heat of the summer and her stolen and then censured glances at men anticipated what the new regime had in store for its women.

In the early days of the revolution, the Islamic government of Iran, much like its royal predecessor, concerned itself with cultural production. Whatever was seen to be oppositional to its specifically Islamic interests was carefully censured. The case of Salman Rushdie has entered the annals of world history. Some writers complied with the government's will and wrote piously about the virtues of the revolution. Others, many of them women, protested the new restrictions; for example, A. Rahmani's "Short Hike" acts out a tense moment of defiance between an Islamic guard and the woman he has just reprimanded for revealing a strand of hair. Milani notes that in the short two-year period between 1983, when compulsory veiling was generally enforced, and 1985 "126 books by or about women were published in Iran." Restrictions had forced women to speak out (Milani, 1992:231).

As previous chapters have explored, it is not only in Iran that Muslims have called for the establishment of an Islamic state. After the abolition of the Ottoman caliphate in 1924 and the consequent secularization of Turkey, Muslims elsewhere in the Middle East became nervous. This was particularly true in Egypt where the first formal association of Muslim revolutionaries was established in 1929. Other such groups formed, and many remain active today in many countries of the Middle East. Their increasing prominence in public life became a theme in literature from the 1970s on. In 1977, during a period spent in exile in Germany, the Egyptian 'Abd al-Hakim Qasim (1935–1990) wrote a story about the attempted conversion to Islam of a poor Coptic umbrella maker. "The Mahdi" explores the new animosities arising between Christians and Muslims who had always lived together peacefully. The story also reveals the growing chasm between young Islamists and more traditional Muslims in rural Egypt (al-Musawi, 2009: 172–177).

The Islamists have played contradictory roles in the history and politics of their countries. In Egypt, for instance, they helped leaders like Nasser come to power, but they have also sought to remove such leaders. During the mid-1960s, Nasser arrested several Islamist leaders. Their years in prison produced several memoirs, of which arguably the most interesting is that of the leader of the Muslim Ladies Association Zaynab al-Ghazali (1912–2004). In 1965, she was incarcerated for a year in the War Prison with her male colleagues. That experience inspired her book *Days from My Life* (1977). Less memoir than inspirational literature, this text recounts the tortures and miracles that mark their subject as especially blessed. It can be read as a model for young women seeking guidance as they try to combine political ambitions with their scripturally defined roles as wives and mothers.

In 1981, a group of Islamists assassinated Egyptian president Sadat. They charged him with making an unpardonable compromise in promoting the Camp David Accords with Israel. The Islamists do not confine their targets to political leaders, however. As seen in Algeria in the 1990s, Islamists are increasingly focusing their attention on intellectuals who are charged with secularism and perversion of the people's morals. In 1992, Egyptian fundamentalists assassinated journalist Farag Foda for his critique of their discourse. Most annoying to them had been his book *Before the Fall* (1992). That summer, they published in paperback format the proceedings of a trial they had conducted, titled *Nawal El Saadawi in the Witness Stand.* With its cover picture of a wild, white-haired woman staring out from behind bars, the book was so widely distributed that it could be found in the streets of Cairo on the blankets of sidewalk book vendors, selling for a few piasters. These echoes of the fatwa (religious opinion) Ayatollah Khomeini had pronounced on February 14, 1989, calling for Rushdie's death for his novel *Satanic Verses* were too loud to be ignored. Moral censure of literature had escalated to the sanction of deadly assaults on authors. Nawal El Saadawi, who is accustomed to threats from governments and Islamists, did not shake this threat off as idle. When the government, which had itself imprisoned her for a few months during Sadat's regime, sent guards to keep watch on her apartment, she realized that she had to leave. She went to Duke University in North Carolina where she spent most of the following four years writing her autobiography, *Daughter of Isis.*

El Saadawi was condemned to death because of two books. *The Fall of the Imam* (1987) is the lyrically told tale of the assassination of the highest authority in the land, a transparent reference to Sadat's assassination, and of the pursuit and execution of his assassin who is also his illegitimate daughter, Bint Allah. *Innocence of the Devil* (1992) takes place in a psychiatric hospital where one of the patients thinks he is God and another that he is Satan. The collapse of the God-Satan tension reveals the vanity of trying to know God through his opposite. The God who is paired with the devil is the God of organized monotheistic religions, a tyrant who must be resisted. These two novels are open attacks on the hypocrisy and emptiness of religions. Unlike El Saadawi's earlier fiction, in which women are confined to the role of victim, these novels explore the ways in which women resist the tyranny of men who use scripture to justify violence against women. Fearing them, these men link women with the devil and then justify their actions in religious terms.

Translation and Recognition

Middle Eastern writers have attracted world attention over the past fifty years. Three writers have won the Nobel Prize for Literature: in 1966, the Israeli Shmuel Yosef Agnon (1888–1970); in 1988, the Egyptian Naguib Mahfouz; and in 2006, the Turkish Orhan Pamuk. In 1989, Moroccan Tahar Benjelloun won the Prix Goncourt, the first Arab to be awarded this coveted French prize. In 1997, Turk Yashar Kemal was recognized with Italy's most prestigious prize, the Nonino Literary Award.

At the same time, more and more Arabic, Hebrew, Persian, and Turkish fiction and poetry are being translated into European languages. Previously the translation process had been idiosyncratic; random works appeared according to individual tastes of translators. By the mid-1980s, however, the translation process became more systematic. For example, in 1981, Palestinian poet and literary critic Salma al-Khadra' al-Jayyusi founded the Project for Translation from Arabic (PROTA) in the United States. At first, these translations were picked up only by marginal presses dedicated to publishing works by writers from the Global South. By the late 1980s, however, major European, US, and even Japanese publishing houses, including some university presses that came to consider Middle Eastern literature as potential textbooks, started adopting Middle Eastern literary series as well as the works of individual authors.

The growth of the translation industry provides readers with unprecedented access to the cultural imaginary of people they had previously known only through the stories of journalists, scholars, and travelers. This is important, above all, for the writers and particularly for those who have already gained a share of recognition abroad. They are writing with the awareness that their works will be translated, and that what they say about their culture will be consumed far from the local readership they originally targeted. Writing thus entails consequences that must be anticipated. Self-criticism must become what Moroccan cultural critic 'Abdelkebir Khatibi has called "double critique." The eye turned in on the injustices of a society must simultaneously look out to discern the contours of the external enemy. Local tyrannies must be held in balance with the dangers of global hegemony, with the understanding that the one interacts with the other. This double critique changes the way people think and write, and this changed writing is cultivating new tastes and creating new markets. Middle Eastern writers of the twenty-first century are seeing their work become part of a global project in which they will play an increasingly visible role.

Notes

The author is indebted to Guven Guzeldere and Erdag Goknar for information, invaluable advice, and stimulating conversations about Turkish culture. Warm thanks to Mohamad Tavakoli-Targhi for a careful reading of the penultimate version of this chapter and for wonderful suggestions concerning Iranian literature.

1. Albert Memmi notes that, between 1947 and 1986, Algerian women published thirty-seven novels and short story collections (1987:6).

2. For example, Nawal El Saadawi first published her autobiography, *My Papers My Life,* in 1995 in *Al-Musawwar,* a magazine that is distributed throughout the Arab world.

Bibliography

Alvi, Sajida. 1984. "Buzurg Alavi's Writings from Prison (1940s)." Pp. 274–291 in Thomas M. Ricks (ed.), *Critical Perspectives on Modern Persian Literature.* Washington, DC: Three Continents Press.

cooke, miriam. 1988. *War's Other Voices: Women Writers on the Lebanese Civil War.* Cambridge: Cambridge University Press.

———. 1997. *Women and the War Story.* Berkeley: University of California Press.

———. 2007. *Dissident Syria. Making Oppositional Arts Official.* Durham: Duke University Press.

Daragahi, Haideh. 1984. "The Shaping of the Modern Persian Short Story." Pp. 104–123 in Thomas M. Ricks (ed.), *Critical Perspectives on Modern Persian Literature.* Washington, DC: Three Continents Press.

Fanon, Frantz. 1967. *Black Skin, White Masks.* New York: Grove Press.

Goknar, Erdag. 2008. "The Novel in Turkish: Narrative Tradition to Nobel Prize." Pp. 472–503 in Resat Kasaba (ed.), *Cambridge History of Turkey.* Vol. 4. Cambridge: Cambridge University Press.

Hafez, Sabry. 1992. "The Modern Arabic Short Story." Pp. 270–328 in Mustafa M. Badawi (ed.), *Modern Arabic Literature.* Cambridge: Cambridge University Press.

Halman, Talat Sait (ed.). 1976. *Modern Turkish Drama. An Anthology of Plays in Translation.* Minneapolis: Bibliotheca Islamica.

———. 1982. *Contemporary Turkish Literature.* Rutherford, NJ: Fairleigh Dickinson University Press.

Lewis, Franklin, and Farzin Yazdanfar. 1996. *In a Voice of Their Own: A Collection of Stories by Iranian Women Written Since the Revolution of 1979.* Costa Mesa, CA: Mazda.

Memmi, Albert. 1987. Introduction to *Anthologie du Roman Maghrebin.* Paris: Nathan.

Milani, Farzaneh. 1992. *Veils and Words: The Emerging Voices of Iranian Women Writers.* Syracuse: Syracuse University Press.

Moayyad, Heshmat (ed.). 1991. *Stories from Iran: A Chicago Anthology, 1921–1991.* Washington, DC: Mage.

al-Musawi, Muhsin. 2009. *Islam on the Street: Religion in Modern Arabic Literature.* Lanham, MD: Rowman & Littlefield.

Najmabadi, Afsaneh. 1998. "Crafting an Educated Housewife in Iran." Pp. 91–125 in Lila Abu-Lughod (ed.), *Remaking Women: Feminism and Modernity in the Middle East.* Princeton: Princeton University Press.

Somekh, Sasson. 1992. "The Neo-Classical Arabic Poets." Pp. 36–81 in Mustafa M. Badawi (ed.), *Modern Arabic Literature.* Cambridge: Cambridge University Press.

Tavakoli-Targhi, Mohamad. 1990. "Refashioning Iran: Language and Culture During the Constitutional Revolution." *Iranian Studies* 23, no. 1:77–101.

———. 1999. November 20. Inteview with author, Durham, NC.

Yudkin, Leon I. 1984. *1948 and After: Aspects of Israeli Literature.* Manchester: University of Manchester Press.

14

Trends and Prospects

Jillian Schwedler

Much of this volume has looked backward, as we traced the imprint of the Middle East on the world and of the world on these twenty-plus countries. In this final chapter I look to the future to assess what might be coming down the line for the peoples of the region. Among the most notable issues are those related to the role of religious actors in the new political institutions of the Arab uprisings, the continued need for economic development that finally alleviates (rather than increases) inequality, continued foreign intervention in political as well as economic realms, and the explosive role of new media in shaping the politics and cultures of the region.

The Arab Uprisings and Popular Mobilizations

It is impossible to now look at the Middle East without thinking about the dramatic events of the Arab uprisings: wholly peaceful protests that brought down repressive regimes in Tunisia and Egypt; a peaceful protest that led to a quasi-transition in Yemen where a religiously conservative female demonstrator, Tuwakkil Karman, was awarded the 2011 Nobel Peace Prize; protests that turned to armed conflict in Libya and Syria; harsh repression of a massive uprising in Bahrain; and numerous other regimes scrambling to deflate opposition movements through bribery or tepid reforms. The short- and medium-term effects of the uprisings are as yet unknown, but it is not an exaggeration to suggest that the Middle East is irrevocably changed.

The impacts of the Arab uprisings are many and complex. The political changes are most evident, as postrevolutionary states struggle against pressures from a range of interests, including those of the former political, military, and economic elites. A wide range of peoples have begun to feel empowered and are expressing that newfound sense of agency while those most threatened by that empowerment are mostly pushing back. But the uprisings were not only about repression and political exclusion. The majority of protesters in Tunisia and Egypt, for example, were most immediately angry over their dismal economic circumstances. From laborers and unions demanding higher wages (or that wages should be paid at all!), to the frustrations of university graduates unable to find even the most humble of jobs, one central grievance was that a tiny elite was flourishing while most people were suffering. Expensive shopping malls and gated communities with swimming pools popped up everywhere while most suffered through routine water shortages and occasional electrical blackouts. Regimes celebrated gleaming neoliberal projects that brought foreign firms to invest in their countries, but few felt positive effects even as they walked past those construction sites daily. The Arab uprisings have not changed the economic inequality of the region, but the now-common demands for greater democratic citizen involvement in governance—in some cases, realized—will not likely be silenced in the near future.

As in most of the developing world, efforts to fundamentally restructure the economy are complicated by accumulated debt from prior failed projects as well as the entrenched elites' intent on increasing their personal wealth at the expense of the country as a whole. The uprisings have opened new spaces for critiques of these practices, but the reality is that powerful domestic as well as international forces have such strong interests in seeing those projects move forward that even postrevolutionary regimes—which have many issues to tackle, including ongoing demonstrations—are unlikely to entirely reverse those projects. Indeed, a conventional characteristic of posttransition societies is a high degree of bargaining among new and old elites hoping to control the direction and degree of reform. We are undoubtedly seeing these dynamics in Egypt, Libya, Yemen, and Tunisia; and, when the Assad regime in Syria finally falls, we can expect power struggles among various factions there as well. The Arab uprisings have not changed the reality that the economic and political legacies of European imperialism in the Middle East have hindered the creation of autonomous industrial programs independent of foreign assistance, external borrowing, or intervention by international organizations, a pattern that is characteristic of historically colonized states throughout the world. Domestic obstacles include burgeoning urbanization and the environmental problems that this often creates as well as rising unemployment and continued restrictions on economic opportunities for women.

Another characteristic of some Middle Eastern economies continues to make them different from most other countries: the role of oil extraction. From Algeria to Yemen to Iran, petroleum has paid for many development projects. Indeed, during the 1970s and early 1980s oil wealth was a major distinguishing feature of the region, and the "oil decade" of 1973 to 1983 left two positive legacies. First, it led to the establishment of a large, indigenous professional class of engineers, bankers, doctors, and educators. Second, even after taking into account failed and inappropriate projects, worthless boondoggles, and greed and corruption, oil revenues did pay for considerable basic infrastructure in much of the region. Both of these factors should facilitate further economic growth and development even as the Arab uprisings shake up long-standing political structures.

New Media

A related way in which the uprisings have changed the region has been to create a sense of empowerment and to open up new spaces to expressing outrage and frustration at the status quo. These spaces include the retaking of public spaces by citizens across the region: Bourguiba Boulevard in Tunisia, Tahrir Square in Egypt, Pearl Square in Bahrain, and Change Square in Yemen. But new media have also created new spaces for personal expression as well as social networking and political mobilization. Many Western observers have romanticized the role of social media in the Arab uprisings, erroneously calling the uprisings Facebook or Twitter revolutions. The vast majority of peoples in the region are not connected to these networks, and in fact most do not even have regular Internet access. At the same time, it is unquestionable that new media in part made the revolutions possible, or at least contributed to their specific dynamics.

With the rise of satellite television stations such as Al Jazeera in the late 1990s, these new means of information exchange meant that governments could no longer dominate the information that reached their populations. The availability of cell phones meant that people no longer had to wait sometimes years for telephone service to be connected, nor did they have to be wealthy enough to bribe the necessary people. Cell phone technology has changed the face of refugee flows, providing a lifeline that keeps scattered family members connected.

On closer inspection, the clash of civilizations that is supposed to characterize the yawning divide between the West and the Middle East (among other regions) is less about religion and culture than it is about inequality and dispossession of the vast majority of the people from their wealthy, privileged political and economic elites. Religious revival movements mobilize and spend vast sums trying to affect the shape of government policies domestically and abroad, just as they do in the United States. Teenage bloggers in Iran, like many of their counterparts in the West, complain that their parents will not let them date whomever they want. This is not to suggest that there are no differences between the Middle East and the West, as there certainly are, but to point out that there are also many similarities, familiar situations, and shared concerns of parents wanting their children to have

*Eyes on the street: Protests throughout the Middle East receive widespread
media attention both domestically and internationally. These photographers
line up to cover an anti-Israeli protest in Amman in June 2010.*

better lives. Thus, the real challenge of understanding the contemporary
Middle East is not one of learning the particularities of a different culture
(although those challenges exist), but of recognizing the precise ways in
which political, social, and economic patterns differ from elsewhere as well
as the ways in which they are similar.

Conclusion

As the contributors to this volume have made evident, the Middle East is
defined not only by state boundaries but also by history, economic interactions, cultural patterns, and natural resources, among other attributes. It is a
highly dynamic place with deep connections to global trends at the macro
level and longings for a better life at the micro level, far from the mysterious, exotic, impenetrable region it is often portrayed to be. It is a region in
which diverse peoples struggle—and have struggled for centuries—to improve their lives, gain the dignity of self-governance, and live by the moral
frameworks that inspire them and give meaning to their lives. They write
novels, watch television, e-mail friends, and pray to God. Every region of
the world faces particular sets of challenges—obstacles that inhibit political, economic, and social reforms. The Middle East is no different, and we
hope that this collection of writings has provided you with the conceptual

frameworks and historical details necessary to help you understand these challenges. We also hope that you do not dwell on what is least familiar and, instead, recognize and explore those issues that you share with the region's peoples and their aspirations. Whether you find that connection through literature, a strong sense of religious identity, Facebook, or elsewhere, recognizing and building on those connections provides the most tangible and effective means of bridging the artificial "cultural" divides on which all conflict and violence are founded.

Acronyms

AAA	American Anthropological Association
AHC	Arab Higher Committee for Palestine
AHDR	Arab Human Development Report
AKP	Justice and Development Party (Turkey)
ARAMCO	Arabian American Oil Company
BBC	British Broadcasting Corporation
BCE	before the common era
BDS	Boycott, Divestment, and Sanctions movement
BP	British Petroleum
CADAW	UN Convention on the Elimination of All Forms of Discrimination Against Women
CE	of the common era
CFP	French National Oil Company
CIA	Central Intelligence Agency (United States)
CNN	Cable News Network
CWP	Coalition of Women for Peace
DFLP	Democratic Front for the Liberation of Palestine
DHS	Demographic and Health Surveys
DNA	deoxyribonucleic acid
EFTA	European Free Trade Association
EFU	Egyptian Feminist Union
ESCWA	Economic and Social Commission for West Asia (UN)
EU	European Union
FBD	father's brother's daughter
FDI	foreign direct investment
FIS	Islamic Salvation Front (Algeria)

FJP	Freedom and Justice Party (Egypt)
FLN	National Liberation Front (Algeria)
GAFTA	Greater Arab Free Trade Area
GAP	Güneydoğu Anadolu Projesi (Turkey)
GCC	Gulf Cooperation Council
GDP	gross domestic product
GLBT	Gay Lesbian Bisexual Transgender
GNI	gross national income
GPC	General Popular Congress (Yemen)
Hamas	Islamic Resistance Movement (Palestine)
HDI	Human Development Index
HTS	Human Terrain Systems
IAF	Islamic Action Front (Jordan)
ICG	International Crisis Group
ICJ	International Court of Justice
IEA	International Energy Agency
IFI	international financial institution
ILO	International Labour Organization
IMF	International Monetary Fund
IOC	international oil company
ISI	import substitution industrialization
JMP	Joint Meetings Party (Yemen)
KOC	Kuwait Oil Company
MDG	Millennium Development Goal
MENA	Middle East–North Africa
NATO	North Atlantic Treaty Organization
NGO	nongovernmental organization
NIOC	National Iranian Oil Company
OAPEC	Organization of Arab Petroleum Exporting Countries
OECD	Organisation for Economic Co-operation and Development
OIC	Organisation of Islamic Cooperation (formerly Organization of the Islamic Conference)
OPEC	Organization of Petroleum Exporting Countries
OPIFG	Iranian People's Fedayeen Guerrillas
PA	Palestinian Authority
PCP	Palestine Communist Party
PDR Yemen	People's Democratic Republic of Yemen (South Yemen)
PFLP	Popular Front for the Liberation of Palestine
PKK	Kurdistan Workers Party (Turkey)
PLO	Palestine Liberation Organization
PMOI	People's Mojahedin Organization of Iran

PNA	Palestinian National Authority
PPP	purchasing power parity
PQBDS	Palestinian Queers for BDS
PROTA	Project for Translation from Arabic
QIZ	Qualifying Industrial Zone
RFFG	Reserve Fund for Future Generations
RP	Refah Partisi (Welfare Party, Turkey)
R2P	responsibility to protect
SAVAK	Sazman-e Ettelaat va Amniyat-e Keshvar (Iran)
SCAF	Supreme Council of Armed Forces (Egypt)
SWF	sovereign wealth funds
TGNA	Turkish Grand National Assembly
UAE	United Arab Emirates
UAR	United Arab Republic
UN	United Nations
UNCTAD	United Nations Conference on Trade and Development
UNDP	United Nations Development Programme
UNEP	United Nations Environment Programme
UNESCO	United Nations Educational, Scientific and Cultural Organization
UNHCR	United Nations High Commissioner for Refugees
UNRWA	United Nations Relief and Works Agency for Palestinian Refugees in the Near East
USAID	US Agency for International Development
USSR	Union of Soviet Socialist Republics
WMD	weapons of mass destruction
WOI	Women's Organization of Iran
WTO	World Trade Organization
WWCC	Wafdist Women's Central Committee

Basic Political Data

The Basic Political Data was updated by Tyler Schuenemann from material originally compiled by David Dolson and Deborah J. Gerner. While the data are based on information from a variety of sources, accurate data on Middle Eastern political events are often difficult to obtain and conflicting accounts and dates are common. Although we have generally used at least three different sources to corroborate each item, readers may nonetheless find discrepancies in other sources, including some material presented in the chapters. All population figures are estimates from United Nations Department of Economic and Social Affairs, Population Division (2011) except for the West Bank and Gaza Strip, which are from the Central Intelligence Agency's *CIA World Factbook* (2012). The United Nations Development Programme's Human Development Index (HDI) is a composite measure based on life expectancy; adult literacy; combined primary, secondary, and tertiary enrollment in school; and adjusted per capita income in each country. The HDI score can range from 0.0 to 1.0, with higher numbers reflecting greater development in terms of longevity, knowledge, and a decent standard of living; n.a. indicates the data is not available.

Democratic and Popular Republic of Algeria
Capital City Algiers
Date of Independence from France July 3, 1962
Population 35,468,000
HDI Score 0.677
Rulers Since Independence
1. President Ahmed Ben Bella, 1962–June 1965
2. President Houari Boumedienne, June 1965–December 1978
3. President Benjedid Chadli, February 1979–1992
4. Five-member High Council of State, headed by Muhammed Boudiaf, fulfilled the function of the head of state until January 1994

5. President Liamine Zeroual, appointed January 30, 1994
6. President Liamine Zeroual, November 16, 1995–April 25, 1999
7. President Abdelaziz Bouteflika, elected on April 15, 1999, after all six rivals withdrew, charging electoral fraud

Kingdom of Bahrain
Capital City Manama
Date of Independence from Great Britain August 15, 1971
Population 1,262,000
HDI Score 0.801
Rulers Since Independence
1. Emir Isa ibn Salmon al-Khalifah, 1961–March 6, 1999
2. Emir Hamad ibn Isa al-Khalifah, March 6, 1999. In February 2002, Bahrain became a constitutional monarchy and Hamad took the title of king

Federal Islamic Republic of the Comoros
Capital City Moroni
Date of Independence from France July 6, 1975
Population 735,000
HDI Score 0.428
Rulers Since Independence
1. President Ahmed Abdallah, July 1975–August 1975
2. Coup led by Ali Soilih, August 1975; president, 1976–1978 (assassinated)
3. President Ahmed Abdallah, reinstated in coup by mercenaries under Robert Denard, 1978–November 27, 1989 (assassinated)
4. Robert Denard, November 27, 1989–December 15, 1989 (removed by French government)
5. Said Djohar, December 16, 1989–March 1996
6. President Mohammad Taki Abdoulkarim, March 1996–April 30, 1999
7. Coup led by Col. Assoumani Azali, April 30, 1999–2002
8. Col. Azali temporarily stepped down, only to be elected president in April 2002–2006
9. President Ahmed Abdallah Sambi, May 15, 2006–May 26, 2011
10. President Ikililou Dhoinine, May 26, 2011–

Republic of Djibouti
Capital City Djibouti
Date of Independence from France June 27, 1977
Population 889,000
HDI Score 0.402
Rulers Since Independence

1. President Hassan Gouled Aptidon, June 24, 1977; reelected June 1981, April 1987, May 1993
2. President Isma'il Omar Guelleh, elected May 8, 1999; reelected April 2005 and April 2011

Arab Republic of Egypt
Capital City Cairo
Date of Independence from Great Britain February 28, 1922
Population 81,121,000
HDI Score 0.620
Rulers Since Independence
1. King Fu'ad I, 1917–1936
2. King Farouk, 1936–1952 (overthrown in coup led by Col. Gamal Abdul Nasser and Abdul al-Hakim)
3. President Mohammed Neguib, June 1953–November 1954
4. Prime Minister Gamal Abdul Nasser, 1954–1956; president, 1956–1970
5. President Anwar Sadat, 1970–October 1981 (assassinated)
6. President Hosni Mubarak, October 14, 1981–February 11, 2011 (overthrown by mass uprising)
7. President Mohammad Mursi, June 30, 2012–

Islamic Republic of Iran
Capital City Tehran
Date of Independence Not colonized
Population 73,974,000
HDI Score 0.702
Rulers During Twentieth and Twenty-first Centuries
1. Qajar dynasty: Muzaffar al-Din, 1896–1907; Muhammad Ali, 1907–1909; Ahmad, 1909–1924
2. Pahlavi dynasty: Reza Shah, 1926–1941; Mohammad Reza Shah, 1941–1979
3. Religious leaders: Ayatollah Ruhollah Khomeini, 1979–1989; Ayatollah Sayyed Ali Khamenei, 1989–
4. Presidents: Mehdi Bazargan, 1979–1980; Abolhassan Bani-Sadr, 1980–1981; Muhammad Ali Raja'i, 1981; Sayyed Ali Khamenei, October 1981–July 1989; Hojatolislam Ali Akbar Hashemi Rafsanjani, July 1989–1997; Mohammad Khatami, 1997–2005; Mahmood Ahmadinejad, elected 2005; reelected 2009

Republic of Iraq
Capital City Baghdad
Date of Independence from Great Britain October 3, 1932
Population 31,672,000

HDI Score   n.a.
Rulers Since Independence
1. King Faisal I, 1921–1933
2. King Ghazi ibn Faisal, 1933–1939
3. King Faisal II, 1939–July 14, 1958 (overthrown)
4. Brig. Gen. Abd al-Karim Qasim, July 14, 1958–February 1963 (overthrown)
5. National Council of Revolutionary Command led by Prime Minister Ahmad Hasan al-Bakr and President Abd al-Salaam Arif, February 1963–November 18, 1963 (overthrown)
6. President Abd al-Salaam Arif, November 1963–April 1966 (died in accident)
7. President Abd al-Rahman Arif, April 1966–July 17, 1968 (overthrown)
8. Revolutionary Command Council led by President Ahmad Hasan al-Bakr, July 17, 1968–July 16, 1979
9. President Saddam Hussein, July 16, 1979–2003 (overthrown by US-led invasion)
10. Interim authority (Coalition Provisional Authority and the Iraqi Governing Council), April 21, 2003–June 28, 2004
11. Iraqi Interim Government headed by Prime Minister Iyad Allawi, June 28, 2004–May 3, 2005
12. Iraqi Transitional Government headed by President Jalal Talabani and Prime Minister Ibrahim al Jaafari, May 3, 2005–May 20, 2006
13. Prime Minister Nouri al-Maliki, May 20, 2006; reelected March 7, 2010

State of Israel
Capital City   Tel Aviv or Jerusalem; contested internationally
Date of Independence from Great Britain   May 15, 1948
Population   7,418,000
HDI Score   0.872
Rulers Since Independence
1. Prime Minister David Ben-Gurion, 1948–1953
2. Prime Minister Moshe Sharett, 1953–1955
3. Prime Minister David Ben-Gurion, 1955–1963
4. Prime Minister Levi Eshkol, 1963–1969
5. Prime Minister Yigal Allon (acting), 1969
6. Prime Minister Golda Meir, 1969–1974
7. Prime Minister Yitzhak Rabin, 1974–1977
8. Prime Minister Shimon Peres (acting), 1977
9. Prime Minister Menachem Begin, 1977–1983
10. Prime Minister Yitzhak Shamir, 1983–1984

11. Prime Minister Shimon Peres, 1984–1986
12. Prime Minister Yitzhak Shamir, 1986–1992
13. Prime Minister Yitzhak Rabin, 1992–1995 (assassinated)
14. Prime Minister Shimon Peres, 1995–1996
15. Prime Minister Benjamin Netanyahu, 1996–1999
16. Prime Minister Ehud Barak, 1999–2001
17. Prime Minister Ariel Sharon, 2001–2006
18. Prime Minister Ehud Olmert, January 2006–2009
19. Prime Minister Benjamin Netanyahu, March 2009–2013; re-elected 2013

Hashemite Kingdom of Jordan

Capital City Amman
Date of Independence from Great Britain May 25, 1946
Population 6,187,000
HDI Score 0.681
Rulers Since Independence
1. Emir then King Abdullah I, 1921–July 1951 (assassinated)
2. King Talal, 1951–1953 (abdicated)
3. King Hussein I, 1953–February 7, 1999
4. King Abdullah II, February 7, 1999–

State of Kuwait

Capital City Kuwait City
Date of Independence from Great Britain June 19, 1961
Population 2,741,000
HDI Score 0.771
Rulers Since Independence
1. Shaikh Abdullah III al-Sabah, 1950–1965
2. Shaikh Sabah al-Salim al-Sabah, 1965–1977
3. Shaikh Jabir al-Ahmad al-Jabir al-Sabah, December 31, 1977–2006
4. Shaikh Saad al-Abdullah al-Sabah, January 15, 2006–January 24, 2006 (forced to step down because of ill health)
5. Shaikh Sabah al-Ahmed al-Jabir al-Sabah, January 29, 2006–

Republic of Lebanon

Capital City Beirut
Date of Independence from France November 22, 1943
Population 4,228,000
HDI Score n.a.
Rulers Since Independence
1. President Bisharaal-Khuri, 1943–1952 (prime ministers: Riyad al-Solh, Sami al-Solh)

2. President Camille Chamoun, 1952–1958 (prime ministers: Abdallah al-Yafi, Sami al-Solh, Rashid Karami)
3. President Fu'ad Chehab, 1958–1964 (prime minister: Rashid Karami)
4. President Charles Hilu, 1964–1970 (prime minister: Rashid Karami)
5. President Sulayman Franjiyya, 1970–1976 (prime ministers: Rachid Anis al-Solh, Rashid Karami, Saeb Salaam)
6. President Elias Sarkis, 1976–1982 (prime minister: Salim al-Hoss)
7. President Beshir Gemayel, 1982 (assassinated)
8. President Amin Gemayel, 1982–1988 (prime ministers: Shafiq al-Wazzan, Rashid Karami, Salim al-Hoss)
9. Gen. Michel Aoun, 1988–1990 (prime minister: Salim al-Hoss)
10. President Elias Hrawi, 1990–1998 (prime ministers: Salim al-Hoss, Umar Karami, Rafiq al-Hariri)
11. President Emile Lahoud, 1998–2007 (prime ministers: Salim al-Hoss [December 2, 1998–October 23, 2000], Rafiq al-Hariri [October 23, 2000–October 21, 2004], Omar Karami [October 21, 2004–April 15, 2005], Najib Mikati [April 15, 2005–June 30, 2005], Fouad Siniora [July 19, 2005–2009])
12. Presidency vacant from November 23, 2007 (prime minister: Fouad Siniora [July 19, 2005–2008])
13. President Michel Sulayman, May 25, 2008– (prime ministers: Saad Hariri [2009–2011]; Najib Miqati [July 7, 2011–])

Socialist People's Libyan Arab Jamahiriyah (Republic)
Capital City Tripoli
Date of Independence from Italy December 24, 1951
Population 6,355,000
HDI Score 0.755
Rulers Since Independence
1. King Idris, 1951–1969
2. Col. Muammar Mohammed Qaddafi, leader of the revolution, September 1969–2011 (overthrown)
3. Libyan Transitional National Council: Prime Minister Abd al-Rahim al-Keeb, September 2011–

Islamic Republic of Mauritania
Capital City Nouakchott
Date of Independence from France November 28, 1960
Population 3,460,000
HDI Score 0.433
Rulers Since Independence
1. President Mokhtar Ould Daddah, 1961–July 10, 1978 (overthrown)

2. Lt. Col. Mustapha Ould Mohammed Salek, July 10, 1978–
   June 1979 (forced to resign)
3. Lt. Col. Mohammed Mahmoud Ould Louly, June 1979–
   January 4, 1980 (overthrown)
4. Lt. Col. Mohamed Khouna Ould Haidalla, January 4, 1980–
   December 1984 (overthrown)
5. Col. Maaouya Ould Sidi Ahmed Taya, 1984–2005 (overthrown);
   elected president in first multiparty elections, January 24, 1992;
   reelected December 12, 1997
6. Col. Ely Ould Mohamed Vall, August 3, 2005–2007
7. President Sidi Ould Cheikh Abdallahi, March 11, 2007–2008
   (overthrown in coup)
8. President Mohamed Ould Abdel Aziz, seized presidency in 2008,
   elected August 5, 2009–

Kingdom of Morocco
Capital City Rabat
Date of Independence from France March 2, 1956
Population 31,951,000
HDI Score 0.567
Rulers Since Independence
1. King Mohammed V, March 2, 1956–1961
2. King Hassan II, March 3, 1961–July 23, 1999
3. King Mohammed VI, July 23, 1999–

Sultanate of Oman
Capital City Muscat
Date of Independence Never officially a colony, but strong British
influence
Population 2,782,000
HDI Score n.a.
Rulers During Twentieth and Twenty-first Centuries
1. Sultan Faisal ibn Turki al-Said, 1888–1913
2. Sultan Tamir ibn Faisal al-Said, 1913–1932
3. Sultan Said ibn Tamir al-Said, 1932–1970
4. Sultan Qaboos ibn Said al-Said, 1970–

Palestinian Territories: West Bank and Gaza Strip
Capital City Jerusalem
Date of Independence The Palestinian Authority gained control
from Israel of most of the Gaza Strip and Jericho areas in May 1994.
Subsequent agreements increased the land under Palestinian or joint
Israeli-Palestinian jurisdiction. Since 2001, however, Israel has retaken
control of many of these areas.

Population West Bank: 2,622,544; Gaza Strip: 1,710,257
HDI Score n.a.
Rulers Since Gaza-Jericho Agreement
1. President Yasser Arafat, January 1996–2003
2. President Yasser Arafat and Prime Minister Mahmoud Abbas, 2003; President Yasser Arafat and Prime Minister Ahmad Qura'i, 2003–2004
3. President Rauhi Fattouh and Prime Minister Ahmad Qura'i, 2004–2005
4. President Mahmoud Abbas and Prime Minister Ahmad Qura'i, January 15, 2005–December 15, 2005; President Mahmoud Abbas and Prime Minister Nabil Shaath, December 15, 2005–December 24, 2005; President Mamoud Abbas and Prime Minister Ahmad Qura'i, December 24, 2005–February 19, 2006; President Mahmoud Abbas and Prime Minister Ismail Haniya, February 19, 2006–June 14, 2007; President Mahmoud Abbas and Prime Minister Salam Fayyad, June 15, 2007–

State of Qatar
Capital City Doha
Date of Independence from Great Britain September 3, 1971
Population 1,759,000
HDI Score 0.803
Rulers Since Independence
1. Emir Ahmad ibn Ali, 1971–1972
2. Emir Khalifah ibn Hamad al-Thani, 1972–June 27, 1995
3. Emir Hamad ibn Khalifah ibn Hamad al-Thani, June 27, 1995–

Kingdom of Saudi Arabia
Capital City Riyadh
Declaration of State September 23, 1932
Population 27,448,000
HDI Score 0.752
Rulers Since Statehood
1. King Abdul Aziz ibn Saud, 1932–1953
2. King Saud ibn Saud, 1953–1964
3. King Faisal ibn Saud, 1964–1975 (assassinated)
4. King Khalid ibn Saud, 1975–1982
5. King Fahd ibn Saud, 1982–2005
6. King Abdullah ibn Saud, 2005–

Somali Democratic Republic
Capital City Mogadishu
Date of Independence from Italy and Great Britain July 1, 1960

Population 9,331,000
HDI Score n.a.
Rulers Since Independence
1. President Aden Abdulla Osman, 1960–1967
2. President Abdirashid Ali Shirmarke, 1967–1969 (assassinated)
3. Maj. Gen. Mohammed Siad Barre, 1969–January 27, 1991
4. No functional government, 1991–2000
5. President Abdikassim Salad Hassan, August 26, 2000–2004
   (prime ministers: Hassan Abshir Farah [2001–2003], Muhammad
   Abdi Yusuf [2003–2004])
6. President Abdullahi Yusuf Ahmed, October 14, 2004–December
   2008 (prime ministers: Ali Muhammad Ghedi [2004–2007], Salim
   Aliyow Ibrow [2007], Nur Hassan Hussein [November 24,
   2007–2009])
7. Interim President Adan Mohamed Nuur Madobe, December 29,
   2008—January 31, 2009
8. Transitional Federal President Sharif Sheikh Ahmed, January 31,
   2009– (prime ministers: Omar Abdirashid Ali Sharmarke
   [2009–2010], Abdiwahid Elmi Gonjeh [2010], Mohamed
   Abdullahi Farmajo [2010–2011], Abdiweli Mohamed Ali
   [2011–])

Republic of South Sudan
Capital City Juba
Date of Independence via Secession from Sudan July 9, 2011
Population 10,625,176
HDI Score n.a.
Rulers Since Independence
1. President Salva Kiir Mayardit, July 9, 2011–

Democratic Republic of Sudan
Capital City Khartoum
Date of Independence from Great Britain January 1, 1956
Population 43,552,000
HDI Score 0.379
Rulers Since Independence
1. Prime Minister Ismail al-Azhari, 1956
2. Prime Minister Abdulla Khalil, 1956–1958
3. Prime Minister Ibrahim Abboud, 1958–1964
4. Prime Minister Sir el-Khatim el-Khalifah, 1964–1965
5. Prime Minister Muhammed Ahmad Mahgoub, 1965–1966
6. Prime Minister Sayed Sadiq el-Mahdi, 1966–1967
7. Prime Minister Muhammed Ahmad Mahgoub, 1967–1969
8. Prime Minister Abubakr Awadallah, 1969

9. President Jaafar Mohammed Nimeiri, May 1969–April 1985 (overthrown)
10. Lt. Gen. Abdel Rahman Swareddahab, chairman, Transitional Military Council, April 6, 1985–1986
11. President Ahmed Ali al-Mirghani and Prime Minister Sadiq al-Mahdi, 1986–June 30, 1989 (overthrown)
12. Prime Minister Omar Hassan Ahmed al-Bashir, June 30, 1989; appointed president October 16, 1993; reelected 1996, 2000–

Syrian Arab Republic
Capital City Damascus
Date of Independence from France April 17, 1946
Population 20,411,000
HDI Score 0.589
Rulers Since Independence
1. President Shukri al-Quwatly, 1946–1949 (overthrown)
2. Gen. Husni al-Zaim, March 1949–August 1949
3. Gen. Sami al-Hinnawi, August 1949–December 1949
4. Col. Adib Shishakli, December 1949–February 1954 (overthrown)
5. President Sabri al-Asali, 1956–1958
6. Gamal Abdul Nasser, president of United Arab Republic (Egypt and Syria), 1958–1961 (Abdul-Hakim was the Syrian supervisor during this time)
7. President Nazim al-Qudsi, 1961–1963
8. Gen. Amin al Hafiz, 1963–1966
9. President Salah al-Jadid, 1966–1970 (overthrown)
10. President Hafez al-Assad, 1970–July 17, 2000
11. President Bashar al-Assad, July 17, 2000–

Republic of Tunisia
Capital City Tunis
Date of Independence from France March 20, 1956
Population 10,481,000
HDI Score 0.683
Rulers Since Independence
1. Prime Minister Habib Bourguiba, 1956–July 1957 (becomes republic)
2. President Habib Bourguiba, July 1957–November 1987 (overthrown)
3. President Zine Abidine Ben Ali accedes to the presidency, November 1987–January 2011 (overthrown)
4. Interim President, Prime Minister Muhammad Ghannouchi, January 14–15, 2011

5. Interim President Fouad Mebazaa, January 15–December 2011
4. President Moncef Marzouki, December, 2011–

Republic of Turkey
Capital City Ankara
Date of Independence from Ottoman Empire October 29, 1923
Population 72,752,000
HDI Score 0.679
Rulers Since Independence
1. President Mustafa Kemal (Atatürk after 1933), 1923–1938
2. President Ismet Inönü, 1938–1950
3. President Mahmud Celal Bayar, 1950–May 27, 1960 (overthrown)
4. General Cemal Gürsel, May 27, 1960–October 1961
5. President Cemal Gürsel, October 1961–1966
6. President Cevdet Sunay, 1966–1973
7. President Fahri Korutürk, 1973–September 12, 1980 (overthrown)
8. General Kenan Evren, September 12, 1980–1982
9. President Kenan Evren, 1982–October 1989
10. President Turgut Ozal, October 1989–April 1993
11. President Suleyman Demirel, April 1993–May 2000
12. President Ahmet Necdet Sezer, May 2000–August 2007
13. President Abdullah Gul, August 2007–

United Arab Emirates
Capital City Abu Dhabi
Date of Independence from Great Britain December 2, 1971
Population 7,512,000
HDI Score 0.815
Rulers Since Independence
1. Shaikh Zayid ibn Sultan al-Nuhayyan, 1971–2004
2. Shaikh Khalifa ibn Zayid al-Nuhayyan, 2004–

Yemen Arab Republic (North Yemen)
Date of Independence from Ottoman Empire 1918
Rulers Since Independence
1. Imam Yahya, 1918–1948 (murdered in an attempted coup)
2. Imam Ahmad ibn Yahya, 1948–1962
3. Muhammad al-Badr, 1962 (overthrown after one week)
4. Brig. Gen. Abdullah Sallal, 1962–1967
5. President Abdul Rahman al-Iryani, 1967–1974
6. President Ibrahim Hamdi, 1974–1977
7. President Ahmad Hussein Ghashmi, 1977–1978 (overthrown)
8. President Ali Abdullah Salih, 1978–1990

People's Democratic Republic of Yemen (South Yemen)
Date of Independent from Great Britain 1967
Rulers Since Independence
1. President Qahtan al-Sha'bi, 1967–1969 (overthrown)
2. President Salim Rubayyi'ali, 1969–1978 (executed)
3. President Abd al-Fattah Isma'il, 1978–1980 (resigned)
4. President Ali Nasser Muhammad, 1980–1986
5. President Haider Abu Bakr al-Attas, 1986–1990

Republic of Yemen
Capital City Sana'a
Date of Unification May 22, 1990
Population 24,053,000
HDI Score 0.439
Rulers Since Independence
1. Interim President Ali Abdallah Salih, 1990–2011 (overthrown)
2. President Abd Rabuh Mansur Hadi, February 2012–

Bibliography

Anderson, Ray R., Robert F. Siebert, and John G. Wagner. 2000. *Politics and Change in the Middle East*. 6th. ed. Englewood Cliffs, NJ: Prentice Hall.

Bosworth, C. E., E. Van Donzel, B. Lewis, and C. Pellat (eds.). 1983. *Encyclopedia of Islam*. Vol. 5. Leiden: E. J. Brill.

Burr, J. Millard, and Robert O. Collins. 1995. *Requiem for the Sudan: War, Drought, and Disaster Relief on the Nile*. Boulder: Westview Press.

CIA (Central Intelligence Agency). 2012. *CIA World Factbook*. Washington, DC: CIA. www.cia.gov.

Collelo, Thomas (ed.). 1988. *Syria: A Country Study*. Area Handbook Series. Washington, DC: Government Printing Office.

———. 1989. *Lebanon: A Country Study*. Area Handbook Series. Washington, DC: Government Printing Office.

Congressional Quarterly. 2000. *The Middle East*. 9th ed. Washington, DC: Congressional Quarterly.

Europa Publications. 2003. *The Middle East and North Africa*. 49th ed. Rochester, Kent, UK: Staples Printers Rochester.

Gordon, April A., and Donald L. Gordon (eds.). 2001. *Understanding Contemporary Africa*. 3rd ed. Boulder: Lynne Rienner.

Handloff, Robert E. (ed.). 1990. *Mauritania: A Country Study*. Area Handbook Series. Washington, DC: Government Printing Office.

Hiro, Dilip. 2003. *The Middle East at Your Fingertips: A Dictionary of the Middle East*. New York: Carroll & Graf.

Korbani, Agnes. 1995. *The Political Dictionary of Modern Middle East*. Lanham, MD: University Press of America.

Legum, Colin (ed.). 1976–1998. *Middle East Contemporary Survey*. Vols. 1–22. Shiloah Center for Middle Eastern and African Studies, Tel Aviv University. New York: Holmes & Meir.

Metz, Helen Chapin (ed.). 1989. *Libya: A Country Study.* Area Handbook Series. Washington, DC: Government Printing Office.

———. 1990. *Iraq: A Country Study.* Area Handbook Series. Washington, DC: Government Printing Office.

———. 1991. *Egypt: A Country Study.* Area Handbook Series. Washington, DC: Government Printing Office.

———. 1991. *Jordan: A Country Study.* Area Handbook Series. Washington, DC: Government Printing Office.

———. 1992. *Sudan: A Country Study.* Area Handbook Series. Washington, DC: Government Printing Office.

———. 1993. *Saudi Arabia: A Country Study.* Area Handbook Series. Washington, DC: Government Printing Office.

———. 1993. *Somalia: A Country Study.* Area Handbook Series. Washington, DC: Government Printing Office.

———. 1994. *Algeria: A Country Study.* Area Handbook Series. Washington, DC: Government Printing Office.

———. 1994. *Persian Gulf States: Country Studies.* Area Handbook Series. Washington, DC: Government Printing Office.

Nelson, Harold D. (ed.). 1985. *Morocco: A Country Study.* Area Handbook Series. Washington, DC: Government Printing Office.

———. 1986. *Tunisia: A Country Study.* Area Handbook Series. Washington, DC: Government Printing Office.

Simon, Reeva S., Philip Mattar, and Richard W. Bulliet (eds.). 1996. *Encyclopedia of the Modern Middle East.* 5 Vols. New York: Simon & Schuster.

Sluglett, Peter, and Marion Farouk-Sluglett (eds.). 1996. *The Times Guide to the Middle East.* London: Times Books.

United Nations Department of Economic and Social Affairs, Population Division. 2011. "World Population Prospects: The 2010 Revision." New York: United Nations.

United Nations Development Programme. 2010. *Human Development Report 2010.* New York: Oxford University Press.

Wright, John W. (ed.). 2003. *The New York Times 2003 Almanac.* New York: Penguin Books.

The Contributors

Mohammed Abu-Nimer is associate professor of international peace and conflict resolution in the School of International Service at American University.

miriam cooke is professor of Arab cultures at Duke University.

Deborah J. Gerner was professor of political science at the University of Kansas, Lawrence.

Arthur Goldschmidt Jr. is professor emeritus of Middle East history at Pennsylvania State University, University Park.

Ryan King is a graduate student in Columbia University's Program on Architecture, Preservation, and Planning.

Laurie King-Irani is a social anthropologist and cofounder of Electronic Intifada.

Ian R. Manners is professor of geography at the University of Texas, Austin.

Valentine M. Moghadam is professor of sociology at Northeastern University.

Agnieszka Paczynska is associate professor at the Institute for Conflict Analysis and Resolution at George Mason University.

Barbara McKean Parmenter is GIS research specialist and lecturer in urban and environmental policy and planning at Tufts University.

Lisa Pollard is associate professor of history at the University of North Carolina.

Philip A. Schrodt is professor of political science at Pennsylvania State University.

Jillian Schwedler is professor of political science at Hunter College and the Graduate Center, City University of New York.

Simona Sharoni is professor of gender and women's studies at State University of New York, Plattsburgh.

Mary Ann Tétreault is Cox Distinguished Professor of International Affairs Emerita at Trinity University.

Index

Abasiyanik, Sait Faik Aziz, 412
Abbas, Mahmoud, 58, 85, 95, 206
Abbasids, 48, 50
Abdulaziz, 421
Abdülhamid II, 58
Abdullah, 62, 66, 100, 104, 110, 119, 120, 142
Abortion, 355
Abou-Saif, Laila, 20
Abraham, 47, 382, 387–389
Absolute poverty, 302
Abu Bakr, 47
Abu-Lughod, Janet, 28–30
Achaemenids, 43
Activism, 391–393; moderate religious, 393–396; religious extremism, 396–398. *See also* Movements
Adivar, Halide Edip, 363, 408
Adnan, Etel, 429
Adonis, 424, 426
Afghanistan: refugees, 123; Soviet occupation, 96; Taliban, 102
Agadir trade agreement, 240
Agnon, Shmuel Yosef, 436
Agriculture: ancient, 41–42; cooperatives, 195, 320; cycle, 21; industry and, 228, 228*tab;* Lebanon, 249; market, 54; MENA, 297; oil and, 148; subsistence, 259, 320; Sudan, 237; Tunisia, 239; water for, 22, 73

AHC. *See* Arab Higher Committee for Palestine
Ahmadinejad, Mahmood, 84, 86, 96, 131, 359, 371
AKP. *See* Justice and Development Party
Alavi, Buzurg, 426
Alawites, 63, 333, 385
Al-e Ahmad, Jalal, 411–412, 417, 433
Alexander the Great, 43, 99
Alexandria Lighthouse, 43
Alfaq, Michel, 114–115, 353
Algeria, 3; bread riots, 235; civil war, 104, 248, 427–428; extremism in, 397; FLN, 70–71, 109; foreign debt, 225; France and, 63, 427; health care, 308; independence, 427–428; intellectuals, 435; oil, 241; poverty, 305; socialism, 228; unemployment, 299; wine, 225
Ali, Ibrahim, 54
Ali, Mehmet, 361
Ali, Muhammad (Egyptian leader), 28, 54–56, 91
Ali, Sabhattin, 415
ibn Ali, Husayn, 60
Aliye, Fatima, 362
Al-Qaeda, 4, 82–83, 93, 96–97, 111, 120, 130, 143, 377, 392, 398
Amin, Qasim, 350, 408
Amirshahi, Mahshid, 433

Amman, 20; expansion, *34;* protesters, *442;* remake, 33; water supply, 25
Anderson, Benedict, 36
Anglo-Iranian Oil Company, 65
Anis, Zeynab, 363
Anjoman of the Ladies of the Homeland, 363–364
Ankara, 29
Another Birth (Farrokhzad), 425
Antoon, Sinan, 431
Apprenticeships, 309
Arab awakening, 112
Arab exceptionalism, 113
Arab Higher Committee for Palestine (AHC), 186
Arab Human Development Report, 293–294, 305, 339
Arab League, 151, 154, 178, 240–241
Arab Maghreb Union, 240
Arab nationalism, 68–69
Arab oil weapon, 159, 265, 266, 274
Arab socialism, 70–71
Arab Spring, 282, 308. *See also* Arab uprisings
Arab uprisings, 1–2, 4–6, 8, 309; Bahrain, 86, 156, 439–440; commemorating, *90;* common good, 321; democracy and, 134; Egypt, 27, 153, 439–440; Green Revolution and, 86; Iran, 85–87; Islam and, 390–391; Islamist groups since, 398–400; Jordan, 86; Kuwait, 86; Libya, 27, 86–87, 440; Middle East economic issues and, 245–246; Middle East historical context, 85–87; Middle East international relations and, 168; in Middle East politics, 101–104; as Middle East trend and prospect, 439–441; Morocco, 86; Oman, 86; Pearl Revolution, 385, 441; Saudi Arabia, 86; sovereignty shaken, 139; Syria, 27, 86–87; transitional democracies emerging, 134; triggers, 139; Tunisia, 27, 101, 153–154, 439–440; unrest, 33; women, *373;* Yemen, 86
Arabesques (Shammas), 419
Arabian American Oil Company (ARAMCO), 65, 263, 267
Arabian Peninsula: independence in, 64–66; monarchies, 121

Arabic alphabet, 64, 407
Arabic language, 405, 406, 436
Arab-Islamic conquest, 16
Arab-Israeli conflict (1950s–1960s), 73–76, 84–85
Al-Arabiya, 103
Arafat, Yasser, 73–74, 80, 81, 95, 178, 190–191, 198, 201, 205, 210
ARAMCO. *See* Arabian American Oil Company
Argo, 2
Ashes and Shrapnel (Al-Mala'ika), 424
Ashkenazi Jews, 182, 331
Assad family, 102, 440
Al-Assad, Bashar, 422
Al-Assad, Hafez, 391
Astarabadi, Bibi, 362
Aswan High Dam, 22, 24, 149
At Home (Amirshahi), 433
Atatürk, Mustafa Kemal, 24, 62, 64–65, 104, 112–113, 116, 350, 352, 360–361, 364, 390, 405, 407, 408, 414, 424
Atatürk Dam, 24
Attiya, Rawya, 354
Avery, Uri, *210*
Away from Home (Amirshahi), 433
Aytaam, 319

Baalbaki, Layla, 410
Baath Party, 73, 83, 110, 114–115, 160, 353–355, 360, 368
Bab al-Saha (Khalifa), 428
Babylonians, 42
Baghdad Yesterday (Somekh), 420
Bahai, 385
Bahrain, 3; Arab uprising, 86, 156, 439–440; economy, 246; fertility rates, 292; free-trade agreements, 241; monarchy, 106, 122–123; oil, 226, 241; Pearl Revolution, 385, 441; protests, 103; Qatar boundary dispute, 145; revolutionary spirit, 5; Shi'i Muslims, 122–123; transfer of power, 101; urbanization, 288
Baker, James, 197
Balfour Declaration, 18, 61, 186, 386
Al-Banna, Hassan, 115, 393–394, 396
Barak, Ehud, 82, 183, 204
Barakat, Halim, 338
Baring, Evelyn, 57–58
Al-Barudi, Mahmud Sami, 423

Barzani, Mullah Mustafa, 157
Bashu, 11
The Battle of Algiers (Pontecorvo), 146
Baudelaire, Charles-Pierre, 424
BDS. *See* Boycott, Divestment, and
    Sanctions movement
Bedouins, 100, 326
Before the Fall (Foda), 435
Begin, Menachem, 76, 192
Behbahani, Simin, 425
Beirut (Al-Samman), 429
Beirut Decentrists, 429
Beirut Nightmares (Al-Samman), 429
Bektas, Habib, 433
Ben Ali, Zine Abidine, 5, 101, 102,
    399
Ben Yiju, Abraham, 35
Beneath the Sun (Shamir), 419
Benjelloun, Tahar, 413, 436
Benvenisti, Meron, 27
*Berji Kristin: Tales from the Garbage
    Hills* (Tekin), 32
Beyatli, Yahya Kemal, 423
Bible, 47, 378, 398
Biculturalism, 414
bin Laden, Osama, 82–83, 120, 167
Al-Bitar, Salah al-Din, 114–115, 353
Blind Owl (Hedayat), 417
Bloggers, 430–431
Bolshevik Revolution, 59
Bonaparte, Napoleon, 16, 54, 91
Bouazizi, Mohamed, 5–6, 86, 101
Boundaries: Mauritania-Morocco
    boundary dispute, 145; Middle East,
    13–19, 442; Qatar-Bahrain boundary
    dispute, 145
Boutros-Ghali, Boutros, 25
Boycott, Divestment, and Sanctions
    movement (BDS), 181, 211
Brain drain, 234
Bread riots, 235
Bremer, Paul, 276
Britain: in Arab affairs, 114; bombing
    by, 274–275; British Mandate, 24,
    142; in Iraq, 225–226; Oman as
    protectorate, 65; Palestine controlled
    by, 386; political structure imposed,
    113; ruling Jerusalem, 75; secularity,
    116
Broken String (Behbahani), 425
Bush, George H. W., 80–81, 274, 430

Bush, George W., 82, 85, 93, 95,
    163–164, 275–276
Butler, Richard, 163
Byzantine Empire, 44

CADAW. *See* Convention on the
    Elimination of All Forms of
    Discrimination Against Women
Cairo, 29, 31, 63; City of the Dead, 32;
    real estate development, 32; reforms,
    362; satellite cities, 33; women's
    groups, 363
Caliphs, 47–48
Camels, 44–45
Camp David Accords, 88, 191–192,
    204, 229, 435
Capitalism, 98, 107
Captive (Farrokhzad), 425
Caravans, 36
Carter, Jimmy, 76, 77
Cell phones, 441
Central Intelligence Agency (CIA),
    114, 118
The Cheapest Nights (Idris), 410
Chedid, Andrée, 414
Chekhov, Anton, 404, 406, 421
Children of Gebelawi (Mahfouz), 416
Children of the New World (Djebar),
    427
Chraïbi, Driss, 413
Christianity, 7, 28, 377; conversions to
    Islam, 50; Egypt Coptic Christians,
    384; historical role of, 379–381;
    Lebanon, 384–385; Mithraism and,
    44; Palestinians and, 179; Peoples of
    the Book, 333; Sudan, 385, 389;
    United States as nation, 116
Chubak, Sadiq, 411, 417
CIA. *See* Central Intelligence Agency
Cities of Salt (Munif), 416
Citizenship, 319, 322
Civil marriage, 316
Civil society, 106
Civil wars: Algeria, 104, 248, 427–428;
    Iraq, 104, 318; Jordan, 191;
    Lebanon, 104, 248–250, 318, 429;
    Libya, 19, 97, 102, 250; Palestine,
    104; Sudan, 250–251; Syria, 19, 102,
    250, 328; Yemen, 102, 247–248, 395
Class, 315–341; economic and political
    differences, 335; ethnicity and,

329–335; historical context of environment, 320–322; key concepts, 310–320; kinship system, 322–327; middle class, 106, 337; Palestinians and, 179; pyramidal, 336; strategies or straitjackets, 338–340; structure, 336; upper class, 337
Cliency, 148–150
Climate change, 277–280
Clinton, Bill, 81, 204
The Clown and His Daughter (Adivar), 408
Coalition for Women for Peace (CWP), 211, 215
"Coalition of the willing," 83
Cohen, Ronald, 330, 332
Cold War, 6, 88, 133, 255; agents, 114; cliency, 149–150; competition, 106; impact, 93; oil policies during, 263; politics, 262
Collective identity, 316
Colonialism, 3, 227, 380; Egypt and, 91; European, 403–406; legacy, 90–92; postcolonial struggles, 425–431
The Colonizer and the Colonized (Memmi), 413
Communism, 409; *aytaam* and, 319; collapse, 103; PCP, 178; Soviet Union model, 113
Comoros Islands, 3
Conflict mediation, 321
Confucian capitalism, 98, 107
Conrad, Joseph, 431
Constantine I, 380
Constantinople, 28, 44
Convention on the Elimination of All Forms of Discrimination Against Women (CADAW), 367
Cooperative education, 309
Cooperative Framework Agreement, 24–25
Cosgrove, Denis, 34
Council of Guardians, 85, 131, 389
Cousins, 323–325; cross-cousins, 324
Crimean War (1853–1856), 55
Cromer, Lord, 349
Crusades, 16, 51, 380
Culture: artificial divides, 443; biculturalism, 414; cultural ferment at turn of twentieth century,

406–409; Greek, 43; Middle East diversity, 12; patterns, 442; subcultures, 330
CWP. *See* Coalition for Women for Peace
Cyrus, 43

Danesh, 363
Daneshvar, Simin, 411, 417, 433
Darwish, Mahmud, 428
Daughter of Isis (El Saadawi), 435
Daughters of the Nile, 365
David, King, 42
Days from My Life (Al-Ghazali), 434–435
The Days (Husayn), 406
de Gaulle, Charles, 70
de Lesseps, Ferdinand, 56
de Maupassant, Guy, 404, 406
Débèche, Assia, 413–414
Decimal number system, 3
Decisionmaking, 321
Declaration of Principles, 81
Dehkhoda, Ali Akbar, 411
Democracy: Arab uprising and, 134; conditional, 125–132; Iran conditional, 129–132; Israel conditional, 127–128; Lebanon conditional, 128–129; prospects for, 104–108; terrorism and, 82–85; transitional, 132–134; Turkey conditional, 126–127; Turkey government, 72
Demographic Health Surveys (DHS), 294
Dependency, 147–148
Description de l'Egypte, 11
Desert, 11, 21, 80
Destour Party, 64
Devshirme, 52–53
Dhimmi, 333–334
DHS. *See* Demographic Health Surveys
Diaspora: of Jews, 379; of Palestinians, 178
Dib, Mohamed, 427
Dickens, Charles, 406
Discrimination: CADAW, 367; in Occupied Territories, 127
Diwan, 117
Djebar, Assia, 427–428
Djibouti, 3, 101

Dostoyevsky, Fyodor, 424
Double critique, 436
Druze, 385
Dubai: "starchitecture," 33; urbanization, 288; worker rebellions, 244
Dutch disease, 281

Ebadi, Sherin, 368
Economic development: indicators, 224*tab;* Iraq, 253; Israel, 99; Middle East politics and, 97–99; Qatar, 107; Sudan, 250; Turkey, 99; United Arab Emirates, 107
Economies: Bahrain, 246; Egypt, 246; Gaza Strip, 252–253; informal, 238*tab;* Iraq, 253–255; Libya, 246; oil and, 440–441; Palestine, 251–252; Qatar, 107; regional, 246–255; Saudi Arabia, 65; shadow, 238; Syria, 246; Tunisia, 246; United Arab Emirates, 107; of worker sending countries, 234; after World War II, 226–230; before World War II, 224–226; Yemen, 246. *See also* Middle East, economic issues; Middle East, oil economy
Edip, Halidé Adivar, 363–364
Education: cooperative, 309; Jordan, 293; MENA, 293; Palestinians, 179; women, 292–294, 306, 354; Yemen, 293
EFTA. *See* European Free Trade Association
Egypt, 3, 6; Arab uprising, 27, 153, 439–440; Assyria rule, 43; bread riots, 235; colonialism and, 91; Coptic Christians, 384; cotton, 225, 240, 337; economy, 246; established regime, 103; exports, 239; extremism in, 397; foreign debt, 225; foreign investment, 236; government downfall, 310; health care, 307; immigrants to Gulf, 231; industrial waste, 25; longtime leadership, 101; megacities, 289–290; migrant workers, 231, 234; Muslim Brotherhood, 394–395, 399; Napoleon in, 16; nationalism beginnings, 56–58; oil, 241; poverty, 303, 308; protests, 5–6; public-sector

jobs, 298; riots of 1977, 229; *shadufs,* 22; socialism, 75, 228; Soviet Union aid, 229; Tahrir Square, 9, 86, 156, 441; transfer of power, 101; travel from, 35; unemployment, 299; United States aid, 229; urbanization, 288; water utility, 26; women of, 348, 350–351, 353–354, 356, 364–365, 370; women's education, 306. *See also* Cairo
Egyptian Earth (Al-Sharqawi), 426
El Saadawi, Nawal, 426, 435
Elephant Hamdi (Nesin), 412
Employment, 7; challenges, 295–298; Kuwait, 296; Qatar, 296; Saudi Arabia, 296. *See also* Labor; Unemployment
Emre, Yunus, 405
Endogamous marriage, 324–326
Enlightenment, 347, 407
Erbakan, Necmettin, 110
Erdo, Recep Tayyip, 127, 360
Eretz Yisrael, 144, 185
Ethnicity, 315–341; analysis, 329–333; class and, 335–338; ethnoconfessional groups, 316, 340; ethnoreligious groups, 332, 333; historical context of environment, 320–322; historical context of identity categories, 333–335; identity and, 330–331, 339; key concepts, 310–320; kinship system, 322–327; political units, 333; socioeconomic differences, 331; strategies or straitjackets, 338–340
EU. *See* European Union
Euphrates river, 20–21, 23–24, 41
European Free Trade Association (EFTA), 241
European Union (EU), 96, 131, 145, 227, 360
Exile, 431–433
Extremism, 396–398
ExxonMobil, 277
The Eye with an Iron Lid (Adonis), 426

Facebook, 1, 2, 103, 139, 152, 443
Faisal I (king of Iraq), 62, 66, 118
The Fall of Imam (El Saadawi), 435
Family planning, 410
Family relationships, 7

Fantasia (Djebar), 427–428
Fanton, Frantz, 431
Farming, 41–42. *See also* Agriculture
Farouk, 67–69, 99, 393
Farrokhzad, Forugh, 425
Fatah, 85, 180, 363
Faud, 67
FDI. *See* Foreign direct investment
Fech'ien, 232
Feminism, 353, 362, 365, 367
Feminism and Islam, of Complete Equality for the World of Womanhood (Hamit), 362
Fertile Crescent, 3, 60; Arab unification, 68; French mandates, 66
Fertility rates, 292–294
Fifty Three Men (Alavi), 426
The Fine Woman's Exhibition of Biographies of Famous Women (Nawfal), 362
Fire Quenched (Daneshvar), 411
FitzGerald, Edward, 3
FJP. *See* Freedom and Justice Party
Flaubert, Gustave, 404, 406
FLN. *See* National Liberation Front
Foda, Farag, 435
Foreign direct investment (FDI), 143, 235–237, 248
Fourteen Points, 60
Fragments of Memory (Mina), 416
France: Algeria and, 63, 427; in Arab affairs, 114; in Fertile Crescent, 66; Lebanon and, 16, 67, 226; political structure imposed, 113; Syria and, 62, 63, 67, 226
Free Officers Movement, 393, 409, 414, 415, 421, 426
Freedom and Justice Party (FJP), 39
Freedom House classifications of countries, 102*tab*
From Sleep Unbound (Chedid), 414
Fugitive methane, 279
Fundamentalism, 96, 392–393, 435

GAFTA. *See* Greater Arab Free Trade Area
Gaza Strip, 177; air access to, 85; Arafat returning, 81; corporate interests in, 212; crowded alleys, 223; demonstrations, *181;* economy, 252–253; elections, 192; fertility rates, 292; Israel occupation, 189; military withdrawal, 95; Palestinians, 74, 178, 195, 214; patrols, 73–74; PNA replacing, 177; poverty, 308; settlements, 183; unemployment, 236, 253, 299
GCC. *See* Gulf Cooperation Council
Gecekondus, 31
Gemayel, Beshir, 193
Gender, 7; Gender and Development Index, 366; Gender and Empowerment Measure, 366; gender-oriented kinship, 329; inequality, 309
General Popular Congress (GPC), 395
Genital cutting, 369
Genizah Documents, 35
Geography, 34
Germany, 19, 433, 434
Ghanouchi, Rachid, 398–399
Al-Ghazali, Zaynab, 434–435
Ghaznavids, 50
Ghosh, Amitav, 35
Gibran, Khalil, 3
Global financial crisis of 2007, 233, 245–246
Globalization, 19
Goitein, S. D., 35
Gökalp, Ziya, 350
Goknar, Erdag, 417
Golan Heights, 73–74; attacks, 75; corporate interests in, 212; Israel occupation, 189
Golden Horn, 31
Good Morning! (Haqqi), 409, 426
Governance: Israel, 112; military, 111; monarchies, 111–112; Ottoman Empire, 333; revolutionary, 111–112; self-governance, 442; tasks of, 111; Turkey, 112
Government: Egypt downfall, 310; legitimization, 110–112; Tunisia downfall, 310; Turkey democratic, 72
GPC. *See* General Popular Congress
Grandmother's Tales (Qalamawi), 410
Great Depression, 113–114
Great Powers: Middle East international relations with, 146–150, 166; politics, 141; World War II, 150

Great Recession, 165
Greater Arab Free Trade Area
(GAFTA), 240
Greek culture, 43
Greek history, 14
Green Line, 192, 428
Green Movement, 371
Green Revolution, 86, 165
Greenhouse gases, 279
Gregorian calendar, 64
Gulf Cooperation Council (GCC),
152–153, 161, 233, 240, 242, 245,
281
Gulf War, 19, 163, 234, 274, 359, 390;
Israeli-Palestinian conflict and,
196–197; writers, 430
Gunpowder, 52
Gypsies, 186

Habibi, Emile, 428
Haddad, Malek, 427
Hajj, 35–36
Al-Hakim, Tawfiq, 409, 421
Halman, Talat Sait, 407
Hamas, 85, 96, 179, 252, 397–398;
election by Palestinians, 180, 206;
Fatah and, 180; suicide bombings by,
208; support for, 201
Hamit, Halit, 362
Hammurabi, 42
Haqqi, Yahya, 409, 426, 431
Haram al-Sharif, 387–389, 390
Harem women, 347–348, 362–363
Al-Hariri, Rafik, 28, 84, 129, 249
Hasbani River, 23
Hasim, Ahmet, 423
Hassan II, 101, 118
Haussman, Georges-Eugène, 29
Hawala, 232
Health care, 307–308
The Heat of the Year Zero (Parsipur),
434
Hebrews, 42–43. *See also* Jews;
Judaism
Hedayat, Sadeq, 411, 417
Hizbullah, 84, 94, 96, 129, 134, 249,
389, 396, 398
Hoca, Nasreddin, 412
Holocaust, 68
Holy Land, 51, 315
Horrible Teheran (Kazemi), 408

Hospitality, 321
Hudson, Michael C., 117
Human development, 303–304; *Arab
Human Development Report,*
293–294, 305, 339; progress and
stagnation, 306; UNDP, 255
Human Rights Watch, 125
Hundred Sermons (Kermani), 349
Husayn, Taha, 406
Hussein (king of Jordan), 75, 101, 119,
124, 142, 153, 390, 394
Hussein, Saddam, 66, 78, 80–81, 83,
93, 100, 102, 109, 150, 158,
160–164, 196, 273–275, 328,
355–356, 359, 390–391, 429–430

IAF. *See* Islamic Action Front
Ibrahim, Samira, 369
ICJ. *See* International Court of Justice
Identity: collective, 316; ethnicity and,
330–331, 339; historical context of
categories, 333–335; Israeli, 177,
182; of Jews, 316; kinship and, 328;
Palestinian, 177–178; Persia
national, 55
Idilbi, Ulfat, 410
Idris, Yusuf, 410, 422
IEA. *See* International Energy Agency
Ikhwan, 119
IMF. *See* International Monetary Fund
Imperialism: defined, 90; European,
55–56; retreat of Western, 66–68;
Western in Arab lands, 63–64
Import substitution industrialization
(ISI), 227
Imports, 264; arms, 109; oil, 264; trade,
243–244, 243*tab*
In an Antique Land (Ghosh), 35
In Search of Walid Mas'ud (Jabra), 433
Independence: Algeria, 427–428;
Arabian Peninsula, 64–66; Jordan,
394; Middle East literature and,
425–431; PLO, 80; Tunisia, 64
India, 35
Industrialization, 277
Inequality: gender, 309; income, 7;
MENA, 305*tab;* poverty and,
302–309
Infitah, 229
Innocence of the Devil (El Saadawi),
435

Innocent III, Pope, 380
Inönü, Ismet, 72
International Court of Justice (ICJ), 18, 145
International Criminal Court, 154
International Crisis Group, 247
International Energy Agency (IEA), 271, 278
International Monetary Fund (IMF), 97–98, 229, 234, 250, 339
International oil companies (IOCs), 149, 259–260, 262–268, 271, 276–277, 279
International system, 143
Internships, 309
Intifada, 80, 85, 95, 179–180, 194–195, 199, 201–202, 233, 397
IOCs. *See* International oil companies
Iqta', 50
Iran, 3; Arab uprising, 85–87; conditional democracy, 129–132; fertility rates, 292, 293, 294; Green Revolution and, 86, 165; health care, 307; independence in, 64–66, 72; Islamic revolution, 77–79; Kurds, 157–158, *159;* megacities, 289; monarchy, 118; mother Iran, 351; novels, 416–417; nuclear program, 132; oil, 149, 166, 226, 227, 241, 262; OPEC pricing and, 268; political Islam, 116; *qanats,* 22; revolutionary transformation, 101, 389; Russia in, 91; salt flats, 11; Shi'i Muslims, 94; snowfall, *20;* social organization, 316; stories, 411–412; unemployment, 299; urbanization, 288; velvet revolution, 164; WOI, 356, 368; women of, 352–353, 355, 357–359, 364, 371
Iran-Contra issues, 78
Iranian Revolution (1978–1979), 270, 358, 368, 388–389
Iran-Iraq War, 80, 159, 246, 253, 270–272, 429–430; background, 160; cost of, 162; oil dimension, 161; women soldiers, *162, 359*
Iraq, 3; brain drain, 254; Britain in, 225–226; civil war, 104, 318; economic development, 253; economy, 253–255; fertility rates, 292; independence, 66; Israel

attacked by, 197; Kurds, 160, 275; Kuwait crisis, 80–82, 162–163; Kuwait invaded by, 273–274; migrant workers, 234; military intelligence, 109–110; National Council for the Awakening of Iraq, 93; nuclear program, 132; oil, 226, 227, 241; OPEC pricing and, 268; poverty, 304; reform, 366; refugees, 123, 254–255; revolutionary transformation, 101; Saudi Arabia attacked by, 197; Shi'i Muslims, 94, 328; Soviet Union aid, 229; state structure, 316; unemployment, 236; United States invasion, 235, 247; United States withdrawal, 93; urbanization, 288; war debts, 273; women of, 355, 359, 364, 369; women's education, 306
Iraq War, 6, 150, 164, 253–254; Middle East oil economy and, 274–277
Irgun Zvai Leumi, 76
ISI. *See* Import substitution industrialization
Islah party, 395–397
Islam, 7, 377; Arab uprisings and, 390–391; Arabs before, 45–46; as autonomous system, 45–53; beliefs and institutions, 47; caliphs and Arab conquests, 47–48; conversions, 50; empire extent, 49*fig;* feminism, 367; first Islamic empire, 48–50; groups since Arab uprisings, 398–400; hajj in, 35–36; historical role of, 381–383; Iran revolution, 77–79; Islamism, 144, 166; literacy and, 382; Muhammad and, 46–47; nominal states, 390–391; pan-Islam, 56; political, 115–117, 319; revivalism, 392, 393, 400; spread of, 3; strong states, 388–389; Sudan, 389; symbolism, 391; Turkey revivalism, 105; vitality of, 19; as whole way of life, 393; women and, 348, 360
Islamic Action Front (IAF), 395
Islamic Refah Party, 110
Islamic Republic, 129–130
Isma'il, 56–57
Isma'il Pasha, 29

Israel, 3; Arab negotiations, 80–82; Arab-Israeli conflict (1950s–1960s), 73–76, 134; border guards, *74;* civil marriage, 316; conditional democracy, 127–128; creation of, 68–69, 379; economic development, 99; foreign workers, 233; free-trade agreements, 241; Gaza Strip occupation, 189; Golan Heights occupation, 189; governance, 112; Iraq attacking, 197; irrigation, 22–23; Israeli identity, 177, 182; Jewish people national home, 18; Kadima Party, 183–184; Knesset, 95, 127–128; Labor Party, 100, 127–128, 182–183, 198; League of Nations mandate for, 92; Likud Party, 182–183; Likud-Beiteinu Party, 184; Mapai, 109; military, 109, 180, 201; in 1990s, 196; novels, 419–420; oil embargo against, 267–268; Palestinian occupation by, 80; Palestinians in, 233; PLO and, 79–82, 134; restricting Arab rights, 105; security policy, 203; social organization, 316; state of, 386–388; transfer of power, 101; United States aid, 229; water development scheme, 73; West Bank and, 22, 85, 189. *See also* Jerusalem; Jews; Judaism; Zionism

Israeli-Palestinian conflict, 7, 159; Al-Aqsa Intifada, 199, 201–202; analysis of parties, 176–184; Camp David Accords and, 191–192; central issues and points of contention, 202–206; David *vs.* Goliath, 195; grassroots resolution efforts, 210–211; Gulf War and, 196–197; history and dynamics, 184–202; international conflicts and, 187–194; Israelis in, 181–184; Lebanon invasion and, 192–194; overview, 175–176; Palestinian uprising (1987), 194–196; Palestinians in, 178–181; peace and, 212–213; resolution attempts, 206–213; self-determination, 213; single-state solutions, 207; top-down and bottom-up resolution, 210; two-state solution, 208, 213; United States

and, 209; Zionism and partition of Palestine, 185–189
Istanbul, 29–31, 419; reforms, 362; squatter settlements, 32
Istanbul: Memories and the City (Pamuk), 419
Istiqlal Party, 64
Italy: Fascism, 68; in Libya, 91, 225

Jabra, Jabra Ibrahim, 433
Jackson, Robert H., 139–140
Jamalzadeh, Ali, 408, 411
Jansen, Hermann, 29
Al-Jayyusi, Salma al-Khadra', 436
Al Jazeera, 10, 19, 103, 441
Jefferson, Thomas, 113
Jerusalem, 20, 42, *387;* Arab rule, 48, 51; Britain rule, 75; Jordan control, 189; judaization of, 199; Palestinians in, *214;* sacred city, 27; separation wall, 214, *214;* symbolism of, 386–388; unified, 190; violence, 186
Jesus, 44, 47, 379, 382
Jevdet Bey and His Sons (Pamuk), 418
Jews, 177, 181–182, 331; Ashkenazi, 182, 331; diaspora, 379; identity, 316; Jewish immigrants, 63, 67, 100, 185; Mizrachim, 182–183, 331; Peoples of the Book, 333; as religious-racial community, 378; United States, 379; view of Zionism, 185
Jihad, 397; extremists and, 398; Ottoman Empire, 59–61; suicide bombings by, 208; support for, 201
Jordan, 3, *44;* Arab uprising, 86; border adjustments, 190; bread riots, 235; civil war (1970), 191; education, 293; elections, 125; exports, 239; health care, 308; independence, 394; Jerusalem controlled by, 189; labor force, 295; loss of West Bank, 124, 394; migrant workers, 231, 234; military, 110; monarchy, 100, 101, 123–125; Muslim Brotherhood, 395; police, *124;* poverty, 303; pumping project, 23; refugees, 255; regime challenge, 6; suppression, 103–104; telecommunications, 237; transfer of power, 101; unemployment, 299;

women pieceworkers, 302; women's education, 306. *See also* Amman

Jordan River, 23, 24

Joseph and the Legend of the Seventh Sleeper, 427

The Journey of Ibn Fattouma (Mahfouz), 416

Judaism, 7, 45, 377; conversions to Islam, 50; historical role of, 378–379

Justice and Development Party (AKP), 105, 127, 372

Justinian, 28

Ka'ba, 45–47

Kabbani, Nizar, *423*

Kafala, 296

Kafka, Franz, 411

Kamil, Mustafa, 58, 72

Kanafani, Ghassan, 432, *432*

Karagoz, 420–421

Karaosmanoğlu, Yakup Kadri, 407, 417

Karman, Tuwakkal, 395

Kazemi, Morteza Moshfeq, 408

Kemal, Namik, 421

Kemal, Orhan, 415, 421

Kemal, Yashar, 418, 421, 436

Kendall, David, 33

Kermani, Mirza 'Abd al-Hosayn Khan, 349

Khalaf, Samir, 340

ibn Khaldun, 422

Khalifa, Sahar, 428

Al-Khalifah, Isa ibn Hamad, 123

Al-Khalifah, Isa ibn Salmon, 122, 156

Khameneh, Mir-Hussein Mosavi, 371

Khatami, Mohammad, 359

Khatibi, 'Abdelkebir, 436

Al-Khattab, Umar ibn, 47

Khomeini, Ayatollah Ruhollah, 77, 129–130, 357, 359, 371, 389, 435

Khoury, Philip, 336

Khuri, Fuad, 324

King-Crane Commission, 61

Kinship, 315–341; class and, 335–338; cousins, 323–325; endogamous marriage in, 324–326; ethnicity and, 329–335; extended families, 325; gender-oriented, 329; historical context of environment, 320–322; identity and, 328; imagery and symbolism, 319; key concepts, 310–320; men's and women's roles, 324, 329; pastoral nomadism, 326–328; patrilineal, 323–324, 326–328; strategies or straitjackets, 338–340; system of, 322–327

Kissinger, Henry, 76

Krak des Chevaliers, 381

Kurds, 18, 24, 143; ethnonational minority, 107; Iran, 157–158, *159;* Iraq, 160, 275; nationalism, 367; oil, 276–277; rights in Turkey, 127, 155; stateless, 157; women, 367, 368, 371

Kuwait, 3; Arab uprising, 86; employment, 296; fertility rates, 292; invasion of, 108; investments, 237; Iraq crisis, 80–82, 162–163; Iraq invading, 273–274; migrant workers, 234; monarchy, 123; oil, 226, 241, 261–262, 272–273, 280; revenue distribution, 281; salami tactics, 153; Saudi Arabia dispute, 152–153; United States liberating, 80–82, 150; urbanization, 288

Labor, 7; Jordan labor force, 295; labor force growth, 295–298; MENA, 297; migration, 230–234, 296–297; Ottoman Empire, 335; remittances, 230–234, 231*tab,* 232*tab;* Saudi Arabia labor force, 19; standards, 310; urban markets, 287

Lahham, Durayd, 422

Lahoud, Emile, 129

The Lamp of Umm Hashim (Haqqi), 431

Language: Arabic, 405, 406, 436; Arabic alphabet, 64, 407; Latin alphabet, 407; Middle East, 12; reform, 405; Roman alphabet, 64

Lashin, Mahmud Tahir, 409

Latife U akligil, 352

Latin alphabet, 407

League of Arab States, 3, 150

League of Nations, 16, 61, 92, 141

Lebanon, 3; agriculture, 249; Beirut Decentrists, 429; carved from Syria, 142; Christians, 384–385; civil marriage, 316; civil war, 104, 248–250, 318, 429; cockpit of rivalry, 79–80;

conditional democracy, 128–129; ethnoconfessional groups, 340; fertility rates, 292; France and, 16, 67, 226; Israel invasion, 192–194; Palestinians and, 79; PLO in, 191–193; poverty, 304; silk, 225; state structure, 316; tourism, 239, 249; United States intervening for, 80; women's education, 306

Lenin, Vladimir, 113

Levi, Jacques Victor, 413

Lewis, Bernard, 14, 19

The Liberation of Women (Amin), 408

Libya, 3; Arab uprising, 27, 86–87, 440; civil war, 19, 97, 102, 250; decentralized military movement, 103; economy, 246; health care, 308; Italy in, 91, 225; monarchy, 118; oil, 149, 241, 262; OPEC pricing and, 268; Qatar supporting, 104; revolutions, 5, 266; sovereignty, 155; urbanization, 288

Literacy: achievements, 308; improvements, 228, 300; Islam and, 382; poverty and, 303; programs, 393, 396; theater and, 421; of women, 254, 356, 361, 368

Literature. *See* Middle East, literature

Locke, John, 113

Madmen on the Loose (Nesin), 412

Mahfouz, Asmaa, 369

Mahfouz, Naguib, 3, 414–416, *415,* 436

Mahmud II, 54–55

Makdisi, Ussama, 315

Al-Mala'ika, Nazik, 424

Mallas, Muhammad, 422

Maqama, 420

Marriage: civil, 316; endogamous, 324–326; Marriage Law of 1931, 353; rights, 355

Marsh Arabs, 26

Marx, Karl, 113

Marxists, 371, 379, 426

Mauritania, 3; Morocco boundary dispute, 145; political Islam, 116

McMahon, Henry, 60

MDGs. *See* Millennium Development Goals

Mecca, 35–36, 45–46

Mehmet II, 28

Mehmet IV, 418

Memmi, Albert, 413, 420

Memoirs from the Women's Prison (El Saadawi), 426

Men in the Sun (Kanafani), 432

MENA. *See* Middle East–North Africa

Mernissi, Fatima, 163

Metric system, 64–65

Midaq Alley (Mahfouz), 415

Middle class, 106, 337

Middle East: aridity and rainfall, 226, 320; boundaries, 13–19, 442; cityscapes, 27–34; coining term, 14, 16; cultural diversity, 12; defining, 1–4, 442; geographical view, 9–11; global linkages, 35; as jigsaw puzzle, 36; languages, 12; layoffs, 298; militarization, 108–109, 247; money in, 280–282; political map, *15,* 16, *17,* 18; population growth, 287–288, 290*tab,* 291–295; Semitic and Indo-Iranian invasions, 42–43; terrorism and democracy, 82–85; UN members, 74; United States policy, 88; urbanization, 7, 13, 29–31, 287–291, 289*tab,* 309, 328, 332. *See also specific topics*

Middle East, economic issues, 223–255; Arab uprisings and, 245–246; conflict and regional economies, 246–255; economic crisis and structural adjustment, 234–239; economies after World War II, 226–230; economies before World War II, 224–226; foreign debt, 225, 229; GDP growth, 237*tab;* global financial crisis of 2007, 233, 245–246; labor migration and remittances, 230–234, 231*tab,* 232*tab;* new oil boom, 244–245; shadow economy, 238; trade and, 239–244. *See also* Unemployment

Middle East, historical context of, 41–88; ancient, 41–45; Arab uprisings, 85–87; East and West invasions, 50–52; Egyptian nationalism, 56–58; European imperialism, 55–56; Greek and Roman rule, 43–45; Islam as autonomous system, 45–53; Ottoman Empire and, 52–53, 58; post–World War I, 61–85; subordination to the West, 57–62; Westernizing reforms, 53–55; during World War I, 59–61

Middle East, international relations, 139–168; Arab uprisings and, 168; cliency in, 148–150; dependency in, 147–148; extraregional intervention, 167; with Great Powers, 146–150, 166; Gulf Wars, 159–165; Middle East in world, 155–159; regionalism, 150–153; sovereignty issues, 144–146

Middle East, literature, 403–436; Arabic novel, 414–416; Arabic stories, 409–410; cultural ferment at turn of twentieth century, 406–409; drama, 420–423; emigration and exile, 431–433; European colonialism and its discontents, 403–406; Francophone novels in North Africa, 413–414; independence and postcolonial struggles, 425–431; Iranian novel, 416–417; Iranian stories, 411–412; Israeli novel, 419–420; language reform, 405; Muslim state, 433–435; poetry, 422–425; short story as literary pioneer, 413; sociorealism, 415; translation and recognition, 436; Turkey storytellers, 412; Turkish novel, 417–419

Middle East, oil economy, 259–283; climate change and world order, 277–280; industry structure, 260–263; Iraq War and, 274–277; Middle East politics and, 269–271; money in Middle East, 280–282; oil revolution, 268–269; politics in, 266–268; posted price system, 264; price bust and, 271–274; system unraveling, 263–265

Middle East, politics, 89–135, 269–271; Arab uprisings, 101–104; changing international context, 92–97; colonial legacy, 90–92; conditional democracies, 125–132; economic development, 97–99; government legitimization and state building, 110–112; informal structures of power, 99–100; military's role in, 108–110; myth of instability, 100–101; nationalist revolutionary republics, 112–117; prospects for democratization, 104–108; traditional and parliamentary monarchies, 117–125; transitional democracies, 132–133. *See also* Middle East, religion and politics

Middle East, religion and politics, 377–401; activism, 391–398; Bahai, 385; experience of minorities, 383–386; fundamentalism, 96, 392–393, 435; historical role of, 278–383; Islamist groups since Arab uprisings, 398–400; states and, 386–391

Middle East, trends and prospects, 439–443; Arab uprisings and popular mobilizations, 439–441; new media, 441–442

Middle East–North Africa (MENA), 287, 288; agriculture, 297; education, 293; fertility rates, 292*tab;* health care, 307; labor, 297; megacities, 290*tab;* population growth, 289*tab;* population policies, 294; poverty and inequality, 305*tab;* unemployment, 301*tab*

Migration, 7, 41–42, 147; labor, 230–234, 296–297; White Paper immigration, 67–68; writers and, 431–433

Mikha'il, Dunya, 430

Milani, Farzaneh, 411

Military: arms imports, 109; Gaza Strip withdrawal, 95; governance, 111; Iraq intelligence, 109–110; Israel, 109, 180, 201; Jordan, 110; Libya, 103; Middle East militarization, 108–109, 247; in Middle East politics, 108–110; Syria, 103, 155; Yemen, 103

Mill, James, 408

Millennium Development Goals (MDGs), 306

Millets, 52, 99, 334

Mina, Hanna, 416

A Mind at Peace (Tanpinar), 417

Mishnah, 387

Mission civilisatrice (civilizing mission), 406, 409

Mitchell, Timothy, 10
Mithraism, 44
Mizrachim, 182–183, 331
Moayyad, Heshmat, 412
Mohammed VI, 118
Molière, Jean-Baptiste, 404, 421
Monarchies: Arabian Peninsula, 121; aspects of Arab kingship, 119–120; Bahrain, 106, 122–123; governance, 111–112; Iran, 118; Jordan, 100, 101, 123–125; Kuwait, 123; Libya, 118; Morocco, 101, 103, 118, 125; Oman, 106, 121–122; Qajar, 113, 118, 389, 407; Qatar, 121; Saudi Arabia, 100, 106, 118, 120–121, 388; traditional and parliamentary, 117–125; United Arab Emirates, 122
Mongols, 51
Montagu, Mary Wortley, 347
Montesquieu, Charles-Louis de Secondat, 348
Moroccan Mirages (Swearingen), 25
Morocco, 3; Agadir crisis, 91; Arab uprising, 86; bread riots, 235; exports, 239; fertility rates, 294; foreign debt, 225; free-trade agreements, 241; health care, 307, 308; layoffs, 298; Mauritania boundary dispute, 145; monarchy, 101, 103, 118, 125; Movement 20 Février, 288; nationalists, 64; poverty, 303, 305, 308; protectorates, 56; public-sector jobs, 298; regime challenge, 6; remittances, 230; transfer of power, 101; travel from, 35; urbanization, 288; women's education, 306
Mosaddeq, Mohammad, 72, 77, 262, 263, 355–356
Moses, 42, 47, 378, 382
Mother State (Tahir), 414
Movements: BDS, 181, 211; Free Officers Movement, 393, 409, 414, 415, 421, 426; Green Movement, 371; Libya decentralized military, 103; Morocco Movement 20 Février, 288; Nahda, 398–400; nationalist, 346–347, 363–364, 368–371; PLO resistance, 190; revivalism, 105, 392–393, 398–400, 441; Syria decentralized military, 103; women's,

365–367; Yemen decentralized military, 103
Mubarak, Hosni, 85–86, 94, 101, 102, 106, 110, 229, 357, 366, 369–370, 391, 399
Mubarak, Shaikh, 146
Muhammad, 46–47, 381–383, 386–387, 390, 398, 406
Mu'izz al-Din, 29
Munif, Abd al-Rahman, 416
Mursi, Mohammad, 370, 399
Musa, Hoda Sha'rawi Nabawiyya, 365
Muslim Brotherhood, 2, 94, 103, 115, 388, 392, 393–397, 399–400
Muslim Ladies Association, 434
Muslim Women (Aliye), 362
Mutran, Khalil, 423
My Michael (Oz), 419
My Name is Red (Pamuk), 418

Nabarawi, Ceza, 365
Nabataeans, *44*
Nahda movement, 398–400
Napoleonic Wars, 225
Nasir al-Din, 55
Nasrallah, Emily, 429, 432, 433
Nasser, Gamal Abdul, 69, 73, 75, 116, 149, 151, 353–354, 356–357, 364–365, 393, 394, 426, 434
National Council for the Awakening of Iraq, 93
National Liberation Front (FLN), 70–71, 109
National Pact of 1943, 111
Nationalism: Arab, 68–69, 73, 144, 151, 392; Egyptian, 56–58; Kurds, 367; nationalist movements, 346–347, 363–364, 368–371; Ottoman Empire, 58; revolutionary republics, 112–117. *See also* Baath Party
Native Larks (Djebar), 427
NATO. *See* North Atlantic Treaty Organization
Nawfal, Maryam Nahhas, 362
Nazis, 67–68, 72, 91, 113, 186
Nedjma (Yacine), 427
Negative peace, 212
Negative sovereignty, 140, 143
Nesin, Aziz, 412, 421
Netanyahu, Benjamin, 82, 128, 183, 184, 199

Neutral Zone, 144
Neutralism, 70
New media, 441–442
NGOs. *See* Nongovernmental organizations
Niblock, Tim, 162
Nile River, 1; basin irrigation system, 21–22; marshes and wetlands, 11; migration, 41; Nile Delta, 13; Nile Waters Treaty, 24–25
Nimeiri, Jaafar, 389
Nixon, Richard M., 150, 160, 267
Nixon Doctrine, 150, 160
Nomadism, 21, 41–42, 118, 320; camel nomads, 44–45; horse nomads, 50–51; pastoral, 326–328
Nongovernmental organizations (NGOs), 106, 154, 167, 211, 300, 368
North Atlantic Treaty Organization (NATO), 72, 104, 150, 282

OAPEC. *See* Organization of Arab Petroleum Exporting Countries
Obama, Barack, 93, 95, 132
Occupied Territories: discrimination in, 127; intransigence, 94; Palestinians, 197, 199, 233; political developments, 176; representatives, 93
OECD. *See* Organisation for Economic Co-operation and Development
OIC. *See* Organisation of Islamic Cooperation
Oil, 7; agriculture and, 148; Algeria, 241; Anglo-Iranian Oil Company, 65; Arab oil weapon, 159, 265, 266, 274; ARAMCO, 65, 263, 267; Bahrain, 226, 241; boom, 230–231, 331*tab;* Cold War policies, 263; consumption skyrocketing, 277; decade, 440–441; economies and, 440–441; Egypt, 241; embargoes, 160, 263, 267–268; exploration, 65; exports, 241; ExxonMobil, 277; Iran, 149, 166, 226, 227, 241, 262; Iran-Iraq War dimension, 161; Iraq, 226, 227, 241; Kurds, 276–277; Kuwait, 226, 241, 261–262, 272–273, 280; Libya, 149, 241, 262; new boom, 244–245; oil shock, 266; Oman, 241; in Persia, 140–141; power and, 282; price
decline, 98, 130, 233, 337; production, *98,* 148; profits, 147; Qatar, 241; revenue increase, 135; revolution of 1970s, 143, 268–269; Saudi Arabia, 226, 241, 272–273; Sinopec, 277; statesmanship, 263; Sudan revenues, 236–237; United Arab Emirates, 241, 273; United States as global power, 278–279; US imports, 264; US tax credits, 264; Venezuelan oil industry, 263–264; Yemen, 241. *See also* International oil companies; Middle East, economic issues; Middle East, oil economy; Organization of Petroleum Exporting Countries
Olmert, Ehud, 184
Oman, 3; Arab uprising, 86; as British protectorate, 65; fertility rates, 292; free-trade agreements, 241; monarchy, 106, 121–122; oil, 241; regime challenge, 6; urbanization, 288
On Pre-Islamic Poetry (Husayn), 406
Once Upon a Time (Jamalzadeh), 408, 411
OPEC. *See* Organization of Petroleum Exporting Countries
Operation Desert Shield, 80
Organisation for Economic Co-operation and Development (OECD), 241
Organisation of Islamic Cooperation (OIC), 151
Organization of Arab Petroleum Exporting Countries (OAPEC), 151, 266, 267
Organization of Petroleum Exporting Countries (OPEC), 75, 97; aims and members, 265; challenging, 268; development, 151–152; formation, 264; Iranian Revolution (1978–1979) and, 270; overproduction, 273; power, 269–270; pricing, 268–269, 271–273
Oslo Accords, 95, 177, 183, 198–199, 200*fig,* 201, 204, 206, 212, 213–214, 246, 251
Othello in the Wonderland, 412
Ottoman Empire: accommodation and cooperation, 335; authority, 16;

collapse, 13, 28, 386, 434; division of labor, 335; governance, 333; historical context, 52–53; jihad, 59–61; liberalism and nationalism, 58; reforms, 336; states carved from, 141; trade, 224–225; women, 346, 351

The Outsider (Karaosmanoglu), 407

Oz, Amos, 419

PA. *See* Palestinian Authority

Palace of Desire (Mahfouz), 415

Palace Walk (Mahfouz), 415

Palestine, 3, 178; Arabs, 18; Britain controlling, 386; civil war, 104; economy, 251–252; fertility rates, 292; League of Nations mandate for Israel, 92; oranges, 225; partition of, 185–189, *187;* refugees, 108; state structure, 316–317; women, *370;* writers, 428–429. *See also* Israeli-Palestinian conflict

Palestine Communist Party (PCP), 178

Palestine Liberation Organization (PLO), 73, 76; Arab League and, 178; establishment, 189; independence declared, 80; Israel and, 79–82, 134; in Lebanon, 191–193; negotiations, 196, 205, 213; Norway meetings, 198; resistance movement, 190; in West Bank, 74

Palestinian Authority (PA), 201, 204–205, 206, 211, 251

Palestinian National Authority (PNA), 177, 179, 198–199

Palestinian Queers for BDS (PQBDS), 211, 215

Palestinians, 67; autonomy, 81; Christians, 179; class and, 179; defined, 178; diaspora, 178; displaced, *188;* education, 179; Gaza Strip, 74, 178, 195, 214; Hamas elected by, 180, 206; identity, 177–178; immigrants to Gulf, 231; in Israel, 233; Israeli occupation, 80; in Israeli-Palestinian conflict, 178–181; in Jerusalem, *214;* Lebanese and, 79; as nation without a state, 157; in 1990s, 196; Occupied Territories, 197, 199, 233; power relations, 176;

refugees, 108, 204; rights, 69, 75, 127; self-rule, 78; status, 76; suicide bombings by, 85, 180, 208; uprising (1987), 194–196; view of Zionism, 185; West Bank, 23, 95, 178, 195, 214

Pamuk, Orhan, 3, 418, 436

Pan-Arabism, 70, 77, 353

Pan-Islam, 56

Papacy, 380

Parallel cousins, 324–325

Paris Peace Conference, 63

Parsipur, Shahrnush, 411, 433–434

Parthia, 44

Pasha, Muhammad Ali, 404

Passover, 387

Patrilineal kinship, 323–324, 326–328

Patron-client relationships, 322, 338–339, 341

PCP. *See* Palestine Communist Party

Peace, 417; CWP, 211, 215; Israeli-Palestinian conflict and, 212–213; negative, 212; Paris Peace Conference, 63; positive, 212; road map to, 82, 206; Rogers Peace Plan, 75; West Bank pipeline, 25

Peace Now, 191, 194

Pearl Revolution, 385, 441

Peoples of the Book, 333

Persia, 51, 417; national identity, 55; oil in, 140–141; renaming, 65; women of, 349–351. *See also* Iran

Persian Requiem (Daneshvar), 417

Petraeus, David, 93

Petrodollars, 281

PFLP. *See* Popular Front for the Liberation of Palestine

Phoenicians, 42

Physicians for Human Rights, 210

Pilgrimages, 45–46. *See also* Jerusalem; Mecca

Pillar of Salt (Memmi), 413

PLO. *See* Palestine Liberation Organization

PNA. *See* Palestinian National Authority

Political Islam, 115–117, 319

Politics: changes in Arab countries, 69–71; Cold War, 262; Great Power, 141; Middle East, 269–271; in Middle East oil economy, 266–268;

Western models, 107. *See also* Middle East, politics; Middle East, religion and politics
Polo, Marco, 35
Polygamy, 362, 363
Pontecorvo, Gillo, 146
Popular Front for the Liberation of Palestine (PFLP), 178
Population growth, 7, 287–288; fertility rates, 292–294; MENA, 289*tab,* 291; urbanization and, 289*tab;* youth bulge, 294–295
Positive peace, 212
Posted price system, 264
Poverty, 7; absolute, 302; Algeria, 305; Egypt, 303, 308; Gaza Strip, 308; inequality and, 302–309; Iraq, 304; Jordan, 303; Lebanon, 304; line, 302–303; literacy and, 303; MENA, 305*tab;* Morocco, 303, 305, 308; relative, 302; Tunisia, 303; Yemen, 308
Power: Bahrain transfer of, 101; Egypt transfer of, 101; Gender and Empowerment Measure, 366; informal structures of, 99–100; Israel transfer of, 101; Jordan transfer of, 101; Morocco transfer of, 101; oil and, 282; OPEC, 269–270; Palestinian relations, 176; Saudi Arabia transfer of, 101; Shi'i Muslim political, 129; superpowers, 93; Syria transfer of, 101; transfer of, 101; United States as global oil, 278–279. *See also* Great Powers
PQBDS. *See* Palestinian Queers for BDS
Praetorianism, 110
Project for Translation from Arabic (PROTA), 436
Protestant Reformation, 380
Puppet Show (Chubak), 411
Pyramids of Giza, 1, *10*

Qaddafi, Muammar, 86, 102, 154, 155, 165, 266
Al-Qaeda, 4, 82–83, 93, 96–97, 111, 120, 130, 143, 377, 392, 398
Qajar monarchy, 113, 118, 361, 389, 407
Qalamawi, Suhayr, 410

Qanats, 22
Qasim, Abd al-Karim, 66, 354, 366, 434
Qatar, 3; Bahrain boundary dispute, 145; economic liberalization, 107; employment, 296; monarchy, 121; oil, 241; supporting Libya, 104; unemployment, 236; urbanization, 288
Qazvini, Safi ibn Wali, 36
Qualifying Industrial Zone (QIZ), 239
Qura'i, Ahmad, 206
Quran, 21, 26, 47, 367, 382–383, 393, 406
Qutb, Sayyid, 396–397

Rabbis for Human Rights, 211
Rabin, Yitzhak, 82, 198, 210
Rafsanjani, Ali Akbar Hashemi, 131
Rahbani, Ziad, 340
Rahnavard, Zahra, 371
Raiders of the Lost Ark, 27
Ramadan, 46
Ramsar Convention, 26
Ran, Nazim Hikmet, 421, 424, 426
Rashid, Fatima, 363
Rashid, Shanez, 369
Reagan, Ronald, 78
Red Line Agreement, 261, 270
Reform: Cairo, 362; Iraq, 366; Istanbul, 362; language, 405; nonviolent, 392; Ottoman Empire, 336; Turkey, 373; Westernizing, 53–55
Refugees: Afghanistan, 123; Iraq, 123, 254–255; Jordan, 255; Palestinians, 108, 204; Syria, 254–255; Syrian, 250; UNHCR, 250
Regionalism, 150–153
Relative poverty, 302
Religion, 332. *See also* Christianity; Islam; Judaism; Middle East, religion and politics
Rentier state, 260, 278, 282
Reserve Fund for Future Generations (RFFG), 280
Revivalism, 105, 392–393, 398–400, 441
Reza Khan, 62, 65, 113, 389
Reza Shah, Mohammad, 72, 77, 106, 113, 352–353, 355–357, 407, 417
RFFG. *See* Reserve Fund for Future Generations

Richard the Lion-Hearted, 380
Rights: Human Rights Watch, 125;
    Israel restricting Arab, 105; Kurds in
    Turkey, 127, 155; marriage, 355;
    Palestinians, 69, 75, 127; Physicians
    for Human Rights, 210; Rabbis for
    Human Rights, 211
Road Map to peace, 82, 206
Rogers Peace Plan, 75
Roman alphabet, 64
Roman history, 14–25
Al-Rumi, Jalal al-Din, 3
Rushdie, Salman, 412, 434, 435
Russia: immigrants, 100; in Iran, 91;
    Road Map to peace, 82; Russian
    Orthodox Church, 116; in Turkey, 91

Al-Sa'adawi, Nawwal, 369
Sacred Night (Benjelloun), 413
Sadat, Anwar, 75, 76, 191, 229,
    356–357, 366, 369, 394, 426
Sadat, Jehan, 356
Sadowski, Yahya M., 247
Al-Sadr, Muqtada, 96
Saedi, Gholam Hosayn, 412
Al-Said, Qaboos ibn Said, 118, 122
Saladin, 51, 380
Salafi groups, 400
Salami tactics, 153
Salih, Ali Abdallah, 86–87, 102, 248,
    395
Salih, al-Tayyib, 431
Al-Samman, Ghanda, 410, 429
Sand Child (Benjelloun), 413
Satanic Verses (Rushdie), 412, 435
Saudi Arabia, 3; Arab uprising, 86;
    arms imports, 109; ecology, 281;
    economic giant, 65; employment,
    296; fertility rates, 292; House of
    Saud, 328; Iraq attacking, 197;
    Kuwait dispute, 152–153; labor
    force, 19; migrant workers, 234;
    monarchy, 100, 106, 118, 120–121,
    388; northern desert, 21; oil, 226,
    241, 272–273; OPEC pricing and,
    268; regime challenge, 6; transfer of
    power, 101; urbanization, 288
ibn Saud, Abdul Aziz (king of Saudi
    Arabia), 65, 119, 120, 147, 388
SAVAK. *See* Sazman-e Ettelaat va
    Amniyat-e Keshvar

Al-Sayyab, Badr Shakir, 424
Sazman-e Ettelaat va Amniyat-e
    Keshvar (SAVAK), 77
Scattered Memories (Taraqqi), 433
Schimmel, Annemarie, 26–27
The School Principal (Al-e Ahmad),
    417
Scrap Papers from Prison (Alavi), 426
Sea of Galilee, 26
Season of Migration to the North
    (Salih), 431
*The Secret Life of Saeed, the Ill-Fated
    Pessoptimist* (Habibi), 428
Selem III, 53–55
Seleucids, 44
Self-determination, 202, 213
Self-governance, 442
Sephardim, 383
September 11, 2001, terrorist attacks, 5,
    82, 96, 167, 201, 209, 397, 398, 430
September Birds (Nasrallah), 432
Sèvres Treaty, 64
Al-Shabbi, Abu Al-Qasim, 424
Shadow economy, 238
Shadufs, 22
Shafik, Doriyya, 365
Shahin, Yusuf, 426
Shaikh Khalifa, 122
Shakespeare, William, 421
Shamir, Moshe, 419
Shammas, Anton, 419–420
Sharia, 383, 390
Al-Sharkawi, Pakinam, 370
Sharon, Ariel, 82, 95, 183–184, 201,
    205–206, 211
Al-sharq al-awsat, 14
Al-Sharqawi, 'Abd al-Rahman, 426
Shawqi, Ahmad, 423
Al-Shaykh, Hanan, 429
Shelley, Percy Bysshe, 406, 424
Sherkat, Shahla, 368
Shi'i Muslims, 18, 26, 50, 142;
    Bahrain, 122–123; Iran, 94; Iraq, 94,
    328; militia, 96; political power, 129
Signposts Along the Road (Qutb), 396
Silk Route, 223
Sims, David, 33
Single-state solutions, 207
Sinopec, 277
Six Day War, 23, 160, 189–190, 394,
    416, 422

The Smell of the Shadow (Bektas), 433
Social class. *See* Class
Social media, 1–2
Social solidarity, 310
Social welfare, 281
Socialism, 69; Algeria, 228; Arab,
    70–71; Egypt, 228; Egyptian, 75;
    Tunisia, 228; varieties, 114; Zionism
    and, 127, 182, 408–409
Sociorealism, 415
Solidarity, 310
Somalia, 3
Somekh, Sasson, 420
Sovereign wealth funds (SWF), 280
Sovereignty, 202; Arab uprisings
    shaking, 139; issues in international
    relations, 144–146; Libya, 155;
    negative, 140, 143
Soviet Union, 5; Afghanistan
    occupation, 96; aid to Egypt, 229;
    aid to Iraq, 229; aid to Syria, 229;
    aid to Yemen, 229; breakup of,
    87–88, 93, 103; communist model,
    113; dominant Middle East player,
    226; expansionism, 77; Nazis
    invading, 72; Suez Canal missiles, 75
The Stage and the Mirrors (Adonis),
    424
Stalin, Joseph, 72, 114
"Starchitecture," 33
States: Arabian Peninsula, 121; Arab
    nation- , 111; building, 110–112,
    113; ideal, 140; Israel establishment,
    386–388; Middle East religion and,
    386–391; Muslim literature,
    433–435; nominally Islamic,
    390–391; from Ottoman Empire,
    141; revolutionary, 111; strongly
    Islamic, 388–389; women in
    building, 349–361; Zionist, 207
The Story of Zahra (Al-Shaykh), 429
The Stray Dog (Hedayat), 411
Structural adjustment policies, 234–239
Subcultures, 330
Sudan, 3; agriculture, 237; Christianity,
    385, 389; civil war, 250–251;
    economic development, 250; Islam,
    389; oil revenues, 236–237; political
    Islam, 116
Suez Canal, 29, 56, 57, 60; closing,
    265; defense of, 68; guarding, 63;
    Nazis and, 91; opening of, 348;

Soviet Union missiles, 75; street
    skirmishes, 369; trade and, 225
Suffrage, 354
Sufi Sheikh of Light (Karaosmanoglu),
    417
Sufism, 50–51
Sugar Street (Mahfouz), 415
Suicide bombings, 85, 180, 208, 211
Sunni, 18, 50, 142, 164, 333, 382–383
Superpowers, 93
Swearingen, Will D., 25
SWF. *See* Sovereign wealth funds
Sykes-Picot Agreement, 61, 91
Symbolism: Islam, 391; of Jerusalem,
    386–388; kinship and, 319; women
    as symbolic, 351, 353, 361, 372, 374
Syria, 3; Arab uprising, 27, 86–87;
    Assyria rule, 43; civil war, 19, 102,
    250, 328; decentralized military
    movement, 103; economy, 246;
    exports, 239; fertility rates, 292;
    France and, 62, 63, 67, 226; Lebanon
    carved from, 142; military, 155;
    Orontes River, 22; refugees, 250,
    254–255; revolutionary spirit, 5;
    Soviet Union aid, 229; transfer of
    power, 101; travel from, 35;
    urbanization, 288; women
    pieceworkers, 302; women's
    education, 306
Syriana, 2

Taayush, 211
Tahir, Kemal, 414
Taif Accords, 249
Taif Agreement, 384
Tala'at Harb, Mohammed, 350
Talbott, John, 146
Talib, Aliya, 430
Taliban, 102, 143
Talmud, 378
Tanpinar, Ahmet Hamdi, 417
Taraqqi, Goli, 411, 433
Tavakoli-Targhi, Mohamad, 404–405,
    412
Tawfiq, 57–58
*Tea Ceremony in the Presence of the
    Wolf* (Parsipur), 433
Tekin, Latife, 32
Terraki, 363
Terrorism, 5, 201; Middle East, 82–85;
    scholarship on, 208; September 11,

2001, terrorist attacks, 5, 82, 96, 167, 201, 209, 397, 398, 430; war on, 82–83, 97, 167

TGNA. *See* Turkish Grand National Assembly

Theodosius I, 380

The Thirst (Djebar), 427

Thorn Theater, 422

Tigris River, 20–21, 23, 41–42

Times Atlas, 13

Tolstoy, Leo, 404, 406

Torah, 378

Tourism, 239

Trade: Agadir trade agreement, 240; ancient patterns, 4; European, 223; exports, 239–241, 242*tab;* imports, 243–244, 243*tab;* international, 225; liberalization, 305; as Middle East economic issue, 239–244; Ottoman Empire, 224–225; Roman, 44; routes, 2–3, 45, 53, 140; Suez Canal and, 225

Transparency International, 94

Treaty of Sèvres, 62, 157

Treaty of Uqair, 144

Tribes, 99

Truman Doctrine, 72, 227

Tudeh Party, 426

Tunisia, 3; agriculture, 239; Arab uprising, 27, 101, 153–154, 439–440; Bourguiba Boulevard, 441; bread riots, 235; economy, 246; established regime, 103; exports, 239; fertility rates, 292, 294; foreign debt, 225; government downfall, 310; health care, 307, 308; independence, 64; infant mortality, 293; layoffs, 298; Nahda movement, 398–400; olive oil, 225; phosphates, 225; poverty, 303; protectorates, 56; protests, 6; socialism, 228; unemployment, 299; voters, *105*

Turgenev, Ivan, 404, 406

Turkey, 3, 50–51; baby boom, 293; Cappadocia region, *12;* conditional democracy, 126–127; democratic government, 72; economic development, 99; established leadership, 101; fertility rates, 292, 294; *gecekondus,* 31; governance, 112; health care, 307, 308; independence in, 64–66; industry,

337; Islamic revivalism, 105; Kurds' rights, 127, 155; layoffs, 298; novels, 417–419; reform, 373; remittances, 230; Russia in, 91; social organization, 316; storytellers, 412; telecommunications, 237; unemployment, 299; United States aid, 227; urbanization, 288; women of, 350–353, 360, 366–367, 372; women pieceworkers, 302. *See also* Istanbul

Turkish Grand National Assembly (TGNA), 360, 367

Tutankhamun, 1

Twitter, 1, 103, 139, 152

Two-state solution of Israeli-Palestinian conflict, 208, 213

UAR. *See* United Arab Republic

Umayyads, 48, 50

Umma, 56, 382

UN. *See* United Nations

UN Human Development Index, 255

Unemployment, 7, 234; Algeria, 299; Egypt, 299; Gaza Strip, 236, 253, 299; insurance, 301; Iran, 299; Iraq, 236; Jordan, 299; MENA, 301*tab;* Qatar, 236; rising, 298–302; Tunisia, 299; Turkey, 299; West Bank, 236, 253, 299; women, 299–301, 301*tab;* Yemen, 236, 299; youth, 236, 299

UNHCR. *See* United Nations High Commissioner for Refugees

United Arab Emirates, 3; economic liberalization, 107; fertility rates, 292; monarchy, 122; oil, 241, 273; revenue distribution, 281

United Arab Republic (UAR), 70

United Nations (UN), 68, 70; Gender and Development Index, 366; Gender and Empowerment Measure, 366; inspection teams, 16; Middle East members, 74; negative sovereignty, 140, 143; Palestine partition and, 188–189; Road Map to peace, 82; Security Council resolutions, 74–75, 84, 154–155, 188, 199, 266–267, 386

United Nations High Commissioner for Refugees (UNHCR), 250

United States: aid to Egypt, 229; aid to Israel, 229; aid to Turkey, 227; antitrust tradition, 262; arms supplying, 117; bombing by, 274–275; as Christian nation, 116; Coalition Provisional Authority, 132; dominant Middle East player, 226; energy crisis of 1973, 266; free-trade agreements, 241; as global oil power, 278–279; intervening for Lebanon, 80; Iran-Contra issues, 78; Iraq invaded by, 235, 247; Iraq War, 83–84; Iraq withdrawal, 93; Israeli-Palestinian conflict and, 209; Jewish population, 379; Kuwait liberated by, 80–82, 150; Middle East policy, 88; monetary policy, 272; oil imports, 264; oil tax credits, 264; political structure imposed, 113; PROTA, 436; Road Map to peace, 82; September 11, 2001, terrorist attacks, 5, 82, 96, 167, 201, 209, 397, 398, 430; undemocratic policies tolerated, 106; Watergate scandal, 267. *See also* Iraq War

Upper class, 337

Urabi, Ahmad, 57

Urban II, 380

Urbanization, 7, 13, 309; Bahrain, 288; Dubai, 288; Egypt, 288; Iran, 288; Iraq, 288; Kuwait, 288; labor markets, 287; Libya, 288; Morocco, 288; Oman, 288; population growth and, 289*tab;* Qatar, 288; rapid and dramatic, 328, 332; Saudi Arabia, 288; social change and, 288; Syria, 288; Turkey, 288; urban life, 31; urban planning, 29–31, 287–291; Yemen, 288

Al-'Uthman, Layla, 430

Veiling, 359, 363, 367, 373; downveiling, 372; unveiling, 352–353

Venezuelan oil industry, 263–264

The Vices of Men (Astarabadi), 362

Vitalis, Robert, 147

Wafd Party, 67

Wafdist Women's Central Committee (WWCC), 364–365

Wahhabism, 96, 388

Wannus, Sa'dallah, 422

Washington Consensus, 235

Water: for agriculture, 22, 73; Amman supply, 25; Egypt utility, 26; Israel development scheme, 73; rainfall, 22, 226, 320. *See also specific rivers*

Watergate scandal, 267

Weapons of mass destruction (WMD), 81, 164, 275, 430

Weizmann, Chaim, 61

West Bank, 20; control of, 73; corporate interests in, 212; demonstrations, *181;* elections, 192; fertility rates, 292; Israel and, 22, 85, 189; Jordan losing, 124, 394; Palestinians, 23, 95, 178, 195, 214; peace pipeline, 25; PLO in, 74; PNA replacing, 177; prestige of, 80; rainfall, 22; security fence, 82; settlements, 183; unemployment, 236, 253, 299

"Westoxification," 411–412

White Castle (Pamuk), 418

White man's burden, 140

White Paper immigration, 67–68

White Revolution, 116, 355

Who Remembers the Sea (Dib), 427

WikiLeaks, 139

Wild Thorns (Khalifa), 428

WMD. *See* Weapons of mass destruction

WOI. *See* Women's Organization of Iran

Women, 433; in Arab uprisings, *373;* Atatürk and, 352–353; Beirut Decentrists, 429; classifications, 345; clothing and, 372; contributions, 373; CWP, 211, 215; downveiling, 372; education, 292–294, 306, 354; of Egypt, 348, 350–351, 353–354, 356, 364–365, 370; elite, 362–365; feminism, 353, 362, 365, 367; harem, 347–348, 362–363; idealized images, 346; of Iran, 352–353, 355, 357–359, 364, 371; Iran-Iraq War soldiers, *162,* 359; of Iraq, 355, 359, 364, 369; Islam and, 348, 360; kinship role, 324, 329; Kurdish, 367, 368, 371; literacy, 254, 356, 361, 368; maternal mortality, 293; mother Iran, 351; Nasser and, 353–354; nationalist

movements, 346–347, 363–364, 368–371; Ottoman Empire, 346, 351; Palestine, *370;* pan-Arabism and, 353; of Persia, 349–351; Personal Status Code, 354; pieceworkers, 302; protection of female body, 357, *358;* protesters, *366;* Reza Shah and, 352–353; role of, 345–374; in state building, 349–361; suffrage, 354; symbolic, 351, 353, 361, 372, 374; of Turkey, 350–353, 360, 366–367, 372; unemployment, 299–301, 301*tab;* unveiled, 352–353; veiled, 359, 363, 367, 373; woman question, 346–351; beyond woman question, 361–372; women's movements, 365–367; writers, 362. *See also* Gender; Marriage
Women Without Men (Parsipur), 433
Women's Organization of Iran (WOI), 356, 368
Wordsworth, William, 424
World Bank, 26, 297, 303, 339
World order, 277–280
World War I, 5; Arab Revolt, 58, 59–61; Ottoman jihad, 59–61; post–, Middle East history, 61–85; victors, 146
World War II, 70, 91; economies after, 226–230; economies before, 224–226; Great Powers, 150
World Zionist Organization, 186
WWCC. *See* Wafdist Women's Central Committee

Yacine, Kateb, 427
Yehoshua, A. B., 420
Yemen, 3, 65; Arab uprising, 86; Change Square, 441; civil war, 102, 247–248, 395; decentralized military movement, 103; economy, 246; education, 293; fertility rates, 292; health care, 307; maternal mortality, 293; migrant workers, 231, 234; Muslim Brotherhood, 395; oil, 241; poverty, 308; revolutionary spirit, 5; Soviet Union aid, 229; superpower support loss, 93; travel from, 35; unemployment, 299; urbanization, 288; women's education, 306
Yemeni Congregation for Reform. *See* Islah party
Yesh Gvul, 193
Yisrael Beiteinu, 100
Yom-Kippur War, 190–191
Young Turks, 58, 62, 350–351, 407, 408
Your Eyes Are My Destiny (Al-Samman), 410
Youth bulge, 287
YouTube, 103
Yushij, Nima, 424

Zanan, 368
Zanoyan, Vahan, 167
Zaydan, Jurji, 406
Zionism, 61, 62; Arab nationalism and, 68–69; emergence, 379; fear of, 63, 67; immigration, 147; Palestinian and Jewish view of, 185; partition of Palestine and, 185–189; socialism and, 127, 182; socialist ideology, 408–409; state building, 207; World Zionist Organization, 186
Zionists, 177, 182
Zoroastrians, 385

About the Book

The fourth edition of *Understanding the Contemporary Middle East* has been fully revised and updated throughout to reflect the still unfolding impact of the Arab Spring, the changing international environment, the impasse in the Israeli-Palestinian conflict, and much more. The book also includes an entirely new chapter on the role of women in the Middle East. Maps, photographs, and details of basic political data enhance the text, widely acknowledged as the best available introduction to the region.

Jillian Schwedler is professor of political science at Hunter College and the Graduate Center, City University of New York. Her publications include *Faith in Moderation: Islamist Parties in Jordan and Yemen* and (with Laleh Khalili) *Policing and Prisons in the Middle East: Formations of Coercion.*